Lecture Notes in Computer Science 15839

Founding Editors

Gerhard Goos
Juris Hartmanis

Editorial Board Members

Elisa Bertino, *Purdue University, West Lafayette, IN, USA*
Wen Gao, *Peking University, Beijing, China*
Bernhard Steffen, *TU Dortmund University, Dortmund, Germany*
Moti Yung, *Columbia University, New York, NY, USA*

The series Lecture Notes in Computer Science (LNCS), including its subseries Lecture Notes in Artificial Intelligence (LNAI) and Lecture Notes in Bioinformatics (LNBI), has established itself as a medium for the publication of new developments in computer science and information technology research, teaching, and education.

LNCS enjoys close cooperation with the computer science R & D community, the series counts many renowned academics among its volume editors and paper authors, and collaborates with prestigious societies. Its mission is to serve this international community by providing an invaluable service, mainly focused on the publication of conference and workshop proceedings and postproceedings. LNCS commenced publication in 1973.

Sven Tomforde · Christian Krupitzer ·
Stéphane Vialle · Estela Suarez · Thilo Pionteck
Editors

Architecture of Computing Systems

38th International Conference, ARCS 2025
Kiel, Germany, April 22–24, 2025
Proceedings

Editors
Sven Tomforde
Christian-Albrecht University of Kiel
Kiel, Germany

Christian Krupitzer
Universität Hohenheim
Stuttgart, Baden-Württemberg, Germany

Stéphane Vialle
Paris-Saclay University, LISN
CentraleSupélec
Gif-sur-Yvette, France

Estela Suarez
SiPEARL
Maisons-Laffitte, France

Thilo Pionteck
Otto-von-Guericke University Magdeburg
Magdeburg, Germany

ISSN 0302-9743   ISSN 1611-3349 (electronic)
Lecture Notes in Computer Science
ISBN 978-3-032-03280-5   ISBN 978-3-032-03281-2 (eBook)
https://doi.org/10.1007/978-3-032-03281-2

© The Editor(s) (if applicable) and The Author(s), under exclusive license to Springer Nature Switzerland AG 2026
Chapter "OpenVADL: An Open Source Implementation of the Vienna Architecture Description Language" is licensed under the terms of the Creative Commons Attribution-NonCommercial-NoDerivatives 4.0 International License (http://creativecommons.org/licenses/by-nc-nd/4.0/). For further details see license information in the chapter.

This work is subject to copyright. All rights are solely and exclusively licensed by the Publisher, whether the whole or part of the material is concerned, specifically the rights of translation, reprinting, reuse of illustrations, recitation, broadcasting, reproduction on microfilms or in any other physical way, and transmission or information storage and retrieval, electronic adaptation, computer software, or by similar or dissimilar methodology now known or hereafter developed.
The use of general descriptive names, registered names, trademarks, service marks, etc. in this publication does not imply, even in the absence of a specific statement, that such names are exempt from the relevant protective laws and regulations and therefore free for general use.
The publisher, the authors and the editors are safe to assume that the advice and information in this book are believed to be true and accurate at the date of publication. Neither the publisher nor the authors or the editors give a warranty, expressed or implied, with respect to the material contained herein or for any errors or omissions that may have been made. The publisher remains neutral with regard to jurisdictional claims in published maps and institutional affiliations.

This Springer imprint is published by the registered company Springer Nature Switzerland AG
The registered company address is: Gewerbestrasse 11, 6330 Cham, Switzerland

If disposing of this product, please recycle the paper.

Preface

The 38th International Conference on Architecture of Computing Systems (ARCS 2025) was hosted at the Wissenschaftszentrum Kiel, in close proximity to the Christian-Albrechts University of Kiel (CAU), Germany, April 22–24, 2025. It was organized by the special interest group on "Architecture of Computing Systems" of the GI (Gesellschaft für Informatik e.V.) and ITG (Informationstechnische Gesellschaft im VDE).

The ARCS conference series has 38 years of tradition reporting leading-edge research in computer architecture, operating systems, and other related low-level system software, and a wide range of software techniques and tools required to exploit and build new hardware systems efficiently. ARCS addresses the complete spectrum from fully integrated, self-powered embedded systems up to plant-powered high-performance systems. It also provides a platform covering new emerging and cross-cutting topics, such as autonomous and ubiquitous systems, reconfigurable computing, mathematical models, neural networks, and artificial intelligence.

ARCS was the basis for the founding of the Organic Computing (OC) Initiative and has been one of the driving forces ever since, so that self-adaptation, learning capability, and distributed control through self-organisation in technical systems have been part of the focus for two decades. Recently, further related topics such as sustainable high-performance computing have become part of the scope of ARCS. In 2025 two new tracks were added to give more visibility to and encourage networking between research groups and PhD students. Each track has a specific Program Committee (PC) constituted by international experts in the respective subjects. Bidding was enabled, allowing the PC to tag potential Conflicts of Interest and to give a preference on the papers she/he would prefer to review. These preferences were considered in the review assignments. Each reviewer was assigned a maximum of three manuscripts and two weeks to review and upload their report to the submission platform.

The ARCS 2025 conference included five basic tracks: Architecture of Computing Systems (ARCS), Organic Computing (OC), Dependability and Fault Tolerance (VERFE), Forum on Research Groups (RG), and PhD Forum (PhD). These were co-organized and coordinated by:

- Architecture of Computing Systems (ARCS): Stéphane Vialle (CentraleSupélec, Paris-Saclay University, LISN, France) and Estela Suarez (SiPEARL, France)
- Organic Computing (OC): Anthony Stein (University of Hohenheim, Germany) and Stefan Wildermann (Friedrich-Alexander Universität Erlangen, Germany)
- Fault Tolerance (VERFE): Peter Sobe (HTW Dresden, Germany)
- Forum on Research Groups (RG): Stefan Lankes (RWTH Aachen, Germany)
- PhD Forum (PhD): Sven Tomforde (Christian-Albrechts University of Kiel, Germany) and Christian Krupitzer (Universität Hohenheim, Germany)

In total, ARCS 2025 attracted 49 submissions from authors in 7 countries, namely Austria, Denmark, France, Germany, Greece, Portugal, and the USA. Each submission was reviewed by a diverse and dedicated Program Committee. Almost all papers received at least three qualified single-blind reviews, leading to a total of 142 reviews, of which 119 were provided by the PC members directly and 23 were delegated to sub-reviewers. Adding up all tracks, the PC selected 36 submissions to be presented at ARCS, which corresponds to a 73% paper acceptance rate. ARCS accepted 13 papers, OC accepted 9, VERFE 2, RG 3, and PhD 9. The accepted papers formed seven entertaining sessions with 25-minute slots per presentation in the ARCS, OC, and VERFE tracks, and 12-minute slots in the RG and PhD tracks.

There is no successful conference without keynote talks. At ARCS 2025, we were delighted to host two very interesting keynotes, on "Digital twins for organic computing systems", by Lukas Esterle (Aarhus University, Denmark), and on "Prototyping non-conventional architectures for HPC: some failure, a few successes, and several byproducts", by Filippo Mantovani (Barcelona Supercomputing Center, Spain).

Thanks to all these individuals and all the many other people who helped in the organization of ARCS 2025. Especial thanks go to the proceedings chair Thilo Pionteck (Otto-von-Guericke University of Magdeburg), the web chair Lars Bauer (Ubitium GmbH, Germany), and the publicity chair Mathias Pacher (DHBW Karslruhe, Germany). We further thank all authors for submitting their work to ARCS and presenting accepted papers. Last, but not least, we thank Springer for sponsoring this year's conference.

April 2025

Sven Tomforde
Christian Krupitzer
Stéphane Vialle
Estela Suarez

Organization

General Chairs

Sven Tomforde University of Kiel, Germany
Christian Krupitzer University of Hohenheim in Stuttgart, Germany

Program Chairs

Stéphane Vialle CentraleSupélec, Paris-Saclay University, LISN, France
Estela Suarez SiPEARL GmbH, Germany

Special Track on Organic Computing Chairs

Anthony Stein University of Hohenheim, Germany
Stefan Wildermann Friedrich-Alexander-Universität Erlangen-Nürnberg, Germany

Special Track on Dependability and Fault Tolerance Chair

Peter Sobe HTW Dresden, Germany

PhD Forum Chairs

Ghassan Al-Falouji University of Kiel, Germany
Elia Henrichs University of Hohenheim, Germany

Research Groups Forum Chair

Stefan Lankes RWTH Aachen University, Germany

Proceeding Chair

Thilo Pionteck   Otto von Guericke University Magdeburg, Germany

Publicity and Web Chair

Lars Bauer   Ubitium GmbH, Germany

ARCS Main Track Program Committee

Lars Bauer	Ubitium GmbH, Germany
Andreas Becher	Technische Universität Ilmenau, Germany
Mladen Berekovic	Universität zu Lübeck, Germany
Andre Brinkmann	Johannes Gutenberg-Universität Mainz, Germany
Uwe Brinkschulte	Goethe-Universität Frankfurt am Main, Germany
Joao Cardoso	Universidade do Porto, Portugal
Thomas Carle	Institut de Recherche en Informatique de Toulouse, France
Pierfrancesco Foglia	Università di Pisa, Italy
Roberto Giorgi	University of Siena, Italy
Georgios Goumas	National Technical University of Athens, Greece
Daniel Gracia-Pérez	Thales Research and Technology, France
Christian Gruhl	University of Kassel, Germany
Jan Haase	Nordakademie - Hochschule der Wirtschaft, Germany
Jörg Hähner	University of Augsburg, Germany
Christian Hochberger	Technische Universität Darmstadt, Germany
Gert Jervan	Tallinn University of Technology, Estonia
Wolfgang Karl	Karlsruhe Institute of Technology, Germany
Jörg Keller	FernUniversität in Hagen, Germany
Peter Kogge	University of Notre Dame, USA
Hana Kubátová	Czech Technical University in Prague, Czech Republic
Stefan Lankes	RWTH Aachen University, Germany
Erik Maehle	Universität zu Lübeck, Germany
Sarah Neuwirth	Johannes Gutenberg University Mainz, Germany
Alex Orailoglu	University of California, San Diego, USA
Mathias Pacher	DHBW Karlsruhe, Germany

Thilo Pionteck	Otto von Guericke University Magdeburg, Germany
Mario Porrmann	Osnabrück University, Germany
Jan S. Rellermeyer	Leibnitz University Hannover, Germany
Reza Salkhordeh	Johannes Gutenberg University Mainz, Germany
Martin Schulz	Technical University of Munich, Germany
Leonel Sousa	Universidade de Lisboa, Portugal
Olaf Spinczyk	Osnabrück University, Germany
Anthony Stein	University of Hohenheim, Germany
Jürgen Teich	Friedrich-Alexander-Universität Erlangen-Nürnberg, Germany
Sven Tomforde	Christian-Albrechts-Universität zu Kiel, Germany
Tomoaki Ukezono	Fukuoka University, Japan
Daniel Versick	Nordakademie - Hochschule der Wirtschaft, Germany
Stéphane Vialle	CentraleSupélec and UMI GT-CNRS 2958, France
Stefan Wildermann	Friedrich-Alexander-Universität Erlangen-Nürnberg, Germany

Special Track on Organic Computing Program Committee

Ghassan Al-Falouji	Christian-Albrechts-Universität zu Kiel, Germany
Kirstie Bellman	Topcy House Consulting, USA
Uwe Brinkschulte	Goethe-Universität Frankfurt am Main, Germany
Martin Hoffmann	Bielefeld University of Applied Sciences, Germany
Christopher Landauer	Topcy House Consulting, USA
Erik Maehle	Universität zu Lübeck, Germany
Gero Mühl	University of Rostock, Germany
Mathias Pacher	DHBW Karlsruhe, Germany
Hella Ponsar	University of Augsburg, Germany
Marc Reichenbach	University of Rostock, Germany
Christian Renner	Hamburg University of Technology, Germany
Jürgen Teich	Friedrich-Alexander-Universität Erlangen-Nürnberg, Germany
Torben Weis	University of Duisburg-Essen, Germany
Sebastian von Mammen	Julius Maximilian University Würzburg, Germany

Special Track on Dependability and Fault Tolerance Program Committee

Fevzi Belli	University of Paderborn, Germany
Michael Gössel	University of Potsdam, Germany
Jörg Keller	FernUniversität in Hagen, Germany
Miroslaw Malek	USI-Lugano, Switzerland
Erik Maehle	Universität zu Lübeck, Germany
Dimitris Nikolos	University of Patras, Greece
Francesca Saglietti	Friedrich-Alexander-Universität Erlangen-Nürnberg, Germany
Martin Schulz	Technical University of Munich, Germany
Janusz Sosnowski	University of Warsaw, Poland
Carsten Trinitis	Technical University of Munich, Germany
Peter Tröger	Technsiche Universität Chemnitz, Germany
Norbert Wehn	Technische Universität Kaiserslautern, Germany
Josef Weidendorfer	Technical University of Munich, Germany

PhD Forum Program Committee

Jürgen Brehm	Leibnitz University Hannover, Germany
Uwe Brinkschulte	Goethe University Frankfurt, Germany
Jörg Hähner	University of Augsburg, Germany
Astrid Nieße	Carl von Ossietzky University of Oldenburg, Germany
Mathias Pacher	DHBW Karlsruhe, Germany
Anthony Stein	University of Hohenheim, Germany
Stefan Wildermann	Friedrich-Alexander-Universität Erlangen-Nürnberg, Germany

Research Group Forum Program Committee

Stefan Lankes	RWTH Aachen University, Germany
Oliver Sinnen	University of Auckland, New Zealand
Carsten Trinitis	Technical University of Munich, Germany

Keynote Talks

Digital Twins for Organic Computing Systems

Lukas Esterle

Aarhus University, Denmark

Abstract. Organic computing systems are defined by their ability to adapt to changing environments and interact with other systems at runtime. Typical characteristics of such systems are their ability to self-organize, self-configure, self-optimize, and self-heal. For all these concepts, models are required for the systems to understand, analyse, and potentially predict their actions and respective consequences. In recent years, the idea of Digital Twins has gained significant interest from the research community. In this keynote, we will first discuss the differences between models, Digital Shadows, and Digital Twins. We will explore how we can employ Digital Twins and Digital Shadows in autononous and organic computing systems and discuss their potential benefits. Afterwards, we will also discuss the different challenges we are facing with employing Digital Twins and operating them on various computing hardware, how to deal with uncertainties, or changing and adapting systems and the respective underlying models at runtime.

Prototyping Non-conventional Architectures for HPC: Some Failure, a Few Successes, and Several Byproducts

Filippo Mantovani

Barcelona Supercomputing Center, Spain

Abstract. Over the past two decades, CPU-centric architectures—dominated primarily by x86—have been the cornerstone of high-performance computing (HPC). However, this dominance has faced challenges from several disruptive, non-traditional technologies. The IBM Cell processor and GPUs, initially driven by the gaming market, represent notable examples. While the IBM Cell processor eventually faded, GPU computing thrived and now powers many of the world's top supercomputers. Similarly, the rise of Arm CPUs, originally designed for smartphones and tablets, marked another paradigm shift. Between 2010 and 2015, Arm architectures demonstrated increasing computational capabilities, culminating in the debut of the first Arm-based supercomputer in the TOP500 in 2018. By 2020, Fugaku, powered by Fujitsu's Arm-based CPUs, secured the top spot in the TOP500 rankings. More recently, geopolitical factors have accelerated investments in RISC-V architectures, with Europe and other regions exploring their potential for HPC. While contributing to the Mont-Blanc and EPI projects, I have been leading the prototyping efforts for pushing both Arm and RISC-V into HPC. This talk offers a personal, biased, and occasionally unfair reflection on the challenges, failures, and successes encountered while prototyping with non-conventional HPC technologies over the past decade. Along the way, we will also explore the unexpected byproducts and insights that have emerged from these endeavors.

Contents

Main Track

Progressing Non-blocking Two-Sided Communication Using BlueField DPUs 3
   Ehab Saleh, Amir Raoofy, and Josef Weidendorfer

Efficient Parallel Fuzzy Dilation for Visual Reasoning on Edge: Leveraging ARM SIMD Extensions and Embedded GPUs Accelerators 18
   Laurent Cabaret, Céline Hudelot, Régis Pierrard, and Jean-Philippe Poli

Ternary Signed Digit Addition on Field Programmable Gate Arrays 34
   Thomas Schlögl and Dietmar Fey

FSST Compression of JSON Data on FPGAs 48
   Tobias Hahn, Jan Hofmann, Stefan Wildermann, and Jürgen Teich

CHaOS: A Persistent Lightweight Cache Hybridization-Aware OS 63
   Nils Wilbert, Matthias Szymanski, Stefan Wildermann, Henriette Herzog, Timo Hönig, and Jürgen Teich

MxGPU: A Case Study on OS-Controlled GPGPU Multiplexing 79
   Marcel Lütke Dreimann and Olaf Spinczyk

Towards Complete Open-Source Environments: FPGA-Based GPU Overlay Controlled by RISC-V 94
   Hector Gerardo Muñoz-Hernandez, Muhammad Ali, Keyvan Shahin, Alireza Siyavashi, Diana Göhringer, Marc Reichenbach, Christian Herglotz, and Michael Hübner

Revisiting Gradient Direction Algorithms in Electrostatic Placers 109
   Meinhard Kissich and Marcel Baunach

ZTL: Enabling Zoned Namespace Support for File Systems 125
   Jan Sass, André Brinkmann, Xubin He, Matias Bjørling, and Reza Salkhordeh

Spend More to Save More (SM2): An Energy and Hardware-Aware Implementation of Successive Halving for Sustainable Hyperparameter Optimization 140
   Daniel Geißler, Mengxi Liu, Bo Zhou, Sungho Suh, and Paul Lukowicz

OpenVADL: An Open Source Implementation of the Vienna Architecture
Description Language 156
  Florian Freitag, Linus Halder, Benedikt Huber, Benjamin Kasper,
  Michael Nestler, Kevin Per, Matthias Raschhofer, Alexander Ripar,
  Johannes Zottele, and Andreas Krall

A SIMD MAC RISC-V Extension with Approximate Multipliers
for Accelerating CNN Inference in Tiny Embedded Devices 172
  José Juan Hernández Morales, Frank Hannig, and Jürgen Teich

Wildcat: Educational RISC-V Microprocessors 189
  Martin Schoeberl

Special Track on Organic Computing (OC)

Location-Based Probabilistic Load Forecasting of Electric Vehicle
Charging Sites: Deep Transfer Learning with Multi-quantile Temporal
Convolutional Network 205
  Mohammad Wazed Ali, Mohammad Asif Ibna Mustafa,
  Md. Aukerul Moin Shuvo, and Bernhard Sick

Unsupervised Anomaly Detection in Cellular Modem Metrics Using Deep
Autoencoders 220
  Nikita Smirnov, Mika Friesenborg, and Sven Tomforde

Hyperparameter Optimization for PSO-Based Energy-Aware Path
Planning for AUV Swarms 236
  Wiebke Frenkel and Bernd-Christian Renner

Process-Level Simulation Testbed for Assessing Field Robot Swarms 252
  Jonas Boysen and Anthony Stein

Neural Rules for Reinforcement Learning with XCSF as Controller
in Organic Computing Systems 268
  Connor Schönberner, Kjell-Matti Rothenburger, Armin Mackensen,
  and Sven Tomforde

Evaluating Adaptive Systems: A Comparative Study of XCS
and Established Reinforcement Learning Algorithms in Noisy Multi-step
Environments 283
  Marco Steinberger, Roman Küble, Michael Heider, and Jörg Hähner

A Measurement Framework at Global and Local Levels for Hybrid
Organic Computing Systems 298
    Jonas Lange, Pia Schweizer, Elia Henrichs, Luna Kaendler,
    Sven Tomforde, and Christian Krupitzer

Exploring Model Quantization in GenAI-Based Image Inpainting
and Detection of Arable Plants 314
    Sourav Modak, Ahmet Oğuz Saltık, and Anthony Stein

Unify: Uncertainty Incorporated Federated Learning for Object Detection 330
    Shang Gao, Bernhard Sick, and Franz Götz-Hahn

Special Track on Dependability and Fault Tolerance (VERFE)

Extension of 2-Bit Error Correcting BCH Codes with Simple Decoding 347
    Alexander Benedict Behrens and Michael Gössel

Reduction of Average-Performance Degradation and Variance in Faulty
CPU Cache Memories 362
    Michail Mavropoulos, Georgios Keramidas, and Dimitris Nikolos

PhD Forum

A System Model for Flexible Multi-objective Adaptation Planning
in Hybrid Self-Adaptive and Self-Organizing Systems 379
    Pia Schweizer

Dynamic Multimodal Cyclist Behaviour Modelling: From Representation
Insights to Federated Collaboration 389
    Shang Gao

Self-Explanation of System Behaviour in Organic Computing Systems 399
    Svea Wisy

Enhancing Dynamic Scene Understanding in Manual Assembly Processes 409
    Chenxi Guo

Situational Awareness by Audio Signals in Maritime Application 419
    Paria Vali Zadeh

A Vision for Deep Reinforcement Learning with a Classifier System 430
    Connor Schönberner

AI-Based Computer Vision Methods to Monitor Emission-Relevant
Parameters in Livestock Barns 440
    Simon Mielke

Open the Black Box: Self-Explainability of AI in Autonomous Marine
Systems 449
    Tom Beyer

Leveraging Application-Specific Knowledge for Energy-Efficient Deep
Learning Accelerators on Resource-Constrained FPGAs 459
    Chao Qian

Research Groups

FORnanoSatellites - Innovations in Nano-satellites - A Bavarian Research
Alliance 471
    Dietmar Fey, K. Schilling, J. Franke, M. Schmidt, and C. Fuchs

Feedback-Guided Dataset Shaping for Automated Downstream Task
Optimization 477
    Lukas Nolte, Marten J. Finck, Sören Pirk, and Sven Tomforde

Disruptive Memory Technologies: An Overview of DFG Priority Program
2377 482
    Marcel Köppen and Olaf Spinczyk

Author Index 487

Main Track

Progressing Non-blocking Two-Sided Communication Using BlueField DPUs

Ehab Saleh[(✉)], Amir Raoofy, and Josef Weidendorfer

Leibniz Supercomputing Centre, Munich, Germany
{ehab.saleh,amir.raoofy,josef.weidendorfer}@lrz.de

Abstract. In the context of the Message Passing Interface (MPI), most implementations employ one of the following three mechanisms to ensure strong communication progress: using a background thread, dedicating a hardware core, or relying on the application to make frequent MPI test calls, such as MPI_Test, MPI_Testany, MPI_Testall, etc.. These mechanisms continuously ensure progress in communication operations by processing pending tasks, updating completion queues, and handling necessary callback functions, resulting in effective computation and communication overlap. However, these methods may lead to hardware resource consumption, which could otherwise be used for computation, while also increasing context switches between the main thread and the asynchronous progress thread. In this paper, we leverage the ARM cores integrated within NVIDIA's InfiniBand BlueField Data Processing Unit (DPU) to offload the communication progress in non-blocking two-sided communication. This approach is implemented using Unified Communication X (UCX), leveraging the Unified Communication Protocols (UCP) API. Compared to Open MPI and MPICH, our results indicate that this approach significantly improves the overlap between communication and computation in scenarios with multiple non-blocking send and receive requests, achieving close to 100% overlap. Additionally, we observed an improvement in the solving time for the Jacobi 2D solver applied to massive grid sizes. This improvement is especially significant when compared to MPICH with asynchronous progress thread enabled, where we achieve more than a 50% reduction in the solving time.

Keywords: High-Performance Computing · Message Passing Interface · UCX · BlueField

1 Introduction

The InfiniBand architecture introduces the zero-copy mechanism, enabling direct data transfers from the network adapter to the application memory, bypassing the kernel memory. This is accomplished through two core InfiniBand semantics: Remote Direct Memory Access (RDMA) and Send/Receive.

RDMA semantics, also referred to as memory semantics, support two operations: RDMA Read and RDMA Write. The incoming data are processed by the adapter without involving the host CPU. In addition, these data include information about their destination, so the receiver side does not need to intervene in data placement in its memory. This lack of intervention is the reason why RDMA is referred to as one-sided semantics. On the other hand, Send/Receive semantics require active participation from both sides of the communication: the source node sends a message, while the destination node specifies where the data should be placed in the memory. This participation on both sides for data transfer is the reason why it is also termed two-sided semantics.

Both InfiniBand RDMA and Send/Receive semantics support zero-copy operations, eliminating extra memory copies, and improving performance. Certain network adapters, such as those from Mellanox, demonstrate similar bandwidth and latency for both semantics [6], leaving the choice of semantics to the developer based on application requirements. However, RDMA is typically favored for large data transfers because of its ability to function without requiring remote side involvement. In contrast, Send/Receive semantics are generally better suited for smaller data transfers [10].

MPI, the de-facto standard for message passing in distributed memory architectures, does not define the low-level semantics of its implementation. However, two common protocols have emerged to match the semantics for data transfer: Eager and Rendezvous. The Eager protocol transmits the entire message from the sender to the receiver, making it well suited for small messages that fit within the sender's buffer. In contrast, Rendezvous is used for larger messages, where the CPU passes only the memory address of the data to the NIC, which then handles the transfer of data from that address to the receiver. This process involves the exchange of control messages prior to transferring the data over the wire. However, progressing rendezvous requests requires continuous monitoring of their status to ensure the progress required by the standard. For blocking communication calls, this can be guaranteed as the call blocks until the communication is completed. However, with non-blocking communication calls, the communication context is divided into two phases: initialization and completion, allowing computation to occur in between. Since the MPI standard does not specify where progress should occur–whether during initialization, completion, or in between–some implementations keep communication blocked until the completion phase, preventing any overlap between communication and computation [9].

Progressing non-blocking MPI calls can be achieved using one of three approaches: employing a background thread alongside the main thread, dedicating one or more hardware cores, or requiring the developer to periodically invoke MPI_Test after initiating communication. However, these methods introduce additional computational overhead, potentially diverting resources from computation tasks, and increase the complexity of the application.

In InfiniBand architecture, Completion Queues (CQs) play a crucial role in managing and tracking the progress of communication operations, particularly for send/receive and RDMA operations. Given that these CQs are exclusively shared between endpoints that use the same InfiniBand's Host Channel Adapter(HCA), and the completion of a send request on the sender side corresponds directly to the completion of the related receive request on the receiver side, this paper introduces a new approach for tracking the status of requests of non-blocking two-sided communication. Our approach leverages ARM cores residing in the BlueField DPUs on the receiver side as progress engines for managing send requests. To do so, we utilize the callback mechanism provided by the UCP API to notify the progress engine with the completion of send requests. This approach eliminates the need for a dedicated progress engine on the sender side for each send request, thereby freeing up computational resources to focus solely on computation. In summary, the key contributions of this paper are as follows.

- Propose a novel approach for progressing non-blocking two-sided communication using BlueField DPUs.
- Utilize the receiver-side DPUs to track the completion status of all sender's requests, eliminating the need for running a progress engine on the sender side.
- Optimize communication and computation overlap by efficiently integrating the proposed design with RDMA-based rendezvous data transfer.
- Evaluate the proposed design against state-of-the-art MPI implementations, including MPICH and Open MPI.

We show that, in applications with multiple non-blocking send and receive operations, the proposed approach optimizes resource utilization, ensuring maximum availability for computational tasks.

2 Related Work

Certain MPI implementations, like Open MPI, MVAPICH, MPICH and Intel MPI, provide users with the option to activate a dedicated background thread that polls for communication progress in a continuous loop[1].

Several studies have proposed new approaches to improve the efficiency of communication progress [3,13], and [1]. Specifically, these approaches focus on managing the communication progress of two-sided communication on the host side, either by utilizing a dedicated hardware core or by minimizing context switches between the main thread and the progress thread.

Significant efforts have been made to utilize Smart NICs to offload networking tasks. The authors of BluesMPI [2] present a high-performance design that offloads the MPI_Ialltoall operations from the host CPU to the Smart NIC, achieving complete overlap of communication and computation, and demonstrating notable performance improvements in benchmarks and applications.

---

[1] The latest versions of Open MPI abstracts the details of its progress thread away, but users can still enable or disable hardware-based tag matching (Hardware Tag Matching) [8], when using RDMA NICs, as the only way to offload part of the communication procedure.

Graham et al. developed the Multi-tenant Intelligent Modular Offload Service Architecture (MIMOSA) [3] [12], which employs a modified version of UCX to offload both blocking and non-blocking collective algorithms in the Unified Collective Communication (UCC) library [11].

3 BlueField Smart NICs

Mellanox was a pioneer in introducing InfiniBand network cards with zero-copy capabilities, notably found in the ConnectX series. In 2016, Mellanox launched the first network card featuring a row of ARM cores integrated alongside other network components on a single chip, known as the Data Processing Unit (DPU). After NVIDIA acquired Mellanox in 2020, they released the BlueField-2 series DPUs [7], aimed at maximizing network bandwidth utilization and reducing communication latency.

Figure 1 shows the functional diagram of the NVIDIA BlueField-2 DPU. The ConnectX adapter is connected to both the ARM subsystem and the host through a physical PCIe switch. This configuration allows the same NIC to be accessed directly from the host or through the ARM subsystem, depending on the DPU operation mode.

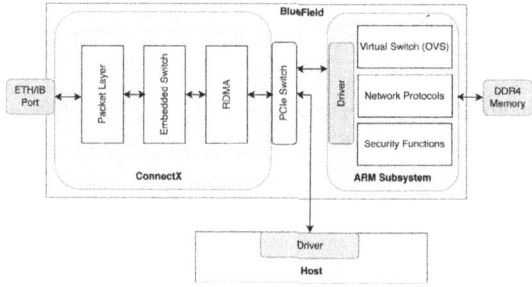

Fig. 1. Functional Diagram of NVIDIA BlueField-2 DPU.

When Ethernet networking is enabled in the DPU, all host traffic is first routed through the virtual switches of the ARM subsystem before reaching the external port. However, Open Virtual Switch (OVS) rules can be offloaded to the embedded switches within the ConnectX adapter, significantly improving latency. In InfiniBand mode, OVS does not handle traffic routing; instead, the host can transmit data directly to the external port, bypassing the ARM subsystem.

4 Proposed Design

The latest MPI standard defines the metadata that must be included within the sent message. This metadata is extracted on the receiver's side to enable selective identification and differentiation of messages. It consists of a fixed set of fields that collectively form the message envelope. These fields are **source**, **destination**, **tag**, and **communicator** [5, p. 35–36]. In all MPI implementations, the destination, tag, and communicator are explicitly specified as parameters in the MPI_Send function, while the source is implicitly determined by the sender's ID. Therefore, when using a lower-level API like UCP for sending or receiving messages, it is essential to embed this information manually if there are no dedicated parameters to specify it.

In UCP library, the simplest form of send and receive operations are as follow:

```
ucs_status_ptr_t
ucp_tag_send_nbx(ucp_ep_h ep, const void *buffer, size_t
    count, ucp_tag_t tag, const ucp_request_param_t *param)
```

```
ucs_status_ptr_t
ucp_tag_recv_nbx(ucp_worker_h worker, void *buffer, size_t
    count, ucp_tag_t tag, ucp_tag_t tag_mask, const
    ucp_request_param_t *param)
```

Both ucp_tag_send_nbx and ucp_tag_recv_nbx are non-blocking operations for sending and receiving messages, respectively. They return NULL if the operation completes immediately (e.g., eager send or eager expected receive, respectively). Otherwise, they return a request handle to the application, which can be used to track the progress of the operation (e.g., rendezvous send/receive).

The receiver acts as a listener for any message that matches a specified tag. As there is no dedicated parameter to explicitly define the source endpoint ID, we can incorporate it within the tag field. Thus, in our UCP-based message-passing send call, the tag field, represented as a uint64_t, should encapsulate all necessary details about the sender, including the tag value, sender ID(endpoint ID), and work ID, structured as follows[2]:

Endpoint ID (32-bit)	Tag Value (20-bit)	Work ID (12-bit)

This tag format ensures that the receiver matches only messages originating from a specific sender, eliminating any possibility of matching messages from senders with different IDs. In our experiments, all tags share the same Work ID but differ in Tag Value and Endpoint ID. The Work ID identifies a group of endpoints working together on a shared task. In MPI, this corresponds to communicators to which the ranks belong.

The proposed approach of offloading communication progress to the DPU is illustrated in Fig. 2. We leverage the RDMA-based rendezvous data transmission, where the sender submits a UCP send request to the HCA. Similarly, it is assumed that the receiver posts a matching UCP receive request (expected receive) to its HCA. The Rendezvous protocol entails the sender initially sending a control message Ready to Send (RTS). The RTS control message includes embedded information such as the virtual

---

[2] In MPI standard, the upper bound value of tag must be at least 32767 [p. 443] [5], which is around 15 bit.

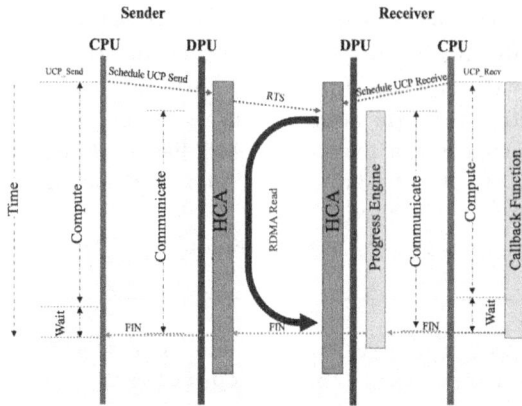

Fig. 2. The proposed offloading sender requests to the DPU.

address and memory handle of the buffer to be sent and once the receiver is ready, the actual data is transferred, typically using RDMA operations.

Each endpoint on the sender side operates with a dedicated thread running on one of the ARM cores of the DPU. The DPU in this setup is selected to be on the receiver side[3]. This thread monitors incoming messages from the receiver's callback function (FIN) and extracts the sender's Tag Value and Endpoint ID from the tag embedded in the FIN notification. After receiving the FIN notification from the callback function, the progress engine prepares another confirmation notification (FIN) to be sent to the corresponding sender's endpoint HCA[4]. The functionality of the progress engine is described in Algorithm 1.

Algorithm 1: Progress Engine Functionality.

Input: Receive Queue with tagged messages
Output: Confirmation message sent to the sender
1 **while** *true* **do**
2   *Polling for Progress()*;
3   **if** *A tagged message exists in the Receive Queue* **then**
4   Extract *tag_number* and *sender_id* from the message;
5   Send a FIN message to *sender_id* with *tag_number*;
6   **end**
7 **end**

It is worth to mention here that the progress engine is specifically designed to notify the sender about the completion of its requests. Unlike traditional progress engines that poll for completions, this design avoids such an approach because the ARM cores lack access to the completion queues of the sender and receiver queues on any HCA.

---

[3] In our design, this selection was made arbitrarily. Alternatively, the progress engine could be placed on the DPU on the sender's side.
[4] On the sender's side, the confirmation message can be checked at any time, such as during the MPI_Wait operation in our case. Furthermore, this confirmation message can be accessed and verified at any point in the execution.

5 Experimental Setup

We implemented and evaluated our proposed approach on a system consisting of four nodes, all having the same CPU architecture and BlueField-2 adapter. As shown in Fig. 3, these nodes are connected in a single-level tree topology using a 200 Gb/s InfiniBand switch.

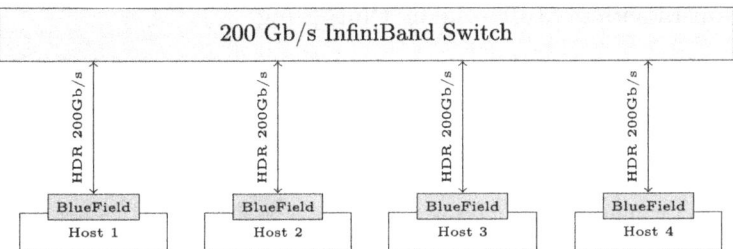

Fig. 3. Computing system composed of four nodes connected through an InfiniBand switch using HDR 200Gb/s cables - hosts include 2 Intel Xeon 8360Y processors each with 36 cores.

We have chosen Open MPI and MPICH, the two prominent open-source MPI implementations, as reference points for evaluating and comparing our approach. All nodes are running the same version of Open MPI (v4.1.7a1) and MPICH(4.3.0b1) built with UCX (Library version: 1.14.0). When running MPI applications, we have chosen the UCX transport layer as Dynamic Connected (DC), which is optimized to provide reliability, low-latency, and high-throughput communication for both one-sided and two-sided operations. To minimize any potential overhead that could affect performance, we have enabled hardware tag matching and offloaded it to the network adapter.

We also evaluated the design against MPICH with the asynchronous progress thread enabled, configuring it to automatically assign available logical CPU cores. In this setup, MPICH determines the affinity of progress threads by dynamically selecting logical CPU cores.

When evaluating our solution (based on the UCP API) we have applied the same UCX configuration as with Open MPI, including the transport layer selection and offloading of tag matching.

We ran the following three main experiments:

5.1 Non-blocking Two-player Ping-Pong

Initially, we measure and record the time required to complete non-blocking send and receive operations, referred to as the pure communication time. This measurement is later used as a reference when conducting a similar experiment that involves a dummy computation following the non-blocking send and receive operations. The dummy computation involves matrix multiplication designed to take approximately the same time as pure communication. This setup facilitates the calculation of the overlap ratio between communication and computation as described in Intel MPI Benchmarks [4]:

$$\text{Overlap\_ratio} = 100 \times \max\left(0, \min\left(1, \frac{t_{\text{Pure\_communication}} + t_{\text{Computation}} - t_{\text{Overlap}}}{\min\left(t_{\text{Pure\_communication}}, t_{\text{Computation}}\right)}\right)\right) \quad (1)$$

where $t_{\text{Pure\_communication}}$ represents the duration of pure communication, $t_{\text{Computation}}$ denotes the time spent on computation, and t_{Overlap} corresponds to the period during which communication and computation overlapped. The message sizes range from 1 MB to 1 GB. Additionally, for each message size, we run the experiment 1000 times, skipping the first 100 iterations to eliminate any overhead caused by initial communication warm-up.

5.2 Non-blocking Multi-player Ping-Pong

This experiment replicates the previous setup, but instead of using just two processes on two nodes, it utilizes all the available nodes in our computing system. As shown in Fig. 4, the processes in this experiment are arranged in a perfect square grid, ensuring that each process has at least two neighboring processes, and some processes have up to four neighboring processes.

The total number of processes is selected as a perfect square to facilitate an even distribution of work among processes, ensuring a balanced workload. Consequently, the number of processes per node (PPN) is set to 1, 4, 9, 16, 36, and 64.

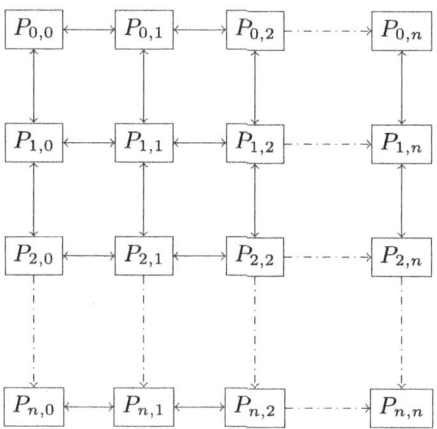

Fig. 4. Organizing processes in a perfect square layout in the Multi-Player Ping-Pong benchmark.

5.3 2D Jacobi Solver

In the previous two non-blocking ping-pong experiments, it was assumed by default that the pure communication time was equal to the computation time. However, this assumption does not always hold in real-world scenarios, where communication time may exceed the workload to be processed or vice versa. In this experiment, we use the same process mapping shown in Fig. 4 to run a 2D Jacobi solver. In this case, the amount of computation is significantly larger compared to communication, and this is because we follow the normal execution of Jacobi 2D, where the volume of data exchanged is limited to the size of a single row (sent/received to the top and bottom) and a single column (sent/received to the left and right).

The experiment was carried out with 64 processes per node, requiring a number of progress threads on the DPU that exceeded the available physical ARM cores. The experiments used grid sizes of 100K × 100K, 150K × 150K, and 200K × 200K, each containing double numbers. In all cases, we run 150 Jacobi iterations.

6 Experimental Evaluation

Figure 5 illustrates the overlapping ratio, pure communication time, and overlapping time observed when running the non-blocking ping-pong benchmark. We note that both the offloading approach and MPICH-Async-Enabled achieve higher overlapping ratios compared to Open MPI and MPICH-Default. Nevertheless, the MPICH-Async-Enabled achieves a higher overlapping ratio compared to our approach for smaller message sizes. In contrast, Open MPI and MPICH-Default failed to guarantee communication overlap, even when offloading tag matching to the network adapter.

The pure communication times across all implementations are nearly identical, confirming that our approach neither introduces additional communication latency nor reduces it even when utilizing a lower-level APIs.

The overlapping time, however, highlights both Open MPI and MPICH-Default inability to progress communication efficiency. The results show that the message delivery latency increases significantly when computation is involved with non-blocking communication.

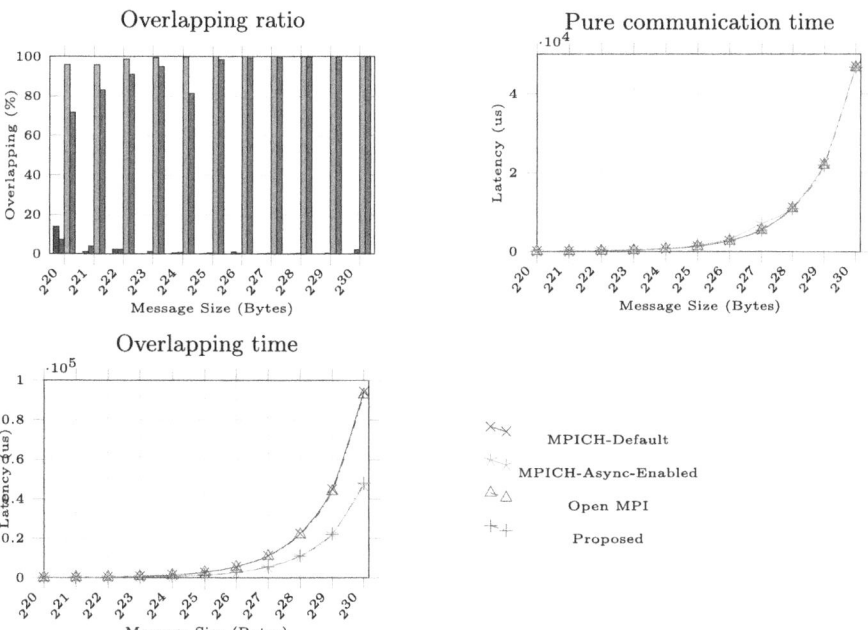

Fig. 5. Pure communication time, overlapping time and overlapping ratio of the non-blocking Ping-pong benchmark

Figure 6 presents the overlapping ratio for the multi-player ping-pong experiment with varying numbers of processes per host in our network. We observe that both the proposed approach and the MPICH-Async-Enabled exhibit a similar trend, achieving 100% overlap across all tested configurations. In contrast, Open MPI and MPICH-Default show lower overlapping ratios. However, as the number of processes per node increases, MPICH-Default begins to approach higher overlapping ratio at the same level of Open MPI.

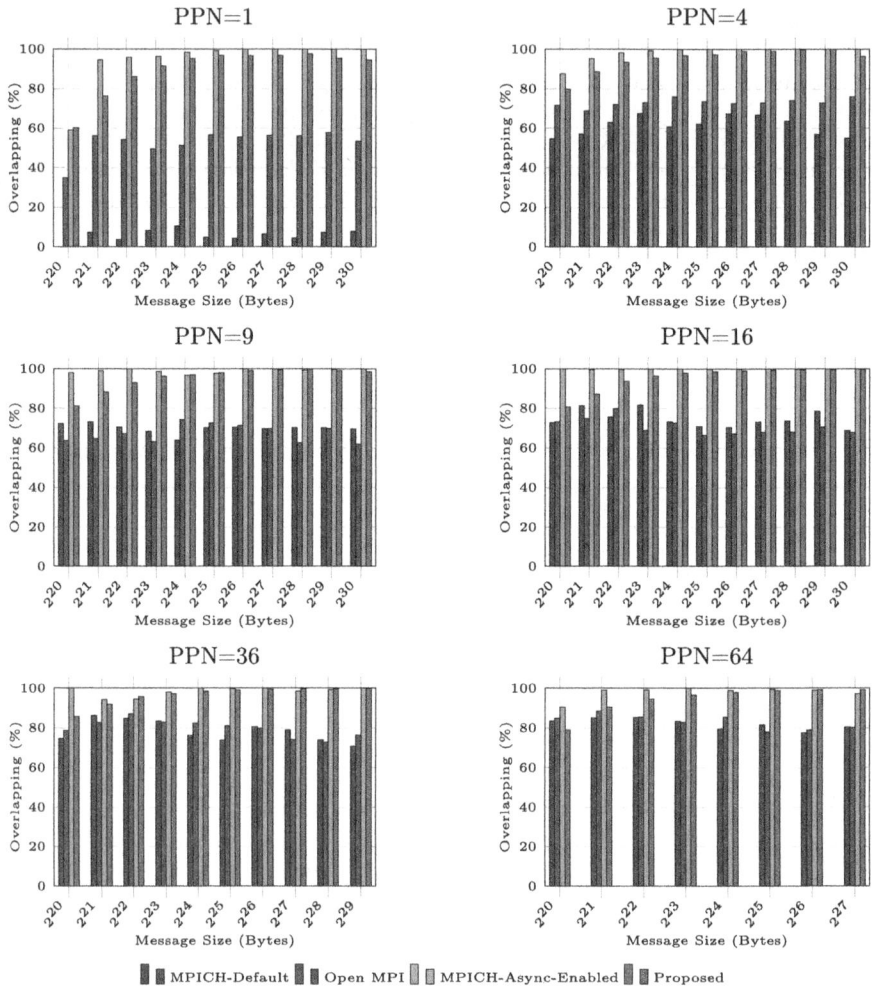

Fig. 6. Overlap ratio of the Multi-player Ping-pong benchmark at varying numbers of processes per node (PPN).

Across all Multi-player Ping-pong experiments, we observe that using our offloading approach keeps the overlapping ratio stable, even as the increasing number of processes on the host side eventually leads to more progressing threads on the DPU than the available ARM cores.

Figure 7 shows the pure communication time when running the same multi-player ping-pong experiments. The proposed method achieves better latency, particularly for larger number of processes per node. However, it is important to note that although our proposed method employs a lower-level API, it does not significantly reduce pure communication time, which is consistent with expected behavior.

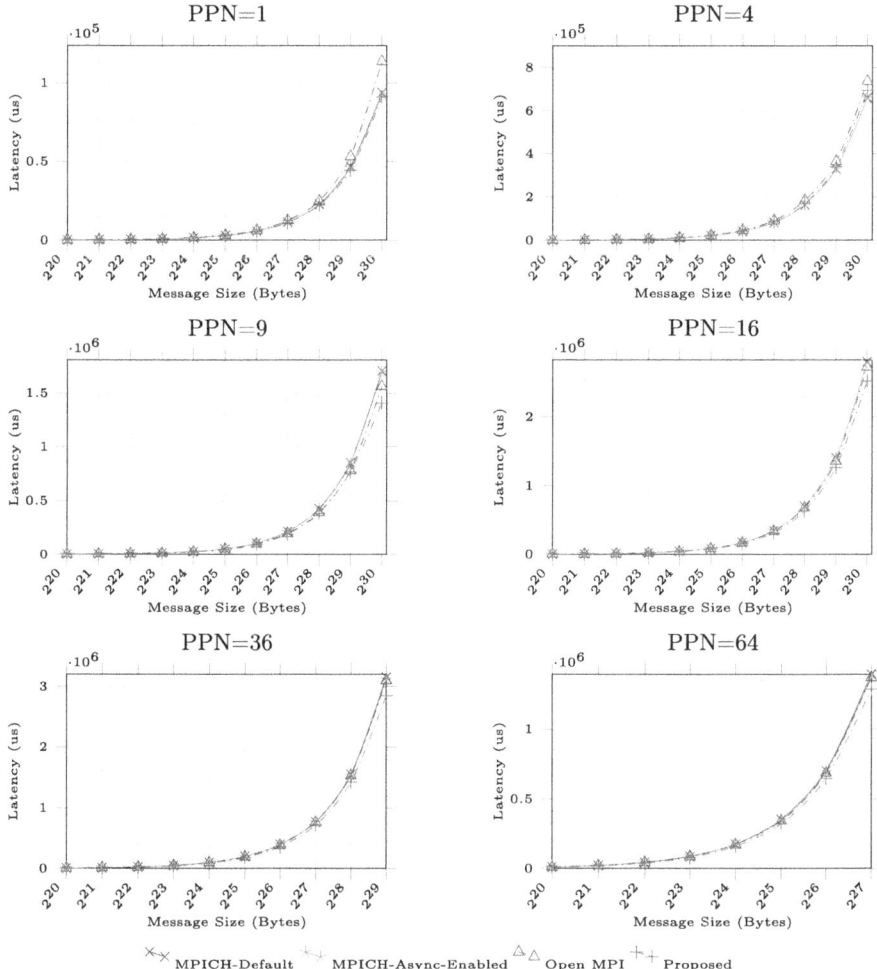

Fig. 7. Pure communication time of Multi-player benchmark at varying numbers of processes per node (PPN).

Figure 8 illustrates the overlapping time across different process counts. We observe that Open MPI and MPICH-Default exhibit similar communication behavior when overlapping with computation. In contrast, both the MPICH-Async-Enabled and our approach achieve better communication performance, with our approach demonstrating a greater reduction in overlapping time compared to the MPICH-Async-Enabled.

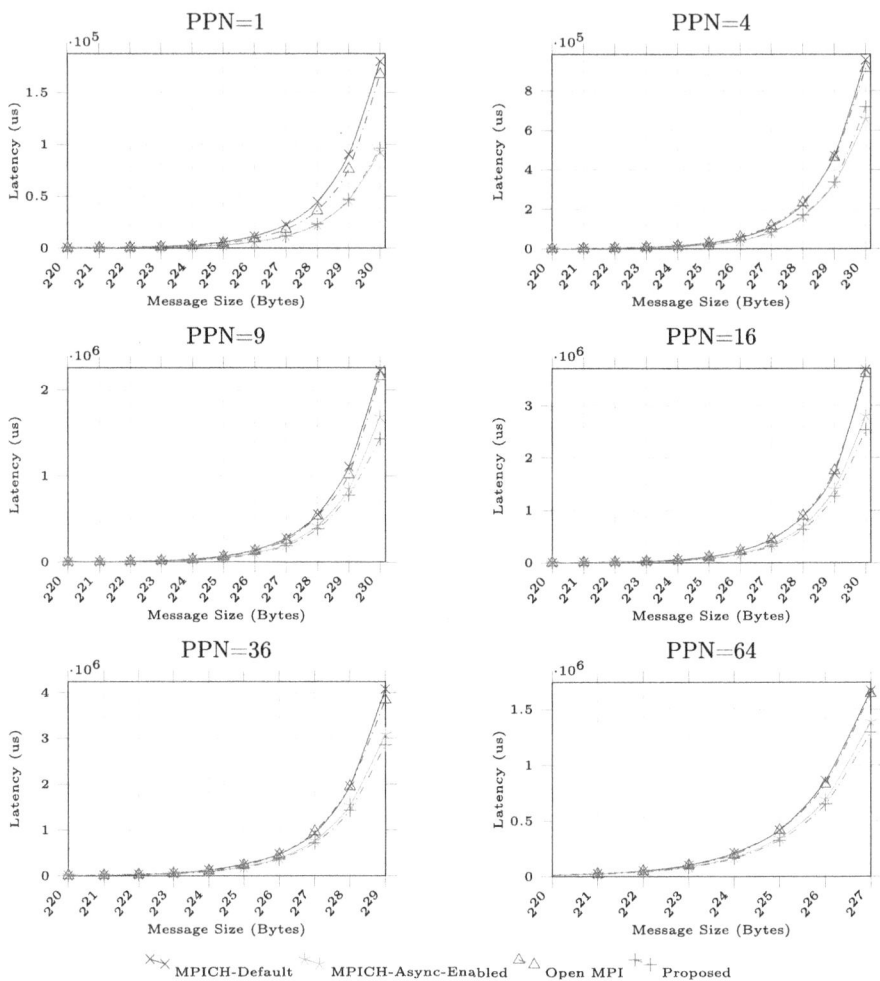

Fig. 8. Overlapping time of Multi-player benchmark at varying numbers of processes per node (PPN).

Based on our observation of Multi-player Ping-pong results, we can conclude that Open MPI does not employ an independent progress thread, as its behavior aligns with that of MPICH-Default, which does not enable the progress thread by default.

Now, when running the Jacobi 2D experiment at the aforementioned grid sizes, we recorded the results shown in Table 1. We can notice that our proposed approach demonstrates significant performance improvements across all tested grid sizes compared to existing MPI implementations. The improvements are particularly notable when compared to the MPICH-Async-Enabled implementation, where our approach achieves substantial reductions in execution time, with improvements reaching up to 54.16% for the largest grid size (200K × 200K). Additionally, for MPICH-Default, our approach achieves up to 14.65% improvement for the 100K × 100K grid and 9.52% for the 150K × 150K grid.

These results highlight that while both our approach and the MPICH-Async-Enabled exhibit similar communication performance in the tested benchmarks, the MPICH-Async-Enabled fails to maintain this performance when the number of processes increases and the computational workload grows relative to the volume of communication exchanged. In such a scenario, when the CPU is fully occupied with computation, the MPICH progress thread receives insufficient cycles to advance large number of communication requests, leading to delayed message processing and higher latency.

Table 1. Jacobi 2D Solving Time (T) Comparison Across Grid Sizes (PPN=64).

Grid Size	MPI Implementation	T (ms)	Proposed (ms)	Improvement (%)
$100K \times 100K$	Open MPI	70,264		2.63
	MPICH-Default	80,157	68,412	14.65
	MPICH-Async-Enabled	143,769		52.39
$150K \times 150K$	Open MPI	154,898		1.61
	MPICH-Default	168,425	152,402	9.52
	MPICH-Async-Enabled	327,869		53.50
$200K \times 200K$	Open MPI	269,975		1.29
	MPICH-Default	278,980	266,493	4.49
	MPICH-Async-Enabled	581,315		54.16

7 Conclusion and Future Work

In conclusion, this paper presented a novel approach for offloading the progress engine for non-blocking two-sided communication using BlueField DPUs. By leveraging the RDMA rendezvous protocol and the low-level UCP API, the proposed approach eliminates the need for the sender to handle progress tasks. Instead, it relies on the advanced UCP callback mechanism on the receiver side to seamlessly notify the offloaded progress engine upon request completion. The results of the implementation validated the efficiency of the approach and demonstrated notable improvements in communication-computation overlap, especially in scenarios with multiple send and receive requests, achieving near-complete overlap.

A more advanced approach can be envisioned as future work, building upon the proposed approach. This would involve running a single daemon to manage progress of all sender requests, while also enabling the sender to directly register requests on the remote DPU. The DPU would subsequently poll these requests to monitor and handle their completion.

Additionally, we suggest providing the sub-system on the DPU that has access to the same HCA as the host, with the functionality to read the completion queues of requests running on the host side. By doing this, the ARM cores can function completely as a hardware progress engine, polling the progress and notifying the host. We leave this proposal to NVIDIA for consideration in future versions of BlueField cards.

Acknowledgment. This paper is funded by the ScalNext project, funding number 16ME0687 from the Federal Ministry of Education and Research (BMBF). This includes funding by the European Union - 'NextGenerationEU. Performance results have been obtained on systems in the test environment BEAST (Bavarian Energy Architecture & Software Testbed) at the Leibniz Supercomputing Centre.

References

1. Bayatpour, M., et al.: Communication-aware hardware-assisted MPI overlap engine. In: Sadayappan, P., Chamberlain, B.L., Juckeland, G., Ltaief, H. (eds.) ISC High Performance 2020. LNCS, vol. 12151, pp. 517–535. Springer, Cham (2020). https://doi.org/10.1007/978-3-030-50743-5_26
2. Bayatpour, M., Sarkauskas, N., Subramoni, H., Maqbool Hashmi, J., Panda, D.K.: BluesMPI: efficient MPI non-blocking Alltoall offloading designs on modern BlueField smart NICs. In: Chamberlain, B.L., Varbanescu, A.-L., Ltaief, H., Luszczek, P. (eds.) ISC High Performance 2021. LNCS, vol. 12728, pp. 18–37. Springer, Cham (2021). https://doi.org/10.1007/978-3-030-78713-4_2
3. Graham, R., et al.: Optimizing application performance with bluefield: accelerating large-message blocking and nonblocking collective operations. In: ISC High Performance 2024 Research Paper Proceedings (39th International Conference), pp. 1–12 (2024). https://doi.org/10.23919/ISC.2024.10528935
4. Intel: Measuring communication and computation overlap (2021). https://www.intel.com/content/www/us/en/docs/mpi-library/user-guide-benchmarks/2021-2/measuring-communication-and-computation-overlap.html. Accessed 24 Jan 2025
5. Message Passing Interface Forum: MPI: A Message-Passing Interface Standard Version 4.1 (2023). https://www.mpi-forum.org/docs/mpi-4.1/mpi41-report.pdf
6. NVIDIA: Why compromise? (2006). https://network.nvidia.com/pdf/whitepapers/WP_Why_Compromise_10_26_06.pdf. Accessed 24 Jan 2025
7. NVIDIA Corporation: Data processing unit (dpu) (2025). https://www.nvidia.com/en-us/networking/products/data-processing-unit/. Accessed 24 Jan 2025
8. NVIDIA Corporation: Tag matching verbs api and implementation example (2025). https://enterprise-support.nvidia.com/s/article/tag-matching-verbs-api-and-implementation-example. Accessed 24 Jan 2025
9. Si, M., Balaji, P.: Process-based asynchronous progress model for mpi point-to-point communication. In: 2017 IEEE 19th International Conference on High Performance Computing and Communications; IEEE 15th International Conference on Smart City; IEEE 3rd International Conference on Data Science and Systems (HPCC/SmartCity/DSS), pp. 206–214 (2017). https://doi.org/10.1109/HPCC-SmartCity-DSS.2017.27
10. Sur, S., Jin, H.W., Chai, L., Panda, D.K.: Rdma read based rendezvous protocol for mpi over infiniband: design alternatives and benefits. In: Proceedings of the Eleventh ACM SIGPLAN Symposium on Principles and Practice of Parallel Programming, PPoPP '06, pp. 32–39. Association for Computing Machinery, New York (2006). https://doi.org/10.1145/1122971.1122978

11. UCC Consortium: Ucc - unified collective communication (2025). https://ucfconsortium.org/projects/ucc/. Accessed 24 Jan 2025
12. Yang, Q., Contributors: Dpu offload service (2023). https://github.com/yqin/dpu_offload_service. Accessed 24 Jan 2025
13. Zhou, H., Latham, R., Raffenetti, K., Guo, Y., Thakur, R.: MPI progress for all. In: SC24-W: Workshops of the International Conference for High Performance Computing, Networking, Storage and Analysis, pp. 425–435. IEEE Computer Society, Los Alamitos (2024). https://doi.org/10.1109/SCW63240.2024.00063. https://doi.ieeecomputersociety.org/10.1109/SCW63240.2024.00063

Efficient Parallel Fuzzy Dilation for Visual Reasoning on Edge: Leveraging ARM SIMD Extensions and Embedded GPUs Accelerators

Laurent Cabaret[1](✉), Céline Hudelot[1], Régis Pierrard[2], and Jean-Philippe Poli[3]

[1] CentraleSupélec, Mathematics Interacting with Computer Science, Paris-Saclay University, 91190 Gif-sur-Yvette, France
{laurent.cabaret,celine.hudelot}@centralesupelec.fr
[2] Hugging Face, New York, USA
regis@huggingface.co
[3] Paris-Saclay University, CEA, LIST, 91191 Gif-sur-Yvette cedex, France
jean-philippe.poli@cea.fr

Abstract. Fuzzy spatial relations are increasingly utilized in visual reasoning tasks, such as semantic annotation and object recognition. However, these tasks often rely on compute-intensive fuzzy morphological operators, leading to significant latency during relation evaluation. Addressing this challenge requires optimized implementations that are tailored to modern architectures. Previous works introduced the Reverse (R) and Parallel Reverse (PR) algorithms for Intel processors, leveraging OpenMP and SIMD intrinsics. In this work, we extend these contributions to embedded systems by targeting ARM-based processors and NVIDIA embedded GPUs. Specifically, we propose three architecture-specific implementations: PR64N, using 64-bit NEON SIMD instructions; PR128N, using 128-bit NEON instructions; and PRGPU, a GPU-optimized version based on CUDA. Our evaluation is conducted on the NVIDIA Jetson Orin Nano Super platform, an advanced ARM-based system-on-chip designed for low-power edge AI applications. The results demonstrate that our CPU implementations achieve near-peak performance by fully exploiting the platform's memory bandwidth. Meanwhile, the GPU implementation efficiently offloads fuzzy spatial relation evaluations, allowing the CPU to manage additional workloads. These findings underline the suitability of our methods for enabling visual reasoning tasks on resource-constrained embedded systems and contribute to the broader discussion on addressing heterogeneous architectures with tailored algorithms.

Keywords: Fuzzy dilation · Fuzzy spatial relations · ARM NEON SIMD · Embedded GPU computing

1 Introduction

Spatial knowledge plays an important role in many computer vision systems, as it is essential for understanding the scene [2,6,10]. With the advent of explainable artificial intelligence (XAI), the need for interpretability and explainability [9,11,12] in such systems has been reinforced. The goal of these XAIs is to solve a task and provide an explanation of the result [15,19], as shown in Fig. 1 where the detection of the liver is explained by its relations with other known anatomical objects. The fuzzy logic framework [26] provides efficient tools to represent and process such spatial information [5,24]. In fact, fuzzy logic allows us to represent in a unified way a wide variety of spatial relations [5,18] by taking into account their vagueness and double nature (quantitative and qualitative). Several of these relations rely on a fuzzy morphological dilation (directional relations [3], distances [4] and more complex relationships like parallelism or alignment [23]). Fuzzy dilation generates a *fuzzy landscape* [3] where the value of each pixel represents to what extent it verifies the relationship under study, as shown in Fig. 1 (top-right image) for the relation *to the left of the liver*. For a given reference object, this fuzzy landscape is generated once and then used to evaluate all relations of the type *x to the left of the liver* with all other objects. To generate explanations as in Fig. 1 on a set of images, the most relevant relations between objects are extracted from a training set of images by computing one landscape per image, per object and per investigated relation. For reference, with six objects as in Fig. 1 and considering 5 relations (*left, right, above, under, close to*), 30 fuzzy landscapes are necessary for one image. With the complexity of the scene and the size of the training set, the number of landscapes to compute can then easily escalate, hence the importance to create new algorithms able to support a real-time usage. Moreover, the standard fuzzy morphological dilation is computationally intensive and, therefore, many approximate methods have been proposed to compute it efficiently [3,25]. In [17], the authors proposed an efficient and exact fuzzy dilation algorithm based on a change of perspective on the algorithm to reduce computations, the adaptation to multiple core programming (using OpenMP) and vector extensions (AVX/AVX2/AVX512) of modern heavy loads X86 processors. The increasing deployment of artificial intelligence (AI) algorithms on edge devices [13] has created a growing demand for Explainable Edge AI (XEdgeAI). To facilitate this paradigm shift, it is essential to develop algorithms that can operate efficiently within the distinct computational and memory constraints inherent to edge devices, which deviate significantly from those of traditional cloud-based servers or desktop computers used in [17].

In this article, we target the embedded AI applications of fuzzy landscapes and provide a NEON optimized set of algorithms PR64N (64-bit SIMD NEON instructions) and PR128N (128-bit SIMD NEON instructions); additionally, we provide a GPU version based on CUDA to both offload fuzzy computations and provide fuzzy spatial relations capabilities to existing GPU context applications.

The remainder of the paper is organized as follows. In Sect. 2, we present the fuzzy dilation operator. In Sect. 3 we present the related algorithms. Our propositions are detailed in Sect. 4 followed by the benchmark description and the discussion of the results in Sect. 5. We conclude in Sect. 6.

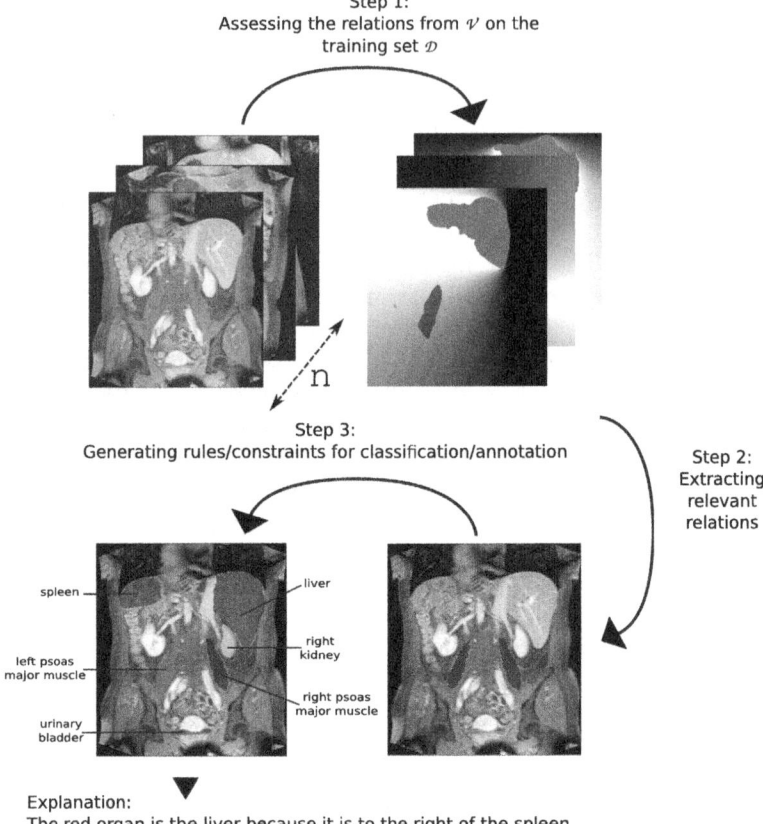

Fig. 1. Example of explainable organ annotation [15]. Given a set of six objects and a set of spatial relations, annotation generation is based on the evaluation of a set of relations between all the objects in the image. The top-left images are the unannotated input images, The top-right images represent how a specific relation between two objects is evaluated. The bottom-right represent a relation between two elements, The bottom-left represent the annotated image based on all the relevant relationships evaluations.

2 Fuzzy Dilation Operator

Like the dilation operator in mathematical morphology [22], the fuzzy dilation operator is the result of set-theoretic operations between an input image (representing the reference object on which the dilation is performed) and a structuring element (specifying the nature of the dilation). The result of the fuzzy dilation is represented by a fuzzy landscape, which is a fuzzy set whose membership function represents to which extent each pixel belongs to the dilation. Objects can also be represented as fuzzy landscapes. For instance, Fig. 2c displays the fuzzy landscape corresponding to the dilation of membership function $D_\nu(\mu)$ (dilation of μ by ν). The membership functions μ and ν associated respectively to the

(a) Fuzzy landscape corresponding to the membership function μ associated to the reference object.

(b) Fuzzy landscape corresponding to the structuring element associated to the relation *close to* and represented by the membership function ν.

(c) Fuzzy landscape corresponding to the dilation of μ by ν associated to the membership function $D_\nu(\mu)$ (μ in red).

Fig. 2. Fuzzy dilation $D_\nu(\mu)$ (Fig. 2c) of the reference object μ (Fig. 2a) by the structuring element ν (Fig. 2b). The spatial relation represented here is *close to*. The intensity of each pixel of $D_\nu(\mu)$ represents to which extent it satisfies the relation. The structuring element needs to be 4 times as big as the reference objet fuzzy landscape.

reference object and the structuring element are displayed in Fig. 2a and Fig. 2b respectively.

Let S be the space of the image. The fuzzy dilation of μ by ν, called $D_\nu(\mu)$, can then be defined as in [3]

$$\forall x \in S, D_\nu(\mu)(x) = \sup_{y \in S} \left[t(\nu(x-y), \mu(y)) \right] \quad (1)$$

with μ and ν crisp or fuzzy objects and t a t-norm. Several t-norms are defined in the fuzzy logic literature. In this paper, we use the most common one, the *Zadeh* t-norm, which is the *minimum*. Besides, since we work on images, S is a finite set so the *supremum* is equivalent to the *maximum*. Thus, the expression we actually implemented is the following

$$\forall x \in S, D_\nu(\mu)(x) = \max_{y \in S} \left[\min(\nu(x-y), \mu(y)) \right] \quad (2)$$

The main advantage of fuzzy dilation is that various spatial relations, such as distances and relative directional positions between objects, can be computed with the same dilation operator by using different structuring elements. For example, in the case of directional relations, a commonly used structuring element is

$$\forall x \in S, \nu(x) = \max\left(0, 1 - \frac{2}{\pi} \arccos \frac{\vec{x} \times \vec{u_\alpha}}{||\vec{x}||}\right) \quad (3)$$

with $\vec{u_\alpha}$ a unit vector in the direction α and $\vec{x}$ the vector from the origin (the center of the structuring element) to x. In Fig. 2, another type of relation is expressed: *close to* μ. To assess if another object of membership function λ is close to μ, a fuzzy pattern matching approach is performed [7]. For instance, in Fig. 1, for a reference object μ (in red) and another object λ (in blue), the relation λ *to the left of* μ can be evaluated as the fuzzy degree of intersection between λ and $D_\nu(\mu)$ thus the degree of realization of the evaluated proposition.

The two main advantages of this fuzzy-landscape-based approach are its ability to manage any relation that can be generated with a fuzzy dilation and the fact that only one landscape has to be generated for a given relation and a given reference object. Thus, in Fig. 1, the relation x *to the left of the liver* (reference object in red) can be computed for all x in the set of 6 objects in Fig. 1 with a single landscape generation.

3 Related Algorithms

3.1 Forward Algorithm the Accuracy Reference

The *Forward* algorithm (Algorithm 1) is the direct application of Eq. 2 as described in the original paper on fuzzy directional dilations [3]. Three data structures representing 2D images (Fig. 2) are involved: D(N×M) which holds the resulting dilated image (fuzzy landscape), μ(N×M) the input image containing the reference object and ν(2N×2M) the structuring element which is 4 times larger than D and μ to generate all configurations of dilated pixels and input pixels. The computation of each pixel of D leads to the application of the structuring element to all pixels of μ, regardless of whether they belong to the contributing object or not. Thus, $(NM)^2$ max/min operations have to be performed, leading to a high computation time. Furthermore, while D is scanned forward (from top left to bottom right), μ is also scanned forward but ν is scanned backwards (line 6 in Algorithm 1), leading to inefficient CPU cache usage and inefficient vectorization.

Algorithm 1. Forward algorithm

Require: μ, D, ν
Ensure: D
1: **for** $i \leftarrow 0$ to $N-1$ **do**
2:    **for** $j \leftarrow 0$ to $M-1$ **do**
3:       **for** $k \leftarrow 0$ to $N-1$ **do**
4:          **for** $m \leftarrow 0$ to $M-1$ **do**
5:             $val \leftarrow \mu[k][m]$
6:             $se \leftarrow \nu[N+i-k][M+j-m]$
7:             $D[i][j] \leftarrow max(min(val, se), D[i][j])$

3.2 Reverse Algorithm

The *Reverse* algorithm (Algorithm 2) reorders the operations to eliminate unnecessary processing: a pixel with a zero value in the input image ($val = \mu(y) = 0$) does not contribute to $D_\nu(\mu)$ as $min(\nu(y-x), \mu(y)) = 0$ (cf. Eq. 2), unlike in the *Forward* algorithm, where those pixels cannot be separated from the contributing ones (active pixels).

Algorithm 2. Reverse algorithm

Require: μ, D, ν
Ensure: D
1: **for** $i \leftarrow 0$ to $N-1$ **do**
2:     **for** $j \leftarrow 0$ to $M-1$ **do**
3:         $val \leftarrow \mu[i][j]$
4:         **if** $val > 0$ **then**
5:             $posx \leftarrow N-i$
6:             $posy \leftarrow M-j$
7:             **for** $k \leftarrow 0$ to $N-1$ **do**
8:                 **for** $m \leftarrow 0$ to $M-1$ **do**
9:                     $se \leftarrow \nu[posx+k][posy+m]$
10:                   $D[k][m] \leftarrow max(min(val, se), D[k][m])$

By processing the computation based on the input image (μ) rather than the dilated image D, one can detect and drop all computations related to these non-contributing pixels (lines 3 and 4 in Algorithm 2). So, based on the same equation (Eq. 2), val is evaluated once per pixel. Then, its contribution to the dilation is evaluated over D with the structuring element centered around the position of the input pixel (line 9 in Algorithm 2). Due to the associative properties of the min and max operators, the final result is exactly the same as that of the *Forward* algorithm. The processing time of the fuzzy landscape does not depend on the fuzziness, position, and shape of the object. Only, the number of pixels of the reference object affects the number of max/min operations. For an object of size p pixels belonging to a $N \times M$ input image, only $p \times N \times M$ max/min operations are executed, providing an immediate acceleration factor based on the object size ratio to the whole image. Furthermore, ν and D are both scanned forward (lines 3 and 9 in Algorithm 2), which induces better cache usage and a direct SIMD alignment.

3.3 PR: Parallel Reverse Algorithm

The high-level code transformation in *Reverse*, allows an efficient usage of multiple cores and vector instructions (SIMD). Reorganizing the computations paves the way for separate processing of different parts of D (the output fuzzy landscape) by different threads, avoiding potential race conditions. It also guarantees coalescent reading of D and ν (the structuring element centered on the current active pixel at the i-th row and j-th column) and coalescent writing of D, putting us in the best possible position for the vectorization. Then, for each pixel where $\mu(i,j) = val > 0$ (active pixels), PR uses the OpenMP parallelization framework [8] to dispatch the computations of D over each core using a strip based spatial decomposition as shown in Fig. 3 and in Algorithm 3 (from line 9 to line 14).

Although auto-vectorization can accelerate straightforward algorithms [1] and was enabled, the authors have shown that explicit vectorization of PR provides substantial performance gains on server architectures supporting AVX (128-bit), AVX2 (256 bit), and AVX-512 (512 bit) instructions. The acceleration provided by explicit vectorization of AVX512 (PR512) over implicit vectorization on the same machine (Intel Xeon CPU 6148 - 20 cores - fixed 2.4 GHz frequency) is: x6.6 for a 4096-pixel centered fuzzy square in a 256×256 image, x8.4 for a 4096-pixel centered fuzzy square in a 512×512 image, and x15.3 for a 4096-pixel centered fuzzy square in a 1024×1024 image. For reference, compared to the forward version, the vectorized accelerations are respectively ($\times(1.4 \times 10^4)$, $\times(19.5 \times 10^3)$, and $\times(15.8 \times 10^4)$).

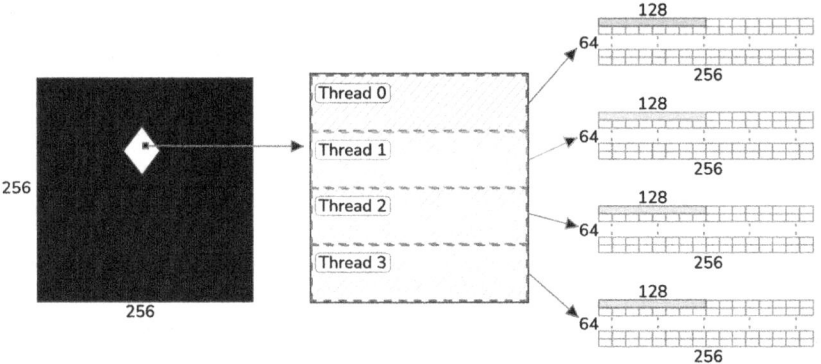

Fig. 3. Contribution to the fuzzy dilation of one active pixel (red square) from the reference object (on the left). For the sake of this illustration, only 4 threads and 128-bit SIMD registers are represented. (Color figure online)

4 Proposed Algorithms

Compared to large HPC servers, embedded architectures present distinct performance trade-offs. The vast majority of these platforms are based on ARM architectures and feature compact, power-efficient GPUs that differ significantly from the high-end GPU cards used in HPC systems. As AI workloads continue to shift towards edge computing, we now present optimized versions of Parallel Reverse for embedded architectures. We introduce three novel variants of Parallel Reverse: PR64N, a specialized version optimized for NEON SIMD 64-bit intrinsics, PR128N, a specialized version optimized for NEON SIMD 128-bit intrinsics, and a GPU-accelerated version built on CUDA designed to leverage the capabilities of embedded GPUs.

4.1 PR64N and PR128N

Auto-Vectorization Reference. The relevant portion of the code candidate for vectorization is situated between lines 12 and 14 of Algorithm 3. The corresponding code, without explicit vectorization, is given in the Listing 1.1. With

Algorithm 3. Parallel Reverse algorithm

Require: μ, D, ν
Ensure: D
1: #omp parallel
2:   **for** $i \leftarrow 0$ to $N-1$ **do**
3:     **for** $j \leftarrow 0$ to $M-1$ **do**
4:       $val \leftarrow \mu[i][j]$
5:       **if** $val > 0$ **then**
6:         $posx \leftarrow N - i$
7:         $posy \leftarrow M - j$
8:         #omp for
9:         **for** $b \leftarrow 0$ to nthreads **do**
10:           $posxb \leftarrow posx + b * (N/nthreads)$
11:           **for** $k \leftarrow 0$ to $N/nthreads$ **do**
12:             **for** $m \leftarrow 0$ to $M-1$ **do**
13:               $se \leftarrow \nu[posxb+k][posy+m]$
14:               $D[k][m] \leftarrow max(min(val, se), D[k][m])$

auto-vectorization enabled at compile time, PR leverage the auto-vectorization capabilities of the compiler (gcc version 11.4.0 on the Jetson Orin Nano Super platform with JetPack6.2). The resulting executable will serve as a performance reference point to evaluate the performance of each explicit vectorization version. All images are 8-bit.

Listing 1.1. PR code without intrinsics for auto-vectorization

```
for (auto m = 0; m < width; m++) {
    auto contrib = std::min(val, nu[xb+k][y+m]);
    D[k+b*(N/PU)][m] = std::max(D[k+b*(N/PU)][m], contrib);}
```

PR64N uses the 64-bit intrinsics NEON extension set. The specific instructions used are listed in the Table 1 and the Fig. 4. The implementation is described in Listing 1.2. Line 1 - Before the loop, for each pixels ou μ where $val > 0$, `val` (8-bit) is broadcast on each lane of `vals` a 64-bit vector (a `uint8x8_t` containing eight 8-bit elements) using `vdup_n_u8`. Line 3 - The loop on m will advance by eight elements at each step according to the number of elements by vector. Line 4 - Eight consecutive values of the structuring element ν are then loaded in one operation in `se` (`uint8x8_t`) using `vld1_u8`. Line 5 - The pairwise minimum is calculated for each element of the vector between `vals` and `se` using `vmin_u8`. Line 6 - 8 consecutive elements of D the fuzzy landscape are loaded into d. Line 7 - The pairwise maximum between d and `contribution` is keep in `contribution` using `vmax_u8`. Line 8 - Then the eight values of `contribution` are stored back into D contiguously using `vst1_u8`. Note: if the width of the images is not a multiple of eight, the end of line can be computed with the same scalar code as the auto version.

Listing 1.2. PR64N using intrinscics (64bits - 8 uint8)

```
auto vals = vdup_n_u8(val); // Before #pragma omp for
...
for (auto m = 0; m < width; m+=8) {
    auto se     = vld1_u8(&(nu[xb+k][y+m]));
    auto contrib = vmin_u8(vals, se);
    auto d      = vld1_u8(&(D[b*(N/PU)+k][m]));
    contrib     = vmax_u8(contrib, d);
    vst1_u8(&(D[b*(N/PU)+k][m]), contrib);}
```

Table 1. NEON SIMD Intrinsics used in the proposed algorithms

Intrinsics	Action	Vector width and return type
vdup_n_u8	Load all lanes of vector to the same literal value	64-bit/uint8x8_t
vld1_u8	Load a single vector from memory	64-bit/uint8x8_t
vmax_u8	Return the pairwize maximum of each element	64-bit/uint8x8_t
vmin_u8	Return the pairwize minimum of each element	64-bit/uint8x8_t
vst1_u8	Store a single vector into memory	64-bit/none
vdupq_n_u8	Load all lanes of vector to the same literal value	128-bit/uint8x16_t
vld1q_u8	Load a single vector from memory	128-bit/uint8x16_t
vmaxq_u8	Return the pairwize maximum of each element	128-bit/uint8x16_t
vminq_u8	Return the pairwize minimum of each element	128-bit/uint8x16_t
vst1q_u8	Store a single vector into memory	128-bit/none

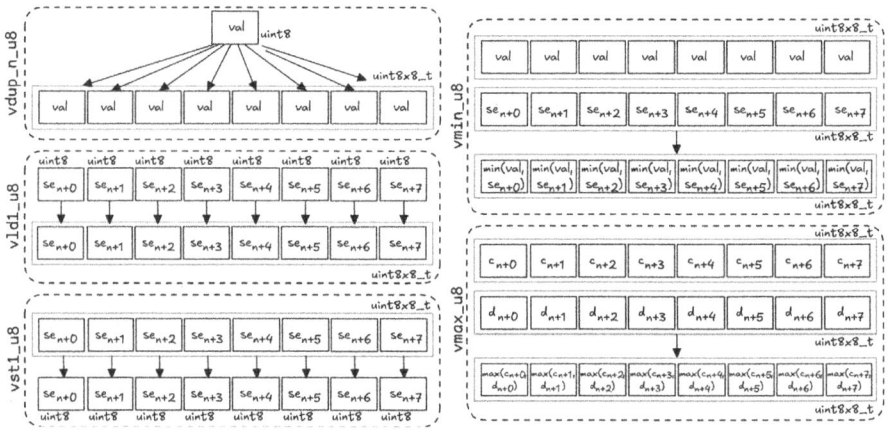

Fig. 4. SIMD NEON intrinsics illustration

PR128N is similar to PR64N. Only the step size ($8 \rightarrow 16$) and the SIMD instructions are modified (Q sized instructions of 128-bit) as represented in Listing 1.3 and described in Table 1.

Listing 1.3. PR128N using Q intrinscics (128bits - 16 uint8)

```
auto vals = vdupq_n_u8(val); // Before #pragma omp for
...
for (auto m = 0; m < width; m+=16) {
    auto se = vld1q_u8(&(nu[xb+k][y+m]));
    auto contrib = vminq_u8(vals, se);
    auto d = vld1q_u8(&(D[b*(N/nthreads)+k][m]));
    contrib = vmaxq_u8(contrib, d);
    vst1q_u8(&(D[b*(N/nthreads)+k][m]), res);}
```

4.2 PRGPU

Designing an efficient GPU algorithm requires careful organization of operations to ensure coalesced data access, minimize access contention, and adequately supply the available threads of the SIMT model. The Reverse modification places us again in a favorable position. As we have observed in CPU algorithms, coalesced data access is achieved for both D and ν reads and D writes. As described in Fig. 5, PRGPU, similarly to PR on CPU, computes the contribution of a pixel to the fuzzy landscape when the pixel is active ($val > 0$). Then the CPU host invokes the kernel responsible for applying the structural element centered on this pixel. The benefits of this process are that the fuzzy landscape then does not have to be transferred back to the host between two kernels and remains resident in the GPU's memory. It is simply updated for each new contributing point and finally processed by the host after the complete procedure. Similarly, the structuring element ν is only sent once to the GPU's memory and can even remain resident to process several images as the two images have a small memory footprint (D-1MB for a 1024×1024 image, ν-4MB for a 1024×1024 image) compared to the 8GB of the Jetson Orin Nano Super.

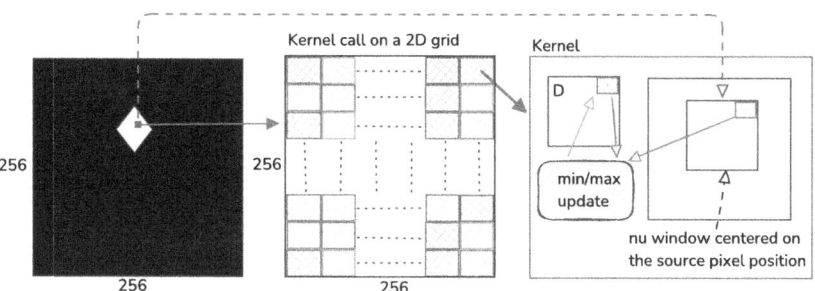

Fig. 5. Contribution to the fuzzy dilation of one active pixel (red square) from the reference object (on the left). The 2D grid division and the kernel are usual. (Color figure online)

As part of this study, alternative parallelization approaches were evaluated. It was found that using OpenMP to process several contributive pixel simultaneously and launch several kernels in parallel in separate streams, did not provide any benefits. In fact, this method needs synchronizations to avoid race conditions. In addition, it was found that the integrated GPU was already being fully exploited for each kernel and that there was no benefit from adding this parallelism to the CPU. As a result, it was decided to proceed from a single CPU thread launching kernels for each contributive pixel, maximizing the CPU availability for other tasks.

Listing 1.4. PRGPU kernel

```
__global__ void gpu_fuzzy(u_char val, u_char *nu, u_char *D,
    unsigned int height, unsigned int width, unsigned int i,
    unsigned int j) {
    int x = blockIdx.x*blockDim.x + threadIdx.x;
    int y = blockIdx.y*blockDim.y + threadIdx.y;
    int ResIndex = x*width+y;
    if ((y<height)&&(x<width)) {
        auto se = nu[(i+y)*2*width + (j+x)];
        if (se>0) {
            auto contrib = min(val, se);
            auto d = D[ResIndex];
            if (d<contrib) {
                D[ResIndex] = contrib;
}}}}
```

5 Benchmark, Results and Analysis

5.1 Dataset

The authors provided in [17] a structured dataset composed of artificial images (available online [16]) and medical images representative of visual reasoning applications like the ones presented in Fig. 1. As PR, was previously demonstrated (and verified in the current work) only dependent on image shape and number of active pixels ($val > 0$), the result presented in this article were obtained using one image of the dataset per evaluated size: a 400 (20×20) pixels square object in a 256×256 image (imageCrispCarre20_52_52.pgm), a 1681 (41×41) pixels square object in a 512×512 image (imageCrispCarre20_102_102.pgm), a 6724 (82×82) square object in a 1024×1024 image (imageCrispCarre20_204_204.pgm).

5.2 Benchmark Configuration

Computing Platform: The NVIDIA Jetson Orin Nano Super is a compact computer system dedicated to small edge devices. Many recent research studies were based on the platform, including video monitoring applications [21],

Lidar based applications [14], and agricultural applications [20]. This board provides a 6-core Arm Cortex-A78AE v8.2 CPU with heterogeneous multiprocessing (HMP) CPU architecture, a NVIDIA Ampere GPU architecture with 1024 CUDA cores, and a unified memory of 8GB 128-bit LPDDR5. The CPU is organized in two clusters: one 4-core cluster (128 KB L1 + 256KB L2 per core + 2MB L3) and one 2-core cluster (128 KB L1 + 256KB L2 per core + 2MB L3) and an additional System Cache of 4 MB shared across all clusters. Power efficiency is a key element for edge computing, Nvidia provides 3 power modes trade-offs named 15 W, 25 W, MAXQ (Table 2). On can remarks that the 25W limits the CPU max frequency to provide more computing power to the GPU.

Table 2. Jetson Orin Nano Super power modes

Power mode	CPU max frequency	GPU max frequency
15W	1.5 GHz	612 MHz
25W	1.35 GHz	918 MHz
MAXQ	1.7 GHz	1020 MHz

Algorithms: Four algorithms were evaluated: PR the parallel version with auto-vectorization, PR64N, PR128N, and PRGPU. As demonstrated in [17], PR and its variations depend only on the object size and image size. All results will be presented for a crisp square. Each power mode was evaluated for both CPU versions and PRGPU using executables generated with -O3 and -march=native -mCPU=native flags by g++ version 11.4.0 included in JetPack6.2 for the Jetson Orin Nano Super platform). For PRGPU the compute capabilities 8.7 where targeted arch=compute_87,code=sm_87 with nvcc (cuda 12.6). As the GPU execution times were fluctuating, we provide minimum and maxiumum execution times out of 10 benchmark executions of an executable that provides the mean value of 100 fuzzy landscape computations. Thermal throttling was never detected (grep "" /sys/class/hwmon/hwmon*/oc*). The best grid configuration was found by experimentation (16 × 16).

5.3 Results

As observed in Intel architectures, explicit vectorization has a significant impact on performance. The PR64N algorithm is accelerated by factors of x4.8, x6.7 and x5.4 for the 256 × 256, 512 × 512 and 1024 × 124 images, respectively, compared to PR with auto-vectorization. Similarly, the PR128N algorithm is accelerated by factors of x6.2, x8.8, and x5.8 under the same conditions. A notable point is the performance of the PR128N algorithm in the 1024 × 1024 configuration.

Table 3. Execution time in ms for one fuzzy landscape computation for the 3 reference images with varying number of active threads in the 15W power mode

Image width	Algorithm	\multicolumn{6}{c}{Number of active threads}					
		1	2	3	4	5	6
256	PR	43.03	23.04	15.36	11.73	9.57	**8.49**
	PR64N	6.14	3.51	2.39	2.00	1.82	**1.78**
	PR128N	4.61	2.71	1.82	1.46	**1.37**	1.37
512	PR	731.9	372.1	251.5	190.0	152.3	**129.1**
	PR64N	103.4	53.0	36.1	27.2	22.8	**19.4**
	PR128N	80.0	39.9	26.9	20.5	16.5	**14.7**
1024	PR	11589	5849	3921	2955	2379	**1998**
	PR64N	1703	844	582	431	369	**366**
	PR128N	1341	652	477	**346**	350	359

The best performance is achieved with 4 active threads, rather than 6 (Table 3). This result holds for all energy modes (Table 4). As indicated in the benchmark section, the processor features a High-Performance Multi-Core (HMP) architecture and is divided into two clusters of 4 and 2 cores. The heavy load on memory bandwidth and caches reaches the limits of bandwidth and highlights a Non-Uniform Memory Access (NUMA) effect between the two clusters. Neither the PR64N nor PR-auto algorithms had reached this limit. PR128N algorithm fully exploits the ARM CPU capabilities. Nvidia allows separate activation of CPU clusters in the card configuration (for example, a 7W mode is available, which only activates the first 4 cores). To minimize power consumption while maintaining maximum performance, the PR128N algorithm can be optimally used with a customized mode that offers maximum frequencies but only 4 cores.

Table 4. Execution times in ms for one fuzzy landscape computation for the 1024×1024 image with different power modes for PR128N and PRGPU

Power mode	PR128N						PRGPU	
	\multicolumn{6}{c}{Number of active threads}			min	max
	1	2	3	4	5	6		
15W	1341	652	477	**346**	350	359	772	1237
25W	1474	729	528	**390**	397	416	715	980
MAXQ	1176	572	418	**304**	313	319	480	922

Table 5. PRGPU execution time in ms for one fuzzy landscape computation for the 3 reference images with different power modes.

Power mode	256×256		512×512		1024×1024	
	min	max	min	max	min	max
15W	4.98	5.18	51.5	51.5	772	1237
25W	3.81	3.88	36.0	36.1	715	980
MAXQ	3.34	3.38	32.4	32.6	480	922

Regarding the PRGPU algorithm, for the 15 W mode, its results are consistently better than the auto-vectorized version and worse than the PR64N and PR128N algorithms. The Table 4 presents the differences between the PR128N and PRGPU algorithms for other power modes, namely x3.0, x1.9, and x2.8 for 15 W, 25 W, and MAXQ, respectively. We observe the effects of Nvidia's trade-off between CPU and GPU frequency according to the mode, as the 25 W mode CPU execution times are higher than for the 15 W and MAXQ modes, due to the lower CPU max frequency. Meanwhile, the MAXQ mode is the best for PRGPU performances (Table 5).

6 Conclusion

In this paper, we proposed three edge computing optimized algorithms based on PR, a fast and exact algorithm for the computation of the fuzzy dilation operator. Two CPU versions, based on multicore and SIMD capabilities of the ARM64 architecture, and a GPU version leveraging CUDA. We found that the optimized 128-bit SIMD algorithm PR128N is the fastest algorithm on ARM64 architecture. At least x5.8 faster than the already multithreaded Parallel Reverse (PR) in any tested configurations. It confirms that small but precise adaptations of algorithms to hardware are highly beneficial and should always be considered in the HPC and/or embedded context. The GPU version is also faster than the PR version but slower than the CPU versions on a Jetson Orin Nano Super. These results enables us to deploy efficiently fuzzy spatial relations on edge. Depending on the application, it is now possible to offload fuzzy landscape computings to a GPU while managing other operations such as flight control or direction in the case of robotic devices. Conversely, in the common case of using a deep learning algorithm on a GPU, it is possible to execute fuzzy landscape computations on the CPU to generate corresponding explanations (XAI). In future work, we plan to develop algorithms that target both the CPU and GPU of Apple silicon devices to address tablet computers and desktop versions.

References

1. Amiri, H., Shahbahrami, A., Pohl, A., Juurlink, B.: Performance evaluation of implicit and explicit simdization. Microprocessors Microsystems **63**, 158–168 (2018). https://doi.org/10.1016/j.micpro.2018.09.002
2. Biederman, I.: On the semantics of a glance at a scene. In: Perceptual Organization, pp. 213–253. Routledge (2017)
3. Bloch, I.: Fuzzy relative position between objects in image processing: a morphological approach. IEEE Trans. Pattern Anal. Mach. Intell. **21**(7), 657–664 (1999)
4. Bloch, I.: On fuzzy distances and their use in image processing under imprecision. Pattern Recogn. **32**(11), 1873–1895 (1999)
5. Bloch, I.: Fuzzy spatial relationships for image processing and interpretation: a review. Image Vis. Comput. **23**(2), 89–110 (2005)
6. Boudet, L., Poli, J.P., Bergé, L.P., Rodriguez, M.: Situational assessment of wildfires: a fuzzy spatial approach. In: 2020 IEEE 32nd International Conference on Tools with Artificial Intelligence (ICTAI), pp. 1180–1185 (2020). https://doi.org/10.1109/ICTAI50040.2020.00179
7. Cayrol, M., Farreny, H., Prade, H.: Fuzzy pattern matching. Kybernetes **11**(2), 103–116 (1982)
8. Dagum, L., Menon, R.: Openmp: an industry standard api for shared-memory programming. Comput. Sci. Eng. IEEE **5**(1), 46–55 (1998)
9. Doshi-Velez, F., Kim, B.: Towards A Rigorous Science of Interpretable Machine Learning. arXiv e-prints (2017)
10. Freeman, J.: The modelling of spatial relations. Comput. Graph. Image Process. **4**(2), 156–171 (1975)
11. Goodman, B., Flaxman, S.: European union regulations on algorithmic decision-making and a right to explanation. AI Mag. **38**(3), 50–57 (2017)
12. Gunning, D.: Explainable artificial intelligence (xai) (2017)
13. Li, W., Liewig, M.: A survey of AI accelerators for edge environment. In: Rocha, Á., Adeli, H., Reis, L.P., Costanzo, S., Orovic, I., Moreira, F. (eds.) Trends and Innovations in Information Systems and Technologies. WorldCIST 2020. AISC, vol. 1160, pp. 35–44. Springer, Cham (2020). https://doi.org/10.1007/978-3-030-45691-7_4
14. Lompado, A., Carvalho, D.R.M., Brown, J.P.: 3D flash lidar object detection and tracking on edge hardware. In: NAECON 2024 - IEEE National Aerospace and Electronics Conference, pp. 25–29 (2024). https://doi.org/10.1109/NAECON61878.2024.10670672
15. Pierrard, R., Poli, J.P., Hudelot, C.: A new approach for explainable multiple organ annotation with few data. In: IJCAI Workshop on Explainable Artificial Intelligence (XAI) 2019 (2019)
16. Pierrard, R., Cabaret, L., Poli, J.P., Hudelot, C.: FuzzySpatialRelationsDataset (2019). https://bit.ly/2QZHqIX
17. Pierrard, R., Cabaret, L., Poli, J.P., Hudelot, C.: SIMD-based exact parallel fuzzy dilation operator for fast computing of fuzzy spatial relations. In: WPMVP'20: Proceedings of the 2020 Sixth Workshop on Programming Models for SIMD/Vector Processing. San Diego, United States (2020). https://doi.org/10.1145/3380479.3380482, https://hal.science/hal-02517053
18. Pierrard, R., Poli, J.P., Hudelot, C.: Spatial relation learning for explainable image classification and annotation in critical applications. Artif. Intell. **292**, 103434 (2021). https://doi.org/10.1016/j.artint.2020.103434

19. Poli, J.P., Ouerdane, W., Pierrard, R.: Generation of textual explanations in xai: the case of semantic annotation. In: 2021 IEEE International Conference on Fuzzy Systems (FUZZ-IEEE), pp. 1–6 (2021). https://doi.org/10.1109/FUZZ45933.2021.9494589
20. Rosales, A.M., Cruz, P.P.: Embedded Computer Vision for Agricultural Applications, pp. 195–222. Springer, Cham (2024). https://doi.org/10.1007/978-3-031-54277-0
21. Scalcon, F.P., et al.: AI-powered video monitoring: assessing the nvidia jetson orin devices for edge computing applications. In: 2024 IEEE Transportation Electrification Conference and Expo (ITEC), pp. 1–6 (2024). https://doi.org/10.1109/ITEC60657.2024.10598994
22. Serra, J.: Image Analysis and Mathematical Morphology. Academic Press Inc., Cambridge (1983)
23. Vanegas, M., Bloch, I., Inglada, J.: Alignment and parallelism for the description of high-resolution remote sensing images. IEEE Trans. Geosci. Remote Sens. **51**(6), 3542–3557 (2013)
24. Vanegas, M., Bloch, I., Inglada, J.: Fuzzy constraint satisfaction problem for model-based image interpretation. Fuzzy Sets Syst. **286**, 1–29 (2016)
25. Wang, X., Ni, J., Matsakis, P.: Fuzzy object localization based on directional (and distance) information. In: 2006 IEEE International Conference on Fuzzy Systems, pp. 256–263 (July 2006)
26. Zadeh, L.: Fuzzy sets. Inf. Control **8**(3), 338–353 (1965)

Ternary Signed Digit Addition on Field Programmable Gate Arrays

Thomas Schlögl[✉] and Dietmar Fey

Department of Computer Science, Chair for Computer Architecture,
Friedrich-Alexander-Universität Erlangen-Nürnberg, Erlangen, Germany
{thomas.schloegl,dietmar.fey}@fau.de

Abstract. Addition using a ternary signed digit (SD) number representation, i.e. using digits –1, 0 and 1, has the advantage of being computable in O(1) compared to O(n) in standard binary addition using ripple carry adders (RCAs). Therefore, in the past proposals were made how to implement SD adders in Field Programmable Gate Arrays (FPGAs). However, this work is some years old and used older FPGAs with only 4-bit input modules.

We propose two different implementations of binary coded ternary SD number additions on Ultrascale FPGAs from Xilinx/AMD and compare them to standard binary addition concerning resource usage and delay. Furthermore, our solutions use newest FPGA technology and improve on previous solutions in literature which are based on less efficient FPGA technology. The first approach is purely based on lookup tables (LUTs). The second one tries to reduce LUT usage by exploiting so called carry chains, which are extremely fast and normally only used to implement binary RCAs. We show that using ternary SD addition increases the resource usage compared to binary RCAs but allows higher addition clock frequencies independent of the number of digits. The implementation incorporating carry chains reduces the number of LUTs compared to our naive LUT based approach and other previously proposed approaches by 50% while maintaining a comparable delay that is better than for standard binary addition.

Keywords: signed digit · number system · ternary addition · carry chain · FPGA

1 Introdcution

Due to the feature of a carry-free addition, signed digit (SD) number representations are of large relevance for the set-up of an arithmetic that offers both low latency and low power consumption. An efficient implementation of an SD arithmetic depends also heavily on the underlying hardware platform. To exploit a fast arithmetic with SD numbers is not only of interest for an application-specific integrated circuit (ASIC) but in particular also for an Field Programmable Gate

Array (FPGA) with its specific architecture constructs. This considers the implementation of Boolean logic with so-called lookup tables (LUTs), in which the result of a Boolean operator is not calculated but stored in advance, and the possibilities of the offered interconnection scheme to cascade these LUTs to realize high-order Boolean functions, e.g. by so-called carry chains.

Therefore, in the past several proposals were published to profit from SD arithmetic in FPGAs, too. The earliest works in this context go back to the 1990s. Ternary number representations for realizing fast carry-free additions in FPGAs were used in [1] and [2], respectively for the implementation of fast division algorithms resp. digit-serial online arithmetic, which is often exploited in cryptography. In [3] the traditional SD algorithm based on Avizienis [4] was extended towards the computation of an additional bit aside the transfer bit to distinguish special cases to limit carry propagation. This avoids cascading of two adders, as used in conventional SD adders, for the price to consider not only two neighboured but three neighboured digits at once. This leads to comparatively complex Boolean function tables that have to be mapped onto multiple by corssbars linked LUTs within the FPGA resulting in high latencies. At the end the break even point at which the SD adder was faster than a normally synthesized two's complement adder was given for a digit length of $n = 24$. With the occurrence of 6-input LUTs in FPGAs radix-4 based SD numbers using the digit set $\{-3, ..., +3\}$ were proposed for the accelerated computation of finite impulse response (FIR) filters in [5]. In [6] it was shown that also 4-input LUTs of a newer FPGA technology can be used for the set-up of a radix-4 based SD arithmetic. An unique SD representation, the so-called canonical signed-digit (CSD) representation [7], which reduces the number of digits unequal to zero in operands, was used in [8] to reduce addition operations in multiplications by converting binary numbers to CSD for the design of efficient filter functions in FPGAs. Most of these cited work did not have in the focus to speed up the signed digit addition itself but wanted to profit from a carry-free addition in filter operations or the advantage of a signed-digit addition became just apparent for relatively large digit lengths.

Approaches that have in mind to speed-up the addition tried to exploit the given so-called fast-carry chains in FPGAs that allow to combine LUTs without transferring signals via latency increasing crossbar structures. In [9] a method was proposed to map arbitrary Boolean functions onto LUTs cascaded with fast carry chains. In [10] the fast-carry chain logic was used for the implementation of high-performance multipliers as soft cores in FPGAs using conventional arithmetic. In contrast to that we pursue a new approach namely to use the fast carry chains for fast and area-efficient low-power signed-digit adders.

The rest of the paper is structured as follows. In Sect. 2 we explain briefly the basic balanced ternary number system we are using for the implementation of a fast signed-digit adder in FPGAs and how the SD adder looks like in principle independent from its technological implementation. Section 3 presents how the generic adder structure is mapped onto the FPGA hardware and in Sect. 4 the implemented results are discussed. Finally, in Sect. 5 we finish the paper with the summary of the most important results.

2 Used Redundant Number System and SD Adder

In the following we explain the basics of the used redundant number system, how it is encoded in a purly binary environment, how to convert between standard binary and SD representation and how a corresponding SD adder using this encoding can be built by using full adder circuitry.

2.1 Ternary Signed Digit Representation

We favour a balanced ternary SD number system, i.e. for the used digits d_i of a SD number holds $d_i \in \{\bar{1}, 0, 1\}$, where $\bar{1}$ stands for -1. Furthermore, the radix is fixed to 2. Using a balanced ternary system has the advantage compared to other ternary representations that the subtraction can be simply reduced to an addition by changing all $\bar{1}'s$ in a SD number to $1s$ and vice versa. On digital systems these three possible states of a digit need to be represented by two bits, which causes one digit to be represented twice. The assignment of the encoding can be freely chosen and differentiates in literature as shown in Table 1. E.g., the coding used in [11] corresponds to a minus-plus-coding, i.e. the left binary digit is interpreted as negative, the second one as positive, and the coded digit is the sum of both, e.g. $-1 = 10_2 = -1 + 0$. The value of a n-digit SD integer $sd = d_{n-1}, ..., d_0$ can be calculated as:

$$sd = d_{n-1}2^{n-1} + d_{n-2}2^{n-2} + \cdots + d_1 2^1 + d_0 2^0, d_i \in \{\bar{1}, 0, 1\}. \quad (1)$$

The number system is called redundant because there are several possible representations for a single integer, e.g. 3 can be represented as $0011 = 2 + 1$, $010\bar{1} = 4 - 1$ or $1\bar{1}0\bar{1} = 8 - 4 - 1$. This has the disadvantage that comparisons become harder to do than for standard binary numbers. E.g., for a binary number given in 2's complement for determining the sign only the first bit needs to be observed whereas for the determination of the sign of a SD number sd the first digit $sd_i \neq 0$ from the most significand digit side has to be searched. The sign of that sd_i is at the same time the sign of sd. The big advantage of the SD number system is the carry-propagation-free addition and subtraction in $O(1)$, as oposed to addition in standard binary which has to be done in $O(n)$ for ripple-carry addition or $O(log(n))$ for the more resource demanding carry-lookadhead addition.

2.2 Conversion from and to Standard Binary Representation

Unfortunatly the conversion is expensive and needs pattern matching, standard binary addition and constant shifts. Therefore it is best to have the whole arithmetic data path in SD and only convert whenever it is necessary, e.g. when the result needs to be store to memory or interaction with other accelerators that expects standard binary representation is necessary. Table 2 shows some examples for the conversion between binary and SD representation.

Table 1. Binary coding of ternary SD number on digital systems

Digit	Coding from [11]	Our Coding
-1	10_2	00_2
0	00_2 & 11_2	01_2 & 10_2
1	01_2	11_2

Conversion from Binary. For positive numbers this step is straight forward: one only has to append a '1' bit per digit. When using our encoding of SD numbers it does not matter if it is appended in front or after the already existing bit.

For negative numbers, which are represented in 2's complement, the conversion is done by substracting 1 from the binary value and appending a zero bit per digit.

Conversion to Binary. The conversion from a SD number to a 2's complement binary number is done in $O(N)$ by checking each digit and applying it by either adding or substracting 1 and constant shifting the result based on the position.

Table 2. Conversion Examples

Number	2's complement	SD encoding
-7	1001	10 00 00 00
-2	1110	10 10 00 10
0	0000	10 10 10 10
3	0011	10 10 11 11
5	0101	10 11 10 11

2.3 Signed Digit Number Addition

Additions involving two ternary SD numbers can be implemented using mainly full adders (FAs). Dependant on the chosen encoding of the digits additional inverters at some inputs at the FA are needed, as for e.g. for the coding from [11] shown in the second column in 1. We developed the encoding shown in the third column in Table 1. Using this encoding for the digits such inverters are not necessary, which would come handy for an ASIC implementation of the SD adder because then just highly optimized standard cells for FA can be used. However, this does not make much of a difference when choosing an FPGA implementation because of the inherent property of LUTs with N inputs to be able to represent any N-input function. Figure 1 shows the adder circuit, where red and green lines indicate the generated carry and sum bits of the corresponding FAs. The inputs are called 'A' and 'B' and the generated addition result is called 'S'. The attached number shows the index of the digit. The most-significant bit (MSB) of the encoded digit is indicated by the letter 'p', the least-significant bit (LSB) by the letter 'n'. E.g., 'Ap1' stands for the MSB of the second digit of input 'A', while 'Sn0' is the LSB of the first digit of the addition result.

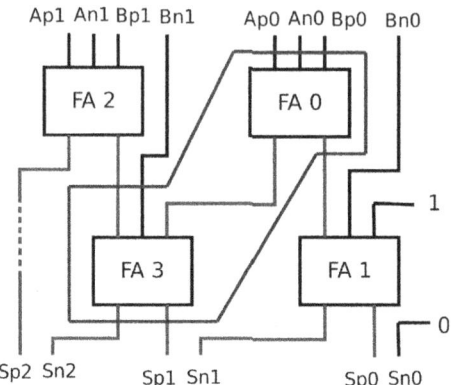

Fig. 1. Signed Digit Adder with SD operands 'A' and 'B' and resulting SD number 'S'. (Color figure online)

It can be seen that the cirtical path of the adder is always through two FAs and that the carry is only propagated to the next FA element and not further, therefore the addition is said to be carry free and computable in $O(1)$ (the delay of two FAs) independent of the number of digits.

3 Implementation

For our implementation the FPGAs of the Ultrascale and Versal series from Xilinx/AMD are used. They offer some unique features that can be used and evaluated when it comes to the implementation of complex logic like ternary adders. In the next section the will first describe the features of the platforms that are used for our implementation and then go into detail on how we used them for an optimized solution.

3.1 Implementation on Ultrascale

The Ultrascale series offers some unique features that can be used and evaluated when it comes to the implementation of complex logic like ternary adders. One of them are dedicated circuits called carry chains (CCs), which are normally used to implement ripple carry additions, but can be repurposed to execute arbitrary logic as shown in [9]. Carry chains consist of blocks that can be instantiated to speed up calculation of sum and carry results in blocks of four or eight bits, called Carry4 and Carry8 blocks respectively [13]. Figure 2 shows an 8 bit carry chain primitive that can also be used as two separate CARRY4 blocks, indicated by the two carry inputs (CI and CI_TOP). Figure 3 shows a snippet of the dedicated circuits inside of such a block. The S-Input of a carry chain can only be used with the corresponding LUT in front of it which needs to implement a two input XOR function in order to realize a full ripple carry adder circuit together with the multiplexer and the XOR gate in the carry chain. It is not possible to use the S inputs of a carry chain without the LUT. For a detailed description on how to use and instantiate carry blocks please consult the corresponding Ultrascale user guides [13] [14].

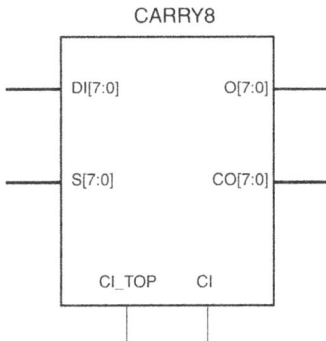

Fig. 2. Carry8 Primitive taken from [13].

Another special feature are six input LUTs called LUT6_2 that can generate two outputs for the same five input signals [14] as illustrated in Fig. 4. To do this the sixth input I5 must be set to constant zero, otherwise the LUT will act like a normal six input one. Functionality is considered to be mapped onto these special LUTs during the implementation step whenever special optimization flags are set, so their use is not directly reliably controllable, but they can also be instantiated manually by structural descriptions. A detailed description on this can be found in [14].

Four different implementations are described in the following sections, consisting of a naive one, two purely LUT based version that incorporates the Ultrascale LUT6_2 lookup tables and a forth one that tries to incorporate the existing fast carry-chain hardmacros.

Naive Implementation. The naive implementation just describes the boolean expression of the SD addition logic on the RTL level using VHDL. This implementation is used as our baseline for the comparison and lets the Vivado synthesis and implementation algorithms have full control over how it realizes the adders on the available LUTs and other resources.

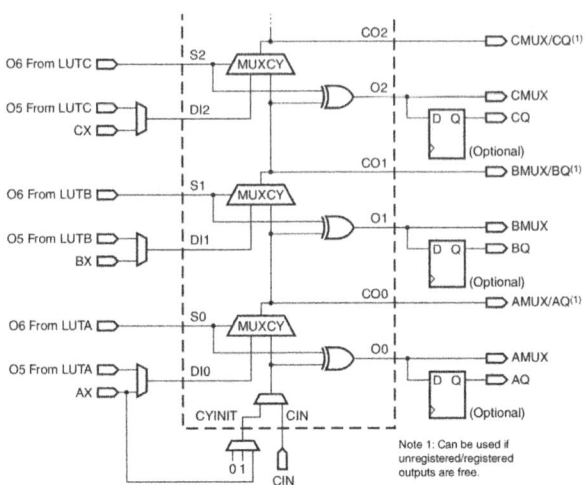

Fig. 3. Snippet of carry logic path and associated elements taken from [13].

LUT6_2 Based Implementation. A LUT based approach is the standard way for logic implementation on FPGAs but a simple realization that just describes the full adder logic is not optimal and leaves little place for optimization and therefore is unlikely to achieve the wished performance gains compared to standard binary addition.

Therefore we chose to carefully handcraft our SD adder by creating a generic description in VHDL that manually instantiates LUT6_2 where possible and does not rely on the implementation tools to do LUT optimizations and compaction.

Here we try two different approaches:

Since one LUT6_2 can produce two outputs for the same five inputs, we map one FA element, that produces the carry and the sum into one LUT6_2. This only makes use of three of the five available inputs but is very simple and fast to realize.

For the second approach, we investigate the adder circuit in depth and come up with a more complex but also more efficient mapping strategy that we explain with the help of the example of a two digit SD adder in Fig. 1. It can be seen that the first two outputs of full adder FA1 can be generated by a single LUT6_2. The functionality inside of the blue box, consisting of full adders FA0 and FA3, can also be mapped to one LUT6_2. The green sum bit of full adder FA2, that feeds this LUT6_2, needs to be generated by a separate three input LUT. This mapping to LUTs is proceeded for all remaining digits by a generate-for-loop. The last output of the SD sum, corresponding to the carry bit of FA2, is calculated by another single three input LUT. This last FA can also be mapped to a LUT6_2 generating both sum and carry bit in a single LUT.

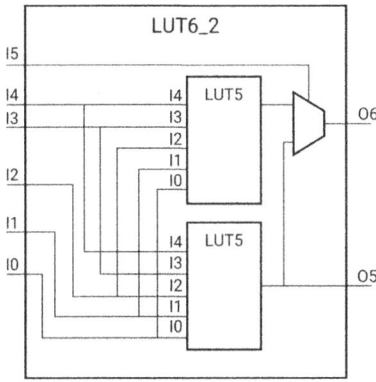

Fig. 4. LUT6_2 Primitive taken from [14].

Carry-Chain-Based Implementation. Next we present an implementation that is based on carry chains. This seems to be an appropriate approach because they inherently contain the full adder functionality needed. The main problem with carry chains is the they can only be instantiated as a whole block that generates 4 or 8 succeeding sum and carry bits. But for the implementation of the SD adder only two succeeding full adder are needed as visible in Fig. 1 and therefore the rest of the calculation capacity of the block is wasted. The Ultrascale architecture offer four bit long carry chains [13], so in our implementation half the functionality is unused. Older architectures just offer eight bit long carry chains, here the loss is greater of course. This should not be a big problem for most applications, since carry chains are only used for adders and are not automatically instantiated when describing arbitrary logic.

A single carry chain is suited to implement the logic that is encapsulated by the blue box in Fig. 1, because the carry is passed here. Since the carry chain can only be instantiated with a LUT in front of the used 'S' inputs as indicated in Fig. 3, logic that generates the sum bit of FA2 can also be incorporated into this LUT, resulting in the function $S0 = Ap_n \oplus Bp_n$ for the first input of the carry chain and $S1 = Ap_{n+1} \oplus An_{n+1} \oplus Bp_{n+1} \oplus Bn_{n+1}$ for the second input, where the lower index n stand for the current digit position. The rest of the S inputs are unused and should be set to '0'. FA1, that generates the first addition result, is mapped to one LUT6_2, as in the purely LUT based approach, with the four bits that represent the first digits to be added as its inputs and the other two set to '0'. The last generated carry bit of FA2 is once again mapped on a single three input LUT.

3.2 Implementation on Versal

The Versal series improved upon the Ultrascale FPGAs by no longer relying on ripple-carry addition but by incorporating hardmacros that can do carry lookahead logic instead of the previously described carry-chains [15]. There was also a redesign in the Configurable Logic Blocks (CLBs): LUT6_2 are still present and it is now possible to directly cascade the output of one LUT the input is its upper neighbor in the CLB without using any external routing mesh. This enables the implementation of larger functions with minimal delay. The use of these fast cascading Paths can not be used by instantiation and is fully dependent on the vivado mapping algorithm (Fig. 5).

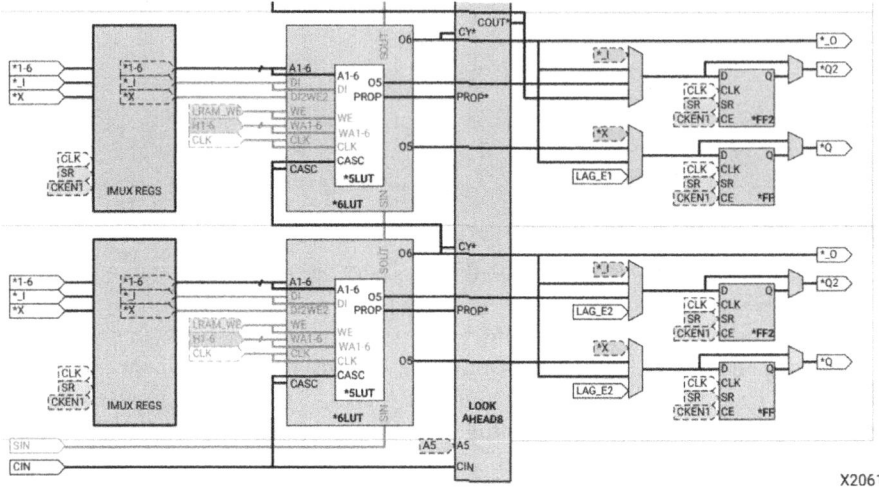

Fig. 5. Snippet of Versal CLB taken from [15].

On Versal the have the same implementation strategies as previously described for Ultrascale for the LUT based approaches, but we did not reimplement a solution for the carry lookadhad hardmacros because this approach already seemed not very promising during the implementation on Ultrascale because of its wastful use of computational resources.

4 Evaluation

This section shows the implementation results obtained on a Ultra96 version 2 board from Avnet and the Versal VCK190 Evaluation Kit. All evaluations were made using Vivado 2021.2.

Table 3 and 4 show the resource usage (number of used Carry8/CLA8 blocks and LUTs) after the implementation step as well as logic delay for standard binary ripple carry addition, our LUT and carry chain based approaches to SD addition using different number of digits.

Each adder is embedded in a wrapper that buffers the in- and outputs in registers and implements no additonal in- and output delays (using-mode out_of_context). The values were aquired by iterativly decreasing the clock period based on the remaining slack until implementation fails (Fig. 7).

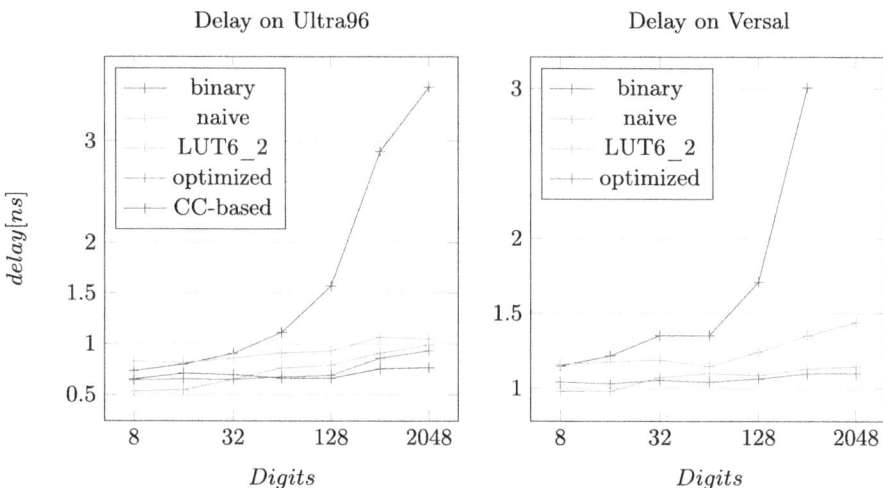

Fig. 6. Circuit Delay for the different implementaton on Ultrascale (left) and Versal (right).

Figure 6 displays the delay for each implementation. It is observable that our implementations have lower delay times than standard binary additions for the number of digits and that the delays stay relatively constant independent of the number of digits, as it is expected.

If we compare the naive implementation where we just described the output functionality of the FAs to the implementation where we just mapped each FA into one LUT6_2 we can see that we just need half the amount of LUTs but increase the delay slightly. We can improve the delay by our more complex mapping scheme that does not increase the resrouce (LUT) usage.

The number of carry chains is given in Carry8 blocks, where a Carry8 block consists of two independently usable Carry4 blocks, which were used for our implementation of the carry chain based SD adder. If older FPGA architectures are used, which only supply inseparatable Carry8 blocks, the number of used blocks would increase from $\lceil N/2 \rceil$ to $N-1$ but the number of LUTs would remain the same. The number of LUTs corresponds to approximately $2*N$ and the the number of used Carry8 blocks is $\lceil N/2 \rceil$. As mentioned during the implementation section, only half of the carry chain is used when Carry4 blocks are available or one forth when using Carry8 blocks.

Table 3. Resource Utilization & Timing on Ultra96

Implementation Sytle	#Digits	Resources		period [ns]
		#LUTs	#Carry Chains[c]	
Ripple Carry[a]	8	11	0	0.733
	16	16	2	0.798
	32	32	4	0.905
	64	64	8	1.111
	128	128	16	1.568
	1024	2792	247	2.896
	2048	5763	500	3.531
naive[b]	8	30	0	0.537
	16	62	0	0.546
	32	126	0	0.653
	64	254	0	0.761
	128	510	0	0.791
	1024	4094	0	0.910
	2048	8190	0	0.987
simple LUT6_2[b]	8	16	0	0.830
	16	32	0	0.815
	32	64	0	0.860
	64	128	0	0.911
	128	256	0	0.931
	1024	2048	0	1.065
	2048	4096	0	1.052
optimized LUT[b]	8	15	0	0.643
	16	31	0	0.653
	32	63	0	0.648
	64	127	0	0.675
	128	255	0	0.689
	1024	2047	0	0.860
	2048	4095	0	0.932
CC-based[b]	8	16	4	0.652
	16	32	8	0.708
	32	64	16	0.697
	64	128	32	0.662
	128	256	64	0.660
	1024	2048	512	0.754
	2048	4096	1024	0.767

[a] Standard binary based Ripple Carry adder using Carry Chains
[b] Ternary SD adder implementations.
[c] Number of Carry8 Blocks.

Table 4. Resource Utilization & Timing on Versal

Implementation Sytle	#Digits	Resources		period [ns]
		#LUTs	#CLA Blocks[c]	
Carry Lookahead[a]	8	11	0	1.147
	16	16	2	1.214
	32	32	4	1.350
	64	64	8	1.350
	128	128	16	1.706
	1024	2582	247	3.006
	2048			
naive[b]	8	23	0	0.979
	16	47	0	0.980
	32	97	0	1.072
	64	191	0	1.098
	128	383	0	1.084
	1024	3073	0	1.128
	2048	6144	0	1.144
simple LUT6_2[b]	8	16	0	1.159
	16	32	0	1.176
	32	64	0	1.188
	64	128	0	1.145
	128	256	0	1.240
	1024	2048	0	1.350
	2048	4096	0	1.438
optimized LUT[b]	8	15	0	1.040
	16	31	0	1.029
	32	63	0	1.052
	64	127	0	1.040
	128	255	0	1.062
	1024	2047	0	1.096
	2048	4095	0	1.098

[a]Standard binary based Carry Lookahead Adder using CLA Blocks
[b]Ternary SD adder implementations.
[c]Number of CLA8 Blocks.

Table 5. Abstract Comparison Implementation Results

Implementation	Resources	
	#CC or #CLA	#LUTs
binary adder[a]	$\lceil N/8 \rceil$	N
Naive[b]	0	$\approx 4*N$
$LUT6\_2$-based[b]	0	$2*N$
optimized LUT-based[b]	0	$(2*N) - 1$
CC-based[c]	$\lceil N/2 \rceil$	$2*N$

[a] Standard binary adder on Ultrascale or Versal.
[b] Ternary SD adder implementations.
[c] Only on Ultrascale Implementation.

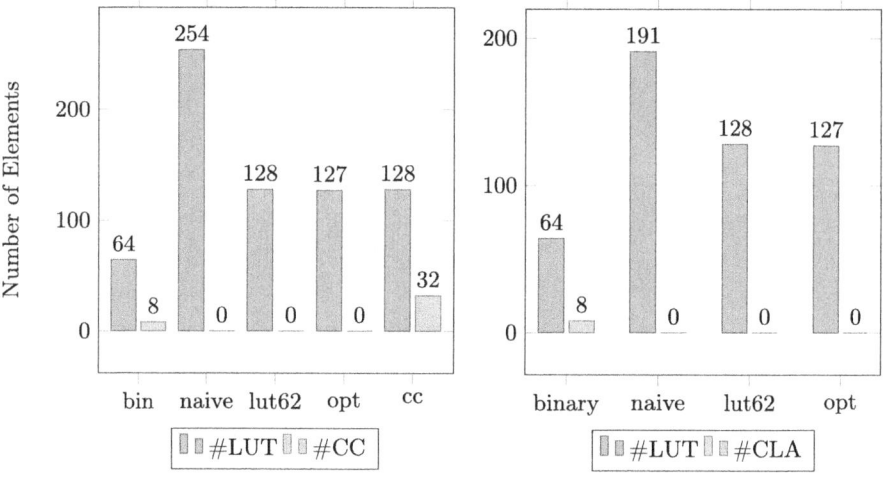

Fig. 7. Resouce Utilization for the different implementatons on Ultrascale (left) and Versal (right) for 64 Digit Adders. The same numbers and and different adder widths can be found in Tables 3 and 4

5 Conclusion

We presented multiple approaches to implementing signed digit ternary number addition on a modern FGPA architecture, namely the Ultrascale and Versal architecture from Xilinx/AMD and evaluated them in comparison with standard binary addition. The first approaches were purely LUT based, while the last one tried to reduce LUT usage by exploiting carry chains. We achieved higher possible clock frequencies by simultaneously moderately increasing the resource usage.

References

1. Morán, J., Rios, I., Meneses, J.: Signed digit arithmetic on FPGAs. In: Selected Papers from the Oxford 1993 International Workshop on Field Programmable Logic and Applications on More FPGAs, pp. 250–261. Abingdon EE&CS Books, Oxford (1994)
2. Turner, L.E., Graumann, P.J.W., Gibb, S.G.: Bit-serial FIR filters with CSD coefficients for FPGAs. In: Moore, W., Luk, W. (eds.) FPL 1995. LNCS, vol. 975, pp. 311–320. Springer, Heidelberg (1995). https://doi.org/10.1007/3-540-60294-1_125
3. Schneider, K., Willenbucher, A.: A new algorithm for carry-free addition of binary signed-digit numbers. In: 2014 IEEE 22nd Annual International Symposium on Field-Programmable Custom Computing Machines, pp. 44–51. IEEE, Boston (2014). https://doi.org/10.1109/FCCM.2014.24.
4. Avizienis, A.: Signed-digit number representations for fast parallel arithmetic. IRE Trans. Electron. Comput. EC **10**(3), 389–400 (1961). https://doi.org/10.1109/TEC.1961.5219227
5. Cardarilli, G.C., Pontarelli, S., Re, M., Salsano, A.: On the use of signed digit arithmetic for the new 6-inputs LUT based FPGAs. In: 2008 15th IEEE International Conference on Electronics, Circuits and Systems, pp. 602–605. IEEE, Saint Julian's (2008). https://doi.org/10.1109/ICECS.2008.4674925
6. Tanaka, Y., Suzuki, Y., Wei, S.: Novel binary signed-digit addition algorithm for FPGA implementation. J. Circ. Syst. Comput. **29**(09), 2050136 (2020). https://doi.org/10.1142/S0218126620501364
7. IEEE aerospace and electronic systems society. IEEE Trans. Aeros. Electron. Syst. AES **11**(5), c2-980a (1975). https://doi.org/10.1109/TAES.1975.307978.
8. Nigam, S.: Hardware implementation of cascaded integrator-comb filter using canonical signed-digit number system. In: Reddy, K.A., et al. (eds.) Proceedings of Fourth International Conference on Computer and Communication Technologies. Lecture Notes in Networks and Systems, vol. 606. Springer, Singapore. https://doi.org/10.1007/978-981-19-8563-8_10
9. Senhadji-Navarro, R., Garcia-Vargas, I.: Mapping arbitrary logic functions onto carry chains in FPGAs. Electronics **11**(1), 27 (2021). https://doi.org/10.3390/electronics11010027
10. Ullah, S., Rehman, S., Shafique, M., Kumar, A.: High-performance accurate and approximate multipliers for FPGA-based hardware accelerators. IEEE Trans. Comput. Aided Des. Integr. Circuits Syst. **41**(2), 211–224 (2022). https://doi.org/10.1109/TCAD.2021.3056337
11. Ercegovac, M.D., Lang, T.: Digital Arithmetic. Section 2.12, pp. 97–112. Morgan Kaufmann Publishers (2004). ISBN: 1-55860-798-6
12. Eason, G., Noble, B., Sneddon, I.N.: On certain integrals of Lipschitz-Hankel type involving products of Bessel functions. Phil. Trans. Roy. Soc. London **A247**, 529–551 (1955)
13. Xilinx. UltraScale Architecture Configurable Logic Block - User Guide. UG574 (v1.5) (2017)
14. Xilinx. UltraScale Architecture Libraries Guide. UG974 v2020.2 (2020)
15. Xilinx. Versal ACAP Configurable Logic Block - Architecture Manual. AM005 (v1.0) (2020)

FSST Compression of JSON Data on FPGAs

Tobias Hahn(✉), Jan Hofmann, Stefan Wildermann, and Jürgen Teich

Friedrich-Alexander-Universität Erlangen-Nürnberg (FAU), Erlangen, Germany
{tobias.hahn,jan.hofmann,stefan.wildermann,juergen.teich}@fau.de

Abstract. Semi-structured data formats, such as JSON, are widely adopted in big data applications to achieve flexibility, fast integration and portability. As these formats are commonly highly sparse, compression is often applied before data is stored or transmitted over networks. However, since semi-structured records often need to be accessed individually, they need to be compressed separately, resulting in low compression factors when applying traditional Lempel-Ziv compression schemes. As a remedy, Fast Static Symbol Table (FSST) was proposed, a lightweight dictionary-based compression scheme specifically designed for short strings. In this paper, we present hardware acceleration techniques for the FSST compression scheme. Moreover, we evaluate the applicability of FSST to semi-structured data, such as JSON, and compare it to other compression schemes. Finally, in the evaluation of the presented accelerator circuits, we report speedups of 1.4 to 2.6 times and a reduction in energy consumption of 6.0 to 10.5 times compared to the open source FSST software implementation.

Keywords: compression · JSON · FSST · FPGA · static dictionary · semi-structured

1 Introduction

In big data applications, especially in the Internet of Things (IoT), applications must constantly adapt their functionality to changing environmental conditions and user requirements. Semi-structured data formats such as JSON have emerged as a solution to support the need for flexibility in data encoding. Due to the sparse information density of many semi-structured formats, especially flexible ones like JSON, compression is often applied before data is transmitted over networks or stored. Several NoSQL databases, such as MongoDB, support compression of ingested semi-structured documents through various Lempel-Ziv (LZ)-based compression schemes. Stream processing applications also frequently rely on compressed semi-structured data [19].

While encoding data in semi-structured formats in combination with compression provides both flexibility and a manageable data footprint, this approach comes at a considerable computational cost. In addition, run-length-based encoding, such as Lempel-Ziv, only achieves high compression factors for long strings since the dictionary is built at runtime. However, semi-structured records often need to be accessible individually, such as in a document store, so they need to be compressed individually, resulting in low compression factors. As a remedy, Boncz, Neumann, and Leis [5] proposed Fast Static Symbol Table (FSST) [5], a lightweight dictionary-based compression scheme specifically designed for short strings. Compared to LZ4, which offers a good trade-off between compression factor and throughput, FSST can achieve significantly higher compression factors while providing slightly higher throughput for strings. FSST achieves this by its simple table-based compression scheme, with a dictionary of just 255 entries with a maximum of 8 bytes per entry, and by utilizing SIMD instructions available on modern x86 CPUs.

To meet the low latency and high throughput requirements of big data applications, FPGA-based accelerator architectures have emerged as a promising solution [18]. Since big data applications often run for very long periods of time, ranging from hours to weeks, it is worth synthesizing perfectly tailored hardware accelerators. FPGA accelerators have proven to be particularly efficient for processing semi-structured data, such as JSON [9,11,12], since the hardware accelerators can take full advantage of the sparsity of the input data. However, many of the proposed solutions do not take into account that such sparse semi-structured data is usually compressed. JSON-CooP [13] thus proposes a parser architecture that can parse JSON directly from an FSST-compressed input, eliminating the need for any additional decompression. The authors also show that FSST is perfectly suited for compressing JSON data and also present adaptations for achieving even higher compression factors for JSON. However, while the parser accelerator can run on compressed input, no hardware accelerator for the FSST compression scheme has ever been presented. In general, little research efforts have been spent into the compression of semi-structured data. This paper aims at closing this gap.

Our main contributions are:

- **Analysis**: We provide a detailed comparative analysis of the suitability of different compression schemes for compressing semi-structured data. Our focus is on the widely used JSON format and its binary equivalent BSON.
- **Architecture**: Two resource-efficient hardware accelerator architectures implementing the FSST compression scheme are introduced. One accelerator core for compression and one for decompression.
- **Evaluation**: The presented accelerators are evaluated, compared with an FSST software implementation as reference in terms of throughput and energy efficiency, and placed in the landscape of existing FPGA accelerators.

2 Related Work

Related work on short string compression mostly relies on dictionary-based deduplication. Binnig et al. [4] propose an order-preserving string compression scheme aimed at compressing column stores. The scheme allows for accessing individual strings in reasonable time as entries can be compressed individually. However, the scheme relies on a large global dictionary, making it unsuitable for hardware implementation. Re-Pair [15] (recursive pairing) recursively constructs a grammar to compress the input. In each recursion the most frequent character pairs are replaced with a new symbol. The compression scheme achieves high compression factors and allows for individual access. Yet creating a grammar is computationally intensive, and its recursive nature is unsuitable for implementation in hardware.

There has been extensive research on FPGA-based compression and decompression, primarily targeting the acceleration of LZ-based compression schemes. Numerous studies in this area have shown that the computationally complex compression and decompression operations are well suited for FPGA acceleration, achieving significantly higher throughput than a CPU counterpart [7]. The widely adopted *deflate* algorithm used in zlib and gzip has been implemented several times as an FPGA accelerator [10,16]. Deflate uses LZ77 compression combined with Huffman coding, resulting in high compression factors. However, this makes the compression scheme highly complex, resulting in high resource requirements for a hardware implementation. Xilinx offers a reference design for accelerating Google Snappy[1], an LZ77-based compression scheme optimized for speed. However, the resource requirements of this reference design are comparable to those of the more complex *deflate* algorithm [16], making it less resource-efficient despite its focus on performance. The LZ4 compression scheme, on the other hand, provides a balanced trade-off between compression factor and computational intensity. [1,3] present LZ4 accelerators with low resource requirements. Liu et al. [17] adapted the LZ4 scheme to allow for a more FPGA-tailored implementation. As a result, the authors were able to achieve high throughput with relatively low hardware requirements. We could not find a hardware accelerator that implements a compression scheme targeted at short strings. Therefore, the evaluation will mainly cover comparisons with LZ-based compression schemes/accelerators.

3 Preliminaries

Fast Static Symbol Table (FSST) [5] is a lightweight compression scheme optimized for short strings. FSST was originally designed to be run on modern CPUs utilizing AVX512 SIMD instructions as provided in an open-source[2] implementation by the authors. However, as will be shown in the following, the compression scheme is also well-suited for being accelerated in hardware.

---

[1] https://xilinx.github.io/Vitis_Libraries/data_compression/2021.1/source/L2/snappy.html.

[2] https://github.com/cwida/fsst.

ex. record (uncompressed)	symbol table		ex. record (compressed)
{"id":123,	00	{	1	00 04 01
"user":{	01	123,	4	06 00
"name":	02	"Doe␣\	6	07
"Doe␣\nJane",	03	Jane",	6	02 FF 6E 03
"id":123,	04	"id":	5	04 01
"in	05	terests"	8	FF 22 FF 69 FF 6E
terests":	06	"user":	7	05 FF 3A
"fpgas,	07	"name":	7	08
animals"	08	"fpgas,	7	09
}}	09	animals"	8	0A 0A
	0A	}	1	

Fig. 1. FSST [5] compresses strings by replacing *code symbols* of length 1–8 bytes by 1-byte *code values*. If a given *code symbol* can not be found in the table, characters are escaped using the reserved *code value* **FF**. *Figure taken from* [13].

FSST is based on the observation that strings in a database column or, as proposed in this work, JSON records in a data stream often contain the same substrings (e.g., JSON attribute names). To exploit this, FSST identifies frequently occurring substrings and replaces them with a *code value*. This concept is illustrated in Fig. 1. The identified strings, also called *code symbols*, are entered in a table with a maximum of 255 entries, allowing the index of each entry to be encoded in 1 byte. This 1-byte index, also referred to as *code value*, can then be used to replace the respective entry during encoding. However, as one byte encodes 256 values, one value remains, which is used as an escape character (i.e., *code value* **FF**). Since *code symbols* can potentially be substrings of each other, e.g., both `{` and `{"id":` could be valid *code symbols*, we will always search for the longest possible table entry for replacement. If no entry to replace the current input can be found in the table, the characters are encoded individually using the escape *code value*. For example, after encoding *code symbol* `123,` to 01 in Fig. 1, the input continues with the characters "interes... . The next 1–8 bytes (" , "i , "in , ..., "interes) are all not included in the table, so we encode the " character by placing the escape *code value* **FF** before the actual character, i.e., **FF 22** (22 being the ASCII hex representation of ").

For efficiency reasons, the *code symbols* in the table are limited to 1–8 bytes, allowing SIMD operations to be used for finding the longest valid *code symbol* during encoding and thus achieving high compression performance. This is also advantageous for our proposed hardware implementation as *code symbols* can at most be 8 bytes long and therefore can be passed via fixed-sized interfaces.

The dictionary is obtained during a training phase, where the *code symbols* with the highest *gain* are identified. The *gain* of a *code symbol* is calculated as the frequency of the *code symbol* multiplied by the length of the *code symbol*. This is repeated for several iterations, each time testing new *code symbols* and selecting the 255 *code symbols* with the highest gain. For more details on the training phase, we refer to the original paper [5]. JSON-CooP [13] extends the FSST scheme by adapting the training phase to JSON data, resulting in higher compression factors for JSON data. This is achieved by restricting JSON structural characters (i.e., `{` , `}` , `[` , `]` , `:` , `,`) to only appear at the end of a *code symbol*. These restrictions provide better alignment of symbols, as frequently repeated strings are typically occurring after structural characters. For example, attribute names are often repeated in JSON records and are typically located after a `,` or `{` character. Similarly, attribute values are often repeated and are always located after a `:` character. Accordingly, since the training does not consider less effective *code symbols* containing different independent JSON parts, higher compression factors can be achieved. In addition, decompression can start at any attribute in the JSON record because attribute values are aligned to *code symbols*.

4 Proposed Compression/Decompression Hardware Architecture

This section introduces two hardware architecture designs, one for compressing and one for decompressing to implement the FSST [5] compression scheme presented in Sect. 3. The accelerator for compression is introduced in Sect. 4.1 and the accelerator for decompression in Sect. 4.2. Both accelerators can be used independently, in parallel on the FPGA, or swapped by partial reconfiguration as described in Sect. 5.2.

4.1 Compressor

The basic architecture of our compressor units is shown in Fig. 2. To recognize which *code symbols* (i.e., table entries) match the input stored in an 8-byte buffer (top), 255 parallel comparators are used, each of which matches one *code symbol*. The buffer is filled with one byte per clock cycle until 8 valid bytes are in the buffer. If a *code symbol* of length $n, 1 \leq n \leq 8$ is matched, the encoded n bytes are taken from the buffer, and it takes n clock cycles until the next match process is started. A priority encoder is used to determine the longest of several matched *code symbols*. For example, in Fig. 2, both entries `12` and `123,` match. As a result, the priority encoder outputs the *code value* 1 because the corresponding *code symbol* is longer.

If none of the comparators match, the nor-reduce connected to all comparator outputs will output a 1, indicating that the most significant byte in the buffer must be escaped. This binary *escaped* signal is used to control a multiplexer to output either the first buffer byte or the *code value* of the priority encoder. In addition, the *escaped* signal itself is also output, as the escape code must be inserted before each escaped byte according to the FSST encoding. Before the escape codes are inserted, the *code value* and the *escaped* signal are buffered in a FIFO to avoid unnecessary stalling of the comparators.

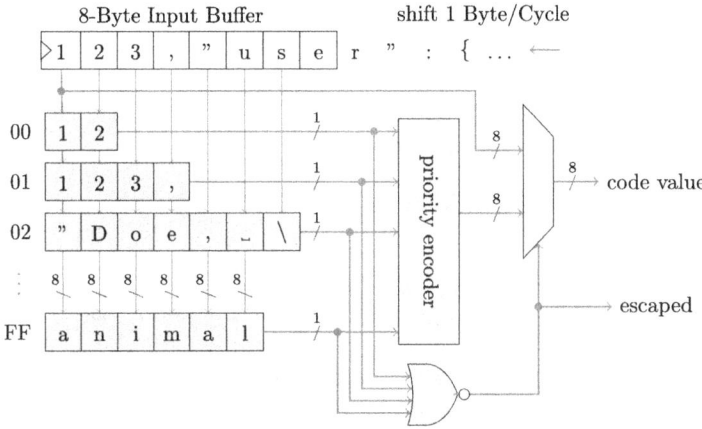

Fig. 2. Basic architecture of a compressor unit.

Since the input buffer is filled with one byte per clock cycle, the throughput of the compressor unit is 1 byte per cycle. However, since the comparators can ideally identify one *code symbol* per clock cycle, the throughput should be equal to the compression factor achieved with a given data set. For example, with a compression factor of 2.5 (cf. the compression factor evaluation in Table 2), an average throughput of 2.5 bytes per cycle could be achieved ideally. For this purpose, the input buffer must be able to be filled with the number of encoded bytes n in each clock cycle. However, since all comparators must be evaluated within one clock cycle to determine n, a long critical path is introduced, preventing high clocking of the accelerator. For this reason, and for the higher predictability (i.e., the accelerator always processes exactly one byte), such an implementation was not pursued any further. In order to achieve higher throughput still, we instantiate several compressor units in parallel. Since the compression scheme is designed for short strings anyway, these short strings can be distributed round-robin to several parallel FIFOs at a higher throughput (e.g., 8 bytes/cycle). The compressor units can then process the inputs of the FIFOs at a low rate but in parallel (e.g., 8 units at 1 byte/cycle). The compressed data is then buffered again, converted to the higher rate and reassembled in the correct order using a round-robin arbiter.

We have also investigated implementing the compressor with a deterministic finite automaton as well as a nondeterministic finite automaton. The idea was to exploit potential overlaps at the beginning of symbol entries (i.e., the first letters of several symbols are identical and can be mapped to the same state). However, the automaton-based solutions turned out to be inferior to the comparator-based solution in terms of both resource requirements and timing, which is why the latter approaches were not pursued any further.

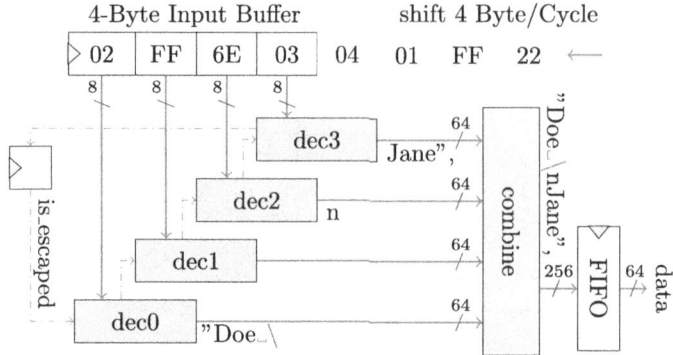

Fig. 3. Basic architecture of a decompressor unit.

4.2 Decompressor

The architecture of the decompressor unit is shown in Fig. 3, consisting of 4 decoder modules, each connected to 1 byte of the input buffer. The decoder modules are responsible for converting the input *code value* back to the corresponding *code symbol*. Since the *code value* is only 1 byte long, the decoder is implemented as a lookup table, as indicated in Fig. 1. *Example: the input for dec0 is 0x02, so a lookup in the table is performed and the corresponding string for index 2, i.e.,* "Doe␣", *as well as its length is output.* If the *code value* contains an escape code, the decoder outputs no *code symbol* and instead outputs the is_escaped wired to the next decoder. This next decoder will just output its input character. *Example: dec1's input is 0xFF, which is the code symbol reserved for escape codes, so dec1 outputs no code symbol and sets the is_ escaped wired to dec2 to 1. Dec2 consequently passes its input byte to the output, i.e.,* n *, since it is the ASCII character corresponding to 0x6E.* The outputs of the decoders are then multiplexed into a continuous 32-byte signal in the combiner using the given length information. This combined signal can contain between 1 and 32 valid bytes, depending on the lengths of the detected *code symbols*. These valid bytes are finally re-sampled in a FIFO to an 8 byte AXI streaming interface.

Unlike the compressor, the decompressor is parallelized at the byte level, i.e., without the need for round-robin arbitration of records. This is possible because each decoder always processes exactly one byte per clock cycle, so there is no critical path to determine the number of bytes consumed. On the other hand, multiplexing the variable number of output bytes into one signal can easily be pipelined. The number of decoders was set to 4, as this allows the output interface to be fully saturated assuming a compression factor greater than or equal to 2.

5 Evaluation

The evaluation first discusses in Sect. 5.1 the applicability of FSST to semi-structured data. Subsequently, the hardware setup is introduced in Sect. 5.2, and finally the presented accelerators are evaluated in Sect. 5.3.

5.1 Compression Factor

In order to evaluate how well the FSST scheme is suitable for compressing semi-structured data, the compression factors achieved on such data will be evaluated in the following. For this purpose, we evaluated 5 different JSON datasets, shown in Table 1. These are the *twitter*[3] dataset, which contains deeply nested and diverse records, the *kostya*[4] dataset, which contains float coordinate values, the *yahoo* [8] dataset, which contains advertising campaign data, the *taxi* [20] dataset, which consists of taxi rides, and the *skyshark* [14] dataset, which contains airplane flight information.

Table 1. Overview of JSON datasets used for evaluation.

name	avg len	example excerpt
twitter	5496	{"metadata":{"result_type":"recent","iso_language_code":"ja"},"created...
kostya	121	{"x":-3.257814207621368e-30,"y":3.554033292114247e+30,"z":0.8135...
yahoo	241	{"user_id":"4ee7888f-f763-48c2-9a45-5a889ff1fa5e","page_id":"0e019c...
taxi	460	{"row_id":0,"vendor_id":1,"tpep_pickup_datetime":"2022-08-01 00:17:...
skyshark	341	{"id":0,"icao24":"ab6fdd","callsign":"AAL1787 ","origin_country":"Un...

The results are shown in Table 2. The FSST [5] scheme, the CooP [13] scheme, and two LZ-based methods, LZ4 and zlib, were evaluated. For the latter, LZ4 is less computationally intensive than zlib, but achieves worse compression factors. The CooP scheme is a variant of the FSST scheme specifically tailored to JSON, thus achieving higher compression factors for such data. The CooP scheme differs from FSST only in the table creation, meaning that the presented accelerator can execute both schemes. The higher compression factors are achieved by restricting valid table entries, thus aligning the table entries to the JSON structure [13]. All compression schemes were evaluated on five different JSON datasets. In addition, all datasets were also encoded in BSON to examine a binary, schema-free data format, as such encodings are also commonly used in document stores (e.g., MongoDB uses BSON). To determine the compression factors, the records were compressed individually in order to be able to read the records individually. For CooP and FSST, half of the dataset was used to create the dictionary (trainset, see Sect. 3) and half for evaluation (testset). Since the LZ schemes create the dictionary at runtime, they were only evaluated on the testset.

---
[3] https://github.com/simdjson/simdjson/blob/master/jsonexamples/twitter.json
[4] https://github.com/kostya/benchmarks.

Table 2. Compression factors of different JSON data sets. Each data set[†] is a 1 MB file.

	CooP[‡]	FSST*	LZ4	zlib	BSON*	BSON* +FSST*	BSON* +LZ4	BSON* +zlib
twitter	1.86	1.67	2.41	**3.72**	1.27	1.56	2.63	3.42
kostya	**2.24**	1.79	0.84	1.07	1.35	2.08	1.08	1.34
yahoo	**2.27**	1.96	0.97	1.38	0.96	1.68	0.94	1.29
taxi	**4.77**	4.34	1.18	1.67	0.94	2.77	1.12	1.48
skyshark	**3.07**	2.88	1.03	1.41	1.02	1.95	1.02	1.20

[†] Due to lack of data the Twitter data set is only 562 KB in size. [‡] [13] * [5]
* BSON values are in relation to the JSON baseline.

In Table 2 it can be seen that the LZ-based compression schemes (i.e., LZ4, zlib) achieve significantly higher compression factors for the longer *Twitter* records (average size 4332 Bytes). For the remaining data sets, however, this trend is reversed due to the smaller record sizes (average sizes 90 bytes - 492 bytes), which make run-length encoding ineffective. For these data sets, FSST, and especially the adapted CooP scheme, achieve significantly higher compression factors. It is particularly interesting that the binary BSON format in combination with compression performs worse than the corresponding JSON variants. Even for the *kostya* dataset, which consists almost entirely of float values and is therefore particularly suited to binary encoding, JSON+CooP achieves the best result. This suggests that converting from JSON to BSON does not reduce the data footprint if the records are to be compressed individually. Since the CooP adjustments could provide a significant improvement over FSST, we also evaluated such symbol restrictions for compressing BSON values. However, in a binary encoding without reserved delimiters, it is substantially more difficult to align code symbols with attributes. We evaluate several possibilities, such as restrictions on null bytes, since these delimit objects and strings in BSON. Unfortunately, due to the presence of null bytes in the remaining value bytes, no significant improvement in compression factors could be achieved.

5.2 System Setup

Figure 4 depicts the overall system architecture, based on [2], consisting of a tightly coupled ARM CPU and programmable logic (PL) into which our compressor design has been integrated and tested. The PL contains several dynamically Reconfigurable Regions (RRs), which are connected to each other and to various interfaces via a crossbar. In each of the RRs resides a DMA engine, managed by the on-chip ARM CPU. The different RRs can be used to compress or decompress simultaneously with different dictionaries, enabling multi-tenant applications. Free regions can also be used to deploy a CooP [13] parser that can parse directly from an FSST compressed input. This allows, for example, a near-data document store to be realized by directly reading compressed data with the CooP accelerator that has been compressed with the FSST accelerator and written to a hardware-attached NVMe.

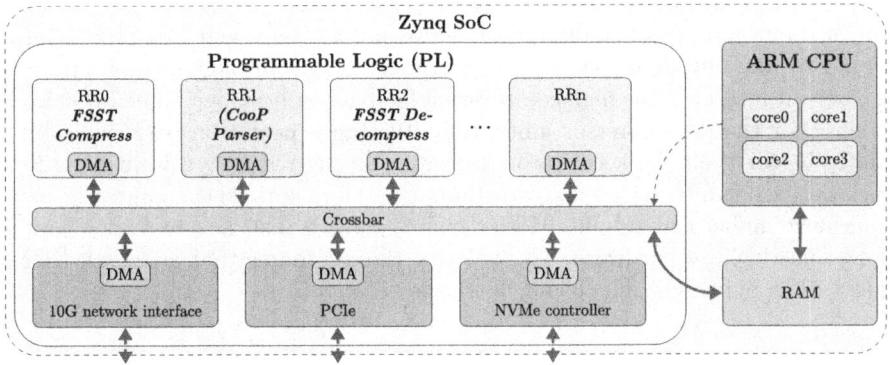

Fig. 4. SoC system architecture used for evaluation.

In our experiments, 31.3 MB of JSON data from the *twitter* data set *(inflated)*, 12.6 MB from the *kostya* data set, 36.9 MB from the *Skyshark* data set, 60.3 MB from the *Yahoo* data set, as well as 4.0 MB from the taxi data set, were preloaded into the RAM and transferred to the respective (de/-)compressor accelerator (blue RR in the figure) using DMA. The results containing the compressed JSON objects were again written back to RAM via DMA.

5.3 Accelerator Evaluation

The results of the hardware resource evaluation are shown in Table 3. The resource usage varies depending on the dataset, as each accelerator is synthesized with a dictionary tailored to the specific schema of the dataset. For example, for the Twitter dataset, the dictionary contains shorter entries on average. This results in smaller comparators and thus fewer LUTs for the compressor unit. On the other hand, the required number of FlipFlops and BRAMs of the compressor units are constant in most cases, since the dictionary only affects the comparators. Only the compressor unit for the Twitter dataset is different in terms of BRAM utilization, due to the larger record sizes. To buffer these larger records, we used UltraRAM instead of BRAM. The decompressor units vary less in LUT consumption because only a small fraction of LUTs are needed for the decoder units. The resource consumption for the decompressor unit is also generally lower (between 2.8% and 3.6%).

The maximum clock speeds achieved for the compressor units range from 250 MHz to 310 MHz. And the achieved maximum clock rates for the decompressor units range from 299 MHz to 351 MHz. For the experiments, the entire system was clocked at 250 MHz, thus with a word width of 64 bits, a maximum throughput of 2 GB/s is achievable in the ideal case. The achieved throughput shown in Table 4 is ~1.95 GB/s for the compressor units. The slight differences to the maximal interface rate are due to some overhead from the DMAs. The CPU, on the other hand, only reached throughput values between 0.76 GB/s and 1.41 GB/s, resulting in a speedup of between 1.4 and 2.6 times. The throughput of the decompressor units ranges between 0.42 GB/s and 1.01 GB/s and is bound by the output interface in most cases. As the throughput is limited by the output interface, the high compression factors result in low input throughput values. For the decompressor units, the CPU implementation performs significantly better than the accelerator. However, as the resource utilization is low, the approach can be scaled up by instantiating more parallel decompressor units to achieve higher throughput. Moreover, [13] showed that decompression can be done selectively in hardware, e.g., only for the attributes that are needed for a query, thus bypassing the output bottleneck.

Table 3. Accelerator synthesis results.

	dataset	resources				max freq. [MHz]
		LUTs	FFs	BRAMs	URAMs	
compress	taxi	48,571 (21.1%)	6,681 (1.4%)	16 (5.1%)	0 (0.0%)	250
	twitter	16,565 (7.2%)	6,825 (1.5%)	0 (0.0%)	16 (16.7%)	310
	yahoo	31,852 (13.8%)	6,681 (1.4%)	16 (5.1%)	0 (0.0%)	294
	kostya	39,806 (17.3%)	6,681 (1.4%)	16 (5.1%)	0 (0.0%)	300
	skyshark	45,314 (19.7%)	6,681 (1.4%)	16 (5.1%)	0 (0.0%)	267
decompress	taxi	8,220 (3.6%)	2,346 (0.5%)	5 (1.6%)	0 (0.0%)	350
	twitter	6,362 (2.8%)	1,947 (0.4%)	5 (1.6%)	0 (0.0%)	351
	yahoo	8,166 (3.5%)	2,364 (0.5%)	5 (1.6%)	0 (0.0%)	344
	kostya	7,801 (3.4%)	2,330 (0.5%)	5 (1.6%)	0 (0.0%)	299
	skyshark	8,056 (3.5%)	2,339 (0.5%)	5 (1.6%)	0 (0.0%)	338

The power measurements were taken using a socket power meter and therefore cover the entire system (i.e., ZCU106 eval board or x86 computer), including all peripherals, memory and power supply. It can be seen in Table 4 that the energy requirements for the compressor accelerators are significantly lower than for the CPU (i.e., 6.0x to 10.5x reduction). For the decompressor units, the energy consumption is almost the same as for the CPU. The power consumption for the accelerator units stays constant at 25 W, which is almost the idle power of the eval board (~24 W). Accordingly, the energy consumption is directly proportional to the throughput. Scaling up the number of units would therefore also increase the energy efficiency.

Table 5 shows a comparison of our presented accelerator architecture with other FPGA-based compression accelerators. As mentioned in Sect. 2, there are no existing hardware accelerators for the FSST compression scheme, so the comparison focuses on Lempel-Ziv schemes. Given that the resource requirements

Table 4. Benchmark results for accelerator and x86 cpu.

	dataset	accelerator				x86 cpu		
		throughput [GB/s]		power [W]	energy [J]	throughput [GB/s]	power [W]	energy [J]
		in	out					
compress	taxi	**1.94** (2.35)	0.41	25	**0.52**	0.83	104	5.07
	twitter	**1.94** (2.31)	1.14	25	**4.03**	0.84	111	41.11
	yahoo	**1.95** (2.56)	1.00	25	**7.74**	0.76	104	81.30
	kostya	**1.95** (1.38)	1.03	25	**1.62**	1.41	112	9.72
	skyshark	**1.95** (1.90)	0.71	25	**4.75**	1.02	109	38.94
decompress	taxi	0.42 (0.15)	1.99	25	0.51	**2.88**	123	**0.43**
	twitter	1.00 (0.31)	1.71	25	4.58	**3.20**	122	4.78
	yahoo	1.01 (0.33)	1.96	25	7.69	**3.08**	122	8.02
	kostya	0.97 (0.30)	1.84	25	1.71	**3.24**	123	**1.62**
	skyshark	0.73 (0.23)	2.00	25	4.62	**3.12**	121	4.32

Table 5. Comparison of compression accelerators.

accelerator	scheme	resources				max freq. [MHz]	throughput [GB/s]
		LUTs	BRAMs	URAMs	DSPs		
ours	FSST	36,422	16	0	0	284	1.95
[17]	LZ4*	573	69	0	4	240	1.92
[1]	LZ4	729	17	0	3	224	n.a.
[3]	LZ4	14,509	82	0	32	156	6.08
Xilinx[†]	LZ4	18,374	19.25	6	0	274	1.66
Xilinx[‡]	Snappy	58,800	48	48	0	299	1.80
[16]	deflate	69,114	260.5	0	0	250	4.00

All accelerators were evaluated on AMD Xilinx Ultrascale+ devices.
[†] https://github.com/Xilinx/Applications/tree/master/data_compression/xil_lz4.
[‡] https://xilinx.github.io/Vitis_Libraries/data_compression/2021.1/source/L2/snappy.html.
modified version.

of our accelerator are dependent on the dataset, the entry depicted in Table 5 is based on the average of all evaluated datasets. In terms of resource utilization, our accelerator has a high LUT requirements, but uses fewer DSPs and BRAMs than the other approaches. For throughput, our accelerator is on par with most LZ4 accelerators.

Many applications rely on storing short strings individually to allow access to individual entries. With the accelerators presented, such data can be compressed within the storage medium using a SmartSSD, reducing the amount of data movement. As data movements have been found to account for the majority of energy consumption in most applications, this approach could lead to further energy savings [6]. In such a setup, our accelerators use similar resources and provide similar throughput as LZ-based accelerators, but achieve significantly higher compression factors. A possible application for such a setup could be a document store where incoming JSON data is compressed directly by the accelerator on the SmartSSD. To retrieve the stored JSON tuples, the JSON-CooP [13] parser accelerator can then be used directly on the SmartSSD to extract relevant information from the compressed data.

6 Conclusion

It was shown that the FSST compression scheme is well suited for compressing semi-structured data. The scheme achieves higher compression factors than LZ-based schemes when compressing JSON or BSON data. The increase in compression factor is particularly pronounced for smaller records.

Based on this observation, we presented hardware architectures to accelerate the FSST scheme. The presented hardware implementation achieves significantly higher throughput and energy efficiency for compression than a CPU-based reference implementation of FSST. For decompression, the CPU implementation is more efficient, but the hardware implementation can be scaled to achieve higher throughputs. In addition, related work [13] shows that decompression can be done selectively in hardware, also achieving higher throughputs. While the throughput and energy efficiency of our compressor accelerator is significantly higher than that of the software reference implementation, the hardware requirements are in the same ballpark as other FPGA-based accelerators for LZ compression schemes.

Acknowledgement. This work has been supported by the German Science Foundation (Deutsche Forschungsgemeinschaft, DFG) as part of the Priority Programme SPP 2037 under project ReProVide (project number 361498444).

References

1. Bartik, M., Ubik, S., Kubalík, P.: LZ4 compression algorithm on FPGA. In: 2015 IEEE International Conference on Electronics, Circuits, and Systems, ICECS 2015, Cairo, Egypt, 6–9 December 2015, pp. 179–182. IEEE (2015). https://doi.org/10.1109/ICECS.2015.7440278
2. Becher, A., Herrmann, A., Wildermann, S., Teich, J.: ReProVide: towards utilizing heterogeneous partially reconfigurable architectures for near-memory data processing. In: Datenbanksysteme für Business, Technologie und Web (BTW 2019), 18. Fachtagung des GI-Fachbereichs "Datenbanken und Informationssysteme" (DBIS), 4.-8. März 2019, Rostock, Germany, Workshopband. LNI, vol. P-290, pp. 51–70. Gesellschaft für Informatik, Bonn (2019). https://doi.org/10.18420/BTW2019-WS-04
3. Benes, T., Bartík, M., Kubalík, P.: High throughput and low latency LZ4 compressor on FPGA. In: Andrews, D., Cumplido, R., Feregrino, C., Platzner, M. (eds.) 2019 International Conference on ReConFigurable Computing and FPGAs, ReConFig 2019, Cancun, Mexico, 9–11 December 2019, pp. 1–5. IEEE (2019). https://doi.org/10.1109/RECONFIG48160.2019.8994794

4. Binnig, C., Hildenbrand, S., Färber, F.: Dictionary-based order-preserving string compression for main memory column stores. In: Çetintemel, U., Zdonik, S.B., Kossmann, D., Tatbul, N. (eds.) Proceedings of the ACM SIGMOD International Conference on Management of Data, SIGMOD 2009, Providence, Rhode Island, USA, June 29– 2 July 2009, pp. 283–296. ACM (2009). https://doi.org/10.1145/1559845.1559877
5. Boncz, P.A., Neumann, T., Leis, V.: FSST: fast random access string compression. Proc. VLDB Endow. **13**(11), 2649–2661 (2020). http://www.vldb.org/pvldb/vol13/p2649-boncz.pdf
6. Boroumand, A., et al.: Google workloads for consumer devices: mitigating data movement bottlenecks. In: Proceedings of the Twenty-Third International Conference on Architectural Support for Programming Languages and Operating Systems, ASPLOS 2018, Williamsburg, VA, USA, 24–28 March 2018, pp. 316–331. ACM (2018). https://doi.org/10.1145/3173162.3173177
7. Chen, J., Daverveldt, M., Al-Ars, Z.: FPGA acceleration of zstd compression algorithm. In: IEEE International Parallel and Distributed Processing Symposium Workshops, IPDPS Workshops 2021, Portland, OR, USA, 17–21 June 2021, pp. 188–191. IEEE (2021). https://doi.org/10.1109/IPDPSW52791.2021.00035
8. Chintapalli, S., et al.: Benchmarking streaming computation engines: storm, flink and spark streaming. In: 2016 IEEE International Parallel and Distributed Processing Symposium Workshops (IPDPSW), pp. 1789–1792 (2016). https://doi.org/10.1109/IPDPSW.2016.138
9. Dann, J., Wagner, R., Ritter, D., Faerber, C., Fröning, H.: Pipejson: parsing JSON at line speed on fpgas. In: International Conference on Management of Data, DaMoN 2022, Philadelphia, PA, USA, 13 June 2022, pp. 3:1–3:7. ACM (2022). https://doi.org/10.1145/3533737.3535094
10. Fowers, J., Kim, J., Burger, D., Hauck, S.: A scalable high-bandwidth architecture for lossless compression on FPGAs. In: 23rd IEEE Annual International Symposium on Field-Programmable Custom Computing Machines, FCCM 2015, Vancouver, BC, Canada, 2–6 May 2015, pp. 52–59. IEEE Computer Society (2015). https://doi.org/10.1109/FCCM.2015.46
11. Hahn, T., Becher, A., Wildermann, S., Teich, J.: Raw filtering of JSON data on fpgas. In: 2022 Design, Automation & Test in Europe Conference & Exhibition, DATE 2022, Antwerp, Belgium, 14–23 March 2022, pp. 250–255. IEEE (2022). https://doi.org/10.23919/DATE54114.2022.9774696
12. Hahn, T., Wildermann, S., Teich, J.: SPEAR-JSON: selective parsing of JSON to enable accelerated stream processing on fpgas. In: 33rd International Conference on Field-Programmable Logic and Applications, FPL 2023, Gothenburg, Sweden, 4–8 September 2023, pp. 189–196. IEEE (2023). https://doi.org/10.1109/FPL60245.2023.00034
13. Hahn, T., Wildermann, S., Teich, J.: Json-coop: a JSON decompression/parsing co-design for fpgas. In: 34th International Conference on Field-Programmable Logic and Applications, FPL 2024, Torino, Italy, 2–6 September 2024, pp. 11–18. IEEE (2024). https://doi.org/10.1109/FPL64840.2024.00012
14. Langohr, M., Vogler, T., Meyer-Wegener, K.: SKYSHARK: a benchmark with real-world data for line-rate stream processing with FPGAs. In: Leyer M, W.J. (ed.) Lernen, Wissen, Daten, Analysen (LWDA) Conference Proceedings, Marburg, Germany, 9–11 October 2023. CEUR Workshop Proceedings, vol. 3630, pp. 98–109. CEUR-WS.org (2023). https://ceur-ws.org/Vol-3630/LWDA2023-paper9.pdf

15. Larsson, N.J., Moffat, A.: Offline dictionary-based compression. In: Data Compression Conference, DCC 1999, Snowbird, Utah, USA, 29–31 March 1999, pp. 296–305. IEEE Computer Society (1999). https://doi.org/10.1109/DCC.1999.755679
16. Ledwon, M., Cockburn, B.F., Han, J.: High-throughput fpga-based hardware accelerators for deflate compression and decompression using high-level synthesis. IEEE Access **8**, 62207–62217 (2020). https://doi.org/10.1109/ACCESS.2020.2984191
17. Liu, W., Mei, F., Wang, C., O'Neill, M., Jr., E.E.S.: Data compression device based on modified LZ4 algorithm. IEEE Trans. Consum. Electron. **64**(1), 110–117 (2018). https://doi.org/10.1109/TCE.2018.2810480
18. Müller, R., Teubner, J., Alonso, G.: Glacier: a query-to-hardware compiler. In: Proceedings of the ACM SIGMOD International Conference on Management of Data, SIGMOD 2010, Indianapolis, Indiana, USA, 6–10 June 2010, pp. 1159–1162. ACM (2010). https://doi.org/10.1145/1807167.1807307
19. Pekhimenko, G., Guo, C., Jeon, M., Huang, P., Zhou, L.: TerseCades: efficient data compression in stream processing. In: 2018 USENIX Annual Technical Conference, USENIX ATC 2018, Boston, MA, USA, 11–13 July 2018, pp. 307–320. USENIX Association (2018). https://www.usenix.org/conference/atc18/presentation/pekhimenko
20. Shukla, A., Chaturvedi, S., Simmhan, Y.: Riotbench: an iot benchmark for distributed stream processing systems. Concurr. Comput. Pract. Exp. **29**(21), e4257 (2017)

CHaOS: A Persistent Lightweight Cache Hybridization-Aware OS

Nils Wilbert[1,2(✉)], Matthias Szymanski[3], Stefan Wildermann[2], Henriette Herzog[3], Timo Hönig[3], and Jürgen Teich[2]

[1] Julius-Maximilians-Universität Würzburg, Würzburg, Germany
nils.wilbert@uni-wuerzburg.de
[2] Friedrich-Alexander-Universität Erlangen-Nürnberg, Erlangen, Germany
{stefan.wildermann,juergen.teich}@fau.de
[3] Ruhr-Universität Bochum, Bochum, Germany
{matthias.szymanski,henriette.herzog,timo.hoenig}@rub.de

Abstract. Computer systems are prone to crashes and power outages, particularly in intermittent computing scenarios where embedded systems rely on unreliable energy-harvesting sources. Hybrid caches, which integrate volatile and non-volatile memory (NVM) sections, offer opportunities for efficient operating system (OS) services to ensure data persistence over power interruptions. However, the lack of OS awareness of hybrid cache structures can result in inefficient backups, data loss and inconsistencies, as well as underutilization of the potential of hybrid caches. This paper introduces the Cache Hybridization-aware Operating System (CHaOS), that is based on a co-design of the OS and the underlying hardware to systematically persist volatile states and data in case of power outages. Our evaluation demonstrates that CHaOS not only proves robust against power outages, but also can significantly reduce the backup latency. In our test of using CHaOS to execute an image processing application on a hybrid-cache system, already with 75% of caches being non-volatile, the backup latency drops to only 8.2% compared to a completely volatile cache. At the same time, the energy demand could be reduced due to lower static power consumption of NVM technology. Our investigations validate the feasibility of CHaOS and establish a strong foundation for future research.

Keywords: Hardware/OS Co-Design · Hybrid Caches · Persistent OS

1 Introduction

Due to the rise of the Internet of Things (IoT), mobile devices have long reached levels of complexity where the use of dedicated Operating Systems (OSs) has become irreplaceable. Mobile devices are mostly battery powered, potentially

---

N. Wilbert—Work completed while at Friedrich-Alexander-Universität Erlangen-Nürnberg.

even making use of energy-harvesting techniques to charge their battery on the go [27]. The occurrence of power outages are thus a possibility, meaning unless dedicated mechanisms are provided by the OS and the hardware, all volatile memory contents can become irrecoverable in such an instance. Early mobile OSs such as Palm OS did not provide any guarantees concerning the persistence of data following a power outage due to, e.g., a depleted battery [26]. Nevertheless, robustness against power failures is naturally a desired property of mobile OSs to enhance the user experience, as even the later Palm PDA's attempted to achieve persistence guarantees through a flash-based non-volatile file system, which required applications to be copied to the volatile RAM before their execution [20]. Concerning the resulting discipline of intermittent computing [14], byte-addressable Non-Volatile Memory (NVM) technology is slowly becoming mature enough to be commercially viable and may one day replace the conventional volatile DRAM and SRAM technology [4,34]. The use of such memories that can guarantee persistence as a hardware property is thus of natural interest. By combining volatile and non-volatile memory technologies at cache level to a hybrid cache design [31,35], a trade-off between the individual technology characteristics can be realized to achieve highly space and energy-efficient caches.

The hybridization of caches has the potential to alleviate the implementation of efficient OS services that guarantee data persistence in the event of power outages and system crashes. However, the challenge is that parts of the memory system still are volatile. Data stored in these volatile regions is not only lost during power failures, but also does the order of memory consistency not have to comply with the order of memory persistency, as highlighted in [21]. Consequently, persistent data can be in inconsistent states. Since caches are typically transparent to the OS, a critical question arises: To what degree must the OS be aware of the underlying hybrid cache architecture to achieve minimal backup and recovery times while reliably providing persistence as a service?

If the OS is not made aware of the hybridized cache, unnecessary backups of non-volatile cache lines, a loss of modified volatile cache lines or generally a poor exploitation of the potential of hybrid caches might be the consequence. On the other hand, a hybrid cache aware OS can generate additional overhead for the backup process. In this paper, we propose and analyze the potential of a lightweight OS based on Unikraft called Cache Hybridization-aware Operating System (CHaOS). The key idea of CHaOS is a cooperation of the OS with the underlying hardware by removing a layer of transparency, thus allowing for the exploitation of the non-volatility property of hybrid caches, in order to efficiently provide robustness against power outages.

With this paper, we make the following contributions:

- **Cache Hybridization Awareness**: We analyze the potential benefits of removing a layer of transparency by making the OS aware of hybrid caches.
- **Hardware/OS Co-Design**: CHaOS achieves data persistence by enabling the OS and hardware to cooperate in performing backups.
- **Advantages of Hybrid Caches**: We demonstrate the advantages and feasibility of OS managed hybrid caches in intermittently powered systems.

– **Foundations for Future Approaches:** We discuss the impact on transactional and security-relevant systems that incorporate hybridized caches.

The structure of the paper is as follows: In Sect. 2, we explain the fundamentals of our approach and discuss related work. The CHaOS approach is presented in great detail in Sect. 3. In Sect. 4, we experimentally evaluate CHaOS. A conclusion and an outlook on future work is provided in Sect. 5.

2 Background

This section lays out fundamentals and related work on non-volatile memory technology and persistence in the context of OSs.

Non-volatile Memory Hierarchies: In the realm of intermittent computing, systems have to handle frequent power outages and in order to reduce the overhead of rebooting and recomputing previous functions, systems should persist the volatile system state across such power outages. Thus, between detecting a power outage and the system losing power, enough energy must be available to back up the volatile memory. This either requires triggering the backup process at a voltage threshold suitable to ensure all volatile memory contents can be saved, or alternatively equipping the system with additional capacitors scaled accordingly [32]. The more (volatile) memory the system provides, the higher the voltage threshold has to be set or the bigger the backup capacitors have to be scaled, respectively. For embedded systems, byte-addressable NVM technologies that do not need to be backed offer great advantages. Phase Change Memory (PCM) and Spin-Transfer Torque RAM (STT-RAM) in particular [4,34], have been identified as promising non-volatile alternatives for DRAM and SRAM, respectively. Both technologies showcase high density and low static power, which can also improve the future scalability of embedded systems [28,29]. However, writing to PCM or STT-RAM cells requires changing the physical state of chalcogenide glass or changing the orientation of a magnetic field, respectively. Thus, the energy and latency requirements for write accesses are much higher compared to DRAM and SRAM.

To further raise the border of persistence in the memory hierarchy, non-volatility can also be introduced on cache level, by hybridizing the caches, i.e., splitting the cache sets into volatile SRAM and non-volatile STT-RAM sections [31,35]. Fully non-volatile caches are generally not considered suitable due to the low endurance of STT-RAM. However, due to its higher density, STT-RAM-based caches can be designed with higher capacities than SRAM caches. They can also enable more energy efficient designs, due to lower static power consumption. As hybrid caches are only partially persistent, the modified SRAM contents have to be backed up in case of a power failure. In contrast to entirely volatile caches, the amount of data that needs to be persisted is reduced. Therefore, a smaller backup capacitor to ensure all data is persisted can be utilized. By incorporating non-volatile flip-flops, the border of persistence can also be raised to the level of the entire CPU, leading to the concept of NonVolatile Processors (NVPs) [30]. However, NVPs are heavily limited in terms of achievable clock rates, thus mainly being of interest for the ultra-low power energy-harvesting domain.

Persistence in Operating Systems: Persistence, especially for larger systems, must also be supported on the system-software level. For traditional systems, the OS takes a key role in persisting data from the volatile main memory to disk. This happens explicitly on a system suspend or shutdown and implicitly as part of the OS' virtual-memory system, when swapping out pages from main memory to disk. Narayanan et al. [17] discuss the potential of utilizing NVM on all memory layers to achieve *whole-system persistence*. Their approach enables fast recovery of applications' main-memory state after power failures. Integrating NVM at the main-memory level is not only beneficial for the recovery of in-memory state, but also allows for new OS functionality. [1] describe several OS components that can be redesigned with NVM. For example, if a system is equipped with NVM in sufficient capacity, the disk layer may become obsolete. This enables improvements in terms of performance, as paging and swapping mechanisms can be removed. Additionally, the reboot process becomes faster and more efficient, when the execution state remains in the persistent main memory across shutdowns.

While NVM offers the possibility of designing more efficient OSs, it can also negatively impact OS security and data consistency. As described by [1], volatility can improve system security. For example, encryption keys or decrypted data is durable in NVM even after the corresponding programs exit execution. Thus, such sensitive data needs to be handled by a non-volatile OS or as part of hardware/OS co-design [11]. Additionally, problems with data inconsistency in non-volatile memories may arise in case of power failures [24]. This is especially relevant when considering intermittently-powered devices for which power outages may occur at any time.

Related Work: Hybrid cache hierarchies have previously been applied to the field of intermittent computing [33,36]. However, these works focus on policies regarding efficient backup and replacement strategies solely on hardware level. On the software side, approaches such as Alpaca [15] provide a programming model to allow for intermittent executions without explicitly setting checkpoints. Nevertheless, this still requires the user to adapt to a new programming model, which we avoid with our approach by providing persistence as a service. On operating-system level, approaches concerning the use of NVM technologies have been researched to a greater extent. For example, Twizzler [6] is an OS that is optimized for systems with hybrid main memory, composed of both NVM and DRAM. By enabling programs to explicitly place objects in NVM, data can be shared not only by different programs, but also across program runs. Twizzler also optimizes persistent memory accesses to improve the system's overall performance. [23] envision a system with *whole-system persistence* and provide the foundation for running general-purpose OSs exclusively with NVM, which allows OS design without performance and energy-intensive persistence measures.

To achieve persistence of a whole system across power outages, a number of approaches that consider the OS level already exist. However, while works such as [16] present techniques that are closely related to our approach, namely writing back the entire volatile system state to a non-volatile location, they do not consider partially non-volatile caches. [3] present a kernel-oriented approach to ensuring continuous operation of intermittently-powered IoT devices. They utilize an interrupt-driven checkpointing mechanism, where the OS stores a backup of the entire main memory to the system's NVM in case a power outage is detected. Furthermore, works such as Mementos [25] or Hibernus [2] provide well-known approaches for placing checkpoints at compile-time or dynamically saving a snapshot of the system on a voltage drop, respectively. However, none of these approaches consider the presence of caches in the system.

When caches are transparent to the OS and without special hardware support, explicit cache line flushes and memory fences (to avoid reordering memory instructions) are required for persistent programming to guarantee that cache contents up until the given instruction have reached a state of persistence. To ensure that caches are part of the persistence domain, Intel's eADR platform and similar works such as [18] propose a "flush-on-fail" approach, where the hardware automatically flushes the cache to a persistent memory on detecting a power failure. In this paper, we follow a similar "flush-on-fail" paradigm, however, we extend the scope to hybrid volatile/non-volatile caches where persistence of parts of the cache is a given property. To our knowledge, none of the previously presented approaches have considered the combined role of the OS and the hardware in an intermittently powered system that incorporates hybrid caches to a greater extent.

3 CHaOS: Combining OS-Level Persistence with HW-Persistence

In this section, we present Cache Hybridization-aware Operating System (CHaOS), a hardware/OS co-design for non-volatile embedded systems that exploit hybrid volatile/non-volatile caches. The CHaOS approach, as illustrated in Fig. 1 (right), focuses on the interaction between the OS and the hardware on cache level. First, we lay out the design and principles of CHaOS in Sect. 3.1 and detail the implementation in Sect. 3.2.

3.1 Hardware/OS Co-design

Hardware Design: Regarding the hardware design, we consider systems with conventional single-core CPUs in this paper, in our case using the ARM ISA, i.e., we explicitly do not require any NVPs for our approach, meaning CHaOS-based systems can be clocked at frequencies up to the GHz domain. The CPU cache is considered to be a hybrid volatile/non-volatile cache. To be precise the

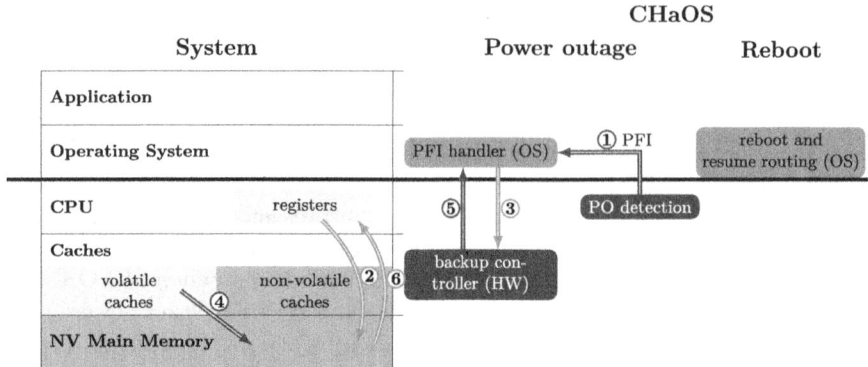

Fig. 1. Overview of interplay between operating system (green) and hardware (blue) in CHaOS. (Color figure online)

hybridization takes place on cache set level, meaning for an n-way associative cache, there are n_0 volatile SRAM and n_1 non-volatile STT-RAM cache lines, wrt. $n_0 + n_1 = n$. To ensure, that a non-volatile cache line can withstand a power outage, the hybridization not only concerns the data array of the cache, but also the tag array and cache flags, as data without the correct tag and flags is invalid to read by design. For this paper, we consider a single-level cache hierarchy, however, the approach can also be applied to multi-level hierarchies. For the base of our memory hierarchy, we consider a non-volatile PCM main memory. While our approach requires a non-volatile main memory, this does not have to be a limitation as PCM main memories in particular have already been shown to provide a feasible, energy-efficient alternative to conventional DRAM main memories [37]. To back up the cache in case of an outage, a dedicated hardware controller, as seen in, e.g., [19] is used. However, for our design the backup controller is integrated into the cache controller itself, as it requires knowledge, whether data is stored in a volatile or a non-volatile cache line. Upon access to the cache, the backup controller will track when data is placed to a volatile cache line and whether the access modifies said data. The backup controller thus keeps track of all volatile, modified cache lines and can, in case of a power outage, directly issue write back requests of the tracked cache lines. As the number of volatile cache lines is limited, so is the number of tracked cache lines. Upon a power outage, the backup controller is powered via an additional capacitor.

Operating System Design: For the OS design, we build upon the principles of Neverlast [9,10]. Neverlast is a lightweight kernel for intermittently powered systems equipped with non-volatile main memory. A key feature to ensure data consistency across power outages is the *Power Failure Interrupt (PFI)*. This interrupt is issued once the supply voltage drops below a certain threshold that is chosen so that all remaining volatile system components can be backed up to NVRAM. This backup routine is further described below. Additionally, Neverlast uses a device configuration log to persist the volatile state of external devices so that on resuming execution, the devices can be restored to their previous configuration. This allows the system to continue program execution without the risk of failures due to uninitialized or misconfigured devices.

The principles of Neverlast are adapted to the unikernel approach chosen for CHaOS. In addition to the device configuration log, CHaOS enables further operating-mode optimizations with regard to energy efficiency. Based on energy models of external devices (such as sensors), we can estimate the energy demand for different functions of these devices. Such models can be obtained through energy measurement campaigns and are configured per device on its initial deployment. With this data and combined with user-provided priorities to individual device functions, the OS can prioritize which functions are executed when limited power supply is available. CHaOS's hardware/OS co-design allows us to further extend the system functionality.

In the following, the design of CHaOS core features, the power-outage handling, system suspend and resume routines specific to CHaOS are described in more detail. Section 3.2 further details their implementation.

Power Outage Handling: To ensure continuous operation with consistent data across power outages, our system requires three key routines: **power outage detection**, **system suspend**, and **system resume**. The design of each step is outlined below, while the implementation is detailed in Sect. 3.2.

Our approach utilizes the **detection of imminent power outages** (*PO detection*) to initiate a consistent system backup and suspend, performed by the OS. Concerning the mechanism of detecting an imminent power outage, multiple approaches are possible. Our hybrid-cache-aware persistent OS designed provides a generic interface that allows a variety of PO-detection mechanism to be included. Related approaches mentioned in Sect. 2, such as [2], make use of a hardware module detecting supply-voltage drops below a pre-determined threshold, in which case an external interrupt is triggered to notify the system.

In CHaOS, the suspend routine consists of a handshake between the OS and the backup controller to switch control back and forth between them. Utilizing both hardware and OS, ensures that all volatile data is persisted. The individual steps followed upon a power failure (PO) as illustrated by numbers in circles in Fig. 1, are explained in detail in the following. Once the PO detection is triggered, the hardware initiates the *Power-Failure Interrupt (PFI)*, which signals the OS to start the power-outage handling ①. For this, the OS halts the current execution and initiates the backup of the remaining volatile system components as part of the *PFI handler*. Once the backup has finished, a handshake with the *backup controller* of the hybrid cache is performed, handing the control of the following backup steps to the hardware ③. The backup controller stalls the system until all cache misses have been served, to ensure that the system is suspended in a consistent state.

Then, the volatile cache lines of each cache hierarchy level are written back to non-volatile memory ④. When the last cache level has been backed up to the main memory, we can safely assume that the whole memory hierarchy has been persisted. Non-volatile or unmodified cache lines require no special handling, as they retain their contents when the hardware loses power. At this point, the second part of the handshake is performed: the backup controller signals the OS that the hybrid-cache backup is complete and OS regains control over the backup process ⑤ and powers down the system.

Once the power supply is established again, the system reboots and the OS checks whether a valid backup is available during its initialization. If such a backup is detected, the OS assumes that the previous execution was halted due to a power outage and initiated the **resume routine**. The OS restores all backed-up volatile data ⑥ and resumes program execution from the point of the PO detection. During the restore routine, no special handling of the caches is required, as all volatile cache lines were written back to non-volatile memory during the suspend and the non-volatile cache lines retained their contents.

Persistence as a Service: CHaOS guarantees persistence, as no progress is lost despite the occurrence of power outages. Applications running with CHaOS can also still make use of caching effects, as they are part of the persistent domain. CHaOS further exploits hybrid volatile/non-volatile caches by performing a selective backup of only the volatile cache lines. This dramatically reduces the overhead compared to approaches that include caches in the persistent domain but without further knowledge of the underlying hardware, which require writing back the entire cache to the main memory. However, to maintain a degree of transparency, we do not require the OS to have full knowledge of the underlying cache hierarchy. Moreover, while exploiting NVM, the CPU can remain volatile with higher clock rates compared to NVPs.

For security applications, NVPs can even be hazardous, as confidential information may be persisted and can become vulnerable to attacks. With a hardware/OS co-design as proposed by CHaOS, users could provide hints in their application code that specify whether certain data should be persisted or not. As the OS acts in cooperation with the cache controller, placement decisions can be guided to avoid storing confidential data in the non-volatile cache section and, thus, avoid persisting this data to the main memory. The CHaOS principle can thus also serve as a base to allow for transactional systems with hybrid caches. By placing transaction start and stop hints in the program, the suspend routine would then not back up the current Program Counter (PC) when the execution is halted within a transactional section. Instead, the position marked with as the starting point is persisted. From this point on, all data is kept in a separate volatile cache section that is excluded from the backup during the suspend routine. During the resume routine, the PC is then restored to the start of the transaction and the remaining instructions are replayed. With our approach, we thus want to emphasize how future OS for systems incorporating hybrid caches may need to remove a layer of transparency regarding caches in order to realize the full potential of the architecture.

3.2 Implementation

Regarding the implementation of hybrid caches, we make use of the gem5 simulator [5]. The modularity of gem5 allows us to extend the simulator towards hybrid caches, allowing us to select different types of memory technologies for implementing each cache line. Additional latency and energy parameters are used in accordance with the memory technology of the accessed cache lines. Furthermore, the cache backup controller is also implemented as a gem5 module. For the OS, we implement the PO detection, suspend and resume routines as outlined in Sect. 3.1 into Unikraft [13], a lightweight unikernel OS suitable for the embedded area. We chose Unikraft due to its efficient execution in regard to boot time and runtime overhead. Additionally, Unikraft is currently under development to include multi-core support, which will allow its use for a wider range of hardware platforms.

Power-Outage detection: For the power-outage detection (PO detection), we assume a hardware module that detects whether the supply voltage falls below a pre-determined threshold. With regard to the implementation, we trigger power outages by setting a specific flag from outside the simulated system.

Suspend Mechanism: Following the detection of an imminent PO, the system has to be suspended in a consistent state. For this, the OS handles the *PFI*, which is triggered by the PO detection, and initiates the backup of the remaining volatile system components. These encompass the general-purpose registers and the stack pointer (SP). The register contents are stored in a secluded non-volatile partition of the system memory that is not available for either stack, heap, or page tables ②. The PC cannot be backed up easily due to its read-/write-protection. However, its backup is redundant due to the information within the frame pointer, the link register, and the stack pointer. Due to the system running in non-volatile main memory, the stack is inherently persistent and does not require a backup. Additionally, a backup flag is stored. Based on this flag, the OS either resumes computation from the backup or performs a clean boot system startup once the power supply is established again.

Once the CPU registers are backed up, the OS hands over control to the backup controller ③. This controller first waits until all Miss Status Holding Registers (MSHRs) of the cache are drained. MSHRs contain information on yet to be served cache misses, meaning the CPU does not have to stall on a cache miss unless encountering data dependencies [12]. Even if the CPU is already drained, the MSHRs may still contain entries on outstanding cache misses. Therefore, to ensure that we halt the system in a consistent state, those misses have to be served before initiating the backup of the cache lines. After the MSHRs are drained, we can commence with writing back the volatile cache content ④. For every modified volatile cache line, a writeback is issued, storing the cache line's content in the write buffer towards the next lower level of the memory hierarchy. For non-volatile or unmodified cache lines, no special handling is required.

Table 1. Characterized read/write latencies and average read/write access energies of the hybrid cache.

	SRAM Cache	STT-RAM Cache
Read Latency	2 Cycles @480 MHz	2 Cycles @480 MHz
Write Latency	2 Cycles @480 MHz	8 Cycles @480 MHz
Read Energy (per access)	0.09 nJ	0.07 nJ
Write Energy (per access)	0.09 nJ	0.56 nJ
Static Power	407.877 mW	22.676 mW

Write buffers naturally have a limited capacity. Therefore, in case the number of necessary writebacks exceed the buffer capacity, writebacks have to be held back temporarily to allow successively feeding the write buffer instead. For multi-level cache hierarchies, the cache backup procedure is repeated for the next lower level of the hierarchy. Once the lowest cache level is backed up, the cache backup is considered complete. At this point, the hardware notifies the OS of the completed backup by setting a register flag, handing back control over the backup process to the OS ⑤. The OS then powers down the system.

Resume Routine: Once the power supply is established again, the system reboots. After the memory initialization, the OS checks the backup flag. If it is set, the OS restores the volatile system state ⑥. For this, the general purpose registers and the stack pointer, including the frame pointer and link register, are restored in reverse order. As outlined above, no special handling of the caches is required following the reboot. Lastly, the backup flag is cleared. After a successful restore process, the program continues its execution right after the point in the suspend routine, where the registers were backed up to NVM. This is right before the handshake with the backup controller. As the backup flag was cleared during the OS restore routine, the handshake is not repeated and the control flow exits the *PFI* handler. With the PC restored, the program execution can resume where it was halted before the power outage.

4 Evaluation

In this section, after explaining our experimental setup, we display a number of statistics for experimental runs of our CHaOS approach, not only validating the concept but further demonstrating the potential of our design paradigm.

For the experiments, we use the gem5 simulator [5], which has been extended as described in Sect. 3.2. Our gem5 extensions further allow configuring hybrid caches with different non-volatility ratios: The non-volatility ratio can be set to any number between 0 and 100 with the value determining the percentage of cache lines per cache set which are treated as non-volatile STT-RAM lines. For our test system, we make use of a 256 kB large 4-way-associative hybrid data

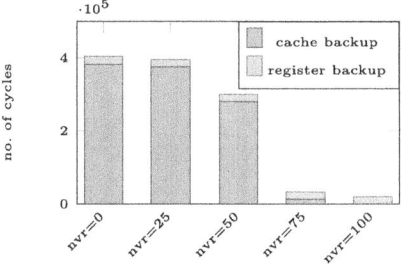
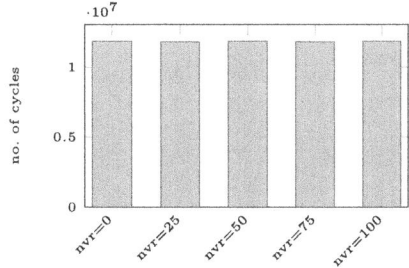

Fig. 2. Number of cycles to backup and suspend the system

Fig. 3. Number of cycles to reboot the system

cache. We run our experiments with non-volatility ratios of 25, 50 and 75 implying one, two and three of the four cache lines to be non-volatile, respectively. Non-volatility ratios of 0 and 100, implying a conventional SRAM and a fully non-volatile cache, respectively, serve as reference points. Least Recently Used (LRU) serves as the cache replacement policy. A pipelined, single core, in-order-issue out-of-order-execution CPU clocked at 480 MHz is used in our simulated system. The non-volatile main memory is simulated in NVMain2.0 [22] and given as a 4 GB PCM as seen in [7]. The latency and energy parameters for the hybrid cache are generated using NVSim [8] and are shown in Table 1. Our experiments are based around the task of 2D convolution for image processing. A 640 × 640 image is first filtered through a 3 × 3 large kernel, after which a power outage is triggered. Parts of the output image might thus still be located in the cache and need to be persisted, as the result is otherwise incomplete. CHaOS will now persist all volatile contents as explained in Sect. 3 and suspend the system. After the reboot, we perform a second convolution on the same input image with a different 3 × 3 large kernel. By using the same input image, we can thus benefit from cache effects in case parts of the input image are located in the non-volatile cache lines, thus remaining cached, even following a power outage. The application is built using Unikraft [13] extended with our CHaOS services (see Sect. 3). While power outages can occur at any point of time, with this setup we ensure the comparability and reproducibility of our results.

In Figs. 2 to 7, we display a number of key measures stemming from our simulation-based experiments using CHaOS. The different non-volatility ratios are denoted as *nvr*.

Looking at the cycles required for the backup in Fig. 2, a clear trend can be observed. For lower non-volatility ratios, the time to suspend the system is dominated by the cache backup. With higher non-volatility ratios, the cycles required to back up the cache are reduced. From our experiments, we can even observe a dramatic reduction in cache backup overhead when switching from a non-volatility ratio of 50 to one of 75. Whereas the analytical worst-case cache backup time would scale down proportionally to the higher non-volatility ratios, due to caches acting as a heuristic the actual backup times can be far

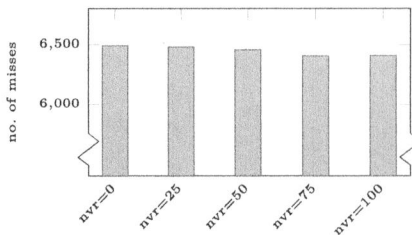

Fig. 4. Number of read misses for the 2D convolution following a power outage

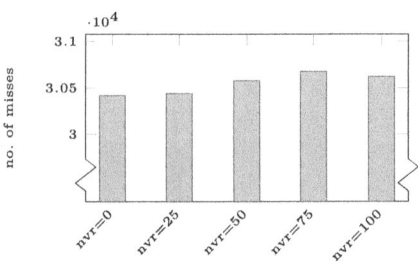

Fig. 5. Number of write misses for the 2D convolution following a power outage

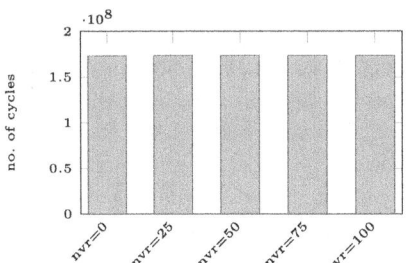

Fig. 6. Number of cycles for performing two 2D convolutions including a power outage occuring inbetween the convolutions

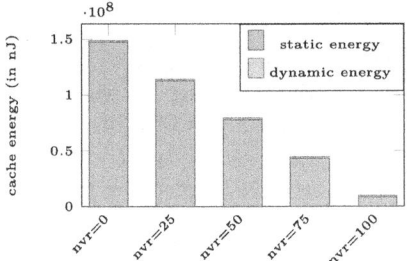

Fig. 7. Energy consumed by the data cache when performing two 2D convolutions including a power outage occuring inbetween the convolutions

below the worst-case. Here, CHaOS allows us to exploit these caching effects, as the cooperation with the hardware allows for a selective backup of only the modified volatile cache lines. CHaOS thus not only provides, but also realizes the potential to achieve far lower backup times compared to the worst case. The time required to back up the registers remains fairly constant throughout all tested non-volatility ratios. As is to be expected, the time required to reboot the system (Fig. 3) also remains fairly constant for all non-volatility ratios.

Concerning the data reuse following the reboot after the power outage, the number of read and write misses for the second 2D convolution are depicted in Figs. 4 to 5, respectively. While the input image, i.e., the data that is accessed via read requests can be reused from the previous convolution, the output image will be written to a newly allocated memory location. In Fig. 4, we can observe that the amount of read misses is reduced with a higher non-volatility ratio. However, the reduction of read misses is only marginal regarding the big picture. In fact, while read misses are reduced for the higher non-volatility ratio due to data remaining cached following the power outage, the number of write misses, visualized in Fig. 5, rises. This can be explained by the higher amount of cache lines remaining valid following the power outage leading to unfavorable decisions by the replacement policy, especially if data withstanding the power outage is not even reused before eventually being evicted. CHaOS can thus realize data reuse following a power outage by exploiting the non-volatile cache lines. However, for bigger working sets, the advantage of a small amount of data withstanding a power outage is only marginal. The main argument for non-volatile caches in the field of intermittent computing is thus not a reduced miss-rate following a power outage, but rather the reduction in the backup overhead.

Considering the overall runtime and cache energy requirements for performing the two successive 2D convolutions, as depicted in Figs. 6 and 7, respectively, the write overhead caused by the STT-RAM sections of the cache proves to be marginal. Latency-wise, this can be explained by the fact, that the increased NVM write latency is mainly of concern when having to wait for a write request to finish due to, e.g., data dependencies. Since data dependencies between instructions are mainly on register rather than on cache level, this is only rarely the case, with the CPU continuing with the next instruction as soon as a write is issued rather than stalling until the write is completed, in case there are no data dependencies. Pipelined out-of-order CPUs (as seen in our test system), can help to hide these latencies even further. Regarding the energy dimension, in our experiments, a fully non-volatile cache leads to an increase in dynamic energy consumption of 11.9% compared to a conventional volatile cache, with the hybridized designs ranging between the two extreme points. As read requests lead to lower energy costs when served in the STT-RAM section of the cache, for read-intensive applications, this can balance out huge parts of the NVM write overhead. However, the lower static power of STT-RAM compared to SRAM provides a clear advantage of higher non-volatility ratios in the total energy consumption, which, especially for larger caches, is dominated by the static energy. Therefore, despite minor disadvantages regarding the dynamic energy consumption, hybrid cache designs can prove to be more energy-efficient than conventional caches.

In summary, in our experiments we have observed that hybrid caches offer a great potential for intermittent computing, as the backup overhead, otherwise limiting the potential use of caches in intermittently powered systems, is greatly reduced with our CHaOS approach. The CHaOS approach further proved robustness against power outages, as no errors could be observed following the interruption by a power outage. Additionally, in our experiments the NVM write overhead has shown to be only of minor concern, therefore validating the feasibility of hybrid caches for future research, with the concept of hybrid-cache awareness in OS further proving to be a suitable direction.

5 Conclusion and Outlook

In this paper, we have proposed CHaOS, an extension to Unikraft providing persistence as a service including awareness for hybrid volatile/non-volatile caches by performing the backup procedure as a hardware/OS co-design. With regard to our results, the CHaOS approach has not only shown to be robust, but we have drastically reduced the backup overhead compared to approaches that do not feature any cache-awareness, thus not being able to exploit partially non-volatile caches. For future research in the field of intermittent computing, dissolving a layer of transparency regarding cache has shown to be a promising direction and may even be a necessity to capitalize on the potential of NVM in caches. Furthermore, hybrid caches in general have shown to be a feasible approach for intermittently powered systems, therefore remaining a research field worth exploring. Looking ahead, the CHaOS approach can further be investigated for the use in transactional systems as the potential of user-provided hints to the OS to realize, e.g., critical sections, is still to be evaluated in greater detail. With CHaOS, we have thus created a foundation for future works extending on the exploitation of persistence provided as an OS service in NVM-based systems. This is not only limited to intermittent computing in embedded systems, but to computing scenarios in general which require performance, consistency, and security guarantees over crashes and power outages.

Acknowledgements. This work is funded in parts by the Deutsche Forschungsgemeinschaft (DFG, German Research Foundation) – project numbers 502213043 (*HYPNOS*) and 502228341 (*Memento*) as part of SPP 2377 and 465958100 (*NEON*) and 539710462 (*DOSS*).

References

1. Bailey, K., Ceze, L., Gribble, S.D., Levy, H.M.: Operating system implications of fast, cheap, non-volatile memory. In: Proceedings of HotOS (2011)
2. Balsamo, D., et al.: Hibernus: sustaining computation during intermittent supply for energy-harvesting systems. IEEE Embed. Syst. Lett. **7**(1), 15–18 (2015)
3. Berthou, G., Delizy, T., Marquet, K., Risset, T., Salagnac, G.: Sytare: a lightweight kernel for nvram-based transiently-powered systems. IEEE Trans. Comput. **68**(9), 1390–1403 (2019)
4. Bhatti, S., Sbiaa, R., Hirohata, A., et al.: Spintronics based random access memory: a review. Mater. Today **20**(9), 530–548 (2017)
5. Binkert, N., Beckmann, B., Black, G., et al.: The gem5 simulator. SIGARCH Comp. Arch. News **39**(2), 1–7 (2011)
6. Bittman, D., Alvaro, P., Mehra, P., Long, D.D.E., Miller, E.L.: Twizzler: a data-centric os for non-volatile memory. ACM Trans. Storage (TOS) **17**(2) (2021)
7. Choi, Y., Song, I., Park, M.H., et al.: A 20 nm 1.8 V 8 Gb PRAM with 40 MB/s program bandwidth. In: Proceedings of ISSCC, pp. 46–48 (2012)
8. Dong, X., Xu, C., Xie, Y., Jouppi, N.P.: NVSim: a circuit-level performance, energy, and area model for emerging nonvolatile memory. IEEE TCAD **31**(7), 994–1007 (2012)
9. Eichler, C., Hofmeier, H., Reif, S., Hönig, T., Nolte, J., Schröder-Preikschat, W.: Neverlast: an NVM-centric operating system for persistent edge systems. In: Proceedings of APSys, pp. 146–153. ACM (2021)
10. Eichler, C., Hofmeier, H., Reif, S., Hönig, T., et al.: Neverlast: towards the design and implementation of the NVM-based everlasting operating system. In: HICSS 2021, Kauai, Hawaii, USA, January 2021, pp. 1–10. ScholarSpace (2021)

11. Krishnan, A.S., Suslowicz, C., Dinu, D., Schaumont, P.: Secure intermittent computing protocol: protecting state across power loss. In: Proceedings of DATE, pp. 734–739 (2019)
12. Kroft, D.: Lockup-free instruction fetch/prefetch cache organization. In: 25 years of the International Symposia on Computer Archived (Selected Papers), pp. 195–201 (1998)
13. Kuenzer, S., et al.: Unikraft: fast, specialized unikernels the easy way. In: Proceedings of EuroSys, pp. 376–394 (2021)
14. Lucia, B., Balaji, V., Colin, A., Maeng, K., Ruppel, E.: Intermittent computing: challenges and opportunities. In: SNAPL. LIPIcs, vol. 71, pp. 8:1–8:14 (2017)
15. Maeng, K., Colin, A., Lucia, B.: Alpaca: intermittent execution without checkpoints. Proc. ACM Program. Lang. **1** (2017)
16. Miemietz, T., Reusch, V., Roitzsch, M., Härtig, H.: An NVM performance study towards whole system persistence on server platforms. In: Proceedings of DIMES, DIMES '23, pp. 45–51 (2023)
17. Narayanan, D., Hodson, O.: Whole-system persistence. In: Proceedings of ASPLOS, ASPLOS XVII, pp. 401–410 (2012)
18. Narayanan, D., Hodson, O.: Whole-system persistence. SIGPLAN Not. **47**(4), 401–410 (2012)
19. Pala, D., Miro-Panades, I., Sentieys, O.: Freezer: a specialized NVM backup controller for intermittently powered systems. IEEE TCAD **40**(8), 1559–1572 (2021)
20. Palm Inc.: What is NVFS? (2005). https://web.archive.org/web/20060218213506/http://kb.palmone.com/SRVS/CGI-BIN/WEBCGI.EXE?New,Kb=PalmSupportKB,ts=Palm_External2001,case=obj(35222). Accessed 15 Jan 2025
21. Pelley, S., Chen, P.M., Wenisch, T.F.: Memory persistency. SIGARCH Comp. Arch. News **42**(3), 265–276 (2014)
22. Poremba, M., et al.: NVMain 2.0: a user-friendly memory simulator to model (non-)volatile memory systems. IEEE Comp. Arch. Letters **14**, 140–143 (2015)
23. Rabenstein, J., et al.: Back to the core-memory age: running operating systems in NVRAM only. In: Proceedings of ARCS, pp. 153–167 (2023)
24. Ransford, B., Lucia, B.: Nonvolatile memory is a broken time machine. In: Proceedings of MSPC. ACM (2014)
25. Ransford, B., et al.: Mementos: system support for long-running computation on RFID-scale devices. SIGARCH Comp. Arch. News **39**(1), 159–170 (2011)
26. Rhodes, N., McKeehan, J.: Palm OS Programming: The Developer's Guide. O'Reilly Media, Inc., Newton (2002)
27. Sanislav, T., Mois, G.D., Zeadally, S., Folea, S.C.: Energy harvesting techniques for internet of things (IoT). IEEE Access **9**, 39530–39549 (2021)
28. Senni, S., et al.: Embedded systems to high performance computing using STT-MRAM. In: Proceedings of DATE, pp. 536–541 (2017)
29. Shao, Z., Liu, Y., Chen, Y., Li, T.: Utilizing PCM for energy optimization in embedded systems. In: Proceedings of ISVLSI, pp. 398–403 (2012)
30. Su, F., et al.: Nonvolatile processors: why is it trending? In: Proceedings of DATE, pp. 966–971. IEEE (2017)
31. Sun, G., Dong, X., Xie, Y., Li, J., Chen, Y.: A novel architecture of the 3D stacked MRAM L2 cache for CMPs. In: Proceedings of HPCA, pp. 239–249 (2009)
32. Umesh, S., Mittal, S.: A survey of techniques for intermittent computing. J. Syst. Architect. **112**, 101859 (2021)
33. Wilbert, N., Wildermann, S., Teich, J.: Hybrid cache design under varying power supply stability - a comparative study. In: Proceedings of MEMSYS (2024)

34. Wong, H.S.P., et al.: Phase change memory. Proc. IEEE **98**(12), 2201–2227 (2010)
35. Wu, X., Li, J., Zhang, L., Speight, E., Rajamony, R., Xie, Y.: Hybrid cache architecture with disparate memory technologies. SIGARCH Comp. Arch. News **37**(3), 34–45 (2009)
36. Xie, M., Pan, C., Zhang, Y., Hu, J., Liu, Y., Xue, C.J.: A novel STT-RAM-based hybrid cache for intermittently powered processors in IoT devices. IEEE Micro **39**(1), 24–32 (2019)
37. Zhou, P., Zhao, B., Yang, J., Zhang, Y.: A durable and energy efficient main memory using phase change memory technology. SIGARCH Comp. Arch. News **37**(3), 14–23 (2009)

MxGPU: A Case Study on OS-Controlled GPGPU Multiplexing

Marcel Lütke Dreimann[(✉)] and Olaf Spinczyk

Universität Osnabrück, Wachsbleiche 27, 49090 Osnabrück, Germany
{marcel.luetkedreimann,olaf}@uni-osnabrueck.de

Abstract. With the growing demand for artificial intelligence and other data-intensive applications, the demand for graphics processing units (GPUs) has also increased. Even though there are many approaches on multiplexing GPUs, none of the approaches known to us enable the operating system to coherently integrate GPU resources alongside CPU resources into a holistic resource management. Due to the history of GPUs, GPU drivers are still a large, isolated part within the driver stack of operating systems. This paper aims to conduct a case study on how a multiplexing solution for GPGPUs could look like, where the OS is able to define scheduling policies for GPGPU tasks and manage GPU memory. We will discuss the architecture of MxGPU, which offers software-based multiplexing of integrated Intel GPUs. MxGPU has a tiny code base, which is a precondition for formal verification approaches and usage in safety-critical environments. Experiments with our prototype show that MxGPU can grant the operating system control over GPU resources while allowing more GPU sessions with less overhead compared to existing work.

Keywords: GPGPU · Multiplexing · Resource Management · Operating System

1 Introduction

GPGPU workloads are becoming increasingly important, especially with the high volume of AI-related workloads [19]. In addition, GPUs are becoming part of safety-critical applications, such as the use of AI in medical applications, infrastructure and autonomous driving [4,5,11]. Server vendors usually offer virtualized GPU environments to customers. Additionally, GPU virtualization of embedded GPUs is also used for automotive platforms [18]. However, with the large software stack involved, it becomes difficult to ensure safety/security, scalability, and flexibility at the same time [20]. As part of the safety and security concern, developers want to reduce the software size in terms of lines of code to minimize the risk of bugs and security issues. For scalability, it is important to offer many virtual GPUs to keep a server profitable: Many customers can share a single GPU server. Also, when serving many applications, the response time of GPU tasks is important. Finally, flexibility is needed to assign customers or applications their respective GPU compute and memory resources. This includes scheduling policies with priorities and constraining GPU memory usage.

This setting leads us to following requirements for multiplexing GPUs:

1. The operating system should control all compute and memory resources, including GPUs to support coherent scheduling policies.
2. GPGPUs should be multiplexed in the same way CPUs are multiplexed, so that each application get its share.
3. The amount of privileged (supervisor-mode) code for enabling GPGPU multiplexing and resource management must be minimized to strengthen safety and security.

In standard general-purpose operating systems, these requirements are not met. For example, the Linux operating system itself is not aware of GPGPU workloads and does not pay attention to priorities for these workloads. We can show this in a simple experiment with the 2 MM benchmark of the Polybenchmark Suite [10]: The matrix multiplication benchmark is executed with OpenCL on the GPU first. After the GPU kernel has finished, the same operation is executed on a single CPU core. Figure 1 shows the execution time of a single instance of 2 MM (left), two instances pinned on the same CPU core with the same priority (middle) and two instances pinned on the same core with different priorities (right). CPU execution time is partitioned according to priority. However, the GPU execution time is not affected by the Linux process priority. The GPU kernels seems get an equal share of the execution time, even though different priorities are applied. This is a clear priority violation. In our opinion it is a design flaw that GPU resource scheduling is controlled by the hardware-vendor's GPU driver instead of the operating system.

In this paper, we want to conduct a case study on how GPGPU multiplexing can be orchestrated so that it meets the given requirements. The presented study will concentrate on multiplexing of the compute component exclusively and therefore not address a GPU's graphic stack. We will use our prototype MxGPU to show a small code base offering a multiplexing environment for execution of GPGPU tasks. Our implementation is based on Genode [8] and makes use of a custom GPGPU driver for integrated Intel GPUs [20]. MxGPU meets our requirements by

1. having a source code complexity much lower compared to existing solutions.
2. supporting any number of GPU sessions as long as enough memory is available.
3. allowing the operating system manage GPU resources by defining scheduling policies and managing GPU memory.
4. having less overhead than Linux.

The rest of the paper is organized as following: We first cover related work in Sect. 2. Next, Sect. 3 introduces the Intel GPU hardware and explains necessary features for multiplexing. Then, we present the MxGPU architecture in Sect. 4. Section 5 describes our evaluation. Finally, Sect. 6 concludes the paper and presents future work.

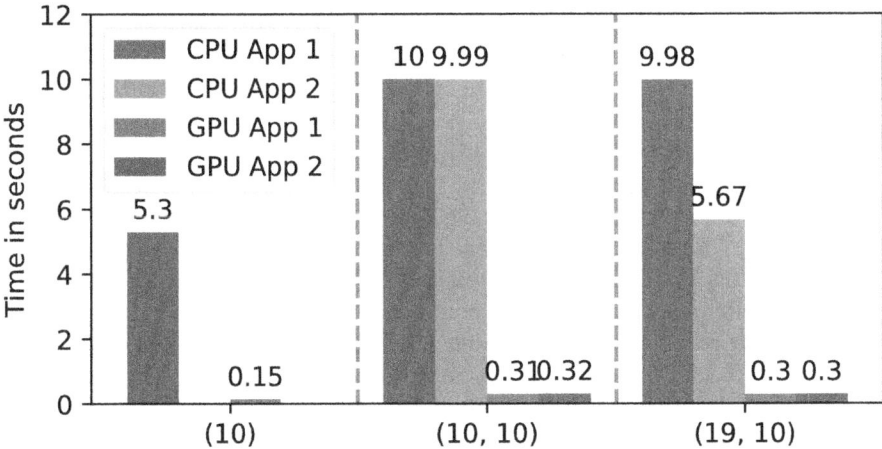

Fig. 1. 2 MM CPU and GPU benchmark of a single Linux process (left), two Linux processes using the same niceness (middle) and two Linux processes using different niceness values (right).

2 Related Work

GPU multiplexing is an integral part of GPU virtualization. Since virtualization of GPUs is already a well-researched area, we will present work on it here. Existing virtualization solutions can be categorized in three different classes: *API forwarding*, *para and full virtualization* and *hardware virtualization* [3,13].

API forwarding implements the virtualization layer at library level. API calls to libraries such as CUDA or OpenCL are redirected and executed in a host OS. This approach has no limitation on the number of virtual GPUs, GPU tasks within a virtual machine are translated into normal GPU tasks within the host OS. An actual virtual representation of the GPU is not required. On the one hand, the key advantage is that any GPU hardware is supported as long as the host OS offers drivers for it. But on the other hand, the required software stack to execute GPU tasks is quite large, because the host OS is usually a full Linux system. Additionally, the incurred overhead can become a problem, because all API calls will be translated into system calls for communication to the host OS. Furthermore, the host OS itself will reserve CPU cores and memory. Lastly, resource management strategies are difficult to implement, because API forwarding bypasses the hypervisor and the host OS is not aware of other virtual machines. Examples of API forwarding are gRemote, FairGV and rCUDA [7,12,25].

Para virtualization and full virtualization virtualize GPUs at the driver level. Full virtualization uses unmodified device drivers, while para virtualization makes use of special device drivers with optimizations for virtualization. Most drivers still require a host OS. Therefore, the aforementioned disadvantages of a host OS still persist. However, due to its implementation at a lower level, the hypervisor is capable of managing GPU resources. The GPU performance highly depends on the drivers' implementation: Trapping GPU instructions from the guest OS into the hypervisor can incur high overhead [3]. Optimized drivers with special support for virtualization are able to offer near-native performance. Examples for full virtualization are [24]. [9,14,24] make use of para virtualization.

Hardware virtualization is implemented below driver level. Hardware features such as IOMMU and SR-IOV are used to present the GPU multiple times within the PCIe bus. This is especially useful for performance isolation, because some GPUs offer additional memory controllers and cache for each device. High-bandwidth usage and cache thrashing of a single virtual machine leaves all other virtual machines unaffected. Because additional hardware components are required, not all GPUs are supported and the number virtual GPUs is limited. The hypervisor can only choose given memory configurations and scheduling policies which are implemented in hardware. These approaches are typically offered by the hardware vendors [2,21].

Our approach could be classified somewhere in between API forwarding and para virtualization. We use a modified library layer to batch library calls into driver calls. The custom driver has special support for OS-controlled resource management and overcomes hardware limitations.

2.1 NVIDIA GPU Partitioning [2]

NVIDIA offers two different approaches for sharing GPUs between virtual machines: *Multi-Instance GPUs* (MIG) and *virtual compute server* (vCS).

MIG is using spatial sharing and supports up to seven concurrent partitions on a single A100 GPU. Partitions are isolated from each other and have their own streaming multiprocessors (SMs), bandwidth, memory and cache. This ensures, that virtual machines can not affect each other's GPU performance, even if a partition fully utilizes its assigned memory controller or thrashes its cache. However, only a fixed number of partitions with a fixed partition size are available (Table 1):

Table 1. MIG configurations for the NVIDIA A100 GPU.

Instances	SMs	Memory
7	14	5 GB
3	28	10 GB
2	42	20 GB
1	56	20 GB
1	98	40 GB

Partitions can be dynamically created and destroyed. The resources of empty partitions can not be used by other partitions.

Virtual compute server is using temporal sharing of resources and allows up to ten virtual GPUs. This improves the utilization compared to MIG if vGPUs are idle. With vCS, idle vGPUs do not get time slices assigned and therefore the whole compute resources are available for active vGPUs. However, during peak demand, the high frequency of context switches incurs additional costs and therefore degrades compute performance. The system administrator can choose one of three scheduling policies, and its time slice if available:

1. Fixed share: Equal time slices for all vGPUs. If a vGPU is idle, compute cycles are not used.
2. Equal share: Equal time slices for all running vGPUs. Compute cycles of idle vGPUs are harvested by active vGPUs.
3. Best effort: Round-Robin based on demand.

Furthermore, NVIDIA MIG and vCS can be combined to allow more flexibility and isolation of partitions. This is for example used in *NVIDIA AI Enterprise*.

3 Intel GPU

In this Section, we present the Intel GPU hardware and explain the necessary features for our multiplexing approach. The first paragraph is about the *Global Graphics Translation Table* (GTT) and *Per Process Graphics Translation Table* (PPGTT), which are used for memory management. The supported preemption modes are presented in the second paragraph.

3.1 GGTT and PPGTT [15]

Integrated GPUs, such as the Intel UHD 630, share their memory with the CPU. In order to access memory, Intel GPUs require a table called *Graphics Translation Table* which is similar to the CPU's page table. A table entry contains an aligned physical memory address and a "valid" bit. The required alignment of the physical address depends on the page size configured. The supported page sizes are 4 KB, 64 KB, 2 MB and 1 GB. Each memory access in a GPU program specifies a GPU address, which can be split into an index and an offset. The index is then used to look up the physical address in the GTT. Every GPU comes with a global GTT (GGTT), which is located in the mapped device memory. Furthermore, the driver can allocate multiple additional GTTs called *Per Process Graphics Translation Table* (PPGTT) anywhere in system memory. The name stems from the i915 Linux driver, where this abstraction is used to isolate the process memory used by the GPU. Only a single PPGTT can be active at any point in time and the driver is responsible to manage its activation. Internal GPU commands can be configured to use either the GGTT or the PPGTT. The same concept can also be used for Intel's dedicated ARC GPU with the difference of an additional bit that determines whether a page can be found in the dedicated GPU memory or not [17]. GPUs of other vendors such as NVIDIA or AMD can also be supported as long as a software-based method for memory isolation is available.

3.2 Preemption [16]

GPGPU programs are typically long-running workloads compared to CPU threads. However, the GPU is also used to render the desktop environment and to handle display output. To enhance the user experience, graphic and compute-workloads have to be scheduled preemptively to avoid freezes or lags in the display output. The GPU makes use of preemption to maintain a stable refresh rate, while concurrently executing a compute-workload. The same concept is used if multiple compute-workloads are executed at the same time (compare Sect. 1). Three different modes of preemption are available for Intel GPUs:

- Command Buffer preemption: Course-grained preemption between GPU commands (s to ms scale)
- Workgroup preemption: Preemption of actual GPU programs on given boundaries (ms scale)
- Thread preemption: Preemption at instruction level (μs scale)

The incurred costs of saving and restoring a GPU context highly depend on the used preemption mode. Preemption can be triggered by the driver by writing to specific MMIO registers. Scheduling decisions can also be handled by the driver. However, as of GEN9 and subsequent architectures, Intel employs a closed-source firmware to run scheduling decisions partially in hardware [1]. While this might reduce the CPU overhead for GPU scheduling decisions, it prevents the operating system from controlling compute resources.

4 MxGPU Overview

This section will start by presenting the architecture of MxGPU at a high level view. Next, we will describe two important components in more detail: The GPU service component and the resource manager.

4.1 Architecture

The MxGPU architecture is build upon the MxKernel architecture, which is optimized for many-core systems with multiple NUMA nodes [6]. Applications are executed in resource containers called "cells", and a resource manager can assign or remove resources from those cells dynamically. For CPU cores, MxKernel supports efficient space sharing by migrating cores between cells depending on their load. For example, if a cell runs a database management system, incoming queries will increase the load of the cell and the resource manager can decide to assign additional CPU cores to that cell. Once the query is completed, CPU cores become idle and can be migrated to other cells.

The same concept is extended to GPUs. However, as the number of GPUs in a system is typically much smaller than the number of applications running on a server, MxGPU is required to support time-sharing. Modern GPUs also support space sharing within a single GPU (see Sect. 2.1), but as we conduct our case study for Intel GPUs, we will not support this technique for compute resources.

Figure 2 shows an overview of our architecture. With MxKernel serving as the foundation and the goal of security and safety, we choose a microhypervisor approach. The microhypervisor *MxVisor* is responsible for CPU management and interrupts. The resource manager, our GPU Service and a PCI driver component operate in userspace as an ordinary cell. In the event of a failure of the GPU Service component, such as a crash or hang, the remaining system remains operational, despite the loss of functionality in the crashed component. Cells, which are also running in userspace, can communicate via Remote Procedure Calls to the resource manager and GPU Service. The resource manager is able to read a cell's CPU or GPU priority and its assigned maximum memory. Furthermore, it can manage CPU resources by configuring the MxVisor and GPU resources by configuring the GPU Service component.

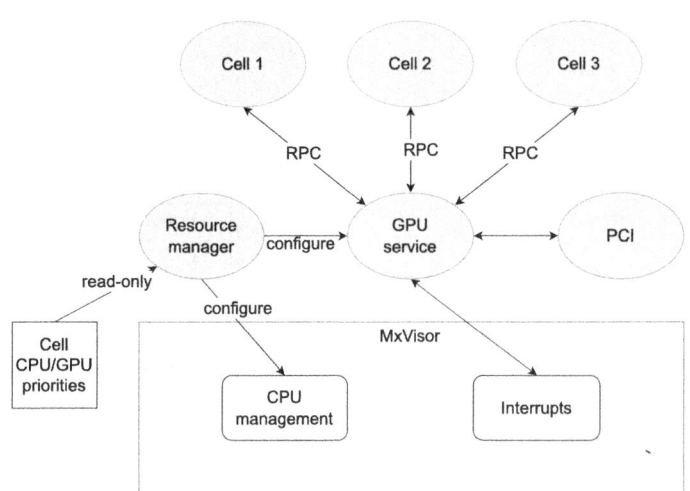

Fig. 2. MxGPU architecture overview

4.2 GPU Service

The GPU service component consists of three subcomponents:

1. GPGPU driver
2. Driver wrapper
3. Multiplexer

The GPGPU driver is a modified version of the open-source UOS-INTEL-GPGPU driver [20]. It is responsible for GPU initialization and offers interfaces to start GPGPU tasks and allocate/free GPU contexts. The GPU is initialized upon creation of the GPU service cell. The driver wrapper implements stubs for the GPGPU driver and registers an interrupt handler for GPU interrupts. GPU interrupts serve to notify the service cell of completion of GPGPU tasks. This enables the service cell to free any CPU cores during a GPGPU task execution. The Multiplexer subcomponent can open up a GPU session for each cell and is responsible for enforcing a scheduling policy. Each GPU session has its own GPU context, PPGTT and a MPSC queue[1] for its tasks. Moreover, the Multiplexer is responsible for providing an interface for scheduling policies and call the respective policy callbacks. In addition to the scheduling interface, the subcomponent also provides an interface for ordinary application cells. This interface is notably compact: An application can sign up for a GPU session and submit GPGPU tasks. A custom OpenCL implementation is able to use our interface to provide a well-defined API for applications. When a GPU session is created, the Multiplexer will create a GPU context with empty PPGTT for it. Furthermore, it will allocate a shared memory region of the size provided by the resource manager (see Fig. 3). The use case for the shared memory region is two-fold: Firstly,

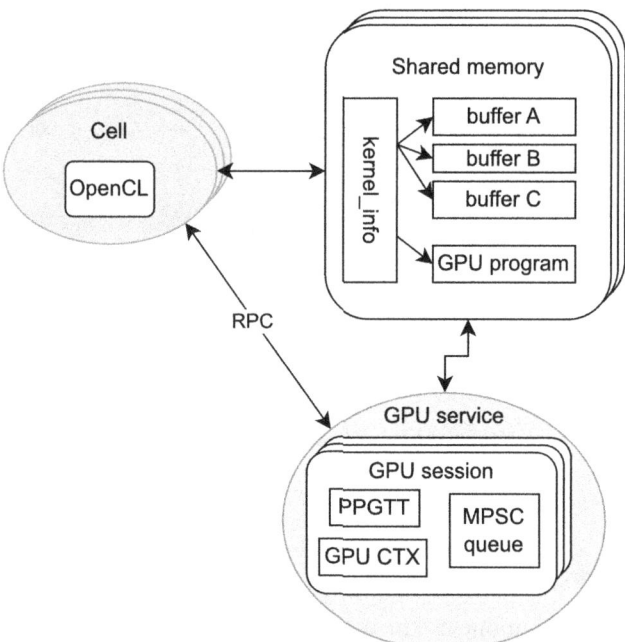

Fig. 3. Interaction between application cell and GPU service using RPCs and a shared memory region.

---

[1] Multiple producer single consumer queue.

it facilitates efficient communication with the cell by storing GPU task objects and merely passing references in RPCs. Secondly, it is used to store GPU buffers such as input/output buffer and the GPU program itself. The memory region is under ownership of the GPU service component to restrict its size for cells and to be able to get the physical memory address of GPU buffer objects for PPGTT entries. For security reasons, a cell can not get the physical memory address of some other cells virtual memory address. This enhances security, but restricts the possibilities for zero-copy memory: Zero-copy memory is only feasible if the cell uses a special allocator, that allocates its memory in the shared memory region instead of ordinary cell memory. If, for example, an input buffer resides in the cell's ordinary memory, it has to be copied to the shared memory region, because the GPU Server component would not be able to the buffers physical memory address.

4.3 Resource Management

The resource manager is the component responsible for CPU migration and memory management. Additionally, it assigns time slices and available memory to each GPU session. It can do so by implementing the policy interface of the multiplexing subcomponent. Figure 4 shows the resource manager with a completely fair scheduler (CFS), for example.

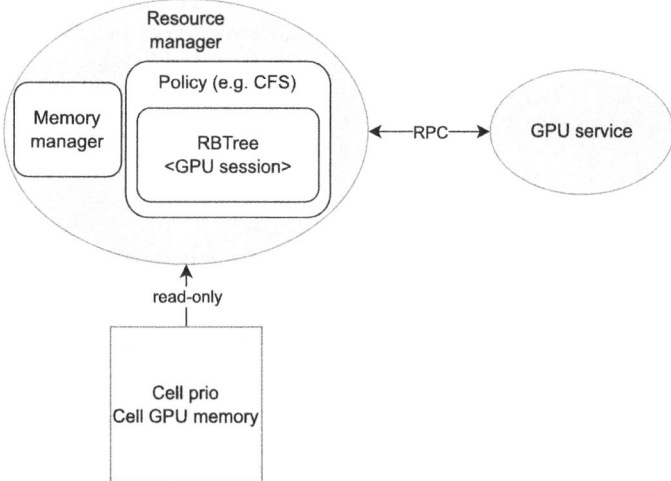

Fig. 4. Resource Manager subcomponents for GPU resource management and interaction to other cells.

Because our architecture shall be able to handle an arbitrary number of GPU sessions, we choose a red-black-tree data structure, which is similar to the Linux CFS scheduler. The red-back-tree can store and update GPU session objects in logarithmic time and efficiently retrieve the session with the lowest virtual runtime. Besides CPU priority and available main memory, the resource manager can also read GPU priority and maximum allowed GPU memory from the cell configuration. A cell's virtual GPU runtime is scaled by its respective GPU priority. Our interface between resource manager and GPU service has also the possibility to choose one of the preemption methods mentioned in Sect. 3.2 and manually trigger the preemption of GPGPU tasks. When it comes to GPU memory management, the resource manager can specify a maximum number of allocated GPU pages for a GPU session. In contrast to NVIDIA's static memory partitioning (Sect. 2.1), this approach offers a more flexible way to assign GPU memory to virtual GPUs.

5 Evaluation

In this section, we compare MxGPU with a recent Linux environment (Ubuntu 24.04.1 with kernel 6.8.0-52 and Intel NEO 23.43), because most of the related work makes use of Linux and its official GPU drivers. Our MxGPU prototype implementation is based on Genode [8] with the NOVA microhypervisor [23]. Furthermore, it employs the UOS-INTEL-GPGPU driver [20]. The system is equipped with an Intel i9-10900K and 4×32 GB of DDR4 memory. The CPU includes an Intel UHD 630 integrated GPU, that shares its memory with the CPU. In Sect. 5.1, we compare the lines of code of our prototype implementation with the i915 driver. Section 5.2 discusses why MxGPU's number of GPU sessions is theoretically unlimited. Next, Sect. 5.3 shows, that the resource manager can actually manage GPU resources, for example by specifying a priority-based scheduling policy. Finally, we compare the overhead of submitting a GPGPU task between MxGPU and Linux.

5.1 Dependability

Our prototype implementation employs the UOS-INTEL-GPGPU driver together with its wrapper and a tailored interface especially for multiplexing. The specific use case allows our software stack to be much smaller compared to Linux. This statistically results in a reduced number of software bugs, and makes it an easier candidate for formal verification of correctness. Figure 5 shows the number of lines of our GPU service subcomponents and the Linux i915 driver.

Note, that this comparison is not completely fair: On the one hand, the UOS-INTEL-GPGPU driver does only support a single GPU generation without graphics stack, and it lacks optional features and performance optimizations. On the other hand, while the i915 driver supports various GPU generations with all their features, it does not support compute workloads. In order to run compute workloads in Linux, the Intel NEO userspace driver is required. Nevertheless, we identified our GPU service component and the i915 driver as the critical point of failure of the system.

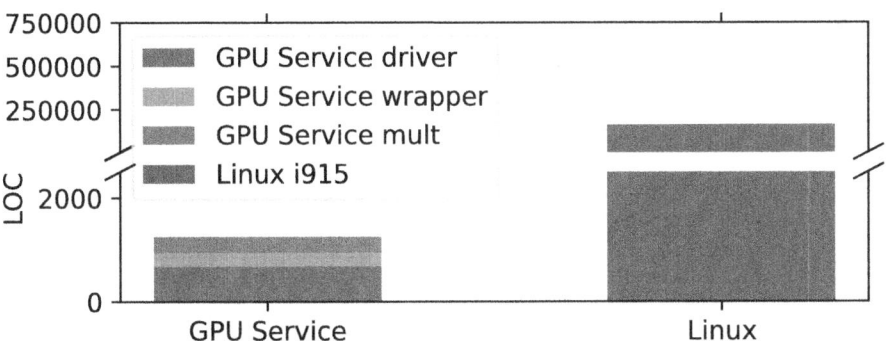

Fig. 5. Lines of code of MxGPU and Linux.

5.2 Scalability

When serving many applications, the same amount of GPU sessions are required. NVIDIA does only support up to seven MIG instances and even if time-sharing (vCS) is used, a maximum number of ten instances can be hosted (see Sect. 2.1). Intel's virtualization approach GVT-G can support only up to 8 vGPUs [22]. In contrast to related work, MxGPU does not rely on constrained hardware resources such as memory controllers or SR-IOV virtual functions. While this degrades performance isolation between cells, it breaks the limitation of a fixed number of GPU sessions and dependencies to special GPU hardware. For each GPU session, a PPGTT table and GPU context consisting of GPU state buffers are allocated. Each state buffer is mapped in the PPGTT of the respective GPU session. As long as ordinary system memory is available, PPGTTs and GPU contexts can be allocated. The hardware itself has no upper limit for the number of PPGTTs. The activation of a GPU context is initiated by writing the physical address of the designated PPGTT into an MMIO register. Experiments show, that our prototype implementation is capable of supporting at least 128 GPU sessions executing the 2 MM benchmark. Theoretically, the number of instances may be increased beyond this value by reducing the matrix size so that all instances fit into system memory.

5.3 Scheduling

To demonstrate that the resource manager has full control over GPU resources, we used our priority-based CFS scheduling policy and executed two instances of 2 MM. The scenario is similar to our Linux experiment in Sect. 1 without the CPU benchmarks. However, to overcome our limitation of missing preemption support, we measured the throughput of multiple 2 MM instances. Figure 6 shows the throughput of the two concurrently running benchmarks for Linux and MxGPU. When using the same priority, each cell/application yields the same throughput. In contrast to Linux, if different priorities are assigned, MxGPU is able to assign GPU compute resources accordingly. In Linux, niceness values

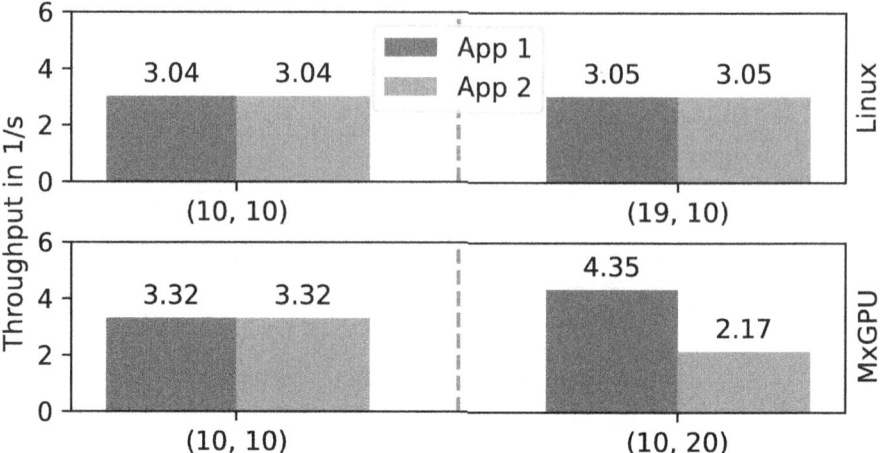

Fig. 6. Throughput of 2 MM GPU-only benchmark in two processes/cells using the same priority (left) and using different priorities (right). The top figure shows the throughput in Linux, whereas the bottom figure shows the throughput in MxGPU.

19 and 10 were assigned and MxGPU uses priority values of 20 and 10. For MxGPU's CFS scheduler, this means that the virtual GPU runtime of one cell runs twice as fast as that of the other cell. The throughput of the cell with higher priority is therefore twice as high as the throughput of the cell with lower priority.

5.4 Overhead

Lastly, we investigate the induced overhead of GPGPU task submission in our prototype and Linux. Therefore, we measured 2 MM's execution time without the actual time the GPU uses to calculate the matrix multiplication (compare Fig. 7). The remaining time is spent on preparing kernel arguments and submitting the kernel object to the driver. In the MxGPU architecture, the time includes RPC communication between the application cell and the GPU service cell. Linux has a similar phase, where the userspace application submits its task to the kernelspace i915 driver. In addition to communication costs, both systems spend time on preparing the task for the hardware by initializing GPU status buffers and switching PPGTTs. Figure 7 shows, that MxGPU requires only half of the CPU cycles for GPGPU task submission. This can be explained by the slimmer and more specialized architecture of MxGPU. According to *strace*, the Intel NEO driver is issuing nine mmap, five munmap and twelve ioctl system calls used for userspace to hardware communication. The sum of the times spent in these system calls adds up to roughly 1.3 million cycles and makes already 87% of the total overhead in Linux.

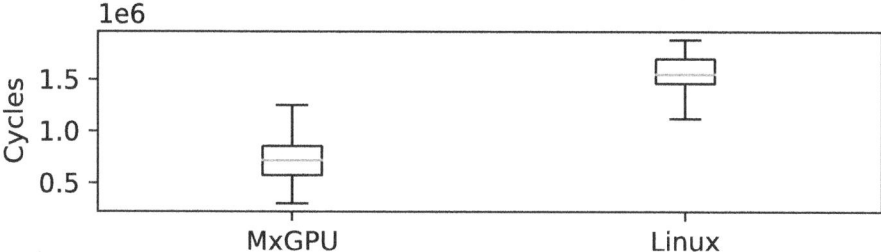

Fig. 7. Overhead of 2 MM benchmark executed in MxGPU and Linux (n = 100).

6 Conclusion and Future Work

In this work, we presented MxGPU, a small code base offering a multiplexed environment for the execution of GPGPU tasks. MxGPU employs a custom GPGPU driver to use hardware features such as PPGTTs to allow the operating system to manage GPU memory. Different modes of preemption can be configured, and task can manually be preempted to manage compute resources. Our concept has no upper limit of GPU sessions as long as there is enough system memory for GPU sessions. Our prototype implementation has less overhead compared to Linux and therefore also outperforms any work which builds on top of the Linux driver stack.

However, MxGPU and our prototype implementation leaves room for improvement. Besides performance optimizations, the UOS-INTEL-GPGPU driver could be extended to support dedicated Intel GPUs. Despite similar hardware features, the overall use case would be more realistic and managing dedicated GPU memory would become more important, because less GPU memory is available and transfers are more costly. Furthermore, actual preemption support of the driver would allow for preemptive scheduling policies and therefore handle compute resource in a more fine-grained manner. Additionally, the MxGPU architecture could be extended to support shared GPU memory between application cells.

Acknowledgments. The work on this paper has been funded by the Deutsche Forschungsgemeinschaft (DFG, German Research Foundation) – 361498541, 502565817.

References

1. Enabling the guc/huc firmware for linux* on new intel gpu platforms. Technical Report 609249-1.0, Intel Corporation (2019). https://www.intel.de/content/www/de/de/content-details/609249/enabling-the-guc-huc-firmware-for-linux-on-new-intel-gpu-platforms.html

2. Nvidia multi-instance gpu and nvidia virtual compute server. Tech. Rep. TB-10226-001_v01, NVIDIA Corporation, 2788 San Tomas Expressway, Santa Clara, CA 95051 (November 2020), https://www.nvidia.com/content/dam/en-zz/Solutions/design-visualization/solutions/resources/documents1/Technical-Brief-Multi-Instance-GPU-NVIDIA-Virtual-Compute-Server.pdf
3. Alyas, M., Hassan, H.: Gpgpu virtualization techniques a comparative survey. VAWKUM Trans. Comput. Sci. **8**(1), 09–22 (2019). https://doi.org/10.21015/vtcs.v15i3.521. https://vfast.org/journals/index.php/VTCS/article/view/521
4. Atzori, A., Barra, S., Carta, S., Fenu, G., Podda, A.S.: Heimdall: an ai-based infrastructure for traffic monitoring and anomalies detection. In: 2021 IEEE International Conference on Pervasive Computing and Communications Workshops and other Affiliated Events (PerCom Workshops), pp. 154–159 (2021). https://doi.org/10.1109/PerComWorkshops51409.2021.9431052
5. Campmany, V., Silva, S., Espinosa, A., Moure, J., Vázquez, D., López, A.: Gpu-based pedestrian detection for autonomous driving. Procedia Comput. Sci. **80**, 2377–2381 (2016). https://doi.org/10.1016/j.procs.2016.05.455. https://www.sciencedirect.com/science/article/pii/S1877050916309395
6. Dreimann, M.L., Mühlig, J., Müller, M., Spinczyk, O., Teubner, J.: MxKernel: A Bare-Metal Runtime System for Database Operations on Heterogeneous Many-Core Hardware, pp. 117–143. Springer, Cham (2025). https://doi.org/10.1007/978-3-031-74097-8_5
7. Duato, J., Peña, A.J., Silla, F., Fernández, J.C., Mayo, R., Quintana-Ortí, E.S.: Enabling cuda acceleration within virtual machines using rcuda. In: 2011 18th International Conference on High Performance Computing, pp. 1–10 (2011). https://doi.org/10.1109/HiPC.2011.6152718
8. Feske, N.: Genode operating system framework (2015)
9. Gottschlag, M., Hillenbrand, M., Kehne, J., Stoess, J., Bellosa, F.: Logv: low-overhead gpgpu virtualization. In: 2013 IEEE 10th International Conference on High Performance Computing and Communications & 2013 IEEE International Conference on Embedded and Ubiquitous Computing, pp. 1721–1726 (2013). https://doi.org/10.1109/HPCC.and.EUC.2013.245
10. Grauer-Gray, S., Xu, L., Searles, R., Ayalasomayajula, S., Cavazos, J.: Auto-tuning a high-level language targeted to gpu codes. In: 2012 Innovative Parallel Computing (InPar), pp. 1–10 (2012). https://doi.org/10.1109/InPar.2012.6339595
11. Haleem, A., Javaid, M., Khan, I.H.: Current status and applications of artificial intelligence (AI) in medical field: an overview. Curr. Med. Res. Pract. **9**(6), 231–237 (2019). https://doi.org/10.1016/j.cmrp.2019.11.005. https://www.sciencedirect.com/science/article/pii/S235208171930193X
12. Hong, C.H., Spence, I., Nikolopoulos, D.S.: Fairgv: fair and fast gpu virtualization. IEEE Trans. Parallel Distrib. Syst. **28**(12), 3472–3485 (2017). https://doi.org/10.1109/TPDS.2017.2717908
13. Hong, C.H., Spence, I., Nikolopoulos, D.S.: Gpu virtualization and scheduling methods: a comprehensive survey. ACM Comput. Surv. **50**(3) (2017). https://doi.org/10.1145/3068281
14. Huang, Y.J., Wu, H.H., Chung, Y.C., Hsu, W.C.: Building a kvm-based hypervisor for a heterogeneous system architecture compliant system. SIGPLAN Not. **51**(7), 3–15 (2016). https://doi.org/10.1145/3007611.2892246
15. Intel Corporation: Intel®Open Source HD Graphics and Intel Iris^{TM} Plus Graphics Programmer's Reference Manual For the 2016 - 2017 Intel Core^{TM} Processors, Celeron^{TM} Processors, and Pentium^{TM} Processors based on the Kaby

Lake Platform, Volume 5: Memory Views (2017). https://01.org/linuxgraphics/documentation
16. Intel Corporation: Intel®Open Source HD Graphics and Intel Iris^{TM} Plus Graphics Programmer's Reference Manual For the 2016 - 2017 Intel Core^{TM} Processors, Celeron^{TM} Processors, and Pentium^{TM} Processors based on the Kaby Lake Platform, Volume 7: 3D-Media-GPGPU (2017). https://01.org/linuxgraphics/documentation
17. Intel Corporation: Intel®Arc^{TM} A-Series Graphics and Intel Data Center GPU Flex Series Open-Source Programmer's Reference Manual For the discrete GPUs code named "Alchemist" and "Arctic Sound-M" Volume 6: Memory Views (2023). https://www.intel.com/content/www/us/en/docs/graphics-for-linux/developer-reference/1-0/overview.html
18. Lee, C., Kim, S.W., Yoo, C.: Vadi: GPU virtualization for an automotive platform. IEEE Trans. Ind. Inf. **12**(1), 277–290 (2016). https://doi.org/10.1109/TII.2015.2509441
19. Li, B., et al.: Ai-enabling workloads on large-scale gpu-accelerated system: characterization, opportunities, and implications. In: 2022 IEEE International Symposium on High-Performance Computer Architecture (HPCA), pp. 1224–1237 (2022). https://doi.org/10.1109/HPCA53966.2022.00093
20. Lütke Dreimann, M., Kessener, D.: Developing bare-metal gpgpu drivers from scratch: What prevents scientists from developing own gpgpu drivers? Tagungsband des FG-BS Frühjahrstreffens 2021 (2021). https://doi.org/10.18420/fgbs2021f-03
21. Shaikh, A., Suresh, A.: Revolutionizing VDI performance: the impact of intel®data center gpu flex series and sr-iov technology. Technical Report 827319, Intel (2024). https://www.intel.de/content/www/de/de/content-details/827319/revolutionizing-vdi-performance-the-impact-of-intel-data-center-gpu-flex-series-and-sr-iov-technology.html
22. Song, J., Lv, Z., Tian, K.: Kvmgt: a full gpu virtualization solution. In: KVM Forum, vol. 2014 (2014)
23. Steinberg, U., Kauer, B.: Nova: a microhypervisor-based secure virtualization architecture. In: Proceedings of the 5th European Conference on Computer Systems, EuroSys '10, pp. 209–222. Association for Computing Machinery, New York (2010). https://doi.org/10.1145/1755913.1755935
24. Suzuki, Y., Kato, S., Yamada, H., Kono, K.: GPUvm: why not virtualizing GPUs at the hypervisor? In: 2014 USENIX Annual Technical Conference (USENIX ATC 14), pp. 109–120. USENIX Association, Philadelphia (2014). https://www.usenix.org/conference/atc14/technical-sessions/presentation/suzuki
25. Tang, D., et al.: gremote: API-forwarding powered cloud rendering. In: Proceedings of the 29th International Symposium on High-Performance Parallel and Distributed Computing, pp. 197–201 (2020)

Towards Complete Open-Source Environments: FPGA-Based GPU Overlay Controlled by RISC-V

Hector Gerardo Muñoz-Hernandez[1]( ), Muhammad Ali[2],
Keyvan Shahin[1], Alireza Siyavashi[1], Diana Göhringer[2],
Marc Reichenbach[3], Christian Herglotz[1], and Michael Hübner[1]

[1] Chair of Computer Engineering, Brandenburg University of Technology
Cottbus-Senftenberg, Cottbus, Germany
{munozher,keyvan.shahin,alireza.siyavashi,
christian.herglotz,michael.huebner}@b-tu.de

[2] Chair of Adaptive Dynamic Systems, Dresden University of Technology,
Dresden, Germany
{muhammad.ali,diana.goehringer}@tu-dresden.de

[3] Institute of Applied Microelectronics and Computer Engineering,
University of Rostock, Rostock, Germany
marc.reichenbach@uni-rostock.de

Abstract. Image and signal processing applications have been widely implemented in Field Programmable Gate Arrays (FPGAs) and Graphical Processing Units (GPUs) due to their energy efficiency and performance, respectively. GPUs provide high data processing parallelism and are usually chosen to accelerate applications where low energy consumption is not a high priority. On the other hand, FPGAs are more tailored to hardware solutions due to their reconfigurability, but they struggle to outperform GPUs in data throughput. Soft IP cores implemented on reconfigurable hardware, are an alternative offering advantages from both worlds.

Some of these soft-core solutions offer an entire environment that includes scripts to automate their implementation, custom compilers, and other diverse tools. Unfortunately, some of these soft-cores are dependent on proprietary Intellectual Property (IP) or require hardware expertise to use properly. In this work, we propose an extended version of a popular open-source soft GPU, which can now run alongside a soft RISC-V core, and with High-Bandwidth memory (HBM2) compatibility. Previously, this soft GPU was only ready to be deployed in boards with a hard ARM core, but now it can be easily used in FPGAs without this requirement. We also provide an evaluation of how the soft GPU performs with respect to the pure RISC-V core, and a hard ARM core achieving geometric mean speed-ups of 114.60x and 19.72x respectively when performing some image and signal processing applications. Finally, we demonstrate how our soft GPU benefits from the HBM integration.

Keywords: FPGA · Soft-core GPU · System-On-Chip · RISC-V · HBM

1 Introduction

In recent decades, image-processing applications have become increasingly prevalent in various industries. The automotive and aerospace sectors, particularly in areas such as autonomous driving and spacecraft systems, critically rely on GPUs that provide high computational power at the cost of high energy consumption [16]. Considering the substantial computational demands of these applications, optimized and open-source GPUs for parallel processing are a big area of opportunity.

Targeted hardware like GPUs and Application Specific Integrated Circuits (ASICs), while very fast and energy efficient, have a hard non-reconfigurable hardware architecture. In case a specific application has different requirements such as space, energy, or speed constraints, the developer has to choose a different GPU or engineer a new ASIC. FPGA is a reconfigurable technology that can be reused for multiple applications [28]. FPGAs nowadays have thousands of Digital Signal Processing (DSP) blocks that support IEEE 754 floating-point computations for versatile applications [21]. This has significantly improved the computational efficiency with which FPGAs can implement arithmetic-intense applications. However, each implementation can take a long time to design and implement, and require hardware expertise [24].

An alternative that offers good trade-offs for performance vs. fast prototyping are soft IP cores. Soft IP cores are processor cores that can be programmed as an overlay architecture into FPGAs. For example, we could have a GPU as a parametrization of an FPGA which can be re-used quickly with different software implementations. On top of this, if a hardware configuration of the soft-core is not ideal for the current set of applications, it can be re-implemented in the same FPGA.

Soft CPUs, although usually not as efficient as hard CPUs, offer flexibility and the opportunity to have such solutions on FPGAs. AMD/Xilinx has such an alternative solution for FPGAs without hard CPUs by using the Microblaze processor [19]. Unfortunately, this core is still proprietary. Another alternative is to use open-source Instruction Set Architectures (ISAs) like RISC-V [33]. There are also popular soft-cores that use RISC-V ISA and maintain their open-source status like RocketChip, CVA6, and RI5CY to name a few [9,17,34].

The goal of this work is to provide an easy-to-use and open-source solution that provides both GPU and CPU soft-cores, in addition to a newly developed HBM integration. The chosen GPU core was **FPGA GPU (FGPU)** [3], which is a Single-Instruction Multiple-Threads (SIMT) processor written entirely on VHDL, which includes AXI4-interfaces as communication buses with a Processing System (PS), making it easy to use in FPGA boards. It comes with its custom compiler which is compatible with OpenCL code. This way we offer compatibility with any FPGA regardless of whether they do or do not have hard-cores, but retain the advantages of controlling the soft-core execution at run-time.

Namely, the main contributions of this work are:

- An extended open-source design that contains a soft-core GPU compatible with FPGAs.

- Integration of said design with an open-source RISC-V core which controls the execution[1].
- Added compatibility with HBM2.
- Evaluation of the proposed design with different benchmarks and metrics like resource utilization and latency.

The paper is structured as follows: Sect. 2 gives an overview of related and state-of-the-art designs. Section 3 presents the architecture of our soft GPU core and the integration with the RISC-V core. Later an evaluation of the proposed design is presented and discussed in Sect. 4. The work closes with Sect. 5 where conclusion remarks and possible directions for future work are presented.

2 Related Work

This section presents some past and ongoing work regarding the two types of cores we are targeting: CPUs and GPUs. First, a short explanation regarding soft CPUs is given in Subsect. 2.1, along with widely used soft-cores. Later some soft GPUs are presented and discussed in Subsect. 2.2. Some of the latest cores are presented as well as their capabilities and how they compare to our proposed design.

2.1 Soft CPU Cores

Soft CPU cores are processors implemented on programmable hardware such as FPGAs. Unlike hard CPU cores with a fixed architecture, soft-cores are flexible and can be modified or customized to fit specific application needs. They offer versatility in prototyping and embedded system development, as designers can reconfigure the core's architecture to optimize performance, power consumption, or area based on the application's requirements. With RISC-V [33] emerging as a popular open-source instruction set architecture (ISA), there is a rise in the development of different CPU architectures. RISC-V was initially developed by the University of California, Berkeley. It supports 32-bit, 64-bit, and 128-bit architecture and a wide range of standard extensions. RISC-V also comes with open-source support for simulators and compilers, making it more feasible to adapt.

Microblaze [19] is a soft-core CPU from AMD Xilinx. The architecture is RISC-based, it is highly configurable and supports both 32-bit and 64-bit architectures. Initially, MicroBlaze had a RISC-based ISA, however recently AMD Xilinx released a new version called MicroBlaze V which supports RISC-V ISA. The current version of MicroBlaze V only supports 32-bit architecture and some standard extensions. The IP is completely integrated in Xilinx Vivado and Vitis which provides programmability and a large range of IPs that can be included.

Another possibility is to use an open-source soft-core CPU to develop system-on-chip (SoC) on FPGA. In this approach, usually, there is less support for

---

[1] https://github.com/CEatBTU/FGPU_RISCV_HBM.git

the IPs and most of the SoC development has to be done manually. OpenHW Group[2] is a non-profit, global organization that offers a wide range of CPU architectures that can be used as soft-core CPUs in FPGAs. The most notable CPUs are CV32E40P (previously known as RI5CY) [17] and CVA6 (Ariane) [34]. CV32E40P is a 4-stage in-order CPU that focuses on 32-bit architecture and standard extensions. On the other hand, CVA6 focuses on 64-bit architecture, with 6-stage, single-issue, in-order architecture. There are different versions with different extension support available for each CPU.

Similarly, CHIPS Alliance [13] also provides open-source hardware designs and tools with a focus on both FPGA and ASICs. Rocket Chip [9] is the CPU provided by the CHIPS alliance which is one of the first RISC-V-based CPUs. This CPU is implemented using Chisel hardware construction language, and the group provides tools and resources to work with it. The CPU is also highly configurable and supports different standard extensions.

2.2 Soft GPU Cores

There have been some advances in executing GPU code in an FPGA [24,25]. Even though it is not extensively documented, each of these works addresses unique hardware and software challenges. As an example, providing custom software for a new General-Purpose GPU (GPGPU) architecture means a big effort in supporting parallel language features like atomic operations [1]. This is because of the complexity of multi-layered soft GPGPUs [1].

Among the few soft GPGPUs, GPU-like cUstomizable Parallel Processor prototYpe (GUPPY) [15] was released in 2012. GUPPY is tailored to accelerate small, integer, and bit-based data sets. This means that this soft-core is not suitable for embedded processors that need floating-point processing. This highly reduces the applications and range on which GUPPY can be used. It is also only compatible with the CUDA programming language, which could be considered a disadvantage because it is a vendor-specific language, and customization to the compiler is not possible. Guppy uses the LEON3 architecture as a host CPU.

MIAOW [10] is an example of an RTL implementation of a GPGPU which is based on the AMD Southern Islands ISA. This platform however is not entirely synthesizable, due to its on-chip networks, register files, and memory controllers being all described using behavioral C/C++. There is also an extension of supported instructions for MIAOW, which is application-specific aware and customizes the CUs accordingly [14]. A downside of this design is that it can not be implemented with a frequency higher than 100MHz. MIAOW uses a Microblaze as a soft CPU to control the execution. This GPGPU project is no longer maintained, and also it does not support HBM.

Another initiative is called FLExible GRaphIcs Processor (FlexGrip) [7] which is written in VHDL, but it is only compatible with a CUDA compiler, as GUPPY. This tool is geared towards simulating the Nvidia F80 microarchitecture, which hinders customization further. FlexGrip has also been used to

---

[2] https://openhwfoundation.org/.

present a fault injection methodology to evaluate the effects of Single Event Upsets in the register files [29]. FlexGrip also uses Microblaze as a soft CPU for controlling purposes.

The latest soft GPU was eGPU introduced in 2023 [22]. This soft GPGPU can be implemented on an FPGA with up to 771MHz as the operating frequency. It is also very resource efficient, claiming 20x less resource consumption than FlexGrip, and 10x less than FGPU with an equivalent number of implemented PEs. eGPU does not support enhanced features like thread divergence and has a less complex memory system without caches [22]. Finally, eGPU is not open-source which means that the design is not open to the public to use and modify.

In summary, some of these solutions rely however on proprietary IPs [7,10]. Some of them use hard-cores to control the soft-core at run-time [20]. This limits the target hardware that can be used in devices such as ZYNQ or MPSoC boards from AMD which house an FPGA alongside ARM cores for instance. Other initiatives do not use hard IP cores, but then they are not very user-friendly as the developer has to know Tool Command Language (TCL)/Joint Test Action Group (JTAG) or Peripheral Component Interface Express (PCIe) commands to communicate with the soft-core [1]. Also, the open-source solutions [7,10] are not compatible with HBM.

3 FGPU-RISC-V Proposed Platform Overview

The FGPU [3] was first released in 2016 by Muhammad Al Kadi [3], and it has been maintained and enhanced at the Brandenburg University of Technology Cottbus-Senftenberg since then. The FGPU has been used broadly by the academic community and some popular use cases have been to evaluate Deep Neural Network (DNN) tasks [23,28], or to test its radiation resilience [11,18,26,27]. It has also been used in more industry-involved projects [12]. In the publications regarding DNNs, it has been demonstrated that the FGPU is a suitable platform for accelerating DNNs such as Convolutional Neural Networks (CNNs). While the performance of the FGPU does not surpass commercial GPUs, after some modifications, it is only 4–7x slower than a Nvidia Volta V100 GPU [23]. Also without any modifications, the FGPU performance surpasses the ARM core that commonly comes inside SoCs boards in some computational-intensive applications like executing convolutional layers [20,28].

The FGPU needs a PS to control and interface with the external memory. For instance, the Zynq PS and MPSoC Zynq from AMD/Xilinx which include hard ARM cores could be used, and also RISC-V cores can be another solution. While the former offers a quick solution for AMD/Xilinx boards, the latter offers a more open-source solution by having all its core components independent from proprietary software, but also offers a good alternative for other boards that do not include hard ARM cores.

Sub-section 3.1 discusses briefly the original architecture of the FGPU, and the extended proposed version is presented in sub-section 3.2, followed by the toolflow in Subsect. 3.3 which is permitted by our open-source contribution.

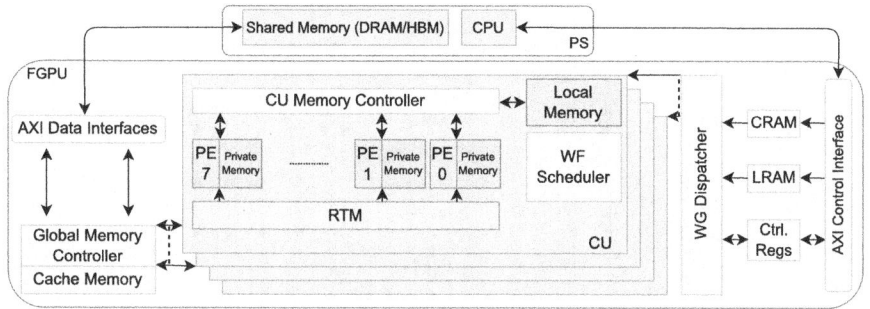

Fig. 1. The architecture of the soft-core FGPU (Adapted from [20]).

3.1 Architecture

Figure 1 shows the basic architecture of the FGPU. The FGPU can have up to 8 Compute Units (CUs), each of which can instantiate up to 8 Processing Elements (PEs). Every CU has a local memory of configurable size that can be accessed by every Work Item (WI) inside it through the CU memory controller [31]. Each PE has its own Arithmetic Logic Unit (ALU) and some register files that can interface with the Runtime Memory (RTM) which holds information like the individual IDs of the WIs, and some other kernel parameters. Every PE has its private memory that can be accessed by every WI inside it. All CUs are governed by the same global memory controller which can have a cache. This global memory controller is connected to the CPU via an AXI-stream interface.

As for the control interface of the FGPU, the CPU is responsible for sending the execution information, analog to what a host code does to a GPGPU. The compiled OpenCL code is sent to the FGPU as Code RAM (CRAM). All the information regarding the execution like the number of WIs and how they should be grouped in WGs, as well as the actual pointers to the data that the FGPU needs to compute, are inside the Link RAM (LRAM). Finally, the control registers are used to signal the FGPU to start the execution, and also the FGPU uses a register to signal the CPU when a kernel has finished the execution. These three elements are handled through the Work Group (WG) dispatcher which forwards them directly to the CUs.

3.2 RISC-V Extension

To enhance the FGPU compatibility with other FPGA platforms, we extended it to be used with FPGAs that do not have a Zynq processing system or a dedicated ARM core. This extension integrates a RISC-V core as a flexible, open-source alternative to control the operation of the FGPU. This basic structure can be seen in Fig. 2. The RISC-V core can send parameters and commands to the FGPU like the compiled OpenCL kernels, and host parameters like the number of WIs in a WG, and it can also send control signals to start the execution of a kernel. In this figure, it can also be seen how the RISC-V core and the FGPU

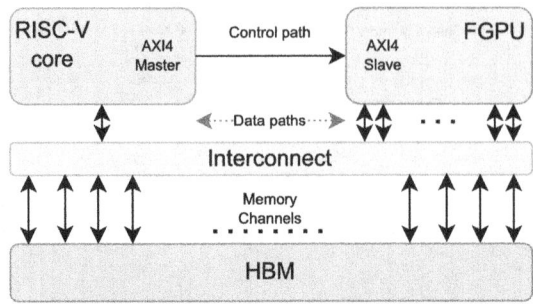

Fig. 2. Block diagram of FGPU in the RISC-V integration using HBM.

both have independent access to the main memory, as opposed to the previous FGPU version, where only the hard ARM core had access to the main memory. In this extended version, the FGPU was extended to have a configurable number of channels ranging from 1 to 16, to match the 16 channels one stack of a HBM2 IP can have. One of the main contributions of this work is the integration of the RISC-V core which makes the FGPU design independent from proprietary hard-core processors and thus widely deployable on different FPGA platforms.

Moreover, the integration of RISC-V, aligns the FGPU more with the open-source movement, enabling the formation of a fully open-source implementation from control logic to processing. In addition, integrating High-Bandwidth Memory (HBM) has taken care of the need for a high-speed data transfer rate in demanding applications and has complemented the design with an option to choose between HBM and DDR as a basic memory resource. This implementation provides a flexible, configurable tool flow that is capable of either supporting a soft RISC-V or hard ARM core and different memory configurations to achieve the best performance for a range of FPGA configurations.

As for the RISC-V core, we used RocketChip [9], an open-source SoC design generator synthesizable at the RTL level and implemented in Chisel hardware construction language. We used the open-source repository [30] as a starting point for the RocketChip generator. With this design is possible to run a Linux-embedded Operating System (OS) on a 64-bit RocketChip processor. But for this work, we focus on a 32-bit RISC-V processor, and the applications are run in a bare-metal fashion.

The chosen configuration for the RocketChip is simple, as we only need the CPU to control the FGPU. The FGPU is only connected to the master IO interface of the RISC-V processor, as seen in Fig. 2, but the chosen RocketChip instance has another AXI interface to connect directly to the main memory. Once the RocketChip instance is compiled, its sources are imported and integrated into a block diagram together with the FGPU.

3.3 Toolfow

Figure 3 shows the toolflow of the proposed design. The flow is divided into two parts: the hardware or bitstream generation, and the software application. The

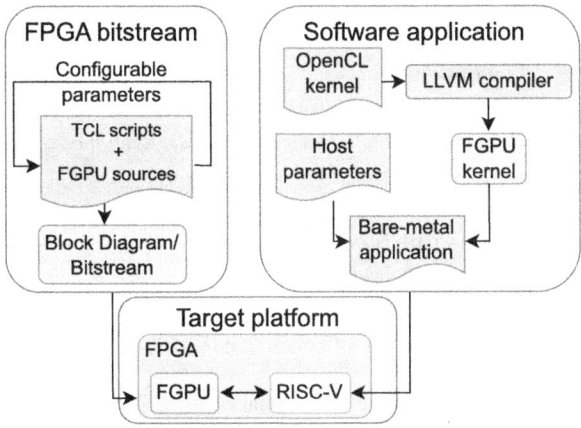

Fig. 3. Toolflow of the FGPU - RISC-V.

scripts and sources provided in the open-source project are designed with ease of use in mind, and so the developer only has to configure a few FGPU parameters like the number of CUs, and number of memory channels to name some. The developer can also choose if the RISC-V should be implemented as a 32- or 64-bit architecture. The scripts synthesize and implement the design, to generate the bitstream.

On the other hand, the OpenCL code has to be compiled using the custom LLVM compiler[3] to generate the FGPU kernel. The first version of our compiler had compatibility with 45 OpenCL instructions. The FGPU was then extended with local memory, WG barriers, and synchronization functions. This increased the number of OpenCL compatible instructions to 52 [31]. The FGPU has also the possibility to use atomic operations, further mitigating racing conditions [2].

The compiled openCL code and other host parameters have to be adjusted as in any GPGPU execution. All of these parameters are part of a bare-metal application that runs on the RISC-V core. In other words, the FGPU executes compiled OpenCL code, and the RISC-V core executes C++ code. After the bitstream is loaded into the FPGA, the bare-metal binaries can be executed.

4 Experimental Evaluation

The Alveo FPGA U55C board [5], provides a very powerful platform for the implementation and optimization of computational workloads. The U250 is equipped with 64 GB of DDR memory and a memory bandwidth of 77 GB/s for fast access and processing of data [4]. The U55C board is designed to increase memory bandwidth and capacity, with a maximum of 16 GB of HBM2 memory and up to 460 GB/s bandwidth, increasing the capacity for heavier workloads

---

[3] https://github.com/CEatBTU/FGPU_Compiler.git.

Table 1. Benchmarks used with description

Benchmark	Description
Bitonic	Implementation of bitonic sort
Copy memory	Copy values in different regions of the main memory
Edge detection	A 3 × 3 Sobel filter for edge detection in images
FIR filter	FIR filter with 12 taps
Floyd-Warshall [32]	Shortest path between all pairs of vertices of a weighted graph finder
Matrix Multiplication	Matrix multiplication
Median filter	A 3 × 3 median filter for images
Parallel Selection	Sort values of an array by reading it completely and do a single write per element
Sharpen filter	A 5 × 5 sharpen filter for images
Xcorr	A sliding dot product of two arrays

Table 2. Benchmark speed-ups for FGPU vs. hard ARM

Benchmark	1CU	8CUs
Bitonic	4.94×	25.27×
Copy Memory	1.47×	7.73×
Edge Detection	6.35×	41.43×
FIR	5.28×	25.46×
Floyd-Warshall	0.81×	5.47×
Matrix Multiplication	7.88×	43.98×
Median	10.87×	48.90×
Parallel Selection	6.11×	41.22×
Sharpen	7.30×	38.76×
Xcorr	2.92×	2.30×
Geometric mean	4.30×	19.72×

requiring fast data movement [5]. This board is based on the advanced architecture of the Xilinx UltraScale+ family and offers a scalable and flexible solution for a wide range of workloads. It allows for the effective implementation of complex algorithms while allowing optimizations relevant to particular application needs, thus being equally suitable for this research and the implemented applications. These boards were chosen to enable a comparison between the two main memory integrations in our design.

4.1 Execution Speed

The chosen applications to evaluate our work cover a wide range of variety from image processing, signal processing, and graph algorithms, to more general processing benchmarks [3]. These applications along with a short description can be

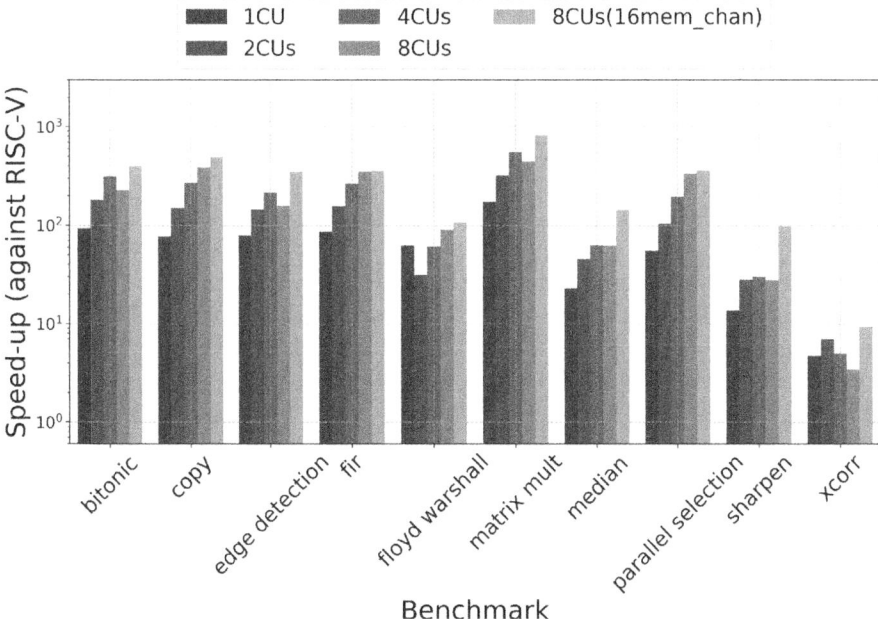

Fig. 4. Speed-up of benchmarks with different configurations FGPU vs. a soft RISC-V core.

seen in Table 1. These benchmarks were run with integer values, and soft floating-point support, as the chosen 32-bit RocketChip instance does not support hard floating-point. It is worth mentioning that bigger RocketChip instances can support this. Table 2 illustrates the performance increase obtained by using the FGPU in comparison to independently using the hard ARM respectively for the chosen applications. The performance is measured as the execution time of the benchmarks. The benchmarks were compiled using all available optimizations for the ARM compiler. Table 2 reports the speed-ups from two different FGPU configurations: 1CU and 8CUs configurations, which are the least and most amount of CUs that can be implemented currently. As demonstrated, most applications show considerable speed-ups based on the nature of the application.

A worth mentioning benchmark is *floyd warshall*, which uses floating-point values. To run this benchmark, the FGPU used soft floating-point support which is included with the LLVM compiler. The ARM-cores have sophisticated hardware floating-point support [8], and this is also why the speed-up is small when comparing the FGPU to the ARM execution.

The target hardware used for these experiments was the ZC706 board from AMD [6]. This board has a DDR as the main memory and a dual ARM Cortex-A9 MPCore. The operating frequency for the ARM and the FGPU was 667.6 MHz and 250 MHz, respectively. These values are the highest operating frequencies our model currently supports.

Table 3. Geometrical mean speedup of FGPU in different configurations vs. CPUs

CPU	FGPU configuration			
	1 CU	2 CUs	4 CUs	8 CUs
ARM	4.30×	8.20×	17.12×	19.72×
RISC-V	46.10×	75.03×	111.89×	114.60×

Figure 4 shows the speed-ups of the FGPU when changing its number of CUs configuration against the soft RISC-V core. The code for the host CPU was compiled using level 3 optimizations. All the benchmarks were run on the RISC-V setup which uses the Alveo U55C-HBM board [5] as target hardware. The operating frequency of the FGPU and the soft RISC-V core shown in Fig. 4 was set to the maximum implementable values: 250 MHz, and 100 MHz respectively.

Generally speaking, the higher the values shown in Fig. 4, the bigger the difference between the FGPU and the CPU. This means that higher values in the graph represent lower performance on the side of the CPU. The FGPU outperformed every benchmark in every configuration.

The *xcorr* kernel reported the lowest speed-up against the RISC-V CPU. This benchmark requires each WI to scan the whole input vectors, which is used to compute a single value, making this benchmark very memory-intensive. As the cache of the FGPU is direct-mapped, the frequency of cache misses is high with these types of benchmarks. This is one reason for the lower performance speed-ups from the FGPU.

There are some benchmarks like *bitonic, edge detection, matrix multiplication, sharpen*, and *xcorr* where a drop in performance is observed for an 8CUs configuration. This can be attributed to the fact that for some memory-intensive applications, the memory bottleneck becomes more evident, and providing more computing power does not necessarily lead to more performance. This is where the attributes from HBM come into play. By increasing the number of memory channels between the FGPU and the main memory in an 8CUs configuration, it is evident how this memory bottleneck starts to dissipate.

And thus, it can be seen in Fig. 4 that some benchmarks like *edge detection, matrix multiplication, median, sharpen*, and *xcorr* greatly benefit from increasing the numbers of memory channels that can be addressed in parallel from the HBM. In this figure, the last bar represents a configuration of 8CUS and 16 memory channels which can be used independently from each other. The first four bars represent a different number of CUs with 1 memory channel, as it is the standard case of an FGPU-DDR configuration. It is worth mentioning though, that efficient and sophisticated memory access patterns were not exploited in this experiment, as efficient use of HBM is out of the scope of this paper.

Table 3 shows in more detail the geometric mean speed-ups of every benchmark. Here we show how fast the FGPU is against the CPUs in different configurations. In this table, it can also be seen how the FGPU has higher speed-ups on average when using the soft-core in contrast to a hard-core CPU. Even if

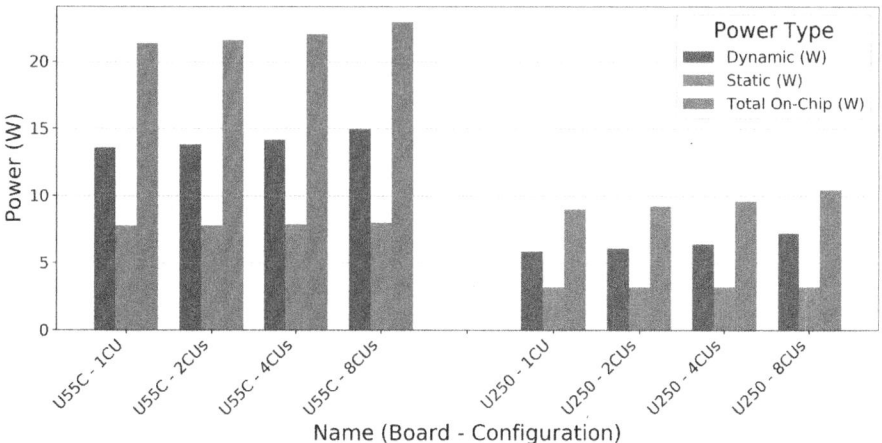

Fig. 5. Power Estimation Metrics for U250 and U55C Configurations

soft-cores like RISC-V showed less performance than hard-cores like ARM in this work, the advantage of using a RISC-V core is the availability. The RISC-V soft-core can be used in any FPGA, even if a hard-core like ARM is not available.

4.2 Power Consumption

Figure 5 shows the power consumed estimations by all layers in each configuration with a different number of CUs for both U250 and U55C Alveo boards. Increasing the number of CUs shows a slight increase in the consumed power of the FGPU-RISC-V combination, however, the platform itself has a much more accented impact on the power consumption. A dominant reason for this is the fact that the HBM itself uses on average 27.25% of the total power consumed in the U55C setup, across its different configurations.

The power estimations demonstrated here were obtained as estimates from the post-implementation reports of the tool itself. Although these measurements might differ from real-life power consumption, we aim to show in theory how different FGPU configurations would scale in this respect.

4.3 Resource Consumption

Table 4 presents the resource utilization of the hybrid FGPU-RISC-V architecture. For these implementations, we chose to scale the number of CUs in the FGPU. Every CU has 8 PEs, and each PE has an ALU. Each ALU in the design utilizes 4 DSP slices, with the DSP slice requirement calculated as follows:

$$\text{DSP Slices} = \text{CUs} \times \text{PE per CU} \times 4 \tag{1}$$

In this equation, CUs and $PE\ per\ CU$ are the number of Compute Units and processing elements per unit, respectively.

Table 4. Resource utilization comparison between FGPU designs using ZYNQ approach vs RISC-V.

Resource	Processing System	1CU	2CUs	4CUs	8CUs
Look-up Tables	ZYNQ	29,918	43,425	66,805	124,951
	RISC-V	91,173	105,154	132,201	188,126
Flip-Flops	ZYNQ	33,940	63,263	114,604	222,472
	RISC-V	97,973	123,179	173,548	274,280
Block RAMs	ZYNQ	47.5	86.5	188.5	436.5
	RISC-V	145.5	198.5	304.5	516.5
DSP Slices	ZYNQ	32	64	128	256
	RISC-V	32	64	128	256

Table 4 also displays other key resources when instantiating our design like LUTs, Flip-Flops, and BRAMs. As expected, the amount of units utilized in these three resources is higher in the RISC-V implementation, when compared to the ZYNQ. This is because the ZYNQ model uses the hard ARM cores as PS, so the FPGA saves the resources that otherwise are used to accommodate a soft RISC-V core.

5 Conclusion and Future Work

In this work, we propose a soft GPU core that can be used as an accelerator by using a soft CPU core, both of which are open-source. This design enables researchers and engineers working on edge-computing devices to configure and optimize any FPGA-based implementation, regardless of whether or not this hardware includes hard CPUs or not. Our approach shows performance improvements in a variety of applications ranging from image and signal processing to graph algorithms, achieving a geometric mean speed-up of 114.60x with respect to pure soft CPU processing. Also, the benchmarks were run on a hard ARM core, yielding up to 19.72x improvements of the soft GPU core against it. It was also shown how the HBM integration can mitigate the latency of memory-bound applications by incrementing the number of memory channels between the FGPU and the main memory.

While this work introduces a versatile open-source soft-core for FPGA implementations leveraging both CPU and GPU capabilities, several future directions could enhance and extend it. One opportunity is to run a Linux-embedded OS on the CPU. In this way, the FGPU could act as an accelerator inside a more complex heterogeneous environment where the OS is orchestrating the execution of tasks. This setup would pave the way to the integration of more complex OS capabilities like advanced communication, and robust multithread, among others. In this scenario, we could start targeting real-time applications as well.

References

1. Ahn, C., et al.: Comparative analysis of executing GPU applications on FPGA: HLS vs. soft GPU approaches. In: IPDPSW, pp. 634–641 (2024). https://doi.org/10.1109/IPDPSW63119.2024.00123
2. Al Kadi, M., Huebner, M.: Integer computations with soft GPGPU on FPGAs. In: FPT, pp. 28–35. IEEE, Xi'an (2016). https://doi.org/10.1109/FPT.2016.7929185
3. Al Kadi, M., Janssen, B., Huebner, M.: FGPU: an SIMT-architecture for FPGAs. In: ACM/SIGDA, FPGA, pp. 254–263 (2016). isbn: 9781450338561. https://doi.org/10.1145/2847263.2847273
4. AMD/Xilinx. Alveo U200 and U250 Data Sheet (DS962) (2023)
5. AMD/Xilinx. Alveo U55C Data Sheet (DS978) (2023)
6. AMD/Xilinx. ZC706 Evaluation Board for the Zynq-700 XC7Z046 SoC User Guide (UG954) (2019)
7. Andryc, K., Merchant, M., Tessier, R.: FlexGrip: a soft GPGPU for FPGAs. In: FPT (2013). https://doi.org/10.1109/FPT.2013.6718358
8. ARM. Cortex - A9 Technical Reference Manual. Revision: r1p0 (2008)
9. Asanović, K., et al. The Rocket Chip Generator. Technical report. UCB/EECS2016-17. EECS Department, Univ. of California, Berkeley (2016)
10. Balasubramanian, R., et al.: Enabling GPGPU low-level hardware explorations with MIAOW: an open-source RTL implementation of a GPGPU. ACM Trans. **12**(2) (2015). https://doi.org/10.1145/2764908
11. Braga, G., et al.: Evaluating softcore GPU in SRAM-based FPGA under radiation-induced effects. Microelectron. Reliabil. 114348 (2021). https://doi.org/10.1016/j.microrel.2021.114348
12. Brandalero, M., et al.: AITIA: embedded AI techniques for industrial applications. In: FPL (2021). https://doi.org/10.1109/FPL53798.2021.00071
13. CHIPS Alliance. FOSS FLows for FPGA (2023). Accessed 29 Oct 2024
14. Duarte, P., Tomas, P., Falcao, G.: SCRATCH: an end-to-end application-aware so-GPGPU architecture and trimming tool. In: MICRO, pp. 165–177 (2017). ISSN: 2379-3155
15. Al-Dujaili, A., et al.: Guppy: a GPU-like soft-core processor. In: FPT, pp. 57–60 (2012). https://doi.org/10.1109/FPT.2012.6412112
16. Furano, G., et al.: Towards the use of artificial intelligence on the edge in space systems: challenges and opportunities. IEEE AESS **35**(12), 44–56 (2020). https://doi.org/10.1109/MAES.2020.3008468
17. Gautschi, M., et al.: Near-threshold RISC-V core with DSP extensions for scalable IoT endpoint devices. IEEE Trans. VLSI Syst. **25**(10), 2700–2713 (2017). https://doi.org/10.1109/TVLSI.2017.2654506
18. Goncalves, M.M., et al.: Investigating floating-point implementations in a softcore GPU under radiation-induced faults. In: ICECS, pp. 1–4 (2020). https://doi.org/10.1109/ICECS49266.2020.9294939
19. Halfhill, T.R.: Microblaze V7 gets an MMU. In: Microprocessor, The Insider's Guide to Microprocessor Hardware (2007)
20. Hernandez, H.G.M., et al.: Edge GPU based on an FPGA overlay architecture using PYNQ. In: SBCCI, pp. 1–6 (2022). https://doi.org/10.1109/SBCCI55532.2022.9893229
21. Langhammer, M., Constantinides, G.A.: A statically and dynamically scalable soft GPGPU. In: ACM/SIGDA, pp. 165–175. ACM, Monterey (2024). https://doi.org/10.1145/3626202.3637567

22. Langhammer, M., Constantinides, G.A.: eGPU: a 750 MHz class soft GPGPU for FPGA. In: FPL, pp. 277–282. IEEE, Gothenburg (2023). https://doi.org/10.1109/FPL60245.2023.00047
23. Ma, R., et al.: Specializing FGPU for persistent deep learning. In: FPL, pp. 326–333 (2019). https://doi.org/10.1109/FPL.2019.00059
24. Ma, R., et al.: DO-GPU: domain optimizable soft GPUs. In: FPL, pp. 140–144 (2021). ISSN: 1946-1488. https://doi.org/10.1109/FPL53798.2021.00031
25. Meyer, M., Kenter, T., Plessl, C.: In-depth FPGA accelerator performance evaluation with single node benchmarks from the HPC challenge benchmark suite for Intel and Xilinx FPGAs using OpenCL. J. Parallel Distrib. Comput. **160**, 79–89 (2022). https://doi.org/10.1016/j.jpdc.2021.10.007
26. Monopoli, M., et al.: Exploiting FPGA dynamic partial reconfiguration for a soft GPU-based system-on-chip. In: PRIME, pp. 181–184 (2023). https://doi.org/10.1109/PRIME58259.2023.10161859
27. Monopoli, M., et al.: Exploring key aspects of soft GPGPU computing for on-board acceleration of artificial intelligence algorithms in space applications. In: EDHPC, pp. 1–6 (2023). https://doi.org/10.23919/EDHPC59100.2023.10396624
28. Munoz Hernandez, H.G., Veleski, M., Brandalero, M., Hübner, M.: Accelerating convolutional neural networks in FPGA-based SoCs using a soft-core GPU. In: Derrien, S., Hannig, F., Diniz, P.C., Chillet, D. (eds.) ARC 2021. LNCS, vol. 12700, pp. 275–284. Springer, Cham (2021). https://doi.org/10.1007/978-3-030-79025-7_20
29. Nedel, W., Kastensmidt, F., Azambuja, J.: Evaluating the effects of single event upsets in soft-core GPGPUs. In: LATS, pp. 93–98. IEEE (2016). https://doi.org/10.1109/LATW.2016.7483346
30. Tarassov, E., et al.: AMD/Xilinx Vivado block designs for FPGA RISCV SoC running Debian Linux distro. GitHub, Inc. (2024)
31. Todaro, G., et al.: Enhanced soft GPU architecture for FPGAs. In: PRIME, pp. 177–180 (2023). https://doi.org/10.1109/PRIME58259.2023.10161749
32. Triana, Y.S., Syahputri, I.: Implementation Floyd-Warhsall algorithm for the shortest path of garage. Int. J. Innov. Sci. Res. Technol. **3**(2) (2018)
33. Waterman, A., Asanovic, K., Division, C.S.: Volume I: Unprivileged ISA RISC-V. EECS Dept., Univ. of CA, Berkeley (2019)
34. Zaruba, F., Benini, L.: The cost of application-class processing: energy and performance analysis of a Linux-Ready 1.7-GHz 64-Bit RISC-V core in 22-nm FDSOI technology. IEEE Trans. VLSI Syst. **27**(11), 2629–2640 (2019). https://doi.org/10.1109/tvlsi.2019.2926114

Revisiting Gradient Direction Algorithms in Electrostatic Placers

Meinhard Kissich(✉) and Marcel Baunach

Graz University of Technology, Graz, Austria
{meinhard.kissich,baunach}@tugraz.at

Abstract. Electrostatic placers are a type of non-linear placers that gained popularity due to their high quality of results. Obtaining an accurate placement solution is crucial in Field-Programmable Gate Arrays (FPGAs), where routing resources are limited and post-placement improvements, such as buffer insertions, are not possible. This paper investigates the electrostatic placer in the open-source place&route framework nextpnr. Driven by the vast interest in machine learning, new gradient direction algorithms emerged. We revisit the choice of gradient direction algorithm and compare Nesterov's method used in ePlace and elfPlace against RMSProp, Adam, Adan, and an adaptive restarting scheme. Further, we add optional initial bi-partitioning and tune the hyper-parameters for two schemes to update the Lagrange multipliers. Initial experiments show that adaptively restarting Nesterov's method can be beneficial and emphasize Adam as a promising candidate besides Nesterov's method due to its high-quality results and fast convergence.

Keywords: Electrostatic Placer · FPGA · Optimizer · VLSI

1 Introduction

Placement algorithms play a crucial role in obtaining a routable and fast physical design implementation for complex and continuously growing digital designs, such as heterogeneous system-on-chip designs. They have a substantial impact on the expected runtime and significantly influence the Quality of Result (QoR) of the whole flow [5,6]. While the placement problems in Electronic Design Automation (EDA) for Application-Specific Integrated Circuits (ASICs) and Computer-Aided Design (CAD) for Field-Programmable Gate Arrays (FPGAs) are related, each domain faces its unique challenges. In FPGAs, some of the difficulties are heterogeneous resources [22], limited routing supply [3], and the lack of buffer insertion ability after placement to post-improve the critical path [6].

The placement problem can be expressed as minimizing the Half-Perimeter WireLength (HPWL) while obtaining a legal placement of all cells, i.e., to find $\mathrm{argmin}_{x,y}(\mathrm{HPWL}(x,y))$ such that (x,y) is legal. x and y are vectors of the x_i and y_i coordinates of each cell i, respectively. In addition to a pure wirelength-driven optimization, further metrics such as criticality (timing-driven) and routing congestion (routability) need to be taken into account. There are various approaches to this. One approach to emphasize critical nets, i.e., nets that contain a connection that is on the boundary of being the limiter for the maximum frequency, is weighting the wirelengths [23] as done by ω_e in (1). However, timing-driven placement and net weighting are not new approaches and date back to early placers [28,40]. $\boldsymbol{E}$ in (1) denotes the set of all nets where e is one net of it. Each net has a maximum spatial expansion of W_{e_x} and W_{e_y} in the x and y direction, respectively. Routability can be accounted for by, e.g., artificially enlarging cells in overpopulated areas [22] based on a congestion estimation [4,37].

$$\text{HPWL}(\boldsymbol{x},\boldsymbol{y}) = \sum_{e \in E} \omega_e (W_{e_x} + W_{e_y}) \\ = \sum_{e \in E} \omega_e \big(\max_{i,j \in e} |x_i - x_j| + \max_{i,j \in e} |y_i - y_j| \big) \tag{1}$$

Placement algorithms can roughly be divided into four categories: (a) stochastic placers such as Simulated Annealing (SA) as in the academic VPR [1,29] tool and Altera's Quartus II [26], (b) min-cut-based placers [27,34], and Analytical Placers (AP) such as (c) quadratic placers [2,9,38], and (d) non-linear placers [22–25]. APs are a promising approach to solve placement for large ASICs and FPGAs in modern VLSI design. While SA-based placers deliver a good QoR, their runtime is a significant burden, and APs lead to faster convergence [38,41].

Among non-linear placers, the category of electrostatic placers has established and shown high-quality results [24,25]. Each design cell is modeled as a charged particle that repels other cells. Numerical methods iteratively progress the system, leading to an equilibrium that gives the placement solution. Details are discussed in Sect. 2. Besides the total system potential energy, also the wirelength is considered in the objective function (4). The method of Lagrange multipliers is taken to solve the constrained optimization problem using unconstrained gradient direction algorithms. The choice and tuning of the algorithms are essential to guarantee fast convergence to a sufficient minimum.

This paper investigates the electrostatic placer in the popular and open-source place&route framework nextpnr [35]. We modify the optimization problem and compare two schemes for updating the Lagrange multipliers. Further, we revisit the choice of gradient direction algorithm proposed in the literature and analyze its impact on convergence and QoR. To the best of our knowledge, this is the first work analyzing the electrostatic placer in nextpnr.

The remainder of this paper is organized as follows: Sect. 2 gives some background and summarizes the key ideas behind electrostatic placers and challenges in FPGAs. Section 3 delves into related work. It is split into related placers and optimization algorithms. The algorithms considered in this work are further examined in Sect. 4. Section 5 lists some of the applications of nextpnr and introduces the most noteworthy modifications we applied in this work. Section 6 discusses the performed experiments and gives details about the used designs, the hyper-parameters that are optimized, and the obtained results. Section 7 discusses the results together with the limitations that we will address in future work. Finally, Sect. 8 summarizes the results and concludes this work.

2 Background

In electrostatic placers, each cell i is modeled as a positively charged particle with charge q_i proportional to its area. The repulsion forces of each cell $\boldsymbol{F}_i = q_i \boldsymbol{\xi}_i = -q_i \nabla \psi_i$ are computed by Lorentz force law and iteratively used to update each cell's position. $\boldsymbol{\xi}_i$ is the local electric field in x and y directions, i.e., $\boldsymbol{\xi}_i = (\xi_{i_x}, \xi_{i_y})$. ψ_i is the electric potential at the position of cell i. The electrostatic system is given by (2a)–(2a), where $\mathcal{R}$ is the placement region and $\partial \mathcal{R}$ describes the boundary. $\rho(x, y)$ is the charge density. The electric potential distribution $\psi(x, y)$ in (2a) is given by Gauss's law and computed using Poisson's equation. The Neumann boundary condition in (2a) prevents cells from moving outside $\mathcal{R}$ as the normal on the boundary $\partial \mathcal{R}$ is zero. Finally, (2a) ensures a unique solution.

$$\Delta \begin{cases} \psi(x,y) = -\nabla \cdot \boldsymbol{\xi}(x,y) = -\rho(x,y) & (x,y) \in \mathcal{R} \quad (2a) \\ \hat{\boldsymbol{n}} \cdot \nabla \psi(x,y) = \boldsymbol{0} & (x,y) \in \partial\mathcal{R} \quad (2b) \\ \iint_\mathcal{R} \rho(x,y) = \iint_\mathcal{R} \psi(x,y) = 0 & (x,y) \in \mathcal{R} \quad (2c) \end{cases}$$

The electrostatic system is efficiently solved using spectral methods on an $m \times m$ grid. However, there are more details about electrostatic placers, such as density smoothing, the removal of DC offset, and filler insertion to achieve optimal placement solutions. Details are well explained by Lu et al. [24].

Placement aims to minimize the HPWL (1) by the constraint that the potential energy Φ becomes zero so that the cells are spread out, i.e., $\min_{x,y} f(\boldsymbol{x}, \boldsymbol{y}) = \text{HPWL}(\boldsymbol{x}, \boldsymbol{y})$ such that $\Phi = 0$. Since the HPWL is not differentiable, it is approximated by a smooth and differentiable function $\widetilde{W}_{e_x}(\boldsymbol{x}, \boldsymbol{y}) \approx W_{e_x}(\boldsymbol{x}, \boldsymbol{y})$. Often, the Weighted-Average (WA) wirelength model (3) is used due to its small modeling error that is upper bounded by $\epsilon(e) \leq \frac{\gamma \Delta x}{1 + \exp \Delta x / n}$ [11] compared to, e.g., the Log-Sum-Exp (LSE) model (upper bounded by $\epsilon(e) \leq \gamma \ln n$ [33]).

$$\widetilde{W}_{e_x}(\boldsymbol{x}, \boldsymbol{y}) = \frac{\sum_{i \in e} x_i \exp(x_i/\gamma)}{\sum_{i \in e} \exp(x_i/\gamma)} - \frac{\sum_{i \in e} x_i \exp(-x_i/\gamma)}{\sum_{i \in e} \exp(-x_i/\gamma)} \quad (3)$$

The optimization problem is usually solved using an (Augmented) Lagrangian Method [14,22,24]. Thus, the constrained optimization objective can be solved by the unconstrained optimization problem in (4). Vector notation is used as FPGAs have multiple parallel systems that are solved concurrently.

$$\min_{x,y} f(\boldsymbol{x}, \boldsymbol{y}) = \widetilde{W}(\boldsymbol{x}, \boldsymbol{y}) + \boldsymbol{\lambda}^T \boldsymbol{\Phi}(\boldsymbol{x}, \boldsymbol{y}) + \frac{\boldsymbol{\mu}^T}{2} \boldsymbol{\Phi}^2(\boldsymbol{x}, \boldsymbol{y}) \quad (4)$$

$\widetilde{W}(\cdot)$ is the smooth and differentiable wirelength approximation, $\boldsymbol{\lambda}$ the Lagrange multipliers, $\boldsymbol{\Phi}(\cdot)$ the current sum of potential energies of the system. $\boldsymbol{\mu}$ is an optional quadratic penalty term to enhance convexity and, thus, convergence [22] of the optimization problem. Modern heterogeneous FPGAs consist of various hard blocks with strongly varying quantities. To circumvent the issue and cope with largely differing electric fields, each group $s \in \mathcal{S}$ is solved as an independent electrostatic system. This leads to a vector of Lagrange multipliers, quadratic penalties, and system energies. Thus, $\boldsymbol{\lambda}^T \boldsymbol{\Phi}(\boldsymbol{x},\boldsymbol{y}) = \sum_{s \in \mathcal{S}} \lambda_s \Phi_s(\boldsymbol{x},\boldsymbol{y})$, where $\mathcal{S}$ is the set of groups in the target FPGA, e.g., $\mathcal{S} = \{\text{LUT}, \text{FF}, \text{BRAM}, \text{DSP}\}$. The wirelength, however, is optimized across the groups.

3 Related Work

Placers. HeAP [9] is a quadratic placer for FPGAs adapted from SimPL [16], a quadratic placer for ASICs. It significantly improves runtime at the cost of some reduction in QoR compared to Altera's Quartus II placer, which is based on simulated annealing. At the same time, it outperformed the academic placer of VPR and is the basis for the quadratic placer implemented in nextpnr [35] (albeit modified in its implementation). Rajarathnam et al. [32] combine the analytical HeAP placer and simulated annealing for further optimization.

In contrast to quadratic placers, which use a quadratic function to model the HPWL that can be optimized efficiently, non-linear placers use a non-linear objective function and have shown promising results despite their higher computational complexity. ePlace [24] proposes a novel placement density function, *eDensity*, paving the way for many placers building on electrostatic system modeling. The authors introduce the analogy of cell instances and charged particles that converge to an equilibrium state over time. The placement problem is converted into a constrained minimization problem (see Sect. 2). As shown in (4), it can be solved by unconstrained optimization through Lagrange multipliers and gradient-based optimization methods. In contrast to the Conjugate Gradient solver used by Kahng et al. [14], Lu et al. [24] propose using Nesterov's method and Lipschitz constant prediction (see Sect. 4) to overcome computationally expensive line search. In addition to the Lipschitz prediction proposed in ePlace, Lu et al. [25] add steplength backtracking in ePlace-MS by performing a bisection search. The authors show that backtracking only introduces a less than 4% runtime overhead, while without backtracking, one design fails and a 43.12% average wirelength overhead is added to the remaining benchmarks.

While these electrostatic placers consider constraints like hard macros, the heterogeneity of FPGA demands further adaptions. elfPlace [22] builds on ePlace and targets the placement of cells onto the basic elements of an FPGA. It uses independent electrostatic systems for each group of cells. In addition, Li et al. introduce a quadratic penalty term in the objective function to enhance convergence (cf. $\boldsymbol{\mu}$ in (4)). Notably, in contrast to ePlace, elfPlace does not start with a pre-computed initial placement but a random placement.

Optimization Algorithms. Recently, much effort has been put into optimizer research due to the vast interest in machine learning. Many new methods emerged, such as RMSProp [20][1], Adam [18], and Adan [43]. The algorithms considered in this work are briefly introduced in the following section.

---
[1] RMSProp originates from Hinton's Coursera class [10] and Tieleman [39].

4 Optimization Algorithms

With the vast interest in machine learning, new gradient direction algorithms emerged that are more adaptive and resilient. This section briefly introduces the optimization algorithms used in the subsequent evaluation in Sect. 6. For readability, the cell positions are combined in one vector, e.g., $\boldsymbol{u}_k = (\boldsymbol{x}_k, \boldsymbol{y}_k)$, where $\boldsymbol{u}_k$ is the cells' $\boldsymbol{x}$ and $\boldsymbol{y}$ positions in the k-th iteration. Note that some notations have been altered from the original works for reasons of consistency.

Nesterov with Lipschitz Prediction. Nesterov's method [30] is a first-order optimization method that achieves a convergence rate of $O(1/k^2)$ for k iterations on a convex objective if the condition in (5) holds. ePlace approximates the Lipschitz constant $\widetilde{L}_k$ using the prediction in (6) to avoid compute-intensive line search. Its reciprocal is used as the steplength, i.e., $\alpha_k = \widetilde{L}_k^{-1}$. While some performance loss is expected by not finding the zero-gradient point exactly, line search has shown to consume 63% runtime in global placement, 50% of the total placement time [24]. The algorithm is summarized in Algorithm 1, where line 1 sets the steplength according to the reciprocal of the Lipschitz approximation in (6). A gradient descent step is taken to compute $\boldsymbol{u}_{k+1}$ in line 2, and the optimization parameter a is updated. Following the naming convention used by Lu et al., a new *reference solution* $\boldsymbol{v}_{k+1}$ is computed in line 4 for steplength prediction. This algorithm builds the basis for the current implementation in nextpnr. → Referred to as *Nesterov* in the subsequent evaluation.

$$f(\boldsymbol{v}_k) - f(\underbrace{\boldsymbol{v}_k - \alpha_k \nabla f(\boldsymbol{v}_k)}_{\boldsymbol{u}_{k+1}}) \geq \frac{1}{2} \alpha_k ||\nabla f(\boldsymbol{v}_k)||^2 \tag{5}$$

$$\widetilde{L}_k = \frac{||\nabla f(\boldsymbol{v}_k) - \nabla f(\boldsymbol{v}_{k-1})||}{||\boldsymbol{v}_k - \boldsymbol{v}_{k-1}||} \tag{6}$$

Algorithm 1. Step: Nesterov with Lipschitz prediction.

Input: objective function f, current solution $\boldsymbol{u}_k$, reference solutions $\boldsymbol{v}_k$ and $\boldsymbol{v}_{k-1}$, parameter a_k
Output: new solution $\boldsymbol{u}_{k+1}$, reference solution $\boldsymbol{v}_{k+1}$, parameter a_{k+1}
1: $\alpha_k = \widetilde{L}_k^{-1}$ ▷ steplength by Lipschitz prediction
2: $\boldsymbol{u}_{k+1} = \boldsymbol{v}_k - \alpha_k \nabla f(\boldsymbol{v}_k)$ ▷ update solution
3: $a_{k+1} = (1 + \sqrt{4a_k^2 + 1})/2$
4: $\boldsymbol{v}_{k+1} = \boldsymbol{u}_{k+1} + (a_k - 1)(\boldsymbol{u}_{k+1} - \boldsymbol{u}_k)/a_{k+1}$ ▷ update reference solution
---

Nesterov with Lipschitz Prediction and Backtracking. Lipschitz prediction as in (6) may overestimate the steplength, which can misguide the solver and reduce the solution quality [25]. Thus, ePlace-MS uses backtracking in addition to Lipschitz prediction. In essence, backtracking finds a temporary steplength by

Lipschitz prediction. This steplength is used to compute a temporary solution and steplength. If the new steplength exceeds the aforementioned one, the algorithm backtracks accordingly. Details can be found in the ePlace-MS paper [25]. The stop condition of the backtracking loop in this work follows the implementation in easyPlace [8] for stable termination. → Referred to as *Nesterov+Bktr* in the subsequent evaluation.

Adaptive Restart. O'donoghue and Candes [31] demonstrate that ripples in the objective value occur in momentum-based gradient methods once the momentum exceeds a critical value. The ripple has a period proportional to the square root of the condition number. They also propose two adaptive conditions to restart the algorithm (i.e., to reset the momentum) and recover linear convergence in many cases. We apply the gradient scheme (7) along with Nesterov's method and Lipschitz prediction. Whenever the reset condition is satisfied, we consider it in the subsequent iteration. Nesterov a is reset (i.e., $a_k = 1$), and the next cell positions are computed without incorporating the momentum term, i.e., set to the gradient descent position. → *Adapt* in the subsequent evaluation.

$$\nabla f(\boldsymbol{v}_{k-1})^T(\boldsymbol{u}_k - \boldsymbol{u}_{k-1}) > 0 \tag{7}$$

RMS Propagation. RMSProp is an extension to Adagrad. Instead of a monotonically decreasing learning rate, a moving average of squared gradients is used [20]. A step is summarized in Algorithm 2. In line 1, $\boldsymbol{n}_{k+1}$ is computed by taking the weighted average of $\boldsymbol{n}_k$ and the element-wise squares of the current gradients. $\beta \in [0, 1]$ is a decay factor. The new solution is computed in line 2, which updates the cell positions. $\odot$ indicates an element-wise multiplication.

Algorithm 2. Step: RMSProp.

Input: objective function f, learning rate α, decay factor $\beta \in [0,1]$, current moving average of squared gradient elements $\boldsymbol{n}_k$, solution $\boldsymbol{u}_k$
Output: updated solution $\boldsymbol{u}_{k+1}$, moving average $\boldsymbol{n}_{k+1}$
1: $\boldsymbol{n}_{k+1} = \beta \boldsymbol{n}_k + (1-\beta)(\nabla f(\boldsymbol{u}_k))^2$ ▷ element-wise squares of gradients
2: $\boldsymbol{u}_{k+1} = \boldsymbol{u}_k - \alpha\left(\epsilon + \sqrt{\boldsymbol{n}_{k+1}}\right)^{-1} \odot \nabla f(\boldsymbol{u}_k)$ ▷ element-wise root and product

---

Adaptive Moment Estimation. Adam [18] estimates first and second gradient moments and computes an adaptive steplength. The algorithm is summarized in Algorithm 3. The complete pseudocode, including initialization, can be found in the original work. In lines 1 and 2, the biased first moment and second raw moment estimates are computed, respectively. They are bias-corrected in lines 3 and 4 before updating the solution vector $\boldsymbol{u}$ by an adaptive steplength.

Adaptive Nesterov Momentum. In Adan [43], the first- and second-order moments are estimated by a Nesterov momentum estimation. A step is summarized in Algorithm 4. Note that the indices are shifted for easier readability, and the decay factors are reversed compared to Adam. In this work, no restart condition is used, which can optionally stabilize optimization and enhance convergence. Further details and initialization can be found in the original work.

Algorithm 3. Step: Adam.

Input: objective function f, decay rates $(\beta_1, \beta_2) \in [0,1)^2$, steplength α, $\epsilon > 0$, current solution u_k, estimates m_k and v_k
Output: updated $m_{k+1}, v_{k+1}, u_{k+1}$

1: $m_{k+1} = \beta_1 m_k + (1 - \beta_1)\nabla f(u_k)$ ▷ biased first moment estimate
2: $v_{k+1} = \beta_2 v_k + (1 - \beta_2)(\nabla f(u_k))^2$ ▷ biased second raw moment estimate
3: $\hat{m}_{k+1} = m_{k+1}/(1 - \beta_1^{k+1})$ ▷ bias-corrected first moment estimate
4: $\hat{v}_{k+1} = v_{k+1}/(1 - \beta_2^{k+1})$ ▷ bias-corrected second raw moment estimate
5: $u_{k+1} = u_k - \alpha \cdot \hat{m}_{k+1}/\left(\epsilon + \sqrt{\hat{v}_{k+1}}\right)$ ▷ update cell positions

---

Algorithm 4. Step: Adan.

Input: objective function f, steplength α, decay rates $(\beta_1, \beta_2, \beta_3) \in [0,1]^3$, $\epsilon > 0$, weight decay λ_k, current solution u_k, previously computed gradient $\nabla f(u_{k-1})$, estimates m_k, v_k, and n_k
Output: updated $m_{k+1}, v_{k+1}, n_{k+1}, u_{k+1}$

1: $m_{k+1} = (1 - \beta_1)m_k + \beta_1 \nabla f(u_k)$ ▷ estimate first momentum
2: $v_{k+1} = (1 - \beta_2)v_k + \beta_2(\nabla f(u_k) - \nabla f(u_{k-1}))$ ▷ estimate second momentum
3: $n_{k+1} = (1 - \beta_3)n_k + \beta_3\bigl(\nabla f(u_k) + (1 - \beta_2)(\nabla f(u_k) - \nabla f(u_{k-1}))\bigr)^2$
4: $\alpha_{k+1} = \alpha/(\epsilon + \sqrt{n_{k+1}})$
5: $u_{k+1} = (1 + \lambda_k \alpha)^{-1}\bigl(u_k - \alpha_{k+1} \odot (m_{k+1} + (1 - \beta_2)v_{k+1})\bigr)$ ▷ update cell positions
6: **if** restart condition holds **then** ... **endif**

---

5 Nextpnr and Modifications in This Work

nextpnr [35] is an open-source place&route framework. Due to its versatility in adopting new architectures via an Application Programming Interface (API), many real-world FPGA architectures are supported and nextpnr established as a widely-used solution in the open-source community to implement for real target hardware. In addition, the flexibility allows to implement for custom architectures [19]. nextpnr currently implements three placers: a simulated annealing placer that is based on nextpnr's predecessor Arachne-pnr [44], a quadratic placer based on HeAP, and an electrostatic placer based partially on ePlace and elfPlace. This work builds upon nextpnr's electrostatic placer in commit `cf42baa`. However, there are some modifications to this implementation, most notably:

Initial Placement. nextpnr initializes all cells randomly around the FPGA's center. We add a bi-partitioner based on Fiduccia-Mattheyses [7] to optionally initialize the cells around two points separated by a heuristic min-cut.

Lagrange Multipliers. We modify the Lagrange multiplier updates.

Fade In. We use a parametrizable sigmoid function to fade in the penalty term, as the strong initial field causes too much spreading. The used fade-in factor is shown in (8), where κ and κ_2 are two hyper-parameters.

$$\eta_k = \frac{1}{1 + \exp(-\kappa_2 \cdot (k - \kappa))} \tag{8}$$

Preconditioning. Preconditioning by a Jacobian is used to enhance convergence. We adopt the approximation of the second derivative of the wirelength function from elfPlace and replace the original preconditioner with the one in (9). E_i denotes nets incident to cell i and $|e|$ the degree of net e.

$$\frac{\partial^2 f(\boldsymbol{x}, \boldsymbol{y})}{\partial x_i^2} \approx \max\left(1, \underbrace{\sum_{e \in E_i} \frac{1}{|e| - 1}}_{\approx \frac{\partial^2 \widetilde{W}(x,y)}{\partial x_i^2}} + \lambda_s q_i\right) \tag{9}$$

Penalty Reset. nextpnr currently does not implement area inflation techniques. However, intermediate legalization is performed. An adjustment of $\boldsymbol{\lambda}$ is added to account for the perturbation through legalization. It is similar to the adaptation of $\boldsymbol{\lambda}$ in elfPlace after instance area adjustment.

Scaling. ePlace uses density scaling to adjust the area of fixed and dark cells and their resulting force to the target density. We apply this concept to dark cells and utilize the same mechanism for fillers to reduce their force by scaling.

Optimization Algorithms. nextpnr uses Nesterov's method as solver. All further algorithms discussed in this work are added.

Finally, instrumentation code is added which is expected to have little impact.

6 Experiments and Results

Update schemes. Besides the effect of the gradient direction algorithm, two schemes for updating the Lagrange multipliers are applied and compared in this work. **(U1)** The first one is influenced by ePlace, where the Lagrange multiplier updates are affected by the HPWL trend. We use an adaptive factor t_k. Its elements t_{k_s} are computed by one group each as in (10). $\boldsymbol{\lambda}$ is increased by the factor α_L if the HPWL is identical to the iteration before. In addition, a decrease in wirelength leads to further incrementing the Lagrange multiplier, whereas an increase in wirelength slows down the Lagrange multiplier growth and, depending on the hyper-parameter values, may even decrease it. The Lagrange multipliers are then updated by an element-wise multiplication $\lambda_{k+1} = t_k \lambda_k$.

$$t_{k_s} = \tanh\left(\gamma_{(U1)} \frac{\text{HPWL}_{s,\text{prev.}} - \text{HPWL}_s}{\text{HPWL}_{s,\text{prev.}}}\right)(\alpha_H - \alpha_L) + \alpha_L \quad (10)$$

The quadratic penalties are set to a constant $\beta/\Phi_{s,k=0}$, scaled by λ similar to elfPlace. In addition, they are faded in by (8). Once the cell overlap threshold of 10% is reached, intermediate legalization is performed, and λ is adjusted. **(U2)** The second scheme is similar to the one in elfPlace. However, the fade-in is also applied to the Lagrange multipliers due to the otherwise high initial spreading. All executions can invoke the initial bi-partitioning by a binary hyper-parameter. In (U1) and (U2), the Lagrange multipliers are not updated for groups that have reached their overlap target. In (U2), these are also not included in the calculation of the sub-gradient norm.

Designs. Two designs are used to show the impact of the choice of gradient direction algorithm and update scheme. **(D1)** The first design is a VexRiscv-based Linux-capable System on Chip (SoC) [12,36] generated with LiteX [15]. It is selected for its popularity in the open-source domain and acts as a typical modern SoC representative, which is extensible by the LiteX framework.

The second design **(D2)** is CoreScore [17] with 150 cores. It provides a different netlist structure, as many tiny RISC-V cores are replicated. Also, it has been used for evaluation in the FPGA'24 routing contest with 500 cores [13]. The pre-packing device utilizations are summarized in Table 1.

Table 1. Pre-packing resource utilization of the two designs used in this work.

ECP5-85k	(D1) linux-on-litex-vexriscv [12]		(D2) CoreScore [17] 150 cores	
Type	Utilization	Relative	Utilization	Relative
Total LUT4s	31717/83640	37%	49506/83640	59%
RAM LUTs	9760/10455	93%	0/10455	0%
RAMW LUTs	4880/20910	23%	0/20910	0%
Total DFFs	7090/83640	8%	42485/83640	50%

Hyper-Parameter Tuning. We find preferable values for the hyper-parameters by optimizing for the HPWL. An ECP5 [21] FPGA in its 85k variant is used as the target in all experiments. The hyper-parameters are tuned within a constrained range using FLAML [42] with 900 execution runs and 50 parallel evaluations on a dual socket AMD EPYC 7F52 machine. Each nextpnr execution is limited to 1000 iterations and has a timeout while tuning. The execution is terminated after placement is performed, and the HPWL is weighted as in (11). Intuitively, the parameters are tuned for the HPWL if the number of iterations is sufficiently low. Once the number of iterations exceeds 750, the HPWL is increasingly penalized such that it must get 7.5% shorter over the remaining 250 iterations for a better score (lower value). The threshold iteration number is chosen to be larger than the number of iterations in the baseline for design (D1) to focus on QoR over runtime. The penalty is added for a smoother transition to the hard timeout that is required to limit the runtime of tuning.

$$\text{Score} = \begin{cases} \text{HPWL} \cdot \left(1 + \max(0, \text{iter} - 750) \cdot \frac{0.075}{250}\right) & \text{if successful} \\ 1e8 & \text{otherwise} \end{cases} \quad (11)$$

Table 2 summarizes the hyper-parameters common to all algorithms. α_L, α_H, and $\gamma_{(U1)}$ determine the increase rate of the Lagrange multipliers, e.g., for (U1) in (10). u_{target} sets the target utilization and, thus, determines the number of filler cells added to the design cells. κ and κ_2 parametrize the fade-in function in (8). β scales the penalty that is faded in. η and η_{legal} scale the Lagrange multiplier initialization and adjustment, respectively. Details can be found in (18) and (27) in [22]. I_{FM} is a flag that sets whether an initial min-cut bi-partitioning is performed. In addition, gradient-algorithm-specific hyper-parameters are added.

Table 2. Hyper-parameters common to all optimization algorithms.

α_L, α_H, $\gamma_{(U1)}$	determine the increase of the Lagr. multipliers, e.g., in (10) for (U1)
u_{target}	target utilization: determines amount of filler cells inserted; see [24]
κ, κ_2	rate of fade-in factor as shown in (8)
β, η, η_{legal}	scales penalty; scales Lagrange initialization; Lagr. multiplier adjust
I_{FM}	$\in \{\text{yes}, \text{no}\}$; whether initial bi-partitioning is performed

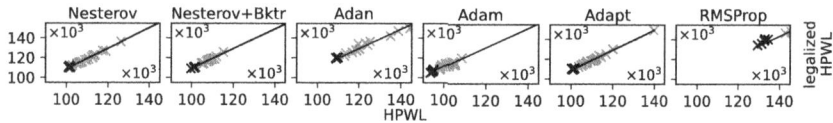

Fig. 1. HPWL (x-axis) vs. legalized HPWL (y-axis) for each gradient algorithm when tuning for (D1) using scheme (U1). The distribution shows the best five runs (black) and a random sampling of runs (grey).

Performed Experiments. For both schemes to update the Lagrange multipliers, (U1) and (U2), the hyper-parameters are tuned for design (D1) in our initial experiments. (D2) is used to evaluate the chosen hyper-parameters with an independent design that has not influenced tuning. Figure 1 plots the correlation between HPWL and post-legalize HPWL after tuning using (U1). As can be seen, the values correlate linearly, and tuning can be done for the pre-legalized placement without considering the legalizer's capabilities and runtime.

Table 3. Best results by tuning using (U1) and (U2) for (D1). The found hyperparameter values are evaluated on (D2). Bold numbers indicate the best-achieved result among these. Gray lines add results with a high QoR on both designs. f_{max} is evaluated on the routed implementation. *Baseline* is the unmodified electrostatic placer.

	(D1) linux-on-litex-vexriscv			→	(D2) CoreScore 150		
Algorithm	HPWL	legalized f_{max}	/MHz Iter.		HPWL	legalized f_{max}	/MHz Iter.
Baseline: static	103 943	111 293	38.4 525		239 020	293 837	33.7 363
(U1) Nesterov	100 895	110 334	40.8 985		**210 689**	258 343	35.8 795
Nesterov+Bktr	99 665	109 175	41.5 838		240 893	294 962	31.3 745
Nesterov+Bktr$_{10}$	101 534	110 424	40.6 878		205 286	257 327	30.5 778
Adan	108 849	120 021	40.2 197		273 467	317 023	37.0 147
Adam	**93 514**	105 010	36.0 254		217 091	271 350	**40.0** 203
Adam$_{10}$	94 317	106 217	41.0 215		207 851	259 268	37.0 162
Adapt	100 307	110 402	**42.8** 700		221 661	269 311	39.5 314
RMSProp	129 411	134 427	38.8 160		339 960	374 166	29.6 106
(U2) Nesterov	100 453	110 254	38.9 596		225 717	289 240	26.9 470
Nesterov$_{10}$	101 941	112 082	39.7 961		217 852	282 409	25.6 839
Nesterov+Bktr	101 317	110 831	42.0 814		265 646	321 110	26.8 665
Nesterov+Bktr$_{10}$	101 995	112 205	36.1 635		232 013	288 242	25.1 485
Adan	112 242	120 909	40.3 858		289 996	335 818	38.4 829
Adam	95 217	107 340	42.1 203		305 213	372 505	26.5 161
Adam$_{10}$	98 231	108 723	40.6 243		241 939	297 577	35.1 216
Adapt	100 480	109 316	38.0 875		226 178	279 248	26.6 798
Adapt$_{10}$	101 993	109 840	40.4 905		221 101	267 526	34.7 855
RMSProp	124 624	130 931	42.0 963		317 934	360 314	27.6 900

Discussion. Table 3 summarizes the results found by tuning for (D1) and the corresponding results on the evaluation design (D2). In addition, it includes parameterizations that do not achieve the shortest HPWL on (D1) but a good overall QoR. They are colored in gray and marked with a suffix. Candidates are selected from the best 10 runs for (D1) and kept if (a) the HPWL for (D2) decreases and outperforms the baseline at a maximum decrease of 15% in f_{max}, or (b) f_{max} increases at least 15% and outperforms the baseline while the HPWL decreases. The one with shortest HPWL for (D2) is kept. This emphasizes tuning for a more extensive set of designs, as discussed in Sect. 7.

In our experiments, (U1) achieves a shorter HPWL on average. By comparing the results of the evaluation design (D2) using the hyper-parameters found by tuning for (D1), Nesterov leads to the shortest HPWL, whereas Adam achieves the highest f_{max} at faster convergence. This is in contrast to the tuning results of (D1), where Adam achieves the shortest HPWL at a lower f_{max}. Taking into account parameterizations that achieve a good QoR on both designs (the gray lines mentioned above), Adam outperforms Nesterov at a higher f_{max}. While this run slightly increases the HPWL for (D1), its $f_{\max}$ improves. Adapt is close to Adam and achieves a high $f_{\max}$ – and the highest for (D1).

Apart from RMSProp, all 10 best sets of hyper-parameters for (D1) also converge for (D2). Among these, Adapt achieves the smallest standard deviation ($\sigma_{HPWL}=10\,017$) for (D2). Adan has the lowest variability for $f_{\max}$ ($\sigma_{f_{\max}} = 2.3$), neglecting RMSProp due to its unfavorable results. However, the average $f_{\max}$ ($\bar{f}_{\max} = 36.3$) is below Adam. Adam has low overall variability ($\sigma_{HPWL}=13\,319$, $\sigma_{f_{\max}} = 2.7$) and the highest average $f_{\max}$ ($\bar{f}_{\max} = 37.9$). It outperforms the baseline in HPWL by 9.2% and achieves an 18.7% higher $f_{\max}$ at fast convergence. The majority of high-ranked executions use initial bi-partitioning.

For (U2), the algorithms achieve comparable results with slightly higher average $f_{\max}$ on (D1) but cannot transfer them to (D2) in the performed experiments. This can specifically be seen by the results of $f_{\max}$, with the notable exception of Adan. Adam achieves the shortest HPWL on (D1) but worse results for (D2).

Summary. Overall, we observe better results for (U1). Using this scheme, Adam achieves a high QoR and fast convergence but has a slightly lower $f_{\max}$ for (D1) on the tuning result. Adapt is close in HPWL and has a higher $f_{\max}$ for (D1). It shows the lowest standard deviation among the 10 best tuning results. Nesterov achieves a shorter (better) HPWL on (D2) but at a lower $f_{\max}$. Table 4 summarizes the hyper-parameters of the best tuning run for these algorithms.

Figure 2 visualizes the progression of the HPWL and total potential energy over the iterations for the three best executions on (D1) using (U1). It shows how energy is successively lowered, interrupted by a bump originating from the perturbation of legalization and adjusting λ. The gray vertical lines mark the final iteration count for each run. Figure 3 plots some exemplary placement solutions. Design cells are colored red, while filler cells are shown in black. Figure 3(a) plots the baseline intermediate solution after 100 iterations. It shows a state where the design cells that are initialized densely around the FPGA's center start to spread in different directions depending on their forces. It also shows how the design cells initially cause a significant repulsion to the filler cells. The final placement is shown in (b), where it can be seen that filler cells mingle into the

Table 4. Hyper-parameters of best run for algorithms which achieved a high QoR.

	Algorithm	u_{target}	α_L	α_H	κ	κ_2	β	η	η_{legal}	I_{FM}	$\gamma_{(U1)}$	Stepl.	β_1	β_2
(U1)	Adam	0.82	1.07	1.23	114	10.13	0.299	0.006	0.065	yes	24.24	10.3	0.89	0.99
	Adapt	0.70	1.02	1.27	495	0.00	0.015	2.677	0.496	yes	28.97	2.4	–	–
	Nesterov	0.68	1.02	1.11	565	89.34	1.156	0.057	0.004	yes	0.60	–	–	–
	Nesterov+Bktr	0.74	1.03	1.18	1106	0.00	1.032	0.005	0.106	no	27.50	–	–	–
(U2)	Adam	0.83	1.01	1.04	128	0.64	0.039	1.247	0.024	yes	–	11.3	0.94	0.98
	Adapt	0.71	1.04	1.13	808	0.02	1.179	1.047	0.046	no	–	15.0	–	–
	Nesterov	0.79	1.03	1.22	437	0.05	0.038	5.027	0.018	yes	–	–	–	–
	Nesterov+Bktr	0.75	1.01	1.17	729	0.01	0.170	0.018	0.327	no	–	–	–	–

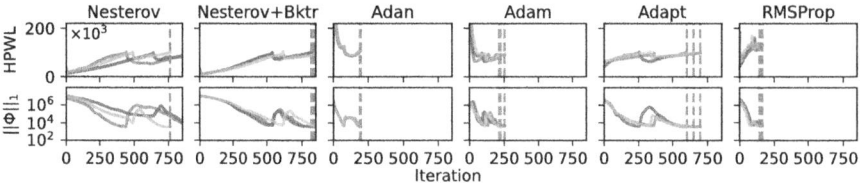

Fig. 2. Progression of HPWL (upper row) and total system potential energy Φ (lower row) of the three best runs while tuning design (D1) using (U1).

accumulation of design cells. In Fig. 3(c), the initial bi-partitioning is used. The rendering displays a state showing some movements between the design cells and repulsion to the filler cells. It leads to the solution in (d), where many fillers enter the accumulation of design cells. Nesterov achieves a visually cleaner solution, as shown in (e). Finally, (f) and (g) show the placement for the larger design (D2). In contrast to (c), (f) indicates an asymmetric spreading likely caused by the allowed imbalance in bi-partitioning.

7 Limitations and Future Work

Adam shows promising results and convergence rate using (U1). However, also Adapt achieves a high QoR, besides plain Nesterov, for this scheme at the cost of slower convergence in the performed experiments. To determine a generic algorithm and associated set of hyper-parameters, a more extensive set of designs needs to be taken into account that also covers borderline device utilization and different FPGA architectures. Table 3 shows that the best parameterizations found for (D1) do not necessarily lead to an optimal HPWL for design (D2) and that the update scheme can have a significant impact. Whereas Adam achieves a desirable HPWL on both designs using (U1), it degrades on the evaluation design using (U2). Also, one set of hyper-parameters may not be optimal in all scenarios, requiring a pre-classification of the design to achieve the optimal results. However, the choice of gradient algorithms has demonstrated the ability to improve the QoR and convergence rate—and is, thus, worth revisiting.

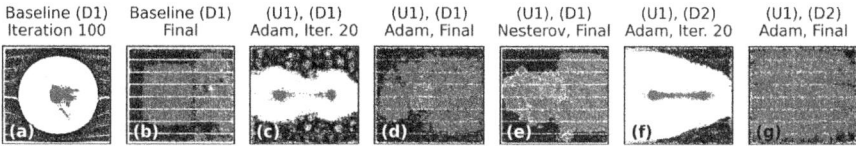

Fig. 3. Placement solutions for different algorithms and different points in time. (Color figure online)

We want to point out that the experiments performed do not imply generality about the capability of the gradient algorithms, and many influencing factors need to be considered. Moreover, algorithmic discrepancies can significantly impact the result, and details such as the chain update between iterations must be explored. Also, decisions such as sizing filler cells or the balancedness of the performed min-cut for initial placement need to be further investigated. While the experiments show a preference for an initial bi-partitioning, its runtime must also be considered in conjunction with the QoR improvement.

We will address the abovementioned limitations in future work and take into account further optimization objectives. These include congestion metrics and net weightings. The latter is currently set as a hard-coded function of the net criticality and acts as a handle to optimize for the critical path and, thus, achieve a higher maximum clock frequency, f_{max}.

8 Conclusion

This paper investigated the electrostatic placer in nextpnr and revisited the choice of gradient direction algorithm. We applied two schemes to update the Lagrange multipliers and tuned the hyper-parameter for each to compare the placement results. Initial experiments emphasized Adam as a promising candidate besides Nesterov and an adaptive restating scheme. However, generality must be proven with a more extensive set of designs covering a broader range of utilizations and congestion. As has been shown, algorithmic choices such as the Lagrange multiplier update scheme can significantly impact the quality of results achieved and generalization capability. Thus, we discussed current limitations and improvements, which we will address in future work.

Disclosure of Interests. The authors have no competing interests to declare that are relevant to the content of this article.

References

1. Betz, V., Rose, J.: VPR: a new packing, placement and routing tool for FPGA research. In: Luk, W., Cheung, P.Y.K., Glesner, M. (eds.) FPL 1997. LNCS, vol. 1304, pp. 213–222. Springer, Heidelberg (1997). https://doi.org/10.1007/3-540-63465-7_226
2. Brenner, U., Hermann, A., Hoppmann, N., Ochsendorf, P.: BonnPlace: a self-stabilizing placement framework. In: Proceedings of the International Symposium on Physical Design, ISPD 2015, pp. 9–16. ACM (2015)
3. Chen, S.C., Chang, Y.W.: FPGA placement and routing. In: Proceedings of the International Conference on Computer-Aided Design (ICCAD), pp. 914–921. IEEE (2017)
4. Cheng, C.L.E.: RISA: accurate and efficient placement routability modeling. In: Proceedings of the International Conference on Computer-Aided Design, pp. 690–695 (1994)
5. Diamantopoulos, D., Siozios, K., Xydis, S., Soudris, D.: GENESIS: parallel application placement onto reconfigurable architectures (invited for the special issue on runtime management). ACM Trans. Embed. Comput. Syst. **14**(1) (2015)

6. Elgamma, M.A., Murray, K.E., Betz, V.: Learn to place: FPGA placement using reinforcement learning and directed moves. In: Proceedings of the International Conference on Field-Programmable Technology (ICFPT), pp. 85–93. IEEE (2020)
7. Fiduccia, C.M., Mattheyses, R.M.: A linear-time heuristic for improving network partitions. In: Proceedings of the Design Automation Conference (DAC). ACM (1988)
8. Ge, Z., Liu, Y.: easyPlace. https://github.com/geziangfinn/easyPlace. Accessed 07 Dec 2024. Commit: 7d91058
9. Gort, M., Anderson, J.H.: Analytical placement for heterogeneous FPGAs. In: Proceedings of the International Conference on Field Programmable Logic and Applications (FPL), pp. 143–150 (2012)
10. Hinton, G., Srivastava, N., Swersky, K.: Lecture 6a Overview of mini-batch gradient descent. https://www.cs.toronto.edu/~tijmen/csc321/slides/lecture_slides_lec6.pdf. Accessed 05 Dec 2024
11. Hsu, M.K., Chang, Y.W., Balabanov, V.: TSV-aware analytical placement for 3D IC designs. In: Proceedings of the Design Automation Conference (DAC), pp. 664–669 (2011)
12. litex hub: linux-on-litex-vexriscv. https://github.com/litex-hub/linux-on-litex-vexriscv. Accessed 07 Dec 2024
13. Hung, E., Lavin, C., Nafziger, Z., Kaviani, A.: Runtime-First FPGA Interchange Routing Contest@ FPGA'24 (2024)
14. Kahng, A.B., Wang, Q.: A faster implementation of APlace. In: Proceedings of the International Symposium on Physical Design (ISPD), pp. 218–220 (2006)
15. Kermarrec, F., Bourdeauducq, S., Lann, J.C.L., Badier, H.: LiteX: an open-source SoC builder and library based on Migen Python DSL. arXiv preprint arXiv:2005.02506 (2020)
16. Kim, M.C., Lee, D.J., Markov, I.L.: SimPL: an effective placement algorithm. IEEE Trans. Comput. Aided Des. Integr. Circuits Syst. **31**(1), 50–60 (2012)
17. Kindgren, O.: CoreScore. github.com/olofk/corescore. Accessed 07 Dec 2024
18. Kingma, D.P.: Adam: A Method for Stochastic Optimization. arXiv preprint arXiv:1412.6980 (2014)
19. Koch, D., et al.: FABulous: an embedded FPGA framework. In: Proceedings of the International Symposium on Field-Programmable Gate Arrays (FPGA), pp. 45–56 (2021)
20. Kochenderfer, M.: Algorithms for Optimization. The MIT Press Cambridge (2019)
21. Lattice Semiconductor Corp: ECP5 and ECP5-5G Family (2024). FPGA-DS-02012-3.3
22. Li, W., Lin, Y., Pan, D.Z.: elfPlace: electrostatics-based placement for large-scale heterogeneous FPGAs. In: Proceedings of the International Conference on Computer-Aided Design (ICCAD), pp. 1–8. IEEE (2019)
23. Liao, P., et al.: Dreamplace 4.0: timing-driven placement with momentum-based net weighting and lagrangian-based refinement. IEEE Trans. Comput.-Aided Des. Integr. Circ. Syst. **42**(10), 3374–3387 (2023)
24. Lu, J., et al.: ePlace: electrostatics-based placement using fast fourier transform and nesterov's method. ACM Trans. Des. Autom. Electron. Syst. (TODAES) **20**(2), 1–34 (2015)
25. Lu, J., et al.: ePlace-MS: electrostatics-based placement for mixed-size circuits. IEEE Trans. Comput. Aided Des. Integr. Circuits Syst. **34**(5), 685–698 (2015)
26. Ludwin, A., Betz, V.: Efficient and deterministic parallel placement for FPGAs. ACM Trans. Des. Autom. Electron. Syst. **16**(3) (2011)

27. Maidee, P., Ababei, C., Bazargan, K.: Fast timing-driven partitioning-based placement for island style FPGAs. In: Proceedings of the Design Automation Conference (DAC), pp. 598–603. ACM (2003)
28. Marek-Sadowska, M., Lin, S.P.: Timing driven placement. In: Proceedings of the International Conference on Computer-Aided Design, pp. 94–95. IEEE Computer Society (1989)
29. Murray, K.E., et al.: VTR 8: high-performance CAD and customizable FPGA architecture modelling. ACM Trans. Reconfigurable Techn. Syst. **13**(2) (2020)
30. Nesterov, Y.: A method of solving a convex programming problem with convergence rate $O(1/k^2)$. Proc. USSR Acad. Sci. **269**, 3 (1983)
31. O'donoghue, B., Candes, E.: Adaptive restart for accelerated gradient schemes. Found. Comput. Math. **15**, 715–732 (2015)
32. Rajarathnam, R.S., et al.: Better together: combining analytical and annealing methods for FPGA placement. In: Proceedings of the Conference on Field-Programmable Logic and Applications (FPL), pp. 43–52 (2024)
33. Ray, B.B., et al.: An optimized HPWL model for VLSI analytical placement. In: Proceedings of the International Conference on Information Technology (ICIT), pp. 7–12 (2015)
34. Roy, J.A., et al.: Capo: robust and scalable open-source min-cut floorplacer. In: Proceedings of the International Symposium on Physical Design (ISPD), pp. 224–226. ACM (2005)
35. Shah, D., et al.: Yosys+nextpnr: an open source framework from verilog to bitstream for commercial FPGAs. In: Proceedings of the Annual International Symposium on Field-Programmable Custom Computing Machines (FCCM), pp. 1–4. IEEE (2019)
36. SpinalHDL: VexRiscv. github.com/SpinalHDL/VexRiscv. Accessed 11 Dec 2024
37. Spindler, P., Johannes, F.M.: Fast and accurate routing demand estimation for efficient routability-driven placement. In: Design, Automation & Test in Europe Conference & Exhibition, pp. 1–6. IEEE (2007)
38. Spindler, P., Schlichtmann, U., Johannes, F.M.: Kraftwerk2-a fast force-directed quadratic placement approach using an accurate net model. IEEE Trans. Comput. Aided Des. Integr. Circuits Syst. **27**(8), 1398–1411 (2008)
39. Tieleman, T.: Lecture 6.5-rmsprop: divide the gradient by a running average of its recent magnitude. COURSERA Neural Netw. Mach. Learn. **4**(2) (2012)
40. Tsay, R.S., Koehl, J.: An analytic net weighting approach for performance optimization in circuit placement. In: Proceedings of the Design Automation Conference (DAC), pp. 620–625 (1991)
41. Vercruyce, D., Vansteenkiste, E., Stroobandt, D.: Liquid: high quality scalable placement for large heterogeneous FPGAs. In: Proceedings of the International Conference on Field Programmable Technology (ICFPT), pp. 17–24 (2017)
42. Wang, C., Wu, Q., Weimer, M., Zhu, E.: FLAML: A Fast and Lightweight AutoML Library. arXiv preprint arXiv:1911.04706 (2019)
43. Xie, X., et al.: Adan: adaptive nesterov momentum algorithm for faster optimizing deep models. IEEE Trans. Pattern Anal. Mach. Intell. **46**(12), 9508–9520 (2024)
44. YosysHQ: Arachne-pnr. github.com/YosysHQ/arachne-pnr. Accessed 06 Dec 2024

ZTL: Enabling Zoned Namespace Support for File Systems

Jan Sass[1]($\boxtimes$), André Brinkmann[1], Xubin He[2], Matias Bjørling[3], and Reza Salkhordeh[1]

[1] Johannes Gutenberg University, Mainz, Germany
{sass,brinkman,salkordeh}@uni-mainz.de
[2] Temple University, Philadelphia, PA, USA
xubin.he@temple.edu
[3] Western Digital Corporation, Copenhagen, Denmark
matias.bjorling@wdc.com

Abstract. A Flash Translation Layer (FTL) hides the intrinsic flash properties of SSDs and provides a block interface to the host. FTLs completely embedded in the firmware of SSDs must therefore duplicate host functionality, such as the translation between logical and physical blocks performed by a file system, introducing performance unpredictability and increasing device cost. Zoned Namespace (ZNS) SSDs overcome these drawbacks by only implementing limited FTL functionality inside the SSD and by exposing a more flash-friendly interface to the host. However, moving away from the block interface means that the storage stack inside the host must be modified for ZNS devices. This requires considerable effort, which is one reason why F2FS is the only Linux file system with reliable ZNS support today.

This paper discusses how the Linux storage stack can be extended to simplify the process of adapting file systems to ZNS devices. It then proposes the host-side Zoned Translation Layer (ZTL), which provides abstractions and functionalities required by many file systems to support ZNS devices. We demonstrate the feasibility of ZTL by providing the first EXT4 implementation for ZNS devices and by comparing our implementation of ZNS support for F2FS with the native ZNS support of F2FS.

1 Introduction

Compared to hard disk drives (HDDs), SSDs offer increased throughput and reduced latency for read and write operations [6,8,13]. Read and write accesses are performed at the granularity of pages, which are grouped into blocks. Each block must be written sequentially. SSDs do not allow in-place updates and erase operations must be performed at block granularity. A dedicated firmware component, the Flash Translation Layer (FTL), hides these flash-specific characteristics and provides a block interface that can be accessed in the same way as HDDs [6,13,31]. The main functions of the FTL include mapping between

© The Author(s), under exclusive license to Springer Nature Switzerland AG 2026
S. Tomforde et al. (Eds.): ARCS 2025, LNCS 15839, pp. 125–139, 2026.
https://doi.org/10.1007/978-3-032-03281-2_9

logical block numbers requested by the host and physical block numbers on the SSD, garbage collection to reclaim invalidated pages, and wear-leveling to reduce the impact of erase operations on the SSD's limited lifetime.

FTLs introduce their own overhead by requiring additional device resources and they operate without semantic information about the pages, resulting in suboptimal performance and increased costs [2,32]. For example, their logical-to-physical page mapping introduces an additional layer of indirection when coupled with a file system, as the file system already maps its contents to logical blocks, which are then again mapped by the FTL to physical pages on the SSD. This page mapping consumes a significant amount of the scarce memory resources on SSDs. In addition, the block interface cannot semantically distinguish between data and metadata of a file system and also cannot infer the hotness of the data, resulting in increased write amplification [22,23].

The Zoned Namespace (ZNS) specification defines a novel way for the host to directly interface with the flash medium, removing the need for a full on-device FTL. Compared to conventional SSDs, ZNS SSDs allow for reduced cost, more consistent performance, and prolonged device lifetime [2,23]. The integration of ZNS SSDs into the storage stack requires moving parts of the FTL into the host. Generic host-side FTL implementations, such as dm-zoned [27] or dm-zap [18], are reimplementations of SSD FTLs and do not utilize the benefits of ZNS. On the other hand, FTLs included in file systems, such as F2FS [12] and BTRFS [24,25], lack portability and spread out development over multiple implementations.

We propose the *Zoned Translation Layer* (ZTL), a host-side flash translation layer that abstracts generic parts of the FTL, such as garbage collection and ZNS management, and provides an interface that allows file systems to control data placement on the device and garbage collection scheduling. ZTL requires no additional translation layer as it integrates tightly with the file system and significantly reduces the effort required to adapt general-purpose file systems to ZNS devices compared to dedicated FTL implementations. We have integrated ZTL with EXT4 and F2FS and evaluated our implementation on physical hardware.

2 Technical Background

Flash pages are grouped into blocks, which need to be written sequentially. Once a block has been fully written, it can only be rewritten after erasing it. The FTL transforms host write operations into sequential write patterns to satisfy these requirements. It operates transparently and employs a mapping to translate the logical block address (LBA) specified by the host into its physical counterpart [6, 8,31]. A page on the device is considered invalid when it is rewritten to a new location or denoted as deleted by the host. In order to reclaim invalid pages, the FTL executes a periodic garbage collection. During this task, valid pages of a selected *victim* block are rewritten to different blocks and then the victim block is erased. The lack of semantic information on the device leads to suboptimal data placement and increased garbage collection overheads [9,14]. Combined with the duplicated mapping efforts, these shortcomings invite alternative concepts in order to replace the FTL [2,10,15].

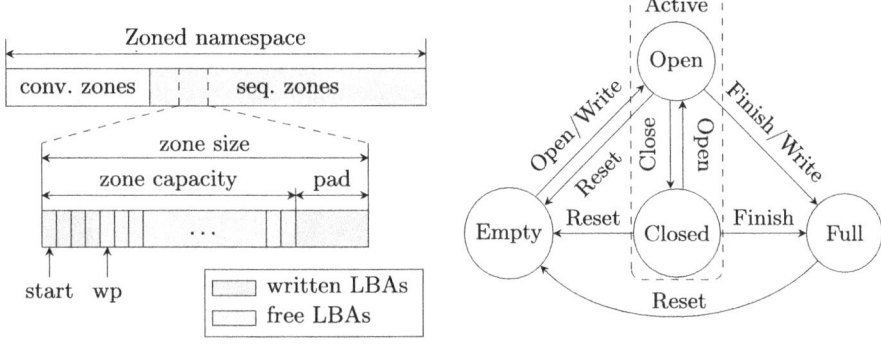

(a) An example for a ZNS SSD.   (b) Simplified zone states and transitions.

Fig. 1. .

ZNS SSDs were introduced to overcome the limitations of standard SSDs by moving most of the FTL to the host [3]. According to the NVMe ZNS specification [21], the LBA range of a ZNS SSD is partitioned into zones of equal size. Each zone must be written sequentially and can only be erased as a whole. Each zone has a write pointer (wp), denoting the next sector to be written. To align the starting sector of every zone to a power-of-two value, address padding is employed. ZNS SSDs require a host-side driver similar to the FTL on conventional SSDs: The host has to align writes with the write pointer of a zone, perform garbage collection to reclaim invalidated pages, maintain metadata for validity information and mapping tables, and handle zone state changes.

Aligning write operations with a write pointer requires the host to enforce strict request ordering throughout its storage stack, reducing flexibility and potentially throughput while increasing implementation complexity [5,16]. The *zone append* operation was added, so that the host can simply append data pages to a selected zone. The device then advances the writer pointer accordingly and returns the physical location in a callback to the host [3,7,21].

Each sequential write zone represents a state machine (Fig. 1b). On an empty device, each zone is in the *Empty* state and its write pointer points to its start sector. Issuing write operations transitions zones implicitly from *Empty* to *Open* and ultimately to *Full*. *Full* zones may be rewritten after an explicit *Reset* operation. While most transitions are performed implicitly by the device, the host can issue explicit transitions to enforce a stricter state policy. The number of concurrently active zones is limited due to device resources [3,11,21].

3 Design and Implementation

ZTL is a kernel space FTL implementation that integrates with file systems, enabling them to utilize the benefits of the ZNS.

We therefore assume that a random-write area is available for metadata operations of the file system. This area can either consist of conventional zones on the ZNS or dedicated storage. We see this as a sensible assumption as writing metadata to append-only logs incurs excessive overheads [12]. F2FS, the only stable file system with ZNS support, follows the same approach [26].

3.1 ZNS Support for File Systems

ZTL transparently implements all file system-independent tasks in the block layer. This includes managing zones, transforming write requests into sequential patterns, and providing a garbage collection routine.

Append-Only Logs and Zone Representation. ZTL abstracts physical zones using append-only logs. The file system can configure the number of logs to match its write patterns, e.g., to separate data with different expected lifetimes. Each log points to an active zone, which ZTL advances automatically once the zone becomes full. Towards the file system, a log is represented by a small integer value, e.g., $l \in \{0, 1, \ldots, n-1\}$ where n is the number of logs.

ZTL obtains zone information (LBA range of the sequential area and zone states) from the device at setup time. Additional metadata is provided by the file system, i.e., validity bitmaps used by the garbage collection, log-to-zone mappings from previous mount times, and each log's migration target.

Transparent Transformation of Write Requests. ZTL attaches to the ZNS block device and integrates with functions inside the block layer that are used by file systems when writing to a device. Upon request creation, the request is limited to the maximum number of pages for a zone append operation. When adding the first page to the request, ZTL redirects the request to the zone currently represented by the selected log. When further pages are added, ZTL clamps the request to zone boundaries. During the request callback after a successful write operation, ZTL state is updated.

The behavior of these functions is fully transparent to the file system, which only needs to configure the request to perform the zone append operation and supply the log number in place of an LBA. ZTL retains the idiomatic workflow of adding pages to a request until either the request is full or, specific to ZNS, a zone boundary is encountered. File systems already align with this routine by submitting the current request and starting a new one. Hence, the submission workflow requires minimal modifications within the file system.

Garbage Collection. ZTL tracks page invalidations in per-zone counters and bitmaps. A background thread periodically checks the page counters of full zones and starts a garbage collection if a zone contains a large fraction (e.g., 75%) of invalid pages. In addition, ZTL can perform a foreground garbage collection when under pressure, i.e., when less than 5% of the zones are empty during log advancements, or when the file system chooses to invoke it.

During garbage collection, the remaining valid pages of a zone are read from the device and written to a different zone using the zone append operation.

Afterwards, ZTL triggers an update of the file system metadata and invalidates the old page locations on the victim zone of the garbage collection. Once all pages have been migrated and their old locations have been invalidated, the victim zone can be reset.

The file system may specify the log target of page migrations in order to prevent repeated page migrations. For example, a file system that uses logs $\{0, 1, 2\}$ to represent cold data, hot data, and directories, may specify a mapping such as $\{0 \rightarrow 0, 1 \rightarrow 0, 2 \rightarrow 2\}$ to indicate migration targets. To ensure garbage collection can always succeed, a small number of zones (depending on the log configuration) are reserved for garbage collection purposes.

3.2 Enabling ZNS Benefits for File Systems

ZTL allows the file system to schedule a garbage collection and provide its own implementation of victim selection strategies. This allows the file system to leverage the advantages of ZNS and reduce write amplification as well as the impact of garbage collection on read and write latencies. By selecting a ZTL log to append to, the file system can attain the physical separation of data with different expected lifetimes, further augmenting this benefits.

3.3 Eliminate Duplicate Translation

The file system maintains a mapping from logical blocks belonging to files or directories to blocks on the device. Traditional FTL implementations, being detached from the host system, perform an additional translation from logical block addresses to flash pages. This extra layer of indirection can be removed by using the integration of ZTL with file systems as no additional translation is required by ZTL. Furthermore, ZTL utilizes the NVMe metadata features [20] to place the physical-to-logical mapping on the device, which is required by the garbage collection to update the file system metadata after page migrations.

3.4 Sustain File System Consistency

A ZTL host must delay metadata updates until a write operation completes and its callback is triggered (Sect. 4.2). If a system failure occurs *after* the write completes and *before* the file system updates its metadata, the pages are already written to the ZNS device while the file system has no information about their location. However, this does not harm consistency, as pages are only marked up-to-date after the metadata update of the file system. The impact of a fault during a zone append operation is the same as with conventional writes. Fault handling at any other time during the lifetime of the file system remains unchanged.

4 File System Integration

Some functionality necessarily remains dependent on the file system and cannot be abstracted by ZTL. In this section, we will describe the required adaptations. Listing 1.1 displays parts of the interface exposed by ZTL.

```
struct ztl_operations {
    int (*gc_bio_begin)(struct block_device *bdev, struct bio *bio,
                unsigned int from_log);
    int (*gc_bio_end)(struct block_device *bdev, struct bio *bio,
                unsigned int to_log);
    int (*fg_find_victim)(struct block_device *bdev, size_t nr_zones,
                struct ztl_zone **zones, struct ztl_zone **victim);
    int (*bg_find_victim)(struct block_device *bdev, size_t nr_zones,
                struct ztl_zone **zones, struct ztl_zone **victim);
    bool (*bg_gc_may_run)(struct block_device *bdev);
};

struct ztl_config {
    log_t nr_logs;                /* Nr of logical logs */
    sector_t *log_zones;          /* Each log's current zone */
    log_t *log_migration_zones;   /* Map of logs to GC target */
    log_t min_op_zones;           /* Minimum OP zones */
    unsigned int gc_inteval;      /* Interval for background GC, in secs */
    bitmap_t **blk_validity;      /* Per-zone validity bitmaps */
};
int ztl_init_context(struct super_block *sb, struct block_device *bdev,
                struct ztl_operations *ops, struct ztl_config *cfg);
void ztl_destroy_context(struct block_device *bdev);
int ztl_run_gc(struct block_device *bdev);
int ztl_invalidate(struct block_device *bdev, ino_t ino, ztl_blk_t block,
                ztl_blk_t count);
```

Listing 1.1. Excerpt of ZTL interface structures, prototypes, and functions. Only the prototype `gc_bio_end` is mandatory.

4.1 Context Lifetime and Super Block Changes

A ZTL context is required for each ZNS used by a file system. Accordingly, ZTL should be set up and removed by the file system when mounting and unmounting a ZNS device (`ztl_init_context` and `ztl_destroy_context`). On initialization, function prototypes and configuration options can be specified by the file system (Listing 1.1). The configuration allows the file system to specify the number of write logs (`nr_logs`), their underlying zones (`log_zones`), and their corresponding garbage collection targets (`log_migration_zones`). If `log_zones` is not provided, ZTL will autonomously select suitable zones. The overprovisioned zones (`min_op_zones`), and the garbage collection interval (`gc_interval`) can additionally be configured. Lastly, zone validity bitmaps from a previous mount time may be supplied (`blk_validity`). ZTL maintains no persistent metadata itself as it does not own any block device itself. Hence, the file system needs to hold ZTL related metadata in order to allow remounts (e.g., block validity information, required for garbage collection).

Additionally, the file system must keep information about the ZNS and its logical block range to maintain consistency. For example, the total available blocks are required to account for the capacity of the device. Lastly, the user space tools that create file system partitions (mkfs) may be needed to be modified to consider ZTL integration. However, this is out of the scope of this work.

4.2 Zone Append Operation

The file system determines which write operations are designated for the random-write area, i.e., metadata or data that relies on a fixed block location. Typically, this data can be identified by examining the inode type and number to distinguish between file data, directories, or special inodes (e.g., containing metadata or journals). All other write operations are designated for the sequential-write area of the ZNS. Some file systems, such as F2FS, already categorize pages into metadata, nodes, and data.

When issuing write operations to the conventional area, no or very little changes to the write workflow are required. For example, some file systems place metadata relative to the data on the device and may need to adjust the target sector for metadata writes accordingly. Despite our efforts to minimize the intrusiveness of ZTL, creation and submission of write operations to the sequential area require minor modifications. First, on request creation, the file system is to set the operation flag to zone append and select the log to append to instead of providing an LBA. Second, the file system needs to update its metadata after the operation, as the physical location of the written pages is provided during the request callback. Lastly, some global file system tasks, such as checkpointing or flushing of journals, may need to wait for the writeback operation on pages to finish in order to prevent deadlocks.

4.3 Block Validity and Garbage Collection

Garbage collection migrates valid pages to a different zone. This task is performed by ZTL, which afterwards notifies the file system about the new physical locations of migrated pages. To this end, the file systems must provide an implementation for the gc_bio_end prototype. ZTL allows the file system to perform additional preparations by providing a definition for the gc_bio_begin prototype. For the file system, the metadata update after a migration is very similar to the update after a non-migration write (Sect. 4.2), allowing the file system to aggregate both update functions.

ZTL holds information about the validity of pages in each zone for use by the garbage collection. The file system must call the ztl_invalidate function to notify ZTL whenever a physical address is no longer used by the file system, e.g., when deleting a file. Otherwise, the garbage collection would migrate pages the file system considers as deleted and trigger a file system metadata update based on outdated information.

The file system can provide implementations for the remaining function prototypes in Listing 1.1. fg_find_victim and bg_find_victim are used to select a zone during foreground and background garbage collections. If no implementation is given, ZTL uses a variant of the greedy victim selection (Sect. 3.1). In order to postpone the garbage collection dynamically, the file system can use the prototype bg_gc_may_run which is called by ZTL at the start of every garbage collection task. The file system can use ztl_run_gc to manually trigger a garbage collection.

5 Case Studies

In this section, we describe the integration of ZTL into EXT4 and F2FS. EXT4 does not natively support ZNS. F2FS, on the other hand, already supports ZNS SSDs, which allows us to compare the effort of our implementation against the native approach.

5.1 EXT4

EXT4 utilizes extents for allocating data on storage devices. Extents only require the starting LBA, the corresponding file offset and the number of consecutive blocks, effectively reducing the metadata overhead and allocation time compared to mapping single blocks [19,30].

During write operations, EXT4 performs four steps. First, for a given page, it traverses its inode's extent tree to look for a previously mapped physical location. If a previous block number is found, allocation stops. Otherwise, a new physical location is selected. The in-memory metadata is then updated for future requests. Second, the page is added to a write request, which is created if it does not already exist. Third, if no more pages are to be written or subsequent pages are not adjacent in the inode's address space, the write request is submitted. Finally, a callback step commits the in-memory metadata to the journal and marks the written pages as up-to-date. EXT4 always only writes pages that belong to a single inode, and all pages in a write request are contiguous in the inode's address space.

We implemented all changes according to Sect. 4. First, we integrated the ZNS device into the EXT4 metadata and added its zones to the available block range of the current EXT4 mount. On context creation, EXT4 registers ZTL with three logs: one for directories, one for data, and a garbage collection target. This extends the standard EXT4 implementation by an approach to reduce the garbage collection impact, based on previous works [12,15]. We provided an implementation for gc_bio_end and left the remaining ZTL settings to the default.

Second, to align with the zone append operation, we modified the write routines and directed data to the sequential part of the ZNS. We set the request operation flag accordingly and selected the appropriate log for the pages to be written. To decide which write operations are designated for the sequential area of the zoned device, we used the inode number of the pages to be written and directed metadata and journal pages to the conventional area. For other pages, we inspected the inode type to distinguish file data from directories.

Third, we integrated metadata updates into the after-write work queue of EXT4, which also frees resources and sets pages up-to-date. Lastly, we added calls to inform ZTL of invalid LBAs when an extent is deleted during removal or overwrite operations.

5.2 F2FS

The Flash Friendly File System (F2FS) [12] is designed to align file system tasks with the FTL as closely as possible and to extend the lifetime of flash storage while improving performance over previous file systems. F2FS appends write operations to different logs, based on the type of data and its expected lifetime. A random-write area is used to store metadata. F2FS requires a garbage collection routine similar to that of the FTL. The unit of garbage collection, called a *segment*, is aligned to the physical blocks of the underlying SSDs. By additionally issuing the *discard* operation to the device, F2FS aims to perform the garbage collection at file system level and leverage host insights to decrease the impact of the FTL. Because of its log-structured design and the use of write-buffers, F2FS does not support direct I/O.

F2FS uses inode indirection blocks to denote the location of data on the device. Inodes and indirection blocks are written to dedicated logs. F2FS uses a node address table to store the location of node blocks in the log. In order to avoid recursive updates, this table is kept in the random-write area next to other metadata [4,12].

When a ZNS device is detected, F2FS adapts the garbage collection unit to fit the size of the zones of the ZNS SSD, replaces the *discard* operation with a zone reset command, and disables in-place updates which are used when the available device capacity is below a given threshold [11]. Additionally, F2FS handles zone states, acquires zone metadata, and translates the device geometry into internal data structures.

The default ZNS support in F2FS does not utilize the zone append operation. Instead, it relies on ordered scheduling throughout the storage stack on the host. Hence, F2FS requires the `mq-deadline` scheduler to be enabled for the zoned device. `mq-deadline` has previously been adapted to submit write requests to zoned devices in ascending order by their target sector [5,7,11]. Support for zone write plugging [16] is currently not implemented in F2FS.

We integrated ZTL within F2FS by setting up the FTL context and related data structures. We configure ZTL logs similar to the native ZNS support and adapted the write workflow to make use of the zone append operation. As data block updates need to be denoted in node blocks, node updates need to be delayed until the corresponding data blocks are written. We handle the request callbacks for node and data separately using dedicated work queues. Lastly, we disabled in-place updates and the F2FS-intrinsic garbage collection and, instead, use the ZTL GC implementation.

F2FS performs periodic checkpointing to maintain file system consistency when a system outage occurs. While doing this, all other writeback operations are temporarily paused. The checkpoint procedure flushes the write buffers to the backing device and causes the associated callbacks to take place. A checkpoint is then written to the metadata region of the device. When a checkpoint is started before a write request is mapped, up-to-date node information is not available and the file system is at risk of being corrupted. Hence, we delayed checkpointing while write operations take place.

In contrast to the strict write ordering that F2FS applies for native ZNS support, our approach uses the zone append operation and removes the previously imposed scheduling restriction.

6 Experimental Results

In this section, we evaluate the impact of ZTL integration in terms of file system throughput, latencies and potential processing overheads. We compare ZTL integrated into EXT4 and F2FS (refered to as EXT4-ZTL and F2FS-ZTL) with stock F2FS and BTRFS on a physical ZNS SSD. While we included BTRFS in our evaluation, we note that tests run with fio [1] produced device errors during execution (i.e., trying to exceed the limit of concurrently opened zones). Despite numerous errors, BTRFS maintained its consistency. We did not compare against host-side FTLs such as dm-zap, dm-zoned, or SPDK as they pursue different goals.

We run all experiments on a machine with a 20 core Intel Xeon Gold 5215 CPU at 2.50 GHz and 128 GiB memory. We used an 8 TB Western Digital Ultrastar DC ZN540 as a physical ZNS SSD. The conventional area of this device is not sufficient for file system metadata and we therefore used a Samsung 983 DCT Series Enterprise SSD for the conventional area. We expect that future generations of ZNS devices come with a larger conventional area and more flexible device partitioning.

The zones of the ZNS are 2048 MiB in size and 1077 MiB in capacity. F2FS, F2FS-ZTL and EXT4-ZTL used the conventional SSD for metadata while BTRFS ran exclusively on the ZNS device. We used Linux kernel version 6.6 for all tests. Garbage collection was enabled during all experiments. F2FS and BTRFS employ their own implementation while F2FS-ZTL and EXT-ZTL utilize the implementation described in Sect. 3.1. Both variants perform the same steps, i.e., reading and writing pages from the ZNS and updating page locations in the file system metadata. Further investigation of garbage collection is out of the scope of this work.

6.1 Microbenchmarks

We conducted microbenchmarks using fio with different request sizes, measuring throughput, latency and CPU load during file system workloads. We tested read and write in random or sequential order (*read-rand*, *read-seq*, *write-rand* and

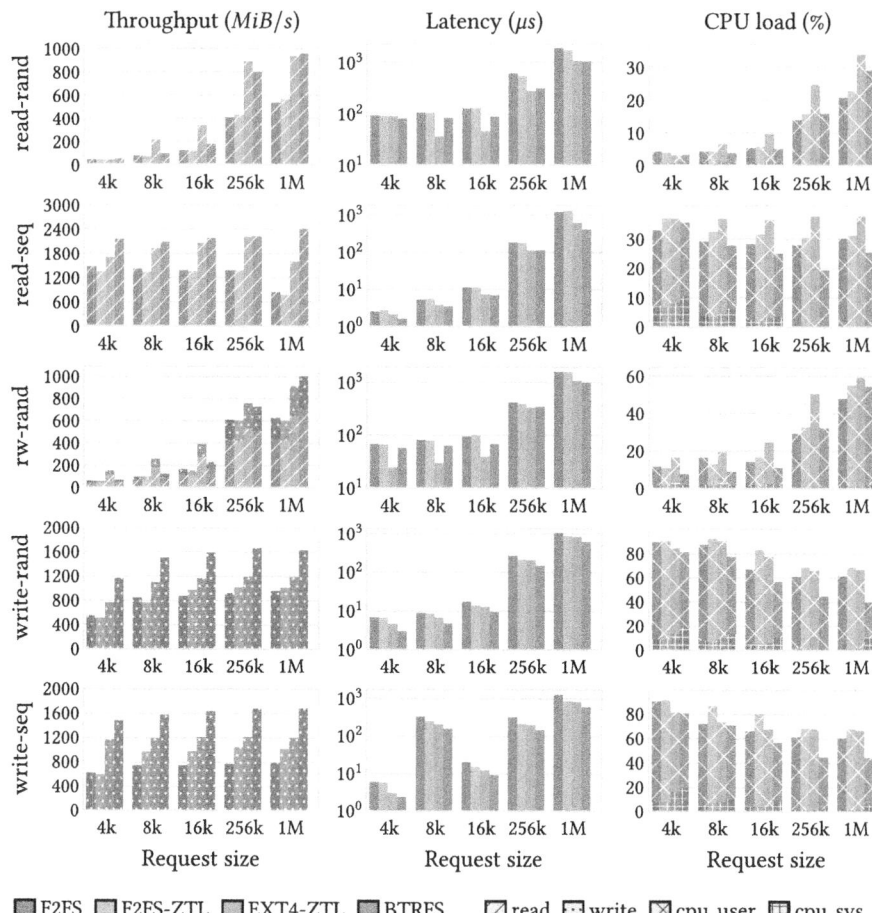

Fig. 2. Microbenchmarks of throughput, average latencies and CPU load (a load of 100% equals one fully-utilized CPU core). CPU load is divided into user space load (cpu_user) and kernel space load (cpu_sys).

write-seq), and a mixed workload of 30% random writes and 70% random reads (*rw-rand*). The results are presented in Fig. 2.

We observed significant performance improvements on write operations when using F2FS-ZTL compared to the native F2FS implementation. The latter employs conventional writes, requiring additional scheduling. By using the zone append operation, F2FS-ZTL circumvents scheduling restrictions and exceeds the write throughput of native F2FS by up to 37% for sequential write workloads, while maintaining compatible or better performance for all other benchmarks.

EXT4 achieves higher throughput than both native F2FS and F2FS-ZTL in all workloads and with all request sizes, due to its more compact metadata layout. BTRFS achieves the highest throughput of all file systems as it maintains the largest number of concurrently opened zones, more effectively saturating the device bandwidth than other file systems. Similar to EXT4, BTRFS also maintains its metadata in extent trees for better cache utilization.

The average latencies measured during the tests show that the zone append workflow and the prolonged writeback period of pages do not incur additional overheads. Instead, due to increased throughput in some cases, the latencies are reduced. During the read-seq workload, all file systems perform readahead operations that lead to average latency values below the access time of the physical device for small request sizes.

CPU usage scales with number of requests processed and hence correlates with increased throughput of file systems. However, we observe that the CPU load increases for F2FS-ZTL even when the performance does not increase compared to native F2FS. This is an expected result of the zone append write workflow and the metadata update after zone append. Optimizing a file system for zone append and towards a lower CPU load is out of the scope of this work.

6.2 Filebench

We used the fileserver, oltp, and varmail personalities of the Filebench file system benchmarking framework [28]. The results of the experiments are shown in Fig. 3a. We observe that F2FS-ZTL yields improvements over native F2FS of 19.8% for fileserver, 20.3% for oltp, and 16.9% for varmail. EXT4 performs similar to F2FS-ZTL for oltp and varmail and better (20.8% compared to F2FS-ZTL) for fileserver. BTRFS fails to maintain competitive throughput for oltp and varmail as frequent fsync calls lead to large metadata overheads and the resulting tree traversals slow the file system down. Additionally, BTRFS does not use a conventional device for metadata, further amplifying the effect of fsync.

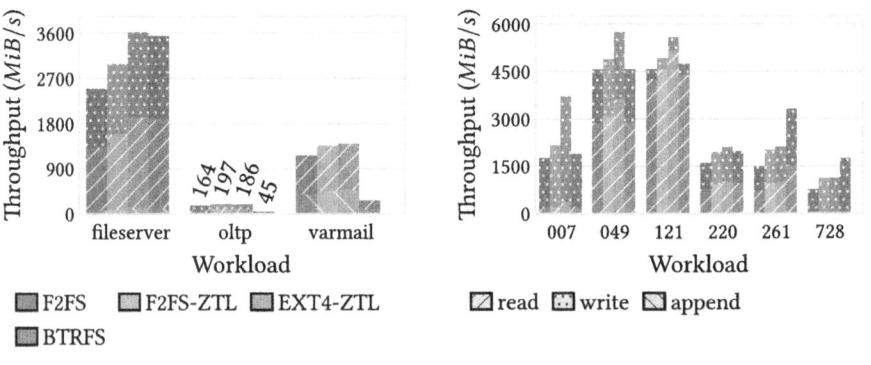

(a) Filebench workloads. (b) Selection of Alibaba block traces [17].

Fig. 3. .

6.3 Block Traces

To evaluate the overall file system performance with ZTL integration, we ran a selection of *Alibaba Block Traces* [17,29]. Block traces are evaluated using fio on a single file, representing the target block device. This evaluation reflects virtual machines workloads. We deliberately select traces with differing working set size (WSS) ratios to evaluate ZTL regarding caching and the writeback period. Our selection is displayed in Table 1. The results of these tests are shown in Fig. 3b.

Table 1. Selected Alibaba Traces [29]. The WSS (Working Set Size) ratio denotes the relative amount of pages used from the device size.

#	Device Size	WSS Ratio	R:W Ratio	I/O Size
007	500 GiB	5.77%	5:95	2328 GiB
049	40 GiB	11.33%	51:49	1226 GiB
121	60 GiB	15.28%	78:22	3396 GiB
220	160 GiB	66.12%	69:31	1212 GiB
261	100 GiB	93.64%	28:72	1744 GiB
728	300 GiB	93.37%	4:96	1190 GiB

Traces with small WSS ratio show large throughput due to caching effects. With larger WSS, the device is accessed more frequently, resulting in less throughput. We notice that F2FS-ZTL shows better overall performance than native F2FS. EXT4 allows better utilization of the page cache compared to F2FS and its performance is better during workloads with a small WSS. During write-heavy workloads, BTRFS shows higher throughput than all other file systems tested, as this allows BTRFS to better utilize the bandwidth of the ZNS.

6.4 Integration Effort

We integrated ZTL into F2FS and EXT4 and changed 547 and 534 lines of code during the process. The native ZNS support for F2FS accumulates to 648 lines changed, however using traditional writes. To adapt to the zone append paradigm, more extensive modifications would have to be made. Native ZNS support for BTRFS required more than 2500 additional lines of code, despite being currently unstable. The implementation of ZTL contains 4000 lines of code.

While these numbers only give an estimate of the implementation effort, we note that even a traditional file system like EXT4 can utilize the advantages offered by ZTL and ZNS. Furthermore, only ZTL needs to be adapted when the kernel API or the ZNS specification evolve, not the file system itself.

7 Conclusions

In this paper, we have proposed ZTL, a compatibility layer that allows arbitrary file systems to implement ZNS support with minimal effort. Our experiments show that ZTL reduces the effort required to add ZNS support while providing in the case of F2FS even better performance than the native ZNS implementation. Additionally, we provided the first ZNS implementation for EXT4, which exceeds the performance of F2FS.

Acknowledgement. This research has been funded by the Federal Ministry of Education and Research within the project "ScalNEXT: Optimierung des Datenmanagements und des Kontrollflusses von Rechenknoten für Supercomputing" (16ME0688).

References

1. Axboe, J.: fio - Flexible I/O tester rev. 3.36. https://fio.readthedocs.io/en/latest/fio_doc.html
2. Bjørling, M., et al.: The necessary death of the block device interface. In: Sixth Biennial Conference on Innovative Data Systems Research (CIDR) (2013)
3. Bjørling, M., et al.: ZNS: avoiding the block interface tax for flash-based SSDs. In: 2021 USENIX ATC (2021)
4. Brown, N.: An f2fs teardown (2012). https://lwn.net/Articles/518988/
5. Corbet, J.: 4.16 Merge window part 1 (2018). https://lwn.net/Articles/746129/
6. Cornwell, M.: Anatomy of a solid-state drive. Commun. ACM **55**(12) (2012)
7. Edge, J.: Zoned storage and filesystems (2023). https://lwn.net/Articles/932748/
8. Gal, E., Toledo, S.: Algorithms and data structures for flash memories. ACM Comput. Surv. **37**(2) (2005)
9. Gupta, A., Kim, Y., Urgaonkar, B.: DFTL: a flash translation layer employing demand-based selective caching of page-level address mappings. In: Proceedings of ASPLOS 2009 (2009)
10. Kim, J., et al.: A space-efficient flash translation layer for CompactFlash systems. IEEE Trans. Consum. Electron. **48**(2) (2002)
11. Le Moal, D., et al.: Zoned Storage. https://zonedstorage.io
12. Lee, C., et al.: F2FS: a new file system for flash storage. In: Proceedings of the 13th USENIX FAST Conference (2015)
13. Lee, S., et al.: Application-managed flash. In: 14th USENIX FAST Conference (2016)
14. Lee, S., et al.: Exploiting sequential and temporal localities to improve performance of NAND flash-based SSDs. ACM Trans. Storage **12**(3) (2016)
15. Lee, S., et al.: LAST: locality-aware sector translation for NAND flash memory-based storage systems. ACM SIGOPS **42**(6) (2008)
16. LeMoal, D.: Zone write plugging (2024). https://lwn.net/ml/linux-block/20240328004409.594888-1-dlemoal@kernel.org/
17. Li, J., et al.: An in-depth analysis of cloud block storage workloads in large-scale production. In: IEEE International Symposium on Workload Characterization, pp. 37–47 (2020)
18. Maisenbacher, D., et al.: dm-zap (2022). https://github.com/westerndigitalcorporation/dm-zap

19. Mathur, A., et al.: The new ext4 filesystem: current status and future plans. In: Proceedings of the Ottawa Linux Symposium (2007)
20. NVM Express®Base Specification v2.1 (2024). https://nvmexpress.org/specifications/
21. NVM Express®Zoned Namespace Command Set Specification v1.2 (2024). https://nvmexpress.org/specifications/
22. Oh, S., et al.: MIDAS: minimizing write amplification in LogStructured systems through adaptive group number and size configuration. In: 22nd USENIX FAST Conference (2024)
23. Purandare, D.R., et al.: Append is near: log-based data management on ZNS SSDs. In: 12th Conference on Innovative Data Systems Research (CIDR) (2022)
24. Rodeh, O., Bacik, J., Mason, C.: BTRFS: the Linux B-tree filesystem. ACM Trans. Storage **9**(3) (2013)
25. Rybczyńska, M.: BTRFs on zoned block devices (2021). https://lwn.net/Articles/853308
26. Seo, D., et al.: Is garbage collection overhead gone? Case study of F2FS on ZNS SSDs. In: Proceedings of the 15th ACM/USENIX Workshop on Hot Topics in Storage and File Systems (HotStorage), pp. 102–108 (2023)
27. Snitzer, M., Reinecke, H.: dm-zoned (2023). https://www.kernel.org/doc/html/latest/admin-guide/device-mapper/dm-zoned.html
28. Tarasov, V., Zadok, E., Shepler, S.: Filebench: a flexible framework for file system benchmarking. Login Usenix Mag. **41**(1) (2016). https://www.usenix.org/publications/login/spring2016/tarasov
29. Wang, Q., Shi, C.: Alibaba Block Traces (2022). https://github.com/alibaba/block-traces
30. Wong, D.J., et al.: ext4 General Information (2023). https://www.kernel.org/doc/html/latest/admin-guide/ext4.html
31. Wu, M., Zwaenepoel, W.: eNVy: a non-volatile, main memory storage system. In: Sixth ASPLOS Conference (1994)
32. Yang, J., et al.: Don't stack your log on my log. In: 2nd Workshop on Interactions of NVM/Flash with Operating Systems and Workloads (INFLOW) (2014)

Spend More to Save More (SM2): An Energy and Hardware-Aware Implementation of Successive Halving for Sustainable Hyperparameter Optimization

Daniel Geißler[1(✉)], Mengxi Liu[1], Bo Zhou[1,2], Sungho Suh[1], and Paul Lukowicz[1,2]

[1] German Research Center for Artificial Intelligence (DFKI), Kaiserslautern, Germany
daniel.geissler@dfki.de
[2] University of Kaiserslautern-Landau (RPTU), Kaiserslautern, Germany

Abstract. A fundamental step in the development of machine learning models commonly involves the tuning of hyperparameters, often leading to multiple model training runs to work out the best-performing configuration. As machine learning tasks and models grow in complexity, there is an escalating need for solutions that not only improve performance but also address sustainability concerns. Existing strategies predominantly focus on maximizing the performance of the model without considering energy efficiency. To bridge this gap, we introduce Spend More to Save More (SM^2), an energy and hardware aware hyperparameter optimization implementation based on the widely adopted successive halving algorithm. Unlike conventional approaches including energy-intensive testing of individual hyperparameter configurations, SM^2 employs exploratory pretraining to identify inefficient configurations with minimal energy expenditure. Incorporating hardware characteristics and real-time energy consumption tracking, SM^2 identifies an optimal configuration that not only maximizes the performance of the model but also enables energy-efficient training. Experimental validations across various datasets, models, and hardware setups confirm the efficacy of SM^2 to prevent the waste of energy during the training of hyperparameter configurations.

Keywords: Energy-Awareness · HPO · Successive Halving

1 Introduction

The rising complexity of Artificial Intelligence (AI) applications solved through advanced deep-learning models continuously increases the energy demand of the whole AI sector. It is estimated that large language models like the popular GPT-4 may require between 52 MWh and 63 MWh of energy for training, whereas inference may account for even more energy consumption over time [24]. This trend is driven by the ubiquity of machine learning applications being present in the majority of our daily lives. Considering the life cycle of an AI model from initial development towards its final deployment possibilities, there are multiple stages involved that may be optimized in terms of energy efficiency, mainly due to the waste of resources [30].

This work accounts for the initial stages of the life cycle, with a focus on optimizing the training process of machine learning models to generate a more energy-aware and efficient solution for AI developers. Besides the quality of the dataset and model architecture fitment to the desired task, hyperparameter optimization (HPO) is an integral part of a well-suited model. Two key hyperparameters, namely batch size and learning rate, significantly affect training convergence quality and speed [13]. However, determining the optimal values for these parameters, often hardware and task-specific, remains a challenging task requiring selection by experienced developers at the first attempt. Various strategies have been developed to improve the HPO problem, yet their only aim is to maximize the model's prediction performance. Additionally, due to trends of supporting AI developers' work with high-performance data centers, usually, due to economic reasons, it is a simple but energy-intensive process to spawn multiple training runs to manually explore the hyperparameter space. While more efficient hardware has continuously been updated to alleviate the training cost of trial and error, there lacks a holistic method that incorporates hardware energy footprint into the model training HPO process.

To resolve this issue, this paper presents Spend More to Save More (SM^2), a novel approach combining HPO and energy consumption tracking to generate a profound strategy to sustainably improve the machine learning training process. To the best of our knowledge, this work is the first work to optimize the hyperparameters while considering energy consumption. Our work makes significant contributions to the field of sustainable HPO and can be summarized as follows:

- Implementing energy-aware training through hardware-based power monitoring.
- Deploying a sequential Successive Halving Algorithm strategy to minimize energy waste.
- Extending the traditional training regime with exploratory components to energy-efficiently explore hyperparameter configurations.
- Evaluating the SM^2 approach across three different scenarios of models and datasets to validate our hypothesis of equal model performance while improving energy efficiency.

2 Related Works

2.1 Hyperparameter Optimization

The landscape of HPO covers multiple different methodologies from different areas to explore and manifest the best-performing hyperparameter setting. In many cases, there is no clear identification of the best-performing strategy possible because the efficiency of the algorithm depends on the respective machine learning problem to solve and the user's preferences. Nevertheless, there is a trend of different HPO categories being fused to elevate the performance compared to the traditional algorithms. [7]

Starting with the classic methods, grid search is the most common and simple strategy next to the manual exploration of hyperparameters. The strategy is based on an initialized grid that covers the range of each hyperparameter [20]. Due to its simplicity, it is commonly used but suffers from inefficiencies in high-dimensional scenarios due to many low-performing training runs and their independence from each other. Another simple but more efficient strategy in this scope is random search [4]. Instead of exploring a fixed grid, the hyperparameter space is randomly sampled to provide a more stochastic exploration. Due to its ease of implementation, it still serves as a baseline benchmark.

Another category involves evolutionary strategies to work out the best hyperparameter setting [6]. Such algorithms explore the hyperparameter space based on the biological concept of evolution. Throughout a fitness function, a population of hyperparameter configurations is evaluated whereas the worst-performing configurations are removed. Instead of proceeding with the most promising configurations, similar to natural evolution, the next iteration consists of crossovers and mutations of the previous configurations. Works like [2] and [8] confirm the usability of evolutionary strategies as state-of-the-art.

Bayesian optimization constitutes another strategy for HPO, introduced in works such as [29]. Such algorithms can efficiently explore the hyperparameter space by constructing probabilistic surrogate models and using acquisition functions to guide the search. Introduced by [3], Tree-structured Parzen Estimators (TPE) is a Bayesian optimization variant that ranks the performance of HPO configurations. TPE has shown impressive results, especially in high-dimensional optimization tasks, making it one of the current state-of-the-art HPO algorithms [12].

Hyperparameter optimization through Reinforcement Learning (RL) was recently introduced through works like [16] and [32]. Instead of systematically exploring the hyperparameter space, RL consists of a sequential decision-making process to find the best configuration based on the policy that guides the RL agent along the desired path. In terms of sustainably and efficiency, this solution is quite complex and requires many training iterations due to the expensive exploration and exploitation trade-off in RL. Moreover, instead of optimizing only the traditional model, also the RL model requires optimization.

Pruning-based methods, such as the common Successive Halving Algorithm (SHA) [23], aim to efficiently allocate computational resources to promising hyperparameter configurations in a parallelized environment. By iteratively terminating less promising configurations, such methods reduce the overall training time while maintaining a focus on high-performing settings. This bandit-based algorithm demonstrates a practical approach to balancing exploration and exploitation, making it well-suited for high-dimensional HPO scenarios.

Throughout extended works like [22], multi-fidelity optimization improves SHA by removing predefined evaluation timestamps. Instead of training all configurations in a synchronized, parallel environment, resources can be reallocated asynchronously to generate a more dynamic training procedure. Works like [21] and [31] are currently considered state-of-the-art in this field. Due to its benefits in terms of efficiency and its overlaps with our ideas to stop less-promising configurations early in the training process, we utilize the SHA approach as our foundation.

2.2 Energy Consumption Tracking

In the AI sector, energy consumption tools are still a niche, especially when it comes to generating awareness about the energy expenditure for training machine learning models. Currently, there is a small but growing list of software available with most of them utilizing the same approach to gather the power consumption data from the hardware manufacturers' utility logging. They are usually designed to capture energy information by building an additional layer between the system's hardware configuration and the user's model training process [15]. Generally speaking, the power consumption of the Graphics Processing Units (GPU) is considered the largest part of the training process as it performs the core work with the parallel processing of mathematical tasks [26]. Nevertheless, other hardware components and even secondary power consumers like the cooling system or the power supply unit (PSU) itself contribute to the overall energy consumption. Therefore, there is great interest in tracking the power consumption of the full system to minimize deviations.

As a general rule, the energy consumption is calculated from the current power consumption and the polling time interval set in the software. The energy per epoch, commonly stated in watt per hour (Wh), is a common metric and follows the calculation of Eq. (1).

$$E_k = \frac{1}{n} \sum_{i=0}^{n} \text{power}(k,n) \cdot \frac{\text{time}(k)}{3600}, \quad \forall k \in [0, T] \tag{1}$$

Works like Carbontracker [1], eco2Ai [9] and Green Algorithms [19] utilize this approach to gather data from the hardware. To handle missing elements in the calculations, software like Carbontracker multiplies its results with an efficiency constant to incorporate untracked secondary power needs and efficiency losses. With an extended focus on user experience, projects like Cloud Carbon [11] or CodeCarbon [10] extend the gathered knowledge and present it in analytic-based dashboards. Based on the calculated energy consumption and the user's location, the average local energy mix from fossil and renewable energy sources is utilized to estimate the carbon emissions in kilograms or even tons [18]. On top of that, since the carbon emissions are difficult to visualize or imagine, the conversion into kilometers driven by car, flights with a plane, or the number of phones charged is a standard practice to make the user aware of the generated carbon emissions amount.

3 Energy-Aware Training

A major goal of this work is to generate energy awareness within the training process to finalize a well-performing model trained through hardware operated in an energy-efficient state. Instead of compromising between performance and sustainability, we envision SM^2 as a strategy to prioritize two objectives at the same time. During our initial tests, we established the energy expenditure per trained epoch as a suitable metric to calculate the efficiency of the current setup. As discussed in Sect. 2.2, a precise solution for tracking the total energy consumption of all involved hardware components is still missing. Consequently, our work focuses on the energy efficiency of the GPU, the primary energy consumer for training deep-learning models in a parallelized and hardware-accelerated environment [26].

To properly monitor the energy consumption of the GPU, we decided to utilize the Carbontracker library [1]. Due to its technical and data-driven approach compared to the other available solutions, it provides an appropriate foundation to consciously track the energy demand of hardware. The library operates as a background service, tracking the GPU power through the hardware's System Management Interface (SMI) over time to calculate the consumed energy. In our implementation, based on version 1.2.5. of Carbontracker, we extended its capabilities to facilitate live tracking of energy consumption instead of logging the data to files. Throughout a callback function, the current power consumption and the energy of the current epoch can be obtained. This integration ensures that SM^2 can directly benefit from the relevant information.

Since different manufacturers offer their unique interface solutions for measuring and they may differ in terms of true and measured GPU wattage, we decided to test SM^2 on CUDA-supported GPUs to provide reproducibility and comparability of results. Currently, SMI provides information only about the total power consumption of the GPU, neglecting the number of processes or threads concurrently running in parallel on the GPU. Therefore, Carbontracker is unable to partition the overall energy consumption to multiple processes, whereas our implementation of SM^2 is based on a sequential architecture to ensure proper tracking within these limitations.

In theory, a more comprehensive implementation could include extended hardware information logging for different manufacturers or other hardware components, such as the Central Processing Unit (CPU) or the PSU. However, the inclusion of such components would necessitate careful validation to ensure the validity of cross-comparable measurements. To the best of our knowledge, including the discussed restrictions, our custom implementation of Carbontracker to forward the power and energy information from the SMI directly into the training loop is currently the first and most promising solution for SM^2.

4 SM^2: Spend More to Save More

HPO algorithms usually form an additional layer throughout a library or framework on top of the traditional training to optimize selected hyperparameters [5].

With the aim to maximize the final model's performance, they usually do not account for the waste of resources to explore the hyperparameter space. As a result, HPO is often connected with time-consuming and energy-intensive training of weak models, especially in terms of rudimentary algorithms like random or grid search. Each setup of hyperparameters is trained, and the best version is taken as the final model. The unpleasant side, which is usually not presented in publications or advertisements, contains the number of less-performing models, trained just for the purpose of exploring the hyperparameter space. Together with the growing size of datasets and the complexity of machine learning models, the wasted energy adds up and further supports climate change if fossil energy resources are utilized [1].

As already introduced in Sect. 2.1, SHA and its variations like ASHA are promising solutions and are considered state-of-the-art to the best of our knowledge. To summarize, SHA is an iterative hyperparameter optimization method in which the number of inspected hyperparameter configurations is pruned exponentially over time until the final, best-performing model remains. The idea of terminating less-performing models early in the training process to decrease the waste of resources supports our idea for sustainable HPO, wherefore we decided to implement SHA as a general basis for "Spend More to Save More". As a motivation, we argue that **spending slightly more energy for a single training run is more sustainable than training models multiple times**, considering that such a strategy can find the optimal hyperparameter configuration satisfactory.

Based on previous research in [13], batch size and learning rate rule the energy efficiency for training a machine learning model, whereas we focus on those two hyperparameters in this work. It is noteworthy that SM^2 is not limited in this regard, however, there is not such a strong influence on efficiency by other hyperparameters. Operating independently of the core training process, custom optimizers, models, and loss functions can still be utilized and provide evidence for universality.

Identifying a suitable batch size lets the GPU run in an efficient power state based on the GPU utilization. For SM^2 we do not utilize the wattage as a metric, the energy per epoch gathered from Carbontracker serves as an indicator of how efficiently the current batch size matches the hardware power state. On the other hand, operating the GPU in its efficiency window may not contribute to the overall efficiency of the training run if too many epochs are necessary to complete the training. Therefore, it is essential to work out a well-performing learning rate to speed up the model's convergence. To solve this, we implement cyclical learning rate exploration within the SHA algorithm to identify the optimal setting [27]. With such process, we aim to set the largest stable learning rate, so that the convergence speed is maximized without disturbing the training.

To generate a more efficient HPO algorithm compared to existing approaches, we split up the training into an alternating process of exploratory training and thorough training. With exploratory training on fewer batches of the dataset and only one epoch duration, SM^2 identifies trends of the current selection with less energy waste to narrow down the hyperparameter space. The thorough training represents the traditional training on the full dataset across multiple epochs.

An objective function finally unites the introduced sustainability considerations with the main aim of the model to maximize its prediction performance.

4.1 Batch Size Optimization

Next to the dataset and model architecture, batch size is a crucial parameter to control the utilization of the GPU [33]. To efficiently utilize the GPU, one might think that maximizing the GPU utilization results in less energy consumption due to the improved training speed. However, depending on the specific hardware, the efficiency window of a GPU usually lies below the maximum utilization due to bottlenecks like data transfer or cooling issues [33]. As such information is not available, calculating the optimal batch size for efficiency beforehand is impossible, wherefore we utilize SHA and the energy per epoch metric as a solution. Throughout the training, our energy-aware implementation tracks the average power and duration of each epoch and calculates the energy consumption for training one epoch. Based on such metrics, energy awareness can be integrated into the training process. Within the exploratory training, the energy per epoch for each batch size configuration is monitored and taken into account with the objective of removing inefficiently trained configurations.

4.2 Learning Rate Optimization

In addition to measuring the energy per epoch to train the model in an efficient environment, the number of epochs trained needs to be minimized to keep the overall energy consumption low. To evaluate the learning rate effectiveness, cyclical learning rate scheduling is embedded into the exploratory training phase [27]. For each batch in the exploration phase being passed through the model, a different learning rate is tested through alternation and the respective loss is documented. As a general rule, low learning rates tend to unnecessarily extend the training process, whereas larger learning rates may increase loss fluctuations [28].

As shown in Fig. 1, we analyze the inspected learning rates computationally by calculating the second derivative to receive the curvature of the loss. Through a sliding window approach, we can identify windows with a low curvature. By sorting the windows based on the curvature and the mean learning rate of the window, we can identify the largest learning rate that maintains stability throughout the training process. In the case of Fig. 1, we marked the selected learning rate window with two dotted lines. Selecting the largest learning rate within the identified window further maximizes the learning rate selection in terms of shrinking the training time.

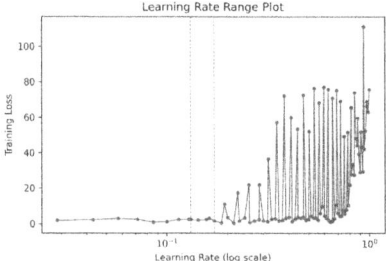 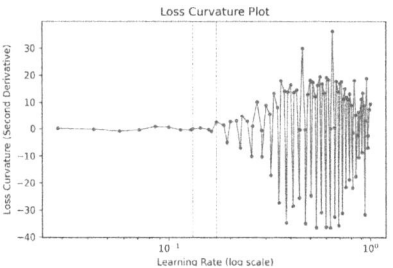

Fig. 1. Computational analysis of loss curvature (blue) through the sliding window to select the area with the largest stable learning rate based on the second derivate (green). The optimal selection range is highlighted in red. (Color figure online)

4.3 Objective Function

To include the individual optimization targets in the training process, we introduce an objective function that determines the best-performing configurations of the current set during the exploratory phase. Following the general SHA rule, the objective is necessary to halve the number of configurations until only one configuration remains. Further, since SM^2 envisions the hyperparameter optimization as a holistic system, especially from the sustainability aspect, it is a key necessity to merge the observations for each hyperparameter to finalize a combination that fulfills the needs.

The introduced objective function in Eq. (2) accounts for the performance metric of the trained model, the consumed energy per epoch, and the selected, stable learning rate. To compare those attributes, we rescale each list of attributes into the range between 0 and 1 across all explored configurations. Thus, the calculated objectives as well as the three attributes themselves are independent of any influences from the specific model and the utilized hardware. Additionally, depending on the nature of the attributes, we invert them to either reward higher values, like for the learning rate, or lower values, for instance, the energy consumption. Two parameters α and β allow the balance between the three attributes. They need to be set beforehand as described in the following Sect. 5.1. For each configuration, the objective is calculated whereas after a full exploratory iteration, the less-performing half is dropped.

$$f(\alpha, \beta) = \alpha \times P + (1 - \alpha) \times (\beta \times E + (1 - \beta) \times LR) \quad (2)$$

$$P = \text{Performance},\ E = \text{Energy},\ LR = \text{Learning Rate}$$

Once there is only one configuration remaining, the SM^2 algorithm remains in thorough training mode, with only a focus on further learning rate optimization. From this point onwards, it can be assumed that the best possible efficiency per epoch has been found for the training and hardware combination and that it is now only possible to optimize the training duration to minimize energy demand.

4.4 Algorithm

The SM^2 algorithm follows the nature of the introduced SHA approach, implemented in a sequential manner due to the energy consumption tracking limitations. As shown in Algorithm 1, SM^2 consists of multiple loops to handle configurations sequentially. The outermost while loop represents the stopping criteria, which can be set depending on the project and the user's preferences. Afterward, the whole training is split up into two training modes, exploratory and thorough training. For the thorough training, we selected the split into test and training data according to the best practices of each dataset, whereas the exploratory training contains a quarter of the training dataset as a randomly selected subset of batches to save resources. While thorough training represents traditional training, the logic and the resulting adaptions to the code of SM^2 happen in the exploratory mode. Iterating through each configuration and the number of epochs to train, exploratory training has the sole benefit of improving training based on the objective function. Both modes are isolated from each other by backing up the models after each iteration, wherefore training and testing in exploratory mode does not contribute to the final model's performance. After selecting the final configuration through the alternating process, the algorithm stays in thorough training mode till the stopping metric is triggered. On the other hand, the independence between SM^2 and the thorough training mode enables custom implementations by the user, for instance, to integrate the desired optimizer or early stopping metric. Even though exploratory training contributes towards increased energy consumption in the short term, the benefit of exploring batch size and learning rate outperforms the computational overhead in the long term observations of the total energy of the project. This strategy again manifests the idea of "Spend More to Save More".

5 Experiments

5.1 Setup

To validate the universality and effectiveness of the proposed SM^2 approach, we conducted experiments on three different machine learning scenarios, each utilizing a distinct model architecture and dataset. Starting with a ResNet-18 model trained on the CIFAR-10 dataset [17] as an initial validation of our approach, we further added an LSTM model trained on the Energy-Household dataset [14] and a Transformer model trained on WikiText2 [25] to check the usefulness of SM^2 for different complexities. The model architectures and their respective hyperparameters were selected following best practices for each scenario. Throughout all experiments, model architectures and dataset preprocessing procedures were maintained consistently. Additionally, all experiments were run three times on different hardware configurations using Nvidia RTX A6000, Nvidia Tesla V100-32GB, and Nvidia GeForce RTX 3090, ensuring hardware independence.

Algorithm 1. SM^2 Algorithm

```
 1: Initialize SM² Setup
 2: while not stop do
 3:    for mode in {expl, thorough} do
 4:       for config in Configs do
 5:          Prepare config-related data
 6:          for epoch in Epochs do
 7:             if mode=expl then
 8:                Exploratory Training (1 epoch)
 9:                Isolated Environment
10:                Dataset Partition (25% random subset)
11:             else
12:                Thorough Training ( 5 epochs)
13:                Full Dataset (According to best practice split)
14:             end if
15:          end for
16:       end for
17:       if mode=expl then
18:          Evaluate Exploration
19:          Drop less performing configs
20:       end if
21:    end for
22:    Update stopping condition
23: end while
24: return model, energy
```

From the implementation side, we utilized PyTorch as the basic framework to thoroughly execute SM^2 in the hardware-accelerated GPU environment. To isolate the energy consumption and overall performance, we added an extended initialization process. Each spawned training setup was initialized with its own model, optimizer, and energy tracker instances. By deep-copying the respective instances and fixing the random seed in PyTorch, we ensured that each configuration could be sequentially executed throughout the same training loop. That being said, the only connection between the configuration is the introduced objective function and the shared dataset.

To minimize energy loss and idling of the GPU due to data transfer, we implemented a flexible batch-size system through a custom data loader. Instead of commonly passing each batch with its respective size to the device depending on the current configuration, we preprocessed the data and preloaded batches into the GPU memory. The preprocessed dataset was divided into batches of the smallest configuration. With a custom iterator, configurations of larger batch sizes were trained on a temporary concatenation of batch sizes within the GPU memory. If the size of the GPU memory cannot retain the full dataset, we utilize a queuing strategy based on a first-in-first-out strategy.

Throughout our initial tests, we experimented with the α and β parameters of the objective function to check if they require any dynamic adaptions depending on the models. Especially for the α value, a balance between performance metrics and sustainability is crucial to consider. It is up to the user to decide how much weight the user wants to put into the energy consumption. However, α parameter value below 0.5 usually tends to prioritize efficiency, whereas the model performance drastically decreases. To strike a balance for including both objectives while allowing performance to keep a benefit against the efficiency,

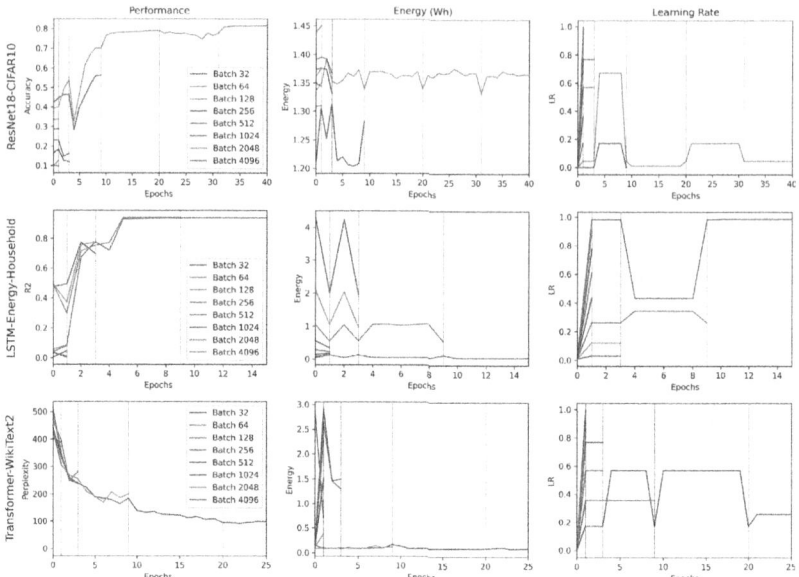

Fig. 2. Evaluation of SM^2: Each row represents a different model and dataset combination; Columns represent Performance, Energy, and Learning Rate; Vertical Lines in the graph highlight exploratory epochs.

an α of 0.75 was found to yield the most promising results base don initial tests ranging from 0.5 to 0.95. Since multiple configurations may achieve the desired performance, such a strategy settles the most efficient configuration out of the best-performing models. For β, controlling the balance between batch size and learning rate schedule, we kept an equal setting of 0.5 since both have an equal possibility to improve efficiency. All the following experiments were therefore conducted with parameters $\alpha = 0.75$ and $\beta = 0.5$.

Since SM^2 is independent of the model architecture or optimizer, users are open to customize and adapt the setup to their desired project. The range and number of batch sizes and learning rates need to be set beforehand next to the number of iterations through exploration and thorough epochs. For our experiments, we set up 8 different batch-size configurations with 20 inspected learning rates in the range of 0.001 to 1 during exploratory training. The exploratory training phase was set to 1 epoch trained only on a quarter of the dataset, whereas the thorough training was set to 5 epochs and extended to 10 epochs after the final configuration was determined.

5.2 SM^2 Evaluation

The results for evaluating the SM^2 approach are visualized in Fig. 2. Each row represents a different scenario, with the ResNet model constituting a medium complexity task, LSTM a low complexity task, and the Transformer model a high complexity respectively. Each column plots the three acquired attributes, performance, energy, and learning rate, which are merged into the objective function as introduced in Sect. 4.3. Vertical dotted lines highlight the exploratory epochs, whereas the rest were conducted in thorough training mode. It is worth mentioning that each plot visualizes the information gathered before normalization across configurations. Further, we present the results for training all scenarios on the Nvidia RTX A6000. Across our experiments, the other two hardware setups shared similar results regarding the objective function decision process while operating on different energy efficiency levels. Due to the restriction on CUDA-based hardware supporting the SMI, we have not been able to test our approach on differing setups from other manufacturers.

Starting with the performance, we visualize the common metrics for each scenario. For the accuracy and R^2 score of the first two plots, higher values indicate increasing model performance, whereas, for the last scenario, lower perplexity values state higher performance. Across all three scenarios, the identified, final configuration selected through successive halving was able to converge the training process.

However, a great explanation can be drawn from the charts when considering the objective function. The large initial range of accuracy in the ResNet scenario from 0.1 for the weakest up to 0.45 for the best-performing scenario rules the decision by passing the best-performing models to the next round. Due to the small differences in energy consumption across the configurations, the slightly higher energy consumption for Batch 64 is tolerated due to the $\alpha = 0.75$ passing more importance to the performance. On the contrary, even though the R^2 range for the second scenario shares similarities to the first scenario, the significantly larger range of the tracked energy, especially due to poor performing smaller batch sizes, leads to an increased impact within the objective function. As a decision of SM^2, training of batch 4096 is continued due to the comparable low energy per epoch and finally outperforms the remaining configurations. For the third, transformer scenario, perplexity does not influence the beginning of the training. Similar to the second scenario, the energy attribute rules the decision towards the smaller, more efficiently performing configurations.

Since energy and learning rate contribute to the final objective throughout the same ratio set with $\beta = 0.5$, also the learning rate, shown in the third column, contributes to the decision process. Even though the selection through the cyclical learning rate process seems coincidental during the first exploratory phase, larger learning rate selections usually support the final configuration decision within later epochs. Therefore, we assess the learning rate as a decision supporter towards the advanced epochs with fewer configurations remaining.

To summarize, for large deviations within the performance, SM^2 neglects efficiency to a certain extent. As a matter of fact, training a model solely based on sustainability aspects may result in another training run with additional energy consumption due to unsatisfactory performance. On the other hand, SM^2 offers great potential to isolate efficient configurations if similar performance is present.

5.3 Energy Compensation

Table 1 presents the total energy demand in watt-hours (Wh) for each experiment, demonstrating the reduction in energy demand between $\alpha = 1.0$ and $\alpha = 0.75$, along with the parity factor. To analyze the results in terms of their sustainability, we executed the scenarios with $\alpha = 1.0$ and a vanilla training without the SM^2 approach. The $\alpha = 1.0$ setting signifies a scenario where the objective function only considers the model performance, whereas the energy efficiency improvement can be calculated across the measurements. The reduction percentage provides insights into how much energy consumption can be saved by incorporating sustainability aspects into the objective function. Parity represents the number of manual HPO explorations, typically in a classic, iterative exploration by the user, that are needed to compensate for the energy investment in SM^2 compared to such vanilla training.

Table 1. Total energy demand (Wh) of SM^2 ($\alpha = 1.0$ and $\alpha = 0.75$) in comparison to traditional vanilla training; parity represents the number of manual user HPO exploration trainings in vanilla mode compared to SM^2.

Experiment	$SM^2(\alpha=1)$	$SM^2(\alpha=0.75)$	vanilla (no SM^2)	parity
ResNet18	49.7	45.8 (−8%)	26.0	1.76
LSTM	28.0	14.8 (−47%)	16.4	1.11
Transformer	48.5	40.7 (−16%)	69.4	1.70

As shown in Table 1, SM^2 managed to reduce the energy demand across all experiments by incorporating the sustainability aspects into the objective function. For the second scenario (LSTM), the decrease in energy consumption of 47% reflects the results depicted in Fig. 2, where the energy-based selection of the larger batch size played a crucial role. In terms of final model performance, the first two scenarios shared the same final performance, while for the third scenario (Transformer), the perplexity was reduced by around 15% points when setting $\alpha = 1.0$. Compared to the vanilla experiment, trained with a traditional training loop while keeping identical parameter setups and early stopping metrics, each setup requires at minimum two manual HPO explorations for compensation. An additional run with a doubled amount of 16 configurations and 40 inspected learning rates resulted in parity between 5 and 6 across the scenarios. Therefore, the parity factor serves as a useful metric to estimate the energy demand and provides evidence for the "Spend More to Save More" concept, emphasizing the reduction of energy waste through inefficient HPO.

6 Conclusion and Future Work

In this paper, we presented "Spend More to Save More (SM^2)", an energy-aware implementation for sustainable hyperparameter optimization. Our approach enables the simultaneous optimization of both model performance and efficiency, addressing the critical need for energy-aware machine learning practices. We presented an objective function as the core of SM^2 to beneficially balance model performance and energy consumption. Although we give more weight to performance, energy efficiency can be the deciding factor, especially in the area of equally performing configurations, to lead the training to its efficient state. Our experiments prove the idea of decreasing the energy demand without significant performance loss, especially when considering the whole development life cycle. As a part of our future work, we envision an improved version of SM^2 to include more energy information from other hardware components and manufacturers. We envision a solution that dynamically adapts to the given hardware setup and fluently scales to parallelized and multi-GPU environments. Extended work should also adapt to less prominent hyperparameters to further maximize energy efficiency. As an outlook, SM^2 can be provided in the form of a library to be integrated to the traditional training workflows, offering a practical solution for researchers seeking to incorporate energy-awareness into their machine learning models.

Acknowledgement. This work is supported by the European Union's Horizon Europe research and innovation program (HORIZON-CL4-2021-HUMAN-01) through the "SustainML" project (grant agreement No 101070408).

References

1. Anthony, L.F.W., Kanding, B., Selvan, R.: Carbontracker: tracking and predicting the carbon footprint of training deep learning models. arXiv preprint arXiv:2007.03051 (2020)
2. Awad, N., Mallik, N., Hutter, F.: Dehb: evolutionary hyperband for scalable, robust and efficient hyperparameter optimization. arXiv preprint arXiv:2105.09821 (2021)
3. Bergstra, J., Bardenet, R., Bengio, Y., Kégl, B.: Algorithms for hyper-parameter optimization. In: Advances in Neural Information Processing Systems, vol. 24 (2011)
4. Bergstra, J., Bengio, Y.: Random search for hyper-parameter optimization. J. Mach. Learn. Res. **13**(2) (2012)
5. Bergstra, J., Yamins, D., Cox, D.D., et al.: Hyperopt: a python library for optimizing the hyperparameters of machine learning algorithms. In: Proceedings of the 12th Python in Science Conference, vol. 13, p. 20. Citeseer (2013)
6. Beyer, H.G., Schwefel, H.P.: Evolution strategies-a comprehensive introduction. Nat. Comput. **1**, 3–52 (2002)
7. Bischl, B., et al.: Hyperparameter optimization: Foundations, algorithms, best practices and open challenges. arxiv 2021. arXiv preprint arXiv:2107.05847 (2021)
8. Bochinski, E., Senst, T., Sikora, T.: Hyper-parameter optimization for convolutional neural network committees based on evolutionary algorithms. In: 2017 IEEE International Conference on Image Processing (ICIP), pp. 3924–3928. IEEE (2017)
9. Budennyy, S.A., et al.: Eco2ai: carbon emissions tracking of machine learning models as the first step towards sustainable AI. In: Doklady Mathematics, vol. 106, pp. S118–S128. Springer, Cham (2022)
10. Code-Carbon: Code carbon (2023). https://github.com/mlco2/codecarbon

11. Cloud-carbon footprint: Cloud carbon footprint (2023). https://github.com/cloud-carbon-footprint/cloud-carbon-footprint
12. Frey, N.C., et al.: Energy-aware neural architecture selection and hyperparameter optimization. In: 2022 IEEE International Parallel and Distributed Processing Symposium Workshops (IPDPSW), pp. 732–741. IEEE (2022)
13. Geißler, D., Zhou, B., Liu, M., Suh, S., Lukowicz, P.: The power of training: how different neural network setups influence the energy demand. In: International Conference on Architecture of Computing Systems, pp. 33–47. Springer, Cham (2024)
14. Hebrail, G., Berard, A.: Individual Household Electric Power Consumption. UCI Machine Learning Repository (2006). https://doi.org/10.24432/C58K54
15. Henderson, P., Hu, J., Romoff, J., Brunskill, E., Jurafsky, D., Pineau, J.: Towards the systematic reporting of the energy and carbon footprints of machine learning. J. Mach. Learn. Res. **21**(1), 10039–10081 (2020)
16. Jomaa, H.S., Grabocka, J., Schmidt-Thieme, L.: Hyp-RL: hyperparameter optimization by reinforcement learning. arXiv preprint arXiv:1906.11527 (2019)
17. Krizhevsky, A., Hinton, G., et al.: Learning multiple layers of features from tiny images (2009)
18. Lacoste, A., Luccioni, A., Schmidt, V., Dandres, T.: Quantifying the carbon emissions of machine learning. arXiv preprint arXiv:1910.09700 (2019)
19. Lannelongue, L., Grealey, J., Inouye, M.: Green algorithms: quantifying the carbon footprint of computation. Adv. Sci. **8**(12), 2100707 (2021)
20. LeCun, Y., Bottou, L., Bengio, Y., Haffner, P.: Gradient-based learning applied to document recognition. Proc. IEEE **86**(11), 2278–2324 (1998)
21. Lee, H., Lee, G., Kim, J., Cho, S., Kim, D., Yoo, D.: Improving multi-fidelity optimization with a recurring learning rate for hyperparameter tuning. In: Proceedings of the IEEE/CVF Winter Conference on Applications of Computer Vision, pp. 2309–2318 (2023)
22. Li, L., et al.: A system for massively parallel hyperparameter tuning. Proc. Mach. Learn. Syst. **2**, 230–246 (2020)
23. Li, L., Jamieson, K., DeSalvo, G., Rostamizadeh, A., Talwalkar, A.: Hyperband: a novel bandit-based approach to hyperparameter optimization. J. Mach. Learn. Res. **18**(185), 1–52 (2018)
24. Ludvigsen, K.G.A.: The carbon footprint of GPT-4 (2023). https://towardsdatascience.com/the-carbon-footprint-of-gpt-4-d6c676eb21ae. Accessed 22 Feb 2025
25. Merity, S., Xiong, C., Bradbury, J., Socher, R.: Pointer sentinel mixture models. arXiv:1609.07843 (2017). https://arxiv.org/abs/1609.07843
26. Mittal, S., Vetter, J.S.: A survey of methods for analyzing and improving GPU energy efficiency. ACM Comput. Surv. (CSUR) **47**(2), 1–23 (2014)
27. Smith, L.N.: Cyclical learning rates for training neural networks. In: 2017 IEEE Winter Conference on Applications of Computer Vision (WACV), pp. 464–472. IEEE (2017)
28. Smith, L.N.: A disciplined approach to neural network hyper-parameters: Part 1–learning rate, batch size, momentum, and weight decay. arXiv preprint arXiv:1803.09820 (2018)
29. Snoek, J., Larochelle, H., Adams, R.P.: Practical Bayesian optimization of machine learning algorithms. In: Advances in Neural Information Processing Systems, vol. 25 (2012)

30. Tornede, T., Tornede, A., Hanselle, J., Mohr, F., Wever, M., Hüllermeier, E.: Towards green automated machine learning: status quo and future directions. J. Artif. Intell. Res. **77**, 427–457 (2023)
31. Wistuba, M., Kadra, A., Grabocka, J.: Supervising the multi-fidelity race of hyperparameter configurations. In: Advances in Neural Information Processing Systems, vol. 35, pp. 13470–13484 (2022)
32. Wu, J., Liu, X., Chen, S.: Hyperparameter optimization through context-based meta-reinforcement learning with task-aware representation. Knowl.-Based Syst. **260**, 110160 (2023)
33. You, J., Chung, J.W., Chowdhury, M.: Zeus: understanding and optimizing {GPU} energy consumption of {DNN} training. In: 20th USENIX Symposium on Networked Systems Design and Implementation (NSDI 2023), pp. 119–139 (2023)

OpenVADL: An Open Source Implementation of the Vienna Architecture Description Language

Florian Freitag[iD], Linus Halder[iD], Benedikt Huber[iD], Benjamin Kasper[iD], Michael Nestler[iD], Kevin Per[iD], Matthias Raschhofer[iD], Alexander Ripar[iD], Johannes Zottele[iD], and Andreas Krall[✉][iD]

Technische Universität Wien, Vienna, Austria
andi@complang.tuwien.ac.at

Abstract. OpenVADL is an open source implementation of the Vienna Architecture Description Language (VADL). VADL is a processor description language (PDL) that enables the concise formal specification of processor architectures. OpenVADL automatically generates an assembler, an LLVM based compiler and a QEMU based instruction set simulator from a single VADL processor specification. Automatic generation of synthesizable specifications in a hardware description language is under development. VADL strictly separates the instruction set architecture (ISA) specification from the microarchitecture (MiA) specification. VADL's MiA specification operates at a higher level of abstraction compared to existing PDLs. This article introduces OpenVADL, describes the generator techniques in detail and shows the performance of the generators in an empirical evaluation. The evaluation demonstrates the capabilities of OpenVADL and its efficiency. An OpenVADL generated instruction set simulator is up to 77% faster than the official human written QEMU frontend for the RISC-V RV64IM instruction set architecture.

Keywords: Processor description language · QEMU generator · Compiler generator · Assembler generator

1 Introduction

OpenVADL is an open source implementation of the Vienna Architecture Description Language (VADL) [8]. VADL is a processor description language (PDL). From a concise VADL processor specification it is possible to automatically generate a QEMU based instruction set simulator, a cycle approximate simulator, a compiler, an assembler and linker and a synthesizable hardware description in a Hardware Description Language (HDL). Unique features of VADL compared to other PDLs are syntactic type safe higher-order macro templates, a Microarchitecture (MiA) specification on a high abstraction level which is strictly separated from the Instruction Set Architecture (ISA) specification, an ISA to MiA mapping by using inherent properties of the instruction's behavior for MiA assignment, and a specification of assembly language by string expressions.

With the experiences gained from the original VADL implementation OpenVADL chooses different design decisions and contributes novel ideas and implementation techniques:

- a highly integrated language frontend
- a sea of nodes [5] based Intermediate Representation (IR)
- a highly optimized mapping from IR to QEMU target code
- effective heuristics to classify instructions for use in compiler generation

2 The Vienna Architecture Description Language

Listing 1.1 shows a complete ISA specification of all RISC-V instructions with immediate operands. In line 3 a constant for the register size is defined. Lines 5 to 9 declare user defined types. VADL supports bit vector types. The basic type is Bits. There exist two subtypes representing signed (SInt) and unsigned (UInt) two's complement integers. Line 12 demonstrates the definition of a register file. Annotations can be used to detail a definition as the specification of a zero register demonstrates (see line 11). An implicitly updated program counter is required in every ISA specification (line 14). A format definition is used to specify bitfields with named and typed member fields (line 16 to 23).

Usually, many instruction definitions are quite similar. VADL supports type safe syntactic macro templates to avoid copying and modifying specifications. A macro definition starts with the keyword model followed by the typed arguments and the result type of the macro. There exist syntactic types like Id (identifier), BinOp (binary operator), Bin (binary constant) or IsaDefs (ISA definitions). An instantiation of a macro or the substitution of a macro argument are indicated by the dollar sign.

An instruction defines the behavior of an instruction (line 27). The encoding sets the fields in an instruction word which are constant for the given instruction (line 29). The assembly specifies the assembly language syntax for the instruction with a string expression (line 30). By packing these three definitions into a macro, we can specify an instruction with immediate operands in one single line. This macro is invoked six times for all RISC-V instructions with immediate operands (lines 33 to 38).

This example only touches the surface of the rich and complex language. VADL supports the definition of multidimensional registers and tensor operations. A detailed description of VADL and its original implementation is contained in [8]. The higher order macro system is described in detail in [9]. OpenVADL extends the language by expressions with operator precedence and by macros which generate macros.

3 OpenVADL Implementation

Figure 1 gives an overview of the OpenVADL architecture. The frontend translates a VADL processor specification into the VADL Intermediate Machine

```
 1  instruction set architecture RV32I = {
 2
 3    constant Size = 32                        // architecture size is 32 bits
 4
 5    using Byte   = Bits< 8 >                  // 8 bit Byte
 6    using Inst   = Bits< 32 >                 // instruction word type
 7    using Regs   = Bits<Size>                 // register word type
 8    using Index  = Bits< 5 >                  // 5 bit register index type for 32 registers
 9    using Addr   = Regs                       // address type is equal to the register type
10
11    [zero : X(0)]                             // register with index 0 always is zero
12    register          X  : Index -> Regs      // integer register file with 32 registers
13    memory            MEM: Addr  -> Byte      // byte addressed memory
14    program counter PC : Addr                 // PC points to the start of an instruction
15
16    format Itype  : Inst =                    // immediate instruction format
17    { imm         : Bits <12>                 // [31..20] 12 bit immediate value
18    , rs1         : Index                     // [19..15] source register index
19    , funct3      : Bits <3>                  // [14..12] 3 bit function code
20    , rd          : Index                     // [11..7]  destination register index
21    , opcode      : Bits <7>                  // [6..0]   7 bit operation code
22    , immS        = imm as SInt<Size>         // sign extended immediate value
23    }
24
25    // macro for immediate instructions with name, operator, type and function code
26    model ItypeInstr (name : Id, op : BinOp, type: Id, funct3 : Bin) : IsaDefs = {
27      instruction $name : Itype =
28        X(rd) := (X(rs1) as $type $op immS as $type) as Regs
29      encoding $name = {opcode = 0b001'0011, funct3 = $funct3}
30      assembly $name = (mnemonic," ",register(rd),","register(rs1),","decimal(imm))
31    }
32
33    $ItypeInstr (ADDI ; + ; SInt ; 0b000)  // add immediate
34    $ItypeInstr (ANDI ; & ; SInt ; 0b111)  // and immediate
35    $ItypeInstr (ORI  ; | ; SInt ; 0b110)  // or immediate
36    $ItypeInstr (XORI ; ^ ; SInt ; 0b100)  // exclusive or immediate
37    $ItypeInstr (SLTI ; < ; SInt ; 0b010)  // set less than immediate
38    $ItypeInstr (SLTIU; < ; UInt ; 0b011)  // set less than immediate unsigned
39  }
```

Listing 1.1. ISA specification of RISC-V instructions with immediate operands

Model VIAM. The architecture synthesis maps all parts of an instruction's behavior to the correct MiA elements (mostly pipeline stages). Now all generators can produce their artifacts.

Architecture synthesis is work in progress in OpenVADL. Therefore, currently no cycle approximate simulator and no hardware description in a HDL are generated. The architecture synthesis will be using an Instruction Progress Graph (IPG) as described in [8], but will become simpler, because the VIAM is closer to the IPG. OpenVADL is implemented in the programming language Java for safe and efficient development. The following sections describe the frontend, the VIAM and the generators for the QEMU simulator, the compiler and the assembler in more detail.

3.1 OpenVADL Frontend

In several passes the OpenVADL frontend transforms a VADL processor specification into the VIAM (see Fig. 2). To keep VADL easily extensible, the VADL parser is automatically generated from a high level grammar. Because of the syntactic macro system the syntax of VADL is context sensitive and only pred-LL(k) parser generators can be used. OpenVADL uses Coco/R [13] as parser generator. Coco/R allows the definition of attributes which are used to generate an Abstract Syntax Tree (AST) directly during parsing. As expressions can be

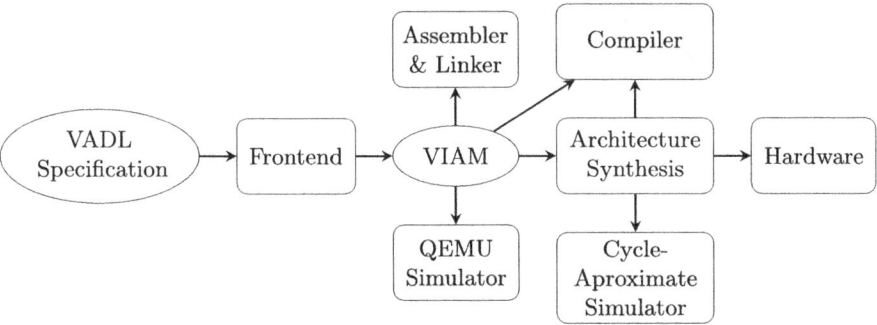

Fig. 1. Overview of the OpenVADL architecture. Generated artifacts are in yellow. (Color figure online)

generated by macros, first a linear left sided tree has to be generated during parsing. When an expression is complete, this linear left sided tree is traversed and reordered into a tree which respects operator precedence [14].

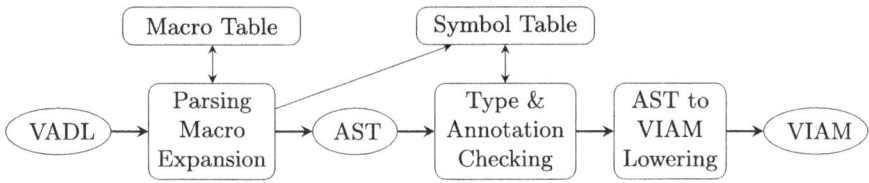

Fig. 2. Overview of the OpenVADL Frontend. Symbol tables are in yellow. (Color figure online)

Macros have to be defined before their first use and recursive instantiations are prohibited. Therefore, macro expansion can be done in a single pass during parsing, and is guaranteed to terminate. When a macro definition is parsed, it is immediately entered into the macro table. When a macro instantiation is parsed, the definition is available in the macro table and an expanded AST can be constructed immediately. Furthermore, all other symbols are collected during parsing and entered into the symbol table.

Now the AST is complete and type inference and type checking can be performed. The type of an expression can depend on the value of a constant expression and the value can depend on the type of an expression. Therefore, the evaluation of constant expressions is done on demand during type checking. Furthermore, symbol resolution of subfields is only possible if the type of the parent is known. Therefore, a part of symbol resolution is deferred until type checking. After the AST is completely typed and all symbols have been resolved, the AST is lowered into the VIAM.

In order to facilitate easy extensibility of VADL, work is in progress to generate parts of type checking and annotation checking from a specification. The descriptions of the type checking rules for the VADL reference manual shall be produced from the same specification.

3.2 VADL Intermediate Architecture Model

The VIAM serves as the IR of OpenVADL, generated by the frontend and processed by various generators. Since different generators have distinct requirements, the VIAM is designed to be generic and extensible, allowing generators to operate directly on it with custom lowerings rather than introducing their own IR. Similar to a VADL specification, the VIAM is divided into two components: one representing definitions, such as `ISA` and `format`, and another describing behavioral aspects, including instruction behavior. The behavioral component is inspired by the Graal IR used in the GraalVM [7].

Definition. The definition component is straightforward, consisting of data structures that facilitate easy access to definitions from the specifications. Certain definitions that encapsulate behavior, such as instructions, also include a graph representing their behavior using the VIAM behavior graph.

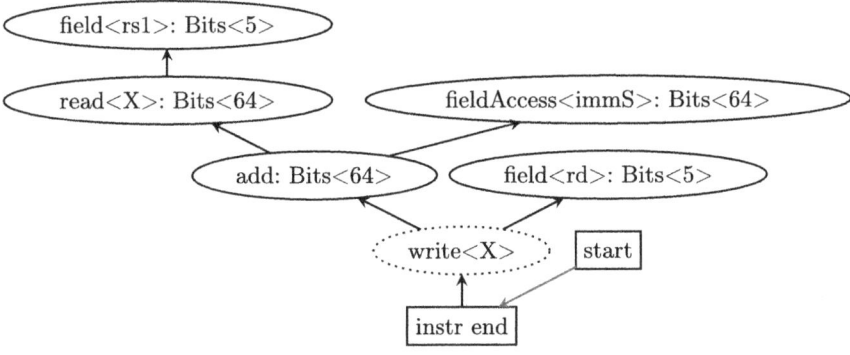

Fig. 3. VIAM behavior graph of the RISC-V `ADDI` instruction, specified in Listing 1.1.

Control Flow Graph (CFG). A VIAM behavior graph is a multigraph that includes both a CFG and a dependency graph. The `ADDI` instruction in Fig. 3 features a minimal CFG, consisting only of a start and end node. More complex instructions may incorporate if-else control flow to represent conditional side effects.

Dependency Graph. To improve readability, VADL behavior follows a sequential reading, while user constraints allow for parallel semantics. This ensures that all resource reads complete before instruction execution begins, and all writes take effect only after execution. This is feasible because VADL instructions cannot write to the same resource twice along the same execution path, preventing undefined behavior between reads and writes.

With parallel semantics, not only expressions but also side-effect nodes, such as register writes, can be incorporated into the dependency graph. As shown in Fig. 3, resource writes are dependencies of a branch end node. If a write is conditional, the branch end node corresponds to the last node of the taken if-branch. Since most generators operate on dependency graphs, this structure enhances flexibility. Additionally, all dependency nodes are unique, ensuring that each side effect or expression appears exactly once in the graph—an inherent optimization.

3.3 QEMU Generator

OpenVADL's generated Instruction Set Simulator (ISS) is based on QEMU [3], an open-source emulator and virtualizer that enables hardware virtualization and full-system emulation for various architectures. It enables fast cross-architecture execution via dynamic binary translation and its Tiny Code Generator (TCG) framework, which translates guest instructions into an IR before converting them into host machine code, as shown in Fig. 4.

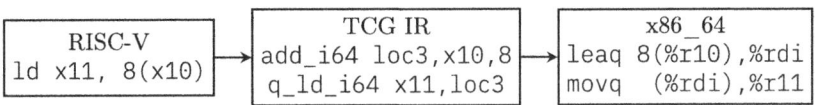

Fig. 4. The TCG translation process involves the guest frontend (e.g., RISC-V) converting instructions into TCG IR, which is then translated by the host backend (e.g., x86_64) into native host instructions for execution.

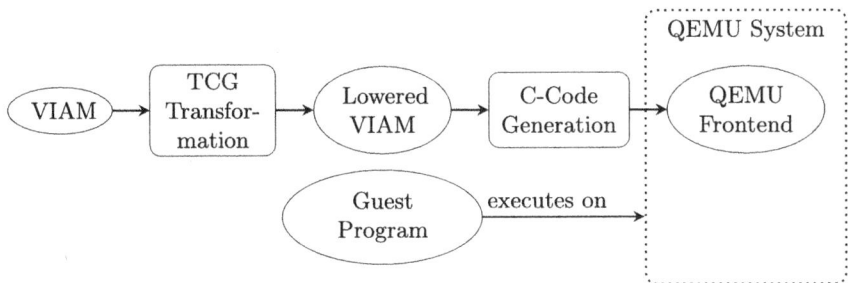

Fig. 5. Overview of the QEMU frontend generation.

To generate an ISS from a given VADL specification, OpenVADL constructs a QEMU frontend based on the specification, as illustrated in Fig. 5. A minimal

QEMU frontend for full system emulation requires defining a CPU state, machine model, instruction decoder, and TCG translation. The CPU state is directly derived from the VIAM, while the machine model remains generic, defining only memory definitions and execution start address.

To support a flexible instruction set encoding, OpenVADL offers a custom implementation for generating an instruction decoder with multiple generation targets in mind, one of them being the ISS based on QEMU. The constructed decode tree is converted to C-Code compatible with the QEMU infrastructure to decode, extract and transform the instruction word according to its specified format.

The core of ISS generation lies in TCG operation translation. Each instruction has a translate function that converts it into strongly typed TCG operations, using input, output, and temporary variables. Registers, immediate values, and temporary values are all represented through these variables.

Several analysis and transformation steps are required to translate an instruction's VIAM behavior graph into a TCG one. Key transformation passes include:

Operation Decomposition: Splits >64-bit operations (e.g., MULH) into QEMU-compatible operations, which are limited to 64 bit.
Side Effect Scheduling: Ensures that register writes and program counter changes occur in the correct order.
Safe Resource Read: Prevents read-write conflicts by scheduling reads before writes.
TCG Expression Scheduling: Determines what is evaluated at translation time vs. runtime. Runtime expressions are marked as TCG operations.
Branch Lowering: Transforms if-else control flow into TCG-compatible branch operations using labels and (un)conditional jumps.
Op Lowering: Transforms previously marked TCG expressions into TCG operations in the CFG.
Variable Allocation: Optimizes temporary variable usage by graph coloring.

Finally, the transformed VIAM behavior graph is converted into a C function `trans_<mnemonic>`, which is called by the instruction decoder during execution.

OpenVADL's cycle approximate simulator will be built on top of the ISS, leveraging QEMU's plugin capabilities to enable fast, cycle approximate simulation of a micro-architecture specification.

3.4 Compiler Generator

The architecture of the compiler generator is extensible to support multiple compiler frameworks. The generation of a compiler is divided into two steps (see Fig. 6). The first step is independent of the chosen compiler framework, the second step depends on the concrete compiler framework. In the first step the Generic Compiler Backend (GCB) performs different compiler independent analyses and transformations and outputs the compiler VIAM. In the second

step a concrete compiler is generated. Currently, OpenVADL only supports the
LLVM framework [11] with the LLVM Compiler Backend (LCB). By supporting
this well established compiler framework, OpenVADL benefits from extensive
compiler research and countless engineering hours dedicated to developing an
industry-standard solution. Unlike LLVM's upstream backends, which are manually crafted, the output of OpenVADL is generated automatically. The resulting
C++ and TableGen files are integrated into a copy of the LLVM source code,
from which the compiler is built. TableGen is LLVM's data structure language
to describe target specific LLVM backends and machine code emitters.

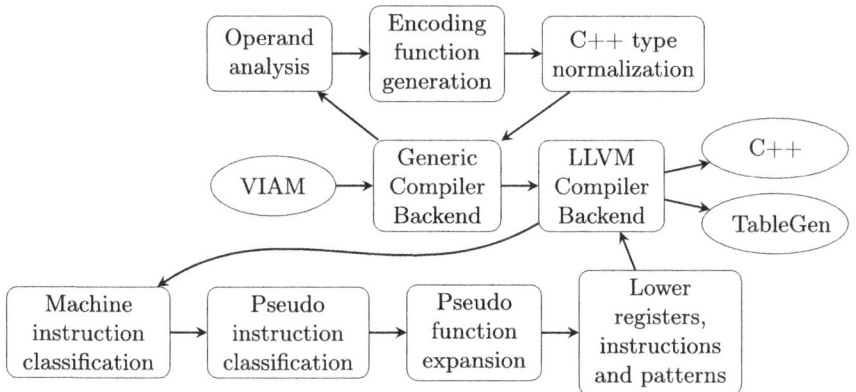

Fig. 6. Overview of compiler generation.

Once compiled, LLVM's frontend *clang* provides a dedicated command-line
option for the target ISA. Figure 6 gives an overview of the steps necessary
to generate a compiler. The input data structure for the GCB is the VIAM.
The input data structure for the LCB is the enriched VIAM output by the
GCB. First, the GCB analyses the instruction's operands. By inspecting the
node type in the VIAM, it determines whether a register or field is written
or read. Second, the GCB generates encoding functions for field accesses that
are not explicitly specified. This feature improves the user experience because
the user can omit these encoding functions. However, the encoding function's
generation is limited to the most common cases. More complicated functions
have to be specified manually. The GCB automatically generates an encoding
function if the decoding function (e.g. immS in line 22 of Listing 1.1)

1. is sign extending or zero extending the field's value,
2. is shifting the field's value or
3. has only addition and subtraction operations.

Lastly, the GCB has to change the node types of encoding and decoding functions. OpenVADL supports arbitrary types, however, compilers are written in

C/C++ with fixed-sized types. Therefore, each type has to be replaced by the next larger type that fits.

Next, the LCB continues to operate on the VIAM output of GCB. At the heart of the compiler generator is the generation of instruction selection patterns for each specified instruction. These patterns are used in the generated compiler in the following way: The compiler frontend translates the input program into LLVM IR. This IR is converted into a dataflow graph which is called SelectionDAG. Each LLVM target has a mapping written in the domain specific language TableGen to map multiple operations from SelectionDAG to machine instructions. The mapping is specified as TableGen patterns. The covering of the SelectionDAG with these patterns, is called instruction selection. LCB's task is to generate those instruction patterns automatically from a given VADL specification.

LCB achieves this by classifying instructions heuristically, based on the dataflow of an instruction's behavior. The classification indicates whether an instruction is an arithmetical, logical, memory, conditional branch, or unconditional branch instruction.

Next, LCB generates C++ functions which expand pseudo instructions. A pseudo instruction is a short notation in the assembly language and represents one or more machine instructions. Since pseudo instructions have no machine code representation, they have to be expanded into their underlying machine instructions. LCB's task is to generate the C++ code for machine instructions to handle immediate operands, register operands and memory operands.

After this step, LCB lowers registers, instructions, and selection patterns. This lowering includes the generation of separate register definitions from register files and the instruction definitions with the encoding, flags and register reads and writes. The result of the lowering is used when the C++ and TableGen files are emitted.

Additionally, the compiler generator has to compensate for missing machine instructions that are nonetheless required by LLVM. In the case of RISC-V, these would be rotate-left, branch-less-or-equal-to or branch-greater-than instructions which are derivable from already existing machine instructions but must be provided automatically. Other tasks for the compiler generator are generating C++ code for frame prologue, frame epilogue and assembly printing.

However, while a lot of optimizations are done on the target independent LLVM IR, they require target specific support functions in the compiler backend which have to be generated automatically.

3.5 Assembler Generator

An assembler's purpose is to translate an assembly language into equivalent machine code. In OpenVADL, assembler generation is part of the LCB, because LLVM's machine code layer (LLVM-MC) offers a large amount of target-agnostic assembler functionality (e.g. lexical analysis, directive handling, expression parsing). In LLVM-MC, this is intuitively represented by two main components: the assembly parser and the machine code emitter, with data structures such as

MCInst serving as the interface between them. Every machine instruction in a VADL specification has an assembly definition, determining how it should be printed. However, this definition is not sufficient for an assembler because an ISA can define additional notations. For example, RISC-V allows `jalr rs` as shortcut for `jalr X1, rs, 0`. VADL allows to define a grammar to handle exactly these cases. Figure 7 gives an overview of OpenVADL's assembler generation.

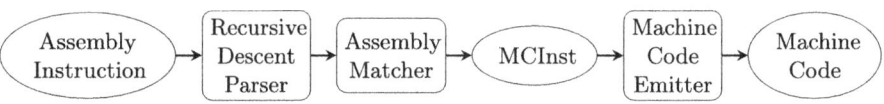

Fig. 7. Overview of the generated assembler.

The parsing of assembly code is managed by a recursive descent parser generated by OpenVADL. It handles the parsing of common statements in assembly languages consisting of instructions, labels and directives.

Recursive Descent Parser. OpenVADL generates the required target-specific functions by constructing a pred-LL(k) recursive descent parser from a formal grammar (see example in Listing 1.2) defined in the assembly description section of a VADL specification. By deploying a pred-LL(k) parsing algorithm OpenVADL improves on the original VADL implementation, which is limited to a strict LL(1) parser. Without compromising on performance, the pred-LL(k) algorithm permits the definition of more expressive grammars.
ïż£

```
grammar = {
  ImmediateInstructions @instruction :
    mnemonic = ImmInstrId @operand
    rd  = Register @operand ","
    rs1 = Register @operand ","
    imm = ImmediateOperand ;
  ImmInstrId :
    "ADDI" | "ANDI" | "ORI" | "XORI" | "SLTI" | "SLTIU" ;
}
```

Listing 1.2. Grammar section with rule definitions for all RISC-V immediate operand instructions as specified in Listing 1.1.

The recursive descent parser utilizes the LLVM-MC provided lexical analysis and creates a vector of operands per parsed instruction statement. This vector stores the instruction's mnemonic along with its other operands such as register names and immediate values.

Assembly Matcher. In the next step, the vector is compared against a table of the target architecture's instructions. If an instruction with matching mnemonic and operands can be found, an instance of `MCInst` containing the parsed values is created and then passed on to the machine code emitter.

Machine Code Emitter. The machine code emitter is responsible for encoding instances of `MCInst` in their machine code representation. The LLVM-MC framework covers the bulk of the transformation process, utilizing encoding information contained in the TableGen files generated by the LCB.

4 Evaluation

4.1 OpenVADL Frontend

Through the reduction of the number of passes and by using Coco/R as parser generator and ahead-of-time compilation with the GraalVM, the OpenVADL parser is up to 150 times faster than the original VADL parser. A detailed evaluation is available in [14].

4.2 QEMU Generator

We evaluated the performance of the generated simulator with the Embench benchmark suite [1] on an x86_64 host. Figure 8 presents the speedup of the QEMU simulator generated from the RV64IM OpenVADL specification relative to the upstream QEMU riscv64 implementation. The OpenVADL generated simulator outperforms the upstream QEMU simulator in all benchmarks.

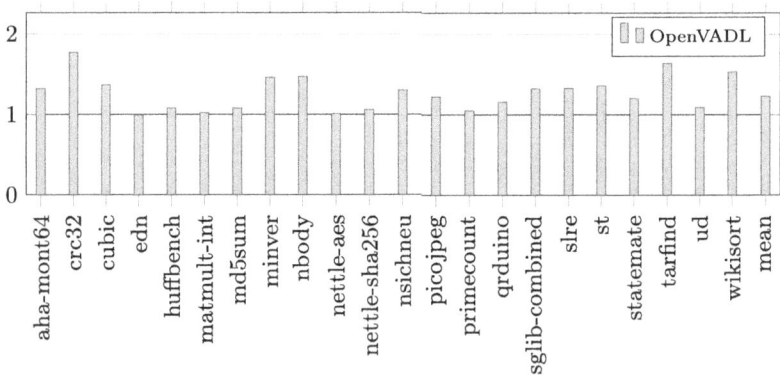

Fig. 8. Performance of generated QEMU relative to upstream (higher is better)

Since the upstream QEMU frontend for riscv64 is human written, it can be considered optimal in terms of generated TCG IR operations. However, the evaluation demonstrates that with the necessary optimizations, the generated TCG operations closely resemble the human written ones.

We attribute the up to 77% better performance of the OpenVADL's QEMU simulator to the inherent complexity of the human written riscv64 guest implementation, which introduces overhead for programs that do not utilize its additional features.

4.3 Compiler Generator

Figure 9 represents the performance evaluation of OpenVADL's LCB using a RISC-V LLVM compiler generated from the VADL specification of RV32IM. As performance metric, we have selected the number of executed instructions reported by the Spike [2] RISC-V simulator. LCB's RISC-V assembler and linker are work in progress. Therefore, we used the upstream LLVM assembler and the GNU linker. The Embench benchmark suite provides 22 benchmarks. Only the cubic benchmark was not run due to a linking issue. As the baseline we used the upstream LLVM compiler. Figure 9 shows that the LCB is on average 14% slower than upstream. All benchmarks were run with the highest optimization level -O3. We suspect that the performance difference comes from specific human written optimizations. These optimizations supplement the instruction selection and automatic generation is work in progress. One of these optimizations is loop invariant code motion on machine instruction level.

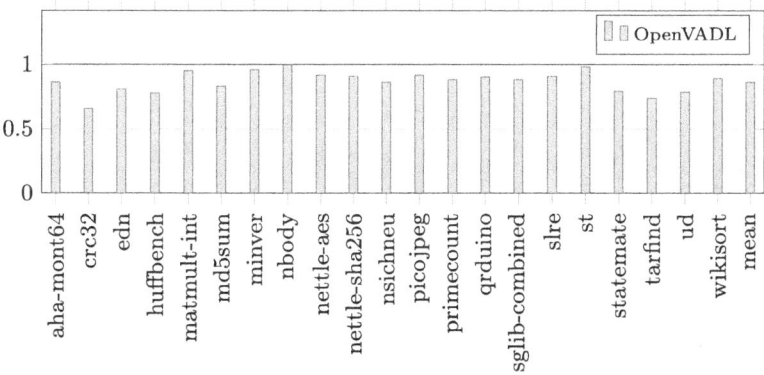

Fig. 9. Performance of generated compiler relative to upstream (higher is better)

5 Related Work

A comprehensive section on work related to VADL and its original implementation can be found in [8]. As a central element, it contains a detailed comparison with other PDLs regarding features and language properties.

This section is about related work relevant for the *implementation* of OpenVADL.

With the VIAM OpenVADL uses a distinctly different IR from the original implementation. While the original implementation uses a quadruple code based IR, OpenVADL's VIAM is graph based. It is inspired by the Graal IR [7], which in turn is based on the *Sea of Nodes* [5]. The Sea of Nodes improves upon a Static Single Assignment (SSA) [6] representation, as it relaxes the order of instructions. The main idea is to combine data dependencies and control dependencies into one graph representation. In OpenVADL, this representation facilitates pattern generation and semantic analysis.

Another SSA based IR is MLIR [12]. Similar to the VIAM an explicit design goal of MLIR is the representation of multiple levels of abstraction. These are called *dialects* in MLIR. MLIR explicitly names these dialects and each dialect has its own name space. An important difference between the VIAM and MLIR is that the VIAM combines both control and dataflow information in its representation.

The frontend of the original VADL implementation is based on Xtext and Xtend [4], OpenVADL uses Coco/R [15] as its parser. While Xtext is suitable for rapid prototyping its performance was not sufficient for the design goals of OpenVADL. Xtext always produces a Concrete Syntax Tree (CST) before making the AST which makes it slower compared to Coco/R. Also Xtext depends on the Eclipse framework. Coco/R has fewer dependencies and is more flexible to work with. This flexibility allows OpenVADL's macro system to expand macros and create the AST in a single pass. This greatly improves performance. Also, the use of Coco/R enables the possibility for ahead-of-time compilation, improving performance even further.

6 Future Work

6.1 QEMU Generator

The QEMU generator is currently less feature-rich and flexible than the VADL language. While QEMU is restricted to 64-bit, VADL specifications are not, requiring special handling for broader compatibility. Planned features include support for floating-point and vector operations, as well as variable instruction lengths.

6.2 Compiler Generator

As reported in Sect. 4.3 the performance of OpenVADL is on average 14% lower than upstream. It is OpenVADL's goal to reduce this number by enabling backend specific optimizations. Furthermore, the quality of an architecture description language is defined not only by the performance of the artifacts it produces but also by the complexity of the architectures it can target. At the moment, the compiler generator only supports RISC-V. Another goal of OpenVADL is to generate a compiler for AArch64 and x86_64. For these architectures it is necessary to support status registers and instructions with multiple results.

Compiler support for Single Instruction Multiple Data (SIMD) and multidimensional tensor instructions is still work in progress. These OpenVADL features will be based on Multidimensional Pattern Matching and Code Replacement (MMTR) presented in [10].

6.3 Hardware Generator

Architecture synthesis and hardware generation are work in progress. Therefore, also instruction scheduling in the compiler and the cycle approximate simulator generator are still under development.

We plan to extend VADL to support multiprocessor systems and specification of buses in the future. As our group is too small to cover all these areas, we are seeking for cooperation in the computer architecture and compiler community to further develop OpenVADL.

7 Conclusion

This article presented OpenVADL, an enhanced and improved open source implementation of VADL. The main contribution is the VIAM, an extensible multiple component, multiple level IR whose behavior component is based on a combined control flow and data flow and dependence graph. In contrast to the original VADL implementation OpenVADL supports an automatically generated QEMU based instruction set simulator which is up to 77% faster than the official human written QEMU simulator. The LLVM compiler generator employs analyses to classify instructions for the use in code generation. The assembler generator implements a more powerful pred-LL(k) parser generator. Finally, OpenVADL is open source and available at openvadl.org.

References

1. Embench: A modern embedded benchmark suite (2024). https://www.embench.org/. Accessed 15 Jan 2024
2. Spike RISC-V ISA Simulator (2024). https://github.com/riscv-software-src/riscv-isa-sim. Accessed 15 Jan 2024
3. Bellard, F.: QEMU, a fast and portable dynamic translator. In: USENIX Annual Technical Conference, FREENIX Track, pp. 41–46. USENIX (2005). https://www.usenix.org/legacy/event/usenix05/tech/freenix/full_papers/bellard/bellard.pdf
4. Bettini, L.: Implementing Domain Specific Languages with Xtext and Xtend - Second Edition, 2nd edn. Packt Publishing (2016). https://dl.acm.org/doi/10.5555/3074444
5. Click, C., Paleczny, M.: A simple graph-based intermediate representation. SIGPLAN Not. **30**(3), 35–49 (1995). https://doi.org/10.1145/202530.202534

6. Cytron, R., Ferrante, J., Rosen, B.K., Wegman, M.N., Zadeck, F.K.: Efficiently computing static single assignment form and the control dependence graph. ACM Trans. Program. Lang. Syst. **13**(4), 451–490 (1991). https://doi.org/10.1145/115372.115320
7. Duboscq, G., Stadler, L., Würthinger, T., Simon, D., Wimmer, C., Mössenböck, H.: Graal IR: an extensible declarative intermediate representation. In: Proceedings of the Asia-Pacific Programming Languages and Compilers Workshop, pp. 1–9 (2013). https://lafo.ssw.uni-linz.ac.at/pub/papers/2013_APPLC_GraalIR.pdf
8. Freitag, F., et al.: The Vienna Architecture Description Language (2025). https://doi.org/10.48550/arXiv.2402.09087
9. Hochrainer, C., Krall, A.: A Pred-LL(*) parsable typed higher-order macro system for architecture description languages. In: Proceedings of the 22nd ACM SIGPLAN International Conference on Generative Programming: Concepts and Experiences, GPCE 2023, pp. 29–41. Association for Computing Machinery, New York (2023). https://doi.org/10.1145/3624007.3624052
10. Huber, B., Krall, A.: Pattern matching, transformation and code replacement on a polyhedral representation of nested loops. In: Varbanescu, A.L., Simmhan, Y. (eds.) International Conference on Computing Frontiers (CF 2025). ACM (2025)
11. Lattner, C., Adve, V.: LLVM: a compilation framework for lifelong program analysis & transformation. In: Proceedings of the International Symposium on Code Generation and Optimization: Feedback-Directed and Runtime Optimization, CGO 2004, p. 75. IEEE Computer Society, USA (2004). https://doi.org/10.1109/CGO.2004.1281665
12. Lattner, C., et al.: MLIR: scaling compiler infrastructure for domain specific computation. In: 2021 IEEE/ACM International Symposium on Code Generation and Optimization (CGO), pp. 2–14 (2021). https://doi.org/10.1109/CGO51591.2021.9370308
13. Mössenböck, H., Löberbauer, M., Wöß, A.: The Compiler Generator Coco/R (2018). https://ssw.jku.at/Research/Projects/Coco/
14. Nestler, M.: Efficient parsing of OpenVADL. Bachelor's thesis, Technische Universität Wien (2024). https://www.complang.tuwien.ac.at/vadl/papers/NestlerFinal.pdf
15. Wöß, A., Löberbauer, M., Mössenböck, H.: LL(1) conflict resolution in a recursive descent compiler generator. In: Böszörményi, L., Schojer, P. (eds.) JMLC 2003. LNCS, vol. 2789, pp. 192–201. Springer, Heidelberg (2003). https://doi.org/10.1007/978-3-540-45213-3_25

Open Access This chapter is licensed under the terms of the Creative Commons Attribution 4.0 International License (http://creativecommons.org/licenses/by/4.0/), which permits use, sharing, adaptation, distribution and reproduction in any medium or format, as long as you give appropriate credit to the original author(s) and the source, provide a link to the Creative Commons license and indicate if changes were made.

The images or other third party material in this chapter are included in the chapter's Creative Commons license, unless indicated otherwise in a credit line to the material. If material is not included in the chapter's Creative Commons license and your intended use is not permitted by statutory regulation or exceeds the permitted use, you will need to obtain permission directly from the copyright holder.

A SIMD MAC RISC-V Extension with Approximate Multipliers for Accelerating CNN Inference in Tiny Embedded Devices

José Juan Hernández Morales[✉][ID], Frank Hannig[ID], and Jürgen Teich[ID]

Friedrich-Alexander-Universität Erlangen-Nürnberg (FAU), Erlangen, Germany
jose.juan.hernandez@fau.de

Abstract. Deploying deep neural networks in ultra-low-power tiny embedded devices has inspired research on compression techniques such as pruning, mixed-precision quantization, and approximation-aware training methods to reduce memory requirements and computational complexity during inference. However, most tiny processors or microcontrollers currently employed for the inference task do not include support for vector or sub-byte integer arithmetic operations, such as those utilized in quantized convolutional neural network (CNN) models. Hence, they need to run programs with additional instructions for packing and unpacking coefficients. Focusing on the multiply-accumulate operations that dominate CNN runtime, we present a SIMD (single instruction, multiple data) accelerator tightly coupled into a RISC-V processor pipeline. This accelerator is capable of receiving packed coefficients in 8-bit and 4-bit formats and outputting their dot product. Moreover, to reduce hardware costs and lower the latency of the SIMD unit, we propose an approximate multiplier structure which considers shared resources for 8×8-bit and 4×4-bit multiplications. Additionally, the level of approximation can be configured at synthesis time to trade hardware resources off with accuracy. The SIMD accelerator has been implemented as a custom function unit within a VexRiscv core synthesized for an FPGA and evaluated by running CNN ResNet models for image classification using the CIFAR-10 dataset.

Keywords: Approximate Computing · RISC-V instruction extension · CNNs

1 Introduction

The use of embedded machine learning (ML) and specifically deep neural networks for inference in resource-constrained applications has been of research and business interest due to many benefits such as privacy and low cost. Its implementation in tiny resource-constrained devices requires the optimization of hardware and software to be able to reach low resources and energy.

Targeting the high number of multiply-accumulate (MAC) operations constituting a high percentage of the total data processing in convolutional neural networks, this work considers the usage of approximate computing to optimize the hardware resources and delay needed for computing the MAC operations of the quantized versions of these neural network architectures. Also, considering the recent exploration of lower-precision weights and activations, the necessity of hardware support for resolutions as low as 4 bits is taken into account.

The contributions of this paper are the following:

- We propose a SIMD MAC hardware custom function unit (CFU) based on approximate multipliers, which can be used as a tightly coupled accelerator within a RISC-V core. It features a selectable precision for 8×8-bit or 4×4-bit signed multiplications. Input weight and activation coefficients are packed into the 32-bit input registers specified in a RISC-V instruction.
- We evaluate the proposed CFU for different image classification CNN architectures, comparing classification accuracy with implementations using exact multiplications. Moreover, to minimize any degradation of classification accuracy, we introduce approximation-aware training (AAT), which takes into account the approximate products of our design.
- The proposed CFU can also be used as a building block for more complex hardware architectures that need to minimize resources and delay when approximate MAC computations are permissible.

2 Background

Approximate computing exploits the error resilience of applications such as image processing and machine learning, so to trade off imprecise computations with area, energy, and performance of a system. When using approximate arithmetic circuits such as adders and multipliers, error metrics must be carefully defined and taken into account. In this paper, let $f : \mathbb{B}^n \to \mathbb{B}^n$ be a Boolean function with n inputs and outputs and $\hat{f}$ a function that approximates f. Further, using the signed number interpretation with two's complement encoding denoted by $\text{val}(f(x))$, $x \in \mathbb{B}^n$, the error metrics mean absolute error (MAE), mean relative error (MRE), and worst-case error (WCE), as defined in Eqs. (2), (3), and (4), respectively, are valuable.

$$e(f(x), \hat{f}(x)) = \text{val}(f(x)) - \text{val}(\hat{f}(x)) \tag{1}$$

$$\text{MAE}(f, \hat{f}) = \frac{1}{2^n} \sum_{x \in \mathbb{B}^n} |e(f(x), \hat{f}(x))| \tag{2}$$

$$\text{MRE}(f, \hat{f}) = \frac{1}{2^n} \sum_{x \in \mathbb{B}^n} \frac{|e(f(x), \hat{f}(x))|}{\text{val}(f(x))} \tag{3}$$

$$\text{WCE}(f, \hat{f}) = \max_{x \in \mathbb{B}^n} |e(f(x), \hat{f}(x))| \tag{4}$$

As described in [1] and [2], the error can be treated as a random variable and characterized by its mean and variance, so to use these metrics in error correction algorithms. Finally, the variance can be defined according to Eq. (5).

$$\text{var}(f, \hat{f}) = \frac{1}{2^n} \sum_{x \in \mathbb{B}^n} \left(\text{e}(f(x), \hat{f}(x)) - \frac{1}{2^n} \sum_{y \in \mathbb{B}^n} \text{e}(f(y), \hat{f}(y)) \right)^2 \quad (5)$$

The use of approximate computing in deep learning and, especially in CNNs, has been growing over the last years, due to its potential for energy efficiency when exploiting the error tolerance of neural networks (NNs) [3]. Significant research has been undertaken to improve image classification tasks with CNNs, with most of its processing made up of MAC operations.

The training process of a neural network (NN) requires high-performance hardware like GPUs to accelerate the forward and back propagation iterations required for error minimization until the convergence of the internal weights. The training phase usually employs 32-bit floating point arithmetic for high-precision computations. After training, the NN architecture and its parameters, which include the fixed weights, are deployed in a processing unit in the field to compute inferences. An inference is the process of feeding input data to the network and computing a forward propagation through all the neurons in the architecture to obtain a single classification at the output neurons. Quantization, the process of reducing the bitwidth of the data with precision scaling, may be applied to the NN parameters to decrease memory usage and simplify the hardware needed for computations during inference. In this regard, quantization techniques have been designed to mitigate the accuracy loss obtained when lowering the precision of the coefficients, like *post-training quantization* (PTQ) and *quantization-aware training* (QAT). The latter involves simulating the quantized inference in the forward pass while keeping the backpropagation in the usual floating-point format [3].

When applying approximate arithmetic to improve area and energy further, the approximate computations can be inserted in QAT to have *approximation-aware training* (AAT). Mrazek et al. employed retraining in their methodology to identify approximate multipliers that minimize the classification accuracy loss [4]. A similar approach was proposed by Ansari et al. [5]. Both works replace accurate multipliers with approximate ones in a pre-trained network and perform retraining for a smaller number of epochs. Some properties of approximate multipliers have been identified that could guide the minimization of classification accuracy loss when applying AAT. In [5], a feature selection algorithm for a predictor anticipating the behavior of an approximate multiplier in a neural network was applied, identifying the error variance and the root mean square error as the most important metrics. Although not employing retraining, Tasoulas et al. applied an error compensation with a constant correction term based on the approximate multiplier mean error, making the accuracy of the convolution operation only subject to the error variance of the multiplier [2].

CNN models like LeNet, AlexNet, and ResNet have been extensively used for the benchmarking of hardware architecture proposals for improvements in performance, area and/or energy in the inference process of this type of neural networks. For instance, Mrazek et al. [6] analyzed the use of approximate multipliers in ResNet architectures to obtain energy savings without high loss in classification accuracy.

3 Related Work

For the deployment of quantized CNNs in tiny embedded devices, integer arithmetic for different precisions has been the target of recent works proposing RISC-V extensions. In [7], Garofalo et al. present a design for a RISC-V extension supporting 4- and 2-bit vector dot product operations. However, resources are not shared, i.e., one separate multiplier instance is used for each precision. Xu et al. [8] proposed a similar approach. In their implementation, the adder trees of the 2-bit and 4-bit dot product operations are distributed among two stages of the RISC-V core pipeline, adding complexity to the reuse of the design in a different core and also without resource sharing among the multiplier instances. In [9], Garofalo et al. propose an architecture using four 17-bit multipliers for parallelization supporting 8-, 4- and 2-bit weights with a fixed size of 8-bit activations. The core clock frequency used for the FPGA implementation is 50 MHz and a multi-pumping scheme with 2x the clock frequency is implemented for the accelerator. Both works mentioned above do not use approximate arithmetic for simplifying hardware. Considering approximate computing applied to CNNs, a focus on approximating the multiplication operation is observed, since this may deliver more resource and energy savings. A complete framework to deploy NNs in a RISC-V core is described in [10], making use of a multiplier design supporting 256 approximation levels by masking the 8 least significant columns of the adder tree. This design allows power savings in an ASIC by gating specific bits to zero. Although the multiplier unit is designed to support SIMD, it does not include the possibility of coefficient packing, i.e., the number of input coefficients is fixed. Similarly, Mrazek et al. propose an exploration framework for multi-objective optimization based on the NSGA-II algorithm for selecting differently approximate multipliers. However, this work includes solely 8-bit multipliers from the EvoApprox library [11].

4 Methodology

Efficient software implementations for deploying small CNN models on low-power microcontrollers have proven their usage even in tiny embedded devices. Yet, lightweight and energy-efficient approaches are crucial to keep pace with the rapidly growing computing demands in ML while meeting the requirements of such tiny devices. One opportunity is the open-source RISC-V instruction set architecture (ISA), which allows custom extensions. This option can be exploited in a low-power processor design to study approximate arithmetic hardware units that could save resources and energy when running error-tolerant applications. Additionally, when using coefficients with a smaller precision than the processor's architecture (e.g., register's width of 32 bits), the hardware unit may be designed to process data in parallel by packing multiple 8-bit or 4-bit values in the registers used as input operands of a SIMD unit.

Mixed-precision CNNs [12] have proven to be an efficient solution for deployment, particularly in resource-constrained systems, while preserving model accuracy. To support mixed-precision CNNs with a SIMD approach, we propose a specific MAC unit design that operates the two input vectors fully packed with either 4-bit or 8-bit coefficients. To diminish the hardware overhead, our proposed MAC vector unit considers shared resources in contrast to the state-of-the-art [8]. Thanks to the reduced number of hardware resources, our design also lowers the critical path through the combinatorial logic. To accomplish the execution of the MAC SIMD instructions even within a single cycle, we propose an approximate multiplier design detailed in Sect. 5.1.

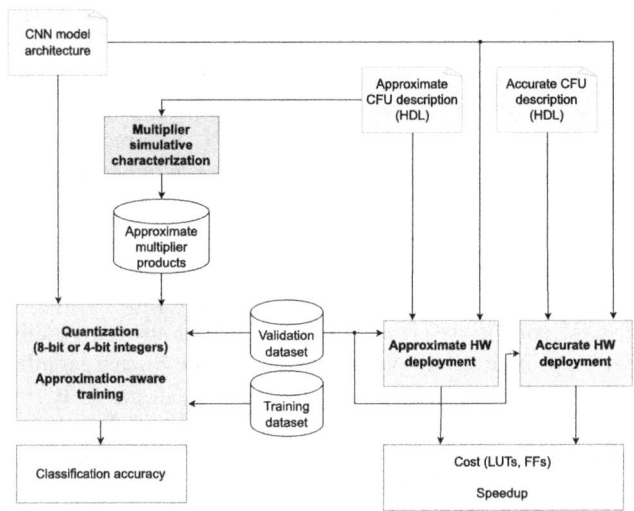

Fig. 1. Flow used for the proposed CFU design and validation.

Employing approximate arithmetic units adds up to other types of approximation typically used in CNNs aimed to be deployed in tiny embedded devices, namely, pruning and quantization. Thus, when applying approximate computing to heavily quantized NNs, its effect on the output accuracy, for instance, in image classification CNNs, is a parameter that should be carefully observed. To counteract such an accuracy degradation, we propose *approximation-aware training*. That is, the multiplications are substituted during the training of the NN by the approximate multiplications being employed during inference on the target device.

Figure 1 shows the flow used for the design and validation of our proposed approximate arithmetic SIMD hardware accelerator. In the proposed flow, two versions of the CFU SIMD architecture are considered, specified at the register-transfer level using a hardware description language: One with accurate and another with approximate multipliers. Both versions have been integrated into a complete hardware/software co-design running CNN inference applications, specifically a RISC-V core executing a C program for deploying a CNN model. For a deployment in FPGAs, we evaluate the resource costs in terms of FPGA look-up tables (LUTs) and flip-flops (FFs). Speedup is calculated with respect to the execution time of the software running in the RISC-V core without the CFU design. For the validation of the classification accuracy recovery, the approximate multiplier design used within the CFU is simulated to obtain the products for all possible inputs. The products are stored in an $n \times n$ array with n the inputs precision bits, which is then used for approximation-aware retraining of the input model.

5 Proposed Approach

A Custom Function Unit (CFU) is defined as a tightly coupled hardware unit inserted within a CPU pipeline [13]. A CFU is able to receive instructions as defined in the RISC-V ISA, thus receiving two 32-bit inputs and outputting one 32-bit result. Using such a configuration, four 8-bit weights and four 8-bit activation values can be packed in the two inputs to compute four multiplications in parallel. In the same way, 4-bit coefficients can be packed to compute 8 multiplications in a single instruction. By using adders that compute the sum of all products within the CFU, a set of instructions can be defined to compute the MAC operation used in dot products and convolutions. In the following, our CFU design and defined instruction extensions are described in detail.

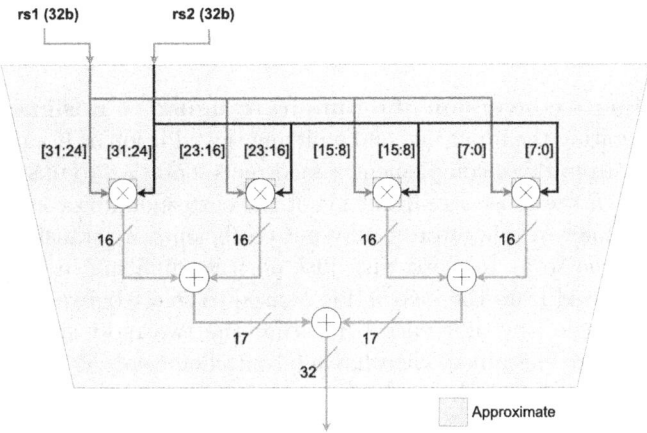

Fig. 2. Proposed SIMD CFU architecture.

5.1 Hardware Design

Considering the *R-Type* instruction format defined in the RISC-V ISA [14], which takes two 32-bit input operands and one 32-bit output, the top level of the proposed accelerator is defined as a SIMD entity splitting the inputs into groups of 8 bits to be input to four multiplier units. The outputs of these multipliers are all summed up to have a single 32-bit accumulated output. Figure 2 depicts the proposed architecture. The multipliers contain internal multiplexers to select between 4×4-bit or 8×8-bit multiplications, depending on the instruction selected. This way, the output of a single multiplier is either the product of two 8-bit coefficients or the sum of the products of two 4×4-bit multiplications. Then, the functionality of the SIMD unit can be described as the dot product of a pair of 32-bit vectors containing 8-bit or 4-bit elements.

Using accurate multipliers and adders, especially when considering 4-bit coefficients, would produce a quite long critical path, as noted in [7]. To alleviate this challenge while considering resource-sharing opportunities between the 8×8-bit and 4×4-bit multipliers, we propose an approximate multiplier design that reduces the critical path delay.

Our approximate SIMD function unit is based on the approximate multiplier design proposed by Liu et al. [15], which requires $\log_2 n$ stages of parallel approximate additions to sum up the partial products of an $n \times n$-bit multiplication. Each of these stages produces a set of approximate sums $\hat{s}$ and errors e (see Fig. 3) so that the accurate sum can be obtained with $s = \hat{s} + e$. By applying a bitwise or operator to all the bits of the same position of the error vectors obtained in all stages, an approximate sum of the error vectors is obtained and added in an error recovery stage to get the final result. A set of q or r most significant bits for error recovery is used, referred to as *error recovery bits* in the following.

Being the case that the coefficients used for the filter's weights and activations in convolutional layers of CNNs are typically signed integers and that the method explained previously was designed for unsigned values, sign conversions have to be implemented at the inputs and outputs of our multiplier design that is explained in detail next.

- **Approximate conversion of inputs from signed to unsigned integers:** By just negating the input bits and omitting the addition of 1, an approximate conversion from two's complement signed representation to unsigned value is applied when the most significant bit of the corresponding coefficient is 1 (a negative value). In other words, all input coefficients are transformed to their absolute value so as to work with just positive numbers in the next steps. A signal derived from the instruction is used to select between 8-bit or 4-bit coefficients logic, the difference being that the two most significant bits (2 coefficients) are contained when having 4-bit coefficients.
- **Generation of partial products matrix:** A partial products matrix of size 8×8 is generated consisting of row vectors $a_n = (rs2[7] \cdot rs1[n], rs2[6] \cdot rs1[n] \ldots rs2[0] \cdot rs1[n])$ with $rs1$ and $rs2$ the input operands (see Fig. 3) and n the row position. Then, a matrix P of size 8×15 with row vectors v_0 to

v_7 containing the a_n vectors is used for the computation of the subsequent steps. Notice that each a_n row vector just covers 8 of the 15 values of v_n while the missing 7 values are set to 0, and that the positions of each a_n vector are shifted to the left by n places.

$$P = \begin{pmatrix} v_0 \\ v_1 \\ v_2 \\ v_3 \\ v_4 \\ v_5 \\ v_6 \\ v_7 \end{pmatrix} = \begin{pmatrix} 0 & 0 & 0 & 0 & 0 & 0 & 0 & a_0[7] & a_0[6] & a_0[5] & a_0[4] & a_0[3] & a_0[2] & a_0[1] & a_0[0] \\ 0 & 0 & 0 & 0 & 0 & 0 & a_1[7] & a_1[6] & a_1[5] & a_1[4] & a_1[3] & a_1[2] & a_1[1] & a_1[0] & 0 \\ 0 & 0 & 0 & 0 & 0 & a_2[7] & a_2[6] & a_2[5] & a_2[4] & a_2[3] & a_2[2] & a_2[1] & a_2[0] & 0 & 0 \\ 0 & 0 & 0 & 0 & a_3[7] & a_3[6] & a_3[5] & a_3[4] & a_3[3] & a_3[2] & a_3[1] & a_3[0] & 0 & 0 & 0 \\ 0 & 0 & 0 & a_4[7] & a_4[6] & a_4[5] & a_4[4] & a_4[3] & a_4[2] & a_4[1] & a_4[0] & 0 & 0 & 0 & 0 \\ 0 & 0 & a_5[7] & a_5[6] & a_5[5] & a_5[4] & a_5[3] & a_5[2] & a_5[1] & a_5[0] & 0 & 0 & 0 & 0 & 0 \\ 0 & a_6[7] & a_6[6] & a_6[5] & a_6[4] & a_6[3] & a_6[2] & a_6[1] & a_6[0] & 0 & 0 & 0 & 0 & 0 & 0 \\ a_7[7] & a_7[6] & a_7[5] & a_7[4] & a_7[3] & a_7[2] & a_7[1] & a_7[0] & 0 & 0 & 0 & 0 & 0 & 0 & 0 \end{pmatrix}$$

- **Three approximate sums stages without carry propagation:** Being i the bit position, j the stage number, and k the vector index within a stage, each bit of each sum vector s and error vector e is computed as:

$$s_{jk}[j] = (x[i] \oplus y[i]) \vee (x[i-1] \wedge y[i-1])$$
$$e_{jk}[j] = (x[i] \oplus y[i]) \wedge (x[i-1] \wedge y[i-1])$$

x and y being the corresponding addend vectors defined in Fig. 3. Since no dependencies exist and approximate sums do not have a carry propagation, all vectors in each stage can be computed in parallel.
- **Error recovery stage:** q error recovery bits are added to the most significant bits of the output result in the 8×8-bit multiplication path. In the 4×4-bit multiplications path, r error recovery bits are also taken from the half positions of the error vectors corresponding to the most significant bits of one 4×4-bit product located at the rightmost position.
- **Approximate conversion of outputs from unsigned to signed integers:** If input factors are of different sign, the products are converted to match the signed integers representation.

As can be seen in Fig. 3, the path for 4×4-bit multiplications takes stage 1 and stage 2 sum and error vectors, but applies an early error recovery stage since the products are already obtained after two stages. However, an approximate unsigned-to-signed conversion and an approximate addition of the products make up the same number of stages for both paths. The approximate addition made in stage 3 of the 4×4-bit multiplications path introduces an additional error with MAE = 31.75 and var = 2048, considering all the 2^{16} possible inputs and that the sum is sign-extended to avoid overflow errors. The sign extension is applied to fill the multiplier's 16-bit output, keeping it in two's complement representation for the further accumulation of the other 3 multiplier products in the SIMD architecture.

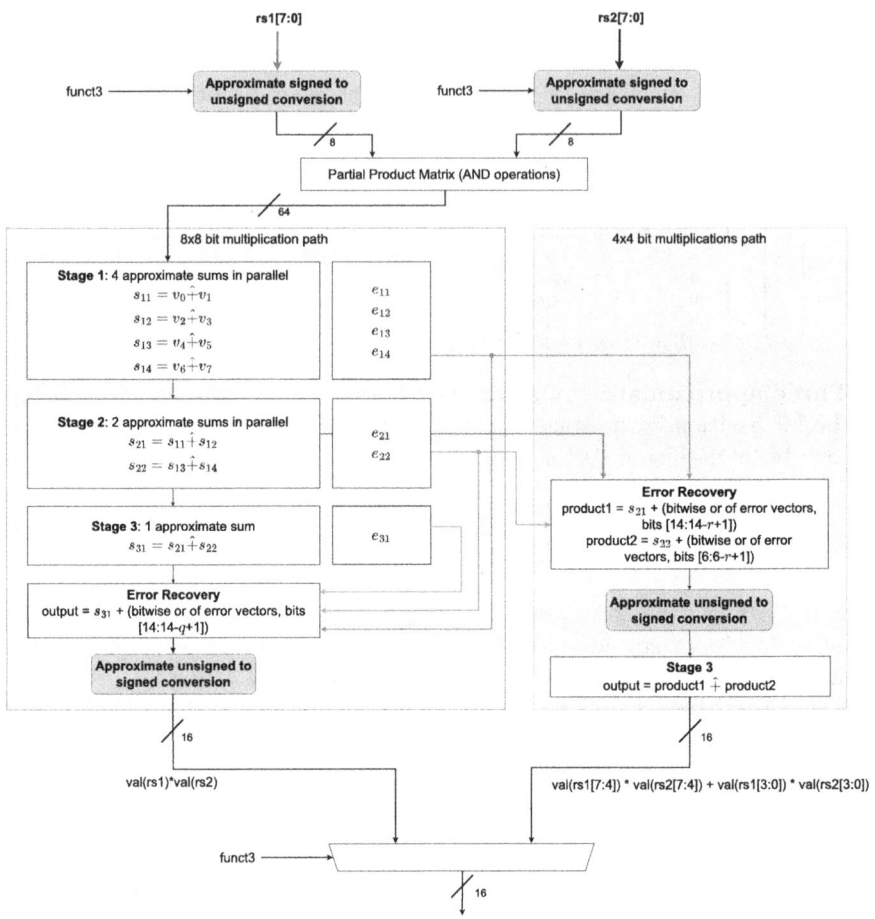

Fig. 3. Approximate multiplier architecture.

5.2 Format of RISC-V Instruction Set Extension

The set of instructions extending the RV32IM RISC-V ISA targets the computation of the MAC operation and, more specifically, its use in quantized convolutional neural networks. Due to the possibility of having these networks as mixed-precision models, the added instructions allow the multiplication of 8- and 4-bit coefficients. This is, for a given convolutional layer, a suitable MAC instruction can be selected to match the precision of its weight and activation coefficients. Table 1 shows all added instructions with the corresponding values for each field of the RISC-V R-Type [14] instruction used. The opcode field is defined with a constant value used for custom instructions according to the ISA, while the funct7 and funct3 fields are the values forwarded to our designed CFU to be decoded to select the instruction to be executed. Table 2 states how the input operands stored in registers rs1 and rs2 are split to compute the corresponding dot product. It can be seen that the coefficients shall be delivered already packed within the register.

Table 1. RISC-V added instructions and formatting with R-Type fields.

Instruction	funct7	rs2	rs1	funct3	rd	opcode
mac8bits	0	4 8-bit coefficients	4 8-bit coefficients	0	MAC result	CUSTOM0
mac4bits	0	8 4-bit coefficients	8 4-bit coefficients	1	MAC result	CUSTOM0

Table 2. RISC-V added instructions description.

Instruction	Description
mac8bits(rs1, rs2)	rd = rs1[31:24]*rs2[31:24] + rs1[23:16]*rs2[23:16] +...+ rs1[7:0]*rs2[7:0]
mac4bits(rs1, rs2)	rd = rs1[31:28]*rs2[31:28] + rs1[27:24]*rs2[27:24] +...+ rs1[3:0]*rs2[3:0]

6 Results

The following sections give insight into the tools used to evaluate our CFU design as well as the cost and performance obtained using the proposed method.

6.1 Experimental Setup

Initial experiments were performed with the MNIST dataset and a CNN composed of two convolutional and two fully connected layers. Further experiments targeted the CIFAR-10 dataset on ResNet8 from the MLPerf Tiny Benchmark [16]. An Arty A7-100T FPGA board was used for deployment. Following the methodology described in Sect. 4, the tools and frameworks used in the evaluation are described next.

Approximation-Aware Training: AdaPT is a PyTorch extension that emulates inference and retraining with approximate multipliers for a pre-trained input model [17]. It incorporates calibration of quantization parameters and quantization-aware training for which approximate multiplications can be used. For the approximate multiplier, a cached aligned C-array with the products for all multiplicand and multiplier combinations is used as a look-up table to accelerate the emulation of multiplications during the quantization-aware training, making it approximation-aware. For our use case, our multiplier design was simulated with a test bench to export the values needed for the C-array used in AdaPT with the targeted CNN models.

Deployment: CFU Playground is a framework developed for the purpose of designing custom RISC-V instructions in an agile process, incorporating tools for the deployment and profiling of CFUs within a RISC-V core [13]. It includes the TensorFlow Lite library and its build process to obtain a binary file containing the program and the NN design parameters. Then, this binary file is used in a Litex SoC containing a VexRiscv core, an open-source RISC-V processor with the designed CFU. For the hardware design, the CFU can be defined using a hardware description language (HDL). In our case, we used Verilog as HDL to specify the proposed SIMD CFU.

Hardware Metrics: For obtaining the quantities of FPGA components used by our design, we utilized the Xilinx Vivado 2023 Design Suite. An implementation was made to obtain the metrics of the standalone CFU, while the project defined in the CFU Playground framework was used to obtain the metrics of the SoC including the VexRiscv core and the CFU.

6.2 Evaluation

Error Analysis of the Approximate Multipliers: Figures 4 and 5 show the error distribution for both the implemented 8-bit and 4-bit multiplications, respectively, where it can be seen that the mean is close to 0 in all cases. Figure 6 shows how the highest errors are presented near the borders of the multiplier and multiplicand ranges. This feature could be beneficial in convolutional layers where the weights have a Gaussian distribution with a mean near 0. Table 3 shows the error metrics defined in Sect. 2 for different numbers q and r of error recovery bits, with $n = 8$ for 8-bit multiplication and $n = 4$ for 4-bit multiplication.

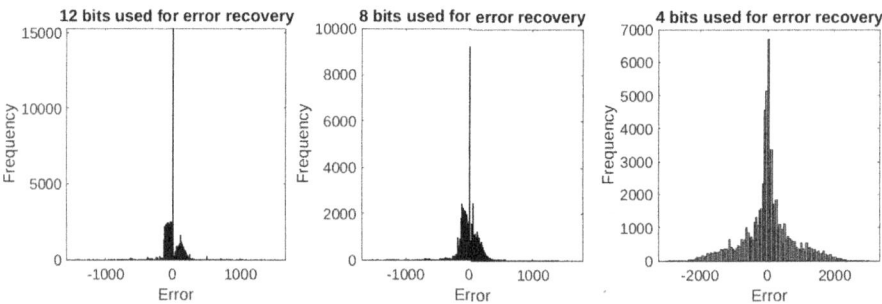

Fig. 4. Histogram of the error (Eq. (1)) of 8-bit multiplications for different numbers of bits used for error recovery.

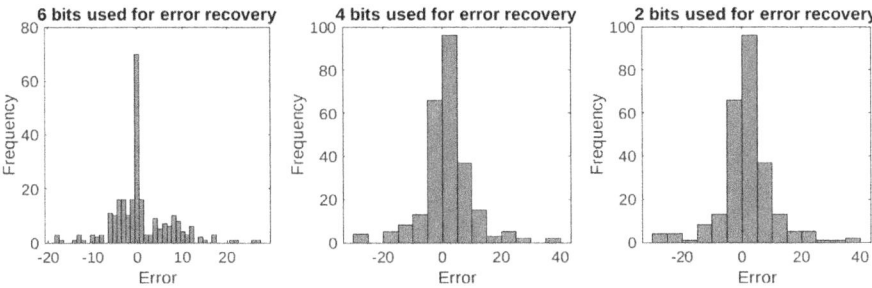

Fig. 5. Histogram of the error (Eq. 1) of 4-bit multiplications for different numbers of bits used for error recovery.

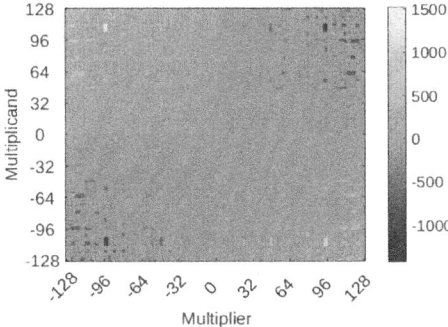

Fig. 6. Errors (Eq. 1) of 8-bit multiplications plotted as a 2D image with the multiplier and multiplicand in each axis.

Table 3. Error and FPGA metrics for the SIMD MAC architecture using the specified recovery bits for 4-bit and 8-bit multiplications. The first row shows the metrics obtained with exact multiplications, while subsequent rows show configurations with different error recovery bits.

8-bit multiplication					4-bit multiplication					FPGA metrics	
q	MAE	MRE	WCE	var	r	MAE	MRE	WCE	var	Delay (ns)	LUTs
–	0	0	0	0	–	0	0	0	0	10.86	590
12	86.5	0.05	1517	21 479	6	4.43	0.27	27	44.4	10.11	684
8	112.6	0.06	1621	29 026	4	5.25	0.29	36	71.1	**9.99**	**555**
4	505.5	0.16	3029	557 960	2	5.50	0.30	39	81.7	**9.65**	**491**
4	505.5	0.16	3029	557 960	7	3.37	0.24	15	23.9	**9.88**	**537**

Resources and Delay of the SIMD Architecture: The SIMD design described in Sect. 5.1 has been synthesized to FPGA, and the results are reported in Table 3. Each row shows the FPGA metrics of the whole CFU design (which includes four multipliers and an adder tree of the 4 products). Considering that

Table 4. Comparison with state-of-the-art proposals implemented in FPGA.

Proposal	Xu et al. [8]	Armeniakos et al. [9]	Ours
FPGA family	Artix-7	Virtex-7	Artix-7
Clock Frequency	100 MHz	50/100MHz	100 MHz
Precisions supported	2/4/8/16	2/4/8 bit	4/8 bit
Resources	1.9K LUTs, 0.2K FFs	1.3K LUTs, 1.9K FFs	0.5K LUTs, 0.1 FFs

using accurate multipliers would result in a synthesized design with 10.86 ns of latency and 590 LUTs, the highlighted values indicate the improved delay of less than 10 ns when using approximate multipliers. For instance, a configuration with $q = 4$ and $r = 7$ error recovery bits already gives a lower delay and number of LUTs. This delay improvement allows to use the SIMD design to operate as a single-cycle instruction given a typical 100 MHz clock frequency for the softcore processor implemented in an FPGA, avoiding the need for additional registers. All configurations, including the accurate one, require 97 flip-flops. The data presented in Table 3 may then be used to perform a design space exploration of a mixed-precision CNN model to be deployed in hardware given specific delay, cost, and classification accuracy restrictions.

The VexRiscv core used for the validation of our CFU can be synthesized with many available configurations varying in cache sizes, single- or multiple-cycle instructions, and branch prediction, among other selectable features. Having used the Litex framework and its available parameters to synthesize a full configuration of the VexRiscv core with our CFU included using an Artix-7 FPGA, a total usage of 3661 LUTs and 1735 FFs was required, which translates on the CFU occupying 15% and 5% of the total LUTs and FFs, respectively. Although the proposed accelerator in [8] introduces a larger set of instructions and support for 16-bit and 2-bit coefficients, an overhead of at least 1762 LUTs, 200 FFs, and 2 DSPs is needed for its implementation in an Artix-7 FPGA, in contrast with our approach focused in accelerating the predominant MAC instructions and typical resolutions used when quantizing CNN models, requiring approximately one-third of the LUTs and half of the FFs with no additional DSPs. A similar design implemented in a Virtex-7 FPGA [9] reports an overhead of 1300 LUTs and 1900 FFs with a system frequency of 50 MHz and a low-resolution multiplications module running at 100 MHz. Table 4 shows the comparison between our design and these proposals.

CNN Speedup Analysis: Speedup for a specific CNN depends on the percentage of MAC operations with respect to the overall processing required. Then, the speedup was computed for the processing of a convolutional layer. Within a layer, a group of k filters $F \in \mathbb{Z}^{k \times w_f \times h_f \times c}$ where w_f is the filter width, h_f is the filter height, and c is the number of channels, are convolved with an activation tensor $A \in \mathbb{Z}^{w_{in} \times h_{in} \times d}$ where w_{in} is the tensor width, h_{in} is the tensor height, and d is the tensor depth. A layer from the ResNet8 architecture tested with

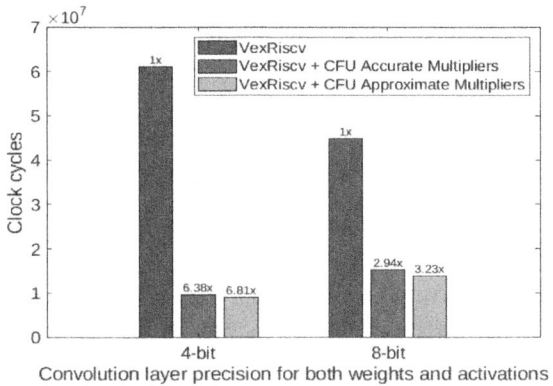

Fig. 7. Speedup for a convolutional layer processing with 4-bit and 8-bit coefficients.

$k = 32$, $w_f = 3$, $h_f = 3$, and $c = 32$ for F; and $w_{in} = 18$, $h_{in} = 18$, and $d = 32$ for A was used for our speedup experiment.

The RISC-V core instructions needed for the control logic and data loading decreases the throughput of the accelerator. For instance, the innermost loop loading 32-bit words for activations, weights and input offsets, consists of 14 instructions created by the compiler, from which 2 are CFU instructions. Then, it is beneficial to apply unrolling to increase the proportion of CFU instructions with respect to control instructions to speed up the execution further. By comparison with a program not using the CFU instructions processing 8-bit coefficients, the innermost loop loading also 32-bit words needs additional instructions for unpacking the coefficients (bitshifts, masking and sign extensions), requiring a total of 42 instructions in our experiment when building with the RISC-V compiler. Considering each instruction takes just one clock cycle, a maximum speedup of $s = 42/14 = 3$ can be obtained without unrolling. The instructions outside the innermost loop, which stay the same in both versions, increment the proportion of sequential instructions, thus the speedup is decreased.

Clock cycle measurements were taken by the program running on the VexRiscv core without the use of the CFU, with the CFU containing accurate multipliers taking 2 clock cycles per instruction, and with the CFU with approximate multipliers taking 1 clock cycle per instruction. For the program using the CFU, an unrolling of 4 words per innermost loop iteration was implemented to increase the speedup of both the accurate and the approximate CFU versions. Figure 7 shows these measurements, for which a speedup of at least 2.94× was obtained with 8-bit quantized weights and activations. Comparing the clock cycles taken between the CFU versions, a speedup of 1.1x is reached with respect to the accurate version when using the approximate multipliers, for both 8-bit and 4-bit coefficients convolutions.

When considering the overall runtime of the ResNet8 architecture where 96% of its processing involves convolutional layers, a speedup of 2.52 was obtained with the use of the CFU with approximate multipliers and 8-bit quantized coefficients.

Classification Accuracy in CNN Models Using AAT: A pair of C-arrays to be used as look-up tables in the AdaPT extension was obtained for the approximate 8-bit multiplier with the computed products with 8 and 4 error recovery bits. An iteration of PTQ and AAT was executed using each of these arrays for multiplications in convolutional layers to obtain the classification accuracy of the CNN models. A simple CNN model consisting of 2 convolutional layers and 2 fully connected layers with 8-bit quantization for weights and activations was implemented as a first experiment for the use of our CFU design with approximate multipliers. The same experiment was performed for the ResNet8 and ResNet18 models classifying the CIFAR-10 dataset. Accuracy results for all models are shown in Table 5. It can be seen that PTQ can introduce a high classification accuracy degradation when using approximate multipliers, observing a decrease of 22.57% in the ResNet8 architecture. However, after AAT, accuracy was improved with respect to just applying PTQ in almost all cases. Overall, the use of the proposed approximate multiplier degraded the classification accuracy at most in 5.66% (in ResNet8) with respect to a quantized model using accurate multiplications.

Table 5. Accuracy results of the tested NN architectures with 8-bit quantization

NN Architecture	Multiplier configuration	Quantized Model (PTQ) Accuracy	Accuracy after AAT
CNN for MNIST	Accurate	98.45	–
	8 error recovery bits	98.46	98.46
	4 error recovery bits	98.46	98.46
ResNet8	Accurate	87.51	–
	8 error recovery bits	77.74	85.94
	4 error recovery bits	64.94	81.85
ResNet18	Accurate	92.93	–
	8 error recovery bits	87.86	92.47
	4 error recovery bits	89.02	91.03

7 Conclusion

We proposed a 4- and 8-bit coefficient configurable and at the same time resource-efficient SIMD MAC hardware accelerator architecture using approximate multipliers that enable a single-cycle operation by avoiding a long critical path of an architecture with accurate multipliers and a long adder tree. According to our evaluations, the level of error can be tolerated in terms of CNN model's accuracy output after approximation-aware training. The ability to support both 4-bit and 8-bit input coefficients further enhances the flexibility and scalability of the proposed design, making it an attractive solution for efficient hardware acceleration in mixed-precision CNNs and error-resilient applications requiring extensive use of MAC operations.

Acknowledgments. This work was partly supported by the Deutsche Forschungsgemeinschaft (DFG, German Research Foundation) under project number 524986327 (NA^3Os).

References

1. Li, C., Luo, W., Sapatnekar, S.S., Hu, J.: Joint precision optimization and high level synthesis for approximate computing. In: Proceedings of the 52nd Annual Design Automation Conference (DAC), pp. 104:1–104:6. ACM (2015). https://doi.org/10.1145/2744769.2744863
2. Tasoulas, Z.-G., Zervakis, G., Anagnostopoulos, I., Amrouch, H., Henkel, J.: Weight-Oriented approximation for energy-efficient neural network inference accelerators. IEEE Trans. Circ. Syst. I Regul. Pap. **67**(12), 4670–4683 (2020). https://doi.org/10.1109/TCSI.2020.3019460
3. Armeniakos, G., Zervakis, G., Soudris, D., Henkel, J.: Hardware approximate techniques for deep neural network accelerators: a survey. ACM Comput. Surv. **55**(4), 83:1–83:36 (2022). https://doi.org/10.1145/3527156
4. Mrazek, V., Sarwar, S.S., Sekanina, L., Vasicek, Z., Roy, K.: Design of power-efficient approximate multipliers for approximate artificial neural networks. In: Proceedings IEEE/ACM International Conference on Computer-Aided Design (ICCAD), pp. 1–7 (2016)
5. Ansari, M.S., Mrazek, V., Cockburn, B.F., Sekanina, L., Vasicek, Z., Han, J.: Improving the accuracy and hardware efficiency of neural networks using approximate multipliers. IEEE Trans. Very Large Scale Integr. (VLSI) Syst. **28**(2), 317–328 (2020). https://doi.org/10.1109/TVLSI.2019.2940943
6. Mrazek, V., Vasicek, Z., Sekanina, L., Hanif, M.A., Shafique, M.: ALWANN: automatic layer-wise approximation of deep neural network accelerators without retraining. In: Proceedings IEEE/ACM International Conference on Computer-Aided Design (ICCAD), pp. 1–8 (2019). https://doi.org/10.1109/ICCAD45719.2019.8942068
7. Garofalo, A., Tagliavini, G., Conti, F., Rossi, D., Benini, L.: XpulpNN: accelerating quantized neural networks on RISC-V processors through ISA extensions. In: Proceedings Conference on Design, Automation and Test in Europe (DATE), pp. 186–191 (2020). https://doi.org/10.23919/DATE48585.2020.9116529
8. Xu, Z., Kang, X., Wang, X., Chen, B., Ye, T.T.: FlexBits: a configurable lightweight RISC-V micro-architecture for flexible bit-width execution. In: Proceedings IEEE 6th International Conference on AI Circuits and Systems (AICAS), pp. 287–291 (2024). https://doi.org/10.1109/AICAS59952.2024.10595975

9. Armeniakos, G., Maras, A., Xydis, S., Soudris, D.: Mixed-precision neural networks on RISC-V cores: ISA extensions for multi-pumped soft SIMD operations. the computing research repository (CoRR) (2024). arXiv: 2407.14274 [cs.AR]
10. Guella, F., Valpreda, E., Caon, M., Masera, G., Martina, M.: MARLIN: a co-design methodology for approximate reconfigurable inference of neural networks at the edge. IEEE Trans. Circ. Syst. I Regul. Pap. **71**(5), 2105–2118 (2024). https://doi.org/10.1109/TCSI.2024.3365952
11. Mrazek, V., Vasicek, Z., Sekanina, L., Jiang, H., Han, J.: Scalable construction of approximate multipliers with formally guaranteed worst case error. IEEE Trans. Very Large Scale Integr. (VLSI) Syst. **26**(11), 2572–2576 (2018). https://doi.org/10.1109/TVLSI.2018.2856362
12. Rakka, M., Fouda, M.E., Khargonekar, P., Kurdahi, F.: A review of state-of-the-art mixed-precision neural network frameworks. IEEE Trans. Pattern Anal. Mach. Intell. **46**(12), 7793–7812 (2024)
13. Prakash, S., et al.: CFU playground: want a faster ML processor? Do it yourself! In: Proceedings of the Conference on Design, Automation and Test in Europe (DATE), pp. 1–2. IEEE (2023). https://doi.org/10.23919/DATE56975.2023.10137093
14. Waterman A., Asanovic K., RISC-V Foundation: The RISC-V Instruction Set Manual Volume I. Unprivileged ISA, Version 20240411 (2024)
15. Liu, C., Han, J., Lombardi, F.: A low-power, high-performance approximate multiplier with configurable partial error recovery. In: Proceedings Conference on Design, Automation and Test in Europe (DATE), pp. 1–4 (2014). https://doi.org/10.7873/DATE.2014.108
16. Banbury, C., et al.: MLPerf tiny benchmark. In: Proceedings of the Neural Information Processing Systems Track on Datasets and Benchmarks (2021)
17. Danopoulos, D., Zervakis, G., Siozios, K., Soudris, D., Henkel, J., et al.: AdaPT: fast emulation of approximate DNN accelerators in PyTorch. IEEE Trans. Comput. Aided Des. Integr. Circ. Syst. **42**(6), 2074–2078 (2023). https://doi.org/10.1109/TCAD.2022.3212645

Wildcat: Educational RISC-V Microprocessors

Martin Schoeberl[✉]

Department of Applied Mathematics and Computer Science,
Technical University of Denmark, Kgs. Lyngby, Denmark
masca@dtu.dk

Abstract. In computer architecture courses, we usually teach RISC processors using a five-stage pipeline, neglecting alternative organizations. This design choice, rooted in 1980s technology, may not be optimal today, and it is certainly not the easiest pipeline for education. This paper examines more straightforward pipeline organizations for RISC processors suitable for educational purposes and for implementing embedded processors in FPGAs and ASICs. We analyze resource costs and maximum clock frequency of various designs implemented in an FPGA, using clock frequency as a performance proxy. Additionally, we validate these results with ASIC designs synthesized using the open-source SkyWater130 process.

Contradictory to common wisdom, a longer pipeline (up to 5 stages) does not necessarily always increase the maximum clock frequency. In two FPGA and one ASIC implementation, we discovered that a four- or five-stage pipeline leads to a slower clock frequency than a three-stage implementation. The reason is that the width of the forwarding multiplexer in the execution stage increases with longer pipelines, which is on the critical path. We also argue that a 3-stage pipeline organization is more adequate for teaching a pipeline organization of a microprocessor.

Keywords: RISC processor architecture · computer architecture education · RISC-V

1 Introduction

When teaching computer architecture, we are used to teaching RISC processors' mechanics in a five-stage pipeline. We ignore entirely other organizations (except teaching out-of-order execution in advanced computer architecture courses).

However, the organization of a RISC processor as a 5-stage pipeline is probably not the best today. It stems from the early RISC processors in the 80' of the last century. Today's technology probably favors different organizations.

In this paper, we explore different and simpler pipeline organizations for RISC processors practicable for teaching computer architecture and probably also useful for the implementation of embedded processors in field-programmable gate arrays (FPGAs) and in ASICs.

The RISC-V instruction set architecture (ISA) was defined by Andrew Waterman in his PhD thesis [21] together with Dave Patterson and Krste Asanovic at the University of California, Berkeley (UCB). Andrew explored three decades of RISC architectures, e.g., MIPS, SPARC, Alpha, and others, to extract the essence of an RISC instruction set. The strongest move in this project was to provide an open-source ISA. Open-source software has been the driver of the Internet's development. However, on the hardware side of computers, a processor's instruction set is a very protected asset. The move to a free ISA will change the way computers are built.

The RISC-V Foundation now maintains the RISC-V instruction set,[1] which was established in 2015. The Foundation has more than 3,100 members across 70 countries. Besides managing the RISC-V ISA specifications, the Foundation regularly organizes RISC-V workshops and summits.

This paper presents Wildcat, an open-source, educational implementation of a RISC-V microprocessor. The name Wildcat was inspired by the nice running area in Tilden Park in Berkeley: the Wildcat area. I started this project in 2015 with a RISC-V ISA simulator after participating in Andrew's PhD defense and a run on the Wildcat Creek Trail. An early version of Wildcat has been presented in [17].

RISC-V is an ISA definition; it does not define an implementation. The "V" stands for the fifth RISC project at UCB and also indicates that vector instructions are a part of the standard. However, in many textbooks, implementations of RISC-V are presented as a 5-stage pipeline.[2]

Educators, the author included, have taught computer architecture with a 5-stage pipeline organization only. I regret my approach to teaching pipeline organizations has been too narrow. This paper aims to argue for a simplified approach with fewer stages, emphasizing efficiency and ease of understanding in contrast to the complexity of longer pipelines.

We start with a simple 3-stage pipeline and extend it to 4 and 5 stages. We then compare these three designs developed in the same language, in the same style, and programmed by the same author. We will show that the additional resource usage of the additional stages does not justify the marginal or non-existing performance gains.

We explore the resource costs and the maximum clock frequency of the different organizations implemented in an FPGA. As the clocks per instructions (CPI) are almost identical for the three designs, the maximum clock frequency is a valid proxy for the performance of the pipeline alone. To validate the results in ASIC designs, we also synthesized the different versions with the open-source OpenLane2 tools using the SkyWater130 process. Our main finding is that a 3-stage pipeline organization is superior to a 4- or 5-stage organization.

The contributions of the paper are: (1) four clean implementations of RISC-V useful for teaching computer architecture, (2) questioning the common wisdom

---

[1] https://riscv.org/.

[2] The author even witnessed a conference participant arguing that the "V" in RISC-V mandates a 5-stage implementation.

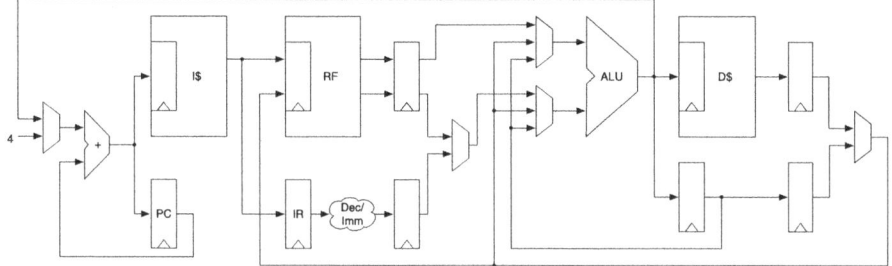

Fig. 1. A textbook style 5-stages RISC-V processor pipeline.

to default to a 5-stage pipeline, and (3) comparing 3, 4, and 5-stage pipeline implementations written by the same person, in the same language, on the same FPGA. To the best of our knowledge, those three organizations have never been compared directly.

This paper is organized into six sections: The following section presents the proposed pipeline organizations. Section 3 describes our implementation of different pipeline organizations. Section 4 evaluates the different organizations on two families of FPGAs and an ASIC synthesis flow. Section 5 presents related work. Section 6 concludes.

2 Pipeline Organizations

In this section, we discuss three different organizations of in-order RISC pipelines. We start with the classic, textbook style 5-stage organization and will argue step-by-step to reduce it to three stages. The arguments are based on my background in FPGA implementations. However, in the evaluation section, we will also explore the three different organizations in the open-source SkyWater130 ASIC technology.

2.1 The Classic 5-Stage Pipeline

The standard textbook organization [9,10] of a RISC pipeline is a five-stage pipeline with the following stages: (1) instruction fetch (IF), (2) instruction decode and register file read (ID), (3) execute (EX), (4) memory access (MEM), and (5) write back (WB). Between each pair of stages, there are the so-called pipeline registers. Figure 1 shows the simplified schematic of the classic 5-stage RISC pipeline. The figure also shows the forwarding paths from MEM and WB to the input of the ALU in the EX stage.

The instruction cache (I$), the register file (RF), and the data cache (D$) can be implemented with synchronous on-chip memories. Synchronous memories have registers at their address and date inputs, and a read operation takes one clock cycle. Therefore, their input registers are part of the pipeline registers between the different stages.

We are all so used to this textbook organization that we seldom question the number of stages. Even Wikipedia does not discuss any other possible organization on the page describing a RISC pipeline.[3] This paper explores different organizations, especially when implementing that RISC pipeline in an FPGA.

In FPGAs, synchronous memories are fast. They are cost-efficient compared to flip-flops. Therefore, the register file should be implemented using synchronous memory. Multiplexers, used for forwarding, are slow compared to on-chip memory in an FPGA. From an earlier design of the Patmos [18] RISC processor, we know that the forwarding path in front of the arithmetic logic unit (ALU) becomes the critical path.

2.2 Do We Need a Write Back Stage?

For a RISC implementation in current technology, we assume for the register file either an implementation in flip-flops or using a synchronous on-chip RAM.[4] Therefore, the input to the register file is the input of a flip-flop.

The write-back stage contains only a 2:1 multiplexer between the forwarded result from the EXE stage and the result of a memory read. The multiplexer sits between the MEM/WB pipeline register and the input of the register file.

This stage performs very little work. However, that 2:1 multiplexer needs to be forwarded to the EXE stage, adding yet another multiplexer to the ALU stage, which is on the critical path.

This multiplexer can be moved into the memory stage. Note that on-chip memories (scratchpad or cache) are faster than an ALU, including forwarding. This leads to a 4-stage pipeline and removes the forwarding path from WB to EXE. Thus reducing the critical path.

2.3 Sharing an Adder for Address Calculation?

In the classic RISC architecture, the address for a memory operation is computed in the EX stage. The adder in the ALU is reused to add an immediate value to a register value to compute the effective address.

This sharing of the adder was probably a good design tradeoff in the 80's where resources were scarce. However, today, adders are cheap (and fast). A 32-bit adder uses 32 LCs in an FPGA. This is in the range of about 2 % of a complete pipeline implementation. Since addition operations are inexpensive and fast, there is no necessity to reuse the ALU for address calculation. Therefore, we propose to have a dedicated adder for the address calculation.

As reading from the register file is fast, we can compute the memory address in the decode stage. Then, we can merge the execution stage with the memory

---

[3] https://en.wikipedia.org/wiki/Classic_RISC_pipeline.
[4] We are aware of other organizations for a register file, e.g., with latches. However, latches are impractical for FPGAs. We might explore other organizations in the future with the SkyWater130 technology. Initial experiments to build a latch-based register file failed with OpenLane as yosys did not like the Verilog code for latches.

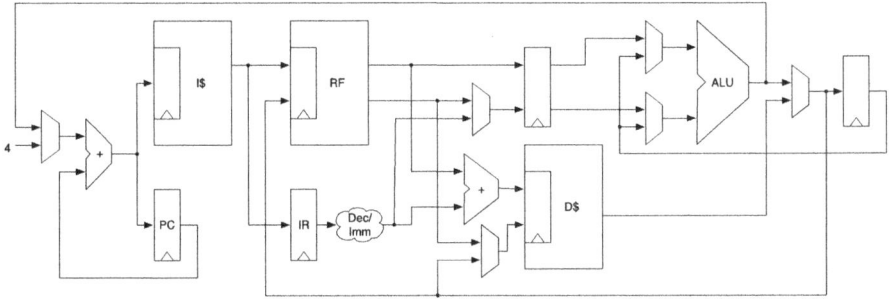

Fig. 2. A 3-stage RISC-V processor pipeline.

stage. This configuration results in a 3-stage pipeline and eliminates another forwarding path. Another benefit of having memory access parallel to the ALU at the same stage is the avoidance of load-use hazards. Data loaded from memory will be available in the next clock cycle and forwarded to the ALU input.

Decoding instructions, particularly those in the RISC architecture, require a relatively small number of gates, and decoding is faster than an ALU operation. Thus, it becomes a viable consideration to relocate that multiplexer responsible for selecting between the register file value and the immediate value into the decode stage. This proposed adjustment represents an additional measure to minimize the critical path within the execution stage.

Figure 2 shows a simplified schematic of the resulting 3-stage RISC-V pipeline. Memory access is merged with a possible ALU operation in the EX stage. One forwarding path from the ALU result or memory read to the next ALU operation exists. Another forwarding path is from the combinational ALU result or memory read to the memory input.

2.4 Branching and Load-Use Hazard

When we assume branch decisions and the branch destination computation in EX, a taken branch takes three clock cycles. The branch can be reduced to two clock cycles by moving the branch decision and computation into the ID stage or implementing a branch predictor. This exploration is out of the scope of this paper.

The 4- and 5-stage pipelines suffer from the so-called load-use hazard. A load-use hazard occurs when an instruction following a load instruction depends on the result of the load. This result cannot be forwarded. We need to stall the pipeline by one clock cycle (or restart the pipeline with the use instruction). Note that the 3-stage pipeline does not suffer from that load-use hazard.

Having only one forwarding path and no load-use hazard simplifies not only the implementation of the pipeline, but also the complexity of teaching a pipelined processor implementation. Even if we start teaching processor organizations with the classic 5-stages pipeline, we should also present other, simpler implementations.

2.5 Is the Proposed Pipeline Organization Controversial?

I am are aware that the classic RISC pipeline is considered to have five stages. I explored several textbooks and slides from computer architecture courses, and they have one thing in common: the RISC pipeline shown consists of five stages.

I have taught computer architecture for around 15 years and have always shown that classic pipeline organization. I even joked with the students that when I wake them up in the middle of the night; they should be able to name those five stages.

Maybe this paper is controversial. Maybe only the teaching is stuck in the "one and only" classic pipeline organization? In related work, we will see that other organizations exist in the wild.

It might be controversial to question about 40-year-old common wisdom. However, this paper tries to do so.

This paper argues that the 5-stages are probably not the sweet spot for short pipeline organizations. This paper does not argue against longer pipelines. It argues for shorter and easier pipelines as a starting point. There will be benefits of 6, 7, or 8 stages in order pipelines. We will consider exploring those benefits and comparing our design with longer pipelines as future work.

3 Implementation

This project aims to provide examples of RISC pipeline implementations for education in computer architecture. Therefore, the code focuses on readability and avoiding distractions by performance or size optimizations. However, clean code does not need to result in a large design with a low clock frequency.

For the design, we use Chisel [2,16], a hardware construction language embedded in Scala. Chisel is a bit more high-level than VHDL or Verilog. However, the more important fact is that it results in better readable code. Furthermore, we switched our education in digital design to Chisel in 2020. Our students are used to writing and reading Chisel code.

3.1 A Simulator

Each non-trivial digital design project should start with a simulation of that design. A processor is a good example. In our computer architecture course, students must write as a final project a RISC-V ISA simulator. Writing a simulator is a good preparation for an optional course of implementing a RISC-V processor in an FPGA.

We wrote a simple instruction set simulator of RV32I. As the pipeline design was planned to be written in Chisel, we used Scala for the simulator. This has two benefits: (1) we can co-simulate the hardware design and the ISA simulator in the same Java virtual machine; and (2) we can share constants between the simulator and the hardware. The ISA simulator is around 300 lines of readable code.

3.2 The Baseline

As a baseline, we implemented the proposed 3-stage pipeline as described before. As we aim for reusable code, we put common functionality, such as decoding, immediate generation, and the ALU code, into Chisel functions. In Chisel, hardware generators, including circuits that contain registers, can be put into plain functions.

The current implementation follows the description of the proposed 3-stages pipeline from the former section. Memory addresses are computed in ID. Branch decision and destination address generation are located in EX. Immediate constant generation is performed in ID. However, the selection between the register value and the immediate value is placed in EX. In future work, we will explore variations in the placement of parts between ID and EX.

The code for the 3-stages pipeline is around 140 lines of code, and additional 250 lines of code for decode, immediate generation, and the ALU are placed in functions for reuse by the other implementations. The number of lines of code is not the only measurement for readability; however, browsing around 400 lines of code is more manageable than reading 3000 lines of code.

We will let others (our students) comment on the readability. Future work will also be to work on the readability and clearness of the code.

3.3 Extending the Baseline

Extending the 3-stage pipeline towards 4 and 5 stages was straightforward. However, this resulted in quite a lot of copied code, which is not good.[5] Our future work will explore ways to share more code without distracting readability.

4 Evaluation

We evaluate the three different designs in two FPGA families and the OpenLane2 open-source ASIC flow for the open-source PDK from SkyWater in 130 nm technology. For the evaluations with FPGAs, we have set the timing constraint for the clock to 200 MHz to push the synthesis tools to optimize for speed. The ASIC flow with OpenLane will not finish when the timing constraint is not met. Therefore, we set it to a frequency of 50 MHz.

After placing and routing in the relevant tools, we derive the results from the reports. We can find those results quickly in the reports using the Quartus (Altera) and Vivado (AMD) tools. The OpenLane flow is a bit more elaborate, consisting of 72 steps with a report and log file for every step. We find the size of the design in report 13 (`floorplan`) when the floor plan is generated. We can find the slack relative to the requested frequency in report 54 (`stapostpnr`). We report the computed maximum frequency for the chip at 25°C at 1.8 V. For the Altera FPGA, we report the timing results for the slow model at 85°C and 1.8 V. Vivado offers only one timing result.

---

[5] Doug Locke stated: "Two copies are never the same".

To provide a baseline, we synthesized two designs targetting Cyclone IV: (1) on-chip memory with registers on the input and output, including forwarding for reads and writes to the same address and (2) our ALU of the 3-stage design, including all forwarding paths and multiplexers for immediate versus register value, the PC for JAL(R), and some more multiplexers. An on-chip memory of 4 KB can be clocked at 587.89 MHz and a 16 KB version at 272.33 MHz. In both cases, Quartus limits the report to 250 MHz due to restrictions of the maximum I/O toggle rate to 250 MHz. The ALU, with inputs and outputs connected to registers, is reported to have a maximum clock frequency of 96.05 MHz. This shows that on-chip memory (in an FPGA) is faster than ALU operations. This observation motivated our pipeline to include some logic after the on-chip memory output, e.g., operations on the register file output and a 2:1 multiplexer at the data memory output.

As we are interested in the pipeline comparison alone, we leave out any instruction and data memories or caches for the synthesis. Our implementation contains two memory interfaces: (1) one for the instruction memory and (2) one for the data memory. A complete processor can attach caches, scratchpad memories, or a shared memory interface. For testing the processor (in simulation and in an FPGA), we use scratchpad memories.

The classic performance equation for in-order pipelines is the instruction count multiplied by the clocks per instruction (CPI) multiplied by the clock period, resulting in execution time. The instruction count for all programs is the same as we use the same ISA. The value of CPI with real benchmarks is missing. However, all three pipelines have a very similar CPI: instructions have a CPI of one, a taken branch has two clock cycle penalty, and on the 4- and 5-stages pipelines, there is one clock cycle penalty for a load-use hazard. The main source of a higher CPI is missing in the caches, which we do not compare in the paper. Therefore, for the performance comparison, we use the maximum clock frequency as a proxy for the performance.

4.1 FPGA Results

For the evaluation, we used an Intel Cyclone IV FPGA. Although a bit dated, it is the FPGA is on the popular Terrasic DE2-115 FPGA board we use at our university. Furthermore, several designs are available with published numbers for this FPGA for a rough comparison. The Java processor JOP [15] needs 2050 LCs for the implementation and can be clocked at 100 MHz. The time-predictable processor Patmos [18] needs 7602 LCs for the implementation and can be clocked at 81.7 MHz. Patmos is also a RISC processor, and the critical path is in the ALU including the forwarding multiplexers.

We synthesize two versions for each design and FPGA: one with the register file built out of flip-flops (FF) and one using synchronous on-chip memory (mem). Table 1 shows the results for the three pipeline organizations for the Altera FPGA. The logic resource usage is reported in logic elements (LE), which consist of a 4-bit lookup table and a flip-flop. The number of flip-flops is also noted in the column flip-flops. RAM bits show the usage of the on-chip memories.

2048 bits of memory (two memory blocks) are needed to support two read ports for the register file. We observe that using on-chip memory for the register file results in a faster implementation in most cases. And the resource usage of LE is reduced. However, the most surprising observation is that most 4- and 5-stage pipelines have a *lower* maximum clocking frequency. This contradicts the very purpose of pipelining, which is to increase the maximum clocking frequency. We explain that the ALU, including the forwarding multiplexers, is the critical path in FPGA technology (memories are fast). Therefore, longer pipelines adding forwarding multiplexers hurt the maximum clock frequency (up to 5 stages).

Table 1. Wildcat results for the Altera FPGA Cyclone IV

Design (Cyclone IV)	max. frequency	logic elements	flip-flops	RAM bits
Three stages (FF)	80.2 MHz	3,130	1,295	0
Three stages (mem)	86.2 MHz	1,756	379	2,048
Four stages (FF)	83.9 MHz	3,040	1,367	0
Four stages (mem)	84.5 MHz	1,727	451	2,048
Five stages (FF)	78.4 MHz	3,107	1,438	0
Five stages (mem)	75.7 MHz	1,813	522	2,048

Furthermore, we synthesize the designs for the AMD (former Xilinx) FPGA Artix 7, the FPGA on the Nexys A7 board. We used the Nexys board to run small example programs on Wildcat on real hardware. Table 2 shows the results for the Artix FPGA. A logic cell (LC) in the Artix FPGA consists of a 6-bit lookup table and a register. Therefore, the numbers are different from the Altera FPGA. This FPGA is a newer generation than the Cyclone IV FPGA, so we observe higher possible clock frequencies. Again, we observe the general trend of slower clock frequency with longer pipelines. The memory-based register file is implemented as a distributed LUT RAMs in the Artix FPGA. Therefore, the number of bits in the block RAMs are zero. Of the 1256 LUTs in the three stages pipeline, 48 are used as distributed RAMs for the register file.

Table 2. Wildcat results for the AMD (former Xilinx) FPGA Artix 7

Design (Artix 7)	max. frequency	logic cells	flip-flops	RAM bits
Three stages (FF)	99.6 MHz	1,744	1,329	0
Three stages (mem)	112.3 MHz	1,270	303	0
Four stages (FF)	107.5 MHz	1,551	1,438	0
Four stages (mem)	111.2 MHz	993	442	0
Five stages (FF)	106.1 MHz	1,724	1,511	0
Five stages (mem)	102.0 MHz	1,158	515	0

4.2 ASIC Results

We use the SkyWater[6] project for the ASIC evaluation. SkyWater is a fab with a 130 nm process and together with efabless[7] they provide a service to run a multi-project wafer design. If the design is open source, Google sponsored the chip production, packaging, and a PCB. However, this sponsorship has been stopped at the time of this writing. Therefore, we submitted Wildcat to run 10 of Tiny Tapeout [20], a very affordable way to produce an ASIC. The Tiny Tapeout project of Wildcat contains a fixed program and fits into 6 Tiny Tapeout tiles.[8]

Although the SkyWater130 process is an old technology, it serves well for comparisons. The process development kit (PDK) of SkyWater130 is available in open source, providing an equal playground for many projects. We expect that the SkyWater130 process will become a reference platform for future publications in computer architecture research.

As we do not have a memory compiler available for this process, we can only implement the register file in flip-flops. Table 3 shows the results for the SkyWater130 ASIC. The ASIC flow results confirm the trend we see in the FPGA results. As expected, the area increases with larger pipelines, and the maximum clock frequency decreases, which was unexpected.

To set the area of the pipeline into context, the area is about $0.2\,\text{mm}^2$. A multi-project waver tile with a user area of $10\,\text{mm}^2$ is available for around $10,000 within the efabless[9] project.

Table 3. Wildcat results with the SkyWater130 ASIC process

Design (SkyWater130)	fmax (MHz)	Size
Three stages (FF)	81.2 MHz	$429 \times 432\,\mu\text{mm}^2$
Four stages (FF)	73.2 MHz	$433 \times 438\,\mu\text{mm}^2$
Five stages (FF)	69.5 MHz	$439 \times 443\,\mu\text{mm}^2$

5 Related Work

David Patterson and John Hennessy coined the term *reduced instruction set computer* (RISC). The first publicly available RISC processor was the RISC I [12,13], designed at UCB and MIPS [11], designed at Stanford University. The IBM 801 predates the two RISC processors from academia, but details have not been disclosed in the early 80's.

---

[6] https://www.skywatertechnology.com/.
[7] https://efabless.com/.
[8] https://github.com/schoeberl/tt10-wildcat.
[9] https://efabless.com/prototyping.

The RISC-V project started with Andrew's thesis [21]. To verify his work on defining *the* RISC instruction set, the research group in Berkeley developed several versions of a RISC-V microprocessor. The initial version was an instruction set simulator called Spike. The hardware implementation following the simulator was called Rocket [1]. Rocket is implemented in Chisel and represents a 5-stage in-order scalar pipeline. The project is also called the Rocket Chip generator, as it is a collection of tools to generate RISC-V-based system-on-chips. Besides the Rocket in-order pipelined core, the generator contains components with the TileLink protocol, several tools, and Diplomacy [3]. Diplomacy is an extension package for Chisel, providing support for two-phase hardware elaboration. This approach enables dynamic negotiation of specific parameters between modules. Rocket was not intended as a reference implementation of a RISC-V microprocessor, but is considered as a reference by many.

As Rocket was a bit too advanced for education, a group in Berkeley developed the Sodor family of RISC-V processors. The Sodor project[10] is an open-source initiative that contains educational RISC-V processor cores. The cores range from a single-stage, 2-stage, 3-stage, up to a classic 5-stage version. Sodor is written in Chisel. However, some of the code is quite advanced, such as Scala code, which is not an easy read for a beginner of computer architecture and Chisel. Furthermore, the Sodor project is no longer self-contained. It needs the The Chipyard SoC generator itself has an elaborate setup. In contrast to Sodor, Wildcat is available in a standalone, and we have put effort into producing readable code instead of showing off with clever but hard-to-read solutions. Furthermore, Sodor cannot easily be used in an FPGA, as it depends on asynchronous memories:

> All processors talk to a simple scratchpad memory (asynchronous, single-cycle), with no backing outer memory.... Programs are loaded in via a Host-target Interface (HTIF) port (while the core is kept in reset), effectively making the scratchpads 3-port memories (instruction, data, HTIF).

YARVI (Yet Another RISC-V Implementation)[11] by Tommy Thorn was probably the first RISC-V implementation that could be synthesized into an FPGA (originally released in 2014). The first implementation was a multi-cycle version, followed by a pipelined version. The current version of YARVI, called YARVI2, is an 8-stage pipeline with an effort on branch prediction. The website reports a maximum clock frequency of over 100 MHz on a Cyclone V. YARVI, with its 8-stage in-order pipeline, shows a path for future versions of Wildcat.

PULPino [6] is a 32-bit RISC-V microcontroller system developed at ETH Zurich. It is written in SystemVerilog in a conservative style (e.g., not using structures but individual signals.) We appreciate that project but consider it too complex for education or research.

---

[10] https://github.com/ucb-bar/riscv-sodor.
[11] https://github.com/tommythorn/yarvi.

Ibex [4][12] is a two-stage pipeline with an additional clock cycle for memory access. Therefore, similar in design to our Wildcat project. The pipeline can be extended with a write-back stage. The documentation states:

> Ibex can be configured to have a third pipeline stage (Writeback), which has major effects on performance and instruction behavior. The details of its impact are not yet documented here.

PicoRV32[13] is a RISC-V implementation optimized for small size and a high clocking frequency but not for execution speed. The application area is as an auxiliary processor in FPGA or ASIC designs. The focus on high clock frequency shall simplify the integration into existing designs without the need for clock domain crossing. The implementation is sequential, with instructions taking between 3 and 14 clock cycles. The single Verilog file picorv32.v is about 3000 lines of Verilog code, which is not an easy read.

VexiiRiscv[14] is a RISC-V implementation in Spinal HDL, which is similar to Chisel. VexiiRiscv is highly configurable with the number of pipeline stages and the RISC-V extensions supported. The configuration is elegantly described in plugins. However, this makes the code base a bit harder to read than the Chisel code of Wildcat. However, comparing the generated VexiiRisc with the "manually" coded Wildcat is an interesting future work.

RISC-V processors are specialized for different domains. For example, MINOTAuR [8] is a time-predictable RISC-V core aiming to be used in real-time systems. Although Wildcat's focus is currently as an educational RISC-V core, we plan to add features from the T-CREST platform [19] to use it in real-time systems.

Ripes [14] is a graphical simulator for different configurations of a RISC-V pipeline. Morten developed Ripes while he was still a student at DTU. We use Ripes to educate students in computer architecture. Ripes seems to have become the most used RISC-V simulator to teach computer architecture. Another RISC-V simulator is WebRISC-V [7]. The simulator was originally developed for MIPS and has been adapted to the RISC-V instruction set.

There are many RISC-V implementations, both open-source and commercial closed-source. Describing them all would result in a long survey paper. A small set of application class RISC-V implementations has been compared [5] concerning performance, area, and power.

5.1 Source Access

Wildcat is available in open source on GitHub: https://github.com/schoeberl/wildcat.

---

[12] https://github.com/lowRISC/ibex.
[13] https://github.com/YosysHQ/picorv32.
[14] https://github.com/SpinalHDL/VexiiRiscv.

6 Conclusion

This paper presents Wildcat, a RISC-V implementation aiming for simplicity and to be used in education. We designed and coded three RISC pipelines with 3, 4, and 5 stages. The 3-stage pipeline is superior to the other version because of lower resource requirements and higher performance (maximum frequency). This result is counterintuitive, as pipelining aims for higher frequencies. However, longer pipelines need more forwarding paths to the ALU, which hurts the critical path in the execution stage. We conclude that the classic 5-stage pipeline organization, taught in computer architecture classes worldwide, is not the sweet spot for short pipeline organizations. Neither for teaching nor for small embedded processors.

Acknowledgment. This work has received funding from the European Union's Health and Digital Executive Agency (HaDEA) with the Edu4Chip project, under grant agreement no. 101123086. I would like to thank Tommy Thorn for the ongoing, inspiring, and enjoyable discussions of RISC pipeline organizations. While this paper explores shorter pipelines, Tommy works towards longer (in-order) pipelines to achieve a high clock frequency. We will follow his direction in future work.

References

1. Asanovic, K., et al.: The rocket chip generator. Technical report UCB/EECS-2016-17, EECS Department, University of California, Berkeley (2016)
2. Bachrach, J., et al.: Chisel: constructing hardware in a scala embedded language. In: The 49th Annual Design Automation Conference (DAC 2012), pp. 1216–1225. ACM, San Francisco (2012)
3. Cook, H., Terpstra, W., Lee, Y.: Diplomatic design patterns: a TileLink case study. In: 1st Workshop on Computer Architecture Research with RISC-V, vol. 23 (2017)
4. Davide Schiavone, P., et al.: Slow and steady wins the race? a comparison of ultra-low-power risc-v cores for internet-of-things applications. In: 2017 27th International Symposium on Power and Timing Modeling, Optimization and Simulation (PATMOS), pp. 1–8. https://doi.org/10.1109/PATMOS.2017.8106976
5. Dörflinger, A., et al.: A comparative survey of open-source application-class risc-v processor implementations. In: Proceedings of the 18th ACM International Conference on Computing Frontiers (2021)
6. Gautschi, M., et al.: Near-threshold risc-v core with DSP extensions for scalable IoT endpoint devices. IEEE Trans. Very Large Scale Integr. (VLSI) Systems **25**(10), 2700–2713 (2017). https://doi.org/10.1109/TVLSI.2017.2654506
7. Giorgi, R., Mariotti, G.: Webrisc-v: a web-based education-oriented risc-v pipeline simulation environment. In: ACM Workshop on Computer Architecture Education (WCAE-19) (2019)
8. Gruin, A., Carle, T., Rochange, C., Cassé, H.: Speculative execution and timing predictability in an open source risc-v core. In: IEEE Real-Time Systems Symposium (RTSS) (2021)
9. Harris, S., Harris, D.: Digital Design and Computer Architecture. Elsevier Science, RISC-V Edition (2021)
10. Hennessy, J., Patterson, D.: Computer Architecture: A Quantitative Approach, 4th ed. Morgan Kaufmann Publishers (2006)

11. Hennessy, J.L., Jouppi, N.P., Baskett, F., Gill, J., Towle, R.: Mips: a microprocessor architecture, pp. 17–22 (1982). https://doi.org/10.1145/1014194.800930
12. Patterson, D.A., Ditzel, D.R.: The case for the reduced instruction set computer
13. Patterson, D.A., Sequin, C.H.: RISC I: a reduced instruction set VLSI computer. In: Proceedings of the 8th annual symposium on Computer Architecture, ISCA 1981, pp. 443–457. IEEE Computer Society Press, Los Alamitos (1981)
14. Petersen, M.B.: Ripes: a visual computer architecture simulator. In: 2021 ACM/IEEE Workshop on Computer Architecture Education (WCAE) (2021)
15. Schoeberl, M.: A Java processor architecture for embedded real-time systems. J. Syst. Architect. **54**(1–2), 265–286 (2008). https://doi.org/10.1016/j.sysarc.2007.06.001
16. Schoeberl, M.: Digital Design with Chisel. Kindle Direct Publishing (2019). https://github.com/schoeberl/chisel-book
17. Schoeberl, M.: The educational risc-v microprocessor wildcat. In: Proceedings of the Sixth Workshop on Open-Source EDA Technology (WOSET) (2024)
18. Schoeberl, M., Puffitsch, W., Hepp, S., Huber, B., Prokesch, D.: Patmos: a time-predictable microprocessor. Real-Time Syst. **54**(2), 389–423 (2018). https://doi.org/10.1007/s11241-018-9300-4
19. Schoeberl, M., Silva, C., Rocha, A.: T-CREST: a time-predictable multi-core platform for aerospace applications. In: Proceedings of Data Systems In Aerospace (DASIA 2014). Warsaw, Poland (2014)
20. Venn, M.: Tiny tapeout: a shared silicon tape out platform accessible to everyone. IEEE Solid-State Circ. Mag. **16**(2), 20–29 (2024). https://doi.org/10.1109/MSSC.2024.3381097
21. Waterman, A.: Design of the RISC-V Instruction Set Architecture. Ph.D. thesis, EECS Department, University of California, Berkeley (2016)

Special Track on Organic Computing (OC)

Location-Based Probabilistic Load Forecasting of Electric Vehicle Charging Sites: Deep Transfer Learning with Multi-quantile Temporal Convolutional Network

Mohammad Wazed Ali[1]({{:}}), Mohammad Asif Ibna Mustafa[1,2], Md. Aukerul Moin Shuvo[3], and Bernhard Sick[1]

[1] Intelligent Embedded Systems (IES), University of Kassel, Kassel, Germany
{wazed.ali,bsick}@uni-kassel.de
[2] Technical University of Munich, Munich, Germany
asif.mustafa@tum.de
[3] Rajshahi University of Engineering and Technology, Rajshahi, Bangladesh
1603061@student.ruet.ac.bd

Abstract. Electrification of vehicles is a potential way of reducing fossil fuel usage and thus lessening environmental pollution. Electric Vehicles (EVs) of various types for different transport modes (including air, water, and land) are evolving. Moreover, different EV user groups (commuters, commercial or domestic users, drivers) may use different charging infrastructures (public, private, home, and workplace) at various times. Therefore, usage patterns and energy demand are very stochastic. Characterizing and forecasting the charging demand of these diverse EV usage profiles is essential in preventing power outages. Previously developed data-driven load models are limited to specific use cases and locations. None of these models are simultaneously adaptive enough to transfer knowledge of day-ahead forecasting among EV charging sites of diverse locations, trained with limited data, and cost-effective. This article presents a location-based load forecasting of EV charging sites using a deep Multi-Quantile Temporal Convolutional Network (MQ-TCN) to overcome the limitations of earlier models. We conducted our experiments on data from four charging sites, namely Caltech, JPL, Office-1, and NREL, which have diverse EV user types like students, full-time and part-time employees, random visitors, etc. With a Prediction Interval Coverage Probability (PICP) score of 93.62%, our proposed deep MQ-TCN model exhibited a remarkable 28.93% improvement over the XGBoost model for a day-ahead load forecasting at the JPL charging site. By transferring knowledge with the inductive Transfer Learning (TL) approach, the MQ-TCN model achieved a 96.88% PICP score for the load forecasting task at the NREL site using only two weeks of data.

Keywords: Electric Vehicle (EV) · EV charging demand · Deep learning for EVs · Location-based EV charging site forecasting ·

Probabilistic EV load forecasting · Multi Quantile regression · Transfer learning · Multivariate Timeseries Analysis

1 Introduction

In recent years, electric car sales and uses have experienced exponential growth, with around 14 million new electric cars sold alone in 2023 and expected to reach 17 million in 2024 [15]. This eagerness to transform the transport sector with EVs and increase the share of renewable energy to meet the Paris Agreement [24] brings unique challenges, such as power outages due to excessive energy demand. Uncontrolled charging and grid instability [9] may result from the lack of fixed charging behavior for EVs. Additionally, integrated renewable energy sources depend highly on weather and other climate-related factors [1]. Therefore, stakeholders such as EV charging station operators, energy traders and energy producers need to know in advance the aggregated energy demand of a charging station at a nearby time or for special occasions such as holidays in order to develop incentive pricing strategies or to charge EVs intelligently [27].

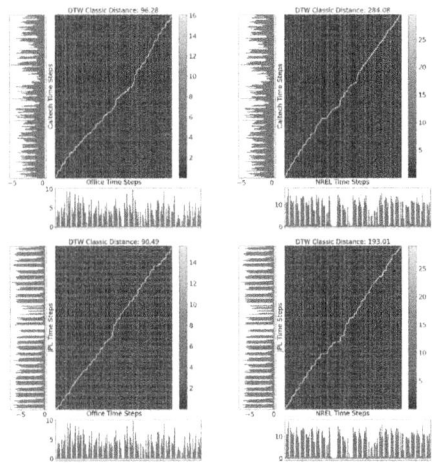 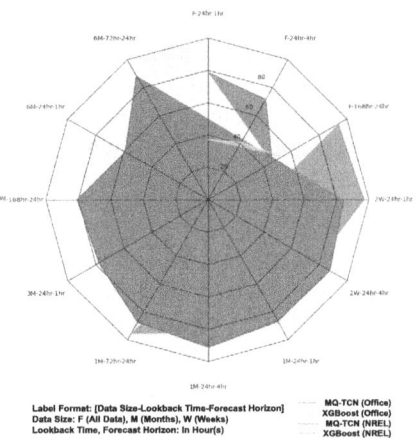

(a) Similarity Distance Measurement between Two EV Charging Sites using DTW method.

(b) Load Forecasting at JPL and NREL EV Charging Sites using Deep MQ-TCN with Inductive Transfer Learning.

Fig. 1. Comparison of DTW Similarity and Load Forecasting Performance at EV Charging Sites.

Many past research works based on statistical or machine learning-based specialized load models failed due to the lack of adaptability and inability to model complex interactions among heterogeneous temporal features and irregular energy usage patterns [12]. Some models are very sensitive to outliers [19], and some can not handle large datasets well [28]. Researchers have recently adopted deep learning (DL) based load models due to their success in related fields. However, much of this DL research relied on large amounts of data and computing power, made predictions without uncertainty, and lacked self-adaptation in different locations. Additionally, these models frequently consider only numerical and temporal features while disregarding informative high-cardinal categorical features.

To address above mentioned limitations of earlier developed models, in this article we consider to follow the approaches and techniques from the field of organic computing (OC) to develop highly self-adaptive, self-optimizing learning models for load forecasting tasks. The main goal of OC is to build systems inspired by natural (biological) systems with self-x properties such as self-adaptive, self-organizing, self-optimizing, self-healing, etc. [20]. Quantile regression combined with an inductive transfer learning approach promotes and exhibits the core principles of OC, like self-adaptation, resilience to noise and uncertainty, etc. Instead of focusing on central tendency or a single best model using mean regression for forecasting, quantile regression provides adaptive modeling by estimating different quantiles via conditional functions. This gives a more detailed and comprehensive view of possible outcomes and can handle heteroscedasticity. We consider inductive Transfer Learning (TL) from a knowledge-transferring perspective among geographically separated charging sites to ensure self-adaptive properties in the models. In this research, we proposed Multi-Quantile TCN (MQ-TCN), an architecture described briefly in Sect. 2 and novel in the e-mobility domain for forecasting load of EV charging sites, incorporating quantile regression techniques and TCN capabilities. We used charging data from four sites (Caltech, JPL, Office-1, and NREL [21]) and the primary dataset, 'ACN' [18]. Experimental evaluation of these datasets using the proposed MQ-TCN architecture in comparison to the XGBoost [8] and Deep Auto-Regressive Recurrent Networks (DeepAR [11]) models leads to the following:

- **Efficient day-ahead load forecasting of EV charging sites** has been achieved with an impressive Prediction Interval Coverage Probability (PICP) score of 93.62% our proposed probabilistic MQ-TCN architecture, as shown in Fig. 1b
- **We are the first** to our knowledge to propose the inductive TL approach with multi-step multi quantile regression and DL architecture (e.g., multivariate TCN) to forecast day-ahead load for geographically separated EV charging sites with few computational resources. Our pre-trained MQ-TCN model achieved a 96.88% PICP score for hourly load prediction at the NREL site and 91.04% for a 4-hour prediction at the Office-1 site using only 2 weeks of historical charging session data.
- **To capture the uncertainty** of the model's generated load forecasts of EV charging sites, our utilized PICP and Winkler Score (WS) metrics efficiently estimate uncertainties jointly by quantifying accurate forecasting within efficient prediction intervals.

– **By investigating the impact** of data size, lookback period, and forecasting horizon time for load forecasting task via experimental evaluation, our proposed MQ-TCN vial TL approach reduces the learnable parameter size upto 72% at Office -1 site compensating accuracy only 5% compared to JPL site.

In this article, Sect. 2 discusses related research in e-mobility. Section 3 gives an overview of the proposed MQ-TCN model and discusses TL settings applied in this research. Section 4 presents details of the experimental settings, evaluation measures with results, and analysis. Section 5 concludes this research article and describes future work.

2 Related Work

E-mobility has become a prominent field in recent years, and forecasting the energy demand of charging sites has become an essential area of research. In this paper [26], EV charging demand forecasting models were developed for a day-ahead horizon and 15-minute resolution. The models incorporated calendar and weather data, and the LSTM model was used. The authors of [23] evaluated the use of deep neural networks (DNNs) and tree-based machine learning models for forecasting energy demand at public EV charging stations and conclude that tree-based models outperform DNNs in accuracy and error metrics. The authors of [23] also studied how traffic, crowd distribution, weather, and charging station distribution affect charging demand [10]. In the deep learning model family, transformers perform better in e-mobility energy demand forecasting [17]. Probabilistic forecasting is an exciting research field that predicts the charging demand for e-mobility. Machine Theory of Mind Based Quantile Forecast Network (MBQFN) framework has proven to perform better than existing DeepAR, ARX-GARCH, DLQR, Persistence, and T-CKDE [14]. Prior to this research article, a comprehensive discussion of the research challenges and potential approaches to adaptive load forecasting has been presented in [1]. In an investigation of [29], Bayesian deep learning and quantile regression methods enhanced load forecasting accuracy in EV charging stations. This approach outperforms traditional methods in dealing with uncertainties. Much earlier research examined electricity load forecasting using convolutional neural networks (CNNs) [7]. Recently, some research has been conducted on the transfer of knowledge in e-mobility, where data is limited in the target domain. The results indicated that using CNN has improved accuracy in predicting EV charging demand and network voltage profiles while reducing computational requirements for power grid operations, but it is unable to handle uncertainty [5]. A novel framework for solving artificial intelligence-supported decision-making, forecasting, and reasoning tasks in the mobility domain is being researched [2]. In [22], XGBoost was used alongside other algorithms on the ACN dataset for both classification and regression tasks with good scores at AUC, F1 Score, R, and RMSE metrics. It lacked adaptability and could not handle uncertainty. In [3], XGBoost predicted single-step charging demand forecasting at public stations.

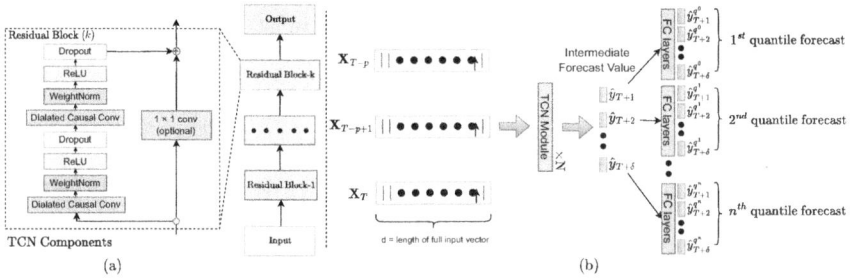

Fig. 2. Architecture of the Multivariate Multi-Quantile Temporal Convolutional Network (MQ-TCN) (a) TCN components [4]; (b) TCN processes input sequences to create intermediate forecasts, followed by Fully Connected (FC) layers for quantile predictions.

3 Methodology

In this section, we define the related terms, methods and then describe our proposed architecture.

3.1 Multivariate MQ-TCN for Multi-step Forecasting

The TCN is a type of Convolutional Neural Network (CNN) designed for sequence modeling. It uses causal and dilated convolutions to ensure predictions rely solely on past data, eliminating future information leakage [4]. Dilated convolutions enhance the receptive field by skipping input values, enabling TCNs to handle long-range dependencies effectively. The architecture features residual blocks with two dilated convolutional layers, Rectified Linear Unit (ReLU) activation, dropout, and optional 1×1 convolutions for dimensionality adjustment as shown in Fig. 2(a) [13]. This design facilitates efficient feature extraction across various time scales, making TCNs ideal for multivariate and multi-step forecasting.

For a multivariate input sequence $\mathbf{X}_{T-p}, \mathbf{X}_{T-p+1}, \ldots, \mathbf{X}_T$, where p represents the number of past observations and $\mathbf{X}_t \in \mathbb{R}^d$ is a d-dimensional non-predictive feature vector at time t, the TCN processes the data through stacked dilated convolutional layers. It generates intermediate forecasting values, which are then passed through fully connected (FC) layers, each specializing in predicting a specific quantile of the forecast distribution. As illustrated in Fig. 2(b), the model performs δ-step forecasting, generating predictions for multiple quantiles at each step. For a forecast horizon of δ, the first quantile forecasts are given by: $\hat{y}_{T+1}^{q^0}, \hat{y}_{T+2}^{q^0}, \ldots, \hat{y}_{T+\delta}^{q^0}$; for the second quantile by $\hat{y}_{T+1}^{q^1}, \hat{y}_{T+2}^{q^1}, \ldots, \hat{y}_{T+\delta}^{q^1}$; and so on, up to the n-th quantile. Here, y_{T+i} is the ground truth target value at time $T+i$ (for $i = 1, 2, \ldots, \delta$), and q denotes the quantile level (e.g., $q = 0.1$ for the 10th percentile, $q = 0.5$ for the median). Then the model is trained using the Pinball Loss function L_{PB}, which penalizes forecast errors based on the quantile level q. The loss for each forecast horizon i is given by:

$$L_{PB}(q, y_{T+i}, \hat{y}^q_{T+i}) = \begin{cases} (1-q) \cdot (y_{T+i} - \hat{y}^q_{T+i}) & \text{if } \hat{y}^q_{T+i} \geq y_{T+i}, \\ q \cdot (y_{T+i} - \hat{y}^q_{T+i}) & \text{if } \hat{y}^q_{T+i} < y_{T+i}, \end{cases} \quad (1)$$

This architecture provides robust probabilistic forecasting, capturing the uncertainty in future values, which is essential for dynamic applications like e-mobility demand forecasting.

3.2 Transfer Forecasting Knowledge with Inductive TL

TL transfers knowledge from one EV load forecasting model, using abundant data, to forecast load at geographically separated charging sites with limited data. Based on existing literature, we define TL and related terms as follows:

A sample data point at time t with d non-predictive features is represented as $\mathbf{X}_t \in \mathbb{R}^d$. A domain D is defined by: (i) the feature space $\mathbf{X} \in \mathbb{R}^{(p \times (d+1))}$, including both non-predictive and target features, and (ii) the marginal probability distribution $P(X)$, where $X = \{x_i \mid x_i \in \mathbf{X}, i = 1, \ldots, d\}$. Thus, a domain can be expressed as $D = \{\mathbf{X}, P(X)\}$. A learning task $\mathcal{T}$ is defined by the label space $\mathcal{Y}$ and a predictive function $f(\cdot)$, represented as $\mathcal{T} = \{\mathcal{Y}, f(\cdot)\}$, where $f(\cdot)$ is learned from training data $\{(\mathbf{X}_i, y_i) \mid \mathbf{X}_i \in X, y_i \in Y\}$. Inductive Transfer Learning (TL) can be defined generally as follows:

Definition (Inductive Transfer Learning): Given a source domain D_{sd} and learning task $\mathcal{T}_{sd}$, and a target domain D_{td} and learning task $\mathcal{T}_{td}$, the goal of inductive TL is to improve learning of the target predictive function $f_{td}(\cdot)$ in D_{td} using knowledge from D_{sd} and $\mathcal{T}_{sd}$, where $\mathcal{T}_{sd} \neq \mathcal{T}_{td}$.

In our research experiment, we focus on a non-linear deep learning model for load forecasting, named MQ-TCN. The source feature space ($\mathbf{X}_{sd} \in \mathbb{R}^{(p \times d)}$) and target feature space ($\mathbf{X}_{td} \in \mathbb{R}^{(\delta \times 1)}$) use a lookback window of length p with d-dimensional predictive source features having δ forecast horizons. The marginal distributions for the source and target variables (future energy consumption) differ: $P_{sd}(\mathbf{X}) \neq P_{td}(\mathbf{X})$. Data from geographically separated EV charging sites leads to non-identical distributions ($D_{sd} \neq D_{td}$) due to varying energy consumption profiles influenced by local factors. The source ($\mathcal{Y}_{sd}$) and target ($\mathcal{Y}_{td}$) label spaces correspond to forecast horizons of length δ. As the predictive function $f(\cdot)$ transfers knowledge in a transfer learning (TL) setting, the source and target forecasting functions remain distinct: $f_{sd}(\cdot) \neq f_{td}(\cdot)$. We investigate both homogeneous and heterogeneous TL, where the target task ($\mathcal{T}_{td}$) involves forecasting horizons of length δ. We employed a 'head replacement' approach in our inductive TL experiments, covering both homogeneous and heterogeneous scenarios. In the heterogeneous cases, the label spaces of source and target domains differ. This method allows for flexibility in experimenting with load forecasting tasks for geographically separated charging infrastructure at various time horizons ($\mathcal{T}_{td} \in \mathbb{R}^{1,4,24}$).

4 Experimental Setup and Evaluation

This section details the datasets, experimental setup, and evaluation metrics used in our research.

4.1 Data

Table 1 summarizes the ACN and NREL datasets. ACN includes EV charging sessions from Caltech, JPL, and Office-1 [18]. Additional data from Caltech Garage-2, N Wilson Garage, and S Wilson Garage added 19,470 sessions and increased the total to 150 charging stations with 13 features. JPL has fewer stations but more sessions, while Office-1 has 8 stations with significantly fewer sessions. NREL, spanning 59 months, includes 141 stations and 16 features for comprehensive data collection [21].

Table 1. E-Mobility Dataset Statistics

Charging Sites	# of Charging Stations	# of Charging Sessions	Duration (Months)	# of Features
Caltech	54	31424	40	13
JPL	50	33638	35	13
Office-1	8	1683	30	13
NREL	141	40979	59	16

Figure 3 illustrates energy consumption trends across locations. Peak usage varies by site (Fig. 3a): Caltech during the day, JPL in the early afternoon, Office-1 at midday, and NREL in the early morning. Figure 3b highlights consumption spikes at NREL on Susan B. Anthony Day and Martin Luther King Jr. Day, and at JPL on Veterans Day, while Office-1 shows low holiday usage. Finally, Fig. 3c shows high variability at NREL and consistent consumption at Office-1 over the years.

To prepare the datasets, we addressed missing values, removed anomalies with Facebook Prophet [25], and standardized hourly samples. We applied sine-cosine transformations for cyclic data and normalized numerical features using Min-Max scaling. We reduced the dimensionality of 'StationID' from 186 to 30 unique values using encoding techniques. Low-dimensional categorical features were handled with one-hot encoding for 2–5 unique values and embedding layers for 5–10 unique values. Data was curated to include only records until March 2020 to avoid COVID-19 disruptions.

4.2 Evaluation Metrics

Metrics like PICP, Pinball Loss, WS Score, and Normalized Deviation (ND) were used to evaluate the model performance. Pinball Loss is defined in the

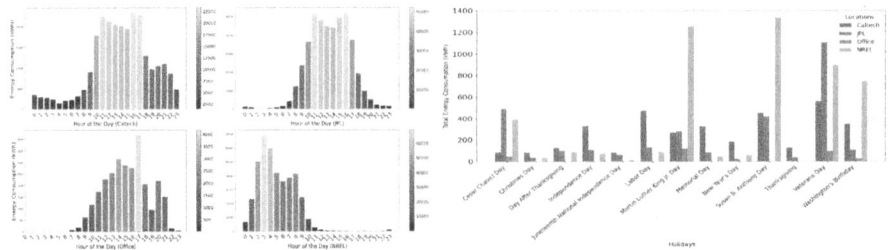

(a) Location-wise Hourly Energy Consumption (KWh).

(b) Location-wise Holiday's Energy Consumption (KWh).

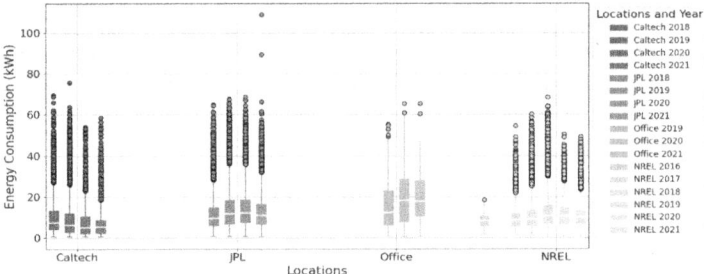

(c) Location-wise Annual Energy Consumption (KWh) Boxplots.

Fig. 3. Energy Consumption Trends and Comparisons for All Locations

Eq. 1, while PICP, WS, and ND are defined as:

$$\text{PICP} = \frac{1}{N} \sum_{i=1}^{N} \varepsilon_i \tag{2}$$

where the variable ε_i is defined as follows:

$$\varepsilon_i = \begin{cases} 1, & \text{if } y_{T+i} \in [L_{T+i,q}, U_{T+i,q}], \\ 0, & \text{if } y_{T+i} \notin [L_{T+i,q}, U_{T+i,q}]. \end{cases} \tag{3}$$

$$WS = \sum_{i=1}^{N} \begin{cases} \gamma, & L_{T+i,q} \leq y_{T+i} \leq U_{T+i,q} \\ \gamma + \frac{2(L_{T+i,q} - y_{T+i})}{\alpha}, & y_{T+i} < L_{T+i,q} \\ \gamma + \frac{2(y_{T+i} - U_{T+i,q})}{\alpha}, & y_{T+i} > U_{T+i,q} \end{cases} \tag{4}$$

$$\text{ND} = \frac{\sum_{i=1}^{N} |y_{T+i} - \hat{y}_{T+i}|}{\sum_{i=1}^{N} |y_{T+i}|} \tag{5}$$

Here, $L_{T+i,q}$ and $U_{T+i,q}$ are the lower and upper bounds of the prediction interval at time $T + i$ for quantile q. The variable ε_i reflects the coverage of prediction intervals, where y_{T+i} is the actual value, and $\hat{y}_{T+i}$ is the forecasted value. N represents the number of evaluation periods, γ is the interval width, and α is set to 0.15.

4.3 Multivariate Multi-step Probabilistic Load Forecasting

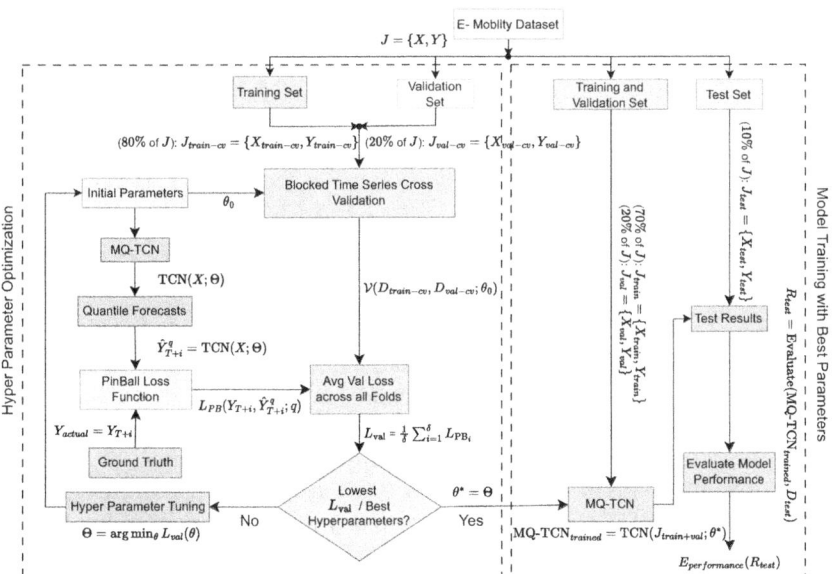

Fig. 4. Experimental Design for MQ-TCN Forecasting in E-Mobility Applications.

We propose the MQ-TCN model and explored XGBoost and DeepAR as baseline forecasting models. Previous research did not consider high cardinal categorical variables along with temporal and numerical features in multivariate, multi-step load forecasting for charging stations. Given our heterogeneous time-series dataset, we modified XGBoost for quantile regression and adjusted the stride size in DeepAR. Our dataset was divided into training, validation, and test sets, as illustrated in Fig. 4. The test set was the last 10% J_{test} of the data, while the remaining data was split into folds for time-series blocked cross-validation, with 80% $J_{train-cv}$ for training and 20% J_{val-cv} for validation. We computed the average validation loss to determine the best hyperparameters, retrained the model using 90% $J_{train+val}$ of $J(X, Y)$, and evaluated the MQ-TCN model on the J_{test} set.

The analysis used lookback periods of 336 and 168 h, and forecasting horizons of 48 and 24 h, resulting in eight configurations for Caltech and JPL, and a total of twelve load forecasting models for three quantiles (0.05, 0.50, 0.90) for source domain. Office-1 was excluded due to very limited samples. XGBoost and DeepAR training used settings based on the best-performing MQ-TCN model, with hyperparameters optimized via Tree-structured Parzen Estimator (TPE) [6]. We compared MQ-TCN and XGBoost using PICP, Pinball Loss, and WS, and MQ-TCN and DeepAR using ND, focusing on 50% quantile predictions.

Table 2. Forecasting Performance Comparison without Transfer Learning (Source Domain).

Caltech							JPL				
Model	PICP	Pin-Ball Loss	WS	ND	Look-back Time	Fore-cast Horizon	Model	PICP	Pin-Ball Loss	WS	ND
MQ-TCN	80.19	3.38	38.90	0.3523	168	24	MQ-TCN	**93.62**	2.28	21.55	0.2226
							XGBoost	64.69	**1.82**	19.58	**0.1770**
							DeepAR	n/a	n/a	n/a	**0.1770**
MQ-TCN	**84.93**	3.47	37.04	0.3602	168	48	MQ-TCN	75.50	2.35	25.04	0.2266
XGBoost	78.96	3.13	33.41	0.3254							
DeepAR	n/a	n/a	n/a	**0.2955**							
MQ-TCN	82.79	3.39	38.94	0.3649	336	24	MQ-TCN	87.85	2.64	20.93	0.2573
MQ-TCN	80.90	**3.04**	**32.37**	0.3261	336	48	MQ-TCN	88.32	1.89	**18.16**	0.1814

Results and Detailed Analysis: Experimental results in Table 2 show significant improvements with our MQ-TCN model compared to the XGBoost baseline across various lookback periods and forecasting horizons. At Caltech site, the MQ-TCN model, utilizing 168 h of historical data to forecast 48 h, achieved a PICP of 84.93%, a 5.97% increase over XGBoost's 78.96% coverage rate. Furthermore, our MQ-TCN model improved a day ahead forecasting by 28.93% at JPL.

4.4 Location Based Load Forecasting Under Data Scarcity

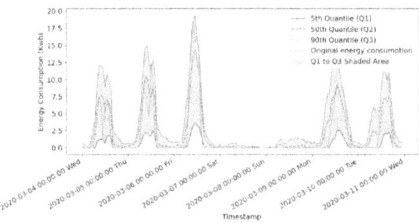
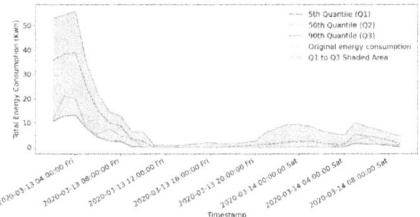
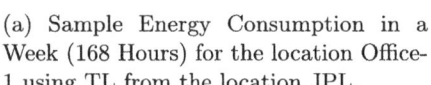

(a) Sample Energy Consumption in a Week (168 Hours) for the location Office-1 using TL from the location JPL.

(b) Sample Energy Consumption in a Single Day (24 Hours) for the location NREL using TL from the location JPL.

Fig. 5. Sample Forecasting of Target Domains: Office-1 and NREL using Transfer Learning.

We conducted experiments to analyze load forecasting task under data scarcity using data from four EV charging stations: Caltech, JPL, Office-1, and NREL. Caltech and JPL have more data than Office-1 and NREL, making knowledge transfer beneficial for load forecasting. In the first stage, we analyzed EV user demographics and charging infrastructure using Dynamic-Time-Warping

(DTW) to assess site similarity, as shown in Fig. 1a. Datasets with lower DTW scores, particularly *JPL-Office-1* and *JPL-NREL*, resemble each other more closely, while higher scores in 'Caltech-Office-1' and *Caltech-NREL* indicate greater dissimilarities. Prioritizing lower DTW scores enhances knowledge transfer and improves model accuracy [16]. Figures 5a and 5b show sample load forecasting results using knowledge transfer, and Fig. 6a indicates that Office-1's prediction errors are closer to zero compared to NREL's. Additionally, Fig. 6b reveals that Office-1 has higher accuracy and less variability in error.

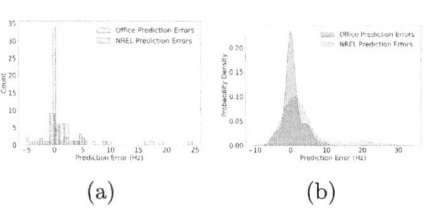 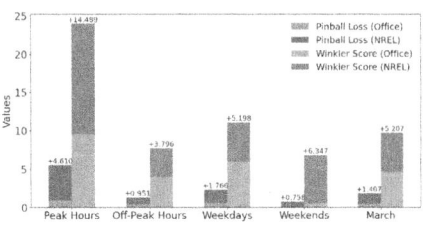

(c) Prediction Error Analysis: Hist. 6a and PDFs 6b.

(d) Pinball Loss and Winkler Score Comparison.

Fig. 6. Comparison of Prediction Error Analysis and Evaluation Metrics for Office-1 and NREL.

Results and Detailed Analysis: Tables 3 and 4 highlight forecasting performance at Office-1 and NREL with inductive TL. The XGBoost model for Office-1 achieved 53.03% PICP in multi-step and 37.24% in single-step forecasting, struggling with shorter data. DeepAR, which does not support single-step forecasting, was outperformed by the MQ-TCN model, achieving 91.04% for multi-step and 86.76% for single-step forecasting using one month of data from Office-1, along with average PICP and ND scores of 83.36% and 0.4813. For NREL, MQ-TCN reached PICP scores of 96.88% for single-step and 95.08% for multi-step, exceeding baseline models.

4.5 Uncertainty Handling and Impact of Variable Data Size, Lookback Period and Forecast Horizon in TL

We experimented with how data size, lookback period, and forecast horizon impact the MQ-TCN model's performance and uncertainty estimation. For Office-1, we used data spans of 6 months, 3 months, 1 month, and 2 weeks, while for NREL, we used 1 month and 2 weeks. We tested lookback periods of 168, 72, and 24 h, and future steps of 24, 4, and 1 for multi-step and single-step predictions.

Table 3. Results of Load Forecasting at Office-1 Site with Inductive TL (Target Domain).

Office-1							
Model	Data Size	Lookback Time	Forecast Horizon	PICP	PinBall Loss	WS	ND
MQ-TCN (JPL-Source)	Full Data	168	24	93.62	2.28	21.55	0.2226
XGBoost		168	24	53.03	0.35	4.27	0.4430
DeepAR				n/a	n/a	n/a	1.0620
XGBoost		72	24	60.45	0.35	3.82	0.4305
DeepAR	Full Data			n/a	n/a	n/a	1.0587
XGBoost		24	4	41.02	0.33	3.48	0.4291
DeepAR		24	1	n/a	n/a	n/a	1.0810
XGBoost		24	1	37.24	0.33	3.62	0.4236
MQ-TCN	2 weeks	24	4	87.50	0.89	8.14	0.4641
		24	1	84.38	0.90	8.83	0.4725
MQ-TCN		72	24	87.30	0.66	6.18	0.4398
	1 month	24	4	**91.04**	0.74	6.03	0.6716
		24	1	**86.76**	0.73	6.21	0.5372
		168	24	80.71	**0.40**	**3.77**	**0.4108**
MQ-TCN	3 months	72	24	86.12	0.61	5.07	0.5862
		24	4	81.02	0.49	5.14	0.4695
		24	1	77.88	0.49	5.44	0.4509
		168	24	**89.23**	0.45	4.67	0.4489
MQ-TCN	6 months	72	24	88.55	0.42	4.25	0.4262
		24	4	84.14	0.45	4.37	0.4434
		24	1	59.08	**0.44**	**4.44**	**0.4353**

Table 4. Results of Load Forecasting at NREL Site with Inductive TL (Target Domain).

NREL							
Model	Data Size	Lookback Time	Forecast Horizon	PICP	PinBall Loss	WS	ND
MQ-TCN (JPL-Source)	Full Data	168	24	93.62	2.28	21.55	0.2226
XGBoost		168	24	46.04	2.04	22.91	0.3112
DeepAR				n/a	n/a	n/a	1.0939
XGBoost		72	24	80.21	1.82	18.74	0.2944
DeepAR	Full Data			n/a	n/a	n/a	1.0562
XGBoost		24	4	71.49	1.73	17.98	0.2681
DeepAR		24	1	n/a	n/a	n/a	1.0520
XGBoost		24	1	78.65	1.74	17.49	0.2718
MQ-TCN	2 weeks	24	4	77.42	3.16	23.26	2.0426
		24	1	**96.88**	1.86	9.78	1.2854
MQ-TCN		72	24	**95.08**	4.28	28.07	0.7647
	1 month	24	4	82.09	**1.92**	**20.07**	**0.5969**
		24	1	85.29	**1.01**	**9.31**	**0.3166**

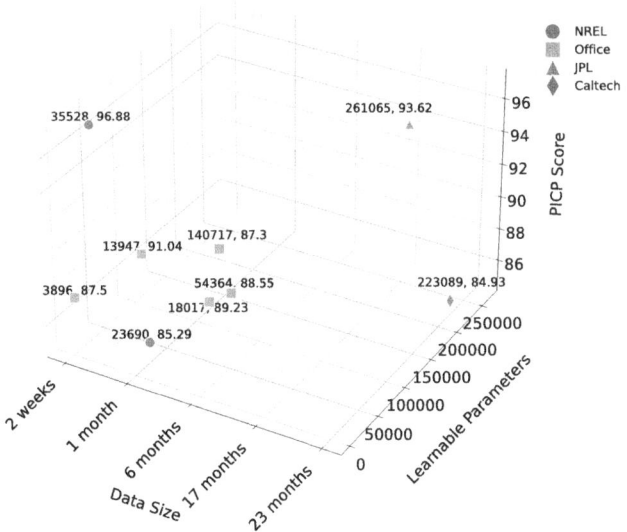

Fig. 7. Comparison of PICP Scores and Learnable Parameters across Different Data Sizes and Locations

Results and Detailed Analysis: The bar chart in Fig. 6d shows the accuracy of energy consumption predictions for Office-1 and NREL. Office-1 has a PICP score of 89.23%, indicating reliable forecasts and a solid energy management strategy. NREL, with a PICP score of 96.88%, shows effective forecasting but less certainty due to a wider prediction interval. Overall, Office-1's model is more precise for its energy management needs. Our analysis found no clear connection between lookback size, forecast horizon, and accuracy. For example, at Office-1, extending the lookback from 72 to 168 h decreased forecast accuracy as shown in 3. The scatter plot in Fig. 7 compares locations (NREL, Office-1, JPL, Caltech) based on data size, learnable parameters, and PICP scores. NREL's scores are 96.88% and 85.29%; Office-1 ranges from 87.3% to 91.04%, JPL scores 93.62%, and Caltech 84.93%. Interestingly, target sites like Office-1 and NREL have fewer learnable parameters than source sites but still achieve competitive PICP scores, reducing computation costs without compromising forecasting efficiency.

5 Conclusion and Future Work

We successfully implemented the MQ-TCN architecture for EV load forecasting across multiple geographically separate charging sites, even with limited data. Our evaluations demonstrated its effectiveness in transferring knowledge among charging stations and its adaptability, achieving accurate forecasts with just two weeks of training data (336 data instances). While the MQ-TCN model showed impressive results under data constraints, it encountered challenges in some novel situations. We plan to address this by exploring continual representation learning and incorporating meta-information in future work.

Acknowledgments. This work results from the project *Selbst-Adaptives Lademanagement für Ladeinfrastruktur* (SALM 01IS20098B) funded by BMBF (German Federal Ministry of Education and Research).

References

1. Ali, M.W.: Deep adaptive knowledge-aware learning for e-mobility. In: Tomforde, S., Krupitzer, C. (eds.) Organic Computing - Doctoral Dissertation Colloquium 2022, p. 139–155. kassel university press (2022)
2. Ali, M.W.: Heterogeneous multi-source deep adaptive knowledge-aware learning for e-mobility. In: IEEE International Conference on Autonomic Computing and Self-Organizing Systems Companion (ACSOS-C), pp. 57–60. IEEE (2022)
3. Almaghrebi, A., Aljuheshi, F., Rafaie, M., James, K., Alahmad, M.: Data-driven charging demand prediction at public charging stations using supervised machine learning regression methods. Energies **13**(16), 4231 (2020)
4. Bai, S., Kolter, J.Z., Koltun, V.: An empirical evaluation of generic convolutional and recurrent networks for sequence modeling. arXiv preprint arXiv:1803.01271 (2018)
5. Banda, P., Bhuiyan, M.A., Hasan, K.N., Zhang, K.: Assessment of hybrid transfer learning method for forecasting EV profile and system voltage using limited EV charging data. Sustain. Energy, Grids Netw. **36**, 101191 (2023). https://doi.org/10.1016/j.segan.2023.101191
6. Bergstra, J., Bardenet, R., Bengio, Y., Kégl, B.: Algorithms for hyper-parameter optimization. In: Advances in Neural Information Processing Systems, vol. 24 (2011)
7. Cai, L., Gu, J., Jin, Z.: Two-layer transfer-learning-based architecture for short-term load forecasting. IEEE Trans. Industr. Inf. **16**(3), 1722–1732 (2020). https://doi.org/10.1109/TII.2019.2924326
8. Chen, T., et al.: Xgboost: extreme gradient boosting. R package version 0.4-2 **1**(4), 1–4 (2015)
9. Clement-Nyns, K., Haesen, E., Driesen, J.: The impact of charging plug-in hybrid electric vehicles on a residential distribution grid. IEEE Trans. Power Syst. **25**(1), 371–380 (2010). https://doi.org/10.1109/TPWRS.2009.2036481
10. Feng, H.J., Xi, L.C., Jun, Y.Z., Ling, Y.X., Jun, H.: Review of electric vehicle charging demand forecasting based on multi-source data. In: 2020 IEEE Sustainable Power and Energy Conference (iSPEC), pp. 139–146 (2020). https://doi.org/10.1109/iSPEC50848.2020.9351008
11. Flunkert, V., Salinas, D., Gasthaus, J.: Deepar: probabilistic forecasting with autoregressive recurrent networks. ArXiv **abs/1704.04110** (2017)
12. Frendo, O., Gaertner, N., Stuckenschmidt, H.: Improving smart charging prioritization by predicting electric vehicle departure time. IEEE Trans. Intell. Transp. Syst. **22**, 6646–6653 (2020)
13. He, K., Zhang, X., Ren, S., Sun, J.: Deep residual learning for image recognition. In: 2016 IEEE Conference on Computer Vision and Pattern Recognition (CVPR), pp. 770–778 (2016). https://doi.org/10.1109/CVPR.2016.90

14. Hu, T., Liu, K., Ma, H.: Probabilistic electric vehicle charging demand forecast based on deep learning and machine theory of mind. In: 2021 IEEE Transportation Electrification Conference & Expo (ITEC), pp. 795–799. IEEE (2021)
15. International Energy Agency (IEA): Global ev outlook 2024 (2024). https://www.iea.org/reports/global-ev-outlook-2024 , https://www.iea.org/reports/global-ev-outlook-2022. Accessed 10 May 2024
16. Ismail Fawaz, H., Forestier, G., Weber, J., Idoumghar, L., Muller, P.A.: Transfer learning for time series classification. In: 2018 IEEE International Conference on Big Data (Big Data), pp. 1367–1376 (2018). https://doi.org/10.1109/BigData.2018.8621990
17. Koohfar, S., Woldemariam, W., Kumar, A.: Prediction of electric vehicles charging demand: a transformer-based deep learning approach. Sustainability **15**(3) (2023). https://doi.org/10.3390/su15032105, https://www.mdpi.com/2071-1050/15/3/2105
18. Lee, Z.J., Li, T., Low, S.H.: ACN-Data: analysis and applications of an open EV charging dataset. In: Proceedings of the Tenth International Conference on Future Energy Systems. e-Energy 2019 (2019)
19. Liang, M., Li, W., Yu, J., Shi, L.: Kernel-based electric vehicle charging load modeling with improved Latin hypercube sampling. In: 2015 IEEE Power & Energy Society General Meeting, pp. 1–5. IEEE (2015)
20. Müller-Schloer, C., Schmeck, H., Ungerer, T.: Organic Computing – A Paradigm Shift for Complex Systems. Springer (2011)
21. Neuman, C., Meintz, A., Jun, M.: Workplace charging data collection and behavior. Technical report, National Renewable Energy Lab.(NREL), Golden, CO (United States) (2021)
22. Ostermann, A., Fabel, Y., Ouan, K., Koo, H.: Forecasting charging point occupancy using supervised learning algorithms. Energies **15**(9), 3409 (2022)
23. Rathore, H., Meena, H.K., Jain, P.: Forecasting of EVS charging behavior using deep neural networks. In: 2023 International Conference on Communication, Circuits, and Systems (IC3S), pp. 1–6 (2023). https://doi.org/10.1109/IC3S57698.2023.10169211
24. Singh, B., Majeau-Bettez, G., Strømman, A.H.: Corrigendum to: Hawkins, t. r., b. singh, g. majeau-bettez, and a. h. strømman. 2012. comparative environmental life cycle assessment of conventional and electric vehicles. J. Ind. Ecol. **17**https://doi.org/10.1111/j.1530-9290.2012.00532.x. Journal of Industrial Ecology **17** (2013)
25. Taylor, S.J., Letham, B.: Forecasting at scale. Am. Stat. **72**, 37–45 (2018)
26. Van Kriekinge, G., De Cauwer, C., Sapountzoglou, N., Coosemans, T., Messagie, M.: Day-ahead forecast of electric vehicle charging demand with deep neural networks. World Electr. Veh. J. **12**(4) (2021). https://doi.org/10.3390/wevj12040178, https://www.mdpi.com/2032-6653/12/4/178
27. Vuelvas, J., Ruiz, F., Gruosso, G.: Energy price forecasting for optimal managing of electric vehicle fleet. IET Electr. Syst. Transp. **10**(4), 401–408 (2020)
28. Xydas, E., Marmaras, C.E., Cipcigan, L.M., Hassan, A.S., Jenkins, N.: Forecasting electric vehicle charging demand using support vector machines. 2013 48th International Universities' Power Engineering Conference (UPEC), pp. 1–6 (2013)
29. Zhou, D., et al.: Using Bayesian deep learning for electric vehicle charging station load forecasting. Energies **15**(17) (2022). https://doi.org/10.3390/en15176195, https://www.mdpi.com/1996-1073/15/17/6195

Unsupervised Anomaly Detection in Cellular Modem Metrics Using Deep Autoencoders

Nikita Smirnov[1,2](✉)🆔, Mika Friesenborg[1]🆔, and Sven Tomforde[1]🆔

[1] Kiel University, Christian-Albrechts-Platz 4, 24118 Kiel, Germany
nikita.smirnov@cs.uni-kiel.de, mika.friesenborg@stu.uni-kiel.de,
st@informatik.uni-kiel.de
[2] ADDIX GmbH, Kaistr. 101, 24114 Kiel, Germany

Abstract. This paper addresses the challenge of unsupervised anomaly detection in key metrics related to data transmission in fourth and fifth-generation (4G and 5G) cellular networks, with the main aim of developing a monitoring service that can alert on abnormal behavior in real-time. The dataset used in this research includes channel and upper-layer performance metrics collected from several cellular modems deployed on a remote-controlled ship. Deep autoencoders (DAE) were selected as the main approach due to their ability to detect point, contextual, and collective anomalies. Several unsupervised machine learning algorithms and preprocessing techniques were applied and optimized to overcome the problem of using DAEs for unsupervised anomaly detection, namely their need for training data containing no known anomalies. Different types of deep autoencoders, including classical, variational, denoising, and robust models, as well as different neural network architectures, consisting of linear and recurrent layers, along with the additional loss function terms, such as contractive and sparse regularizations, have been explored. The presented approach is evaluated using anomalies generated by unsupervised algorithms and special samples that introduce noise and shuffling into normal data, thus affecting the data distribution. Finally, a post-analysis is performed by adding contextual information to the data to help interpret the detected anomalies introducing another layer of validation to the presented approach.

Keywords: anomaly detection · deep autoencoders · unsupervised learning · cellular networks · wireless router · 5G networks · remote-controlled unit · organic computing

1 Introduction

Organic Computing (OC) is a research area dedicated to enhancing the controllability and resilience of complex technical systems by enabling them to self-adapt, self-organize, and even self-heal. In OC systems, the responsibility for managing unforeseen conditions shifts from human operators to the systems themselves, which leverage technologies such as machine learning (ML) and deep learning (DL) to make autonomous decisions based on defined objective functions [14].

A highly topical application area for OC technologies is autonomous systems, such as autonomous shipping. In this paper, the OC entity is represented by the remote-controlled research ship "MS Wavelab" (see Fig. 1) that sails in a dense port area as a prototype for future autonomous public water transportation [4]. As part of the research projects, this ferry is equipped with fifth-generation (5G) wireless communication devices to transmit its sensor data to the land-based remote control center. The main research goal is to use the capabilities of the **public 5G networks** for more effective and reliable transmission of various sensor data.

The unit has multiple wireless 4/5G-capable modems that enable data transmission over cellular channels. These modems continuously aggregate channel performance metrics such as signal characteristics and various 5G-specific quality indicators, augmented by transmission statistics from the network packet interceptors. Given the dynamic and sometimes unpredictable cellular environment, the characterization of network behavior is critical. Implementing a robust, unsupervised anomaly detection model addresses this need, allowing proactive identification of irregularities that may compromise the communication link. By identifying these anomalies in real-time, the monitoring system can alert operators to take timely corrective action, improving overall system reliability and security.

This research contributes to the field of OC by advancing real-time anomaly detection in cellular data, a critical factor improving the reliability and control of remote units within increasingly complex networked systems. Specifically, we:

1. Propose a novel anomaly detection approach based on deep autoencoders (DAEs) with unsupervised pre-training. It effectively detects both point and

Fig. 1. The research ship "MS Wavelab".

contextual anomalies and is rigorously evaluated for robustness under distribution shifts, demonstrating adaptability in dynamic network conditions.
2. Conduct a comprehensive analysis of detected anomalies using expert knowledge and statistical techniques to associate them with a defined set of realtime, observable events, thus increasing the practical applicability of the detection system.
3. Perform empirical data analysis on real-world cellular modem metrics collected from multiple devices installed on a remotely operated research vessel, validating the system in an operational environment.

This paper is organized as follows: Sect. 2 reviews the related work, Sect. 3 presents the dataset, Sect. 4 describes the proposed approach, Sect. 5 addresses evaluation and results and Sect. 6 briefly recaps the content of previous parts and concludes the paper with possible future work.

2 Background and Related Work

Unsupervised Anomaly Detection. attempts to identify unusual patterns in data without labeled examples, i.e., without knowing which samples represent "normal" and "abnormal" behavior. The most common approach is to identify outliers using a particular distance metric. It is further subdivided into density-based methods such as Gaussian mixture models (GMM) or local outlier factor (LOF), neighbor-based approaches such as k-nearest neighbors (kNN), and clustering techniques such as k-means or density-based spatial clustering of applications with noise (DBSCAN). Another group of methods consists of statistical approaches such as principal component analysis (PCA), which reduces dimensionality to highlight variance-driven patterns in the data. The final group is defined as classification-based and includes popular ML algorithms such as isolation forests (IF), which create partitions to isolate outliers, or support vector machines (SVM), which separate outliers by defining boundaries in the feature space [3,8]. These traditional techniques have limitations with high-dimensional, non-linear data, and often require assumptions about data distribution [15].

Autoencoders. (AE) have received considerable attention for their ability to model normal behavior by learning compact representations and to detect anomalies based on reconstruction errors. They represent an artificial neural network, whose architecture consists of an encoder that compresses input data into a low-dimensional representation and a decoder that reconstructs the original input from this compressed form, producing noticeable reconstruction errors for anomalous inputs.

Several types of autoencoders have been proposed in the literature to improve their anomaly detection capabilities. Variational autoencoders (VAE) model data variability probabilistically [10], while denoising autoencoders (DNAE) are designed to handle noisy data by learning to reconstruct clean versions of corrupted inputs [25].

Deep learning has emerged as a powerful alternative to traditional methods due to its ability to learn complex data patterns when they are intricate and non-linear [27]. Deep autoencoders extend the standard AE architecture by stacking multiple layers and sometimes using convolutional (CNN), long short-term memory (LSTM), or other advanced layers instead of fully-connected ones [11].

Despite their advantages, autoencoders face a significant challenge in unsupervised settings, as they rely on the assumption that the training data predominantly represents normal behavior to learn accurate reconstruction. A common solution is to incorporate an additional term into the loss function that iteratively updates an internal measure of sample-wise "normality" to refine the model's focus on "normal" patterns [5,9]. Alternatively, some methods derive "normality" from external contextual information to guide and enhance the AE's training process [7].

Cellular Data Applications actively use deep learning to optimize data transmission in cellular networks, such as traffic prediction [2] and fault detection [21], addressing the complex and dynamic nature of such networks. Studies on anomaly detection in cellular networks focus primarily on real-time monitoring and alerting. A widely used approach combines CNNs and LSTMs to integrate anomaly detection with prediction for early warning in massive multiple-input multiple-output (MIMO) systems [12]. It could be further enhanced by transfer learning, which adapts models across datasets [16], and self-organizing networks, which enable autonomous network management in dense deployments [17]. AE-based anomaly detection has also gained prominence, particularly in IoT networks, balancing system responsiveness and detection accuracy [22]. In addition, CNNs and LSTMs integrated with AEs have proven effective for unsupervised anomaly detection in latency-critical systems [7]. Variational AEs offer another approach, using interpretable latent representations of features to detect and explain anomalies [23].

3 Dataset

The dataset used in this paper covers regular voyages in the dense maritime area, where the ship sent different amounts of data over different protocols (raw UDP/TCP, WebRTC, QUIC) in the uplink direction and received the control commands in the downlink direction. We used a subset of the full dataset limited to: a) the period from January to November 2024, b) certain features described in Table 1, and c) three of the four 5G modems using the same network provider[1]. The full dataset has been collected and published by Denizer and Landsiedel [6].

The features can be divided into three groups: identifiers, channel metrics of the cellular connection[2], and aggregated transmission statistics at the output

---

[1] All devices are from the MikroTik Chateau 5G family: https://www.mikrotik-store.eu/en/wlan-lte-5g-iot-60ghz/5g/chateau, last accessed: October 14, 2025.
[2] The signal characteristics represent the downlink direction, as the uplink metric is calculated at the base stations, which are usually inaccessible in public networks.

Table 1. Features of the cellular modem dataset. The ^{e} symbol means that the values were encoded into numeric categories and initially represented raw strings.

Name	Type	Values	Description
identity	categorical	$\{0, 2\}^e$	Unique ID for the device
phy_cell_id	categorical	$\{0, 148\}^e$	Unique ID of the physical cell the device is connected to
data_class	categorical	$\{0, 2\}^e$	Type of data connection (LTE, 5G NSA, 5G SA)
cqi	categorical	$\{1, 15\}$	Channel Quality Indicator
ri	categorical	$\{1, 4\}$	Rank Indicator representing spatial streams
mcs	categorical	$\{0, 31\}$	Modulation Coding Scheme index representing the quality of the radio link
modulation	categorical	$\{0, 3\}^e$	Modulation Scheme for the input signal (QPSK, 16QAM, 64QAM, 256QAM)
rsrp	integer	$[-156, -31]$	Reference Signal Received Power in decibels-milliwatts (dBm)
rsrq	integer	dev-specific	Reference Signal Received Quality in decibels (dB)
sinr	integer	$[-23, 40]$	Signal-to-Interference-plus-Noise Ratio in decibels (dB)
rx_packets	integer	$[0, \infty)$	Number of received packets
rx_bits	integer	$[0, \infty)$	Number of received bits
rx_drops	integer	$[0, \infty)$	Number of packets dropped in the receive direction
rx_errors	integer	$[0, \infty)$	Number of received packets with errors
tx_packets	integer	$[0, \infty)$	Number of transmitted packets
tx_bits	integer	$[0, \infty)$	Number of transmitted bits
tx_drops	integer	$[0, \infty)$	Number of packets dropped in the send direction
tx_queue_drops	integer	$[0, \infty)$	Number of packets dropped due to queue overflow
tx_errors	integer	$[0, \infty)$	Number of transmission errors

gate of the ship's network. The channel metrics represent the measurements made at the physical layer of the 5G device and are defined according to the 3rd Generation Partnership Project (3GPP) specifications TS 38.133, TS 38.212, TS 38.214, and TS 38.215 [1]. SINR and RSRQ measurements are considered to be implementation-specific. The modems used in this research use the standard SINR ranges, but the RSRQ ranges are non-standard and vary even between models within the same family. In the case of a non-standalone 5G connection (5G NSA), the 5G values were taken.

3.1 Preprocessing

The preprocessing pipeline involves four main steps in the following order:

1. Exclusion features from the raw data that represent spatial and temporal information, navigational characteristics of the ship, and certain device-specific details. Although some of these features are later utilized, they are omitted during training to ensure the models remain agnostic to the current activity, focusing on data transmission and enabling easier transfer to new maritime areas.
2. Conversion of categorical features with non-integer values into integer representations using the OrdinalEncoder from the scikit-learn library [19]. This simple integer label encoder can handle unknown values to avoid throwing exceptions during real-time inference.

3. Fill in missing features using the IterativeImputer from the same library. This multivariate imputer models each feature with missing values as a function of other features in a round-robin fashion. The IterativeImputer was chosen for its ability to impute values in a time-efficient manner during real-time inference compared to alternative multivariate methods. The encoder and imputer were serialized as binary objects and uploaded with the dataset.
4. Filtering out-of-range samples. Samples with out-of-range metrics, such as an SINR value of -3276, are marked as **technical anomalies** and reported separately to the end-user. These samples, typically indicative of hardware malfunction, are deliberately excluded during training and inference to allow the models to focus on meaningful data patterns.

4 Approach

The initial motivation for using DAEs in this research is their ability to capture complex, nonlinear patterns and detect contextual anomalies [26]. As discussed in Sect. 2, a major challenge of DAEs for anomaly detection is their reliance on clean training samples, which means that the dataset should have ground truth (GT) labels to distinguish normal samples from anomalies, so that only normal samples are used for training. To address the lack of GT, our hybrid approach uses various unsupervised machine learning techniques to partition the dataset into normal and abnormal subsets with a manually set anomaly rate.

The trained DAE models are evaluated through a three-step process: (a) testing against a set of anomalies generated by the same ML algorithm, (b) cross-evaluating anomalies identified by other algorithms, and (c) challenging the models with "attacking samples" designed to simulate distributional shifts and contextual anomalies. In addition, the best models are applied to the unseen data, and the detected anomalies are thoroughly inspected. This comprehensive evaluation ensures the ability of the models to generalize and detect anomalies in different scenarios.

4.1 Models

Clean Data. To obtain the normal and anomaly subsets, three distinct unsupervised ML techniques were applied to the initial training dataset: isolation forests (IF), Gaussian mixture model (GMM), and robust principal component analysis (RPCA) with their implementations in the scikit-learn library [19].

Each technique was chosen for its unique ability to highlight different aspects of the data. IF excels at identifying outliers based on feature space isolation, GMM provides probabilistic clustering to detect data points in low-density regions, and RPCA identifies anomalies as deviations from a low-rank data representation. The overlap of the resulting anomalies, shown in Fig. 2, was also examined to assess the power of the chosen ML method and to understand whether the structure of the original dataset is scattered or cohesive.

Applying these methods, the anomaly detection threshold remains consistent across all methods with 2%. The rationale behind this value is rooted in expert knowledge and empirical observations, which suggest that anomalous events in cellular network data when the remote-controlled agent moves at high speed are rare yet not as negligible as usual due to the cellular network's fast-changing environment and stochastic nature.

Architectures. A typical AE architecture has symmetric encoder and decoder blocks with more than one layer in the case of DAE, with a low-dimensional bottleneck layer (latent space) to learn compact representations of the input data to reconstruct it with the decoder back, see Fig. 3. We have used three main types of DAE architectures:

– Linear: A standard DAE consisting of a series of fully connected linear layers, typically with dimensions halved at each layer until reaching the bottleneck.
– LSTM: A sequential DAE with LSTM layers encoding temporal dependencies in the input and symmetric decoding layers for reconstruction.
– Variational (VAE): A probabilistic DAE that learns a latent representation as a distribution rather than a fixed vector and approximates the posterior distribution using techniques such as the reparametrization trick [10].

The model can be extended to DNAE by adding noise to the input data to reconstruct the denoised original input [25]. Two additional loss regularizations were investigated to improve robustness: sparse loss promotes sparsity in the latent representation, helping the model to focus on the most critical features [13], while contractive loss promotes smoothness in learned representations by penalizing sensitivity to small input changes and improving resilience

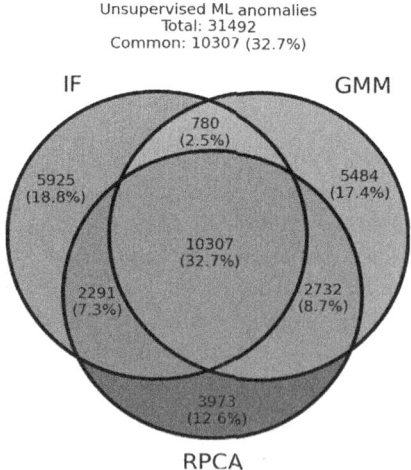

Fig. 2. Overlap of anomalies detected by unsupervised ML algorithms.

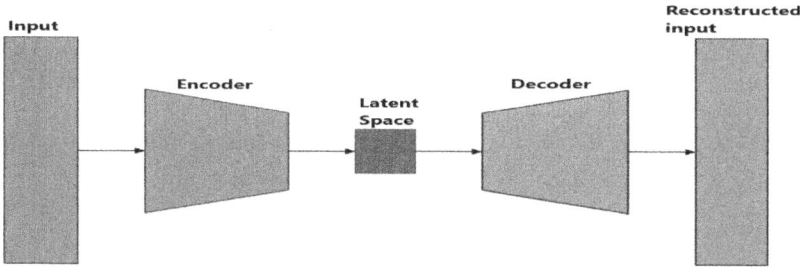

Fig. 3. A generic autoencoder architecture.

to noise [20]. CNN-based architectures were deliberately excluded due to the lack of spatial relationships in the time series dataset.

Training. The model training process was implemented using the PyTorch library [18] and incorporates standard training techniques. Early stopping triggered by no validation loss improvement with configurable patience was applied to avoid overfitting and ensure generalization. In addition, two custom learning rate decay methods were used to aid convergence: "halved," which divides the learning rate by two, and cosine annealing, which gradually reduces the learning rate along a cosine curve. The data was standardized for all models except VAE and normalized for VAE.

For linear and LSTM DAEs, the standard Mean Squared Error (MSE) reconstruction loss was used to measure the difference between the input and its reconstruction. VAE combines Binary Cross-Entropy loss with Kullback-Leibler divergence to regularize the latent space and ensure smoothness [10]. If contractive or sparse regularization was enabled, its term was added to the total loss with the selected weight. The loss value was calculated and stored for each sample or sequence in a batch. The thresholds for anomaly detection were dynamically computed using a configurable percentile in the loss distribution. Specifically, the 98th percentile was selected to match the ML threshold of 2%.

For the LSTM layers, the samples were packed into sequences, introducing two hyperparameters: sequence length and overlap. Zero overlap maximizes the diversity of the training data but was ultimately set to half the sequence length to speed up real-time inference. This configuration was chosen because reports from each cellular modem are generated only once per second.

Hyperparameters. The hyperparameters of all models were optimized by grid search to achieve the best validation loss performance, and the final values are presented in Table 2.

Table 2. Final hyperparameters.

Name	Value	Description
linear_layer_sizes	[128, 64, 32, 16, 8]	Sizes of the linear layers (encoder)
lstm_hidden_size	128	Number of neurons in the LSTM layers
lstm_num_layers	2	Number of the LSTM layers
batch_size	64	Batch size
learning_rate	10^{-3}	Initial learning rate
lr_decay_type	cosine	Learning rate decay type
patience	3	Max epochs without validation loss improvement
noise_sigma	0.5	Standard deviation of noise added to input
sparsity_weight	10^{-4}	Weight for sparsity regularization
contractive_weight	10^{-4}	Weight for contractive regularization
seq_len	8	Sequence length
seq_overlap	4	Overlap between sequences
vae_hidden_size	128	Number of neurons in the VAE layers
vae_latent_dim	32	Dimensionality of the VAE latent space

5 Results

5.1 Results on ML-Partitioned Datasets

Following the evaluation strategy presented in Sect. 4, all models are first evaluated on the ML-partitioned datasets. The models are trained on one of the normal subsets and assessed on all anomalies. The results are averaged over 10 different seeds. We tried linear and LSTM architectures coupled with noise, contractive, and sparse regularization combinations, while also evaluating the VAE. The model without any modifications is denoted as "base" and with all as "all". The results are shown in Fig. 4.

From these results, the VAE outperforms all models on all datasets. Next, the four best models for each dataset are selected: two from the linear and two from the LSTM architectures. The scores on their own anomalies were doubled and summed with two other cross-evaluations. The final selected models for the next evaluation phase are presented in Table 3.

5.2 Results on Attacking Samples

To evaluate the robustness of the models, two groups of "attacking samples" are introduced: "noise" and "variance". Both are designed to test models with typical anomaly detection metrics when labels are known: precision, recall, F1 score, and Matthews correlation coefficient (MCC) with their implementations from the scikit-learn library [19]. Precision ($[0, 1]$) measures the accuracy of positive predictions, recall ($[0, 1]$) evaluates the model's ability to identify all true positives, the F1 score ($[0, 1]$) harmonizes precision and recall, and MCC ($[-1, 1]$)

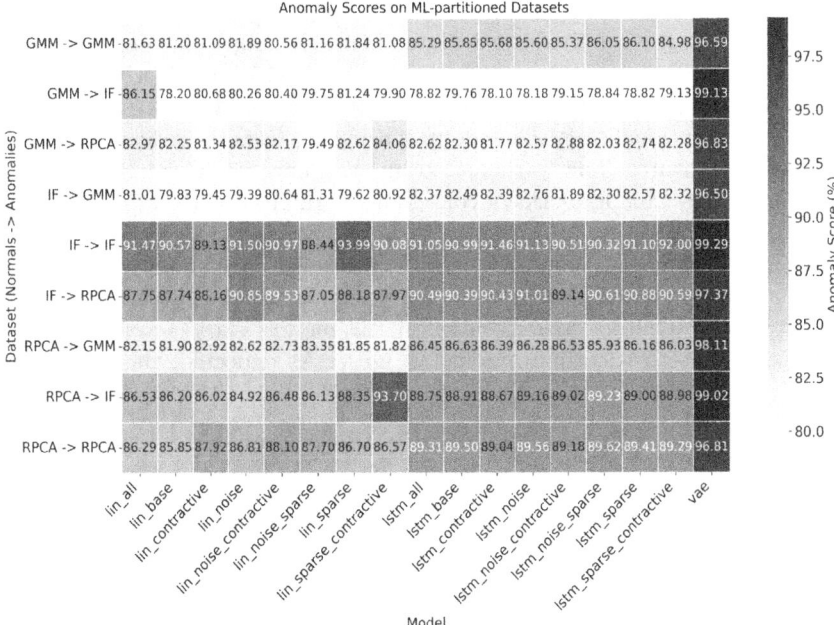

Fig. 4. Anomaly scores on ML-partitioned datasets. The rows indicate the algorithms whose normal and anomaly data were evaluated, and the columns indicate the DAE models that were used.

Table 3. Best models for each ML-partitioned dataset.

Dataset	Architecture	Model Name	Total Score
IF	VAE	vae	392.45/400
IF	LSTM	lstm_sparse_contractive	356.92/400
IF	LSTM	lstm_noise	356.03/400
IF	Linear	lin_sparse	355.77/400
IF	Linear	lin_noise	353.24/400
GMM	VAE	vae	392.45/400
GMM	LSTM	lstm_sparse	333.75/400
GMM	LSTM	lstm_base	333.75/400
GMM	Linear	lin_all	332.38/400
GMM	Linear	lin_sparse	327.54/400
RPCA	VAE	vae	390.75/400
RPCA	LSTM	lstm_noise	354.56/400
RPCA	LSTM	lstm_base	354.55/400
RPCA	Linear	lin_sparse_contractive	348.65/400
RPCA	Linear	lin_noise_contractive	345.41/400

evaluates the overall confusion matrix in a balanced way. For the LSTM models, the individual score (label) was calculated for each sample in a sequence.

In the "noise" group, 100 normal samples detected by all algorithms are augmented with 1000 anomalies by adding noise to the numerical features and introducing a distributional shift. This group specifically tests the resilience of models to perturbed features. The "variance" group combines 550 normal samples with 550 anomalies by mixing blocks of contiguous normal samples, targeting contextual anomalies. Both groups increase the noise and shuffle every 100 samples.

The evaluation results for these attacking samples are summarized in Table 4. While most models achieve near-perfect precision, their recall performance sometimes struggles. On the "noise" samples, the models show acceptable performance, coping with a certain amount of noise. As expected, the LSTM mod-

Table 4. Results on "attacking samples".

Type	Dataset	Model	Normals	Anomalies	Precision	Recall	F1 Score	MCC
noise	if	lstm_noise	100	1000	1.00	0.717	0.8352	0.4327
noise	if	lstm_sparse_contractive	100	1000	1.00	0.706	0.8277	0.4233
noise	if	lin_sparse	100	1000	1.00	0.694	0.8194	0.4134
noise	if	lin_noise	100	1000	1.00	0.694	0.8194	0.4134
noise	if	vae	100	1000	0.91	0.979	0.9418	−0.0441
noise	gmm	lstm_sparse	100	1000	1.00	0.511	0.6764	0.2945
noise	gmm	lstm_base	100	1000	1.00	0.510	0.6755	0.2940
noise	gmm	lin_noise_sparse_contractive	100	1000	1.00	0.513	0.6781	0.2956
noise	gmm	lin_sparse	100	1000	1.00	0.513	0.6781	0.2956
noise	gmm	vae	100	1000	0.91	0.999	0.9519	−0.0095
noise	rpca	lstm_base	100	1000	1.00	0.735	0.8473	0.4487
noise	rpca	lstm_noise	100	1000	1.00	0.706	0.8277	0.4233
noise	rpca	lin_noise_contractive	100	1000	1.00	0.694	0.8194	0.4134
noise	rpca	lin_sparse_contractive	100	1000	1.00	0.675	0.80597	0.3985
noise	rpca	vae	100	1000	0.91	0.983	0.9443	−0.0159
variance	if	lstm_sparse_contractive	550	550	1.00	0.125	0.2229	0.2587
variance	if	lstm_noise	550	550	0.97	0.116	0.2078	0.2373
variance	if	lin_sparse	550	550	1.00	0.056	0.1067	0.1703
variance	if	lin_noise	550	550	1.00	0.045	0.0870	0.1525
variance	if	vae	550	550	0.31	0.455	0.3704	−0.6124
variance	gmm	lstm_sparse	550	550	1.00	0.049	0.0936	0.1586
variance	gmm	lstm_base	550	550	1.00	0.049	0.0936	0.1586
variance	gmm	lin_noise_sparse_contractive	550	550	1.00	0.042	0.0803	0.1461
variance	gmm	lin_sparse	550	550	1.00	0.038	0.0736	0.1395
variance	gmm	vae	550	550	0.37	0.585	0.4529	−0.5113
variance	rpca	lstm_base	550	550	1.00	0.084	0.1544	0.2089
variance	rpca	lstm_noise	550	550	1.00	0.082	0.1513	0.2065
variance	rpca	lin_noise_contractive	550	550	1.00	0.053	0.1002	0.1646
variance	rpca	lin_sparse_contractive	550	550	1.00	0.047	0.0903	0.1556
variance	rpca	vae	550	550	0.34	0.516	0.4110	−0.5591

els outperform the linear models on the "variance" samples, but the joint recall remains relatively low due to the increasing degree of shuffling. The VAE models show negative MCC values, indicating performance close to random label assignment, so they were excluded. Based on this evaluation, three final models were selected: **lin_sparse** (IF), **lstm_sparse** (GMM), and **lstm_base** (RPCA), highlighting the importance of sparse regularization on this dataset.

The goal is to build an ensemble of best-performing models, including at least one linear model that can provide immediate results for real-time inference. The selected linear model has the highest performance. Meanwhile, the selected LSTM models, trained on clean GMM and RPCA datasets, leverage their superior F1 and MCC values to provide sequential anomaly detection with probabilistic and statistical slopes inherited from the original ML algorithms.

5.3 Explaining the Detected Anomalies

The final evaluation focuses on explaining the detected anomalies using the three best models selected in the previous subsection: point-base (DAE IF), seq-prob (LSTM DAE GMM), and seq-stat (LSTM DAE RPCA). These have been tested on unseen data to identify real-time events hypothesized to cause anomalies. The hypotheses are based on expert knowledge and practical observations. The events are as follows:

1. Location and time correlations. The anomalies were analyzed for spatial and temporal patterns using contextual information omitted during preprocessing (see Sect. 3.1). Correlations were found that could highlight dense areas of anomalies that could be marked in advance, enabling real-time alerts for RCU operators.

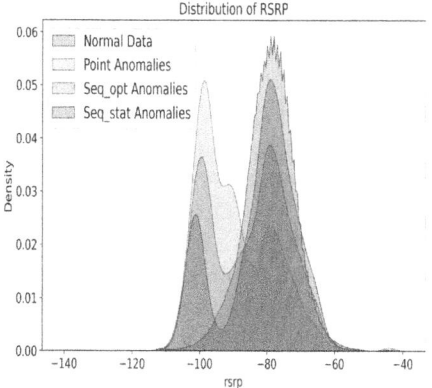

Fig. 5. RSRP distribution.

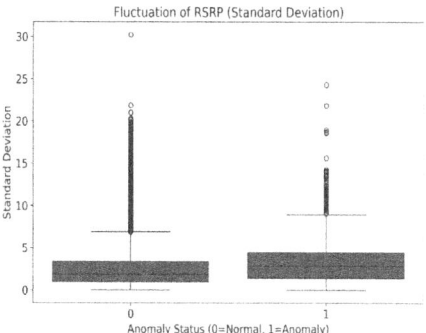

Fig. 6. RSRP standard deviation distribution (line → median, edges → Q1, Q3 quartiles, whiskers → interquartile range.

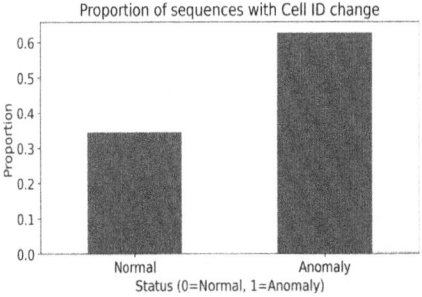
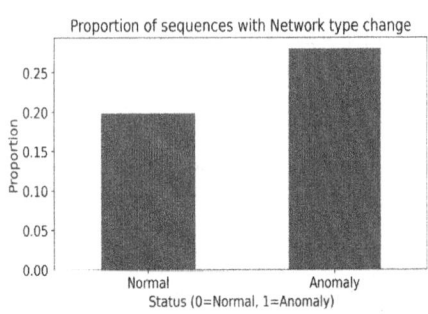

Fig. 7. Cell ID change proportions.

Fig. 8. Network type change proportions.

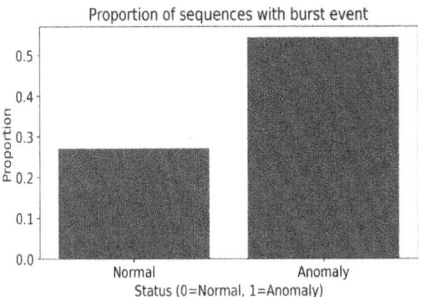
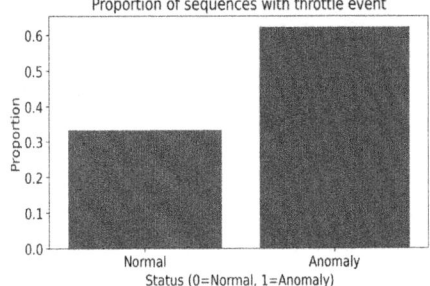

Fig. 9. Burst event proportions.

Fig. 10. Throttle event proportions.

2. Fluctuations in signal characteristics. Anomalies showed distinct patterns in signal metrics, as illustrated for RSRP in Fig. 5. There are three possible sub-events: a) short-term fluctuations, b) altered correlations, and c) asymmetric changes. As shown for RSRP in Fig. 6, anomalies show a larger spread, as reflected by a higher median or a larger range. All sub-events are detectable in real-time by comparing the short-term sequences with the baselines computed for the normal samples from the training and test datasets.
3. Cell and network switches. Cell identifier and network type switches (LTE ↔ 5G NSA ↔ 5G SA) were more frequent in anomalies, especially during handovers involving base station changes, which often cause lost packets and higher latencies. Figure 7 and Fig. 8 show that cell changes occur twice as often in anomalies as the network changes only slightly more often. The additional analysis of cell IDs in anomalies shows that edge IDs between the coverage areas of two base stations are the most frequent.
4. Transmission outliers. This event is represented by burst and throttle sub-events, where the bitrate per second in a sequence is more or less than two standard deviations from the mean. These events are identified in the same way as switch events, and the required statistics can be calculated in real-time using the baselines. Figure 9 and Fig. 10 show that these events are more common in anomalies.

6 Summary

This paper investigates unsupervised anomaly detection in cellular modem metrics using DAEs with different architectures and regularization techniques. The preprocessed dataset was divided into normal and abnormal parts using several unsupervised ML algorithms. DAE models were trained on the normal sets and evaluated on the resulting abnormal sets and attacking samples designed to simulate distributional shifts and contextual anomalies.

The results demonstrate that well-regularized DAEs effectively reconstructed normal patterns while identifying anomalies. Analysis of detected anomalies on an unseen dataset revealed a group of meaningful events within anomalies, which could be identified in real-time providing a possible on-site explanation. The implementation achieves a maximum inference latency of **10 milliseconds** when there are missing values in the raw input.

This work contributes to the field of OC by developing an unsupervised anomaly detection system that monitors and responds to dynamic environments, thus improving real-time decision-making and situational awareness. Our advances extend existing OC systems on the MS "Wavelab" vessel [24] and support the transition from remotely operated to autonomous ferry operations. Future work will investigate advanced architectures, such as attention-based models, and extend the methodology to larger and more diverse datasets to further improve scalability and adaptability.

Acknowledgments. This research has been partly funded by the German Federal Ministry for Digital and Transport (Bundesministerium für Digitales und Verkehr) within the project "CAPTN Förde 5G", funding guideline: "5G Umsetzungsförderung im Rahmen des 5G-Innovationsprogramms", funding code: 45FGU139_H. The authors acknowledge the financial support of the BMDV.

References

1. 3GPP: 3rd Generation Partnership Project; Technical Specification Group Radio Access Network. Technical report, 3GPP (2017). https://portal.3gpp.org/#/. Accessed 25 July 2025
2. Azmin, T., Ahmadinejad, M., Shahriar, N.: Bandwidth prediction in 5G mobile networks using informer. In: 2022 13th International Conference on Network of the Future (NoF), pp. 1–9. IEEE (2022)
3. Bouman, R., Bukhsh, Z., Heskes, T.: Unsupervised anomaly detection algorithms on real-world data: how many do we need? J. Mach. Learn. Res. **25**(105), 1–34 (2024)
4. CAPTN Fjord5G (Förde5G): https://captn.sh/en/foerde-5g-englisch/. Accessed 25 July 2025
5. Cheng, Z., Wang, S., Zhang, P., Wang, S., Liu, X., Zhu, E.: Improved autoencoder for unsupervised anomaly detection. Int. J. Intell. Syst. **36**(12), 7103–7125 (2021)
6. Denizer, B., Landsiedel, O.: Fjord5G: A comprehensive 5G dataset for coastal maritime connectivity. In: 2025 IEEE 101st Vehicular Technology Conference (VTC2025-Spring), pp. 1–5 (2025)

7. Han, J., Liu, T., Ma, J., Zhou, Y., Zeng, X., Xu, Y.: Anomaly detection and early warning model for latency in private 5G networks. Appl. Sci. **12**(23) (2022)
8. Han, S., Hu, X., Huang, H., Jiang, M., Zhao, Y.: ADBench: anomaly detection benchmark (2022). https://arxiv.org/abs/2206.09426
9. Kim, M., Yu, J., Kim, J., Oh, T.H., Choi, J.K.: An iterative method for unsupervised robust anomaly detection under data contamination. IEEE Trans. Neural Netw. Learn. Syst. **35**(10), 13327–13339 (2024)
10. Kingma, D.P., Welling, M.: Auto-encoding variational bayes (2013). https://arxiv.org/abs/1312.6114
11. Li, P., Pei, Y., Li, J.: A comprehensive survey on design and application of autoencoder in deep learning. Appl. Soft Comput. **138** (2023)
12. Liao, Y., Yao, H., Hua, Y., Li, C.: CSI feedback based on deep learning for massive MIMO systems. IEEE Access **7**, 86810–86820 (2019)
13. Makhzani, A., Frey, B.: k-sparse autoencoders (2014). https://arxiv.org/abs/1312.5663
14. Müller-Schloer, C., Tomforde, S.: Organic Computing - technical systems for survival in the real world. Birkhäuser (2017)
15. Munir, M., Chattha, M.A., Dengel, A., Ahmed, S.: A comparative analysis of traditional and deep learning-based anomaly detection methods for streaming data. In: 2019 18th IEEE International Conference On Machine Learning And Applications (ICMLA), pp. 561–566 (2019)
16. Noonari, N., Corujo, D., Aguiar, R.L., Ferrao, F.J.: Multi-scale convolutional LSTM with transfer learning for anomaly detection in cellular networks (2024). https://arxiv.org/abs/2410.03732
17. Oğuz, H.T., Kalaycıoğlu, A.: Anomaly detection in multi-tiered cellular networks using LSTM and 1D CNN. EURASIP J. Wirel. Commun. Netw. **2022**(1) (2022)
18. Paszke, A., et al.: PyTorch: an imperative style, high-performance deep learning library. In: Advances in Neural Information Processing Systems, vol. 32, pp. 8024–8035. Curran Associates, Inc. (2019)
19. Pedregosa, F., Varoquaux, G., Gramfort, A., Michel, V., Thirion, B., Grisel, O., et al.: Scikit-learn: machine learning in python. J. Mach. Learn. Res. **12**, 2825–2830 (2011)
20. Rifai, S., Vincent, P., Muller, X., Glorot, X., Bengio, Y.: Contractive auto-encoders: explicit invariance during feature extraction. In: Proceedings of the 28th International Conference on Machine Learning, ICML 2011 (2011)
21. Sangaiah, A.K., Rezaei, S., Javadpour, A., Miri, F., Zhang, W., Wang, D.: Automatic fault detection and diagnosis in cellular networks and beyond 5G: Intell. Netw. Manage. Algorithms **15**(11) (2022)
22. Savic, M.: Deep learning anomaly detection for cellular IoT with applications in smart logistics. IEEE Access **9**, 59406–59419 (2021)
23. Singh, A., Weber, M., Lange-Hegermann, M.: Interpretable anomaly detection in cellular networks by learning concepts in variational autoencoders (2023). https://arxiv.org/abs/2306.15938
24. Smirnov, N., Tomforde, S.: Real-time data transmission optimization on 5G remote-controlled units using deep reinforcement learning. In: Architecture of Computing Systems: 36th International Conference, Athens, Greece, June 13–15, 2023, pp. 274–289. Springer, Cham (2023)
25. Vincent, P., Larochelle, H., Bengio, Y., Manzagol, P.A.: Extracting and composing robust features with denoising autoencoders. In: Proceedings of the 25th International Conference on Machine Learning, ICML 2008, pp. 1096–1103 (2008)

26. Xu, Z., Saleh, J.H.: Machine learning for reliability engineering and safety applications: review of current status and future opportunities. Reliab. Eng. Syst. Saf. **211** (2021)
27. Zamanzadeh Darban, Z., Webb, G.I., Pan, S., Aggarwal, C., Salehi, M.: Deep learning for time series anomaly detection: a survey. ACM Comput. Surv. **57**(1), 1–42 (2024)

Hyperparameter Optimization for PSO-Based Energy-Aware Path Planning for AUV Swarms

Wiebke Frenkel(✉) and Bernd-Christian Renner

Institute for Autonomous Cyber-Physical Systems, Hamburg University of Technology, Harburger Schloßstr. 28, 21079 Hamburg, Germany
{wiebke.frenkel,christian.renner}@tuhh.de
https://www.tuhh.de/acps/

Abstract. In missions using autonomous underwater vehicles (AUVs), reaching predefined waypoints is essential, e.g., for seabed mapping and infrastructure monitoring. The primary objective is to minimize energy consumption to reduce the risk of failure, avoid long (re)charging times, or maximize the number of successfully visited waypoints. If the AUVs can visit the waypoints in any order, we can frame this as a Travelling Salesperson Problem (TSP). However, finding the global optimal solution to the TSP becomes computationally infeasible even for relatively small sets of waypoints. To address this challenge, we utilize Particle Swarm Optimization (PSO) as a lightweight alternative, allowing us to obtain energy-efficient routes that closely approximate the global solution. Choosing the corresponding hyperparameters is fundamental, as poor selections can lead to local optima. Our analysis shows significant differences in the sensitivity of hyperparameters between the two PSO-based approaches, which only differ in initialization. However, there is a consistent range of hyperparameters where both methods yield comparable results. We identify this range by optimizing hyperparameters to improve solution quality. Simulative evaluations in real-world-inspired scenarios demonstrate that optimized hyperparameter selection improves the energy efficiency of the AUV swarm and ensures reliable mission execution using a minimal number of AUVs.

Keywords: Particle Swarm Optimizer · Hyperparameter Optimization · Travelling Salesperson Problem · AUV Swarm

1 Introduction

Autonomous underwater vehicles (AUVs) are a common choice for a plethora of applications and use cases, e.g., ocean exploration or environmental monitoring. In particular, they have become an essential tool in scientific research, where institutions employ AUVs to gather critical data, as noted in [7]. AUV designs vary based on specific applications, e.g., [20] mentions the deployment of different AUVs for various missions. In [1], AUVs are used for polar and marine research, operating in challenging environments such as the Arctic Ocean. They can estimate underground oil plumes and concentrations, facilitating long-range pollution monitoring, as described in [5]. Similarly, AUVs are utilized for inspecting offshore infrastructure [14] and dam inspections [18]. Moreover, they can assist in predicting environmental disasters using underwater measurements, as highlighted in [18].

In the examples discussed, AUVs collect data simultaneously or over time and navigate to various waypoints. As the number of waypoints increases, deploying a swarm of AUVs to work together can be an effective strategy to enhance operation time and robustness. Mission planning involves determining which AUV will handle each task, including the waypoints and their order, to maximize mission duration and ensure success. We previously addressed this challenge in [9] by framing it as a Traveling Salesperson Problem (TSP) and optimizing the route using a Particle Swarm Optimizer (PSO).

The PSO is inspired by the natural dynamics of flocks of birds or schools of fish and uses self-organized swarm behavior to find an energy-optimal solution. Due to its stochastic nature, PSO offers advantages over other optimization techniques, such as ease of implementation and efficient exploration of large solution spaces. It can deliver near-optimal solutions quickly, making it ideal for real-time applications and resource-limited situations. While PSO provides a practical and flexible optimization routine, its results depend on the choice of configuration parameters, such as population size or number of generations, as we have already discussed in [9]. These parameters influence convergence speed and solution quality, making their sensible choice crucial. Traditional empirical tuning is often time-consuming and suboptimal, especially when dealing with complex, real-time applications. To address this challenge, we adopt a systematic approach by treating these configuration variables as hyperparameters and applying hyperparameter optimization (HPO) techniques widely used in machine learning to enhance algorithmic performance. By leveraging HPO, we aim to improve the robustness and efficiency of PSO-based mission planning for AUVs. In particular, we have identified the following research questions that we address in the paper:

- **How can hyperparameter optimization enhance the PSO-based AUV mission planning?**
  We systematically apply HPO to optimize PSO parameters for swarm-based AUV mission planning. Unlike empirical tuning, where parameters are selected based on manual adjustments or heuristics, our method accelerates the process while improving robustness by considering energy constraints and mission success rates.
- **How does hyperparameter sensitivity affect the stability and energy efficiency of PSO-based AUV mission planning?**
  We conduct an extensive statistical analysis to determine the impact of hyperparameter configurations on PSO performance. This allows us to establish well-defined boundary conditions for stable and energy-efficient mission execution.

- **How can energy-aware optimization reduce AUV swarm size while ensuring mission feasibility?**
  Our framework optimizes mission plans to reduce the number of AUVs required while ensuring energy-efficient waypoint allocation. This leads to lower operational costs and improved mission feasibility in resource-limited environments.
- **How does the optimized PSO-based planning perform under simulated real-world constraints?**
  We evaluate our optimized PSO-based planning approach through simulations that mimic real-world constraints, demonstrating its practical applicability in marine operations such as environmental monitoring and underwater infrastructure inspection.

We review PSO-based AUV path planning in Sect. 2, highlighting strengths and the need for systematic HPO. To address this, we integrate energy-aware AUV allocation into HPO. We formulate the mission planning problem as an asymmetric TSP in Sect. 3, optimizing waypoints and routes under energy constraints. Our cascaded framework in Sect. 4 uses HPO to tune PSO hyperparameters for better convergence and energy efficiency. We evaluate the approach in Sect. 5, analyzing convergence, energy use, and robustness across missions. Finally, Sect. 6 summarizes findings and future work.

2 State of the Art

PSO is a widely used tool in ongoing research on optimization algorithms, which is also described in [11]. The authors use the PSO to solve the discrete optimization problem of the TSP, focusing on a balanced behavior in exploration and exploitation. Classical PSO is effective but often gets stuck in local optima. To improve this, [13] created an enhanced PSO for three-dimensional path planning for AUVs. This version features adaptive nonlinear weight adjustments and a modified velocity function that uses the average of particle positions to improve movement and reduce dispersion. Additionally, it incorporates Darwin's "survival of the fittest" concept to boost convergence speed and optimization performance. The updated parameters were empirically determined and validated through simulations. The article [16] presents an AUV path-planning strategy using a combination of constrained sampling A* and an adaptive quantum-behaved PSO to minimize energy consumption during single AUV diving processes in the presence of ocean currents. The algorithm's effectiveness is demonstrated through validation and comparison with other algorithms using six test scenarios in a simulation. However, some parameters, such as population size and generations, are determined empirically.

The improvements make the original PSO more complex and thus contradict the idea of [10], who introduced the algorithm in 1995, of a simple mathematical description that can be implemented with just a few lines of code.

In all of the mentioned applications, the PSO's hyperparameters, such as population size or generation, were determined empirically. Setting these hyperparameters is anything but trivial and often involves a large number of time-consuming simulation runs, especially with a large number of interrelated hyperparameters. A better way than an empirical setting is to use an optimization technique to find the best set of these parameters. In machine learning, the optimization of hyperparameters has already been established in practice. As [21] pointed out, the direct impact on the model's performance makes appropriate optimization methods to determine the best model parameters essential to avoid time-consuming trial and error. We can also define hyperparameters for the PSO, which we can then determine using a suitable HPO. In addition to standard PSO parameters such as population size or generations, we can also set the number of AUVs as a hyperparameter. Compared to [9], we map the number of AUVs to the waypoints instead of setting them empirically and hoping that the energetically minimum route can be navigated with the selected number.

3 Problem Statement

A fully autonomous swarm of AUVs can enhance underwater exploration, environmental monitoring, and infrastructure inspection. We propose a multi-layered system architecture consisting of a base station, the AUV swarm, and the environment, as illustrated in Fig. 1. Using environmental data like nautical charts, the base station is responsible for the global, coarse-grained mission planning, which includes preliminary path planning and assignment of waypoints. The AUV swarm takes charge of executing the mission autonomously. The swarm members optimize their local paths and adjust to real-time environmental conditions, such as dynamic obstacles and unknown changes in terrain, using their onboard sensors. Real-time decision-making is essential for modifying mission parameters, like altering routes or reassigning waypoints, based on immediate sensor data and predefined mission goals. Additionally, ad-hoc communication between AUVs is crucial for coordinating tasks, sharing important information, e.g., obstacles and changes in conditions, and ensuring efficient swarm behavior while avoiding collisions and redundancy.

This paper addresses the resource-efficient operation of near-optimal path planning at the base station. Therefore, we pre-plan routes at the base station and communicate them to the AUVs, allowing for local adjustments based on real-time factors like energy consumption and environmental changes. We break down mission planning and execution into two main tasks to achieve high-quality solutions with computational efficiency:

1. Assign waypoints to AUVs: Distribute N waypoints among M AUVs, ensuring each waypoint is visited once while balancing the energy consumption.
2. Determine energy-optimal routes: Solve the TSP for each AUV to find the most energy-efficient route for its assigned N_i waypoints, considering environmental factors.

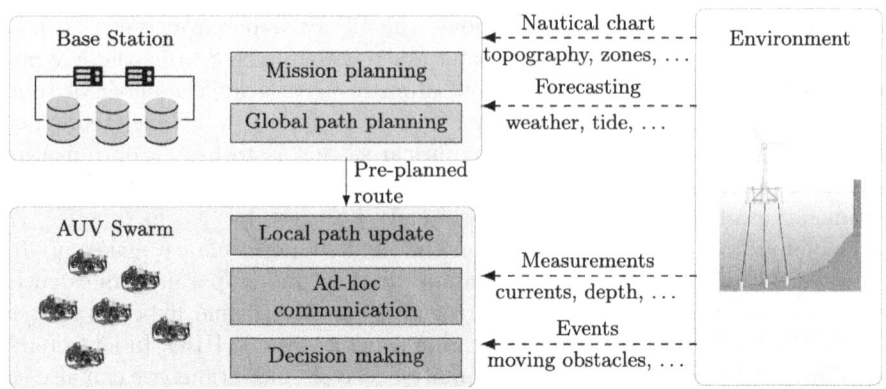

Fig. 1. Overview of the AUV swarm mission setup.

3.1 Energy Model

AUVs are limited by their energy supply, typically from Li-ion batteries. While advancements in battery technology have improved operational duration, energy remains a finite resource that impacts mission feasibility. We use the energy consumption model from [9], which incorporates location-dependent factors like ocean currents, hydrodynamic drag, and vehicle dynamics, demonstrating that energy consumption is influenced by more than just distance, as described in [8].

In Fig. 2, we present the AUV's energy consumption model, consisting of mechanical and electrical components. As noted in [9], AUVs can improve energy efficiency by utilizing natural ocean currents. We define a cost function, where Θ^* represents the set of optimal parameters derived through the optimization process, given by

$$f(\Theta^*) = \sum_{i=0}^{N-1} E_i \quad \text{with } E_i = \mathbf{F} \cdot |\mathbf{x}| \tag{1}$$

that we use to minimize energy consumption by considering the interaction between the AUV and its environment. The differential displacement $\mathbf{x} = \begin{bmatrix} dx & dy & dz \end{bmatrix}^T$ and the force $\mathbf{F}$, which includes environmental factors like ocean currents and hydrodynamic resistance, are both included in the cost function. The energy consumption is adjusted based on the AUV's relative velocity $\mathbf{v}_r = \mathbf{v} - \mathbf{v}_c$, where $\mathbf{v}$ is the velocity of the AUV from a global perspective, and $\mathbf{v}_c$ is the velocity of the ocean current. The energy use is reduced when the AUV moves with the current and increased when moving against it.

A Li-ion battery provides the electrical power to drive the propulsion unit. Similar to [9], we make a statement about mission fulfillment with the estimation of the time derivative of the state of charge SoC

$$\dot{\sigma}(t) = -\frac{1}{C_{\text{bat}}} \cdot i(t) \tag{2}$$

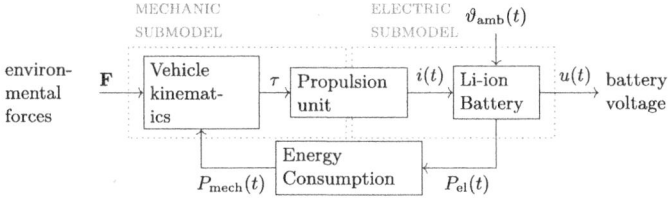

Fig. 2. Energy consumption model of an AUV.

with the capacity C_{bat} and the electric current $i(t)$ of the battery using the nonlinear differential equation system as proposed in [17]. The authors use an electrical equivalent circuit model to describe the electrochemical behavior of the battery, which influences the system dynamics.

3.2 Complexity

As noted in [6], we tackle the problem by converting it into an asymmetric TSP, where energy consumption, influenced by direction-dependent external forces, replaces distance. For an asymmetric TSP with more than two cities, the maximum number of valid tours is $(N-1)!$, leading to an exponentially growing search space that makes complete searches impractical, even for a few cities.

The brute force approach [15], which determines all possible permutations of routes, calculates their associated costs, and selects the lowest-cost route, is an exact method. The number of possible solutions is given by $\sum_{i=0}^{M-1}(N_i - 1)!$ for a uniform distribution of locations. While theoretically sound, this method becomes computationally expensive for larger problem instances.

In practice, metaheuristics such as PSO, genetic algorithms, or simulated annealing are often employed to efficiently approximate near-optimal solutions. In the case of PSO, the search space is limited to $M \cdot P \cdot G \cdot \frac{N}{M}$, determined by the population size P and the number of generations produced G. In practice, these methods are efficient because they can achieve valuable results faster than exact algorithms, such as the brute force approach, by iteratively improving a population of solutions.

4 Optimization Process

We structure the entire optimization process in Fig. 3 into a cascaded framework, where HPO serves as the outer optimization, and the PSO-based TSP solver functions as the inner optimization. As a result, the HPO provides the hyperparameters, which serve as the configuration for the PSO. We embedded the energy model of the AUV in an underlying simulation, which provides values for the object function of the HPO. We solve the AUV swarm's underlying TSP in each iteration step and simulate the energy consumption and battery dynamics.

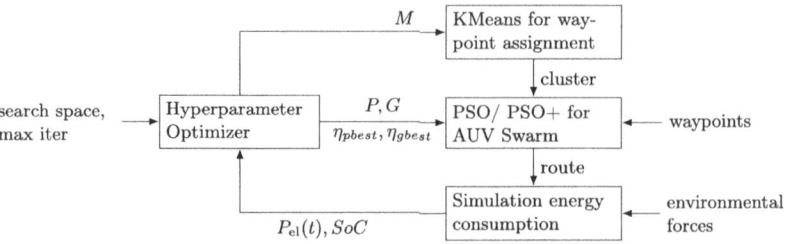

Fig. 3. Block diagram of the cascaded optimization process.

4.1 PSO and PSO+ for TSP

The PSO, introduced by [10], combines elements of genetic algorithms and evolutionary computation. Inspired by flocking behavior in nature, PSO simulates decentralized systems where simple individual actions lead to collective intelligence. Each particle represents a potential solution, moving in an n-dimensional search space and adjusting its trajectory based on personal experiences and the swarm's collective knowledge. The optimal solution is determined by modifying the distances between particles through a stochastic process. The new position of a particle

$$X_i^{k+1} = V_i^k + X_i^k \tag{3}$$

is determined from the current position X_i^k and the corresponding velocity calculating with the discrete differential equation

$$V_i^{k+1} = \omega \cdot V_i^k + \eta_1 \cdot \mathrm{R} \cdot (P_{\text{best}}^k - X_i^k) + \eta_2 \cdot \mathrm{R} \cdot (P_{\text{global}}^k - X_i^k) , \tag{4}$$

whereby ω is the inertia factor and $\eta_1 \cdot R$ weights the best position of the particle P_{best} and $\eta_2 \cdot R$ weights the global best position P_{global}. We define the optimization problem

$$P_{\text{global}}^k = \arg\min_{X_i^k} f(\Theta^*), \tag{5}$$

by minimizing the cost function Eq. 1 with the position of the particles X_i^k in the search space.

In [19], the PSO was adapted for discrete problems like the TSP. We initialize each AUV_i with $i \in \{0, \ldots, M-1\}$, assigning a particle swarm P_i to solve the TSP, with each particle representing a randomized route. Instead of distances between waypoints, we use energy levels based on the energy consumption required for an AUV to travel between points. This energy consumption depends on the distance traveled, the AUV's speed, and the water current, see Sect. 3.1, while we assume a constant speed for our problem. As particles exchange information, the best global solution with the lowest energy level is identified.

To enhance PSO for the TSP, the authors in [12] introduce a greedy initialization for each particle, called PSO+. Instead of random initialization, PSO+ selects the next point with the lowest energy level from a starting point. This method improves convergence speed but may also lead to getting stuck in a local optimum.

4.2 Hyperparameter Optimizer

Selecting hyperparameters for PSO-based algorithms is challenging as their values significantly affect convergence speed and solution quality. The complex interactions between hyperparameters, such as population size and inertia weight, make manual tuning time-consuming and error-prone. To find an optimal configuration, we use HPO. Open-source libraries like Hyperopt for Python [4] facilitate HPO, employing methods such as Random Search (RS) and the Tree-structured Parzen Estimator (TPE). RS tests hyperparameters randomly and is more efficient than grid search, as shown in [3]. In comparison, in [2], TPE models the conditional probability distribution of hyperparameters based on observed target values by separating the result space into areas with high and low probabilities of valuable outcomes. It approximates separate densities for the best and worst results and aims to maximize the ratio of these densities.

Impact of the Hyperparameters. We analyzed the influence of the different hyperparameters on the quality of the result. For this purpose, we conducted a case study with $N \in \{3, 4, \ldots, 10\}$ waypoints in which we configure the PSO and PSO+ with varying hyperparameters $\lambda \in \{G, P\}$, which differ in the initialization. We compare the results of the algorithms against a global solution obtained with brute force methods (BF) through

$$d(P_{\text{global}}^k) = \frac{|P_{\text{global,alg}}^k - P_{\text{global,BF}}^k|}{P_{\text{global,BF}}^k} \text{ with alg} \in \{\text{PSO, PSO+}\} \quad (6)$$

as the normalized difference.

In Fig. 4, we illustrate the influence of the hyperparameters on the result. The PSO+ algorithm performs significantly better than the PSO. We recognize a correlation between the number of generations produced and the population size increases exponentially as the number of waypoints rises. This illustrates that selecting hyperparameters is not a simple task. It requires a careful balance between the number of generations, the population size, and the number of waypoints. While a higher number of generations can improve the chances of finding a global solution, it also increases computation time. Therefore, keeping these values as small as possible is crucial without compromising the search for a global solution. Both tested algorithms, particularly the PSO algorithm, can achieve high accuracy within a certain range despite variations from the global solution. Notably, their minimum plateaus are similar, indicating that a common set of hyperparameters can lead to similarly effective results for both PSO-based algorithms.

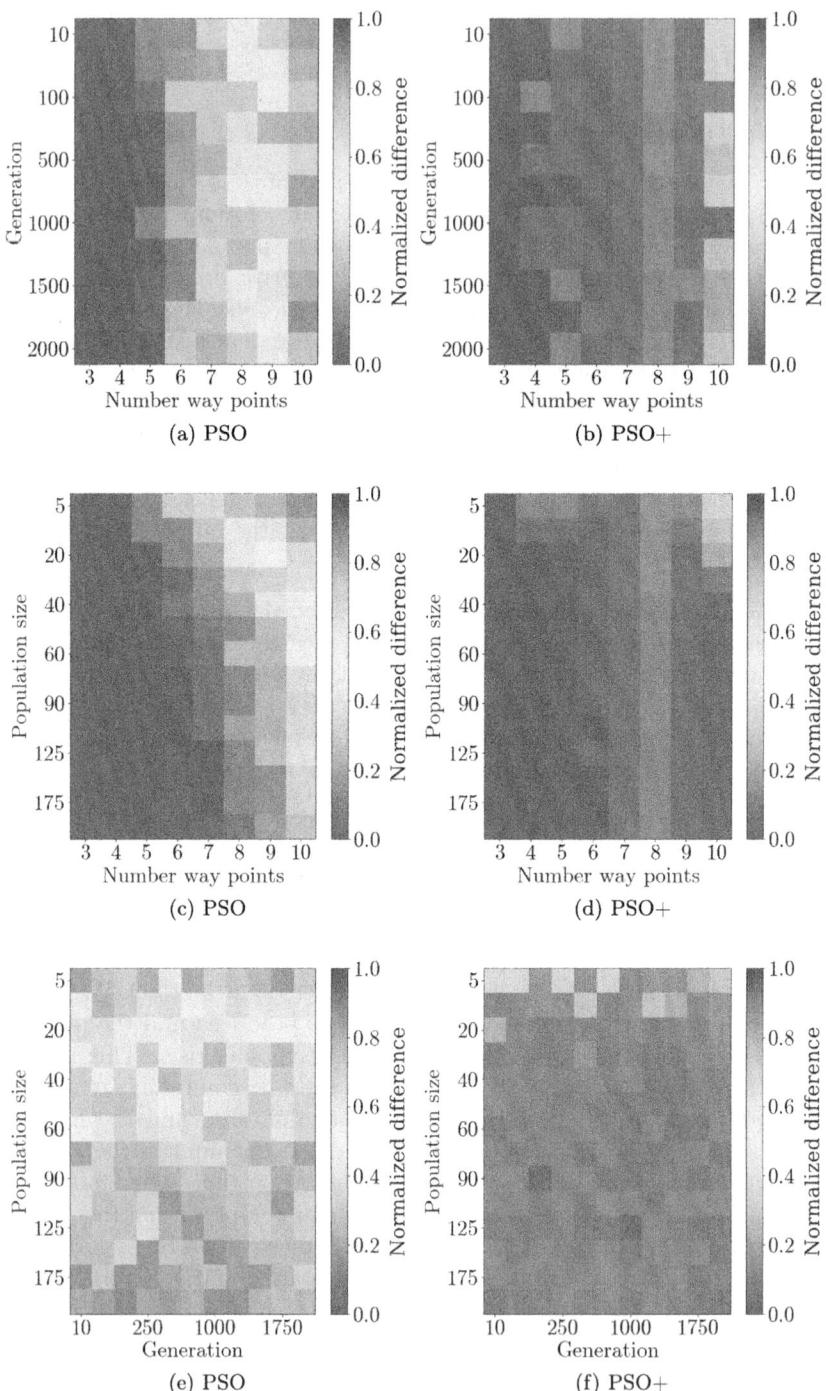

Fig. 4. Dependency of the hyper-parameter for the PSO-based algorithms.

Choice of HPO-Algorithm. We conduct an additional analysis to determine which of the possible algorithms, RS or TPE, is most suitable for our use case. We define the following hyperparameters: population size P, number of generations G, and the probabilities for the best local solution η_{pbest} and the best global solution η_{gbest}. Additionally, we are interested in the number of AUVs, which effectively corresponds to the number of waypoints assigned per AUV for a given total number of points.

To address this, we extend our set of hyperparameters, where M denotes the number of AUVs,

$$\lambda = \{P, G, \eta_{pbest}, \eta_{gbest}, M\} \;, \tag{7}$$

allowing us to formulate the optimization problem as follows:

$$\lambda^{(*)} \equiv \arg\min_{\lambda \in \Lambda} \Psi(\lambda) \;. \tag{8}$$

We aim to minimize the hyperparameter response function over the search space Λ defined as $\lambda \in \Lambda$. With the information presented in Sect. 4.2, we select the configuration such as the search space Λ shown in Table 1. We optimize the parameters for different sets of waypoints and missions to ensure the optimized hyperparameters apply beyond a specific problem. This approach enhances the robustness against the sensitivity of the number of waypoints that each AUV must navigate.

We define the objective function $\Psi(\lambda)$ as

$$\Psi(\lambda) = P_{el}(t) + \omega_1 \cdot M + \omega_2 \cdot \overline{\sigma} + \omega_3 \cdot \sigma_{scale} \tag{9}$$

the simulated electric power $P_{el}(t)$ used from the Li-ion battery, the mean of the state-of-charge (SoC) at the end of the mission, and σ_{scale} is a scaled version of the SoC

$$\sigma_{scale} = \sum_{0}^{N-1} \sum_{0}^{M-1} \frac{\sigma_i - min(\sigma_i)}{max(\sigma_i) - min(\sigma_i)} \;. \tag{10}$$

Since the individual components of the objective function have different units and magnitudes, we apply weighting factors ω_1, ω_2, and ω_3 to balance their contributions. These factors ensure that each term appropriately influences the optimization process, preventing any single term from dominating due to scale differences.

The choice of these weighting factors is motivated by the need to prioritize specific aspects of the mission, depending on the application context. For instance, in specific scenarios, minimizing the number of AUVs (i.e., reducing energy usage) might be more critical, while in others, maximizing the state-of-charge (SoC) could be the key objective. The weightings thus serve as a control parameter that allows for flexible optimization based on the mission's priorities, which we can adjust according to the specific needs of the task.

Table 1. Overview of the HPO configuration, optimal hyperparameters, and computational time for each algorithm variant, including the number of waypoints, missions, and key parameters.

	HPO		RS-PSO	TPE-PSO	RS-PSO+	TPE-PSO+
Max. iter (HPO)		500				
number of waypoints	$N \in \{80, 100\}$	$N \in \{70, 75, 80, 85, 90, 95, 100, 105\}$				
number of missions	$K = 2 \cdot N_{AUV}$	$800 \to 100$ per setup				
	Search space	Optimal hyperparameter				
P	rand(5, 250)	7	72	103	172	
G	rand(100, 500)	207	271	286	301	
η_{gbest}	uniform(0.7, 1.0)	0.83	0.82	0.94	0.93	
η_{pbest}	uniform(0.7, 1.0)	0.73	0.88	0.9	0.96	
M	rand(5, 20)	12	10	10	11	
		Computational time T_{comp}				
mean(T_{comp}) [s]		0.899	1.917	2.28	3.149	
var(T_{comp}) [s^2]		0.243	0.403	0.459	0.486	
var^2(T_{comp}) [s^4]		0.059	0.163	0.211	0.236	

5 Evaluation

When applying HPO to both PSO-based algorithms, the maximum number of iterations alongside the objective function was necessary. This is crucial because, on the one hand, it allows for a more accurate approximation of the global optimum. On the other hand, it helps to limit iteration and avoid unnecessary resource consumption. The convergence plot in Fig. 5(a-d) shows the minimum objective function value at each iteration across 1000 iterations of the HPO. This allows for a visual assessment of how quickly the optimization approaches the global optimum. The advantage of the PSO+ approach becomes apparent since its greedy initialization enables the HPO algorithm to start with a lower objective function value. Although TPE-PSO begins with the highest initial cost, it achieves the lowest objective function value by the end of the optimization process. After approximately 500 iterations, further improvements stagnate, indicating diminishing returns in prolonged optimization. However, since each iteration incurs a computational cost, and we are considering future applications where PSO may serve as a local planner for AUVs, we need to evaluate whether achieving results with fewer iterations, which approach the minimum, is sufficient.

To evaluate this more precisely, we use an internal simulation routine. We consider the AUV failures and the SoC as a function of the maximum iterations, shown in Fig. 5(e-f). The resultn's robustness, we generated 100 missions with $N \in \{70, \dots, 105\}$ waypoints. Since we aim to determine hyperparameters that generalize beyond a specific problem instance, we deliberately varied the

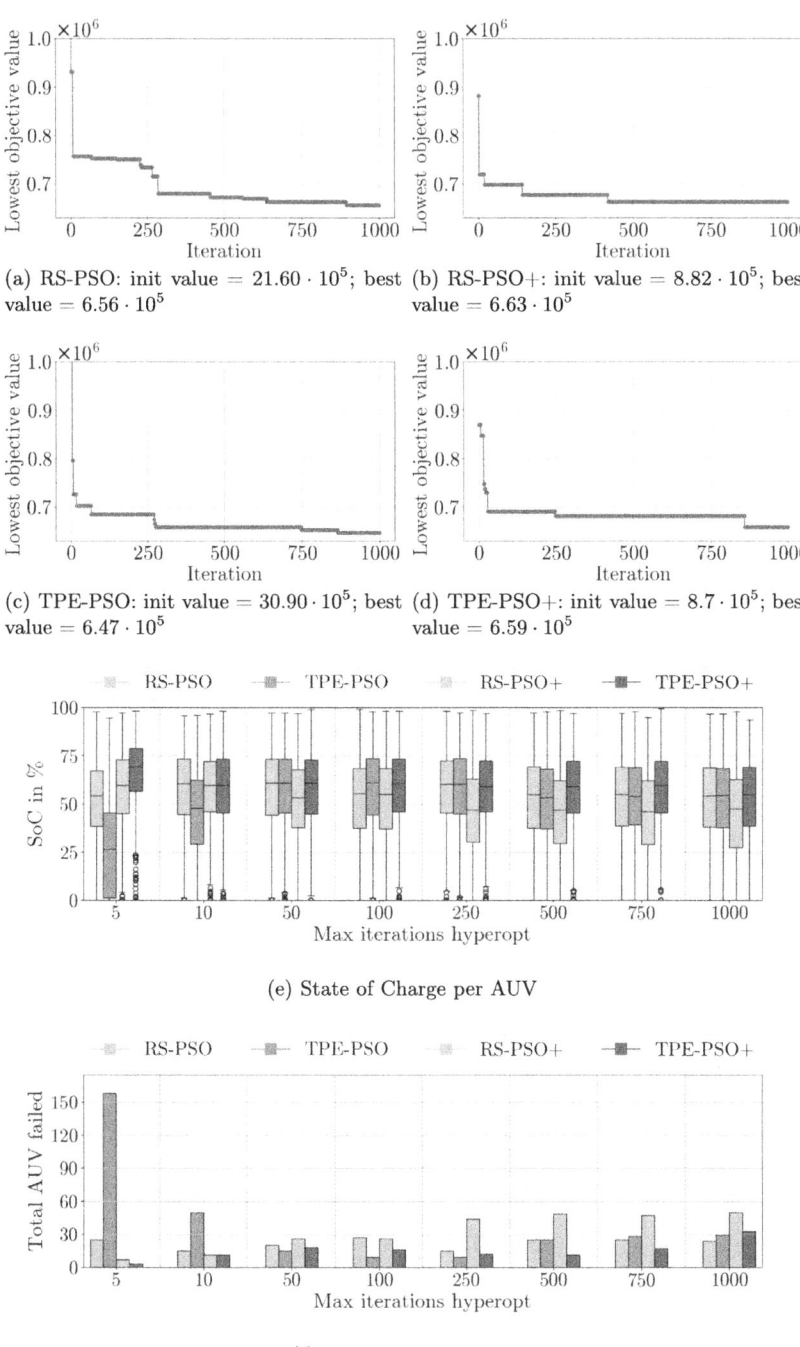

Fig. 5. Results of the HPO: (a-d) Outer Optimization, Convergence plot of the different algorithms as a function of the maximum iterations; (e-f) Inner Optimization, AUV's *SoC* and total number of failure depending on the chosen maximal iterations.

number of waypoints. This allows us to assess the robustness of the selected hyperparameters across different mission sizes. Specifically, we aim to test the transferability of the results by expanding the range of waypoints from 70 to 105 while we initially determine the HPOs for missions with 80 and 100 waypoints. Both plots confirm the observations made in the convergence analysis. Overall, the failure rate is lower for PSO than for PSO+. However, this is mainly due to RS-PSO+, which performs significantly worse than the other variants. In contrast, TPE-PSO+ delivers results comparable to TPE-PSO. Additionally, as the maximum number of iterations increases, the failure rate of AUVs remains lower for PSO, and their SoC stays higher than in PSO+, indicating more efficient energy utilization. However, improvements stagnate after approximately 500 iterations, suggesting diminishing returns from further optimization.

Considering the reduced computation time, we now aim to conduct a more in-depth evaluation to assess how well this configuration performs across different test scenarios under different distributions:

1. Grid: An arrangement typical to pattern tracing methods, where the coordinates are evenly spaced in a square field.
2. Random: Randomly distributed coordinates in the field that follow a regular distribution.
3. Hotspot: Coordinates distributed randomly around three centers.

We test the determined hyperparameters for robustness against deviations in the number of waypoints and the type of distribution in the field. The evaluation plot shown in Fig. 6 presents the outcomes for the SoC and mission failures across three test cases using the hyperparameters at 500 iterations for the HPO. We define a mission as failed if any AUVs do not complete their assigned tasks.

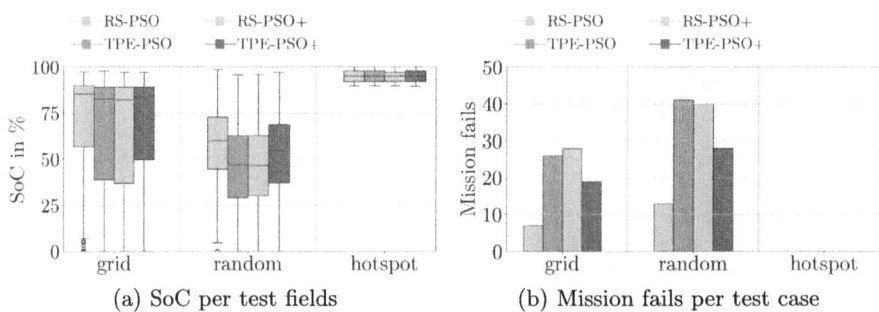

(a) SoC per test fields   (b) Mission fails per test case

Fig. 6. SoC and mission failure rate for all algorithm variants across three test scenarios with HPO over 500 iterations.

Furthermore, we averaged the computational time across all simulation test scenarios, as shown in Table 1. The computational times were measured on a Dell Latitude 7430 laptop, equipped with an Intel Core i7 processor and 16 GB of RAM, running Ubuntu 22.04. We perform the experiments by running each scenario 240 times to ensure statistical significance. The results indicate that all algorithms achieve similar solutions with few mission failures. RS-PSO delivers the best results in mission fulfillment and energy consumption, with the smallest population and fewest generations, leading to the lowest computational time, making it ideal for resource-limited applications. However, it requires the highest number of AUVs, increasing costs. In contrast, RS-PSO+ and TPE-PSO+ have higher computational times but use fewer AUVs, making them more cost-effective when AUVs are limited.

In the hotspot field scenario, shorter routes result in surplus energy, suggesting that fewer AUVs would be sufficient. This highlights a potential improvement for HPO by incorporating waypoint distribution into the optimization process.

In conclusion, with optimized parameters, traditional PSO performs as well as the enhanced versions, suggesting that improvements may not be necessary. Despite using fewer iterations than indicated by the convergence plot, the results remain robust. A good strategy would involve many iterations for global path planning and fewer for local adjustments, thereby reducing computational effort.

6 Conclusion and Outlook

In this work, we investigated how HPO can improve the robustness and resource utilization of PSO for energy-aware AUV mission planning. Our study focused on determining optimal hyperparameters to balance exploration and exploitation, ensuring that PSO delivers energy-optimal solutions for waypoint assignment and path planning. Defining PSO configuration parameters as hyperparameters allows for a systematic optimization process rather than relying on trial-and-error tuning. Through real-world-inspired simulations, we validated that our HPO-driven approach enhances mission success rates, reduces energy consumption, and enables a more precise estimation of the minimum required number of AUVs for a given mission.

A key finding from our simulations is that with optimized hyperparameters, the traditional PSO performs almost as well as the improved PSO+ variant. This suggests that, under the proper parameter settings, the added complexity of PSO+ may not always be necessary. Additionally, while a high number of iterations is beneficial for determining the global path at the base station, significantly fewer iterations are sufficient for local adjustments on the AUVs. This insight can help reduce computational effort in real-world setups.

This work enhances energy-efficient path planning and lays the groundwork for future autonomous swarms. Adaptive configurations for local path planning allow the system to respond dynamically to environmental changes. Additionally, swarm intelligence strategies could enable AUVs to redistribute waypoints in case of individual failures, improving mission robustness. Validation through real-world missions is essential to assess practical applicability and refine optimization based on actual ocean conditions.

References

1. Alfred-Wegener-Institut, Helmholtz Zentrum für Polar- und Meeresforschung: Tiefsee-Ökologie und -technologie (2024). https://www.awi.de/forschung/biowissenschaften/tiefsee-oekologie-und-technologie/technologie.html
2. Bergstra, J., Bardenet, R., Bengio, Y., Kégl, B.: Algorithms for hyper-parameter optimization. In: Advances in Neural Information Processing Systems, vol. 24 (2011)
3. Bergstra, J., Bengio, Y.: random search for hyper-parameter optimization. J. Mach. Learn. Res. **13**(2) (2012)
4. Bergstra, J., Komer, B., Eliasmith, C., Yamins, D., Cox, D.D.: Hyperopt: a python library for model selection and hyperparameter optimization. Comput. Sci. Discovery **8**(1), 014008 (2015)
5. Conmy, R.N., et al.: Advances in underwater oil plume detection capabilities. In: International Oil Spill Conference, vol. 2021, p. 1141330 (2021)
6. Cormen, T.H., Leiserson, C.E., Rivest, R.L., Stein, C.: Introduction to Algorithms. MIT press, Cambridge (2022)
7. FONA - Forschung für Nachhaltigkeit: Unterwasserfahrzeuge der deutschen Meeresforschung (2024). https://www.fona.de/de/massnahmen/forschungsinfrastrukturen/unterwasserfahrzeuge.php
8. Fossen, T.I.: Handbook of Marine Craft Hydrodynamics and Motion Control. John Wiley & Sons, Hoboken (2011)
9. Frenkel, W., Renner, B.C.: Towards energy-aware path planning for AUV swarms. In: 2024 18th ICARCV, pp. 1106–1111. IEEE (2024)
10. Kennedy, J., Eberhart, R.: Particle swarm optimization. In: ICNN 1995, vol. 4, pp. 1942–1948. IEEE (1995)
11. Kuehner, I.: Swarm intelligence for solving a traveling salesman problem. eKNOWN (2020)
12. Liu, X., Su, J., Han, Y.: An improved particle swarm optimization for traveling salesman problem. In: Huang, D.-S., Heutte, L., Loog, M. (eds.) ICIC 2007. LNCS (LNAI), vol. 4682, pp. 803–812. Springer, Heidelberg (2007). https://doi.org/10.1007/978-3-540-74205-0_84
13. Lu, C., Yang, J., Leira, B.J., Chen, Q., Wang, S.: Three-dimensional path planning of deep-sea mining vehicle based on improved particle swarm optimization. J. Mar. Sci. Eng. **11**(9), 1797 (2023)
14. Martin-Abadal, M., Oliver-Codina, G., Gonzalez-Cid, Y.: Real-time pipe and valve characterisation and mapping for autonomous underwater intervention tasks. Sensors **22**(21), 8141 (2022)
15. Messon, D., Verma, D., Rastogi, M., Singh, A.: Comparative study of time optimization algorithms for traveling salesman problem. In: AICTC 2021, pp. 555–566. Springer (2022)
16. Qu, N., Chen, G., Shen, Y.: A Three-dimensional path planning system for AUV diving process considering ocean current and energy consumption. In: OCEANS 2021: San Diego–Porto, pp. 1–7. IEEE (2021)
17. Reuter, J., Mank, E., Aschemann, H., Rauh, A.: Battery state observation and condition monitoring using online minimization. In: 2016 21st MMAR, pp. 1223–1228. IEEE (2016)
18. Villwock, A., Kersten, C.: From the deep sea to the atmosphere: GEOMAR Helmholtz Centre for Ocean Research Kiel (2015)

19. Wang, K.P., Huang, L., Zhou, C.G., Pang, W.: Particle swarm optimization for traveling salesman problem. In: Proceedings of the 2003 International Conference on Machine Learning and Cybernetics (IEEE cat. no. 03ex693), vol. 3, pp. 1583–1585. IEEE (2003)
20. Woods Hole Oceanographic Institution: AUVs (2025). https://www.whoi.edu/what-we-do/explore/underwater-vehicles/auvs/
21. Yang, L., Shami, A.: On hyperparameter optimization of machine learning algorithms: theory and practice. Neurocomputing **415**, 295–316 (2020)

Process-Level Simulation Testbed for Assessing Field Robot Swarms

Jonas Boysen(✉) and Anthony Stein

Department of Artificial Intelligence in Agricultural Engineering,
University of Hohenheim, 70599 Stuttgart, Germany
{jonas.boysen,anthony.stein}@uni-hohenheim.de

Abstract. Agricultural mechanization so far has increasingly led to larger machines with large working widths to optimize their area output and which can be considered a single point of failure. Contrastingly, swarms of smaller machines provide an alternative for a better scalable and more resilient agricultural technology. Following the principles of swarm intelligent systems, the resulting decentralization promises improved robustness, i.e., through the possibility of the swarm to compensate for single failing machines in a self-organizing manner. In this paper, we propose a swarm simulation testbed for assessing the potential of robot swarms in agricultural fields at the process-level. In initial experiments to demonstrate the suitability of our testbed, we explore the scaling potential of a robot swarm compared to a single conventional machine during the process of seeding. We compared three coordination approaches to intelligently control the robot swarm. The approaches vary between: 1) A centralized control unit coordinating the swarm, 2) a decentralized swarm coordination, and, 3) a hybrid variant. The algorithms comprise combinations of the meta-heuristics simulated annealing, a genetic algorithm and a simple rule-based heuristic followed by the individual robots. Our experiments showcase the suitability of our swarm simulation testbed to explore the potential of swarm robotic solutions in agricultural field logistic problems. They also indicate that the decentralized swarm coordination approach results in a higher area output for higher number of machines working on small fields.

Keywords: Swarm robotics · Multi-robot system · Agriculture · In-field logistic optimization · Organic Computing · Artificial intelligence

1 Introduction

Digitization of the agricultural sector progresses as farmers increasingly use smart or digital farming applications. The introduction of AI is expected to further increase the efficiency and productivity of precision farming by developing applications which are capable of processing large amounts of data produced by smart sensors or IoT-devices [8]. Moving towards such complex technologies, however, is associated with the risk to develop vulnerabilities in a critical infrastructural sector such as agriculture. Smart agricultural applications are linked with a strong 'digital dependency' on technology across multiple scales (from machine level, over farm and inter-farm level up to cloud level) which demands resilient architectures to prevent failures in the agricultural processes [4]. Systems with a single point of failure, where the whole process stops if a single machine fails, are highly critical. Recently, agricultural mechanization has shifted to the use of single machines of increasing sizes [2], to achieve higher productivity. However, an increasing size of individual machines also leads to an increasing dependence of the farmer on the proper functioning of these machines, as well as poorer scalability and negative effects on soil health [12]. One current area of research is the replacement of a large machine with multiple smaller robots [9]. This results in advantages in terms of soil compaction, robustness in case of single failures and scalability and enables the use of possible future cropping systems such as spot farming [23]. In order for such a multi-robot system to be used and coordinated effectively, however, swarm robotic algorithms are required. These algorithms need to be tested in simulation before real-world application since a limitation of swarm robotics is the logistical complexity caused by the need to coordinate several machines with low seed or battery capacity.

Organic Computing (OC) focuses on equipping technical systems with lifelike properties through the incorporation of nature-inspired mechanisms to work reliably in complex real-world problems. It is a systems engineering paradigm for the design of intelligent technical systems by endowing lifelike properties such as flexibility, robustness and self-organization. The latter is specifically important for swarm robotics [10,14,15]. While swarm robotics may be coordinated by a centralized control unit [3], it can utilize the full advantage of swarm intelligence by operating through decentralized coordination. Decentralized coordination is a perfect fit for OC systems with multiple agents communicating through a collaborative layer and showing emergent behavior [19]. Recently, OC has been discussed to provide a promising approach to built future intelligent agricultural technology systems in [22]. The presented work takes another step in that direction and provides a simulation tool to explore the adoption of swarm intelligent system approaches to coordinate multi-robot systems in agricultural fields.

In this paper, we propose a process-level simulation testbed to analyze the potential of robot swarms in crop production settings for various swarm coordination approaches. To this end, in Sect. 2, we provide a brief overview on related works investigating swarm robotic applications in agricultural fields. In Sect. 3, we describe our simulation's architecture in detail and report observed results from initial experiments in Sect. 4 to showcase the suitability of our testbed for exploring the scaling potential of robot swarms under different coordination approaches in comparison to a single conventional machine. For this purpose we developed and adopted five different algorithms from the domain of metaheuristic optimization. The algorithmic variants, comprising simulated annealing, genetic algorithms as well as simple rule-based heuristics, can be categorized into three coordination approaches: 1) A centralized control unit coordinating the swarm, 2) a decentralized swarm coordination, and, 3) a hybrid variant. Finally, we discuss the limitations and extensibility of our results along with a possible use in higher education (cf. Sect. 5) and conclude our work.

2 Related Work

Swarm robotics is an active research field for mechanized agricultural operations [2]. Herlitzius et al. [11] propose the Field Swarm (in German 'Feldschwarm') concept. A system with modular, autonomous, interconnected units that can perform multiple agricultural tasks. Another example are the Agbots [16] which are a coordinated multi-agent weeding swarm implemented in simulation that share information to efficiently weed fields with heterogeneous weed growth. The performance of the Agbots approach has been enhanced in Agbots 2.0 [17] and Agbots 3.0 [18] by utilizing improved decision algorithms which, e.g., also function in partial observable environments comparable to fully observable environments and improved the environment dynamics of weed growth. A further multi-robot weed mapping approach has been proposed in the SAGA project by utilizing a swarm of drones for weed mapping [1]. In contrast to their simulation framework, we add the infield logistics specifically the loading of seed and energy at logistic points. Opposed to decentralized coordination, agricultural robot swarms have also been utilized for a real world seeding task in a centralized approach of a seeding task within the MARS project [3]. While concepts, complex real-world machines and simulations have already been proposed in research, a simulation testbed to analyze scalability and test different swarm algorithms in a seeding task including its logistic complexity has not been included in research, yet.

3 Swarm Simulation Architecture

Our simulation targets to simulate the seeding process of multiple machines on agricultural fields. The aim of this process is that machines need to cover the field with seeds. For this propose, the field is divided in headland areas where the machines are turning or navigating and in the fieldwork where the machines are seeding. The fieldwork is split to single straight lanes which are as wide as the working width of the machines. During the field operations, machines need to fill their seed tank and possibly their batteries at specified logistic points in the field. For the simulation of this process, we propose a swarm simulation software which is written in Python (3.10.12) and contains a graphical user interface (GUI) which is created with tkinter (python standard library) using forest-tkk-theme[1]. The GUI is implemented to comprehend and retrace agent behavior within the simulation and allows to monitor machines and fieldwork progress. Fields are implemented as a directed graph using the networkx (3.1) python package and the simulation utilizes shapely (2.0.1) for path generation

---
[1] https://github.com/rdbende/Forest-ttk-theme (last accessed 31.03.2025).

and collision avoidance. Initially, lanes that cover the fieldwork are generated from field boundaries using the python interface of Fields2Cover version 1 [20]. The architecture of our framework is displayed in Fig. 1. In general, orange fields indicate inputs to the framework while green fields are outputs from the simulation. The simulation is tick-based to allow to simulate e.g. time delays resulting from collision avoidance or in future work machine failures. For faster and parallel computation, the GUI can be disabled in a headless mode.

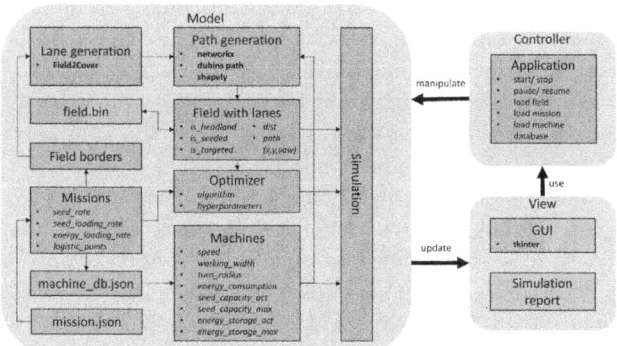

Fig. 1. Architecture of the swarm robotic simulation testbed.

Machines. In this framework machine types can be specified with a json file. The possible attributes for our initial experiments which cover the most essential parameters of a seeding task can be seen in Fig. 1. For each tick in the simulation, a machine can be in one of the following states: 1) seeding within a lane, 2) navigating on headland, 3) waiting anywhere while being blocked by another machine, 4) loading energy and/or seed at a logistic point or 5) stopping at a logistic point when all lanes are seeded or targeted. These states allow the simulation model to update machine positions as well as machine and field information. By design, machines always have a navigation target except if they are in the state of being stopped and no work is left to do (state 5) or if they are loading energy and/or seed (state 4). A target can be to finish seeding the current lane (state 1), to navigate to a targeted lane for seeding or to navigate to a logistic point for loading or stopping (state 2). Machines will always start and end their jobs on logistic points since these are considered as access points to the field, e.g., for the farmer to pick up the robots. Furthermore, machines will only target a lane for seeding if it has sufficient seed to cover the whole lane and if it has sufficient energy to reach the lane, seed the lane and reach a logistic point from the end of the lane. This rule prevents machines from becoming stuck in the middle of the field or seeding only part of lanes.

Missions. Another json file describes the mission. In a mission, the number of machines and the machine types are specified. All generated lanes (by the Field2Cover package) of the fieldwork have the same working width. For this reason, missions must select machines with the same working width. Furthermore, a mission describes the number of logistic points and their attributes as stated in Fig. 1. Additionally, other parameters specific for the job can be set in the mission. In case of a seeding job, the seeding rate is set in $\frac{kg}{ha}$.

Fields. A field corresponds to a directed graph that is created from field borders for machines with a specific working width. The same field borders can be used to generate fields for machines of different working widths. The Field2Cover package will optimize lane arrangement for various cost functions, e.g. the number of generated lanes, in the fieldwork. Furthermore, the minimal turning radius and working width of the machines must be set. The Field2Cover package can create random field borders by specifying the number of field sides and the field area. Although the Field2Cover package includes a number of functionalities to optimize the path of a single machine, our implementation only uses field and lane generation since we target multiple machines in a tick-based simulation. After path generation (cf. Sect. 3), fields can be saved or loaded as binary files as displayed in Fig. 1. Edges of the field graph can either be a headland for navigation or a lane that needs seeding. All edges have a path which is precomputed based on the turning radius of machines. This path is used by the machines for driving. Lanes can have the status of either be seeded, not seeded or targeted by a machine. This information is shared between machines.

Path Generation. The representation of the fields as directed graphs are chosen to reflect the movement direction of a machine in the field and avoid sudden 180∘ turning. A machine driving to a certain navigation point can only leave the navigation point in the opposite direction. For this reason, two nodes are created at the ends of each lane, resulting in a total of four nodes per lane. One of the nodes at a single end corresponds to the entrance of this lane, the other node to the exit of this lane. For each lane, an edge is connected from both entrance nodes to the opposite exit nodes, resulting in two edges per lane. For navigation between different headlands, two navigation nodes are placed in each corner of the field. One of them with a clockwise exit (and an anticlockwise entrance) and the other node with an anticlockwise exit (clockwise entrance). All entrance and exit nodes that end between the same two field corners share a headland and are connected to the navigation nodes at the specific corners. For this connection, the entrance and exit of the navigation nodes in the corners of the field that point to the shared headland are connected with the exit and entrance of each lane ending at the same shared headland.

In Fig. 2a an exemplary headland navigation corner is displayed. The exit node (blue dot) of a lane (brown line) is connected to the entrance node of the navigation point. The blue line represents a headland navigation line, in this case for anticlockwise navigation on the headland, which corresponds to

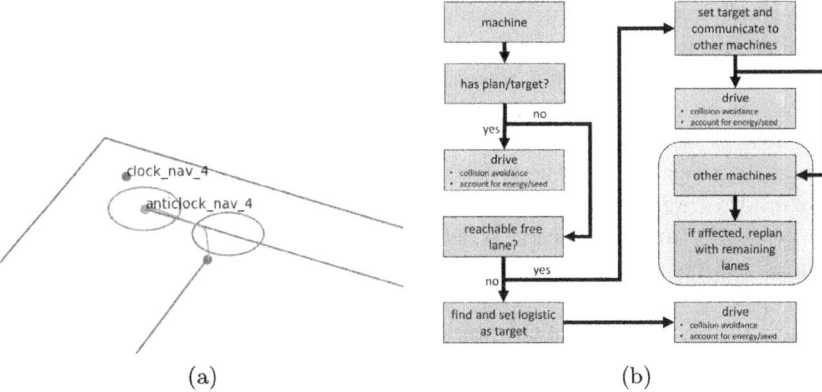

Fig. 2. Navigation path generation at an exemplary field corner (a) and the loop at a simulation tick of a machine (b). (Color figure online)

left-hand traffic. The orange line highlights the robots' path when exiting the brown lane and heading for the navigation node. This path is based on multiple uses (traveling via intermediate points) of the Dubins path algorithm [7] using the implementation of [21]. The intermediate navigation points are created to directly guide the robot to the headland navigation line to avoid disturbing oncoming traffic. The path is generated by first finding the closest point on the respective headland navigation line to the end point of the lane (center of the green circle). From there, we create a point on the line in a distance of $2 \times turn\_radius$ to ensure that the machine can reach the newly created point with its turning radius. A similar point is created at the other end of the headland navigation line (purple circle). The same procedure is used to connect lanes that share a headland and connect logistic points that are placed anywhere on the field border but directly in close proximity to field corners.

Navigation. On each simulation tick, the simulation iterates over all machines and performs movements. The simulation loop of a single machine is shown in Fig. 2b. When a machine is traveling on an edge (states 1–3), the progress on the edge is increased depending on the machines' working speed while the stored energy is decreased depending on the specified energy consumption while driving (state 2). If the current edge is a lane (state 1), the energy storage is decreased depending on the specified energy consumption while working and the stored seed is decreased depending on the machines' working speed as well as seeding rate as specified in the mission file. When the machine is blocked by other machines (state 3), stored energy and seed are not decreased.

When a machine finishes its progress on an edge, additional excess travel distance is saved as a surplus and will be added to the progress on the next edge. As specified before, machines almost always have at least one target (a targeted lane or a logistic point). To reach their target, machines search for the shortest path in the graph with the dijkstra algorithm [6]. This headland navigation must be performed on headland edges only. Machines that do not have a target, will try and find a lane that is not seeded and also not already targeted by another machine. As mentioned before, machines will filter lanes for which they have sufficient seed and energy while also being able to reach a logistic point after finishing the navigation to the lane and to a logistic point from the lane. If they cannot find a target, they will search for a path to the closest logistic point to recharge energy and load seed. When they find multiple possible target lanes, machines will choose the closest lane to reduce navigation distance. They will create a path containing the navigation nodes to the lane, the entrance node to the lane and the exit node of the lane. This rule-based approach where machines globally communicate targets and already seeded lanes is further called swarm.

On the other hand, the framework also allows to assign navigation plans of lane sequences and logistic stops to machines which allows prior optimization of lane to machine allocation and lane sequence optimization. When assigning such plans to machines, the limitations of current as well as maximum energy and seed are taken into account. Machines with such a plan will communicate their immediate target to other machines by setting this lane as targeted. When a machine finishes its plan, it falls back to the rule-based navigation pattern and will globally communicate to find a reachable, close and neither seeded nor targeted lane. These lanes can be part of the plan of a different machine that has not finished its workload yet, e.g., due to a malfunction or an non-optimal plan. In case a machine successfully acquires a free lane that is part of the plan of a different machine, the machines communicate the exchange of the lane and the other machine will replan with the remaining assigned lanes. The (re)planning algorithm expects a lane sequence, the graph, a start node and machine information which includes current and maximum of energy and seed fill. The algorithm will create a navigation plan to seed all lanes in the lane sequence and maintain sufficient energy and seed to not run out between visits of logistic points. This is guaranteed by recursively injecting logistic stops between lanes starting from the end of the plan and where necessary (cf. Algorithm 1). These logistic stops are also optimized by a heuristic that considers seed and energy fill levels as well as the distance to logistic points at each possible interrupt.

Collision Avoidance. A collision avoidance procedure is implemented to simulate that machines cannot pass through each other. For this purpose, machines can reserve area on the 2D-plain field that other machines are not allowed to enter. Machines will always reserve a circular area with a diameter of their working width around them. When driving, the machines will also try to reserve area along their path in front of them. This area is a line of the navigation path buffered by a diameter of the machine's working width. If this area collides with already reserved area of other machines, the machine will stop and not drive during this simulation tick. Consequentially, the machine will not reserve any area of the path but only reserve the circular area around it. Since collisions

Algorithm 1. Recursively add logistic stops to a plan based on a heuristic

1: **function** ADDLOGISTICSTOPS(*path, machine, graph*)
2:    *costs* ← INITEMPTYCOSTS()
3:    **for** *edge* in REVERSED(*plan*) **do**
4:       *costs*.INSERT(0,GETCOSTSTOEND(*graph*))
5:    **end for**
6:    **if** CHECKIFSUFFICENTRESSOURCES(*machine, costs*) **then**
7:       **return** *path*   ▷ Termination of recursion
8:    **end if**
9:    *interrupts* ← REACHABLEEDGESFROMEND(*costs, graph, machine*)
10:    **for** *interupt* in *interrupts* **do**
11:       *interrupt*.ADDUTILITY(DISTSTORAGEHEURISTIC(*graph, machine*))
12:    **end for**
13:    *interupt_at* ← *interupts*.GETBESTINTERUPT()
14:    *remaining_path* ← EXTRACTREMAININGPATH(*path, interupt_at, graph*)
15:    *resulting_path* ← CONSTRUCTRESULTINGPATH(*path, interupt_at, graph*)
16:    *path* ← ADDLOGISTICSTOPS(*remaining_path, machine, graph*)
17:    **return** *resulting_path*.EXTEND(*path*)
18: **end function**

can only occur during headland navigation, area reservations are only applied to path segments that are on headlands. Headland navigation lines as described in Sect. 3 and left-hand traffic reduce the collisions by separating two-way traffic on headlands. However, to reach or leave these headland navigation lines, machines may pass the path of other machines driving in opposite directions. This may result in deadlocks where both machines cannot navigate anymore. Since this simulation is targeting process-level navigation, these deadlocks are resolved by removing collision avoidance for a certain period after machines are blocked for a specified duration, freeing any deadlocks after a penalizing time.

4 Experiment: Field Logistic Optimization

4.1 Experimental Setup

In our experiments, we want to showcase the suitability of our simulation to evaluate the performance of five different coordination approaches (cf. Table 1) of the robot swarm against a conventional machine. The coordination approaches include a rule-based based navigation (swarm), two centralized approaches with lane sequence optimization performed with *simulated annealing* (SA) and a *genetic algorithm* (GA) and two hybrid variants using the central plan only to some extend and will discard any plan after the first logistic stop (hybrid SA and hybrid GA) to analyze the capabilities of the rule-based (swarm) approach when picking up a swarm in the middle of a plan. SA and the GA are used to optimize lane allocation to machines and the sequence of lanes allocated to machines with the target to reduce the total amount of time until completion of the field. We use our directed graph network with a recursive algorithm to inject logistic stops as an oracle to estimate the theoretical simulation time of the worst performing machine of a solution candidate. This way, we calculate the utility or fitness needed for SA or the GA. Alternatively, the tick-based simulation could be run which would require more time. The code is available on github[2].

Table 1. Controlled values of the parameters varied in the experiments and the hyperparameters set for the optimization (SA/GA) of lane sequences and lane to machine allocation.

parameter	values	hyperparameter	SA	GA
logistic points	{1}	epochs 1ha	25k	2.5k
field sizes	{1ha, 5ha, 10ha}	5ha	35k	2.5k
machines	{2r, 4r, 8r, 16r, 32r, 1t}	10ha	45k	3.5k
algorithms	{swarm, SA, GA,	patience	250	200
	hybrid SA, hybrid GA}	mutation rate	-	hard:0.05, soft:0.2
repetition seeds	{0, 1, 2, 3}	population size	-	32 seeds
field generation seeds	{1, 10, 19}	cooling scheme	linear	-
		max. temperature	5	-

Our experiments cover robots that are based on the Phoenix, a conventional machine based on a tractor with a power harrow, three field geometries of different complexity (cf. Fig. 3) scaled to three different sizes, five different robot numbers and one tractor-implement combination, displayed as ($2^{1..5}$r) for robots and (1t) for the tractor setting in Fig. 4, respectively, as well as five navigation algorithms and four repetitions per experiment (cf. Table 1). The number of logistic nodes is set to one throughout our experiments. The swarm algorithm is only covered by one repetition since it is for our current setting deterministic. This could change in the future when considering, e.g., a soil-machine interaction model [5] or machine failures. This results in a total of 918 simulations performed (54 for the swarm approach and 864 for SA/GA and hybrid SA/GA approaches). We evaluate the performance based on the *area output* = $\frac{covered\ area}{working\ time}$ and the *field efficiency* = $\frac{effective\ time}{overall\ time}$.

Hyperparameters of SA and the GA were tested and determined based on preliminary studies. The resulting hyperparameters are reported in Table 1. For the optimization of simulation time, solution candidates are represented by matrices with $n\_machines$ rows and n_lanes columns. If a lane is allocated to a machine, the index of the lane will appear in the row of the respective machine. Unassigned values are set to -1. The assigned lane sequence of a machine is interpreted from left to right ignoring values of -1. An example solution candidate **s** with two machines on a field with four lanes is displayed in Eq. 1. The GA utilizes ranked selection with elitism and includes two different mutations.

---

[2] https://github.com/AI4AgEng-Lab/FieldSwarmSimTestbed.

Fig. 3. The three different field geometries that are generated using the field generation seeds during our experiments. Field work is colored in dark brown and headlands are colored in light brown. Seeded lanes of the field work are colored in green and targeted lanes are colored in light blue. The logistic point is indicated as a purple dot. (Color figure online)

During hard mutation, the complete matrix of a solution candidate is randomized while during soft mutation the values of a row (a single machine) in the solution candidate are randomized. Otherwise one-point crossover at a random point is performed between two rows of one solution candidate. For SA neighbors are generated by swapping the position of neighboring lanes (in the field) and if assigned to different machines also the machine allocation.

$$\mathbf{s} = \begin{bmatrix} -1, & 3, & 0, & -1 \\ 2, & 1, & -1, & -1 \end{bmatrix} \begin{matrix} machine_1 \\ machine_2 \end{matrix} \qquad (1)$$

4.2 Results

The simulation results are displayed in Fig. 4. One bar in Fig. 4 represents the average over repetitions together with field geometries resulting in $N = 12$ for SA, GA and hybrid SA and GA (cf. Table 1) and $N = 3$ for the swarm approach. The error bars represent one standard deviation. We analyze selected measured values of the blocked or loading time before evaluating the performance based on area output and field efficiency as displayed in Fig. 4.

Blocked and Loading Time. The blocked occupation of machines describes the time that a machine waits for other machines in their path. During our experiments, we observe that blocked occupation increases with machine density. The blocked occupation is especially high for 32 robots in the smallest field size (1 ha) where it reached up to $22 \pm 3.4\%$. Navigation with the swarm approach leads in average to comparably lower blocked occupation for large swarms that navigate on larger fields ($10.6 \pm 5.2\%$ (swarm) compared to $15.0 \pm 3.0\%$ (others) on 5 ha and $9.0 \pm 2.5\%$ (swarm) compared to $12.5 \pm 3.1\%$ (others) on 10 ha fields). The loading time describes the relative amount of time spent at a logistic point for loading seed or energy. The experiments show that only smaller machine

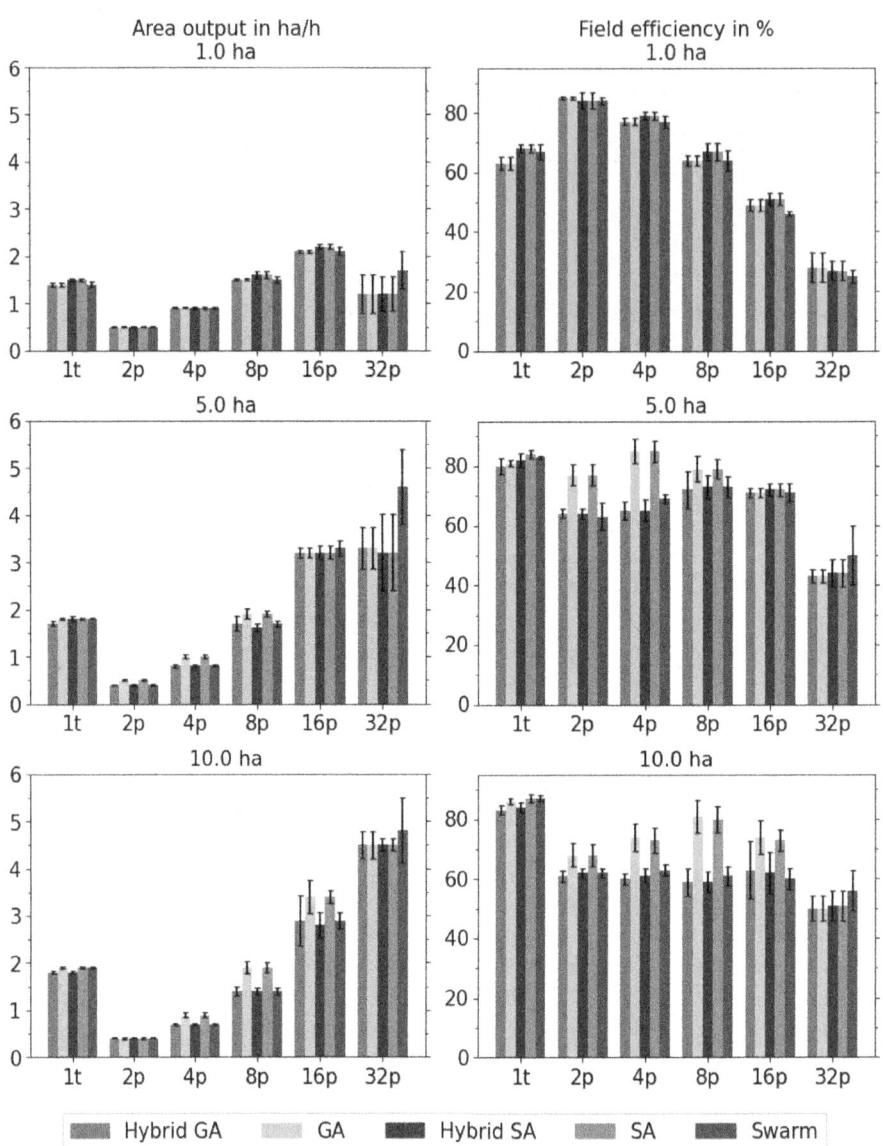

Fig. 4. Mean area output in ha/h (y-axis of left column) and field efficiency in % (y-axis of right column) of the experiments over repetitions and different geometries. Displayed are the five navigation algorithms (colored legend) for different machine numbers (x-axis) including one tractor (1t) and 2^1 to 2^5 phoenix (2p to 32p). One plot corresponds to a certain field size of 1 ha (first row), 5 ha (second row) and 10 ha (third row). The error bars indicate the standard deviations with $N = 12$ except for swarm with $N = 3$.

numbers on larger fields (5 and 10 ha) require loading energy which significantly effects the loading occupation in contrast to loading seed which mostly increased navigation time (smaller capacity and higher loading rate). In general and on 1 ha or 5 ha fields with four to 32 robots and on 10 ha fields with 32 robots, loading occupation is zero or close to zero. We conclude that only loading energy really affected the robots loading occupation since loading energy takes much longer then filling the seed tank. We find that creating a plan with the GA and SA algorithm greatly decreases loading times (e.g. for four robots on a 10 ha field from 23.2% to 13.4% in average). This is achieved because of the knowledge on future energy and seed that is needed to fulfill their plan is used to avoid loading any spare energy or seed that they would not need at the end of the simulation.

Area Output. The left column of Fig. 4 represents the measured area output in ha/h for three different field sizes. The colors indicate different navigation variants while the x-axis attributes the number and type of machines in the simulation run. In general, the area output increases with the swarm size. In contrast, the mean area output of 32 robots on the 5 ha fields (3.2 to 4.6 ha/h with mean std. of 0.7 ha/h) does not increase compared to 16 robots. The mean area output of 32 machines even decreases on the 1 ha fields for approaches except for the swarm approach (1.2 to 1.7 ha/h with mean std. of 0.4 ha/h) due to increased blocking. The swarm approach outperforms in average the other approaches for large robot swarms (32) by 42% in 1 ha fields, 39–42% in 5 ha fields and 7% in 10 ha fields. This observation relates to the blocked occupation which leads to the conclusion that at least some of this performance originates from avoiding being blocked. On 5 ha fields with four to eight operating robots as well as 10 ha fields with four to 16 operating robots, SA and GA outperform the hybrid variants and the swarm approach. Both hybrids show similar performance to the full SA and GA. The single tractor achieves an area output comparable to eight Phoenix robots for all three field sizes. In general, increasing the swarm size is not always leading to a similar increase in area output since the robots start blocking each other more often.

Field Efficiency. The measured mean field efficiency of our experiments is displayed in the right column of Fig. 4. In 5 ha fields and 10 ha fields, the tractor shows the highest mean efficiency (80–84 % with mean std. of 1.6% and 83–87% with mean std. of 1.4% respectively). In 1 ha fields, the tractors' mean field efficiency (63–67% with mean std. of 2.0%) is lower than the field efficiency of two to four robots (77–84% with mean std. of 1.4%). Especially for the experiments on the 1 ha fields, the field efficiency decreases with larger swarms where 32 Phoenix only reach 25 to 28% mean field efficiency. In 5 ha fields with two to eight operating robots as well as 10 ha fields with two to 16 operating robots, SA and GA outperform the hybrid variants and the swarm approach in terms of field efficiency. During these runs, the robots energy demand exceeds the maximum capacity. The SA and GA approaches follow a central plan which is predetermined and bears information of future need of seed and energy which is not provided for the swarm approach. Therefore, they can limit energy charging to a minimum which is sufficient to fulfill their assigned plan. For 32 robots, the swarm approach achieves a higher mean field efficiency than other approaches in the 5 and 10 ha fields (a difference of 6–7% and 5–6% respectively), which is related to the reduced blocked occupation of the swarm approach. Generally, the robot swarm has an advantage in terms of field efficiency on smaller fields (if not too many machines) which decreases on larger fields as the distances to the logistic point increases. Additionally, the field efficiency drastically decreases when the robots need to charge energy to cover the field work.

5 Discussion

The robot parameters are based on the Phoenix platform [13] and not on specific empirical measurements of a seeding task. To achieve precise results, empirical data of the Phoenix during seeding should be recorded. Furthermore, the tractor performs secondary tillage and seeding in a combined workflow, while the Phoenix robot only seeds. In addition, a wider working width of the tractor can be considered when performing secondary tillage without a power harrow in the same workflow. In relation to this, a measure of working quality is not included in the simulation, as smaller machines with lower working speeds have been found to reach higher working quality [9]. Still, the applicability of robot swarms in agricultural fields requires more research regarding, e.g., seeding quality under hard conditions with uneven terrain where the small weight of robots may present a disadvantage or the real-world implementation of a reliable local communication structure. Furthermore, the optimizations are created for multi-agent approaches and not to optimize the navigation of a single machine and statistical tests could underline the significance of simulation results. In further experiments, repetitions with more than one logistic point should be included since this could possibly increase the area output and field efficiency by reducing the blocked amount of time during navigation from and to the logistic point where all machines are gathered. It may also decrease navigation time on large fields where small robots have the disadvantage of traveling long distances to logistic points more often due to their smaller seed capacity.

The framework is written in Python and allows to implement different algorithms for path planning optimization as we proposed with SA and GA. The optimization algorithms performance could further be improved by allowing them to use the simulation as an oracle/ fitness function instead of just the underlying graph which would include blocking events in their performance measure during optimization. On the other hand, information on lanes that need seeding could improve the performance of the swarm approach when provided as, e.g., a heuristic on how much seed/energy to load. Furthermore, failing machines can be implemented to evaluate in addition to the scaling potential also the robustness of decentralized swarm robotic approaches. Currently, machines operate with a constant machine configuration. Different soil conditions, field elevation or the machine-level effects of soil-machine interaction [5], e.g., increased power demand, could be included in such a simulation. The simulation is written for seeding and can further be enhanced by implementing more generic tasks. Furthermore, machine communication on energy and seed load could be added to improve logistic stops of the swarm approach.

The simulation framework is perfect for teaching as it offers a good application interface for the work with basic artificial intelligence algorithm such as classical search or meta-heuristics (single agent). It provides an intuitive example for agronomists of how basic algorithms can tackle complex problems in agricultural engineering. Moreover, it allows further in depth studies to frame even more complex solutions (i.e. multi-agent simulations).

6 Conclusion

In this work, we proposed a simulation testbed for assessing the scaling potential of field robot swarms at the level of agricultural processes. Being initially developed to assess the capability of swarm robotic systems to tackle infield-logistic problems during the crop establishment process of seeding, the simulation framework can be extended to allow an analysis of further agricultural processes such as weed regulation or harvesting. Furthermore, we deem our proposed simulation a great application for interactive and application-oriented teaching of the robustness of robot swarms and contrasting different algorithms to coordinate multi-robot systems. The observed results from our simulation experiments reveal a threshold of eight Phoenix-like robots to reach an area output comparable to a conventional machine. The tractor shows a comparably lower field efficiency on small fields while deploying large swarms on smaller fields also bears the risk of a decreased field efficiency (due to blocking). Area output, however, does not consider working quality, which has been found to be higher for smaller machines with lesser working speeds. Furthermore, concepts for future sustainable cropping systems, e.g., spot farming [23] depend on high precision machines such as those that swarms of small robots could provide in the future.

Acknowledgments. The project is supported by funds of the Federal Ministry of Food and Agriculture (BMEL) based on a decision of the Parliament of the Federal Republic of Germany. The Federal Office for Agriculture and Food (BLE) provides coordinating support for artificial intelligence (AI) in agriculture as funding organization, grant number 28DK109A20.

Disclosure of Interests. The authors have no competing interests to declare that are relevant to the content of this article.

References

1. Albani, D., IJsselmuiden, J., Haken, R., Trianni, V.: Monitoring and mapping with robot swarms for agricultural applications. In: 2017 14th IEEE International Conference on Advanced Video and Signal Based Surveillance (AVSS), pp. 1–6 (2017)

2. Albiero, D., Pontin Garcia, A., Kiyoshi Umezu, C., Leme de Paulo, R.: Swarm robots in mechanized agricultural operations: a review about challenges for research. Comput. Electron. Agric. **193**, 106608 (2022)
3. Blender, T., Buchner, T., Fernandez, B., Pichlmaier, B., Schlegel, C.: Managing a mobile agricultural robot swarm for a seeding task. In: IECON 2016 - 42nd Annual Conference of the IEEE Industrial Electronics Society, pp. 6879–6886 (2016)
4. Bökle, S., Paraforos, D.S., Reiser, D., Griepentrog, H.W.: Conceptual framework of a decentral digital farming system for resilient and safe data management. Smart Agric. Technol. **2**, 100039 (2022)
5. Boysen, J., Zender, L., Stein, A.: Modeling the soil-machine response of secondary tillage: a deep learning approach. Smart Agric. Technol. **6**, 100363 (2023)
6. Dijkstra, E.W.: A note on two problems in Connexion with graphs. Numer. Math. **1**(1), 269–271 (1959)
7. Dubins, L.E.: On curves of minimal length with a constraint on average curvature, and with prescribed initial and terminal positions and tangents. Am. J. Math. **79**(3), 497–516 (1957)
8. Fountas, S., Espejo-García, B., Kasimati, A., Gemtou, M., Panoutsopoulos, H., Anastasiou, E.: Agriculture 5.0: cutting-edge technologies, trends, and challenges. IT Professional **26**(1), 40–47 (2024)
9. Griepentrog, H.W., Stein, A.: Comparison of robot concepts for new sustainable crop production systems. Smart Agric. Technol. **8**, 100499 (2024)
10. Hamann, H., von Mammen, S.: Swarm Robotics, pp. 525–534. Springer International Publishing, Cham (2017)
11. Herlitzius, T., Hengst, M., Grosa, A., Fichtl, H.: Fieldswarm technology for tillage and crop care: Paradigm change in agricultural technology: Bigger, faster, wider is going to change towards smart, connected and modular. at - Automatisierungstechnik **69**(4), 316–324 (2021)
12. Keller, T., Sandin, M., Colombi, T., Horn, R., Or, D.: Historical increase in agricultural machinery weights enhanced soil stress levels and adversely affected soil functioning. Soil Tillage Res. **194**, 104293 (2019)
13. Lüling, N., et al.: Development and evaluation of a self-adaptable planting unit for an autonomous planting process of field vegetables. Smart Agric. Technol. **9**, 100578 (2024)
14. von Mammen, S., Tomforde, S., Hähner, J.: An organic computing approach to self-organizing robot ensembles. Front. Robot. AI **3**, 67 (2016)
15. von Mammen, S., et al.: Ocbotics: an organic computing approach to collaborative robotic swarms. In: 2014 IEEE Symposium on Swarm Intelligence, pp. 1–8 (2014)
16. McAllister, W., Osipychev, D., Davis, A., Chowdhary, G.: Agbots: weeding a field with a team of autonomous robots. Comput. Electron. Agric. **163**, 104827 (2019)
17. McAllister, W., Whitman, J., Axelrod, A., Varghese, J., Chowdhary, G., Davis, A.: Agbots 2.0: weeding denser fields with fewer robots. In: Proceedings of Robotics: Science and Systems. Corvalis, Oregon, USA (2020)
18. McAllister, W., Whitman, J., Varghese, J., Davis, A., Chowdhary, G.: Agbots 3.0: adaptive weed growth prediction for mechanical weeding Agbots. IEEE Trans. Robot. **38**(1), 556–568 (2022)
19. Merkle, D., Middendorf, M., Scheidler, A.: Organic Computing and Swarm Intelligence, pp. 253–281. Springer Berlin Heidelberg, Berlin, Heidelberg (2008)
20. Mier, G., Valente, J., Bruin, S.: Fields2cover: an open-source coverage path planning library for unmanned agricultural vehicles. IEEE Robot. Autom. Lett. **8**(4), 2166–2172 (2023)

21. Sakai, A., Ingram, D., Dinius, J., Chawla, K., Raffin, A., Paques, A.: Pythonrobotics: a python code collection of robotics algorithms. arXiv preprint arXiv:1808.10703 (2018)
22. Stein, A., Boysen, J.: Organic computing for intelligent agricultural technology: perspective and case study. Agric. Eng. EU **80**(1) (2025)
23. Wegener, J.K., et al.: Spot farming-an alternative for future plant production. J. Cultivated Plants/Journal für Kulturpflanzen **71**(4) (2019)

Neural Rules for Reinforcement Learning with XCSF as Controller in Organic Computing Systems

Connor Schönberner[✉][ID], Kjell-Matti Rothenburger, Armin Mackensen[ID], and Sven Tomforde[ID]

Intelligent Systems Group, Kiel University, Kiel, Germany
{cos,st}@informatik.uni-kiel.de, {stu222808,stu224177}@mail.uni-kiel.de

Abstract. Organic Computing (OC) systems tend to incorporate a self-adaptation mechanism allowing them to learn from perceptions of their environment. The hereby used self-learning component is typically a variant of the XCS Classifier System (XCS). XCS is seen as the most researched Learning Classifier System (LCS) which are rule-based Machine Learning systems. LCSs evolve and train populations of classifiers, also called rules, represented as condition-action-evaluation mappings, forming their knowledge base. For their rules, XCS variants employ conditions covering the state space of an environment based on static assumptions about the geometry or structure of the state niches. We take a closer look at using neural networks as so-called neural rules and neural conditions that should be able to evolve to cover state niches of arbitrary structure. While neural rules are far from novel, we modernise the approach and seek to improve the application of neural conditions to Reinforcement Learning problems. XCSF using neural rules and neural conditions was applied to different multi-step Reinforcement Learning environments. Our reported experiments show that they outperform the previous variant of neural rules in all cases, including a traditional XCSF using hyperrectangles in almost all environments.

Keywords: XCS · Learning Classifier Systems · Rule-based Machine Learning · Reinforcement Learning · Deep Learning · Organic Computing

1 Introduction

Organic Computing (OC) [17] describes a paradigm for the development of self-adaptive and learning technical systems. Based on fundamental design concepts such as Observer/Controller [32] or MAPE-K (Monitor-Analyse-Plan-Execute-Knowledge-Cycle from the related field of Autonomic Computing [11]), the productive behaviour of systems is supplemented by an adaptation mechanism that controls the system behaviour based on the current perception of the environmental conditions and optimises this adaptation behaviour independently via learning mechanisms.

In OC systems, this self-learning controller component is typically implemented as a variant of an XCS Classifier System (XCS) [28]; examples can be found in the areas of traffic control [21], network control [31], software testing [22] or in power distribution systems [15]. The process is based on a representation of the input space and the dynamic derivation of rules, so-called classifiers, which are represented as condition-action-evaluation mapping. The condition is usually a hyper-rectangle-based representation in an n-dimensional real-valued space.

A major advantage of XCS and this representation is the interpretability of the current knowledge base and of its decision-making process due to relying on well-understood Machine Learning mechanisms [8,26]. At the same time, it can be observed that neural methods perform on average dramatically better than traditional approaches, especially in the field of Reinforcement Learning (RL) [16].

Classic conditions in Learning Classifier Systems (LCSs) rely on the idea that their condition representation can approximate the structure of the state niches within the state space of an environment at least with sufficient accuracy. For this purpose, those representations usually tend to make static assumptions about the nature of the state niches. For example, the aforementioned hyperrectangle conditions assume that all state niches are coverable using n-dimensional hyper-rectangles. As neural networks are universal approximators, conditions relying on them do not rely on such assumptions and can potentially cover niches of arbitrary form and also evolve to match entirely different forms of state-niches in the same environment. We call such conditions neural conditions and neural rules if they additionally compute the appropriate action for their state niche. While this concept was first proposed in 2002 by Bull et al. [2] it pre-dates the deep learning revolution noticeably. Therefore, most publications for this topic focus solely on shallow one-layer neural networks with small unit sizes.

Modernised neural conditions were applied successfully in one case each to autoencoding [20] and classification [18] and were at least investigated once for multi-step RL problems [23] which are especially relevant for OC systems [30]. In the latter case, the results were inconclusive. In addition, deep neural rules and neural conditions have been not examined, yet. This paper therefore aims to alleviate this and re-examines modernised neural rules and deep neural rules integrated in the classifiers of an XCSF for applying them to multi-step RL problems without severely compromising the advantages of the system and its performance.

In the following, Sect. 2 re-iterates and explains XCS as the used underlying system. Furthermore, it summarises related work on neural rules, neural conditions and related approaches integrating artificial neural networks (ANNs) into classifiers. Section 3 describes and explains in greater detail the semantics of neural rules and conditions, how we alter and use them. Section 4 details the utilised XCS implementation and introduces the targeted environments and the experimental design of this paper. Next, the conducted experiments in the selected multi-step RL environments are reported in Sect. 5. The results and implications of the latter are discussed in Sect. 6. Lastly, a summary and outlook are provided in the concluding Sect. 7.

2 Background

This paper builds on XCS and its subsequent extensions XCSR and XCSF. Following, the important aspects of these systems are re-iterated in Sect. 2.1. This paper focuses on replacing the condition and action mechanisms of the classifiers with an ANN, the origin of this idea and related work are elaborated in Sect. 2.2.

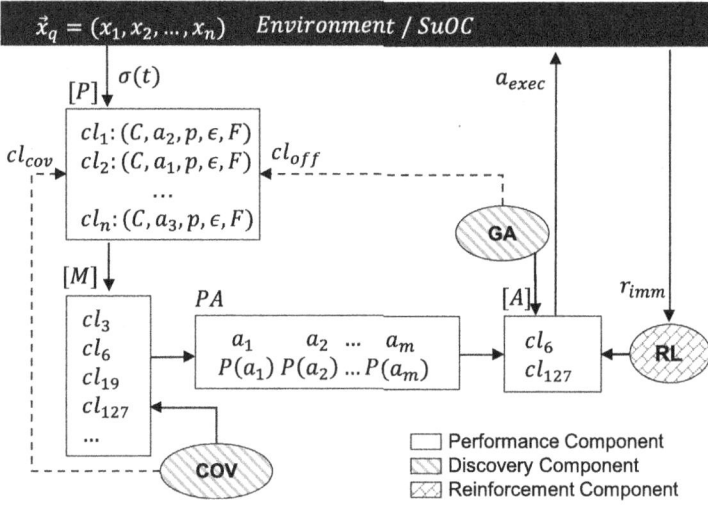

Fig. 1. Schematic of the general XCS architecture, cf. [28]. For simplicity's sake, only the variant for single-step problems is given.

2.1 XCS and Common Extensions

XCS is seen as the most prominent system among Michigan-style LCSs [28]. From the perspective of meta-heuristic systems, XCS and its derivatives are online single-solution LCS, meaning that the system updates itself using single data points or experiences and the whole population forms the solution [8]. XCS combines a population-based evolutionary algorithm (EA), more specifically a Genetic Algorithm (GA), with a Q-Learning-like RL scheme that is used to update subsets of the population sharing the same selected action called action-sets. Due to the combination and intertwined work of the GA and the RL components of XCS, we additionally categorise XCS and related LCS using both components as Evolutionary RL methods.

Classifiers, also called rules or localised models, are the core elements of XCS. One such classifier is defined as $cl = (C, a, p, \varepsilon, F, \ldots)$ and consists of a *condition* C, the *action* a it advocates, the *prediction* p of the payoff, the current prediction *error* ε as an error estimation for the previous predictions, its accuracy-based fitness value F, which is defined an inverse relationship to the prediction error [34], and additional bookkeeping parameters. All currently alive classifiers are collected in the population $[P]$. From a Machine Learning (ML) perspective, the population corresponds to the global model consisting of local models in the form of the classifiers containing the learnable parameters of the system.

The original XCS utilised ternary conditions restricting it to binary input. Wilson [35] alleviated this with XCSR by introducing hyperrectangle conditions in the so-called centre-spread representation making XCS applicable to real-valued problems. Following, Stone et al. [29] introduced the Unordered-Bound Representation (UBR), showing experimental evidence of its superiority over the centre-spread representation.

Furthermore, the constant prediction of XCS was replaced with a computed prediction in XCSF [36] allowing XCS to learn more complex problems. Its Normalised Least Means Squares (NLMS) update formula was later exchanged against the Recursive Linear Least Squares (RLS) update [14]. Nowadays it is the de-facto standard for XCSF.

Figure 1 shows a schema of XCS' structure and sketches its main loop with arrows. For each new time-step t, XCS forms a *match set* $[M]$ out of all classifiers whose condition matches the current observation $\sigma(t)$. If $|[M]| = 0$ or the number of unique actions in $[M]$ is less than the given threshold θ_{mna} the *covering* mechanism adds new classifiers to $[P]$ and $[M]$ matching $\sigma(t)$. Following this, the match set is used to calculate the *prediction array* PA. It has one entry per action. The entry of an action a, called *system prediction* for a, is computed as a fitness-weighted average of all prediction values of those classifiers advocating a. Formalised this means

$$PA(a) = \frac{\sum_{cl \in [M] | cl.a = a} cl.p \cdot cl.F}{\sum_{cl \in [M] | cl.a = a} cl.F}.$$

PA is utilised to select the system response, more precisely the action for the current time step, following an exploration/exploitation strategy which is also called an *action selection regime*. This is usually either done by a variant of epsilon greedy or by an alternating exploration/exploitation strategy, alternating between one pure exploration, meaning selecting the action randomly, and one pure exploitation, meaning selecting the currently best action, episode. All actions that advocate this action are then collected in the *action set* $[A]$. The same action is passed to the environment, which executes it and passes the resulting reward back to the XCS. Next, the RL component updates the classifiers of the current action set $[A]$ or the preceding action set depending on whether XCS is faced with a single- or multi-step problem.

The steady-state niche GA of XCS operates on action sets and is usually activated after the RL update. It is roughly called if the mean time difference to its last call exceeds the given threshold θ_{GA}. It follows the same case distinction as the RL update. First, the GA (usually) selects two parent classifiers using roulette or tournament selection, copies them and applies to a certain probability a crossover and a mutation operator on them. By doing this, the GA exerts evolutionary pressure on the population of XCS, which enables the system to evolve maximally general and accurate classifiers. This is encompassed by Wilson's generalisation hypothesis [34]. In their formal investigations, [3] identified several pressures active within the population and confirmed the hypothesis theoretically.

For more details about the implementation of a canonical XCS, including update formulas, the GA, and hyperparameters, the reader is referred to the algorithmic description of Butz and Wilson [4]. For simplicity's sake, we treat XCS as an umbrella term for all XCS variants but we will exclusively examine an extended XCSF in this paper.

2.2 Related Work - Integrating Neural Networks in Classifiers

This paper is concerned with the idea of integrating neural networks into the classifiers of XCS. The historically most covered variant are neural rules originally introduced by Bull et al. [2] which corresponds to introducing an ANN into each classifier that replaces the condition and computes the action. Several follow-ups [7,9,10] were published advancing different aspects of applying neural rules or combining them with another concept. This ceased after Howard et al. [9] improved their approach of neural rules using spiking neural networks in 2015. Spiking neural networks have fallen out of favour in the ML community, as a result, we do not cover them. If solely the condition is replaced by an ANN, we term this neural condition following Preen et al. [20]. Applying neural conditions to RL problems was so far covered sparingly by publications. Initial experiments were contributed by Schönberner et al. [23] stating inconclusive results.

One related approach originally by Dam et al. [7] replaces the action of a sUpervised Classifier System (UCS) with a shallow ANN. The condition of the system is left as is. It should be noted that actions in UCS correspond to classes or other labels, but not to actions in the original sense derived from RL. Due to that and the focus on supervised learning, we argue it is substantially different and we do not cover it in this paper. Recent works built on this approach by replacing the shallow ANN with Deep Neural Networks (DNNs) [5,12].

Building on XCSF, Lanzi et al. [13] proposed neural prediction replacing the weight vector of a classifier with a sigmoid-activated shallow ANN with one output and updating it with Stochastic Gradient Descent (SGD). Preen et al. [18, 20] integrated neural conditions and neural prediction with DNNs with multiple outputs into their classifiers for autoencoding and classification. Schönberner et al. [23,24] re-examined a modernised variant of the original single-output neural prediction for RL. While neural conditions could be combined with neural prediction, it would reduce the interpretability of the system and is not the focus of this paper.

3 Approach - The Semantics of Neural Rules

Neural rules and neural conditions are ANNs replacing the condition within the classifiers of an LCS. Neural rules also introduce action computation to the system, re-assessing the most appropriate action for their classifiers. Analogous to Preen et al. [19], our neural rules only recompute their actions when a neural rule computes the matching in the match set creation procedure before the covering check is processed to ensure that match sets appropriately cover the action space.

The input layers of both types correspond to the length of the state vector. Classically, the output layer of neural rules and neural conditions corresponds to one unit per action and an additional output unit determining the matching behaviour. Classic neural rules match a state if its final output unit does not have the highest activation. As a result, we call it a non-matching unit. These original neural rules use Sigmoid activation for their hidden layer, their output unit is linearly activated and the weights are uniformly random initialised in $(0, 1)$.

Neural conditions match a state if the activation of their final output unit is higher than θ_{match} with exemplary values of 0 or 0.5, hence we call it a matching unit. In addition, Preen et al. [19] provide an altered variant of neural rules: Their variant uses the matching unit semantics. The action computation also differs due to the output layer of their neural rules consisting of $\max(1, \lceil \log |A| \rceil) + 1$ units and different semantics. The action of their type of neural rules is computed by interpreting the activations of all output units but the last as bits of a binary number that are set if the activation is larger than 0. They clamp the result of this computation in $[0, |A| - 1]$ to allow applying this type of neural rules to scenarios with $|A| \neq 2^k$ with $k \in \mathbb{N}$. We call this type binary (action) neural rules. In our experiments, refer to Sect. 5, we use neural rules as well as binary neural rules with Kaiming initialisation and Rectified Linear Unit (ReLU).

The further semantics of all three variants are equivalent. The GA of the utilised LCS copies the current weights and biases, i.e. the parameters, of a neural rule or condition in the parent selection from parent to offspring classifier and evolves them using solely mutation operators such as parameter mutation, mutating the mutation rates and potentially zeroing and freezing weights of the neural rules. For these aspects, we follow the semantics of Preen et al. [18–20]. Consequently, we also include self-adaptive constructivism for the mutation rates [10]. Arguably, the key operator in the GA is parameter mutation, adding random noise drawn from a Gaussian distribution to the weights and biases. Note that we do not apply the aforementioned freezing operator, to reduce the complexity of the GA.

Neural rules and conditions can be aimed to optimise not only their ability to cover their state niche but also their architecture. They can conduct evolutionary neural-architecture searches by mutating the number of units in their hidden layers. This has the disadvantage of increasing the size of the search space for the evolutionary optimisation potentially requiring a longer time for convergence. Aside, it remains to be demonstrated that evolving a neural rule architecture starting from a very low amount of units per layer leads to better eventual performance than using well-chosen static architecture. We assume that this is not the case. Consequently, we solely focus on evolving the weights and biases of neural rules and conditions and search appropriate architectures manually.

As implied, no crossover and no subsumption operator are applied. While implementing a classic uniform or point crossover operator is possible for ANNs of equal architecture by interpreting them as a sequence of weights and biases, we assessed this approach as not fruitful since it has the high potential to disrupt learned behaviour because it is based on non-linear dependencies between parameters in the same and over multiple layers. Subsumption, on the other hand, is hard to implement since it would need to approximate whether the covered niche of one neural rule or condition is fully included in that of another neural rule or condition. So far, we and others have not investigated this aspect.

4 Experimental Setup

The general setup for the experiments summarises the components of the experiments and the overall methodology. First, the utilised XCS implementation is described in Sect. 4.1. The conducted experiments apply the introduced extended XCS implementation to different multi-step RL environments. Our experiments are conducted in the following environments: Maze6, a map of the maze problem, see Sect. 4.2, the Gymnasium environment Frozen Lake, see Sect. 4.3, and the "Empty" map of the Minigrid environment, see Sect. 4.4. Last, the design of the conducted experiments and the methodology of the evaluation is outlined in Sect. 4.5.

4.1 XCSF Implementation

The implementation used for the experiments of this paper is an adjusted and extended fork of the Python-based XCSF implementation xcsfrl by Bishop[1] which is an improved variant of their XCSF implementation Piecewise[2] [1].

Neural rules and conditions, as introduced in Sect. 3, are implemented in this fork using the PyTorch library. It includes support for classic and binary (action) neural rules as well as neural conditions with arbitrary fully connected layer architecture. Aside from classic neural rules, the implementation of neural rules and their GA operators is inspired by Preen et al. [19].

4.2 The Maze Problem

Maze problems are popular in recent LCS research in RL using XCS variants [23,25,33] since they can be seen as a simplified and approximated simulation of real-world navigation problems [25]. The implementation of the used maze

---

[1] https://github.com/jtbish/xcsfrl (Last Accessed 04.04.2025).
[2] https://github.com/jtbish/piecewise (Last Accessed 04.04.2025).

environment is inspired by that of Preen et al. [19], re-using their collection of classic maze maps and optimal values. The maps are stored as sequences of strings encoding each field as a char following a historically grown notation. Those chars are mapped to discrete floats when simulating the mazes.

The starting position of the agent is a random empty field and we only allow a preconfigured maximal number of steps in one episode - combining these two options is also called teletransportation. The states of the environment correspond to the 8-neighbourhood of a position in which the agent is also allowed to move.

We examine Maze6 which is one of the classic Markov maze maps from LCS literature, has a size of 9×9 and an average optimal step amount of 5.19 [19].

4.3 Frozen Lake

Frozen Lake is a grid world-based Gymnasium environment where an agent has to move over a frozen lake from a fixed start position to a goal position moving in its four-neighbourhood while avoiding holes in the ice. An episode ends, if the goal is reached with a reward of 1 or with a reward of 0 if the time limit is exceeded or the agent falls in a hole.

The states of Frozen Lake correspond to integers indicating the agent is on the i-th position of the map enumerating the positions left-to-right starting in the upper-left corner which is also the start position. As a result, each state is globally unique and has a deterministic optimal action ensuring the Markov property and avoiding aliasing. By default, Frozen Lake has stochastic actions modelled as "slipperiness": An agent moves only with a probability of 0.33 in the direction it intended and with a probability of 0.33 each in one of the directions perpendicular to the desired direction.

ANNs usually do not learn well on discrete integers and the same seems to be the case for XCS when using hyperrectangles. Therefore, the state of the environment, and its position on the lake, is first translated to x, y-coordinates with $x = i$ mod map-size and $y = i$/map-size following the documentation of Frozen Lake. These coordinates are then hot-encoded and concatenated. The resulting array is used as the state representation.

4.4 Minigrid

The Minigrid environment [6] is maintained by Farama, the foundation behind the Gymnasium library. Among others, Minigrid includes grid world maps similar to those used in LCS research [13] such as a classic grid world as "Empty". The reward in this environment is computed as $1 - 0.9(\texttt{steps}/\texttt{maxsteps})$ if the goal position is reached and 0 otherwise. An agent by default starts on the upper-left position with the aim to find the goal position by moving in its 4-neighbourhood allowing the actions to turn left or right and to move forward. We extended the environment with an additional state representation: It consists of the x- and y-coordinates and the current view direction of the agent. Those integers are hot-encoded and the resulting arrays are concatenated.

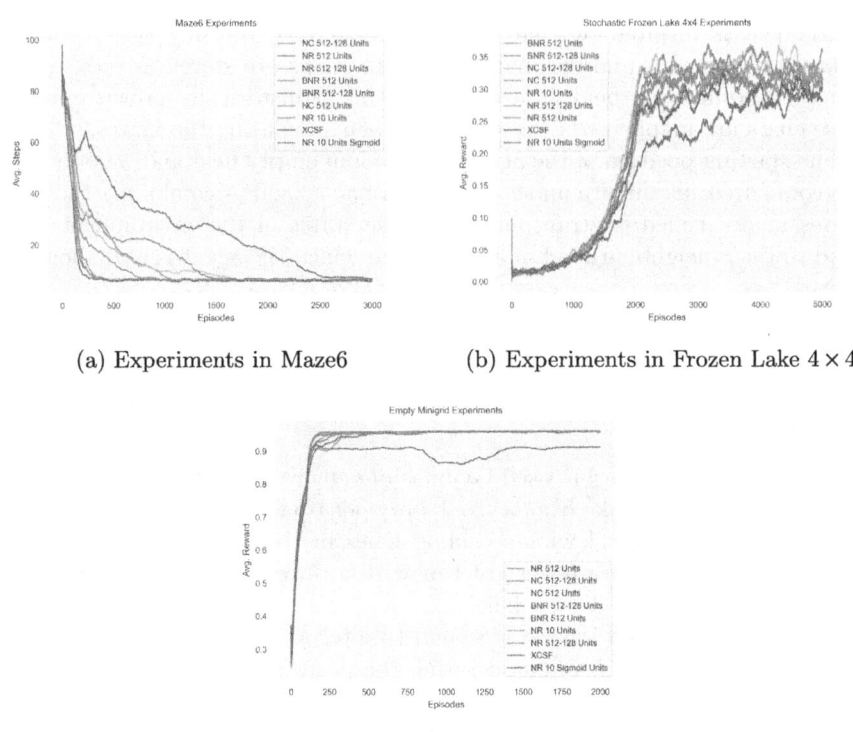

Fig. 2. Neural conditions and neural rules compared to XCSF.

4.5 Experimental Design

Each of our experimental series consist of 20 or 30 separate experimental runs with configured fixed sequences of seeds that use the same environment specific hyperparameters. As the targeted performance metric, we report the average reward or the average steps in 100 episode sliding windows.

During the experiments, the learning performance of each entire episode from start to finish regardless of whether the agent is exploring or exploiting is tracked similarly to related work applying XCS variants to RL [25,27,33]. After collecting the results, the tracked quantities are meant for each time-step over all runs leading to one meant time series used for our showcased plots. The means of the individual experimental runs serve as samples for statistical tests using a two-sided Wilcoxon Signed-Rank test with a significance level of 0.05. We compute the means over the whole experiment's length and the first and last 25% of episodes. The former is chosen to indicate the sample efficiency and the latter to assess the performance for a longer period after convergence. We chose this quantile because we argue that if the training converges it usually has happened before the last 25% of episodes have been reached. We report the mean of the experimental runs' means together with the standard deviation between the means of the experimental runs in tables.

All experimental series re-use the hyperparameters $\theta_{ga} = \theta_{del} = 50$, $\theta_{match} = 0$, $\alpha = 0.1$, $\chi = 0.8$, $\tau = 0.5$, $\delta = 0.1$, $\nu = 5$, $\mu = 0.04$, $\epsilon_I = 0.0001$, $\text{fitness}_I = 0.1$, $\upsilon = 0.5$, $\epsilon_0 = 0.001$, the mutation spread $m_0 = 0.1$ and the covering spread $r_0 = 1$ as fractions of the respective dimensional span. RLS prediction utilises the hyperparameters $\delta_{\text{rls}} = 1000$ and $\lambda_{\text{rls}} = 1.0$ and no covariance matrix resetting following Preen et al. [19]. As usual for linear prediction, the state vector x is augmented with $x_0 = 1$ as a prefix to serve as bias. The GA selects parent classifiers via tournament selection, while the deletion utilises the usual roulette wheel deletion. The chosen hyperparameters are based on common settings found in related literature [1,27,34,36] and the XCSF of Preen et al. [19].

Neural rules support no subsumption and prior experiments indicated potential instability due to subsumption, hence we also deactivated it for hyperrectangles. We apply linearly decaying epsilon greedy as our action-selection strategy for all experiments as done in previous work [23,24]. Plots and tables in this paper abbreviate neural conditions as NC, neural rules as NR and binary neural rules as BNR to allow short descriptors. This paper mainly reports on experiments with neural rules, binary neural rules and neural conditions with one hidden layer with 512 units and two hidden layers with 512 and 128 units since prior experiments indicated good performance for these architectures. We test these against classic neural rules with uniform initialisation in $(0, 1)$ with 10 units and sigmoid activation [10] and a baseline XCSF using hyperrectangles in UBR. We also test configurations with 10 units and ReLU for comparison to the classic neural rules baseline.

5 Experiments

In the following, we report our conducted experiments in the respective environments: Those in Maze6 in Sect. 5.1, those in Frozen Lake in Sect. 5.2, and those using the Empty Minigrid map in Sect. 5.3.

5.1 Maze6 Experiments

Our experiments in Maze6 use the environment-specific hyperparameters $N = 1000$, $\gamma = 0.9$, $\beta = 0.1$, 100 maximum number of steps before terminating the episode, minimal ε_{explr} of 0.01 and decay until episode 100. The weights of the classifiers are initialised with 0 and the bounds for the hyperrectangles are set to $[0, 1]$.

As can be seen in Fig. 2a and Table 1, Neural Rules and Neural Conditions perform in general significantly worse in this environment compared to XCSF while reaching observably similar and significantly not different performance in the case of binary neural rules and neural conditions with one hidden layer and 512 units. On the flip side, the modernised neural rules and conditions outperform the classic neural rules baseline with only 10 units and sigmoid activation

Table 1. Average steps over 100 episodes in the experimental series in Maze6. The results are the means of 30 run means over all 3000 episodes, the first and the last 750 episodes. The quantity behind the "±" is the standard deviation of the run means. Bold indicates the best result in a comparison. A star indicates a significant difference to the XCSF and a circle to the classic neural rule baseline.

Maze6	All	First 750	Last 750
NR 10 Units	15.783 ± 10.788*°	35.496 ± 24.554*°	6.112 ± 0.404*°
NR 512 Units	12.658 ± 6.39*°	31.009 ± 21.793*°	5.864 ± 0.338*°
NR 512 128 Units	13.009 ± 8.513*°	30.142 ± 20.782*°	5.838 ± 0.248*°
BNR 512 Units	8.735 ± 0.931*°	17.456 ± 3.165*°	5.65 ± 0.228°
BNR 512-128 Units	9.012 ± 0.99*°	18.397 ± 3.516*°	5.682 ± 0.229*°
NC 512 Units	9.094 ± 1.172*°	18.865 ± 4.094*°	5.637 ± 0.262°
NC 512-128 Units	10.573 ± 4.067*°	24.373 ± 15.636*°	5.727 ± 0.261*°
XCSF	**8.113 ± 0.586**	**15.421 ± 2.096**	**5.561 ± 0.212**
NR 10 Units Sigmoid	27.061 ± 20.6	51.81 ± 26.475	7.876 ± 4.596

in each case significantly. This is even true for neural rules with one hidden layer and 10 ReLU-activated units, showing that the initialisation and activation function lead to a disadvantage.

5.2 Frozen Lake Experiments

We focused our Frozen Lake experiments on the preconfigured stochastic 4 × 4 map, using the environment-specific hyperparameters $N = 800$, $\gamma = 0.95$, $\beta = 0.2$, 100 maximum number of steps before terminating the episode, minimal ε_{explr} of 0.05 and decay until episode 2000. The weights of the classifiers are initialised uniformly random in $(0, 1)$ and the bounds for the hyperrectangles are set to $[-1, 2]$.

As Table 2 and Fig. 2b indicate, neural conditions and the modernised neural rules, even those with only 10 units in a single hidden layer, outperform the classic variant significantly in the overall mean performance as well as in the last 1250 episodes of the experiments. In comparison to XCSF all variants achieved a better average reward, for four this contributes a significant improvement. The performance in the first 1250 episodes is largely similar between all variants with the exception of the neural conditions showing a small but significant improvement to both baselines. The best and second best overall and last 1250 episode performance in this environment is achieved by neural conditions consisting of two hidden layers consisting of 512 and 128 units and one hidden layer with 512 units. Additionally, the top configuration also has the lowest standard deviation of all other variants.

5.3 Empty Minigrid Experiments

Our experiments on the Empty map of the Minigrid package consist of 20 runs per tested variant and used the environment-specific hyperparameters $N = 1000$,

Table 2. Average rewards over 100 episodes in stochastic Frozen Lake 4 × 4. The results are the means of 30 run means over all 5000 episodes, the first and the last 1250 episodes. The quantity behind the "±" is the standard deviation of the run means. Bold indicates the best result in a comparison. A star indicates a significant difference to the XCSF and a circle to the classic neural rule baseline.

FL4x4	All	First 1250	Last 1250
NR 10 Units	$0.2 \pm 0.022°$	$0.024 \pm 0.006°$	$0.302 \pm 0.038°$
NR 512 Units	$0.209 \pm 0.021^{*°}$	0.025 ± 0.005	$0.308 \pm 0.035°$
NR 512 128 Units	$0.207 \pm 0.016^{*°}$	0.025 ± 0.004	$0.322 \pm 0.037^{*°}$
BNR 512 Units	$0.215 \pm 0.015^{*°}$	0.027 ± 0.006	$0.313 \pm 0.035°$
BNR 512-128 Units	$0.216 \pm 0.017^{*°}$	0.026 ± 0.005	$0.319 \pm 0.029^{*°}$
NC 512 Units	$0.228 \pm 0.018^{*°}$	$\mathbf{0.028 \pm 0.004}^{*°}$	$0.337 \pm 0.032°$
NC 512-128 Units	$\mathbf{0.229 \pm 0.013}^{*°}$	$0.027 \pm 0.006^{*°}$	$\mathbf{0.339 \pm 0.025}^{*°}$
XCSF	0.194 ± 0.019	0.026 ± 0.005	0.293 ± 0.033
NR 10 Units Sigmoid	0.171 ± 0.026	0.024 ± 0.006	0.28 ± 0.055

$\gamma = 0.9$, $\beta = 0.1$, 144 maximum number of steps before terminating the episode, ε_{explr} of 0.01 and decay until episode 100. The weights of the classifiers are initialised with 0 and the bounds for the hyperrectangles are set to $[-1, 2]$.

Noticeably, the XCSF baseline shows a substantially increased higher standard deviation in all three means. One substantial contributor is a run that failed to converge, noticeable at a very low average reward that was unable to solve the environment. We attribute this to the well-known stochastic nature LCSs, in particular of XCS variants. As a result of their higher stability and having no diverging runs, the average performance of neural conditions and modernised neural rules is observably better in all three means, as can be assessed in Table 3 and Figure 2c. In the case of the variants using neural conditions, neural rules and binary neural rules with one hidden layer with 512 units the performance is also significantly better in the last 500 episodes. Only the aforementioned neural conditions outperform the XCSF baseline significantly in the overall performance. All neural conditions and modernised rules significantly outperform the classic neural rules except neural rules with one hidden layer and 10 ReLU activated units. The best performance overall and the best last 500 episodes performance is achieved by using neural conditions with one hidden layer with 512 units, other variants are tied but have a higher standard deviation. For the first 500 episodes, only neural conditions and binary neural rules with one hidden layer and 512 units significantly outperform the XCSF baseline. The latter also achieves the highest performance.

6 Discussion

Neural conditions and the two types of modernised neural rules, refer to Sect. 3, outperformed classic neural rules with low unit counts in all examined environments.

Table 3. Average rewards over 100 episodes in the Empty Minigrid environment. The results are the means of 20 run means over all 2000 episodes, the first and the last 500 episodes. The quantity behind the "±" is the standard deviation of the run means. Bold indicates the best result in a comparison. A star indicates a significant difference to the XCSF and a circle to the classic neural rule baseline.

Empty	All	First 500	Last 500
NR 10 Units	0.931 ± 0.011	0.852 ± 0.044	$0.959 \pm 0.002°$
NR 512 Units	$0.936 \pm 0.004°$	0.867 ± 0.013	$0.96 \pm 0.002^{*°}$
NR 512-128 Units	$0.935 \pm 0.005°$	0.864 ± 0.018	$0.959 \pm 0.002°$
BNR 512 Units	$0.941 \pm 0.003°$	$\mathbf{0.885 \pm 0.01^{*°}}$	$0.96 \pm 0.002^{*°}$
BNR 512-128 Units	$0.939 \pm 0.003°$	$0.877 \pm 0.009°$	$0.96 \pm 0.002°$
NC 512 Units	$\mathbf{0.941 \pm 0.002^{*°}}$	$0.883 \pm 0.009^{*°}$	$\mathbf{0.96 \pm 0.001^{*°}}$
NC 512-128 Units	$0.938 \pm 0.003°$	$0.876 \pm 0.01°$	$0.959 \pm 0.002^{*°}$
XCSF	0.884 ± 0.2	$0.847 \pm 0.153°$	0.909 ± 0.214
NR 10 Sigmoid Units	0.93 ± 0.008	$0.854 \pm 0.028°$	0.957 ± 0.003

Turning to the baseline XCSF: In Maze6, it achieved observably better performance compared to neural rules and neural conditions. The performance difference is significant for all neural conditions and rules aside from two: Neural conditions and binary neural rules with one hidden layer and 512 units achieved no significantly different performance compared to XCSF in Maze6, despite achieving higher average step means. Summarised, there is no indicated advantage to using neural rules or neural conditions in Maze6. One reason for this might be the comparably small state space of the Maze Problem that also does not scale with the map size.

For the Empty Minigrid map and stochastic Frozen Lake 4 × 4, at least one configuration of neural rules or neural conditions significantly outperformed the XCSF baseline. Neural conditions were the best variant in the overall mean performance and the last 25% of episodes in those two environments. Partially, the binary neural rules performed not much worse. In all tested environments, the neural rules using a non-matching unit for their matching logic are consistently outperformed by neural conditions and binary neural rules. This indicates that using a matching neuron leads to better results. The better performance of neural conditions in the latter two environments indicates that classifiers changing their action has additional negative side-effects on the performance, aside from the small computational overhead. Consequently, neural conditions are the preferable option due to their superior performance and simplicity.

7 Conclusion

In this paper, we re-examined neural conditions and neural rules, applying neural conditions and two modernised types of neural rules to three multi-step RL environments. This closes the gap on how neural conditions and modernised neural rules perform in such environments. The reported results showed that all three types outperformed classic neural rules, whereas binary neural rules in general outperform neural rules. In contrast to prior work, neural conditions performed admirably in multi-step environments and outperformed the baseline XCSF in Frozen Lake and Empty Minigrid. The same holds true for neural rules. Only in Maze6, this was not the case. However, the results of these two variants were not significantly different compared to the baseline XCSF. All in all, neural conditions appear to be an adequate condition for XCS that can outperform hyperrectangles in multi-step environments and we recommend it over neural rules due to their simplicity and achieving significantly better or not significantly different performance to them. The worse performance of binary neural rules using the same matching mechanism requires further analysis. After affirming the viability of neural conditions, an XCSF with neural conditions should be integrated as a controller into an actual OC system. Following further work would benefit this proposition: It remains open to assess neural conditions for more complex state niches. In addition, it should be analysed how neural conditions and neural rules explicitly partition the state space of environments. Further work could investigate the behaviour of neural rules in dynamic environments featuring change over time or other actors in the environment that coexist or compete with the neural XCSF-driven agent.

References

1. Bishop, J., Gallagher, M.: Optimality-based analysis of XCSF compaction in discrete reinforcement learning. arXiv:2009.01476 (2020)
2. Bull, L., O'Hara, T.: Accuracy-based neuro and neuro-fuzzy classifier systems (2002)
3. Butz, M., Kovacs, T., Lanzi, P.L., Wilson, S.W.: Toward a theory of generalization and learning in XCS. IEEE Trans. Evol. Comput. (2004)
4. Butz, M., Wilson, S.W.: An algorithmic description of XCS. In: Revised Papers from IWLCS 2000. Springer-Verlag (2000)
5. Buu, S.J., Kang, H.B., Cho, S.B.: Ensemble of deep convolutional learning classifier system based on genetic algorithm for database intrusion detection (2022)
6. Chevalier-Boisvert, M., Dai, B., Towers, M., de Lazcano, R., et al.: Minigrid & miniworld: modular & customizable reinforcement learning environments for goal-oriented tasks. CoRR abs/2306.13831 (2023)
7. Dam, H., Abbass, H., Lokan, C.: Xin Yao: Neural-based learning classifier systems. IEEE Trans. Knowl. Data Eng. (2008)
8. Heider, M., Pätzel, D., Stegherr, H., Hähner, J.: A metaheuristic perspective on learning classifier systems. In: Metaheuristics for Machine Learning. Springer Nature Singapore (2023)
9. Howard, D., Bull, L., Lanzi, P.L.: A cognitive architecture based on a learning classifier system with spiking classifiers. arXiv:1508.07700 (2015)
10. Howard, G.D., Bull, L., Lanzi, P.L.: Self-adaptive constructivism in neural XCS and XCSF. In: Proceedings of the GECCO 2008. ACM Press (2008)
11. Kephart, J.O., Chess, D.M.: The vision of autonomic computing. Computer **36**(1), 41–50 (2003)
12. Kim, J.Y., Cho, S.B.: Exploiting deep convolutional neural networks for a neural-based learning classifier system (2019)

13. Lanzi, P.L., Loiacono, D.: XCSF with neural prediction. In: Proceedings of the ICEC 2006. IEEE (2006)
14. Lanzi, P.L., Loiacono, D., Wilson, S.W., Goldberg, D.E.: Generalization in the XCSF classifier system: analysis, improvement, and extension. Evol. Comput. (2) (2007)
15. Loeser, I., Braun, M., Gruhl, C., Menke, J.H., Sick, B., Tomforde, S.: The vision of self-management in cognitive organic power distribution systems. Energies (2022)
16. Mnih, V., Kavukcuoglu, K., Silver, D., Rusu, A.A., et al.: Human-level control through deep reinforcement learning. Nature (2015)
17. Müller-Schloer, C., Tomforde, S.: Organic computing - technical systems for survival in the real world. Birkhäuser (2017)
18. Preen, R.J., Bull, L.: Deep learning with a classifier system: initial results. arXiv:2103.01118 (2021)
19. Preen, R.J., Pätzel, D.: XCSF. Zenodo (2024)
20. Preen, R.J., Wilson, S.W., Bull, L.: Autoencoding with a classifier system. IEEE Trans. Evol. Comput. (2021)
21. Prothmann, H., Tomforde, S., Branke, J., Hähner, J., Müller-Schloer, C., Schmeck, H.: Organic traffic control. In: Organic Computing — A Paradigm Shift for Complex Systems. Springer Basel (2011)
22. Rosenbauer, L., Pätzel, D., Stein, A., Hähner, J.: An organic computing system for automated testing. In: Proceedings of the ARCS 2021. LNCS, Springer (2021)
23. Schönberner, C., Tomforde, S.: Deep reinforcement learning with a classifier system – first steps. In: Proceedings of the ARCS 2022. Springer (2022)
24. Schönberner, C., Tomforde, S.: XCS: Is covering all you need? In: Proceedings of the GECCO 2024 Companion. ACM, Melbourne VIC Australia (2024)
25. Siddique, A., Browne, W.N., Grimshaw, G.M.: Frames-of-reference-based learning: overcoming perceptual aliasing in multistep decision-making tasks. IEEE Trans. Evol. Comput. (2022)
26. Siddique, A., Heider, M., Iqbal, M., Shiraishi, H.: A survey on learning classifier systems from 2022 to 2024 (2024)
27. Stein, A., Maier, R., Rosenbauer, L., Hähner, J.: XCS classifier system with experience replay. In: Proceedings of the GECCO 2020. ACM (2020)
28. Stein, A., Rauh, D., Tomforde, S., Hähner, J.: Interpolation in the eXtended classifier system: an architectural perspective. J. Sys. Arch. (2017)
29. Stone, C., Bull, L.: For real! XCS with continuous-valued inputs. Evol. Comput. (2003)
30. Tomforde, S., Brameshuber, A., Hähner, J., Müller-Schloer, C.: Restricted on-line learning in real-world systems. In: Proceedings of the CEC 2011 (2011)
31. Tomforde, S., Hähner, J.: Organic network control. In: Biologically Inspired Networking and Sensing - Algorithms and Architectures, pp. 11–35. IGI Global (2012)
32. Tomforde, S., Prothmann, H., Branke, J., et al.: Observation and control of organic systems. In: Organic Computing — A Paradigm Shift for Complex Systems. Springer Basel (2011)
33. Uwano, F., Browne, W.N.: Cognitive learning system for sequential aliasing patterns of states in multistep decision-making. In: Proceedings of the GECCO-C 2024. ACM (2024)
34. Wilson, S.W.: Classifier fitness based on accuracy. Evol. Comput. (1995)
35. Wilson, S.W.: Get real! XCS with continuous-valued inputs. In: Learning Classifier Systems. Springer Berlin Heidelberg (2000)
36. Wilson, S.W.: Classifiers that approximate functions. Nat. Comput. (2002)

Evaluating Adaptive Systems: A Comparative Study of XCS and Established Reinforcement Learning Algorithms in Noisy Multi-step Environments

Marco Steinberger[(✉)], Roman Küble[ID], Michael Heider[ID], and Jörg Hähner[ID]

Organic Computing Group, University of Augsburg, Am Technologiezentrum 8, Augsburg, Germany
marco.steinberger@uni-a.de

Abstract. In the age of advanced technology and automation, self-organizing systems capable of adapting flexibly to diverse situations are becoming increasingly critical. *Organic Computing* (OC) addresses this challenge by drawing inspiration from biological processes to develop systems that respond autonomously and robustly to environmental changes. Within such systems, decision-making plays a pivotal role, with the *XCS classifier system* (XCS) emerging as a prominent method. Another category of algorithms that fits this requirement is reinforcement learning (RL). However, a comprehensive comparison of XCS and RL remains scarce. This paper bridges this gap by presenting an extensive empirical analysis of XCS and various RL algorithms across 51 problem instances from five established RL benchmarks of varying complexity. The results show that while XCS performs competitively on simpler problems, it fails completely on two of the benchmarks, making RL a more suitable alternative to XCS in selected OC systems. While XCS is robust in noisy environments, this trait is not unique. Other algorithms exhibit comparable stability and significantly outperform XCS in complex scenarios with larger state and action spaces.

Keywords: Reinforcement Learning · Organic Computing · XCS · Gymnasium Benchmarks

1 Introduction

As systems grow increasingly complex, *Organic Computing* (OC) [3,12,13] has gained prominence as an approach to developing autonomous systems with *self-x properties*, such as *self-organisation, self-configuration,* and *self-adaptability*. Inspired by biological processes, these systems can respond autonomously and robustly to environmental changes, with decision-making as a central focus. Within this context, reinforcement learning (RL) [20] has emerged as a key method, enabling agents to learn optimal decisions through interaction with their environment. By relying on a reward system, RL allows agents to adapt to new challenges and develop strategies without explicit programming.

In the field of OC, the *XCS classifier system* [26] and its further developments [22] have established themselves as the most common methods (e.g. in [16,21], and [23]) for decision making. XCS combines principles of evolutionary algorithms with RL to create rule-based systems that are human-readable by nature and therefore especially popular for developing OC-like systems.

Despite the popularity of XCS in the OC research community, its comparison to other RL algorithms has been limited, raising questions about its suitability. This paper provides a comprehensive comparison between XCS and four widely-used RL algorithms: *Q-Learning* [25], *SARSA* [19], *DQN* [11], and *Deep SARSA* [27]. The study evaluates their performance and robustness across five multi-step benchmark problems from the Gymnasium library [5], while also examining their resilience to stochastic noise in state and action spaces. A total of 51 problem instances forms the basis for this analysis.

The overall goal of this study is to show whether alternative RL algorithms can provide better performance and robustness compared to XCS. Through a detailed analysis, we hope to diversify research in the field of OC and demonstrate the advantages of different RL methods. Ultimately, this work should help to improve the efficiency and adaptability of autonomous learning systems and open up new perspectives for the development of future OC systems.

The remainder of this paper is structured as follows: Sect. 2 provides background information on XCS and RL in general, illustrates the relevance of RL to OC, and reviews the current state of research. Section 3 specifies the objective of this work and describes the general test procedure, including the implementation of parameter optimisation. Section 4 presents a detailed evaluation of the experiments conducted. Finally, the paper concludes with a summary of the findings and a roadmap for future work.

2 Background and Related Work

This section provides an overview of XCS and reinforcement learning as a foundation for the comparison in this paper. It first examines XCS, including its principles, advantages, and applications in Organic Computing, as well as implementation challenges. RL is then introduced, focusing on its core mechanisms and role within OC. Finally, the section discusses how established RL approaches enhance OC systems in terms of diversity, robustness, and adaptability, and reviews existing comparative studies on XCS.

2.1 XCS

The XCS Classifier System (XCS) [26] is a machine learning approach that combines *evolutionary algorithms* with the principles of *reinforcement learning*. It belongs to the family of *learning classifier systems* (LCS), which operate on populations of classifiers. Each classifier consists of a condition part, which defines the states under which a rule is applicable, and an action part, which determines the respective reaction in these states. At the core of XCS is the continuous adaptation and selection of rules using evolutionary operators. Classifier fitness, which measures their suitability for solving the given learning task, guides this process. In addition to generalisation and adaptive learning, XCS also offers transparency, as individual rules can often be interpreted and understood by humans. The combination of these advantages makes XCS a versatile and effective approach for applications.

This applicability has been demonstrated, for example, by Sommer et al. [16] in their work on resilient traffic control. The authors investigated a decentralised system for the dynamic adaptation of traffic lights. This system is based on the principles of OC and uses XCS to adjust signal control to changing traffic conditions, thereby optimising traffic flow adaptively.

Von Mammen et al. [23] explored the use of OC technologies to control autonomous, adaptive robot ensembles. Using XCS and simulation techniques, the system dynamically adapted to changing goals and conditions.

In another application, Tomforde et al. [21] developed the Organic Network Control system, which employs XCS for the dynamic adaptation of network protocol parameters at runtime. This system, as evidenced in a TCP-based case study, enhances the robustness and efficiency of data communication by continuously adjusting to evolving network conditions.

While XCS has positive attributes and wide applicability, it also has drawbacks that can sometimes outweigh its strengths. While it generally produces interpretable rules, this does not guarantee that the overall model will be human-comprehensible. Heider et al. [2,8] showed that XCSF, a variant for continuous values, achieves solid accuracy but often at the cost of increased model complexity, resulting in a large number of rules. This complexity hampers interpretability, undermining XCS's primary advantage over other RL approaches for real-world applications.

Another disadvantage of XCS is the need to configure 21 parameters, even in its standard version [6]. This complexity requires extensive parameter studies, which are time-consuming and resource-intensive. Insufficient tuning can harm performance, raising doubts about XCS's suitability for continuously learning systems in dynamic environments.

Despite the aforementioned challenges related to model complexity and the large number of required parameters, it is important to consider whether XCS might compensate for these disadvantages. Its ability to generalise and provide theoretically readable models has led to its continued use in a variety of applications [15].

2.2 Reinforcement Learning in the Context of OC

Reinforcement learning [20] is a machine learning paradigm in which an agent learns to make optimal decisions by interacting with its environment. In contrast to other learning methods, such as supervised learning, in which models are trained using predefined input-output pairs, RL is based on the principle of reward and punishment. A key challenge in RL is balancing exploration and exploitation: the agent must explore the environment to discover optimal strategies while exploiting known strategies to maximize rewards.

This trade-off is particularly important in OC systems, where agents must continuously adapt to dynamic and evolving environments. RL offers a particularly valuable methodology in this context, as it enables agents to learn autonomously and adapt to different environments without the need for an explicit model of the environment. This ability to continuously adapt and optimize makes RL a central tool for the implementation of OC principles. In OC systems, RL algorithms can be used to develop adaptive controls, intelligent decision-making processes and robust behaviors that flexibly adapt to changing environments and requirements.

In real-world applications, environments are often noisy, with uncertainty in the states or actions due to external disturbances or imperfect sensing. RL algorithms must therefore be robust enough to handle noise and still learn effective policies. This ability to operate under uncertainty is particularly crucial in OC systems, where the environment is often dynamic and unpredictable. Noise in multi-step environments can make it challenging for an agent to accurately estimate long-term rewards, yet RL algorithms have proven (e.g. in [28]) effective in developing strategies that account for such stochasticity, making them suitable for OC systems that must thrive in noisy and dynamic conditions.

The use of different RL algorithms as self-adaptation deciders in OC systems offers the advantage of diversification. Each RL method has specific strengths and weaknesses. By employing a variety of algorithms within the OC domain, systems can become more robust and flexible, leveraging the individual strengths of each algorithm. A typical OC system is structured according to the Multi-Layered Observer/Controller (MLOC) architecture [13], where RL methods play a crucial role in online learning (Layer 1) and offline simulations (Layer 2). Recent advances, such as semi-model-based RL [24] approaches, further enhance OC systems by blending model-based and model-free techniques, enabling efficient learning in dynamic and complex environments. This diversification of decision makers in OC systems helps to increase robustness and adaptability and improves the system's ability to perform in different and dynamic environments.

2.3 Comparative Studies on XCS

XCS has played an important role in numerous empirical studies, although the focus has predominantly been on its comparison with other learning classifier systems. In contrast, direct evaluations against RL algorithms on typical RL benchmarks have been conducted less frequently.

Gaines and Pakath [7] examined the performance of a general learning classifier system in comparison to XCS in the context of the iterated prisoner's dilemma. In their simulations, XCS was tested against both a deterministic opponent (tit-for-tat) and a completely random antagonist to evaluate its ability to process delayed feedback and deal with unpredictable environments.

In another study, Stone and Bull [18] compared the performance of ZCS (zeroth order classifier system) and XCS in noisy online environments with continuous states and both deterministic and stochastic reward functions. They found that XCS is superior in deterministic environments, while ZCS is more robust in stochastic environments and can even outperform XCS in some cases.

Inoue et al. [9] also investigated the adaptability of XCS, but in multi-agent environments simulated in a simplified football match. They compared different XCS variants that were evaluated either by prediction accuracy or by the reward received. The results show that the original, accuracy-based version of XCS performs better in certain stochastic environments than the alternative, reward strength–based version.

Bishop and Gallagher [4] applied XCSF to the FrozenLake8x8 environment from the OpenAI Gym, in both a deterministic and a stochastic variant. They compared the performance of XCSF in terms of approximating the optimal Q-function and the accuracy of the learnt policy with the optimal solutions obtained by dynamic programming.

Stein et al. [17] extended XCS by integrating Experience Replay (ER) and investigated its influence in different scenarios. They compared the performance of XCS with and without ER as well as a Deep-Q network in single-step and multi-step benchmarks of the OpenAI Gym environment. Their results showed that ER can significantly increase the efficiency of XCS in single-step tasks, while it further increases existing challenges in multi-step environments. This general assessment was extended by Rosenbauer et al. [14], who confirmed the challenges of ER in multi-step environments for the specific context of test case prioritization. They showed that ER is not necessarily advantageous and can even negatively affect performance under certain conditions.

Lanzi et al. [10] used XCSF to solve multi-level RL problems with continuous inputs and compared it with a version of tabular Q-learning adapted for continuous values. The benchmarks used were one-dimensional linear corridors and two-dimensional continuous gridworld environments. The results showed that XCSF converges faster and provides more compact solutions than tabular Q-learning, especially in less explored problem spaces.

However, all these studies still do not provide a comprehensive comparison between XCS and other widespread RL algorithms using typical multi-step benchmarks. The *general absence* of evaluations of XCS on well-known RL problems was already pointed out by Stein et al. [17] in 2020. Since then, to the best of our knowledge, no scientific work has been published that addresses this issue in detail, leaving the situation unchanged. The aim of this article is to close this research gap by conducting a comprehensive comparison and verifying the robustness of these algorithms.

3 Experimental Design

This study aims to systematically and empirically evaluate XCS in comparison to established RL algorithms in noisy multi-step environments. An epsilon-greedy exploration strategy was used for all algorithms to ensure consistency in the exploration-exploitation trade-off. The study examines whether XCS can compete in more challenging RL scenarios or if other RL algorithms prove superior due to their flexibility and robustness. Based on this, the underlying hypothesis of this article is:

XCS is only competitive for simpler RL problems, and is expected to perform significantly worse than the investigated RL algorithms on more complex tasks with large action and state spaces, as well as stochastic noise.

The following sections outline the experimental framework, including the benchmark selection, stochastic environment setup, and algorithm parameterisation, as well as the evaluation strategy.

3.1 Algorithms and Benchmarks

Besides XCS, Q-Learning, SARSA, DQN, and Deep SARSA (all in their basic versions without extensions) were selected, as they represent fundamental and widely used RL approaches with differing strategies. While Q-Learning and SARSA are table-based methods suited for simpler state spaces, DQN and Deep SARSA leverage neural networks to handle larger and continuous state spaces. This selection enables a comprehensive comparison, covering a spectrum from classical to modern RL algorithms, and highlights XCS's position within this range.

For the evaluation of our hypothesis, five benchmark problems from the Gymnasium library [5] that cover a wide range of RL challenges were selected as the basis of our evaluation scenarios. The tasks range from simple gridworld environments such as *Frozen Lake* (in 4x4 and 8x8) and *Cliffwalking*, where the agent has to find safe paths, to more complex scenarios such as *CartPole*, which was discretised (`discretization_bins=10`) to make it solvable for discrete algorithms. In addition, *Blackjack* and *Taxi* were used to test short- and long-term decision strategies. Although *Blackjack* may seem far from classical OC scenarios, it captures key aspects relevant to OC systems—most notably, the need for decision-making under uncertainty and handling delayed rewards. These benchmarks were chosen because they reflect key challenges faced in OC, such as the need for adaptability, robustness, and efficient decision-making in dynamic and stochastic environments. By incorporating tasks with varying complexity, action spaces, and state spaces, the benchmarks provide a representative testbed for evaluating algorithms intended for OC systems. The detailed descriptions of these environments are available in the Gymnasium documentation[1].

To verify the robustness of the algorithms against stochastic influences, a noise component was added to each benchmark problem. Two types of noise were introduced:

---
[1] https://gymnasium.farama.org/environments/.

- **Action noise** - With a probability of x percent, the agent performs an action different from the one originally selected.
- **State noise** - With a probability of y percent, the agent perceives an altered state instead of the actual one.

The noise levels were set to $x, y \in \{0, 5, 10\}$. For the Taxi, Frozen Lake, Cliffwalking, and CartPole benchmarks, all combinations of state and action noise were tested to simulate different levels of stochastic influences. In the Taxi, Frozen Lake, and Cliffwalking benchmarks, action noise forces the agent to execute an orthogonal movement instead of the intended direction (e.g., moving left or right instead of upwards). In CartPole, action noise causes the agent to randomly select between moving left or right.

State noise, on the other hand, results in the agent perceiving a neighboring field as its current state in the Taxi, Frozen Lake, and Cliffwalking environments. Invalid states or states that would immediately terminate the episode are excluded. In CartPole, state noise shifts two of the four state dimensions randomly by 1 to 4 bins to the left or right. For the Blackjack benchmark, only state noise was applied, as altering the available actions (hit or stick) would likely result in losing the episode. Furthermore, the `natural` parameter was varied, with `natural = True` granting a bonus reward for achieving a direct blackjack (ace and ten). In this setting, state noise causes the agent to perceive a slightly modified state ($+/-$ 1 or 2). A total of six problem instances were created for Blackjack by combining the different values for y and the `natural` parameter. Therefore, the agents were evaluated on a total of 51 learning tasks.

The used state encoding varied depending on the algorithm: For *DQN* and *Deep SARSA*, decimal or one-hot encoding was used, as these representations allow deep neural networks to generalise more efficiently. Gray code, a binary numeral system in which adjacent values differ by only a single bit, was used for *XCS* as it efficiently encodes related states. In contrast to conventional binary encodings, this property improves generalisability and ensures that similar states activate similar rules. For *Q-Learning* and *SARSA*, the encoding of the states is not relevant, since these algorithms store the state space in tabular form; here it was only important that the states are uniquely represented.

3.2 Parameter Tuning

To ensure a fair comparison of algorithm performance, a comprehensive hyperparameter optimisation was conducted. For Q-Learning, SARSA, DQN, and Deep SARSA, the learning rate (α), discount factor (γ), and epsilon value for the epsilon-greedy strategy (ϵ) were optimised. For XCS, the target error (e_0) and maximum population size (N) were additionally tuned, as they strongly affect learning behaviour and generalisability. Other XCS parameters followed default values from Butz et al. [6]. Optimisation was performed using Optuna [1], with the `TPESampler` (Tree-structured Parzen Estimator Sampler) generating configurations. Due to the larger parameter space, 125 configurations were tested per XCS instance, while 75 were evaluated for other agents.

Based on preliminary studies, the number of iterations varied between 100 and 4000, depending on the complexity of the tasks and the degree of stochastic noise, with each iteration comprising 30 training episodes and 30 evaluation episodes conducted without exploration. To ensure a fair basis for comparison, all algorithms were tested under identical conditions. The optimisation method maximised the cumulative reward, favouring configurations that could ensure success consistently across multiple seeds. To ensure fairness and comparability, a simple neural network with three fully connected layers and ReLU activation was used for DQN and Deep SARSA.

Table 1 provides the value ranges for the parameter configurations of each algorithm and benchmark. Note that the learning rate for the XCS algorithm is denoted by β rather than α. The parameter ranges for XCS are based on recommendations from [6]. For a detailed overview of the specific parameter configurations used for each problem instance and algorithm, please refer to the associated GitHub repository[2].

Table 1. Parameter ranges for the individual algorithms and benchmark environments. For consistency, the exploration rate ϵ and discount factor γ were standardized across all algorithms and benchmarks, with values ranging from 0.2 to 0.4 for ϵ and from 0.85 to 0.99 for γ.

Algorithmus	Benchmark	Parameter	Min	Max
DQN, Deep SARSA	All	α	0.0001	0.05
Q-Learning, SARSA	All	α	0.005	0.1
XCS	All	β	0.05	0.35
	Taxi	ϵ_0	0.01	0.2
		N	500	2000
	Blackjack	ϵ_0	0.005	0.025
		N	704	2000
	CartPole	ϵ_0	0.001	0.02
		N	5000	20000
	Frozen Lake	ϵ_0	0.001	0.02
		N	64	1000
	Cliff Walking	ϵ_0	0.01	0.2
		N	500	2000

3.3 Evaluation Strategy

The evaluation approach ensured comparability between problem instances while optimizing resource utilization. Preliminary studies guided the choice of iteration numbers, ensuring sufficient learning time and accounting for varying levels of stochasticity. To ensure robustness, a buffer was added to the iteration numbers from these experiments. Deterministic environments were trained for 400

---
[2] https://github.com/stemarco95/xcs_vs_rl.

iterations, whereas stochastic environments with up to 10% noise required up to 5000 iterations. In the Blackjack environment, the number of iterations ranged between 400 and 1500, depending on the noise level. Additionally, thresholds terminated training early when no significant improvements were observed. These thresholds were adjusted based on the noise level: lower thresholds were used for high-noise scenarios, as agents had limited chances of achieving the maximum score over 30 episodes, minimizing unnecessary computational overhead.

Performance evaluation relied on the aggregation of data from 30 independent seeds for each of the 51 problem instances. Average evaluation scores were calculated as the mean episode reward across all seeds, minimizing the impact of random fluctuations. Alongside average scores, the number of successful episodes served as an additional performance metric. To enable comparability across problem instances, the aggregated results underwent min-max normalization. Subsequently, the successful episodes were aggregated across all problem instances within each benchmark to compute the cumulative success rate, serving as the primary indicator of overall performance.

As the performance differences between agents are quite clear based on visual inspections, we do not present additional statistical testing.

4 Evaluation

In our evaluation, we focus on abstract findings rather than detailed case-by-case analyses, presenting the most relevant results in a structured manner. All supporting data, including detailed plots and materials, are publicly available on Zenodo[3] to promote transparency and reproducibility.

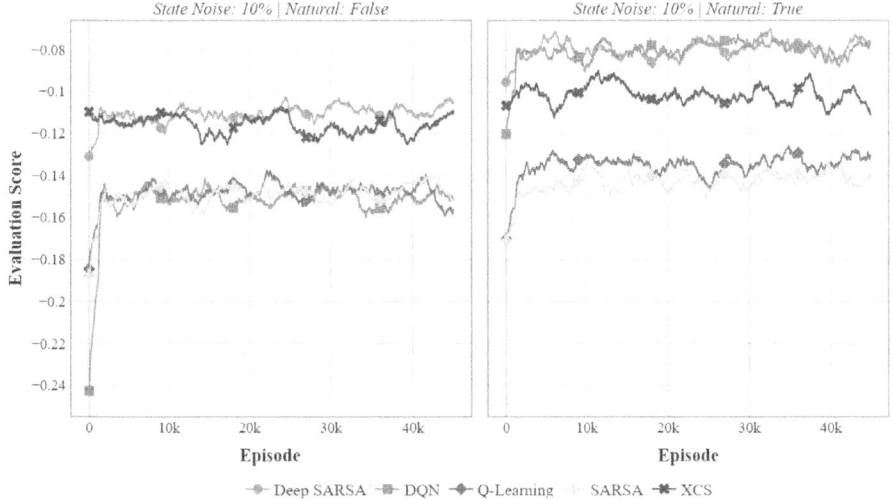

Fig. 1. Blackjack performance with noise and under the two Natural settings.

---
[3] https://doi.org/10.5281/zenodo.14735822.

We begin by analyzing line charts that depict the progression of evaluation scores over training episodes, offering insights into the agents' learning dynamics and adaptation speed.

Figure 1 shows the performance of the agents in the Blackjack environment under the most complex scenario (10% state noise probability) for the two configurations of the Natural parameter: Natural=False and Natural=True.

All agents solve the problem quickly, achieving similar performance levels despite Blackjack's stochastic nature. XCS, DQN, and Deep SARSA show a slight advantage, but these differences are likely insignificant due to the environment's randomness. Performance trends remain consistent across configurations, with higher ratings when Natural=True, driven by additional rewards for starting with a natural blackjack.

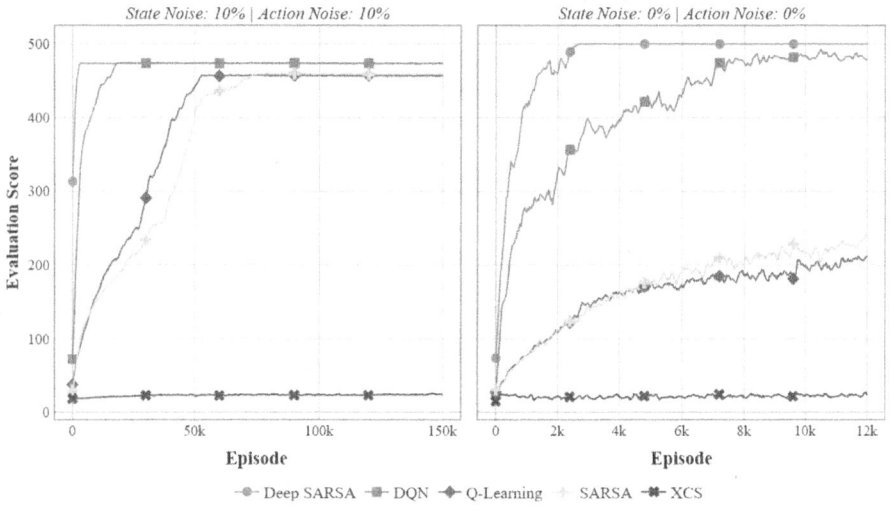

Fig. 2. Performance of CartPole with (left) and without (right) noise.

Figure 2 summarizes the evaluation results for the CartPole environment under two conditions: noisy (State Noise: 10%, Action Noise: 10%) and noise-free. Deep SARSA achieves the best performance in both cases, converging rapidly to the optimal score, followed closely by DQN, which requires slightly more episodes to reach similar performance.

Q-Learning and SARSA show slower learning rates, struggling particularly in the noise-free environment and requiring significantly more episodes to achieve competitive scores. In the noisy environment, their performance improves, likely due to greater exposure to diverse states during training. XCS fails to solve the task in either condition, maintaining consistently low evaluation scores. This poor performance is likely due to the large state space of the CartPole environment, which exceeds its capacity to generalize effectively.

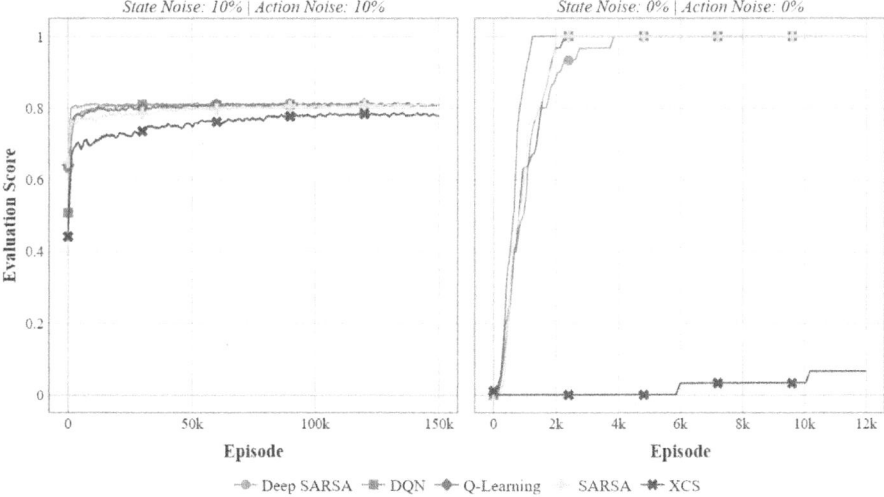

Fig. 3. Performance of Frozen Lake 4x4 with noise (left) and Frozen Lake 8x8 without noise (right).

In the Frozen Lake environment, all algorithms are able to solve the 4x4 scenario despite high levels of noise (State Noise: 10%, Action Noise: 10%), as shown in Fig. 3.

While eventually converging to stable performance, XCS achieves slightly lower scores than the other approaches and requires the most episodes to stabilize. In the 8x8 scenario without noise, the contrast is clear: all algorithms except XCS solve the task despite the increased complexity, achieving high final scores. XCS, however, struggles throughout and shows no meaningful improvement, remaining far behind the others. This contrasting performance highlights a trend: XCS seems better suited to smaller, noisy environments like the 4x4 scenario, where less long-term planning is needed. Larger state spaces, like the 8x8 scenario, pose a greater challenge, even without noise.

The results of the various algorithms are shown as distributions in Fig. 4. The plot visualizes the range of measured values and their distribution for each algorithm. The individual points represent the results of different problem cases and provide information on the variability of the performance of the individual algorithms. To enable direct comparability, all results were normalized to a uniform value range using min-max normalization.

Deep SARSA and DQN show a high concentration of results in the upper range, indicating consistent and reliable performance. Both algorithms exhibit low dispersion and achieve strong results in most cases. Q-Learning and SARSA, on the other hand, show significantly greater variability, including negative values. XCS, while providing medium to good results in some instances, exhibits considerable scatter and a plateau in the lower part of the distribution in specific instances, indicating weaknesses in certain scenarios.

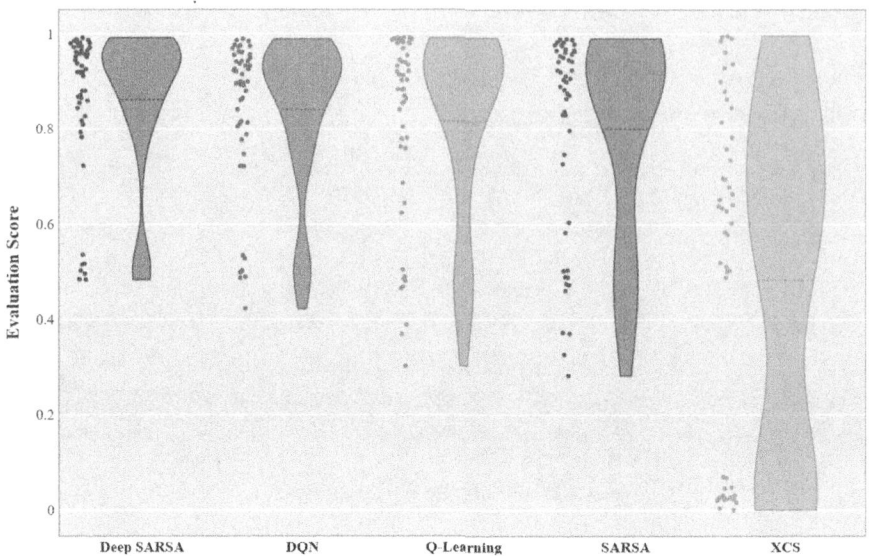

Fig. 4. Distributions of algorithm performance across problem instances, visualized with normalized values for comparability.

This representation offers an abstracted view and shows general trends, but cannot provide detailed conclusions about performance on specific benchmarks. To analyze these differences in more detail, an overview of the successful episodes is presented in Fig. 5, providing a deeper insight into the performance of the algorithms on individual problem instances.

The chart illustrates the number of successful episodes achieved by each algorithm across the different benchmarks, with values aggregated and normalized by the best result for each benchmark to ensure comparability.

The results show consistently strong performance in the Blackjack and Frozen Lake 4x4 benchmarks, aligning with trends observed in the line graphs. SARSA and Q-Learning performed well overall but struggled with the CartPole benchmark, while DQN showed robust results across most tasks but exhibited weaknesses in the Taxi benchmark. XCS faced significant challenges in the CartPole and Taxi benchmarks and achieved lower success rates on Frozen Lake 8x8 compared to other algorithms. However, XCS performed relatively well in the Cliff Walking benchmark, even if it did not reach the level of other algorithms.

These findings support the hypothesis that XCS is mainly competitive in simpler RL problems. In complex tasks with larger state and action spaces, it shows clear weaknesses, particularly in generalization and long-term planning. While DQN and Deep SARSA demonstrated consistent robustness in both noise-free and noisy scenarios, XCS often lagged behind.

The results also highlight that noise does not always hinder learning. In some cases, it promotes exploration and alleviates the exploration/exploitation

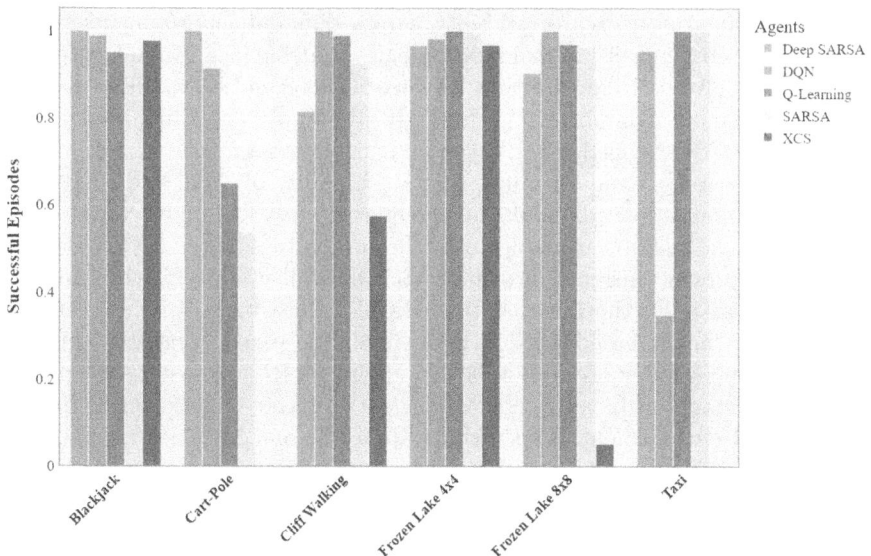

Fig. 5. Sum of successful episodes across all instances of all benchmarks for each algorithm, normalized by dividing each value by the value of the best-performing agent, resulting in a maximum of 1.

dilemma, though higher noise levels can slow learning due to the need for more episodes to achieve stability.

Although XCS uses the same update mechanism as Q-Learning, Q-Learning outperformed it in almost all tested problems. This raises questions about the value of XCS's additional components and parameters, which, while intended to increase flexibility, offered no clear advantages in the evaluated scenarios.

Finally, the findings emphasize the potential for OC systems to benefit from diverse decision algorithms. Leveraging the strengths of different approaches through hybrid methods could enhance their efficiency and robustness in solving complex and varied tasks.

5 Conclusion

This study demonstrates that, compared to established RL algorithms, XCS is primarily suitable for simpler RL problems. In complex scenarios with large state and action spaces or long-term planning requirements, XCS faces significant limitations. Although it showed robustness in smaller, noisy environments—similar to other algorithms—its overall performance lagged behind, even compared to Q-Learning, which shares the same update mechanism with XCS.

These findings suggest that robustness to noise and efficiency in large state spaces are key factors in the success of RL algorithms. While XCS incorporates mechanisms designed to improve flexibility, they did not provide a significant advantage in the evaluated tasks. Instead, algorithms like DQN and Deep

SARSA demonstrated greater stability across different environments, underscoring the need for decision-making strategies that balance generalization and scalability. The results indicate that RL algorithms could be valuable decision-makers in Organic Computing, particularly in complex and high-dimensional tasks where XCS struggled.

Future research should examine the transferability of these findings to real-world applications, especially in domains requiring noisy and multi-step decision-making. It could also be valuable to further evaluate advanced XCS variants, as this may provide insights into improving flexibility and efficiency in high-dimensional tasks. Furthermore, as the MLOC architecture combines reinforcement learning for online adaptation with simulation-based decision-making, an interesting avenue for exploration is how model-based RL can sustain an adaptive environment model in Layer 2 while the agent in Layer 1 continues to interact with the real environment. This hybrid approach refines decision policies by combining real-world experiences with simulations, improving sample efficiency and robustness in dynamic settings. Finally, extending evaluations to continuous action spaces could help clarify the scalability and adaptability of both XCS and RL method.

References

1. Akiba, T.e.a.: Optuna: a next-generation hyperparameter optimization framework. In: Proceedings of the 25th ACM SIGKDD International Conference on Knowledge Discovery & Data Mining, pp. 2623–2631. KDD '19, Association for Computing Machinery, New York, NY, USA (2019)
2. et al., M.H.: Suprb in the context of rule-based machine learning methods: a comparative study. Appl. Soft Comput. **147**, 110706 (2023)
3. et al., S.T.: Organic computing in the spotlight. CoRR **abs/1701.08125** (2017)
4. Bishop, J.T.e.a.: Optimality-based analysis of XCSF compaction in discrete reinforcement learning. In: Parallel Problem Solving from Nature – PPSN XVI, pp. 471–484 (2020)
5. Brockman, G.e.a.: Openai gym. arXiv preprint arXiv:1606.01540 (2016)
6. Butz, M.V.e.a.: An algorithmic description of XCS. In: Advances in Learning Classifier Systems, pp. 253–272. Springer Berlin Heidelberg (2001)
7. Gaines, D.A.e.a.: An examination of evolved behavior in two reinforcement learning systems. Decis. Support Syst. **55**(1), 194–205 (2013)
8. Heider, M.e.a.: Investigating the impact of independent rule fitnesses in a learning classifier system. In: Bioinspired Optimization Methods and Their Applications, pp. 142–156 (2022)
9. Inoue, H.e.a.: Exploring XCS in multiagent environments. In: Proceedings of the 7th Annual Workshop on Genetic and Evolutionary Computation, pp. 109–111 (2005)
10. Lanzi, P.e.a.: Xcs with computed prediction in continuous multistep environments. In: 2005 IEEE Congress on Evolutionary Computation, pp. 2032–2039, vol. 3 (2005)
11. Mnih, V.e.a.: Human-level control through deep reinforcement learning. Nature **518**(7540), 529–533 (2015)
12. Müller-Schloer, C.e.a.: Organic computing—a paradigm shift for complex systems. Springer Science and Business Media (2011)

13. Müller-Schloer, C.e.a.: Organic Computing-Technical Systems for Survival in the Real World. Springer (2017)
14. Rosenbauer, L.e.a.: XCS as a reinforcement learning approach to automatic test case prioritization. In: Proceedings of the 2020 Genetic and Evolutionary Computation Conference Companion, pp. 1798–1806. ACM, Cancún Mexico (2020)
15. Siddique, A.e.a.: A survey on learning classifier systems from 2022 to 2024. In: Proceedings of the Genetic and Evolutionary Computation Conference Companion, pp. 1797–1806. GECCO '24 Companion, Association for Computing Machinery, New York, NY, USA (2024)
16. Sommer, M.e.a.: An Organic Computing Approach to Resilient Traffic Management, pp. 113–130. Springer International Publishing, Cham (2016)
17. Stein, A.e.a.: XCS classifier system with experience replay. In: Proceedings of the 2020 Genetic and Evolutionary Computation Conference, pp. 404–413 (2020)
18. Stone, C.e.a.: Comparing XCS and ZCS on noisy continuous-valued environments. ETechnical Report. UWE **15** (2005)
19. Sutton, R.S.: Generalization in reinforcement learning: Successful examples using sparse coarse coding. Adv. Neural Inf. Process. Syst. **8** (1995)
20. Sutton, R.S.: Reinforcement learning: an introduction. A Bradford Book (2018)
21. Tomforde, S.e.a.: Cooperative self-optimisation of network protocol parameters at runtime. In: 2015 12th International Conference on Informatics in Control, Automation and Robotics (ICINCO), pp. 123–130 (2015)
22. Urbanowicz, R.J.e.a.: Learning classifier systems: a complete introduction, review, and roadmap. J. Artif. Evol. Appl. **2009**(1), 736398 (2009)
23. Von Mammen, S.e.a.: An organic computing approach to self-organizing robot ensembles. Front. Rob. AI **3**, 67 (2016)
24. Von Pilchau, W.P.e.a.: Semi-model-Based Reinforcement Learning in Organic Computing Systems. In: Schulz, M., Trinitis, C., Papadopoulou, N., Pionteck, T. (eds.) Architecture of Computing Systems, vol. 13642, pp. 241–255. Springer International Publishing, Cham (2022), series Title: Lecture Notes in Computer Science
25. Watkins, C.J.e.a.: Q-learning. Mach. Learn. **8**, 279–292 (1992)
26. Wilson, S.W.: Classifier fitness based on accuracy. Evol. Comput. **3**(2), 149–175 (1995)
27. Zhao, D.e.a.: Deep reinforcement learning with experience replay based on sarsa. In: 2016 IEEE Symposium Series on Computational Intelligence (SSCI), pp. 1–6 (2016)
28. Zhao, Y.e.a.: Dynamic Reward-Based Dueling Deep Dyna-Q: Robust Policy Learning in Noisy Environments. Proc. AAAI Conf. Artif. Intell. **34**(05), 9676–9684 (2020)

A Measurement Framework at Global and Local Levels for Hybrid Organic Computing Systems

Jonas Lange[1](✉), Pia Schweizer[2](✉), Elia Henrichs[2], Luna Kaendler[1], Sven Tomforde[1], and Christian Krupitzer[2]

[1] Intelligent Systems Group, Kiel University, Kiel, Germany
{jla,st}@informatik.uni-kiel.de
[2] Department of Food Informatics and Computational Science Hub, University of Hohenheim, Stuttgart, Germany
{pia.schweizer,elia.henrichs,christian.krupitzer}@uni-hohenheim.de

Abstract. Organic Computing (OC) systems adapt to changes in the system or environment to maintain system performance. Therefore, those systems integrate a control part, which can be implemented centralized (globally) or decentralized (locally)—mixed (hybrid) approaches are feasible. When determining the performance of such a system, various metrics can be observed, which generally cluster in system-specific and adaptation metrics. Whereas the first category is domain-specific and measures the system's performance, the second measures the adaptation performance and can be used system-independently for evaluating OC systems. In this paper, we present a measurement framework that takes into account this split in quality attributes. We show how to apply the measurement framework in a hybrid OC system based on the example of platooning coordination.

Keywords: Organic Computing · Measurement Framework · Performance Metrics · Platooning · Coordination · Platoon Formation

1 Introduction

Organic Computing (OC) [16] is a field that focuses on designing self-organizing, adaptive, and robust systems inspired by biological principles to autonomously manage their behaviour in dynamic environments. Therefore, these systems have two main parts: the system itself, called the System under Observation and Control (SuOC), and the adaptation part. The adaptation part usually follows the Observer-Controller Architecture [16], a framework that ensures the adaptability and self-management of systems. The Observer continuously monitors the system and its environment to collect data and identify deviations or patterns, while the Controller uses this information to make decisions and adjust the system's behavior to meet goals or maintain optimal performance. The Observer-Controller elements might be concentrated into a centralized system part (global control) or decentralized in the different sub-systems (local control). Also, mixed (hybrid) architectures are feasible.

However, the question arises of how differences between the architectures can be assessed and what an integrated measurement and evaluation approach for OC systems might look like. In this paper, we present a measurement framework to compare the quality of adaptation for different control architectures. As a complete discussion of the metrics for all aspects of adaptation quality is out of the scope of this work, we focus on relevant metrics for distributed systems, such as trust, benefits, costs, and emergence. We discuss the framework's application by conducting a simulation-based systematic evaluation of available global and local metrics within a platooning system. Platooning is the context-related coordination of vehicles to convoys in order to primarily exploit safety, capacity, and slipstream effects. The coordination of platoons can be centralized (i.e., external infrastructure services), decentralized (i.e., between the participating vehicles themselves), and hybrid as a combination. The basic problem of coordination decision-making is highly dynamic and, with this dynamic as well as the combination of (partially) autonomous local units and a system-wide objective function, it raises fundamental questions of OC [16]. For platooning as an OC example, the same challenges apply as for other use cases: As platooning is a multi-objective problem [20], there is no single objective function that could be optimized directly. This problem is also visible for the generic class of Self-Adaptive and Self-Organizing (SASO) systems, for which OC systems are one example. Corresponding efforts can be mapped to the overarching question of how the potentials and limitations of SASO systems can be made measurable and assessable, especially in comparison to conventional, purely centrally coordinated approaches. As both centralized and decentralized SASO systems come with challenges in cooperative multi-agent scenarios, the underlying project aims to build a hybrid SASO system, combining global optimization with autonomous subsystems [18]. Therefore, a top-down and a bottom-up approach converge towards the hybrid SASO system. Hence, this work focuses on examining the differences between centralized and decentralized control architectures.

The remainder of this work is structured as follows: Sect. 2 introduces the measurement framework. Section 3 describes the simulation environment and the general experimental setup for the platooning application. Section 4 presents the results of applying the relevant metrics from the measurement framework to the platooning application. Finally, Sect. 5 closes this paper.

2 Measurement Framework

The demands of SASO systems are diverse, extending beyond safety concerns to include the quality of their adaptation outcomes and the overhead required to make the adaptation decisions [2,6]. The following outlines a selection of metrics suited to evaluate the key properties of trust in Sect. 2.1, benefit and cost in Sect. 2.2, as well as emergence in Sect. 2.3. While metrics evaluating trust and emergence can be applied use-case independent, metrics evaluating the benefits and cost of a system are mostly use-case specific and require an explicit transformation to the particular application scenario. We also distinguish whether metrics are relevant at the global, local, or both levels simultaneously.

2.1 Trust

Trust in a system builds on a reliable, robust, and resilient performance. This includes consistently fulfilling its intended functions in stable and changing environments, even if unexpected changes occur (e.g., [15]). In particular, Stability, Robustness, and Unavailability are metrics that support the assessment of these three attributes and enable a comparison of trustworthiness between different systems. The three metrics are explained in the following.

Stability. At the local level, the Stability metric focuses on the total time an agent spends in a desired state. Thus, the longer the total time, that the agents spent in the desired state, the more stable a system is considered. In [8], the stability of self-adaptation processes is assessed as how consistently a system selects expected configurations over time. Depending on the system's implementation, this can be on a global or local level. A system is stable if it frequently chooses high-probability configurations, reflecting normal behavior. Instability occurs when low-probability configurations are repeatedly chosen, signalling disturbances or failures. To detect undesired behavior in SASO systems, the authors use measures proposed by Kinoshita, that is, an activity factor and the fluctuation variance of the activity factor [12]. Generally, high stability is desirable because it indicates that the system maintains its structure and functionality consistently over time, showcasing greater reliability. However, frequent recalibrations could be favorable if they lead to a higher-quality outcome.

Robustness. reflects the ability of the system to maintain a stable behavior when faced with unpredictable changes. It can be measured by the system's ability to maintain functionality during perturbations, with minimal variation in solution quality, by the new state of the system being close to the previous state, or by minimal changes within the system between the state during the perturbation and the new stable state [10]. In [11], the authors distinguish between a system's robustness under attack and long-term robustness. If a system never drops below a pre-defined baseline utility, it is considered to exhibit robustness.

Unavailability. measures the time during which the system is not operational or unable to meet the required functionality. Following the work of [3], Unavailability U, i.e., the downtime of a system, can be derived as

$$U = \frac{MTTR}{MTTF + MTTR} \qquad (1)$$

with $MTTR$ representing the *mean time to recover* and $MTTF$ being the *mean time to fail*. For systems with a fully centralized level of control, which represents a potential single point of failure, this metric is crucial and serves as a measure of the system's reliability.

2.2 Benefit and Cost

Achieving high-quality outcomes typically involves higher processing time or resource use, requiring trade-offs between benefit and cost. While understanding benefits aids in assessing costs, systems with strict time constraints must balance optimality and feasibility [23]. In the following, we consider two metrics for each attribute. We assess the benefit by applying the Situation Performance and Fairness, while the Latency and Overhead metrics serve to evaluate the cost.

Situation Performance. SP serves as a measure of the quality of the final adaptation outcome and evaluates whether and how effectively the system fulfills its intended purpose. The higher the SP, the higher the quality or benefit, the lower the connected cost. In [22], the authors derive the Situation Performance of a system by comparing the actual cost for an adaptation decision C_{subsit} to the maximum possible cost $C_{\max}$. Therefore, they divide a situation *sit* into numerous sub-situations *subsit*.

$$SP = 1 - \frac{\sum_{\text{subsit} \in \text{sit}} C_{\text{subsit}}}{\sum_{\text{subsit} \in \text{sit}} C_{\max}} \quad (2)$$

The cost thereby represents a use-case-specific measure that requires an appropriate transfer depending on the system's purpose.

Fairness. can be categorized into various dimensions, such as resource fairness, i.e., equally distributed access to resources, benefit fairness, or responsibility fairness. Focusing on the example of benefit fairness, the metric evaluates how profits are distributed among agents. The authors of [13] determine the fairness among all individuals n by determining the Gini coefficient G.

$$G = \frac{2\sum_{i=1}^{n} ix(i)}{n \sum_{i=1}^{n} nx(i)} - \frac{n+1}{n} \quad (3)$$

Here, n refers to the total number of individuals in the group being analyzed, composed of single individuals i, and their corresponding values $x(i)$, representing a measurable attribute. A G of 0 indicates maximum fairness among individuals, where no single agent or group of agents consistently gains or suffers disproportionately, while an index of 1 refers to minimum fairness.

Latency. generally refers to the delay in system response. It reflects a time cost associated with the system's decision-making and adaptation processes when encountering disturbances. Latency L can be measured by comparing the time the system requires to adapt to changing environments T_{change} to the time it takes to perform its usual functionality without disturbances T_{usual} [10].

$$L = \frac{T_{change}}{T_{usual}} \quad (4)$$

A lower L indicates that the system is able to react more quickly to changes, enhancing responsiveness. However, a higher L may suggest a more detailed search for optimal solutions, which, while introducing delays, can lead to a higher quality of the final adaptation outcome, but may also result in conflicts with time constraints. This trade-off between speed and quality is a key consideration in systems with time-sensitive constraints.

Overhead. For adaptation decisions to take place, information about the participating agents is required. The gathering and processing of information represents, among others, a form of overhead, which grows as the number of agents increases or as more detailed information about each agent is required. In general, overhead creates cost, but in turn, is a prerequisite for benefits. The authors of [21] further distinguish between communication, computation, memory, and monitoring overhead.

2.3 Emergence

Emergence describes a phenomenon where systems evolve from chaotic conditions to higher-order levels without being explicitly programmed beforehand. It arises from the interaction of many individuals who operate without central control [7]. Different ways to detect and measure emergence are presented below, comprising the Interaction, Entropy, and Oscillation Detection metrics.

Interaction. can be assessed by counting the number of effective interactions I_t that take place for every individual i at a given time t [4].

$$I_t = \sum_{\forall i} \delta_{i,t} \tag{5}$$

$\delta_{i,t}$ changes from 0 to 1 for an effective interaction, which means that the interaction resulted in a state change. An emergent behavior can thereby be detected if the results over time deviate from normality.

Entropy. reflects the degree of disorder. Among various types of entropy, Shannon's Entropy is a prominent example in the field of information theory and enables the evaluation of a system's information content [5]. For Shannon's Entropy SE, the possible system states x of a system X follow a probability distribution $P(x)$. SE can be calculated using Eq. 6.

$$SE = -\sum_{x \in X} P(x) \log P(x) \tag{6}$$

A system with a low entropy represents a high certainty regarding the probability of specific system states to occur; thus, the information content of the system is low. Conversely, a high entropy indicates a high information content as the probability of a specific system state occurring is low, resulting in a high uncertainty regarding predictions about system states.

Oscillation Detection. OD represents the interval k after which a system state S_t at time t has already occurred before [2], . The degree of similarity between system states necessary to result in a detected reoccurrence depends on the use-case and the definition of stability.

$$OD = \begin{cases} k & \text{if } S_t \leftrightarrow S_{t-k} | k \geq 1, t \geq 0 \\ 0 & \text{else} \end{cases} \quad (7)$$

It equals zero if there was no repeated state observable and otherwise results in the respective time interval in between the states' occurrence. The repeated occurrence of an OD of 1 describes a steady state. Transferring this to the local system layer, one could study the frequency with which agents change their state and identify persistent fluctuations where the agents struggle to settle into a stable configuration.

2.4 Further Metrics

The metrics presented here provide only a partial view, which is far from exhaustive. Other relevant literature providing further metrics includes the work of Kaddoum et al. [10]. The authors propose several measures for evaluating the adaptive properties of selfâĂŞ*systems, introducing metrics that focus on methodological, architectural, intrinsic, and runtime evaluation criteria. Eberhardinger et al. [6] focus on the key metrics for assessing the performance of self-organization algorithms, with particular emphasis on time and solution quality. Furthermore, Birdsey et al. [2] present a compilation of metrics that enable the evaluation of the two properties, self-adaptation and self-organization, in isolation.

3 Experimental Setup

As for evaluating the performance of SASO and OC systems, adaptation metrics and system-specific metrics must be considered. The experiments aim to integrate domain-specific use case metrics and to show differences between centralized and decentralized control architectures. The experiments were conducted using the example of platoon coordination, which describes a highly dynamic multi-agent environment. For simulating the vehicles and traffic, we rely on the open-source SUMO (Simulation of Urban MObility, [1]) simulator. For simulating the platooning functionality, we use the Python API of Plexe [19], an open-source SUMO extension. In the following, Sect. 3.1 explains the applied traffic situations. Section 3.2 illustrates the implementation of two platooning algorithms, one with a centralized and one with a decentralized control architecture.

3.1 Traffic Scenarios

Some parameters were set statically to keep the number of variable traffic scenarios in check.

Table 1. Platooning parameters

Parameter	Value
Platooning spacing	5 m
Vehicle headway	1.5 s
Max. platoon size	5 Vehicles

Table 2. Vehicle parameters

Parameter	Value
Min. speed	80 km/h
Max. speed	160 km/h
Vehicle length	4.3 m

Table 1 shows the parameters for the platoons, while Table 2 shows the static parameters for the individual vehicles. For simplicity, all vehicles are of the same dimensions and equipped with the same engines, only their desired velocity differs, which is set to a random value between 80 and 160 km/h. We test three different traffic densities on three maps with three different platooning participation rates. Hence, we evaluate the two platooning algorithms on 27 different traffic scenarios. Each scenario simulates exactly 65 min of traffic, of which the first 5 min are not considered for evaluation since the environment is set up with vehicles on an empty highway.

Each of the three maps represents a unique challenge that can occur on highways. For all scenarios, the cars spawn at the beginning of a one-kilometer-long startup section and despawn when they reach the end of the one-kilometer-long cool-down section. Yet only the 10 km long main road section is evaluated, as spawning and de-spawning vehicles (on the startup- and cool-down sections) might disrupt the natural traffic flow. In the *Straight* map, the cars drive on a straight, three-lane highway. The second map is the *Lane Reduction* map, which starts with a straight highway, but at 5 km, the rightmost lane ends; thus, the 4-lane highway turns into a 3-lane highway. This leads to an increased traffic density from that point onward. The third map is called the *Y-map*, which starts with a straight section. After 5 km, the road splits into two, resembling the letter "y" turned by 90°. This introduces a novel challenge to platooning, as platoons might need to split up to ensure that each vehicle reaches its destination.

Traffic Density. will likely influence the performance of platooning coordination systems. We therefore consider the following scenarios: Low Density, Medium Density, and High Density. Traffic density should not be too low, resulting in high inter-vehicle distances and no opportunity for platoons to form. Traffic density should also not be too high, resulting in a traffic jam. The High Density is set to 5400 vehicles per hour (v/h) as this is estimated to be the maximum capacity of a three-lane highway [17]. The Low Density was set to 1200 v/h to ensure that, on average, there are 10 vehicles within a 1 km stretch of highway. The Medium Density is set to 3300 which is the average of Low Density and High Density.

Platooning Participation. is seen as voluntary for vehicles. Hence, we consider that half of the vehicles (50%) want to join platoons. For comparison, we also include scenarios without (0%) and with forced platooning (100%).

3.2 Platoon Coordination

As a general architecture for platoon coordination, we consider two possibilities. Nearly all proposed platooning coordination systems follow one of these two architectures [14]. In a **centralized** architecture, a central control unit is in place to make platooning decisions. In a **decentralized** architecture, individual vehicles coordinate the formation of platoons. In real-world applications, the feasibility of either of these architectures depends on the infrastructure in place (e.g., communication infrastructure). In [18], we further discuss the advantages and disadvantages of the two architectures. As the inter-vehicle communication within platoons (e.g., keeping correct inter-vehicle gap, platoons changing lanes, etc.) is handled by Plexe, the centralized and decentralized platoon coordination algorithms are mainly concerned with assigning vehicles to platoons. Figure 1 shows the three main states of the platooning coordination task.

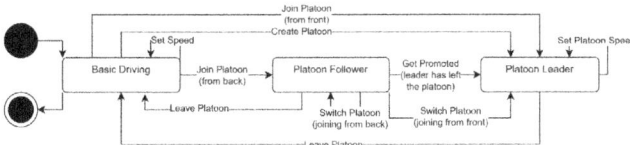

Fig. 1. State machine for the platooning coordination task from the perspective of an individual vehicle. Vehicles can join, leave, and switch platoons. Vehicles not in a platoon control their own speed and lane, while platoon leaders set these for the group.

The authors of [9] propose two static platoon coordination algorithms. The proposed centralized and decentralized algorithms have only three parameters (α, r, and m). This fits well into the experimental design because it focuses on the metrics in relation to the traffic scenarios rather than optimizing algorithm parameters. In assigning vehicles to platoons, the algorithms try to minimize two values: One is the physical distance between the candidate vehicles c and the target platoons' t current position $d_p(c, t)$. The other is their difference in speed $d_s(c, t)$. These two values are weighted against each other using the parameter α, which we set to its default value $\alpha = 0.5$:

$$f(c, t) = \alpha \cdot d_s(c, t) + (1 - \alpha) \cdot d_p(c, t) \tag{8}$$

In the decentralized algorithm, each candidate vehicle applies Eq. 8 individually to find the best target platoon inside its search radius $r = 500$ m. In addition, platoons with a traveling speed outside of the maximum speed deviation $m = 0.2$ are not considered (e.g., a vehicle with a desired speed of 100 km/h would only consider platoons traveling at speeds 80–120 km/h). Vehicle c then selects the candidate platoon t, which minimizes $f(c, t)$. If there are no platoons within r and m, the vehicle creates a new platoon (only containing itself). If two vehicles want to join the same platoon, first-come, first-served is applied.

In the centralized algorithm, a central controller first collects all possible assignments $(c_i, t_j, f(c_i, t_j))$ of candidate vehicles c_i to target platoons t_j. Like the decentralized algorithm, possible assignments outside the search range $r = 500$ m, and the maximum speed deviation $m = 0.2$ are not considered. The central controller then assigns each vehicle to the corresponding optimal platoon. The optimal platoon t_i for a candidate vehicle c is the one that minimizes $f(c, t_i)$. During the assignment, the centralized controller applies a greedy approach. It finds the best target platoon for each candidate vehicle in random order while removing possible assignments $(c_i, t_j, f(c_i, t_j))$ if a vehicle has already been assigned to platoon t_j in this iteration.

We adopted and adapted these two algorithms for our experiments. Our major changes to the original algorithms are twofold: First, in the original implementation [9], vehicles were only searching for platoons in front of them to join them from behind. In our implementation, vehicles search for platoons in front and behind and can join platoons from the back or front. This effectively increases the number of joinable platoons for each vehicle and, thus, the likelihood of finding better-matching platoons. Second, in contrast to the original implementation, our variant allows vehicles to change platoons.

4 Results and Discussion

To quantify the potentials and limitations of SASO systems, we derived use case-specific measures from the metrics of Sect. 2. We focused on those metrics that specifically highlight the differences between the centralized and decentralized algorithms, providing insights into their respective strengths and limitations.

4.1 Trust

The *Robustness* metric measures the ability of a system to maintain functionality during perturbations. While there are no sudden and unexpected perturbations in the evaluated traffic scenarios, there are static perturbations, namely the lane reduction and the y-split. At these points, the systems must adapt as the environment suddenly changes. The platoon coordination system aims to assign as many vehicles to adequate platoons as possible. Therefore, we interpret the functionality of the system to be the number of vehicles driving in platoons.

Figure 2 shows the number of vehicles driving in platoon formations at different points of the road. The straight map can be seen as the baseline, as there are no disturbances on the road. Here, the number of platooning vehicles per 100 m rises steadily for both the centralized and the decentralized algorithms. However, the centralized algorithm, in general, has a higher platooning density. This general performance difference is relevant to consider when evaluating the recovery after the disturbances for the Robustness metric because the focus here is on robustness, not on general performance. On the lane reduction map, the centralized and decentralized algorithms start out similarly. Just before the 5 km

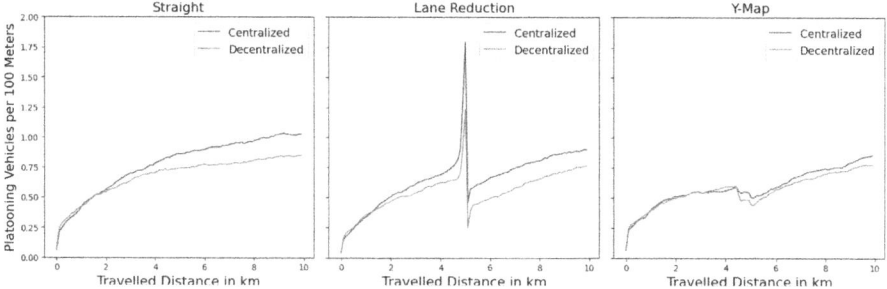

Fig. 2. Robustness as the number of vehicles in a platoon over the length of the map. The scenarios selected are with medium traffic and 50% platooning participation.

mark, the number of platooning vehicles suddenly spikes. This is due to a general high traffic density before the lane reduction point, where some vehicles need to merge, causing a slowdown of the following traffic. The main difference is visible after the lane reduction; here, the centralized system recovered to a higher platooning density than the decentralized system. But when compared to the straight scenario, this difference can be attributed to the better general performance of the centralized system. Thus, for the lane reduction scenario, the two systems are similarly robust. Finally, on the y-map, both systems perform similarly. The functionality drops slightly at the y-split as some vehicles split up from their current platoons. Here, the difference between the centralized and decentralized systems is much smaller than in the straight scenario. This indicates that the decentralized approach, while being, in general, less effective, is more robust in this scenario.

Robustness reflects a system's ability to recover and return to a stable or desired state after a disturbance, ensuring long-term operational continuity. The proposed metric allowed us to assess system robustness under different types of disturbances. The results showed that the robustness varies depending on the disturbance type, revealing potential weak points that could ultimately reduce trust in the system. Explicitly identifying these vulnerabilities enables targeted improvements to enhance system resilience. Therefore, we consider this metric highly relevant within our framework, particularly in the *Trust* category.

4.2 Benefit and Cost

The *Situation Performance* describes the quality of the final adaptation outcome. Concerning the use case, one of the main purposes favoring platooning is the reduction of fuel consumption [24]. Thus, we assume a higher Situation Performance if all vehicles that had the intention to participate in platooning achieve fuel savings compared to a scenario without platooning, where the SASO system was not active. Therefore, we calculate the individual Situation Performance using Eq. 2, and consider the mean fuel consumption of a vehicle that wanted to platoon as C_{subsit}, while the maximum cost C_{max} represents the mean fuel

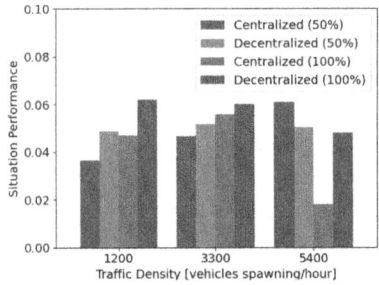
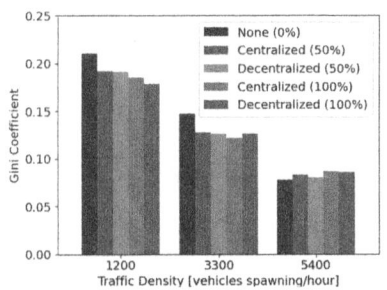

Fig. 3. Situation Performance of platooning vehicles at different platooning participation rates, depending on the traffic density on the lane reduction map.

Fig. 4. Gini Coefficient regarding the fuel consumption of all vehicles at different platooning participation rates, depending on the traffic density on the lane reduction map.

consumption of the same vehicle in the scenario without platooning. This follows the assumption that platooning leads to fuel savings. If this assumption does not hold, the Situation Performance yields a negative value.

Figure 3 illustrates the resulting Situation Performance of both centralized and decentralized systems operating in scenarios with 50% and 100% platooning participation, respectively, depending on the traffic density in vehicles spawning per hour. Here, we chose to focus on the results of the lane reduction map as the static disturbance of the road bottleneck led to traffic congestion for high traffic densities, which represents a disturbance. The road split in the Y-map also represents a disturbance, but did not result in congestion. Despite the challenge, the results show that platooning—regardless of traffic density—yielded a higher Situation Performance and thus improved fuel consumption. At a low and medium traffic density, a higher participation rate led to a higher Situation Performance, and the decentralized system outperformed the centralized one. Conversely, with high traffic density, the trend reversed, making a lower participation rate favorable, as those scenarios resulted in a higher Situation Performance. It additionally came to a switch in performance for the centralized and decentralized approaches at the medium platooning participation rate. The results indicate that high platooning participation especially benefits low and medium traffic densities, as it increases the number of potential platooning partners, enhancing the opportunity to save fuel. With a dense distribution of platoons on a crowded road segment, the inflexibility of all road users increases, reducing the positive effects of platooning and, thus, the Situation Performance. These observations indicate that with the current approaches in place, too-high traffic counteracts the effect of platooning while emphasizing the presence of a sweet spot marking the optimal fuel savings at a specific traffic density and participation rate.

On a local level, one can assess the *Fairness* among the participating agents with respect to their fuel consumption. This fairness, expressed as the Gini coefficient Eq.(3), is presented in Fig. 4 depending on the traffic density in vehicles spawning per hour. For space reasons, we again focus on the results of the lane reduction map, without platooning (0% platooning participation) as well as 50% and 100% platooning participation with a centralized or decentralized coordination algorithm. The results show that a higher vehicle density resulted in a higher equality among the agents, with the Gini coefficient getting closer to a value of zero. While at low and medium traffic levels, a higher participation rate led to greater equality, at high traffic, higher participation resulted in decreased equality. This shows that an increasing vehicle load increases fairness, as fewer vehicles profit from platooning.

The benefit of improved fuel efficiency when platooning comes with necessary pre-investments in the form of, among others, time cost. Therefore, we determined the *Latency* of both approaches, centralized and decentralized, at a maximum platooning participation rate, as here, we assumed the highest computational effort. The lane reduction and y-split seen as a disturbance resulted in no significant difference between the centralized and decentralized approaches when taking the straight scenario as a baseline. However, a larger impact on both system's Latency proved to have the traffic density. With higher throughput, the delay of both systems increased, with the decentralized system having a maximum Latency of 5.25 and, thus, less than half that of the central system with 13.65. This significant difference can be explained by the fact that the centralized approach always tries to find a solution for every vehicle at once, whereas the decentralized approach considers each vehicle individually, resulting in a lower calculation effort.

While the Situation Performance metric provided valuable insights regarding the quality of the final adaptation outcome on a global level, the Fairness metric enabled the performance assessment on a local level. A benefit on a global level is necessary to reason for the system as a whole, whereas understanding the distribution of those benefits on a local level helps identify potential dissatisfaction or even agent withdrawal from participation. Therefore, independent of the SASO system's architectural approach, both perspectives must be considered, making these metrics crucial to our measurement framework. Closely linked to the benefits are the associated costs. The Latency metric, which captures cost in the form of delay, allowed us to compare centralized and decentralized approaches in terms of the time required for adaptation. A key question is whether these incurred costs are justified by the benefits gained, highlighting an inherent trade-off, one that is evaluated differently depending on whether the perspective is global or local. Furthermore, although not explicitly evaluated in this work, assessing the overhead in terms of message exchanges could be a valuable metric for future research. It may provide insights into local-level costs, particularly enabling the evaluation of the effort required for an agent to participate.

4.3 Emergence

Here, we apply the *Interaction* metric, which counts the number of effective interactions between vehicles. The vehicles are constantly communicating in order to advertise and find platoon opportunities. An effective interaction takes place if a state change occurs. In the platooning scenario, a state change equates to a change in driving strategies for at least one of the vehicles involved. A strategy change happens, for example, when a vehicle joins a platoon, switches platoons, or the vehicles' platoon changes lanes.

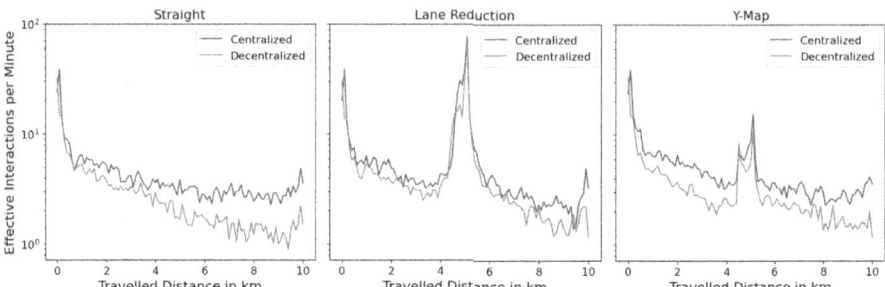

Fig. 5. Interaction as vehicles' strategy changes over the length of the map. The scenario is considering 100% platooning participation at a high traffic density.

Figure 5 shows how many effective interactions took place mapped over the length of the highway. We selected the scenarios with high traffic density and 100% platooning participation because the differences between the centralized and decentralized systems are most clear. In scenarios with lower platooning participation and/or lower traffic density, the trends described below are similar, but the differences between the algorithms are less pronounced. On all three maps, the number of interactions spikes initially as vehicles immediately try to find available platoons and join them. The system then stabilizes as vehicles find adequate platoons and state-changing interactions decrease. In the lane reduction map and the y-map, the number of effective interactions then spikes around the traffic obstacle (at 5 km), as the vehicles need to reorganize to navigate the obstacle. In general, the centralized controller seems to facilitate more effective interactions. This could lead to a better overall performance but also to a higher overhead.

The results of the Interaction metric indicate an emergent behavior of both approaches, centralized and decentralized, when participants encounter disturbances, forcing them to reorganize. We found that out of the three proposed metrics for emergence, the interaction metric is most applicable to our application. Yet the Entropy and Oscillation Detection metrics, might be more suitable for future application scenarios. Hence, we considered all three metrics within our proposed framework for an extensive assessment of a SASO system's emergence: the Interaction metric—to detect emergence, Entropy—to evaluate the degree of (dis)order, and the Oscillation Detection metric—to measure fluctuations and, consequently, the stability of the established order.

4.4 Discussion

Our results have shown that the centralized and decentralized algorithms perform differently in different situations and relative to different metrics. The *Interaction* metric shows that the centralized algorithm facilitates more effective interactions due to its globalized view. On the upside, this leads to a generally higher platooning density (as shown by the *Robustness* metric). On the downside, the *Latency* metric shows that this globalized view also requires more resources, especially when the traffic density increases. When measuring the benefit of applying the centralized vs. the decentralized algorithm, the *Situation Performance* metric shows that there is no clear winner, and the performance is situation-dependent. In some scenarios, the higher general platooning density leads the centralized system to perform better. In other scenarios, savings in overhead and general robustness lead the decentralized system to perform better.

The results show that rather than applying static algorithms, it is necessary to apply intelligent systems that learn to recognize different situations and act accordingly. The decentralized algorithm could be improved by applying Reinforcement Learning. While the centralized algorithm could benefit from optimization techniques that improve the coordination. The results also reinforce the necessity for a hybrid system [18], which combines the strengths of centralized and decentralized systems. Our proposed measurement framework aims at a comprehensive evaluation of SASO systems. We identified three key metric categories: *Trust*, *Benefit and Cost*, and *Emergence*. Our findings demonstrate that no single metric can fully assess an entire category; instead, a combination of metrics is required to capture a system's strengths and weaknesses. Moreover, evaluating both the global and local levels is essential, as their distinct interests influence the system as a whole. Different metrics are needed for each level to ensure a well-rounded assessment. By incorporating both perspectives, our framework not only provides a holistic evaluation but also enables a direct comparison of different approaches. We see two main limitations of this work. First, the proposed measurement framework is far from exhaustive. While this work aims to include the most relevant metrics, we recognize that some excluded ones could round off the framework. Second, with the platooning application, we aim to highlight the ability of the measurement framework to showcase the differences between centralized and decentralized architectures. Yet, one application scenario is not sufficient to show the general applicability of the proposed measurement framework.

5 Conclusion

When it comes to measuring the effects of SASO and OC systems, there is rarely one singular metric that is able to fully capture a system's complexity and overall impact. In this work, we propose a measurement framework to assess such systems' dynamics. Our framework provides diverse measures from the areas of *Trust*, *Benefit and Cost*, as well as *Emergence*. We evaluated the measurement framework on the example of platooning, applying two coordination strategies—centralized and decentralized. None of the two approaches was preferable over all scenarios and the performance was situation-dependent. This work has shown that the framework, while not exhaustive, is able to highlight the strengths and weaknesses of centralized and decentralized systems. Thus, it is in a good position to be useful in evaluating hybrid approaches, which is the main objective of our future work.

Acknowledgments. This work is part of the InHOSaS project which is funded by the Deutsche Forschungsgemeinschaft (DFG, German Research Foundation)—516601628.

References

1. Alvarez Lopez, P., et al.: Microscopic traffic simulation using sumo. In: IEEE ITSC, pp. 2575–2582 (2018)
2. Birdsey, L., Szabo, C., Falkner, K.: Identifying self-organization and adaptability in complex adaptive systems. In: SASO, pp. 131–140 (2017)
3. Candea, G., Cutler, J., Fox, A.: Improving availability with recursive microreboots: a soft-state system case study. Perform. Eval. **56**(1–4), 213–248 (2004)
4. Chan, W.K.V.: Interaction metric of emergent behaviors in agent-based simulation. In: WSC, pp. 357–368 (2011)
5. Crutchfield, J.P., Young, K.: Inferring statistical complexity. Phys. Rev. Lett. **63**, 105–108 (1989)
6. Eberhardinger, B., Anders, G., Seebach, H., Siefert, F., Reif, W.: A research overview and evaluation of performance metrics for self-organization algorithms. In: SASO Workshops, pp. 122–127 (2015)
7. Goldstein, J.: Emergence as a construct: history and issues. Emergence **1**(1), 49–72 (1999)
8. Goller, M., Tomforde, S.: On the stability of (self-) adaptive behaviour in continuously changing environments: a quantification approach. Array **11**, 100069 (2021)
9. Heinovski, J., Dressler, F.: Where to decide? Centralized versus distributed vehicle assignment for platoon formation. T-ITS (2024)
10. Kaddoum, E., Raibulet, C., George, J.P., Picard, G., Gleizes, M.P.: Criteria for the evaluation of self-* systems. In: ICSE SEAMS, pp. 29–38. SEAMS, Association for Computing Machinery, New York, NY, USA (2010)
11. Kantert, J., Tomforde, S., Müller-Schloer, C., Edenhofer, S., Sick, B.: Quantitative robustness – a generalised approach to compare the impact of disturbances in self-organising systems. In: ICAART, pp. 39–50. INSTICC, SciTePress (2017)
12. Kinoshita, T.: Basic characteristics of a macroscopic measure for detecting abnormal changes in a multiagent system. Sensors **15**(4), 9112–9135 (2015)
13. Kohler, T., Steghöfer, J.P., Busquets, D., Pitt, J.: The value of fairness: trade-offs in repeated dynamic resource allocation. In: IEEE SASO, pp. 1–10. IEEE (2014)
14. Lesch, V., Breitbach, M., Segata, M., Becker, C., Kounev, S., Krupitzer, C.: An overview on approaches for coordination of platoons. T-ITS **23**(8), 10049–10065 (2022)
15. Moskowitz, F., McLean, J.B.: Some reliability aspects of systems design. IRE Trans. Reliab. Qual. Control **PGRQC-8**, 7–35 (1956)

16. Müller-Schloer, C., Tomforde, S.: Organic Computing - Technical Systems for Survival in the Real World. Birkhäuser (2017)
17. Ober-Sundermeier, A.: Entwicklung eines Verfahrens zur Stauprognose an Engpässen auf Autobahnen unter besonderer Berücksichtigung von Arbeitsstellen. Ph.D. thesis, University of Kassel (2003)
18. Schweizer, P., Lange, J., Henrichs, E., Tomforde, S., Krupitzer, C.: Towards a hybrid architecture for self-adaptive and self-organizing systems. In: IEEE ACSOS-C, pp. 41–46. IEEE (2024)
19. Segata, M., Lo Cigno, R., Hardes, T., Heinovski, J., Schettler, M., Bloessl, B., Sommer, C., Dressler, F.: Multi-technology cooperative driving: an analysis based on PLEXE. TMC **22**(8), 4792–4806 (2023)
20. Sturm, T., Krupitzer, C., Segata, M., Becker, C.: A taxonomy of optimization factors for platooning. T-ITS **22**(10), 6097–6114 (2021)
21. Szabo, C., Sims, B., Mcatee, T., Lodge, R., Hunjet, R.: Self-adaptive software systems in contested and resource-constrained environments: Overview and challenges. IEEE Access **9**, 10711–10728 (2021)
22. Taranu, S., Tiemann, J.: On assessing self-adaptive systems. In: PERCOM Workshops, pp. 214–219 (2010)
23. Van Der Donckt, J., Weyns, D., Iftikhar, M.U., Buttar, S.S.: Effective decision making in self-adaptive systems using cost-benefit analysis at runtime and online learning of adaptation spaces. In: ENASE, pp. 373–403. Springer (2019)
24. Zabat, M., Stabile, N., Frascaroli, S., Browand, F.: Drag forces experienced by 2, 3 and 4-vehicle platoons at close spacings. SAE Transactions, pp. 1173–1181 (1995)

Exploring Model Quantization in GenAI-Based Image Inpainting and Detection of Arable Plants

Sourav Modak[✉], Ahmet Oğuz Saltık, and Anthony Stein

Department of Artificial Intelligence in Agricultural Engineering and Computational Science Hub, University of Hohenheim, 70599 Stuttgart, Germany
{s.modak,ahmet.saltik,anthony.stein}@uni-hohenheim.de

Abstract. Deep learning-based weed control systems often suffer from limited training data diversity and constrained onboard computation, impacting their real-world performance. To overcome these challenges, we propose a framework that leverages Stable Diffusion-based inpainting to augment training data progressively in 10% increments—up to an additional 200%, thus enhancing both the volume and diversity of samples. Our approach is evaluated on two state-of-the-art object detection models, YOLO11(l) and RT-DETR(l), using the mAP50 metric to assess detection performance. We explore quantization strategies (FP16 and INT8) for both the generative inpainting and detection models to strike a balance between inference speed and accuracy. Deployment of the downstream models on the Jetson Orin Nano demonstrates the practical viability of our framework in resource-constrained environments, ultimately improving detection accuracy and computational efficiency in intelligent weed management systems.

Keywords: Weed Detection · Stable Diffusion · Quantization · Edge AI

1 Introduction

Automated weed control systems, such as robots and smart sprayers, play a vital role in enhancing weeding efficiency, improving crop health, and increasing yields. In contrast, manual weed management is both costly and time-consuming, typically eliminating only 65–85% of weeds [9]. However, achieving viable real-world agricultural performance requires a high-quality, diverse, and balanced dataset. Traditional image augmentation techniques (e.g., image manipulation, geometric transformations, copy-paste, and mixup) often fall short in generating the necessary diversity, as they depend heavily on the input data. In contrast, synthetic images produced by Generative Adversarial Networks (GANs) [6] and Diffusion Models [4] provide highly diverse and realistic representations while preserving natural variations [16,25]. In our previous study, synthetic data augmentation based on the Stable Diffusion Model [19] has been found to potentially improve the performance of downstream models on a sugar beet weed detection task [14]. Notably, replacing only 10% of real-world images with synthetic ones was observed to be sufficient to enhance training efficiency [15] in the investigated case of weed detection. Yet, this approach was limited by its sole reliance on synthetic data generation without the ability to manipulate existing images. To overcome this limitation, we extend our methodology by incorporating inpainting techniques [24]. This extension not only enables precise spatial manipulation, weed size control, and class imbalance reduction within existing images but also seamlessly integrates synthetic augmentation into real-world datasets. In this paper, we evaluate our enhanced approach by progressively incorporating synthetic images during the training of state-of-the-art models such as YOLO11(l) and RT-DETR(l). While these techniques achieve substantial performance gains in contrast to nano and small models, deploying real-time capable deep learning models in practical setups such as agricultural machines for weed detection without sacrificing detection accuracy is still challenging since larger models with higher predictive capability demand considerable higher computational power [18]. To address these challenges, we investigate model quantization techniques purposefully reducing the numerical precision of neural network weights and activations (e.g., *FP16* and *INT8* precision) within a generative AI-based weed detection pipeline introduced earlier [16] which integrates a newly developed image inpainting method and downstream weed detection models. To explore the performance impacts on resource-constrained edge devices as presumably used in future intelligent weed control systems, we deploy our downstream detection models on an NVIDIA Jetson Orin Nano[1]. The contributions of this paper are two-fold and can be summarized as providing initial answers to the following two research questions:

1. What is the effect of post-training quantization on GenAI inpainting and downstream weed detection accuracy?
2. To what extent does post-training quantization enhance inference efficiency while balancing computational trade-offs in the Stable Diffusion and downstream models?

2 Background

2.1 Related Work

Recent advances in generative AI have enabled new data augmentation techniques that boost performance in object detection tasks, but there are limited studies in the agricultural domain. Techniques such as text-prompt-based image generation, image inpainting, and image-to-image translation have been widely adopted. For instance, [2] demonstrated a 1.5% improvement in mAP50-95 scores through enhanced image augmentation. Similarly, [14] showed that applying Stable Diffusion to crop-weed images improved YOLO model performance more

---

[1] https://developer.nvidia.com/embedded/learn/get-started-jetson-orin-nano-devkit (accessed on February 14, 2025).

effectively than traditional augmentation. Moreover, domain adaptive data augmentation using diffusion models has been reported to benefit vineyard shoot detection [8]. In parallel, model quantization techniques have emerged as a promising strategy to reduce computational demands while preserving inference speed and detection accuracy. INT8 quantization offers an effective compromise by optimizing computational requirements without significant sacrifices in performance [7].

2.2 Diffusion Model

Diffusion models, a subclass of generative models, operate by corrupting training data with Gaussian noise (known as *forward diffusion*) and learning to recover the original information through step-by-step denoising (known as *reverse diffusion*). Given an initial data distribution $x_0 \sim q(x)$, the forward process adds Gaussian noise via a Markovian transition:

$$q(x_t|x_{t-1}) = \mathcal{N}(x_t; \sqrt{1-\beta_t}x_{t-1}, \beta_t I), \tag{1}$$

where β_t is a variance schedule controlling noise addition. Reparameterizing, the noisy data at timestep t is:

$$x_t = \sqrt{\alpha_t}x_0 + \sqrt{1-\alpha_t}\epsilon, \quad \epsilon \sim \mathcal{N}(0, I), \tag{2}$$

where $\alpha_t = \prod_{s=1}^{t}(1-\beta_s)$ represents the cumulative noise factor. The model aims to reverse this process by learning the posterior:

$$p_\theta(x_{t-1}|x_t) = \mathcal{N}(x_{t-1}; \mu_\theta(x_t, t), \Sigma_\theta(x_t, t)), \tag{3}$$

where the mean function is parameterized as:

$$\mu_\theta(x_t, t) = \frac{1}{\sqrt{1-\beta_t}} \left(x_t - \frac{\beta_t}{\sqrt{1-\alpha_t}} \epsilon_\theta(x_t, t) \right). \tag{4}$$

A U-Net with sinusoidal time embeddings approximates $\epsilon_\theta(x_t, t)$. The model is trained by minimizing the MSE loss:

$$L(\theta) = \mathbb{E}_{x_0, t, \epsilon} \left[\|\epsilon - \epsilon_\theta(x_t, t)\|^2 \right]. \tag{5}$$

The Stable Diffusion Model, based on the Latent Diffusion Model (LDM), enables conditional text-to-image generation using CLIP text embeddings. Performing the diffusion process in latent space instead of pixel space significantly boosts efficiency. A trained encoder maps high-resolution images to a lower-dimensional latent representation, which is then reconstructed by a decoder. Stable Diffusion's conditioning mechanism allows for text prompts, input masks, and layouts, supporting tasks including text-to-image generation, inpainting, and super-resolution. To enhance computational efficiency during inference, various sampling schedulers, such as Denoising Diffusion Implicit Models (DDIM) and the Euler Ancestral sampler, are used [19].

2.3 Object Detection Models

YOLO11. Evolving from the YOLO family, YOLO11 is a state-of-the-art real-time object detector model. It enhances object detection speed and accuracy with key architectural innovations. The model uses initial convolutional layers for downsampling, followed by the C3k2 block for improved computational efficiency. Features including Spatial Pyramid Pooling-Fast (SPPF) and a new Cross Stage Partial with Spatial Attention module enhance focus on salient regions, improving small object detection. In the neck, features from various scales are fused, while the head refines them through additional C3k2 and CBS layers, ultimately producing bounding boxes, objectness scores, and class predictions [5].

RT-DETR. In contrast to convolution-based architectures, RT-DETR uses a transformer-based backbone to analyze the entire image, allowing it to capture the global context for detecting complex scenes and small objects. It eliminates the need for non-maximum suppression (NMS) by using a one-to-one matching strategy with the Hungarian algorithm, resulting in unique predictions and faster detection. The architecture features a hybrid encoder that combines Attention-based Intra-scale Feature Interaction (AIFI) with CNN-based Cross-scale Feature Fusion (CCFF) for effective multi-scale feature extraction. Additionally, a query selection mechanism improves the quality of initial queries, enhancing overall detection accuracy [26].

Object Detection Metrics. Object detection models are typically evaluated using metrics such as *precision, recall, mAP50,* and *mAP50–95*. *Precision* measures the proportion of correctly identified positives among all predicted positives, while *recall* measures the proportion of actual positives that are correctly detected. Moreover, localization accuracy is crucial in detection tasks. *Intersection over Union (IoU)* quantifies the overlap between predicted and ground-truth bounding boxes, with detections considered correct if IoU $\geq t$ (t is a predefined threshold). *Precision-recall (PR) curves* illustrate the trade-off between precision and recall, with the *area under the curve (AUC)* indicating overall performance. *Average Precision (AP)* computes AUC for a single class, while *Mean Average Precision (mAP)* averages AP across classes. *mAP50* is evaluated at IoU $= 0.50$, whereas *mAP50–95* averages *mAP* over thresholds from 0.50 to 0.95.

2.4 Quantization

Deep learning models typically use 32-bit floating-point (FP32) arithmetic, while lower-precision formats (FP16 & INT8) are often employed for efficiency.

FP32 Representation. FP32 (single precision) uses 32 bits – 1 bit for the *sign*, 8 bits for the *exponent* (bias 127), and 23 bits for the *mantissa*. A floating-point number x in FP32 is:

$$x = (-1)^s \times 2^{e-127} \times \left(1 + \frac{m}{2^{23}}\right), \qquad (6)$$

where s is the sign bit, e is the exponent, and m is the mantissa.

FP16 Representation. FP16 (half precision) uses 16 bits – 1 bit for the *sign*, 5 bits for the *exponent* (bias 15), and 10 bits for the *mantissa*. The FP16 representation of a number x is:

$$x = (-1)^s \times 2^{e-15} \times \left(1 + \frac{m}{2^{10}}\right), \tag{7}$$

where s is the 1-bit sign, e is the 5-bit exponent, and m is the 10-bit mantissa.

INT8 Quantization. INT8 quantization maps a full-precision weight w to an 8-bit integer q. In a signed INT8 representation ($[-128, 127]$), the conversion follows:

$$q = \text{clip}\left(\text{round}\left(\frac{w}{s}\right) + z, -128, 127\right), \tag{8}$$

where s is the scaling factor, z is the zero-point, and clip ensures q remains in range:

$$\text{clip}(x, a, b) = \max(a, \min(b, x)). \tag{9}$$

The original weight is approximately recovered as:

$$\hat{w} = s \cdot (q - z). \tag{10}$$

These quantization methods apply in both post-training quantization and Quantization-Aware Training (QAT), where the loss accounts for quantization error:

$$L_{\text{total}} = L(\hat{w}) + \lambda \|w - \hat{w}\|^2, \tag{11}$$

with λ balancing task loss and quantization error. While FP32 and FP16 explicitly represent numbers using separate fields for sign, exponent, and mantissa, INT8 uses an integer representation with a scaling factor and zero-point. These quantization techniques trade numerical precision for efficiency, which is critical for real-time object detection models [10,12].

3 Material and Methods

Accurate weed identification is vital for intelligent agricultural weed management systems and depends on high-quality data. Our method addresses real-world data challenges, including the under-representation of certain weed classes due to factors, namely seasonal changes, weather, and seed availability. To address these challenges, we utilize an image augmentation strategy derived from our previous data augmentation work [16], which employs an inpainting technique (refer to Fig. 3). This strategy augments the dataset by generating images of underrepresented weed classes, enhancing its diversity and volume. YOLO variants offer a good balance of accuracy and speed, while RT-DETR achieves higher accuracy with slower inference [1,20]. Our previous work [1] shows that YOLO(l) and RT-DETR(l) match their YOLO(x) and RT-DETR(x) counterparts in accuracy while improving increasing efficiency. Thus, we validated our augmented images by fine-tuning YOLO11(l) and RT-DETR(l) on original and synthetic datasets. The proportion of augmented data varied, ranging from 10% to 200%

of the original dataset size, with a 10% increment. However, both the inpainting image generation and subsequent weed detection are computationally intensive. We addressed this by applying post-training quantization (see Sect. 2.4) to speed up inference and lower resource demands (see Fig. 1). For training Stable Diffusion, YOLO11(l), and RT-DETR(l), we used an NVIDIA A100-SXM4-40 GB GPU alongside an AMD EPYC 75F3 32-core processor with 12 GB of memory. Our quantized, fine-tuned downstream models were then deployed on an NVIDIA Jetson Nano 8 GB variant, featuring an 8-core ARM Cortex-A78AE CPU and a 1024-core Ampere GPU with 8 GB of unified memory.

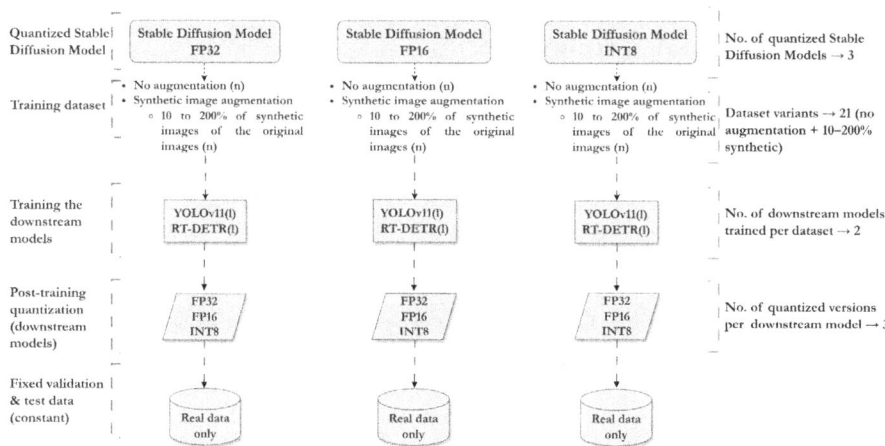

Fig. 1. Workflow of the quantization process and training of downstream models. Images are generated via Stable Diffusion at various precisions and used to augment data (10%–200%). YOLOv11(l) and RT-DETR(l) are trained per data set and then quantized and evaluated on fixed real validation/test data.

3.1 Dataset

The dataset was collected from a test site using a *field camera unit (FCU)* mounted on a smart sprayer attached to a tractor moving at 1.5m/s. The imaging system featured a 6 mm *effective focal length (EFL)* and 2.3 MP RGB sensors, with a dual-band lens filter for near-infrared (NIR) and red wavelengths. Post-processing included projection correction and pseudo-RGB image generation from NIR and red wavelengths. Images were captured from 1.1 m above ground at a 25-degree tilt. The dataset, comprising 2074 images, includes *Sugar beet* as the main crop and four weed types: *Cirsium, Convolvulus, Fallopia,* and *Echinochloa* under diverse soil conditions. These images were precisely annotated by field experts with a background in agronomic studies for object detection purposes. Each image has a resolution of 1752 × 1064 pixels (see Fig. 2).

Fig. 2. A representative sample of pseudo-RGB images highlighting sugar beet crops distributed with various weed species on the euro-pallets.

3.2 Experimental Settings

Pipeline Architecture. The proposed pipeline comprises two main components: dataset transformation and image generation (cf. Fig. 3). The dataset transformation stage is derived from our preceding study [16]. Originally intended for object detection purposes, the dataset is transformed into a zero-shot setting using the Segment Anything Model (SAM) [11], specifically the *SAM ViT-H* variant, which converts bounding box annotations into polygonal masks. The plant and weed shapes are then isolated, and the images are standardized by zero-padding. During the image generation phase, the Stable Diffusion Model v1.5 is fine-tuned on the extracted plant and weed classes using the diffusers [17] library, employing a specific technique denoted as *multi-subject Dreambooth*. Table 1 outlines the hyperparameters utilized during the training process. Given the constraints on GPU memory, a batch size of 1 was used, along with gradient checkpointing. For stable and smooth convergence, a learning rate 5×10^{-6} was applied with a cosine learning rate scheduler. Moreover, to enhance memory usage and computational efficiency, a dynamic quantization method, also known as FP16 mixed precision training, was implemented. Additionally, a text encoder was trained with a unique identifier, namely, HoPla[2], alongside subject classes, including *Sugar beet, Cirsium, Fallopia,* and *Convoluvulus*.

Table 1. Hyperparameter configuration for Stable Diffusion Model training using the diffusers library.

Hyperparameter	Value	Hyperparameter	Value
Image resolution	512	Epoch	2
Batch size	1	Gradient checkpointing	True
Learning rate	5×10^{-6}	Learning rate scheduler	cosine
Maximum training steps	60000	Mixed precision	FP16

---

[2] https://www.photonikforschung.de/projekte/sensorik-und-analytik/projekt/hopla.html (accessed on February 28, 2025).

During inference, we utilized a fine-tuned Stable Diffusion model for inpainting on real-world images (see Fig. 4). A binary image mask specified the region for synthesizing a new object, such as a plant or weed, while a concise text prompt (e.g., *a photo of HoPla Fallopia*) defined the target weed type. Initially, random binary masks were generated dynamically; however, this occasionally caused inpainted regions to overlap with existing objects. To mitigate this, we integrated a fine-tuned object detector (YOLO11X, pre-trained on the COCO dataset [13]) to exclude predicted regions of interest (ROIs) during mask generation. The same detector was later employed for automatic annotation of the synthetic inpainted images. During image generation, we initially classified weeds into four species: *Cirsium, Convolvulus, Fallopia,* and *Echinochloa*. However, for labeling and weed detection, we reclassified them into two broader botanical categories—dicotyledons (*Cirsium, Convolvulus, Fallopia*) and monocotyledons (*Echinochloa*)—to align with herbicide targeting strategies, which focus on botanical groups rather than individual species. Image generation parameters are detailed in Table 2. We employed the Euler Ancestral Discrete scheduler to optimize the trade-off between image quality and computational efficiency. The inference process was configured with 150 steps for optimal image fidelity, and a *strength* parameter of 0.5 to control noise, balancing quality, and generation speed. The output resolution was standardized to 768 × 512 pixels to maintain consistency with input dimensions. Additionally, we explored post-training quantization using FP16 and INT8 to reduce memory overhead and accelerate inference.

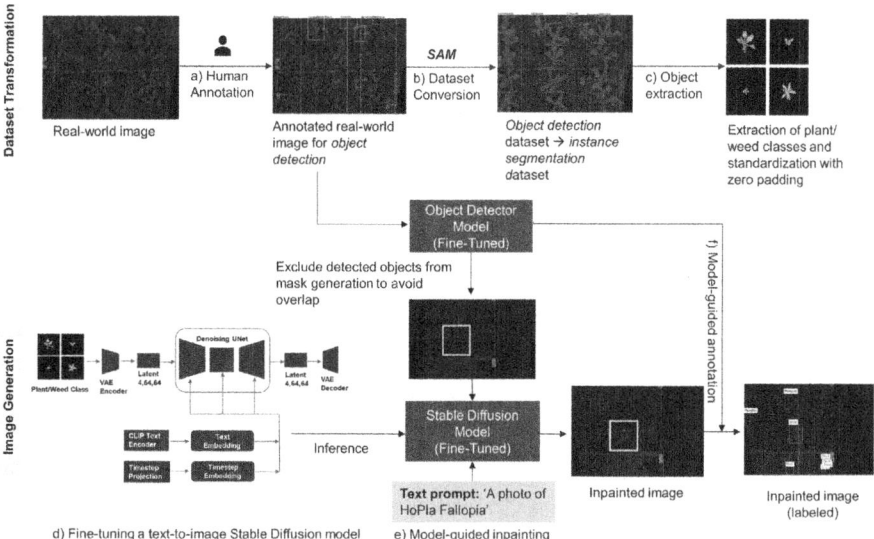

Fig. 3. Overview of the proposed inpainting pipeline. (a) Real images are manually annotated. (b) SAM converts bounding boxes into precise masks, enabling object extraction in (c). (d) A Stable Diffusion model is fine-tuned using extracted plants and weeds. (e) A novel inpainting method inserts new elements using text prompts and dynamic masks, while an object detector model (fine-tuned with real-world images) prevents overlap. (f) The same object detector model is used to auto-label the inpainted images.

Table 2. Properties of inference stage of the fine-tuned Stable Diffusion Model.

Property	Value	Property	Value
Scheduler	Euler Ancestral Discrete	Strength	0.5
Inference steps	150	Image size ($width \times height$)	768 × 512
Guidance scale	16	Post-training quantization	FP16, INT8

Fig. 4. Visualizing image inpainting, highlighted regions show inpainted areas. Left– original image; right–synthetic image generated from the text prompt.

Downstream Model Training. Our approach follows a three-stage pipeline: dataset augmentation using quantized Stable Diffusion models, fine-tuning of state-of-the-art object detectors, and post-training quantization with deployment on an edge computing device (cf. Fig. 1). We begin by quantizing the Stable Diffusion model into three precision formats: FP32, FP16, and INT8. These models generate synthetic images, expanding the original training dataset in controlled increments from 10% to 200% with a 10% increment of its initial size (n). Two dataset configurations are considered: one using only the original images (n), and another incorporating synthetic augmentation at various levels. The original and augmented datasets are then used to fine-tune two state-of-the-art object detection models, YOLO11(l) and RT-DETR(l), both pretrained on the COCO dataset. Each dataset configuration is trained separately to analyze the impact of data augmentation on model performance. The training was carried out with 300 epochs, with early stopping to reduce overfitting, with a patient of 30. We use the learning rates 0.01 and 0.001 for the YOLO11(l) and RT-DETR(l) models, respectively, with a cosine learning rate schedule for a dynamic adjustment for smooth training. Besides, the online augmentation technique was turned off to maintain training consistency and avoid bias.

Deployment. After fine-tuning, the trained models undergo post-training quantization into different bit formats to evaluate the effects of reduced precision. The produced FP32 Torch models coming from downstream detection tasks were converted into *TensorRT* through FP32, FP16, and INT8 quantizations. Prior to deployment, the NVIDIA Jetson Orin Nano was configured to run exclusively the target application by eliminating interfering background processes. Specifically, MAX Power Mode was enabled to ensure that all CPU and GPU cores were active and the system clocks were set to their maximum frequency. The quantized *TensorRT* models were then deployed on this optimized, resource-constrained edge computing device to assess the real-time capability of the downstream detection models. All models were tested for unbiased evaluation using a fixed validation and test dataset composed of real-world images.

4 Results

We begin by evaluating the impact of various quantization techniques on Stable Diffusion models. To accomplish this, we measured two key metrics: inference time, which indicates the duration taken by the model to generate output, and peak memory usage, which represents the maximum memory consumed during the inference process. The results of our evaluation are summarized in Table 3.

Table 3. Performance comparison of different quantization techniques of the Stable Diffusion Model. The best results are highlighted in bold.

Quantization	Inference time (Mean ± SD)	Peak memory (Mean ± SD)
FP32	16.55 ± 0.02 s	6829.98 ± 0.005 MB
FP16	4.50 ± 0.033 s	3683.45 ± 0.005 MB
INT8	**4.4 ± 0.05 s**	**3683.42 ± 0.003 MB**

The results indicate that the quantization of *FP16* achieves a substantial reduction in inference time, decreasing latency by approximately 72.8% compared to *FP32* and lowering memory consumption by 46.1%. *INT8* quantization results in a 73.4% reduction in inference time compared to *FP32*, while maintaining nearly identical memory efficiency to *FP16*. However, *INT8* exhibits slightly higher variability in inference time, as indicated by its larger standard deviation.

We evaluated the effect of quantized inpainting augmentation on two downstream models, *YOLO11(l)* and *RT-DETR(l)*, across three quantization settings (*FP32*, *FP16*, and *INT8*). Model performance was assessed using the mAP50 metric. The mean and standard deviation (SD) of mAP50 values across augmentation conditions were computed for each inpainting precision setting (FP32, FP16, INT8) across all quantized downstream models, excluding the 'No Augmentation' baseline. A Friedman test confirmed significant differences among precision settings ($p < 0.05$). Post-hoc Wilcoxon signed-rank tests with Bonferroni correction identified pairwise differences. Statistical grouping labels (a, b, c, etc.) indicate settings that are not significantly different (same letter) or significantly different (different letters) (see Tables 4 and 5). In *YOLO11(l)*, employing high-precision inpainting techniques (FP32 and FP16) resulted in the YOLO11(l) FP32 and FP16 models attaining their peak mAP50 scores of 0.932 with a 200% augmentation, which marks a modest 0.54% enhancement compared to the baseline without augmentation. However, the YOLO11(l) INT8 model exhibited a much larger improvement of 6.64% (from 0.798 to

0.851), indicating that high-precision inpainting helped mitigate the accuracy loss caused by lower model precision. A similar pattern was observed with FP16 inpainting, where the YOLO INT8 model improved by 5.04% (from 0.814 to 0.855), confirming that augmentation can help compensate for lower-precision models. With INT8 inpainting, the YOLO11(l) INT8 model achieved its peak mAP50 score of 0.862 at 120% augmentation, reflecting an 8.02% increase over the no-augmentation baseline (0.798). Interestingly, the YOLO11(l) FP32 and FP16 models reached their highest scores at 200% augmentation (0.935 mAP50), representing a 1.63% improvement over the baseline. Statistical tests on quantized YOLO11(l) variants revealed significant differences across inpainting precision settings (Friedman test, $p < 0.05$). Post-hoc Wilcoxon tests indicated no significant difference between FP32 and FP16 ($p > 0.05$), while INT8 exhibited significantly lower performance ($p < 0.05$). Consequently, FP32 and FP16 were grouped together (A), with INT8 in a separate group (B). Inpainting precision did not affect YOLO11(l) performance, as these groupings remained consistent across all settings. The *RT-DETR(l)* model exhibited greater sensitivity to inpainting precision settings. With FP32 inpainting, the RT-DETR(l) FP32 and FP16 models achieved their highest mAP50 scores at 40% and 90% augmentation (0.915 and 0.916, respectively), representing an improvement of approximately 1.55%. The RT-DETR(l) INT8 model showed a slightly higher gain of 5.20% (from 0.795 to 0.837) at 100% augmentation, suggesting that moderate augmentation is beneficial. When inpainting was performed at FP16 precision, performance gains were more pronounced, with the RT-DETR(l) FP32 model improving by 3.87% (from 0.879 to 0.913) and the RT-DETR(l) FP16 model improving by 3.75% (from 0.880 to 0.913). These results indicate that RT-DETR(l) benefits from FP16 inpainting but does not require as much augmentation as YOLO11(l). Moreover, the RT-DETR(l) INT8 model showed a 9% improvement (from 0.762 to 0.832) at 140% augmentation, suggesting that increased augmentation can notably enhance performance in lower-precision settings. With INT8 inpainting, both the RT-DETR(l) FP32 and FP16 models reached their highest performance of 0.917 at 170% augmentation, demonstrating the effectiveness of augmentation in stabilizing performance under lower-precision inpainting. However, the RT-DETR(l) INT8 model exhibited variability despite achieving a 6.64% improvement at 130% augmentation (from 0.782 to 0.834). In statistical tests, RT-DETR(l) shows a pattern similar to YOLO11(l), with quantized variants divided into distinct groups: FP32 and FP16 in group (A) and INT8 in group (B), regardless of inpainting precision settings. Similar to YOLO11(l), variations in inpainting precision did not significantly affect RT-DETR(l) performance, maintaining consistent statistical groupings.

Table 4. Performance of the quantized YOLO11(l) model is evaluated across various inpainting precision settings and augmentation levels (no augmentation to 200%), using original (Or.) and synthetic (Syn.) data. Results are reported in **mAP50**, with the highest scores highlighted in **bold**. Statistical groups (superscripts) and Mean ± SD indicate differences and variability across settings.

Augmentation	Inpainting FP32			Inpainting FP16			Inpainting INT8		
	FP32	FP16	INT8	FP32	FP16	INT8	FP32	FP16	INT8
No Augmentation	0.927	0.926	0.798	0.927	0.927	0.814	0.920	0.920	0.818
Or. + Syn. (10%)	0.924	0.924	0.808	0.921	0.922	0.825	0.928	0.928	0.821
Or. + Syn. (20%)	0.919	0.919	0.819	0.922	0.922	0.833	0.923	0.923	0.826
Or. + Syn. (30%)	0.923	0.923	0.815	0.927	0.927	0.836	0.923	0.923	0.828
Or. + Syn. (40%)	0.927	0.927	0.828	0.921	0.921	0.800	0.926	0.927	0.834
Or. + Syn. (50%)	0.931	0.931	0.851	0.927	0.927	0.840	0.926	0.926	0.853
Or. + Syn. (60%)	0.929	0.929	0.848	0.930	0.930	0.841	0.929	0.929	0.831
Or. + Syn. (70%)	0.901	0.901	0.822	0.929	0.928	0.845	0.893	0.893	0.798
Or. + Syn. (80%)	0.924	0.924	0.843	0.899	0.899	0.810	0.930	0.929	0.855
Or. + Syn. (90%)	0.921	0.921	0.832	0.929	0.929	0.849	0.929	0.929	0.847
Or. + Syn. (100%)	0.924	0.923	0.832	0.925	0.925	0.850	0.930	0.930	0.845
Or. + Syn. (110%)	0.927	0.928	0.849	0.929	0.928	0.822	0.931	0.931	0.857
Or. + Syn. (120%)	0.930	0.930	0.849	0.929	0.929	0.847	0.930	0.930	**0.862**
Or. + Syn. (130%)	0.926	0.926	0.834	0.927	0.927	0.850	0.927	0.926	0.832
Or. + Syn. (140%)	0.920	0.920	0.841	0.910	0.910	0.835	0.925	0.925	0.848
Or. + Syn. (150%)	0.927	0.927	**0.851**	**0.932**	**0.931**	**0.855**	0.931	0.931	0.858
Or. + Syn. (160%)	0.925	0.925	0.842	0.930	0.930	0.827	0.922	0.922	0.825
Or. + Syn. (170%)	0.931	0.931	0.840	0.929	0.929	0.843	0.929	0.928	0.858
Or. + Syn. (180%)	0.927	0.927	0.845	0.906	0.906	0.823	0.930	0.931	0.856
Or. + Syn. (190%)	0.915	0.915	0.816	0.928	0.928	0.850	0.929	0.929	0.847
Or. + Syn. (200%)	**0.932**	**0.932**	0.851	0.909	0.909	0.820	**0.935**	**0.935**	0.859
Mean ± SD (Aug. only)	0.924[a] ± 0.007	0.924[a] ± 0.007	0.837[b] ± 0.015	0.923[a] ± 0.009	0.923[a] ± 0.009	0.835[b] ± 0.015	0.926[a] ± 0.008	0.926[a] ± 0.008	0.842[b] ± 0.017

Furthermore, We evaluate the post-quantization model size and latency on the NVIDIA Jetson Orin Nano device intending to deploy in the real-world environment (see Table 6). The inference time and model size results for YOLO and RT-DETR across FP32, FP16, and INT8 precisions (trained on no augmentation and augmentation data) are summarized in Table 6. YOLO11(l) consistently outperforms RT-DETR(l) in inference time, with YOLO11(l)-INT8 achieving the fastest execution at 21.75 ± 1.17 ms, compared to RT-DETR(l)-INT8 at 45.13 ± 5.12 ms. A similar trend is observed in FP32 and FP16, where YOLO11(l)-FP32 and YOLO-FP16 achieve 63.87 ± 4.01 ms and 32.48 ± 2.68 ms, respectively, while RT-DETR(l)-DETR-FP32 and RT-DETR(l)-FP16 remain slower at 88.06 ± 5.40 ms and 51.55 ± 1.97 ms. In terms of model size, INT8 compression achieves the highest reduction, where YOLO11(l)-INT8 (30.8 MB) is smaller and faster than RT-DETR(l)-INT8 (47.4 MB).

5 Discussion

The reported results highlight the impact of quantization on the computational efficiency and performance of the Stable Diffusion model and its downstream models, including YOLO11(l) and RT-DETR(l). In the Stable Diffusion Model, quantization techniques such as FP16 and INT8 substantially reduce inference time and peak memory usage in comparison to FP32 (cf. Sect. 3). However, the difference in peak memory usage and inference time between FP16 and INT8 in the Stable Diffusion model is minimal. Several factors contribute to this observation. First, the model's complex operations, such as attention mechanisms

Table 5. Performance of the quantized RT-DETR(l) model is evaluated across various inpainting precision settings and augmentation levels (no augmentation to 200%), using original (Or.) and synthetic (Syn.) data. Results are reported in **mAP50**, with the highest scores highlighted in **bold**. Statistical groups (superscripts) and Mean ± SD indicate differences and variability across settings.

Augmentation	Inpainting FP32			Inpainting FP16			Inpainting INT8		
	FP32	FP16	INT8	FP32	FP16	INT8	FP32	FP16	INT8
No Augmentation	0.901	0.902	0.795	0.879	0.88	0.762	0.908	0.908	0.782
Or. + Syn. (10%)	0.896	0.896	0.789	0.904	0.905	0.815	0.883	0.884	0.758
Or. + Syn. (20%)	0.896	0.897	0.802	0.901	0.9	0.781	0.893	0.893	0.78
Or. + Syn. (30%)	0.909	0.909	0.808	0.906	0.907	0.808	0.903	0.904	0.824
Or. + Syn. (40%)	**0.915**	0.915	0.819	0.9	0.901	0.785	0.904	0.904	0.749
Or. + Syn. (50%)	0.909	0.909	0.722	0.909	0.909	0.753	0.882	0.882	0.765
Or. + Syn. (60%)	0.911	0.911	0.785	0.9	0.901	0.82	0.908	0.909	0.81
Or. + Syn. (70%)	0.898	0.899	0.739	0.901	0.899	0.819	0.911	0.911	0.833
Or. + Syn. (80%)	0.904	0.904	0.798	0.911	0.91	0.811	0.909	0.909	0.768
Or. + Syn. (90%)	0.915	**0.916**	0.829	0.908	0.908	0.82	0.906	0.905	0.737
Or. + Syn. (100%)	0.907	0.907	**0.837**	0.909	0.909	0.781	0.878	0.878	0.772
Or. + Syn. (110%)	0.901	0.902	0.779	0.91	0.911	0.818	0.91	0.91	0.793
Or. + Syn. (120%)	0.911	0.912	0.827	**0.913**	**0.913**	0.781	0.906	0.906	0.757
Or. + Syn. (130%)	0.873	0.874	0.767	0.907	0.907	0.77	0.906	0.907	**0.834**
Or. + Syn. (140%)	0.901	0.901	0.82	0.901	0.901	**0.832**	0.903	0.904	0.832
Or. + Syn. (150%)	0.906	0.906	0.817	0.905	0.905	0.817	0.903	0.903	0.83
Or. + Syn. (160%)	0.906	0.906	0.798	0.91	0.911	0.766	0.835	0.835	0.759
Or. + Syn. (170%)	0.913	0.914	0.834	0.91	0.911	0.797	**0.917**	**0.917**	0.794
Or. + Syn. (180%)	0.906	0.906	0.826	0.908	0.908	0.744	0.908	0.908	0.821
Or. + Syn. (190%)	0.907	0.908	0.758	0.904	0.904	0.824	0.903	0.903	0.782
Or. + Syn. (200%)	0.900	0.900	0.794	0.902	0.902	0.805	0.903	0.903	0.796
Mean ± SD (Aug. only)	0.904^a ± 0.009	0.905^a ± 0.009	0.797^b ± 0.032	0.906^a ± 0.004	0.906^a ± 0.004	0.797^b ± 0.026	0.899^a ± 0.018	0.899^a ± 0.018	0.790^b ± 0.032

Table 6. Inference Time (Mean ± SD) & model size comparison of YOLO11(l) and RT-DETR(l) trained on both non-augmented and augmented data, evaluated on NVIDIA Jetson Orin Nano.

Model	Inference Time ($Mean \pm SD)(ms)$			Model Size (MB)		
	FP32	FP16	INT8	FP32	FP16	INT8
YOLO11(l)	63.87 ± 4.01	32.48 ± 2.68	21.75 ± 1.17	98.8	51.7	30.8
RT-DETR(l)	88.06 ± 5.40	51.55 ± 1.97	45.13 ± 5.12	125.0	64.6	47.4

and residual connections, do not fully exploit the benefits of INT8 quantization. Additionally, INT8 quantization introduces computational overhead due to frequent dequantization and re-quantization steps, which counteract its potential performance improvements [3]. Furthermore, modern hardware optimizations are often designed to favor FP16, as many GPUs and NPUs are better optimized for mixed-precision computations, which might lead to almost similar performance between FP16 and INT8 [27]. Furthermore, this study indicates that inpainting augmentation can help improve performance lost due to quantization. The effectiveness of this approach depends on the inpainting precision (FP32, FP16, INT8) and the model architecture used. On the downstream models, high-precision settings(FP32 and FP16) provide slight improvements. In contrast, in the INT8 setting, the accuracy is more affected by quantization degradation, which shows a much greater recovery in performance when using synthetic data in all quantized variations of the Stable Diffusion Model. Moreover, our findings further reveal that the benefits of inpainting augmentation are architecture-specific. The YOLO11(l) model appears to leverage synthetic augmentation more effectively, especially in its INT8 configuration, whereas RT-DETR(l) demonstrates more gradual and sometimes variable improvements. However, the relationship between the augmentation and the detection accuracy is varied. This could be a reason of the automated annotation without further checking, which aligns with the findings of [15]. Nevertheless, this experiment was conducted on a single training run using a randomly selected subset of synthetic images for each augmentation combination. To improve statistical reliability and reduce bias, future experiments will incorporate stratified subsampling across at least 10 independent sets for more robust evaluation. Besides, the practical advantages of quantization and inpainting augmentation are evident in the reductions in model size and inference latency-particularly for the INT8 configuration. These efficiency gains are critical for deploying models in resource-constrained environments, where minimizing memory and computational requirements is essential. By effectively combining the benefits of quantization and synthetic inpainting, we can achieve high-performance models that are well-suited for real-time applications.

6 Conclusion

This study explores the potential of quantizing the Stable Diffusion Model and downstream models (YOLO11(l) and RT-DETR(l)) integrated into a GenAI-based weed detection pipeline as introduced in [16]. Post-training quantization of the incorporated Stable Diffusion Model to FP16 and INT8 can substantially reduce latency and computational cost without degrading downstream performance during augmentation. Additionally, quantization improves the inference speed of downstream models, while synthetic image augmentation has been observed to be able to mitigate the performance loss associated with INT8 quantization in YOLO11(l) and RT-DETR(l). Our findings also suggest that the effectiveness of inpainting augmentation varies when looking at different models. Moreover, performance variability appears to be linked to the quality of automated annotations, suggesting that refined annotation strategies could further enhance results. Future research will investigate other quantization strategies of the Stable Diffusion Model, such as BF16, FP8, and FP4 to reduce latency on resource-constrained devices, enabling deployment on platforms such as the NVIDIA Jetson Orin Nano or NPUs. If augmentation pipeline latency is reduced, our method could be integrated into intelligent systems architectures, such as the MLOC [23] from Organic Computing, for applications in intelligent agricultural robots. These architectures include reflection layers that monitor adaptation layers controlling the system (SuOC). When performance drops are detected, reflection layers trigger reconfigurations, such as triggering continual learning to compensate for lacking robustness in corner cases or new environmental conditions [22], to restore performance by addressing knowledge gaps [21] through on-demand synthetic data training.

Acknowledgments. This research was conducted within the scope of the project "Hochleistungssensorik für smarte Pflanzenschutzbehandlung (HoPla)" (grant no. 13N16327), supported by the Federal Ministry of Education and Research (BMBF) and VDI Technology Center based on a decision by the German Bundestag.

Conflicts of Interest. The authors declare no conflict of interest.

References

1. Allmendinger, A., Saltık, A.O., Peteinatos, G.G., Stein, A., Gerhards, R.: Assessing the capability of YOLO- and transformer-based object detectors for real-time weed detection. Precis. Agric. **26**(3), 52 (2025)
2. Deng, B., et al.: Weed image augmentation by ControlNet-added stable diffusion for multi-class weed detection. Comput. Electron. Agric. (2025)
3. Dettmers, T., et al.: Llm.int8(): 8-bit matrix multiplication for transformers at scale (2022). https://arxiv.org/abs/2208.07339
4. Dhariwal, P., et al.: Diffusion models beat GANs on image synthesis. In: Advances in Neural Information Processing Systems, vol. 34, pp. 8780–8794 (2021)
5. Ghosh, A.: YOLO11: faster than you can imagine! LearnOpenCV (2024). https://learnopencv.com/yolo11/
6. Goodfellow, I., et al.: Generative adversarial nets. In: Advances in Neural Information Processing Systems, vol. 27 (2014)
7. Herterich, N., Liu, K., Stein, A.: Accelerating weed detection for smart agricultural sprayers using a neural processing unit. Comput. Electron. Agric. **237**, 110608 (2025) Accelerating weed detection for smart agricultural sprayers using a neural processing unit. Comput. Electron. Agric. **237**, 110608 (2025)
8. Hirahara, K., et al.: D4: text-guided diffusion model-based domain adaptive data augmentation for vineyard shoot detection. Comput. Electron. Agric. **230**, 109849 (2025)
9. Hu, R., et al.: Real-time lettuce-weed localization and weed severity classification based on lightweight yolo convolutional neural networks for intelligent intra-row weed control. Comput. Electron. Agric. **226**, 109404 (2024)
10. IEEE Computer Society: IEEE standard for floating-point arithmetic (2008)
11. Kirillov, A., et al.: Segment anything (2023). arXiv:2304.02643
12. Krishnamoorthi, R.: Quantizing deep convolutional networks for efficient inference: a whitepaper (2018). arXiv:1806.08342
13. Lin, T., et al.: Microsoft COCO: common objects in context. CoRR **abs/1405.0312** (2014). http://arxiv.org/abs/1405.0312
14. Modak, S., Stein, A.: Enhancing weed detection performance by means of GenAI-based image augmentation. In: European Conference on Computer Vision, pp. 252–266. Springer Nature Switzerland, Cham (2024)
15. Modak, S., et al.: Generative AI-based pipeline architecture for increasing training efficiency in intelligent weed control systems (2024). arXiv:2411.00548
16. Modak, S., et al.: Synthesizing training data for intelligent weed control systems using generative AI. In: Architecture of Computing Systems, pp. 112–126. Cham (2024)
17. von Platen, P., et al.: Diffusers: state-of-the-art diffusion models (2022). https://github.com/huggingface/diffusers

18. Rai, N., et al.: Applications of deep learning in precision weed management: a review. Comput. Electron. Agric. **206**, 107698 (2023)
19. Rombach, R., et al.: High-resolution image synthesis with latent diffusion models. In: Proceedings of the IEEE/CVF Conference on Computer Vision and Pattern Recognition (CVPR), pp. 10684–10695 (2022)
20. Saltık, A.O., Allmendinger, A., Stein, A.: Comparative analysis of YOLOv9, YOLOv10 and RT-DETR for real-time weed detection. In: European Conference on Computer Vision, pp. 177–193. Springer Nature Switzerland, Cham (2024)
21. Stein, A., et al.: A concept for proactive knowledge construction in self-learning autonomous systems. In: 2018 IEEE 3rd International Workshops on Foundations and Applications of Self* Systems (FAS*W) (2018)
22. Stein, A., et al.: Reflective learning classifier systems for self-adaptive and self-organising agents. In: 2021 IEEE International Conference on Autonomic Computing and Self-Organizing Systems Companion (ACSOS-C), pp. 139–145 (2021)
23. Stein, A., et al.: Organic computing for intelligent agricultural technology: perspective and case study. agricultural engineering. EU **80**(1) (2025)
24. Tao, H.: Erasing-inpainting-based data augmentation using denoising diffusion probabilistic models with limited samples for generalized surface defect inspection. Mech. Syst. Signal Process. **208**, 111082 (2024)
25. Tudosiu, P.D., et al.: Realistic morphology-preserving generative modelling of the brain. Nat. Mach. Intell. **6**(7), 811–819 (2024)
26. Zhao, Y., et al.: DETRs beat YOLOs on real-time object detection. In: Proceedings of the IEEE/CVF Conference on CVPR, pp. 16965–16974 (2024)
27. Zhou, Y., et al.: ETBench: characterizing hybrid vision transformer workloads across edge devices. IEEE Trans. Comput. (2025)

Unify: Uncertainty Incorporated Federated Learning for Object Detection

Shang Gao(✉), Bernhard Sick, and Franz Götz-Hahn

Intelligent Embedded Systems, University of Kassel, Kassel, Germany
{sgao,bsick,franz.goetz-hahn}@uni-kassel.de

Abstract. Federated Learning (FL) has demonstrated promise for collaborative training on decentralized data while preserving privacy. However, applying FL to object detection remains challenging due to non-IID data distributions and domain shifts that can degrade performance with standard aggregation methods. To address these issues, we propose the <u>U</u>ncertainty <u>I</u>ncorporated <u>F</u>ederated Learning for Object Detection (Unify) framework, a novel FL framework that leverages Evidential Learning (EL) to estimate both epistemic and aleatoric uncertainties. By integrating these uncertainty estimates into the aggregation process, Unify down-weights unreliable client updates, leading to improved cross-domain generalization and enhanced stability. Built upon a lightweight YOLOX detector, our approach achieves detection performance that closely approaches centralized training while significantly outperforming conventional FedAvg under heterogeneous conditions. Evaluations on the KITTI and nuImages datasets demonstrate that Unify improves mean Average Precision (mAP) and yields uncertainties. The findings highlight the potential of uncertainty-incorporated FL in developing resilient, adaptive, and self-organizing computing systems.

Keywords: Federated Learning · Evidential Learning · Uncertainty Estimation · Object Detection · Self-Adaptation · Non-IID Data · Cross-Domain Generalization · Decentralized Systems

1 Introduction

Object detectors for autonomous driving must perform reliably in diverse environments. In a decentralized fleet of vehicles, FL offers a privacy-preserving way to train a shared model without centralizing data. However, a core challenge is that data from different vehicles or locations can have domain shifts, such as variations in weather, lighting, or geography lead to non-identically distributed (non-IID) data across clients [11,22]. Traditional FL algorithms like FedAvg [19] struggle under such heterogeneity: client models trained on divergent data may drift apart, and naive averaging can degrade the global model's accuracy [14]. In safety-critical applications like autonomous driving, these issues are compounded by the need to know when the model might be wrong. Standard object detectors output point estimates but do not quantify uncertainty, often becoming overconfident on unfamiliar scenarios. This lack of uncertainty incorporatedness can be dangerous, as the system cannot detect when conditions fall outside the training distribution.

Uncertainty estimation is crucial for robust decision-making in autonomous systems [20]. By capturing both aleatoric uncertainty, which arises from sensor noise or inherently ambiguous data, and epistemic uncertainty, which results from limited knowledge or novel situations, a model can effectively assess its confidence in each prediction [13]. For instance, heavy rain or glare can induce high aleatoric uncertainty in object detection [2], whereas encountering an unseen object type yields high epistemic uncertainty. Yet, conventional FL methods and even centralized training rarely incorporate uncertainty estimation; they optimize for accuracy assuming all data is equally reliable. This motivates an evidential FL approach for object detection. By endowing the model with uncertainty estimation and using that information during federation, we aim to improve robustness to data heterogeneity and out-of-distribution inputs. In this paper, we propose Unify framework that jointly addresses the challenges of non-IID data, domain shift, and model uncertainty. We develop an EL variant of the YOLOX [9] detector, and a novel federated aggregation strategy that uses uncertainty as a guide for model aggregation, as shown in Fig. 1. The implementation of our study is made publicly available[1] to facilitate further research.

In summary, our key contributions are:

- **Evidential YOLOX for Uncertainty Estimation:**
  We design an EL-based YOLOX detector that can estimate both epistemic and aleatoric uncertainty for each predicted object. Our model outputs belief distributions instead of deterministic outputs. This single-forward-pass uncertainty estimation provides a principled measure of prediction confidence, without resorting to costly Monte Carlo dropout [7] or ensembles [15].
- **Uncertainty-incorporated (UI) Federated Aggregation:**
  We introduce a novel FL aggregation method incorporating predictive uncertainty into the server's model update. By weighting each client's contribution based on the uncertainty of its local model, our method mitigates the impact of skewed or out-of-domain client data. This improves global model convergence and accuracy under severe non-IID settings, outperforming standard FedAvg in heterogeneous object detection tasks.
- **Robustness to Data Heterogeneity and Domain Shifts:**
  Through experiments on multi-domain autonomous driving datasets, we demonstrate that our approach yields superior performance and robustness under domain shift compared to conventional baselines. Our framework handles scenarios with distribution skew, imbalanced data, and unseen domains

---
[1] https://github.com/Andy-ggg/Unify.

more gracefully, showing improved mAP and more calibrated confidence under domain mismatches. This highlights the potential of combining FL, evidential uncertainty, and domain adaptation techniques in a unified object detection model.

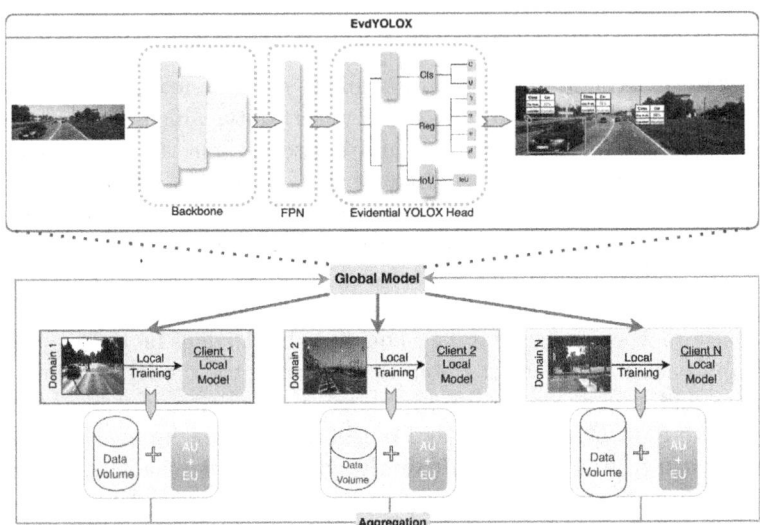

Fig. 1. Unify Framework. The upper section illustrates the Evidential YOLOX model, which enhances object detection by predicting bounding boxes while estimating aleatoric and epistemic uncertainties for more reliable decision-making. The lower section depicts the FL workflow, where the global Evidential YOLOX model is distributed to clients for local training. Unlike standard FL, model aggregation considers both data volume and uncertainty-aware weighting, ensuring a more robust and adaptive global model across diverse domains.

2 Related Work

2.1 FL for Object Detection

FL enables collaborative model training across decentralized data sources while preserving privacy [14]. The FedAvg algorithm averages local model updates but faces notorious difficulties when client data distributions diverge. In such non-IID settings, local models can converge to very different optima, leading to a deteriorated global model [22]. A number of works have proposed improvements to handle data heterogeneity. For instance, adaptive aggregation and optimization methods (FedProx [16], SCAFFOLD [12], FedOpt [23], etc.) introduce server-side momentum, proximal regularization, or variance reduction to stabilize training on skewed data. Personalization techniques [14] train a shared feature extractor while allowing parts of the model to adapt per client, addressing domain-specific needs. However, most FL research has focused on image classification or simple tasks, whereas object detection in FL poses additional challenges: the data tend to be more complex and highly imbalanced. Recent studies have started tackling federated object detection. Quéméneur et al. [22] examine federated optimization of YOLO models for real-time vehicle detection under data imbalance and concept drift. Li et al. [17] and others explore federated detection with domain-specific normalization to cope with client shifts. A semi-supervised FL approach by Diao et al. [4] combines unlabelled data to boost detection performance on non-IID clients. These efforts report that naive FedAvg underperforms significantly in detection tasks with heterogeneous data, and specialized training strategies or architectures are needed to narrow the gap with centralized training. Our work differs in that we explicitly incorporate uncertainty estimation into the FL process. This adds a new dimension to handling heterogeneity: rather than purely algorithmic fixes, we leverage the model's own uncertainty estimates to guide training.

2.2 EL and Uncertainty Estimation

Deploying object detectors in safety-critical applications calls for not only high accuracy but also calibrated confidence in the predictions [20]. Uncertainty estimation in deep learning is typically categorized into aleatoric and epistemic uncertainty [13]. Aleatoric uncertainty represents the irreducible noise in the data, and is present even if the model is perfect. For example, heavy fog or glare can make object localization inherently uncertain [2]. Epistemic uncertainty stems from limited knowledge. The model is unsure because it hasn't seen enough similar data or is encountering an out-of-distribution scenario [13]. Epistemic uncertainty can in principle be reduced with more data or a better model, and is particularly important for identifying domain shift or novel situations. Capturing both types of uncertainty helps improve the reliability of a detector. The system can know when to trust a detection and when to trigger caution or request human intervention.

A variety of approaches have been proposed to quantify uncertainty in deep vision models. Bayesian neural networks and Monte Carlo dropout sample multiple forward passes to estimate epistemic uncertainty, but these methods are often computationally expensive and hard to deploy in real-time detection [2]. An attractive alternative is evidential deep learning (EDL), which learns to predict a distribution over outputs in a single forward pass. For classification, one can replace the softmax output with parameters of a Dirichlet distribution, as introduced by Sensoy et al. [24]. The network thus produces a Dirichlet prior over class probabilities. A high-confidence prediction corresponds to a Dirichlet with sharp concentration on one class, whereas uncertain predictions result in a flatter distribution. For regression tasks, recent works propose to output parameters of conjugate distributions to estimate both a mean and uncertainty interval [1]. The key benefit of EL is that the model learns uncertainty from the data: during training it is penalized not only for prediction errors but also for being overconfident on wrong predictions. This yields well-calibrated uncertainties without needing multiple model samples or ensemble models.

In object detection, uncertainty estimation techniques are emerging. Gasperini et al. [8] introduced a distance-based uncertainty head for object detectors, enabling sampling-free confidence estimates for bounding boxes. Nallapareddy et al. [20] proposed EvCenterNet, an evidential version of CenterNet [5], to jointly estimate classification and localization uncertainties for 2D detection. They devise a combination of evidential loss with focal loss and show that leveraging predicted uncertainty can improve detection performance on challenging out-of-distribution datasets. Similarly, in 3D object detection, Durasov et al. [6] apply an evidential loss on bird's-eye view detection models, reporting 10âĂŞ20% improvement in identifying unreliable detections and out-of-distribution scenes. These works demonstrate that modelling uncertainty can significantly enhance a detector's robustness and provide valuable information for downstream decision-making. Our contribution lies in integrating such evidential uncertainty estimation into a FL setting. This integration is non-trivial because we must ensure that uncertainty estimates remain meaningful across distributed training and that the aggregation method can exploit these estimates to handle client diversity.

2.3 Domain Adaptation in FL

When federated clients reside in differing environments or capture different data domains, the global model can suffer from domain shift issues [11]. In autonomous driving, for instance, cameras on cars in one city might see mostly urban traffic, while others in rural areas see different scenery; a model trained federatively on all vehicles could generalize poorly to each specific domain if not properly adapted. Domain adaptation techniques aim to bridge the gap between domains, and several researchers have started incorporating them into FL. One line of work is Federated Domain Adaptation, where the goal is to adapt a global model to a new target domain without direct access to source data. Peng et al. [21] introduce FADA (Federated Adversarial Domain Adaptation), using adversarial training to disentangle domain-invariant features from domain-specific ones. In this approach, a discriminator is trained to distinguish which client a feature comes from, and the feature extractor is adversarially trained to fool it, thus learning representations that are common across domains. Another strategy is to adjust the aggregation mechanism itself. Lu et al. [18] propose FedDAD (Federated Domain Adaptive Detection), an algorithm that weights and fuses model parameters with dynamic attention based on domain relevance. By focusing more on domain-aligned features, FedDAD achieved significant gains in detection performance under domain shift, improving average precision by over 10% compared to FedAvg on certain classes. There are also approaches like Federated Prototype Learning (FPL) [25] which align class-centric feature prototypes between clients to ensure the global model has a balanced understanding of each class across domains.

Despite these advances, current domain adaptation techniques in FL do not leverage uncertainty estimates. They predominantly rely on feature distribution alignment, specialized aggregation rules, or personalized models to handle domain discrepancies. Our work fills this gap by using predictive uncertainty as an indicator of domain mismatch and model reliability. Intuitively, if a client's model exhibits high epistemic uncertainty on certain inputs, it may signal that those inputs are outside the client's training distribution. This information can help the server adjust its aggregation strategy and prioritize areas that require more focused learning. By combining UI aggregation with evidential modelling, our method provides an implicit domain adaptation effect: the global model becomes less biased by any single domain and more attuned to the trustworthiness of each client's knowledge. This leads to improved generalization across all participating domains, as we will show in our experiments.

3 Methodology

Our Unify framework consists of two main components: (1) a FL algorithm with uncertainty-guided model aggregation, and (2) an evidential object detection model that produces uncertainty estimates for its predictions. In this section, we describe these components and how they interact. We focus on the core methodology and defer implementation details and hyperparameter settings to later sections.

3.1 UI Federated Aggregation

In a standard FL setting, a server coordinates K clients (e.g., vehicles or edge devices), each with local dataset D_i. At each communication round t, clients train a local model on their D_i (initialized from the global model) and send updates back to the server, which aggregates them to update the global model. FedAvg performs this aggregation as a weighted average of client parameters:

$$\mathbf{w}^{(t+1)} = \sum_{i=1}^{K} \frac{n_i}{\sum_j n_j} \cdot \mathbf{w}_i^{(t+1)}. \tag{1}$$

where $n_i = |D_i|$. In our approach, we modify this step by incorporating an uncertainty-based weight for each client. Each client i not only trains a local model $\mathbf{w}_i^{(t+1)}$, but also evaluates its model's uncertainty on the validation set to produce an uncertainty score $U_i^{(t)}$. This score reflects how confident or uncertain the model is on data representative of the global distribution.

Given these scores, the server aims to reduce the aggregation weight of clients that exhibit high uncertainty while encouraging those with larger data sizes. We adopt an exponential decay scheme based on a normalized uncertainty score. Specifically, let $\widehat{U}_i^{(t)}$ be the min–max normalization of the uncertainty values at round t.

$$\widehat{U}_i^{(t)} = \frac{U_i^{(t)} - \min_j U_j^{(t)}}{\max_j U_j^{(t)} - \min_j U_j^{(t)} + \epsilon} \tag{2}$$

Then we define a reliability factor

$$R_i^{(t)} = \exp(-\alpha \widehat{U}_i^{(t)}), \tag{3}$$

where $\alpha > 0$ is a hyperparameter controlling the sensitivity to uncertainty. To account for the data size n_i in a manner similar to FedAvg, we further multiply by a normalized sample-size term:

$$\gamma_i^{(t)} = \frac{n_i}{\sum_{j=1}^{K} n_j} \times R_i^{(t)}. \tag{4}$$

As a result, clients with higher uncertainty scores see their weights decayed exponentially, while those with larger data sizes or lower uncertainties retain larger weights. The overall global update rule becomes:

$$\mathbf{w}^{(t+1)} = \frac{\sum_{i=1}^{K} \gamma_i^{(t)} \mathbf{w}_i^{(t+1)}}{\sum_{j=1}^{K} \gamma_j^{(t)}}. \tag{5}$$

This exponential decay framework offers an additional knob (α) for tuning how aggressively we penalize uncertain clients, which can be advantageous in scenarios where uncertainty varies substantially across participants.

This UI aggregation ensures that if a client's model is unsure about its predictions, its parameters will have a smaller impact on the global model. Conversely, a client that achieves low uncertainty is trusted more in shaping the global parameters. We emphasize that $U_i^{(t)}$ represents a combination of epistemic and aleatoric uncertainty for client i at round t, which is crucial for assessing both the novelty of the information contributed by the client and the quality of its data. In practice, $U_i^{(t)}$ can be a vector of multiple uncertainty measures, including classification and localization uncertainties. For clarity, here we describe it as a single scalar per client per round.

In the absence of a global model in the first round, we further leverage this mechanism by selecting the client with the lowest uncertainty as the initial model for aggregation, ensuring that training starts from a more reliable foundation. This method not only enhances model stability but also provides an implicit self-adaptive alignment strategy-trusting more in the updates that are confident while holding back those that might steer the model off track. As we will show, this results in more stable convergence and higher final accuracy compared to standard FedAvg, particularly in federated object detection tasks where data heterogeneity is significant.

3.2 Evidential YOLOX Head

To enable the above aggregation and to improve detection reliability, we need each client model to estimate its prediction uncertainties. We achieve this by extending the YOLOX object detector with an EL head. YOLOX is a high-performance one-stage detector that eliminates the need for anchor boxes and uses a simplified, decoupled head architecture for classification and regression. In a typical YOLOX head, for each candidate location the network outputs: (a) a set of class probabilities, (b) an objectness score indicating the confidence that an object is present, and (c) bounding box regression offsets (center $\Delta x, \Delta y$ and size w, h). In our Evidential YOLOX, we modify the output representation for both classification and regression to include uncertainty quantification.

Evidential Classification Head. Instead of directly outputting class probabilities, our model outputs an evidence vector $\mathbf{e} = [e_1, e_2, \ldots, e_C]$ for C classes. This evidence is transformed into the parameters of a Dirichlet distribution:

$$\alpha_c = \exp(e_c) + 1, \quad c = 1, \ldots, C. \tag{6}$$

To integrate uncertainty estimation into classification, we extend the standard YOLOX classification loss with evidential learning (EL) terms. The loss consists of three components:

1) Single-Label NLL. For each positive sample with ground-truth class c, we minimize

$$\mathcal{L}_{\text{DirNLL}} = \log \sum_{i=1}^{C} \alpha_i - \log \alpha_c. \tag{7}$$

This term encourages the evidence for the true class to be large, while limiting the overall sum of evidence from other classes.

2) KL Divergence. To prevent over-confident outputs when evidence is insufficient, we introduce a KL regularizer with respect to the Dirichlet$(1, \ldots, 1)$ prior:

$$\mathcal{D}_{\text{KL}}(\boldsymbol{\alpha} \,\|\, \mathbf{1}) = \log \Gamma\Big(\sum_{i=1}^{C} \alpha_i\Big) - \sum_{i=1}^{C} \log \Gamma(\alpha_i)$$
$$- \log \Gamma(C) + \sum_{i=1}^{C} (\alpha_i - 1)\Big[\psi(\alpha_i) - \psi\Big(\sum_{j=1}^{C} \alpha_j\Big)\Big], \tag{8}$$

where $\Gamma(\cdot)$ is the Gamma function and $\psi(\cdot)$ is the Digamma function. This encourages larger uncertainty (i.e., smaller α_i) whenever the model lacks sufficient evidence.

Evidential Regression Head. For each box coordinate (e.g., Δx), we output a tuple $(\hat{v}, \hat{\alpha}, \hat{\beta})$ and map them to positive space:

$$v = \exp(\hat{v}), \quad \alpha = \exp(\hat{\alpha}) + 1, \quad \beta = \exp(\hat{\beta}) > 0. \tag{9}$$

Together with the predicted offset $\hat{\mu}$, these form NIG parameters for an evidential regression framework. We minimize:

$$\mathcal{L}_{\text{NLL}} = \frac{1}{2} \ln(\pi) - \ln(\beta) + \alpha \ln\Big(1 + \frac{\|\mathbf{e}\|^2}{2\beta}\Big), \tag{10}$$

where $\|\mathbf{e}\|^2$ is the squared error between the decoded box and ground truth. In addition, a KL regularization term imposes a prior (e.g., α_0, β_0), encouraging larger uncertainty for difficult samples:

$$\mathcal{D}_{\mathrm{KL}}(\{\alpha,\beta\} \,\|\, \{\alpha_0,\beta_0\}) = \alpha \ln\left(\frac{\beta}{\beta_0}\right) - \ln\Gamma(\alpha) + \ln\Gamma(\alpha_0) \\ + (\alpha_0 - \alpha)\,\psi(\alpha) + \frac{\beta - \beta_0}{\beta_0}. \quad (11)$$

Integrated Loss and Implementation. We add these evidential losses to the standard YOLOX losses for classification, bounding box offsets, and objectness. Specifically, let $\mathcal{L}_{\mathrm{YOLOX}}$ represent the original YOLOX detection loss, which combines BCE/Focal loss for classification, IoU or L1 loss for box offsets, and objectness loss. We define:

$$\mathcal{L}_{\mathrm{total}} = \mathcal{L}_{\mathrm{YOLOX}} + \lambda_{\mathrm{reg}}\Big[\mathcal{L}_{\mathrm{NLL}} + \gamma \mathcal{D}_{\mathrm{KL}}(\mathrm{NIG})\Big] \\ + \lambda_{\mathrm{cls}}\Big[\mathcal{L}_{\mathrm{DirNLL}} + \gamma \mathcal{D}_{\mathrm{KL}}(\mathrm{Dirichlet})\Big]. \quad (12)$$

where λ_{reg} and λ_{cls} control the relative weighting of the regression and classification evidential terms, while γ can be an annealing coefficient to gradually increase the weight of KL divergences.

At inference time, no sampling or ensembling is required; the network directly outputs bounding box coordinates (and their uncertainties) and class logits (along with evidential parameters for uncertainty estimation). Thus, this design provides uncertainty quantification with minimal extra computational overhead.

4 Experiments and Results

We evaluate Unify on two autonomous driving datasets, KITTI [10] and nuImages [3]. The KITTI dataset consists of street-view images collected from a vehicle in urban and highway scenarios. It provides 7481 training images, with the most common dimension being 1242 × 375. In contrast, nuImages is a large-scale dataset derived from the nuScenes collection, featuring 67279 annotated images with 23 distinct object classes, all samples being of size 1600 × 900. Together, KITTI (with its focused set of classes and smaller size) and nuImages (with diverse classes and large scale) allow us to test Unify's performance under different data scales and category distributions. We use the official training splits of each dataset for our experiments, and report results on their validation sets following standard protocols.

4.1 Data Partitioning for FL

To simulate a realistic federated learning scenario with heterogeneous data, we partition the KITTI and nuImages datasets into four clients, ensuring a

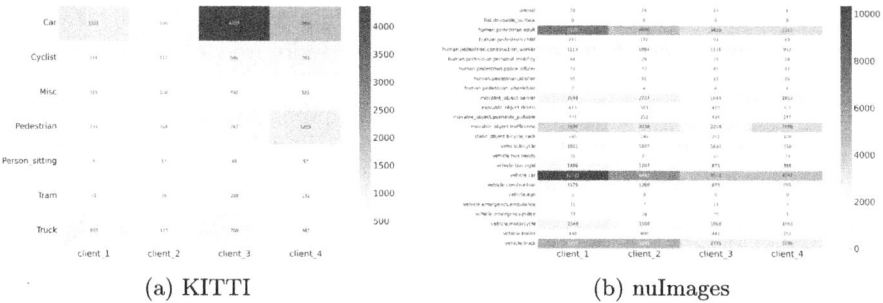

(a) KITTI (b) nuImages

Fig. 2. Comparison of Client-wise Data Distribution in different datasets, darker means more samples. (a) The KITTI dataset primarily consists of categories such as vehicles, pedestrians, and cyclists, with relatively simple data partitioning. (b) The nuImages dataset has a larger variety of categories, leading to more complex client data distributions.

non-i.i.d. distribution of object categories. Some clients predominantly contain vehicles (e.g., car, truck), while others have more pedestrians or cyclists, reflecting real-world data silos due to different road environments and sensor placements. Figure 2 illustrates the category distribution per client. The left heatmap (KITTI) shows $client3$ heavily skewed toward cars (4,359 instances) while $client2$ has significantly fewer (536). Similarly, pedestrians and cyclists are unevenly distributed. The right heatmap (nuImages) highlights even greater category diversity, with $client1$ dominating vehicle.car (10,322 instances) and $client3$ containing more human.pedestrian.adult and $movable\_object.trafficcone$. Such imbalances challenge standard federated learning, as local models overfit dominant classes while struggling with underrepresented ones. These non-uniform distributions rigorously test Unify's ability to aggregate knowledge effectively across skewed clients, underscoring the need for uncertainty-aware aggregation.

4.2 Implementation Details

Our implementation builds on the YOLOX object detector as the base model, extended to produce evidential uncertainty estimates for each prediction. The training hyper-parameters are kept consistent across clients: each local model is trained with a batch size of 8, an initial learning rate of 0.01, and uses the SGD optimizer with momentum. We train with input image sizes 640×640 (as per YOLOX default). The training schedule consists of 300 total epochs of local training, distributed across multiple communication rounds.

We simulate a synchronous federated learning process with a central server and $N = 4$ clients. We experiment with different federation configurations denoted as R-E, where R is the number of global rounds and E is the number of local epochs per round for each client. Given the slow convergence of YOLOX, we set a larger number of local epochs and evaluate five representative settings, ranging from $R5E60$ (5 global rounds, 60 local epochs each) to

$R2E150$ (2 rounds, 150 local epochs each). All schedules result in 300 total local epochs of training per client, but $R5E60$ involves more frequent model aggregation. Specifically, each client first trains a small number of epochs in isolation, and we select the client model with the lowest predictive uncertainty (evaluated on a small validation set) to serve as the initial global model. This ensures that the starting point for federation is a well-conditioned model that is already relatively confident, thereby avoiding the risk of immediate divergence when averaging disparate random models.

4.3 Experimental Results and Analysis

We report quantitative results in Table 1 and provide qualitative examples in Fig. 3 to demonstrate Unify's advantages over baseline methods. We compare three approaches: (i) Centralized YOLOX, including its evidential variant Centralized Evidential YOLOX. (ii) FedAvg baseline, without uncertainty weighting or special initialization. (iii) Our proposed Unify. For fairness, all methods use the same total number of training epochs and identical model architecture.

4.4 Overall Performance

As shown in Table 1, Unify achieves the highest detection performance among the federated methods, significantly outperforming FedAvg and narrowing the gap between federated and centralized training. On the KITTI dataset, Unify (R2E150) attains an mAP of 56.1%, compared to 35.2% with FedAvg and 56.9% with centralized YOLOX. This trend holds on the nuImages dataset, where Unify consistently outperforms standard FedAvg but still lags behind centralized YOLOX trained on the full dataset. Notably, data volume alone does not determine a client's contribution or the final model's accuracy. As shown in Table 2, the client with the largest dataset does not exhibit the lowest uncertainty, primarily due to class imbalance and domain bias in its local distribution. FedAvg, which relies on data volume for weighting and directly averages model parameters for initialization, struggles in such non-i.i.d. settings. In contrast, Unify initializes the global model using the least uncertain client and adjusts aggregation weights based on uncertainty, down-weighting noisier updates while up-weighting more confident updates from smaller but more representative clients. This results in a more balanced global model with improved performance across all categories. These findings highlight the importance of uncertainty in federated aggregation, demonstrating that data volume alone is insufficient for effective weighting, while uncertainty-aware aggregation significantly enhances model generalization.

Centralized YOLOX (upper bound) unsurprisingly yields the highest detection accuracy since it sees the entire training data; however, Unify's performance is quite close, in some cases within a few percentage points of mAP, despite the data remaining siloed. This indicates that our federated training with uncertainty guidance not only preserves accuracy but can sometimes surpass a naive evidential model that doesn't benefit from federation. It is also worth noting

Table 1. Comparison of centralized and federated learning results. Bold values show the best in Centralized and Federated columns.

Dataset	Centralized		Federated				
	YoloX	EvdYoloX	Method	R5E60	R4E75	R3E100	R2E150
KITTI	**56.9%**	55.6%	FedAvg	30.2%	21.6%	35.0%	35.2%
			Unify	47.5%	51.7%	52.5%	**56.1%**
nuImages	21.1%	**21.2%**	FedAvg	14.6%	15.3%	15.6%	16.2%
			Unify	15.8%	16.6%	17.0%	**17.8%**

that the evidential version of YOLOX has a slight drop in mAP compared to the standard YOLOX when trained centrally, due to the added task of uncertainty estimation. Unify, however, manages to match the centralized Evidential YOLOX performance, showing that federated uncertainty learning does not sacrifice accuracy.

Table 2. Comparison of Uncertainty and Performance Across Clients on KITTI and nuImages Datasets. Metrics include Epistemic and Aleatoric uncertainties, mAP, and sample sizes for each client. Bold values indicate the best in each dataset.

Dataset	KITTI				nuImages			
	Client 1	Client 2	Client 3	Client 4	Client 1	Client 2	Client 3	Client 4
Epistemic	0.5738	0.6318	0.4232	**0.3574**	**0.4702**	0.5318	0.4758	0.5124
Aleatoric	1.1412	1.6309	0.8079	**0.7193**	**0.9269**	0.9991	1.0318	1.1442
mAP	0.311	0.232	**0.478**	0.460	**0.159**	0.147	0.137	0.128
Samples	1178	605	**4434**	2381	**11378**	7280	5226	5114

4.5 Federated Configuration Impact

Among the four federated training configurations we tested, increasing the number of local epochs led to a moderate performance improvement. Given the slow convergence of YOLOX, longer local training helped stabilize the model. However, regardless of the specific configuration-whether $R5E60$ or $R2E60$ remained consistently stable and significantly outperformed the FedAvg baseline. Moreover, we did not observe any training divergence or instability with Unify, whereas standard FedAvg occasionally exhibited gradient instability in early rounds, likely due to conflicting updates from highly heterogeneous local models. This stability can be attributed to Unify's uncertainty-aware initialization, which provides a well-calibrated starting point, and its robust aggregation strategy, which prevents any single client from disproportionately influencing the global model with high-uncertainty updates. As a result, Unify facilitates a more stable global model evolution, effectively integrating the strengths of each client while mitigating their limitations.

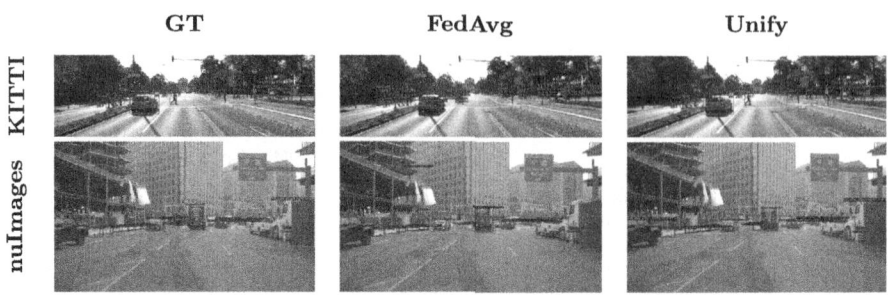

Fig. 3. Qualitative results of FedAvg and Unify on testing data.

4.6 Qualitative Results

Figure 3 highlights example detection outputs from Unify compared to FedAvg. We show sample images from KITTI and nuImages with bounding boxes predicted by Unify. The detections are accurate and cover small distant objects and occluded objects that the FedAvg model often missed. We see that in challenging cases (e.g., a heavily occluded pedestrian or an indistinct object at long range), Unify still detects the object but with a higher uncertainty, whereas the centralized YOLOX might output a hard prediction with less interpretability. This is particularly valuable in a federated context: the model can indicate when it's less sure, which could be leveraged by an autonomous vehicle to trigger caution or query further information. In summary, our experiments validate that the Unify framework effectively combines evidential uncertainty estimation with federated learning to achieve robust object detection. It addresses the key challenges of data heterogeneity and model divergence in FL, leading to performance that rivals centralized training while preserving the benefits of data privacy and distribution. The results in Table 1 and the examples in Fig. 3 collectively show that Unify's uncertainty-aware strategy yields a more reliable and generalizable model than conventional FedAvg, confirming our core hypothesis that incorporating uncertainty into federation can significantly enhance learning in distributed environments.

5 Conclusion

In this paper, we introduced Unify, a novel uncertainty-incorporated federated learning framework designed for robust object detection under non-IID, domain-shifted conditions. By extending YOLOX with evidential learning, our approach quantifies both aleatoric and epistemic uncertainties and leverages these uncertainty metrics to guide model aggregation across heterogeneous clients. Through experiments on KITTI and nuImages, we demonstrated that Unify outperforms standard federated baselines in terms of detection accuracy and adaptation to shifting domains. Beyond the immediate performance gains, our results suggest that uncertainty-aware strategies can fundamentally improve how federated systems reconcile conflicting data distributions and handle unseen scenarios. By reducing the impact of uncertain updates and amplifying contributions from clients whose models exhibit lower uncertainty, Unify achieves more stable and convergent global training-often matching or approaching centralized training accuracy. This highlights the broader value of incorporating model uncertainty in safety-critical FL applications.

Future research will extend this approach to unsupervised or semi-supervised FL scenarios, where labelled data are sparse in each client's silo. We also plan to explore various uncertainty estimation techniques to further improve calibration and model interpretability. Additionally, integrating personalization strategies may help balance global performance with local specialization. By pursuing these directions, we aim to further advance the robustness and adaptability of federated learning for real-world, large-scale autonomous systems.

References

1. Amini, A., Schwarting, W., Soleimany, A., Rus, D.: Deep evidential regression (2020). https://arxiv.org/abs/1910.02600
2. Araújo, B., Teixeira, J., Fonseca, J., Cerqueira, R., Beco, S.: The road to safety: a review of uncertainty and applications to autonomous driving perception. Entropy **26**, 634 (2024). https://doi.org/10.3390/e26080634
3. Caesar, H., et al.: nuscenes: a multimodal dataset for autonomous driving, pp. 11618–11628 (2020). https://doi.org/10.1109/CVPR42600.2020.01164
4. Diao, E., Ding, J., Tarokh, V.: Semifl: semi-supervised federated learning for unlabeled clients with alternate training (2022). https://arxiv.org/abs/2106.01432
5. Duan, K., Bai, S., Xie, L., Qi, H., Huang, Q., Tian, Q.: Centernet: keypoint triplets for object detection (2019). https://arxiv.org/abs/1904.08189
6. Durasov, N., et al.: Uncertainty estimation for 3d object detection via evidential learning (2024). https://arxiv.org/abs/2410.23910
7. Gal, Y., Ghahramani, Z.: Dropout as a Bayesian approximation: representing model uncertainty in deep learning (2016). https://arxiv.org/abs/1506.02142
8. Gasperini, S., et al.: CertainNet: sampling-free uncertainty estimation for object detection. IEEE Robot. Autom. Lett. **7**(2), 698–705 (2022). https://doi.org/10.1109/lra.2021.3130976
9. Ge, Z., Liu, S., Wang, F., Li, Z., Sun, J.: Yolox: exceeding yolo series in 2021 (2021). https://arxiv.org/abs/2107.08430
10. Geiger, A.: Are we ready for autonomous driving? the kitti vision benchmark suite, pp. 3354–3361 (2012)
11. Huang, W., Ye, M., Shi, Z., Li, H., Du, B.: Rethinking federated learning with domain shift: a prototype view, pp. 16312–16322 (2023). https://doi.org/10.1109/CVPR52729.2023.01565

12. Karimireddy, S.P., Kale, S., Mohri, M., Reddi, S.J., Stich, S.U., Suresh, A.T.: Scaffold: Stochastic controlled averaging for federated learning (2021). https://arxiv.org/abs/1910.06378
13. Kendall, A., Gal, Y.: What uncertainties do we need in Bayesian deep learning for computer vision? (2017). https://doi.org/10.48550/arXiv.1703.04977
14. Kim, T., Lin, E., Lee, J., Lau, C., Mugunthan, V.: Navigating data heterogeneity in federated learning a semi-supervised federated object detection (2024). https://arxiv.org/abs/2310.17097
15. Lakshminarayanan, B., Pritzel, A., Blundell, C.: Simple and scalable predictive uncertainty estimation using deep ensembles (2017). https://arxiv.org/abs/1612.01474
16. Li, T., Sahu, A.K., Zaheer, M., Sanjabi, M., Talwalkar, A., Smith, V.: Federated optimization in heterogeneous networks (2020). https://arxiv.org/abs/1812.06127
17. Li, X., Jiang, M., Zhang, X., Kamp, M., Dou, Q.: FedBN: federated learning on Non-IID features via local batch normalization (2021). https://arxiv.org/abs/2102.07623
18. Lu, P.J., Jui, C.Y., Chuang, J.H.: FedDAD: federated domain adaptation for object detection. IEEE Access **11**, 51320–51330 (2023). https://doi.org/10.1109/ACCESS.2023.3279132
19. McMahan, H.B., Moore, E., Ramage, D., Hampson, S., y Arcas, B.A.: Communication-efficient learning of deep networks from decentralized data (2023). https://arxiv.org/abs/1602.05629
20. Nallapareddy, M.R., Sirohi, K., Drews-Jr, P.L.J., Burgard, W., Cheng, C.H., Valada, A.: Evcenternet: uncertainty estimation for object detection using evidential learning (2023). https://arxiv.org/abs/2303.03037
21. Peng, X., Huang, Z., Zhu, Y., Saenko, K.: Federated adversarial domain adaptation (2019). https://arxiv.org/abs/1911.02054
22. Quéméneur, C., Cherkaoui, S.: Fedpylot: navigating federated learning for real-time object detection in internet of vehicles (2024). https://arxiv.org/abs/2406.03611
23. Reddi, S., et al.: Adaptive federated optimization (2021). https://arxiv.org/abs/2003.00295
24. Sensoy, M., Kaplan, L., Kandemir, M.: Evidential deep learning to quantify classification uncertainty (2018). https://arxiv.org/abs/1806.01768
25. Tan, Y., et al.: FedProto: federated prototype learning across heterogeneous clients (2022). https://arxiv.org/abs/2105.00243

Special Track on Dependability and Fault Tolerance (VERFE)

Extension of 2-Bit Error Correcting BCH Codes with Simple Decoding

Alexander Benedict Behrens$^{(\boxtimes)}$ and Michael Gössel

University of Potsdam, An der Bahn 2, 14476 Potsdam, Germany
{alexander.behrens,michael.goessel}@uni-potsdam.de

Abstract. In this paper, a new 2-bit error correcting (DEC) linear code is presented as a modification of a corresponding 2-bit error correcting (DEC) BCH code. Compared to an unchanged BCH code in $GF(2^m)$ with $2 \cdot m$ check bits and a code length of $2^m - 1$, the number of data bits can be increased by at least $m + 1$ bits. The number of check bits only needs to be increased by 1.

New columns and a single new row are added to the parity check matrix of the unchanged BCH code. The added columns are determined according to the columns of a parity check matrix of any 2-bit error correction code with only m check bits. The bits of the added row distinguish between the columns of the unchanged BCH code and the columns of the added columns. The proposed method is particularly interesting for longer code lengths.

Decoding remains simple even with long code lengths, as the known algebraic methods for decoding BCH codes can be used for most of the bits. A small look-up table is only required for the relatively small number of bits added.

Keywords: Error correction · DEC codes · BCH code extension · Maximal code length · Simple decoding

1 Introduction

Until now, 1-bit error correction and 2-bit error detection codes such as the Hsiao code has mainly been used for error correction in memories [4, pp. 435–443]. With the shrinking dimensions and especially for emerging memories, 2-bit error correction is becoming increasingly important, particularly for safety-critical applications [12–14, 16, 18].

The most important 2-bit error correction code is the 2-bit error correction BCH code [8, 11] with approximately twice the number of check bits of the Hsiao code. The well-known BCH codes are also used for decoding long code lengths. The code length of a BCH code with the Galois field $GF(2^m)$ is $2^m - 1$ with $2 \cdot m$ check bits. The number of data bits is limited to $2^m - 1 - 2m$. To protect 2^l data bits, i.e. a power of 2 of data bits, m has to be greater than l. A 2-bit error correcting BCH code cannot be extended by adding an additional column to the H-matrix of the BCH code without adding also a check bit as proven in [6]. The proof is based on the property of the 2-bit error correcting BCH code that the code is quasi-perfect [10].

For example, the Galois field $GF(2^8)$ with its 256 elements is too small to protect 256 data bits. Only $2^8 - 1 - 16 = 239$ data bits can be protected. To encode 256 data bits as a code word of a 2-bit error correcting BCH code, the Galois field $GF(2^9)$ with $2^9 - 1 - 18 = 492$ possible data bits is required. Of the 492 possible data bits, only 256 data bits are then used and 18 check bits have to be added.

To reduce the coding overhead, a new method for modifying 2-bit error correction BCH codes with simple decoding is proposed in this paper. New linear 2-bit error correction codes with $2m + 1$ check bits and a code length greater $2^m - 1 + m$ are derived. The maximum number of data bits of the new codes is for $m \geq 4$ at least $m + 1$ bits greater as the maximum number of data bits of the corresponding BCH code. Only one additional check bit is to be added.

With the proposed method, for example, 256 data bits can be encoded with 17 additional check bits instead of 18 check bits for the unchanged BCH code.

Of particular interest for decoding is that the parity check matrix, also called H-matrix H_{BCH} of the BCH code, remains an unchanged sub-matrix of the H-matrix H_{new} of the modified code. This makes the construction of H_{new} simple and the decoding possible and also simple for longer code lengths. Contrary to 2-bit error correcting codes completely determined by computer search to most of the bits of a code word the known algebraic methods for decoding BCH codes can be used [3, pp. 283–307] [15]. Only for the relatively small number of added bits small lookup tables are needed.

The H-matrix H_{new} is determined by adding $r + 1$ additional columns and a single row of ones to H_{BCH}. The added columns consist of an (m, r)-H-matrix H_2 of any linear 2-bit error correction code and supplemental zeros above and below H_2. To maximize the number $r + 1$ of added columns, arbitrary optimal or near-optimal matrices H_2 with m check bits and a maximal code length r can be used for the proposed modification. Since the number m of check bits of the H-matrix H_2 is small compared to $2 \cdot m$ the matrix H_2 can be effectively determined by a computer search as described in [6]. An H-matrix of a 2-bit error-correcting BCH code can also be used as the H-matrix H_2 as described in Sect. 3.

The bits of the added row distinguish between the columns of H_{BCH} and the newly added columns. As already pointed out most of the columns of the new H-matrix H_{new} are columns of the H-matrix H_{BCH} and only a relatively small number $r + 1$ of additional columns are added to H_{BCH}, and decoding remains simple. This approach makes it possible

- to determine modified large 2-bit error correction codes that cannot be determined in a reasonable time by computer search
- and also to implement effective decoding methods for these new large codes.

Some time ago in [5,7,17] many different theoretical results for combining codes to derive longer codes were already described. But till now no simple decoding methods which can be practically implemented also for the longer codes length for these extended codes are known to the authors. This may be the reason that the extended codes are not yet applied for error correction for instance for memories.

The simplicity of the newly proposed method of extending a 2-bit error correcting BCH codes by adding new columns to the H-matrix of the BCH code allows a simple decoding. This simplicity makes practical application realistic. Decoding remains for most of the bits the same decoding as for the unmodified BCH code. Only for errors in the additional bit special small additional look-up tables are needed.

2   DEC BCH Codes

In this section a short description of 2-bit error correction BCH codes will be given. A 2-bit error correction BCH code C_{BCH} over the Galois field $GF(2^m)$ is described in this paper by its H-matrix H_{BCH}

$$H_{BCH} = \begin{pmatrix} \alpha^0 & \alpha^1 & \alpha^2 & \ldots & \alpha^{n-1} \\ \alpha^0 & \alpha^3 & \alpha^6 & \ldots & \alpha^{3(n-1)} \end{pmatrix} \quad (1)$$

where $n \leq 2^m - 1$ and the exponents of α are to be interpreted $modulo(2^m - 1)$ and α is a generating element of $GF(2^m)$. In its vector representation, α^i can be represented as a m-dimensional binary column vector, and the H-matrix H_{BCH} in its binary form has $2m$ rows and n columns. The number of check bits is $2m$. The code distance of C_{BCH} is 5 and 2-bit errors can be corrected. The length of the code is n. In [6] it is shown that for the same number of check bits $(2 \cdot m)$ it is impossible to increase the code length of a 2-bit error correcting BCH code by adding another column to the H-matrix H_{BCH} in Eq. 1.

If an additional parity bit is used, an additional row of ones is to be added and the H-matrix becomes

$$H_{BCH_P} = \begin{pmatrix} \alpha^0 & \alpha^1 & \alpha^2 & \ldots & \alpha^{n-1} \\ \alpha^0 & \alpha^3 & \alpha^6 & \ldots & \alpha^{3(n-1)} \\ 1 & 1 & 1 & \ldots & 1 \end{pmatrix}. \quad (2)$$

The code distance is now 6 and therefore 2-bit errors can be corrected and 3-bit errors can be detected. The number of check bits is now $2m+1$. To the H-matrix H_{BCH_P} (Eq. 2) a column $\underbrace{(0,0,\ldots,0,1)}_{2m+1}{}^T$ can be added [9][1, pp. 223–228] [2, p. 82] and the resulting H-matrix

$$H_{BCH_{P0}} = \begin{pmatrix} \alpha^0 & \alpha^1 & \alpha^2 & \ldots & \alpha^{n-1} & 0 \\ \alpha^0 & \alpha^3 & \alpha^6 & \ldots & \alpha^{3(n-1)} & 0 \\ 1 & 1 & 1 & \ldots & 1 & 1 \end{pmatrix} \quad (3)$$

describes a 2-bit error correcting and 3-bit error detecting code with code distance 6 and the maximal code length $n + 1 = 2^m$. It is also shown in [6] that no additional column of $2 \cdot m + 1$ bits with the parity bit 1 can be appended to this H-matrix, to enlarge this code as a 2-bit error correcting and 3-bit error detecting code with code distance 6.

For example, with the Galois field $GF(2^4)$ and $n = 2^4 - 1$ the H-matrix $H_{BCH_{P0}}$ with included parity and with an added column $\underbrace{(0,0,\ldots,0,1)^T}_{2m}$ the

H-matrix

$$H_{BCH_{P0}} = \begin{pmatrix} \alpha^0 & \alpha^1 & \alpha^2 & \ldots & \alpha^{14} & 0 \\ \alpha^0 & \alpha^3 & \alpha^6 & \ldots & \alpha^{12} & 0 \\ 1 & 1 & 1 & \ldots & 1 & 1 \end{pmatrix} \quad (4)$$

is in its binary representation

$$H_{BCH_{P0}} = \begin{pmatrix} 1&0&0&0&1&0&0&1&1&0&1&0&1&1&1&0 \\ 0&1&0&0&1&1&0&1&0&1&1&1&1&0&0&0 \\ 0&0&1&0&0&1&1&0&1&0&1&1&1&1&0&0 \\ 0&0&0&1&0&0&1&1&0&1&0&1&1&1&1&0 \\ 1&0&0&0&1&1&0&0&0&1&1&0&0&0&1&0 \\ 0&0&0&1&1&0&0&0&1&1&0&0&0&1&1&0 \\ 0&0&1&0&1&0&0&1&0&1&0&0&1&0&1&0 \\ 0&1&1&1&1&0&1&1&1&0&1&1&1&1&0 \\ 1&1&1&1&1&1&1&1&1&1&1&1&1&1&1&1 \end{pmatrix}. \quad (5)$$

The different representations of the elements of the Galois field $GF(2^4)$ are given in Table 1.

Table 1. Possible representations of elements of the finite body GF(2^4)

exponential	polynomial	vector
0	0	$(0,0,0,0)$
α^0	1	$(1,0,0,0)$
α^1	x	$(0,1,0,0)$
α^2	x^2	$(0,0,1,0)$
α^3	x^3	$(0,0,0,1)$
α^4	$1+x$	$(1,1,0,0)$
α^5	$x+x^2$	$(0,1,1,0)$
α^6	x^2+x^3	$(0,0,1,1)$
α^7	$1+x+x^3$	$(1,1,0,1)$
α^8	$1+x^2$	$(1,0,1,0)$
α^9	$x+x^3$	$(0,1,0,1)$
α^{10}	$1+x+x^2$	$(1,1,1,0)$
α^{11}	$x+x^2+x^3$	$(0,1,1,1)$
α^{12}	$1+x+x^2+x^3$	$(1,1,1,1)$
α^{13}	$1+x^2+x^3$	$(1,0,1,1)$
α^{14}	$1+x^3$	$(1,0,0,1)$

In the first column of Table 1, the elements are given in exponential notation. The second column shows the polynomial representation and the third column is the vector representation. The first $n = 15$ columns of rows one to four and five to eight of the H-matrix $H_{BCH_{P0}}$ in Eq. 5 represent the elements of the Galois field in their vector representation, as shown in Table 1. These eight rows and 15 columns, which result in an H-matrix of a regular BCH code, are extended by a column with eight zeros and a 9th row with 16 ones. This row forms the parity and only with this row the zero column can be added.

3 Description of the Method

This section explains how an extended 2-bit error correction code C_{new} can be determined from a known BCH code C_{BCH} with $2 \cdot m$ check bits and a further 2-bit error correction code C_2 with m check bits. The code length of C_{BCH} is $n = 2^m - 1$, of C_2 is $r \geq m$ and of C_{new} is $n + r + 1$.

The number of check bits of the new code C_{new} is $2m+1$. The H-matrix H_{new} of C_{new} is determined from the H-matrix H_{BCH} of the 2-bit error correcting BCH code C_{BCH}, the columns of the H-matrix H_2 of C_2 and the column of zeros. The H-matrix H_2 has r columns and m rows. The code distance of the BCH code C_{BCH} and the code distance of the code C_2 are both 5.

For $m \geq 4$ the code length r of the code C_2 is at least m. The first m columns of the H-matrix H_2 can be assumed to be unit vectors, in which case H_2 has a systematic form. The following column must have a weight of at least four, i.e. requires at least four ones. Any four of these $m + 1$ columns cannot be added to zero and therefore r for $m \geq 4$ is greater m.

Now the determination of the H-matrix H_{new} of the new code will be described.

- In a first step of modification, a column $(\underbrace{0, 0, \ldots, 0}_{2m})^T$ and a row $(\underbrace{1, 1, \ldots, 1, 1}_{n+1})$ are added to the H-matrix H_{BCH} with $2m$ rows and n columns resulting in an $(n + 1, 2 \cdot m + 1)$-matrix $H(n + 1, 2m + 1)$.
- In the second step the $(n + 1, 2m + 1)$-matrix $H(n + 1, 2m + 1)$ is modified. r additional columns with $2 \cdot m + 1$ components are now added to $H(n + 1, 2m + 1)$. The first m bits of these $2m + 1$ bits are zeros, the second m bits of these $2m + 1$ bits are the m bits of the r columns of H_2. The last bit in each of these added columns is zero.

After this modification the last bit of the first $n + 1$ columns is 1 and the last bit of the following r columns is 0. The last bit of the columns of H_{new} indicates whether the column belongs to the first $n+1$ columns or to the last r columns. If the last bit is 1, the column belongs to the first $n + 1$ columns and if the last bit is 0, the column belongs to the last r columns. The resulting H-matrix H_{new} is

$$H_{new} = \begin{pmatrix} & & 0 & 0 \cdots \cdots 0 \\ & & \vdots & \ddots \\ & H_{BCH} & \vdots & 0 \cdots \cdots 0 \\ & & \vdots & H_2 \\ & & 0 & \\ \hline & 1 \cdots \cdots 1 & 1 & 0 \cdots \cdots 0 \end{pmatrix} \qquad (6)$$

We mention here that it is also possible to swap the ones and zeros in the last row of H_{new}, and the resulting H-matrix H_{new_a} is then

$$H_{new_a} = \begin{pmatrix} & & 0 & 0 \cdots \cdots 0 \\ & & \vdots & \ddots \\ & H_{BCH} & \vdots & 0 \cdots \cdots 0 \\ & & \vdots & H_2 \\ & & 0 & \\ \hline & 0 \cdots \cdots 0 & 1 & 1 \cdots \cdots 1 \end{pmatrix} . \qquad (7)$$

In a more explicit form, the H-matrix is now

$$H_{new} = \begin{pmatrix} & & & 0 & 0 \cdots \cdots 0 \\ \alpha^0 & \alpha^1 & \cdots \cdots \alpha^{n-1} & \vdots & \ddots \\ & & & \vdots & 0 \cdots \cdots 0 \\ \hline \alpha^0 & \alpha^3 & \cdots \cdots \alpha^{3(n-1)} & \vdots & V_1 \cdots \cdots V_r \\ & & & 0 & \\ \hline 1 & 1 & \cdots \cdots 1 & 1 & 0 \cdots \cdots 0 \end{pmatrix} \qquad (8)$$

where the r columns of H_2 are denoted as V_1 to V_r. These column vectors also result in a 2-bit error correcting linear code with a code length of r.

To determine the longest possible code it is essential to know the H-matrices of the best possible or near optimal linear 2-bit error correcting codes for the different numbers of check bits. These codes were determined in [6] for up to 10 check bits and the results are listed in the Table 2.

Table 2. The maximum code length for 4–7 check bits and near maximum code length for 8–10 check bits for linear DEC codes.

check bits	4	5	6	7	8	9	10
code length	5	6	8	11	17	23	33

The number of check bits is given in the first row of Table 2 and the corresponding maximal code length for a linear code is presented in the second row. The maximum code length r is specified for up to 7 check bits. The authors are not aware of any longer code lengths for 8, 9 and 10 check bits of a linear code of code lengths 17, 23 and 33. For example, in the first column of Table 2 it is shown that with 4 check bits the maximal code length of a linear 2-bit error correcting code is 5.

As a concrete example we consider the extension of the BCH code in $GF(2^4)$ of length $n = 15$ and an appended 0-column with the H-matrix $H_{BCH_{P0}}$ given in Eq. 5. The code $C_{BCH_{P0}}$ can be enlarged by 5 bits. The H-matrix H_2 of the code C_2 with 4 check bits is

$$H_2 = \begin{pmatrix} 1 & 0 & 0 & 0 & 1 \\ 0 & 1 & 0 & 0 & 1 \\ 0 & 0 & 1 & 0 & 1 \\ 0 & 0 & 0 & 1 & 1 \end{pmatrix}. \tag{9}$$

The H matrix H_2 is first extended by rows of zeros so that the matrix H_3 is generated in Eq. 10.

$$H_3 = \begin{pmatrix} 0 & 0 & 0 & 0 & 0 \\ 0 & 0 & 0 & 0 & 0 \\ 0 & 0 & 0 & 0 & 0 \\ 0 & 0 & 0 & 0 & 0 \\ 1 & 0 & 0 & 0 & 1 \\ 0 & 1 & 0 & 0 & 1 \\ 0 & 0 & 1 & 0 & 1 \\ 0 & 0 & 0 & 1 & 1 \\ 0 & 0 & 0 & 0 & 0 \end{pmatrix}. \tag{10}$$

We append the matrix H_3 in Eq. 10 to the H-matrix $H_{BCH_{P0}}$ given in Eq. 5 and the resulting H-matrix H_{new} is

$$H_{new} = \begin{pmatrix} 1 & 0 & 0 & 0 & 1 & 0 & 0 & 1 & 1 & 0 & 1 & 0 & 1 & 1 & 1 & 0 & 0 & 0 & 0 & 0 & 0 \\ 0 & 1 & 0 & 0 & 1 & 1 & 0 & 1 & 0 & 1 & 1 & 1 & 1 & 0 & 0 & 0 & 0 & 0 & 0 & 0 & 0 \\ 0 & 0 & 1 & 0 & 0 & 1 & 1 & 0 & 1 & 0 & 1 & 1 & 1 & 1 & 0 & 0 & 0 & 0 & 0 & 0 & 0 \\ 0 & 0 & 0 & 1 & 0 & 0 & 1 & 1 & 0 & 1 & 0 & 1 & 1 & 1 & 1 & 0 & 0 & 0 & 0 & 0 & 0 \\ 1 & 0 & 0 & 0 & 1 & 1 & 0 & 0 & 0 & 1 & 1 & 0 & 0 & 0 & 1 & 0 & 1 & 0 & 0 & 0 & 1 \\ 0 & 0 & 0 & 1 & 1 & 0 & 0 & 0 & 1 & 1 & 0 & 0 & 0 & 1 & 1 & 0 & 0 & 1 & 0 & 0 & 1 \\ 0 & 0 & 1 & 0 & 1 & 0 & 0 & 1 & 0 & 1 & 0 & 0 & 1 & 0 & 1 & 0 & 0 & 0 & 1 & 0 & 1 \\ 0 & 1 & 1 & 1 & 1 & 0 & 1 & 1 & 1 & 1 & 0 & 1 & 1 & 1 & 1 & 0 & 0 & 0 & 0 & 1 & 1 \\ 1 & 1 & 1 & 1 & 1 & 1 & 1 & 1 & 1 & 1 & 1 & 1 & 1 & 1 & 1 & 1 & 0 & 0 & 0 & 0 & 0 \end{pmatrix}. \tag{11}$$

of a 2-bit error correcting code with a code length of 21 and nine check bits. The optimal or near-optimal H-matrices of the codes C_2 from 4 to 10 check bits are given in the Appendix A.

Other 2-bit error-correcting linear codes can also be used for the extension for the new method presented, such as 2-bit error-correcting BCH codes. The BCH code C_a to be expanded has the H-matrix H_a with elements α from the Galois field $GF(2^{m_a})$ and is expanded with an H-matrix H_b with elements β from $GF(2^{m_b})$ of another BCH code C_b. The code C_a has a maximal code length of $n_a = 2^{m_a} - 1$ and the code C_b has a maximal code length of $n_b = 2^{m_b} - 1$ with $m_b = \lfloor \frac{m_a}{2} \rfloor$. The resulting code C_{new_2} has the H-matrix

$$H_{new_2} = \begin{pmatrix} & & & 0 & 0 \cdots\cdots\cdots 0 \\ \alpha^0 \; \alpha^1 \cdots\cdots \alpha^{n_a-1} & \vdots & \ddots \\ & & & \vdots & 0 \cdots\cdots\cdots 0 \\ & & & \vdots & \beta^0 \beta^1 \cdots\cdots \beta^{n_b-1} \\ \alpha^0 \; \alpha^3 \cdots\cdots \alpha^{3(n_a-1)} & \vdots & \beta^0 \beta^3 \cdots\cdots \beta^{3(n_b-1)} \\ & & 0 & & \\ 1 \; 1 \cdots\cdots\cdots 1 & 1 & 0 \cdots\cdots\cdots 0 \end{pmatrix}. \quad (12)$$

In the red box on the left the H-Matrix H_a from the initial BCH code C_a is shown. It has $2m_a$ rows and n_a columns in its binary representation. Just next to it is the column of zeros as explained previously. The blue box on the right side displays the second BCH code C_b with its H-matrix H_b. It has m_a rows and n_b columns in its binary representation in the case that m_a is even. If m_a is odd the number of rows of H_b in binary representation is $m_a - 1$ or in a general form $2 \cdot \lfloor \frac{m_a}{2} \rfloor$. If m_a is odd, the Galois field $GF(2^{\frac{m_a-1}{2}})$ is used for the second BCH code and a row with zeros is added to the H-matrix H_b before constructing the H-matrix H_{new_2} of the new code. The code length of the resulting Code C_{new_2} is $n_a + n_b + 1$.

4 Decoding

Now the error correction for 1-bit and 2-bit errors will be described. Here the decoding is referring to a code with an H-matrix in the form of the H-matrix given in Eq. 8. The error positions of 1-bit and 2-bit errors are easily determined by s_1, s_3 and P. The proposed code is derived from an ordinary 2-bit error correcting BCH code in $GF(2^m)$ with a code length of $n = 2^m - 1$ by appending $(r + 1) > m$ additional bits. This results in the code length $N = n + r + 1$. If an error occurs most of the correction values can be determined in the same "algebraic" way as for the BCH code, to which the bits are added. Only if errors occur also in the relatively small number of $r+1$ added bits look-up tables with m inputs are necessary. This makes decoding for large code length possible and simple. The decoding explained in this paragraph can be also applied if a smaller BCH code is appended to the unmodified BCH code. In this case decoding can be simplified for the 2-bit-errors which are only located within the appended bits. This will be shortly explained at the end of this paragraph.

First, the **correction of 1-bit errors** will be explained. Every column of the H-matrix is unique and different from every other column. For

$$s_1 \neq 0, \; s_1^3 = s_3, \; P = 1$$
$$eUnALT$$

α^i is determined as

$$\alpha^i = s_1$$

and for $0 \leq i \leq n-1$ the position of the error is determined as the exponent of α^i. If we have

$$s_1 = 0, \; s_3 = 0, \; P = 1$$

the position of the error is n. For

$$s_1 = 0, \; s_3 = V_j, \; P = 0$$

the error position j with $n < j < N$ is uniquely determined by a look-up table or a combinatorial function $f_1(s_3)$ with m inputs only.

Now, the **correction of 2-bit errors** will be explained. Most of the errors can be determined as for an ordinary BCH code. As already pointed out only for errors within the appended bits small look-up tables are needed. For

$$s_1 \neq 0, \; s_3 \neq s_1^3, \; P = 0$$

the solutions $x_1 = \alpha^i$ and $x_2 = \alpha^j$ of the quadratic equation

$$s_1^3 + s_3 + s_1 x^2 + s_1^2 x = 0 \tag{13}$$

determine the positions i and j as the exponents of α^i and α^j respectively. Equation (13) is the locator polynomial of the 2-bit error correcting BCH code with the H-Matrix H_{BCH} in Eq. 1. For

$$s_1 \neq 0, \; s_3 = s_1^3, \; P = 1$$

the error positions i and j are determined by $\alpha^i = s_1$ and $j = n$ where i is the exponent of s_1. For

$$s_1 \neq 0, \; s_3 \neq s_1^3, \; P = 1$$

the error positions i and j are determined by $\alpha^i = s_1$ and $V_j = s_3$ and i is the exponent of s_1 and j is uniquely determined by look-up table or a combinatorial function $f_1(s_3)$ with m inputs. For

$$s_1 = 0,\ s_3 \neq 0,\ P = 0$$

the error positions i and j are determined by $V_i + V_j = s_3$ and i and j are uniquely determined by a look-up table or a combinatorial function $f_2(s_3)$ with m inputs. Since the columns of H_2 of C_2 are forming an H-matrix of a 2-bit error correcting code of length r with m check bits i and j are uniquely determined by f_2.

The simplification for decoding of a BCH code C_{big} that has been extended by another BCH code C_{small} is now explained if both the erroneous bits are located in the added bits. Then s_3 equals

$$s_3 = [s_1^{small}, s_3^{small}]$$

where s_1^{small} and s_3^{small} are the components of the syndrome of C_{small}. The erroneous bit positions can be determined as the roots of the locator polynomial

$$(s_1^{small})^3 + s_3^{small} + (s_1^{small})^2 x + s_1^{small} x^2 = 0$$

of the small BCH code C_{small} and no look-up table is needed. This makes decoding possible also for very large values of m.

5 Results

For the different Galois fields $GF(2^m)$ for $m = 1, \ldots, 10$ the obtained code lengths for C_{new} are presented in Table 3. The value m the size of the Galois field GF(2^m) is given in column GF, the length $2^m - 1$ of the corresponding BCH code C_{BCH} is given in column total (BCH), the number $2^m - 1 - 2 \cdot m$ of data bits of C_{BCH} is given in column data (BCH), the number $2 \cdot m$ of check bits of C_{BCH} is given in column check (BCH), the redundancy $(check/total) \cdot 100$ is given in column red. (BCH), the length $2^m + r$ of the new code C_{new} is given in column total (NEW), the number of data bits $2^m + r - (2 \cdot m + 1)$ of the new code is given in column data (NEW), the number of check bits $2 \cdot m + 1$ of the new code is given in column check (NEW), and the redundancy is given in column red. (NEW).

For instance in row 3 it is presented, that for the Galois field $GF(2^5)$ the length of the BCH code is 31 with 21 data bits and 10 check bits. The length of the code C_{new} is 38 since the length r of the code C_2 is 6 and an additional column with the first $2 \cdot m$ components equal zero and a 1 in the last component is added. Therefore 7 bits can be added to form the code H_{new}. Since H_{new} has $2 \cdot 5 + 1 = 11$ check bits the number of data bits $2^5 + 6 - 2 \cdot 5 - 1 = 27$.

Extension of 2-Bit Error Correcting BCH Codes with Simple Decoding 357

Table 3. The maximal code length, number of data bits and check bits are compared between the (DEC) BCH code and the new (DEC) code for a given Galois field $GF(2^m)$.

GF	BCH				NEW			
m	total	data	check	red.(%)	total	data	check	red.(%)
3	7	1	6	85.7	11	4	7	63.3
4	15	7	8	53.3	21	12	9	42.9
5	31	21	10	32.3	38	27	11	29.0
6	63	51	12	19.1	72	59	13	18.1
7	127	113	14	11.0	139	124	15	10.8
8	255	239	16	6.3	273	256	17	6.2
9	511	493	18	3.5	535	516	19	3.6
10	1023	1003	20	2.0	1057	1036	21	2.0

For the Galois fields $GF(2^8)$, $GF(2^9)$ and $GF(2^{10})$ 256, 512 and 1024 data bits can be protected with 17, 19 and 21 check bits instead of 18, 20 and 22 check bits when encoded by an unmodified corresponding BCH code.

The obtained code lengths for C_{new_2} are displayed in Table 4. This table has the same structure as Table 3 and is therefore not explained again. The Code C_{new_2} with an H-matrix H_{new_2} is a BCH code extended by another BCH code. Compared to the results presented in Table 3 one check bit is saved for Galois fields $GF(2^m)$ with $m \geq 10$ here.

Table 4. The maximal code length, number of data bits and check bits are compared between the (DEC) BCH code and the new_2 (DEC) code for a given Galois field $GF(2^m)$.

GF	BCH				NEW$_2$			
m	total	data	check	red.(%)	total	data	check	red.(%)
3	7	1	6	85.7	9	2	7	77.8
4	15	7	8	53.3	19	10	9	47.4
5	31	21	10	32.3	35	24	11	31.4
6	63	51	12	19.1	71	58	13	18.3
7	127	113	14	11.0	135	120	15	11.1
8	255	239	16	6.3	271	254	17	6.3
9	511	493	18	3.5	527	508	19	3.6
10	1023	1003	20	2.0	1055	1034	21	2.0
11	2047	2025	22	1.1	2079	2056	23	1.1
12	4095	4071	24	0.6	4159	4134	25	0.6
13	8191	8165	26	0.3	8255	8228	27	0.3
14	16383	16355	28	0.2	16511	16482	29	0.2
15	32767	32737	30	0.1	32895	32864	31	0.1
16	65535	65503	32	0.1	65791	65758	33	0.1

For example, if the initial BCH code uses the Galois field $GF(2^{10})$ the extended code can encode 2^{10} data bits with 21 check bits, which the initial BCH code can't. For 2^{10} data bits an unmodified BCH code with 22 check bits is needed.

6 Summary

In this paper a new method to derive new linear 2-bit error correcting codes with an increased code length and a simple decoding from 2-bit error correction BCH codes was presented.

It was explained how the $(2 \cdot m, 2^m - 1)$-parity-check matrix H_{BCH} of a BCH code with $2 \cdot m$ check bits $r+1$ additional columns ($r \geq m$) can be appended to determine the $(2 \cdot m + 1, 2^m + r)$-parity-check matrix H_{new} of the new code. The code length of this new code is increased by $r+1$ to $2^m + r$, and the number of check bits by 1.

It was explained how the added columns can be determined from the columns of the (m, r)-parity-check matrix of any linear 2-bit-error correction code with m check bits and code length r. Thereby codes with m check bits determined by computer search or 2-bit error correcting BCH codes can be used.

Decoding was described in detail for the different errors in different error positions. It is of special interest that decoding remains simple even for longer code length since the unmodified parity check matrix H_{BCH} of the BCH code remains a sub-matrix of the parity-check matrix H_{new} of the new code and most of the eventually erroneous bits can be corrected by use of the known algebraic methods for decoding BCH codes.

It was shown that the new codes can save in real applications a check bit. For instance if the number of data bits is a power of 2, i.e. 256, 512 or 1024, the data bits can be protected by 17, 19 or 21 check bits instead of 18, 20 or 22 check bits when an unmodified BCH code would be used.

The simplicity of the proposed method for increasing the code length as well as for decoding is of special interest.

Acknowledgments. The authors would like to express their sincere gratitude to the reviewers for their valuable feedback and insightful comments. We greatly appreciate the time and effort they have invested in reviewing our paper.

A Appendix

H-matrices $H_2 = M_{m,r}$ for the Galois fields $GF(2^m), m = 4, \ldots, 10$ are given in this appendix. They were determined as H-matrices of an 2-bit error correction code with m check bits and maximal length r by an algorithmic search program [6]. For $m = 4, 5, 6, 7, 8, 9, 10$ and $r = 5, 6, 8, 11, 17, 23, 33$ these matrices are:

$$M_{4,5} = \begin{bmatrix} 1 & 0 & 0 & 0 & 1 \\ 0 & 1 & 0 & 0 & 1 \\ 0 & 0 & 1 & 0 & 1 \\ 0 & 0 & 0 & 1 & 1 \end{bmatrix}, \tag{14}$$

$$M_{5,6} = \begin{bmatrix} 1 & 0 & 0 & 0 & 0 & 1 \\ 0 & 1 & 0 & 0 & 0 & 1 \\ 0 & 0 & 1 & 0 & 0 & 1 \\ 0 & 0 & 0 & 1 & 0 & 1 \\ 0 & 0 & 0 & 0 & 1 & 0 \end{bmatrix}, \tag{15}$$

$$M_{6,8} = \begin{bmatrix} 1 & 0 & 0 & 0 & 0 & 0 & 1 & 0 \\ 0 & 1 & 0 & 0 & 0 & 0 & 1 & 0 \\ 0 & 0 & 1 & 0 & 0 & 0 & 1 & 1 \\ 0 & 0 & 0 & 1 & 0 & 0 & 1 & 1 \\ 0 & 0 & 0 & 0 & 1 & 0 & 0 & 1 \\ 0 & 0 & 0 & 0 & 0 & 1 & 0 & 1 \end{bmatrix}, \tag{16}$$

$$M_{7,11} = \begin{bmatrix} 1 & 0 & 0 & 0 & 0 & 0 & 0 & 1 & 1 & 0 & 1 \\ 0 & 1 & 0 & 0 & 0 & 0 & 0 & 0 & 1 & 1 & 1 \\ 0 & 0 & 1 & 0 & 0 & 0 & 0 & 1 & 0 & 1 & 0 \\ 0 & 0 & 0 & 1 & 0 & 0 & 0 & 0 & 0 & 1 & 1 \\ 0 & 0 & 0 & 0 & 1 & 0 & 0 & 1 & 1 & 0 & 0 \\ 0 & 0 & 0 & 0 & 0 & 1 & 0 & 0 & 1 & 0 & 1 \\ 0 & 0 & 0 & 0 & 0 & 0 & 1 & 1 & 0 & 1 & 1 \end{bmatrix}, \tag{17}$$

$$M_{8,17} = \begin{bmatrix} 1 & 0 & 0 & 0 & 0 & 0 & 0 & 0 & 1 & 1 & 1 & 1 & 0 & 1 & 0 & 0 \\ 0 & 1 & 0 & 0 & 0 & 0 & 0 & 0 & 1 & 1 & 0 & 0 & 0 & 1 & 1 & 0 & 1 \\ 0 & 0 & 1 & 0 & 0 & 0 & 0 & 0 & 1 & 1 & 0 & 1 & 1 & 0 & 1 & 1 & 1 \\ 0 & 0 & 0 & 1 & 0 & 0 & 0 & 0 & 1 & 0 & 1 & 0 & 1 & 1 & 1 & 1 & 1 \\ 0 & 0 & 0 & 0 & 1 & 0 & 0 & 0 & 1 & 1 & 1 & 0 & 0 & 1 & 0 & 1 & 0 \\ 0 & 0 & 0 & 0 & 0 & 1 & 0 & 0 & 0 & 1 & 1 & 0 & 1 & 1 & 0 & 0 & 1 \\ 0 & 0 & 0 & 0 & 0 & 0 & 1 & 0 & 0 & 1 & 1 & 1 & 0 & 1 & 1 & 1 & 1 \\ 0 & 0 & 0 & 0 & 0 & 0 & 0 & 1 & 0 & 0 & 1 & 1 & 1 & 0 & 0 & 1 & 1 \end{bmatrix}, \tag{18}$$

$$M_{9,23} = \begin{bmatrix} 1 & 0 & 0 & 0 & 0 & 0 & 0 & 0 & 0 & 1 & 0 & 0 & 1 & 0 & 1 & 1 & 0 & 1 & 1 & 1 & 0 & 0 & 0 \\ 0 & 1 & 0 & 0 & 0 & 0 & 0 & 0 & 0 & 0 & 0 & 1 & 1 & 1 & 1 & 1 & 1 & 0 & 1 & 0 & 0 & 1 & 1 \\ 0 & 0 & 1 & 0 & 0 & 0 & 0 & 0 & 0 & 1 & 0 & 1 & 0 & 0 & 1 & 0 & 0 & 1 & 0 & 0 & 1 & 1 & 1 \\ 0 & 0 & 0 & 1 & 0 & 0 & 0 & 0 & 0 & 1 & 1 & 0 & 1 & 0 & 0 & 1 & 0 & 1 & 1 & 0 & 1 & 1 & 1 \\ 0 & 0 & 0 & 0 & 1 & 0 & 0 & 0 & 0 & 1 & 1 & 1 & 0 & 0 & 0 & 0 & 1 & 0 & 1 & 0 & 1 & 1 & 0 \\ 0 & 0 & 0 & 0 & 0 & 1 & 0 & 0 & 0 & 0 & 1 & 0 & 0 & 1 & 1 & 1 & 1 & 1 & 0 & 0 & 1 & 1 & 1 \\ 0 & 0 & 0 & 0 & 0 & 0 & 1 & 0 & 0 & 1 & 1 & 0 & 1 & 0 & 1 & 0 & 0 & 0 & 1 & 1 & 0 & 1 \\ 0 & 0 & 0 & 0 & 0 & 0 & 0 & 1 & 0 & 0 & 1 & 1 & 0 & 0 & 0 & 1 & 1 & 1 & 1 & 0 & 1 & 1 \\ 0 & 0 & 0 & 0 & 0 & 0 & 0 & 0 & 1 & 0 & 0 & 0 & 1 & 1 & 0 & 1 & 0 & 1 & 0 & 1 & 1 & 1 & 0 \end{bmatrix} \text{ and} \tag{19}$$

$$M_{10,33} = \begin{bmatrix} 1&0&0&0&0&0&0&0&0&0&1&0&0&1&0&0&0&1&1&1&0&1&0&1&1&1&1&1&1&0&0&1&0 \\ 0&1&0&0&0&0&0&0&0&0&0&0&1&1&0&1&0&0&1&1&1&0&0&1&0&1&1&1&1&1&0&0&1 \\ 0&0&1&0&0&0&0&0&0&0&1&0&0&1&1&0&1&0&1&1&1&1&1&0&0&0&1&1&1&1&1&0&1 \\ 0&0&0&1&0&0&0&0&0&0&1&0&1&0&1&0&1&0&0&0&1&0&0&0&1&1&1&1&1&1&0&0&0 \\ 0&0&0&0&1&0&0&0&0&0&1&1&1&1&0&1&1&0&0&1&1&0&0&0&0&1&0&0&0&1&1&1&1 \\ 0&0&0&0&0&1&0&0&0&0&0&0&1&1&0&1&1&1&0&0&1&1&1&1&1&1&0&0&1&0&0&1&0 \\ 0&0&0&0&0&0&1&0&0&0&0&0&1&0&1&1&0&0&1&0&0&1&1&1&0&0&1&1&0&1&1&1&0 \\ 0&0&0&0&0&0&0&1&0&0&0&1&1&0&0&0&1&0&1&0&1&1&1&0&0&1&0&0&1&1&0&0&1 \\ 0&0&0&0&0&0&0&0&1&0&0&0&0&0&0&1&1&1&1&1&0&0&1&0&0&1&1&0&1&0&1&1&0&0 \\ 0&0&0&0&0&0&0&0&0&1&1&1&1&0&1&0&0&0&1&1&0&1&0&1&1&0&0&1&0&0&0&1&0&1 \end{bmatrix} \quad (20)$$

References

1. Berlekamp, E.R.: Algebraic Coding Theory (revised edition). World Scientific (2015)
2. Lin, S., Costello, D.J.: Error Control Coding: Fundamentals and Applications. Prentice Hall, Englewood Cliffs (1983)
3. Peterson, W.W., Weldon, E.J.: Error-Correcting Codes. MIT Press (1972)
4. Wicker, S.B.: Error Control Systems for Digital Communication and Storage. Prentice Hall, Englewood Cliffs (1995)
5. Alltop, W.: A method for extending binary linear codes (corresp.). IEEE Trans. Inf. Theory **30**(6), 871–872 (1984)
6. Behrens, A.B., Gössel, M.: Determination of optimal h-matrices for 2-bit error correcting codes. In: International Conference on Architecture of Computing Systems, pp. 344–357. Springer, Cham (2024)
7. Bierbrauer, J., Edel, Y.: Extending and LengtheningBCHCodes. Finite Fields Appl. **3**(4), 314–333 (1997)
8. Bose, R.C., Ray-Chaudhuri, D.K.: On a class of error correcting binary group codes. Inf. Control **3**(1), 68–79 (1960)
9. Charpin, P.: Weight distributions of cosets of two-error-correcting binary BCH codes, extended or not. IEEE Trans. Inf. Theory **40**(5), 1425–1442 (1994)
10. Gorenstein, D., Peterson, W.W., Zierler, N.: Two-error correcting Bose-Chaudhuri codes are quasi-perfect. Inf. Control **3**(3), 291–294 (1960)
11. Hocquenghem, A.: Codes correcteurs d'erreurs. Chiffers **2**, 147–156 (1959)
12. Li, J., et al.: Low delay single error correction and double adjacent error correction (SEC-DAEC) codes. Microelectron. Reliab. **97**, 31–37 (2019)
13. Neale, A.: Design and analysis of an adjacent multi-bit error correcting code for nanoscale SRAMs (2014)
14. Neale, A., Jonkman, M., Sachdev, M.: Adjacent-MBU-tolerant SEC-DED-TAEC-yAED codes for embedded SRAMs. IEEE Trans. Circuits Syst. II Express Briefs **62**(4), 387–391 (2014)
15. Okano, I.: A construction method of high-speed decoders using ROM's for Bose–Chaudhuri–Hocquenghem and Reed-Solomon codes. IEEE Trans. Comput. **100**(10), 1165–1171 (1987)
16. Rahul, K., Yachareni, S.: Deterministic algorithm to generate SEC-DED-DAEC H-matrix for SRAMS in FPGAs for reliable space applications. In: 2020 5th International Conference on Computing, Communication and Security (ICCCS), pp. 1–5. IEEE (2020)

17. Sloane, N.J.A., Reddy, S.M., Chen, C.-L.: New binary codes. IEEE Trans. Inf. Theory **18**(4), 503–510 (1972)
18. Tripathi, S., Jana, J., Samanta, J., Raj, A., Ranjan, D., Singh, M.P.: Design and evaluation of Neale-based multi-bit adjacent error-correcting codec for SRAM. In: Kundu, S., Acharya, U.S., De, C.K., Mukherjee, S. (eds.) Proceedings of the 2nd International Conference on Communication, Devices and Computing. LNEE, vol. 602, pp. 259–268. Springer, Singapore (2020). https://doi.org/10.1007/978-981-15-0829-5_26

Reduction of Average-Performance Degradation and Variance in Faulty CPU Cache Memories

Michail Mavropoulos[1], Georgios Keramidas[2](✉), and Dimitris Nikolos[1]

[1] Department of Computer Engineering and Informatics, University of Patras, Patras, Greece
{mavropoulo,nikolosd}@ceid.upatras.gr
[2] Department of Informatics, Aristotle University, Thessaloniki, Greece
gkeramidas@csd.auth.gr

Abstract. Cache memory is a critical resource for performance, and as is well known, faults in it can significantly impact processor efficiency. In our everyday life, in non-critical real-time applications, it is desirable for quality of service that performance remains high, and that the worst-case execution time is as close to the average as possible.

In this paper, we demonstrate that neither disabling only the faulty cache sub-blocks [1] nor disabling entire blocks that contain at least one faulty sub-block [23] yields optimal results in terms of average performance and performance variance in faulty CPU caches. Instead, we show that selectively disabling blocks with more than N faulty sub-blocks, while disabling only the faulty sub-blocks in all other blocks, leads to better average performance and lower performance variance. The optimal value of N depends on both the fault percentage and the granularity of the sub-block.

Keywords: CPU Cache Memory · Re-configurable Caches · Graceful Degradation

1 Introduction

Geometry shrinkage allows doubling the number of transistors per area unit in every new CMOS technology node [31], leading to higher power density. Also, smaller transistors degrade faster if Vcc is not scaled down because the electric field density increases. This necessitates a decrease in Vcc. However, lowering Vcc leads to greater static [7] and dynamic [8] process variations. These variations become more significant as the silicon industry moves towards the near-threshold region, leading to a higher fault percentage (pfail) [17].

On-chip cache memories, since they constitute a large percentage of the processor area, are built using minimum-size bit-cells. As a result, they are particularly vulnerable to process variations [6], significantly increasing the likelihood of malfunctioning bit-cells.

To cope with this problem several techniques have been proposed which can be classified into four main categories. The first category aims to enhance bit-cell robustness against process variations and includes circuit-level techniques, such as bit-cell redesign using a larger number of transistors or Schmitt-trigger transistors [9,10,19]. However, these approaches incur large area overheads.

The second category is based on the use of error detecting and correcting codes (ECC) to detect/correct the errors caused by the malfunctioning cells [2,36]. Unfortunately, the large storage overhead combined with long error correction times renders the multibit ECC techniques impractical for first-level caches.

The third category relies on redundancy and tries to substitute the defective cache parts e.g., bit-lines, word-lines, blocks, with functional spare elements [3, 4,25,27,35]. However, due to the limited redundancy that can be afforded, the number of defects that can be tolerated by these methods is relatively small.

The techniques of the fourth category are based on the fact that the cache is a performance related resource that does not affect the functionality of the system. Thus, they propose the disabling of the faulty cache regions at various levels of granularity, such as way, block, or sub-block. Some approaches also introduce supplementary techniques to mitigate the average performance degradation caused by the reduced effective cache area [13–16,21,22,24,26,28,30,32,33,37].

Beyond average performance, the variance of performance is also an issue. Variance arises due to the use of different regions of memory by the same application in different periods of time or among different applications, and disparities among cores of the same design due to the unique distribution of faults in each cache. This variance is undesirable, even for non-critical real-time applications in everyday life, as maintaining consistent performance is essential for quality of service. Ideally, worst-case performance should be close to the average. While many techniques have been proposed to improve average performance, relatively few address both average performance and the variance of performance caused by faults in the CPU cache [1,23].

For a given fault percentage, disabling defective cache parts at the sub-block granularity (e.g., 1/2, 1/4, or 1/8 of a block) preserves a larger effective cache area compared to block-level disabling. However, the performance of executing applications is influenced not only by the percentage of faulty (sub)blocks but also by their specific locations [1]. To address this, the authors of [1] proposed the False Hit (FH) technique, which is based on: i) Disabling at the sub-block granularity to minimize average performance degradation. ii) Periodically cycling the cache addressing map to reduce performance variance (referred to as external permutation in this paper, illustrated in Fig. 1 with a counter). However, each time the cache address mapping is altered, the cache must be flushed, leading to a decrease in average performance. As a result, while this technique reduces performance variance, it does so at the cost of lower average performance.

In [16], logic permutations at both the sub-block and block granularity were proposed to minimize the number of faulty blocks and distribute them more evenly across the cache sets. In this paper, we refer to this approach as internal

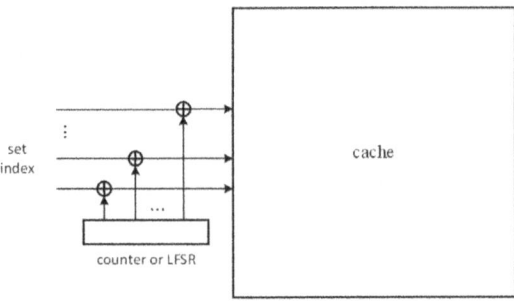

Fig. 1. External permutation. i. Counter is used in [1], ii. LFSR is used in [23].

permutation. After applying the method proposed in [16], some blocks contain only a few faulty sub-blocks, while others have all their sub-blocks faulty. In [23], it was suggested that following the application of the method in [16], all faulty blocks should be disabled-even those with only a single faulty sub-block. Additionally, a periodic random permutation of the addressing map was introduced to reduce performance variance. In the following sections, we refer to this as external permutation (illustrated in Fig. 1 with an LFSR). A Linear Feedback Shift Register (LFSR) is used to generate the random mapping. Furthermore, [23] proposed metrics and thresholds to determine when the LFSR should remain unchanged, thereby reducing the number of cache flushes and improving average performance.

The technique proposed in [1] disables all faulty sub-blocks, while the technique of [23] disables all blocks containing even a single faulty subblock. The techniques of [1] and [23] constitute two extreme approaches, disabling occurs only at sub-block level [1] and at block level [23]. The FH technique [1] introduces some overhead compared to block level disabling [23], however, it preserves a larger effective cache area.

The contributions of this work are:

- A new hybrid approach is proposed. Disabling occurs at block level or sub-block level depending on the number z of the faulty sub-blocks in each block. We disable all blocks with z or more faulty sub-blocks, while we disable only the faulty sub-blocks in the remaining blocks.
- The effectiveness of the hybrid approach with respect to average performance degradation and performance variance across a wide range of pfail scenarios and two sub-block sizes is investigated.
- Extensive experimental results are given comparing the effectiveness of the proposed hybrid approach against those of [1] and [23].

Structure of the Paper. Section 2 provides essential background information. Section 3 outlines our evaluation framework, while Sect. 4 presents the experimental results. Finally, Sect. 5 concludes the study.

2 Background

In this study, we focus on the average performance and performance variance of faulty caches.

We begin by reviewing two existing techniques that have addressed these aspects. Additionally, this section provides essential background information on the internal cache permutation scheme [16], which serves as the foundation for the baseline cache architecture in [23].

The studied techniques assume that the cache is equipped with the ability to disable physical cache portions (blocks or subblocks) that contain malfunctioning cells. With each sub-block an extra bit is connected, called fault bit. When a fault bit is equal to 0, then the associated subblock is fault free, else the sub-block contains one or more malfunctioning cells. All the fault bits constitute the cache fault map. The fault map is generated during production testing and can be updated periodically using a cache built-in-self-test (BIST) circuitry [20].

As mentioned in [1] a sub-block disabling scheme, referred to as False Hit (FH-X) hereafter (where "X" denotes the number of sub-blocks per block), was proposed. In this scheme, to each sub-block is assigned a fault bit, which indicates its status: a value of 1 signifies the presence of one or more malfunctioning cells, while a value of 0 indicates no faults. The advantage of this approach is its low storage overhead-only one fault bit per sub-block. For example, in the FH-4 scheme, a 64B block requires just four additional bits. Compared to cache block disabling techniques, this method preserves a larger effective cache area.

In this scheme [1], each cache access follows the standard process of reading tags and comparing them against the requested address. However, a new scenario may occur: a false hit. A false hit happens when the tag matches, but the corresponding fault bit is set to 1, indicating a faulty sub-block. In this case, the hit/miss signal reports a miss, while the false hit signal is activated.

Whenever a false hit occurs:

1. A miss is reported because the data is not present.
2. The cache line is evicted and dirty data is updated in upper cache levels for write-back caches. Only valid sub-block must be updated. Those bits indicating whether each sub-block is valid or not are retrieved together with the tag. Write-through caches get the cache line evicted for loads, and update upper cache levels for stores.
3. Then, the request is treated as a normal miss. If the instruction causing the false miss is a load, upper cache levels will provide the data. The appropriate data will be bypassed to the petitioner when it arrives. Simultaneously, a cache line will be filled. Since programs exploit temporal locality quite often, the physical cache line where the data was stored is marked as the most recently used line in the set to prevent the fill to happen in the same physical line. Thus, the data is allocated into a different cache line. Such cache line is very likely to have a fault-free sub-block in the location where the datum is to be stored, thus improving temporal locality.

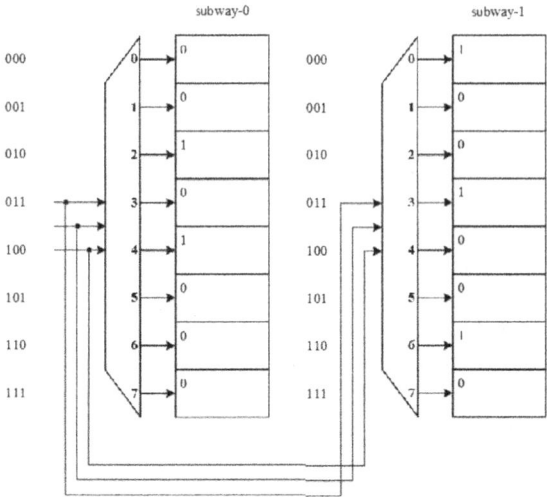

Fig. 2. An example of the internal organization of a way.

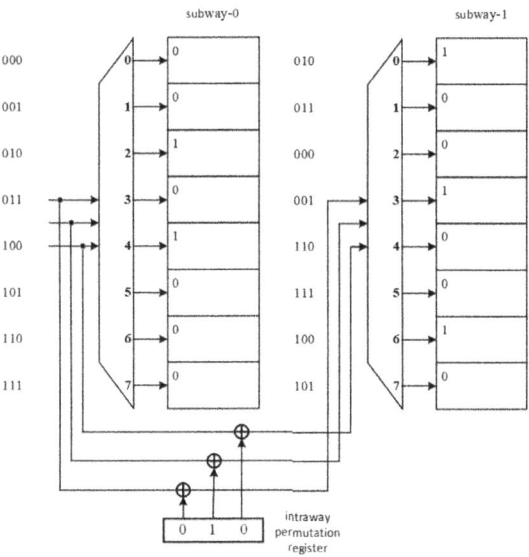

Fig. 3. Sub-block permutation in subway-1.

As the fault percentage increases, the number of cache blocks containing faulty sub-blocks also rises. For large percentages of faults, the FH technique described above results in a large number of misses, because the content of the cache is renewed quickly with consequence the limited exploitation of the temporal locality of the data.

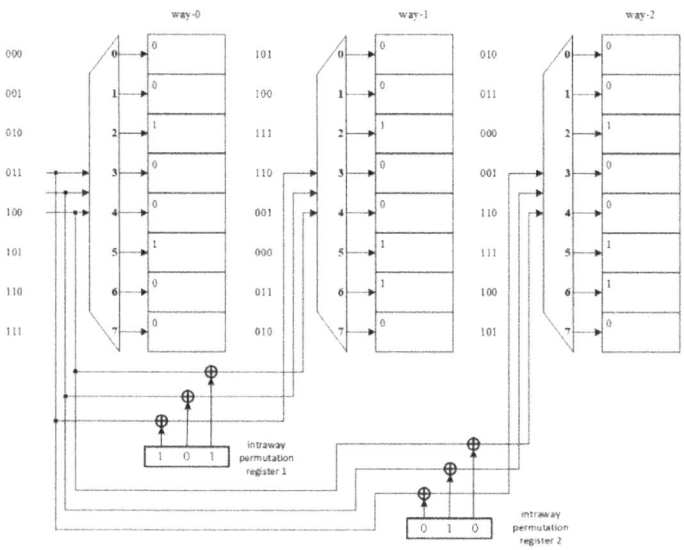

Fig. 4. Block permutation in way-1 and way-2.

The internal permutation technique [16] consists of two permutation algorithms: the sub-block permutation algorithm and the block permutation algorithm. The goal of the sub-block permutation algorithm is to consolidate faulty sub-blocks into the smallest possible number of faulty blocks. To achieve this, each block is divided into 2^i sub-blocks (where i = 1, 2, ...). Each sub-block is supplied with an extra bit, known as the fault bit, which indicates its status: 1 for a faulty sub-block and 0 for a fault-free sub-block. Permutation is carried out using permutation registers. In [16], a systematic method was proposed for determining the contents of these registers, ensuring efficient sub-block reorganization.

In Fig. 2, we assume that each way consists of two sub-ways, with two decoders used to address subway-0 and subway-1, respectively [34]. Each block of the way consists of one sub-block in sub-way-0 and one in sub-way-1. In the upper left corner of each sub-block of Fig. 2 we give the value of the fault bit, while the 3-bit number to the left of each decoder indicates the set of the specific frame to which the sub-block belongs. Figure 3 illustrates the distribution of faulty sub-blocks after applying the permutation register. As shown, the number of faulty blocks is reduced from five in Fig. 2 to only three (blocks with addresses 2, 4, and 0) in Fig. 3. The same technique is applied to the tag array of the cache, in order to assign faulty tags to faulty blocks.

The goal of the block permutation algorithm [16] is to rearrange the addresses of cache blocks within each way so that every set contains almost the same number of faulty blocks. In Fig. 4, we observe that without permutation registers, sets 2 and 5 would be entirely faulty, while set 6 would contain two faulty blocks.

Table 1. System configuration

Parameter	Setting
ROB/IQ/LQ/SQ/Regs	64/48/48/48/256
Fetch/Issue/Commit	2/2/2 instructions per cycle
L1 data cache[a]	16/32 KB, 64B, 4-way, LRU, 4-MSHRs, 2-cycle
L1 instruction cache	8KB, 64B, 4-way, LRU, 4-MSHRs, 2-cycle
L2 cache	256KB, 64B, 8-way, LRU, 20-MSHRs, 20-cycles
DRAM	4 GB, 50 ns, 12.8 GB/s
Process Technology	14 nm
Nominal Operation	2.5 GHz, 1 V
Studied SRAM percentages of malfunctioning cells (pfails) [17]	pfail1: 2.5E−03[b] (651 mV) pfail2: 3E−03 (649 mV) pfail3: 3.5E−03 (646 mV) pfail4: 4E−03 (644 mV) pfail5: 4.5E−03 (642 mV) pfail6: 5E−03 (639 mV) pfail7: 5.5E−03 (637 mV) pfail8: 6E−03 (635 mV)

[a]The caches in gem5 simulator are physically-tagged/physically-indexed.
[b]A pfail of 2.5E−03 indicates that 2.5 out of every 1000 cells will malfunction.

However, by applying permutation registers with the specific configuration, the faulty blocks are redistributed more evenly: sets 0 and 7 each contain two faulty blocks, while sets 2, 3, 4, and 5 each have one faulty block. This ensures a more uniform distribution of faults across the sets.

3 Evaluation Framework

Simulation Infrastructure. Our experimental framework is based on gem5 [5] configured for the x86 ISA, although our approach does not depend on a specific ISA. The core and memory system parameters are illustrated in Table 1. In this work, we considered faults only in first-level data cache memory.

Benchmarks. The whole Malardalen benchmark suite [18] is used to evaluate the proposed approach. This suite consists of 35 benchmarks that are considered representative of real-time applications and suitable for worst-case execution time analysis.

Failures. We consider faults only in the memory arrays of the cache because process variations affect memory structures orders of magnitude more than the logic elements [29]. Things are getting worse under low voltage operation [12]. Random process variations (e.g. random dopant fluctuation) cause malfunctioning cells at random locations in the memory arrays of the cache [13,37].

The application of the discussed techniques requires a bit, called fault bit, to be assigned to each sub-block of the memory array of the cache. All fault bits of the cache array constitute its fault map. The fault map of a memory array is derived during production testing and can be updated by periodic testing (for example when the processor boots as it was proposed in [37]) if we want to consider aging caused malfunctioning cells too [11].

For non-stop systems, the frequency of applying periodic testing depends on the Mean Time Between Failures. Malfunctioning cells can be part of both tag and data arrays of the cache. We consider that the valid bits, the fault bits, and the replacement bits are not affected by process variation induced errors because they have been implemented using SRAM cells that are less sensitive to process variations [9,10,19].

Besides this, if a fault is detected in these bits within a core during production testing, the core could be deactivated. Given the small percentage of these bits relative to the total number of cache bits and the fact that they are implemented using SRAM cells less sensitive to process variations, we conclude that the number of cores deactivated due to faults in these bits will be minimal. As a result, their impact on the yield of the manufacturing process is negligible.

Finally, since defective sub-blocks in the cache are disabled, there is no need to apply a specific fault model (such as the stuck-at fault model or others). The selected fault percentages (pfail) and their associated voltage/frequency levels are described in Table 1. We produce 100 random fault maps and run simulations.

4 Experimental Results

We define the following terms:

- A: adaptive technique (use of the metrics and thresholds of [23] in the external permutation).
- EP: external permutation.
- IPx: internal permutation, the sub-block permutation algorithm is based on sub-blocks of size $1/x$ of the block.
- BDz: only the blocks with z or more faulty sub-blocks are disabled. In the blocks with less than z faulty sub-blocks, only the faulty sub-blocks are disabled.
- FHx: false hit, disabling sub-blocks with size $1/x$ of the block.

By combining the above definitions, we are able to refer to all the methodologies employed in this work:

- EP-FHx: false hit, disabling sub-blocks with size $1/x$ of the block and external permutation.
- EP-IPx-BDz: Block level disabling in cache blocks with z or more faulty sub-blocks, combined with internal permutation with sub-block size $1/x$ of the block and external permutation.
- A-EP-IPx-BDz: Block level disabling in cache blocks with z or more faulty sub-blocks, combined with internal permutation with sub-block size $1/x$ of the block and external permutation triggered based on the adaptive technique presented in [23].

The results presented in this section are illustrated as boxplots. In particular, in each box, the central red line indicates the median value, the displayed data

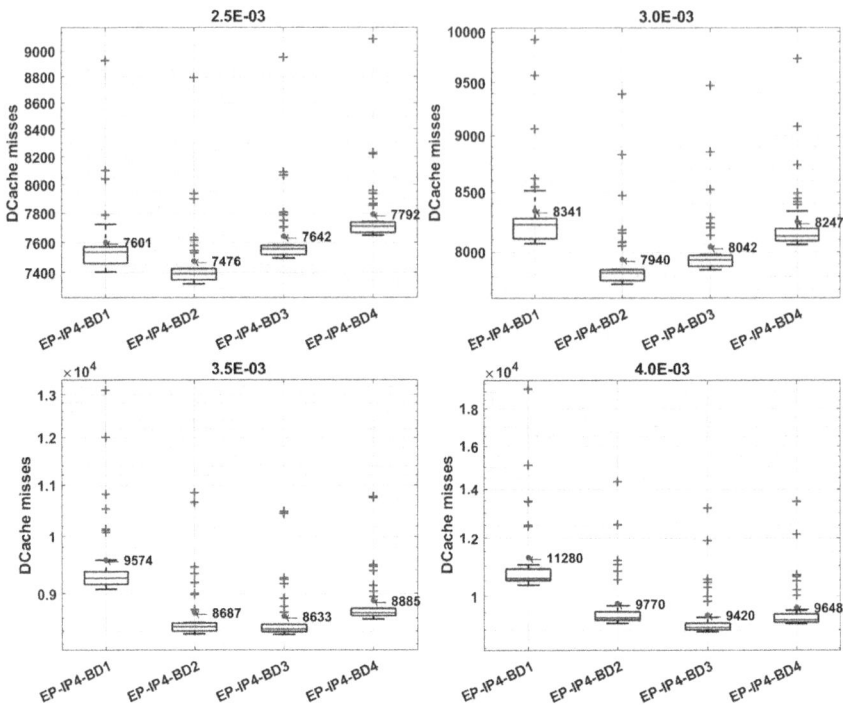

Fig. 5. Baseline: Distribution of misses for blocks with 4 sub-blocks.

value shows the mean value, and the bottom and top edges of each box correspond to the 25% and 75% of the value distribution. The whiskers represent extreme data values that are not considered outliers. Finally, the outliers are plotted individually marked with the '+' symbol.

Figures 5 and 6 compare the method proposed in this paper with the baseline method of [23]. Specifically, Figs. 5 and 6 depict the numbers of cache misses when the internal permutation scheme is configured to operate with sub-blocks that are equal to 1/4 and 1/8 of the block size respectively.

As Fig. 5 indicates, for percentages of faults (pfails) equal to 2.5E−03 (i.e., 2.5 malfunctioning cells per 1000 cells) and 3.0E−03 the policy EP-IP4-BD2, (i.e., all blocks with at least 2 faulty sub-blocks are disabled, while in the blocks with 1 faulty sub-block only the faulty sub-block is disabled) offer better results than the policy EP-IP4-BD1 (the baseline in [23]). While for pfails equal to 3.5E−03 and 4.0E−03 the EP-IP4-BD3 provides the better results.

As we can see in Fig. 6 for pfails, 3.5E−03 and 4.0E−03 the policy EP-IP8-BD3 give the best results, for pfails 4.5E−03, 5.0E−03 and 5.5E−03 the best results are given by the policy EP-IP8-BD4, while for pfail 6.0E−03 the best results are given by the policy EP-IP8-BD5. Therefore, as the percentage of faults increases, the value of z in the EP-IP4-BDz as well as the EP-IP8-BDz

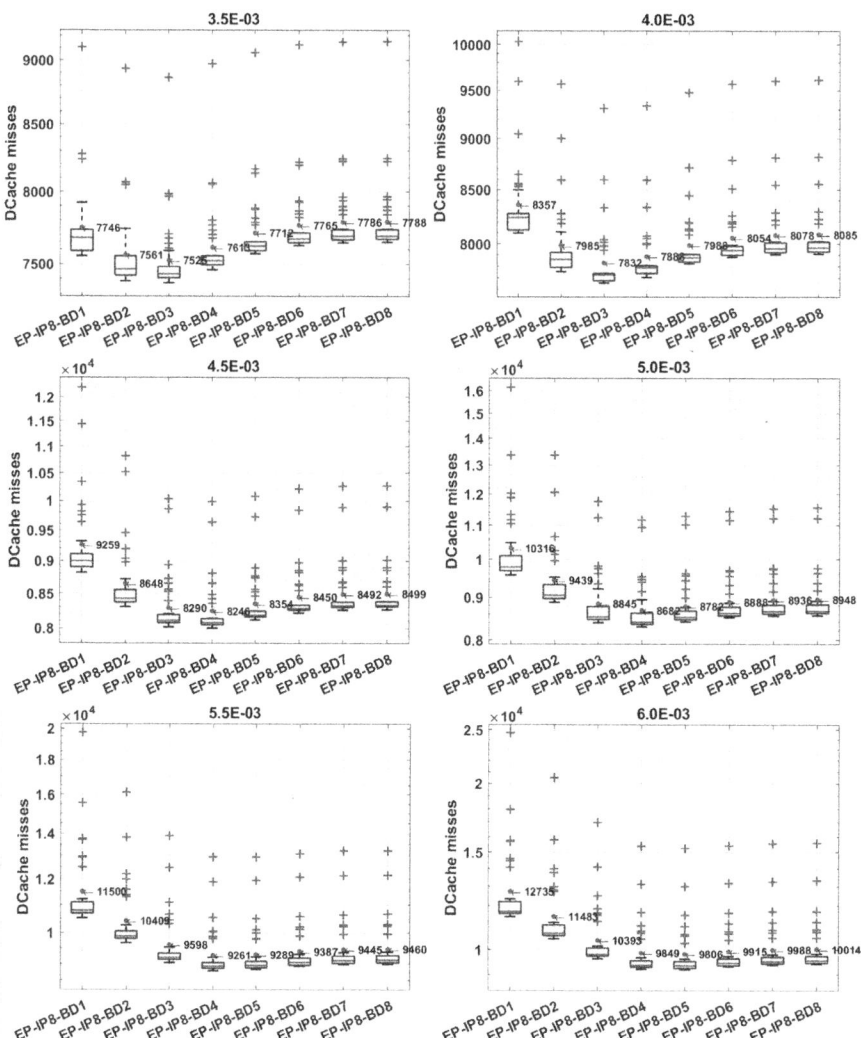

Fig. 6. Baseline: Distribution of misses for blocks with 8 sub-blocks.

technique, which achieves the best results in terms of the average number of misses and variance of misses, also increases.

In Figs. 7 and 8, using in the technique proposed in this paper with the metrics and thresholds from [23], we compare this technique with the methods presented in [1] and [23].

From Fig. 7 we can see that for all pfails the policy A-EP-IP4-BD2/3 gives better results than the FH4 [1], EP-FH4 [1] and A-EP-IP4-BD1 [23] up to 38.7%, 40.1%, 10.2% for the average and 74.3%, 69.5%, 10.2% for the worst case respectively.

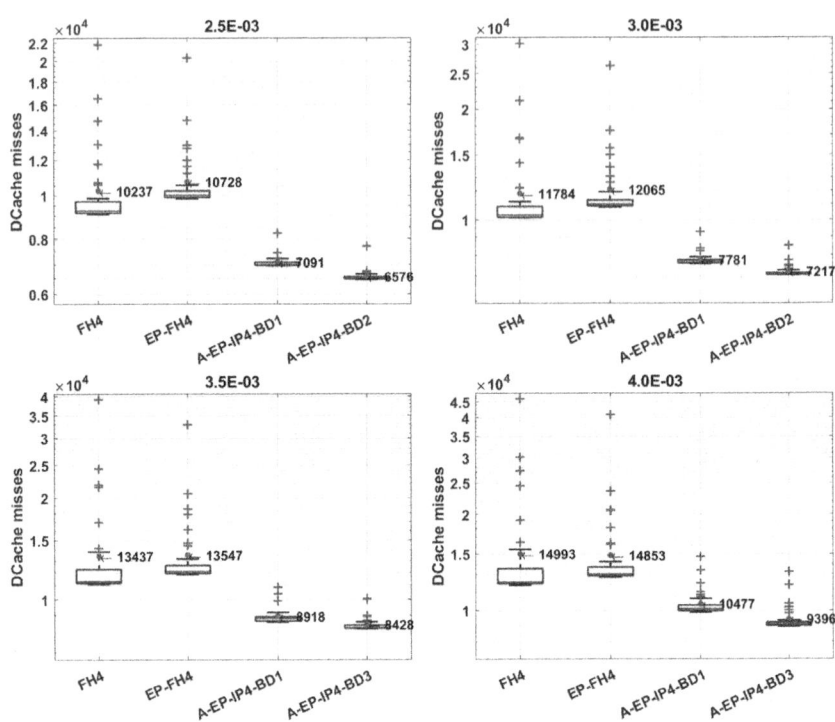

Fig. 7. Adaptive: Distribution of misses for blocks with 4 sub-blocks.

In Fig. 8 we can see that the corresponding adaptive policies A-EP-IP8-BDz, with $z = 3$ for pfails 3.5E−03 and 4.0E−03, $z = 4$ for pfails 4.5E−03, 5.0E−03 and 5.5E−03 and $z = 5$ for 6.0E−03 give better results than the FH8 [1], EP-FH8 [1] and A-EP-IP8-BD1 [23] up to 39.9%, 42.1%, 12.1% for the average and 72.4%, 71.1%, 10.3% for the worst case respectively. Therefore, in all cases, the proposed in this paper technique A-EP-IPx-BDz achieves the best results with respect to the average number of misses as well as their variance.

From Figs. 7 and 8, we can conclude that in the technique proposed in this paper, for the same value of z (where only blocks with z or more faulty sub-blocks are disabled, while in the remaining blocks, only the faulty sub-blocks are disabled), an increase in x (where the sub-block permutation algorithm is based on sub-blocks of size $1/x$ of the block) leads to better results in terms of both the average number of misses and its variance.

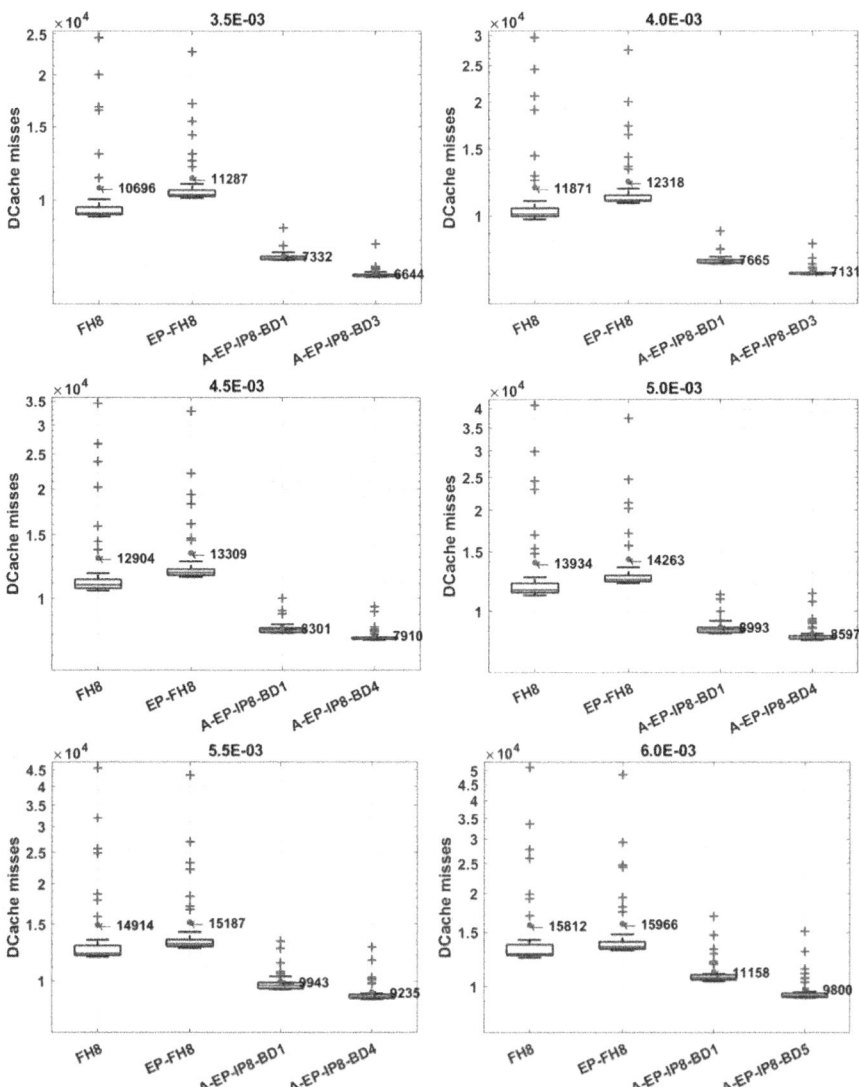

Fig. 8. Adaptive: Distribution of misses for blocks with 8 sub-blocks.

5 Conclusion

In this paper, we have shown that neither the disabling of the faulty sub-blocks [1], nor the disabling of all the blocks containing at least one sub-block [23] yields the best results in terms of average performance and performance variance in faulty CPU caches. We have shown that disabling only the blocks that have z or more faulty sub-blocks and only the faulty sub-blocks in the remaining blocks, results in better average performance and reduced performance variance.

The value of z depends on both the fault percentage and the granularity of the sub-blocks.

References

1. Abella, J., Carretero, J., Chaparro, P., Vera, X., Gonzalez, A.: Low vccmin fault-tolerant cache with highly predictable performance. In: Proceedings of International Symposium on Microarchitecture (2009)
2. Alameldeen, A.R., Wagner, I., Chishti, Z., Wu, W., Wilkerson, C., Lu, S.-L.: Energy-efficient cache design using variable-strength error-correcting codes. In: ISCA 2011 (2011)
3. Ansari, A., Gupta, S., et al.: Zerehcache: armoring cache architectures in high defect density technologies. In: Proceedings of International Symposium on Microarchitecture (2009)
4. Ansari, A., Gupta, S., Feng, S., Mahlke, S.: Maximizing spare utilization by virtually reorganizing faulty cache lines. IEEE Trans. Comput. (2010)
5. Binkert, N., et al.: The gem5 simulator. ACM SIGARCH Comput. Archit. News (2011)
6. Borkar, S.: Design Perspectives on 22 nm CMOS and beyond. In: Proceedings of Design Automation Conference (2009)
7. Borkar, S., Karnik, T., Narendra, S., Tschanz, J., Keshavarzi, A., De, V.: Parameter variations and impact on circuits and microarchitecture. In: Proceedings of Design Automation Conference (2003)
8. Bowman, K., et al.: Circuit techniques for dynamic variation tolerance. In: Proceedings of Design Automation Conference (2009)
9. Chang, L., et al.: A 5.3 GHz 8T-SRAM with operation down to 0.41V in 65 nm CMOS. In: Proceedings of Symposium on VLSI Circuits (2007)
10. Chang, I.J., Kim, J.J., Park, S.P., Roy, K.: A32kb 10T subthreshold SRAM array with bit-interleaving and differential read scheme in 90 nm CMOS. ISSCC Dig. Tech. Papers (2008)
11. Chen, Q., Mahmoodi, H., Bhunia, S., Roy, K.: Modeling and testing of SRAM for new failure mechanisms due to process variations in nanoscale CMOS. In: Proceedings of VLSI Test Symposium (2005)
12. Chishti, Z., Alameldeen, A.R., Wilkerson, C., Wu, W., Lu, S.L.: Cache lifetime reliability at ultra-low voltages. In: Proceedings of International Symposium on Microarchitecture (2009)
13. Choi, Y.G., Yoo, S., Lee, S., Ahn, J.H., Lee, K.: MAEPER: matching access and error patterns with error-free resource for low Vcc L1 cache. Trans. Very Large Scale Integration Syst. (2013)
14. Choudhury, A., Sikdar, B.K.: CIFR: a complete in-place fault remapping strategy for CMP cache using dynamic reuse distance. In: Proceedings of International Symposium on Embedded Computing and System Design (2017)
15. Choudhury, A., Mondal, B., Sikdar, B.K.: ReMiT: redundancy migration for latency aware faulty tolerant cache design in multicore. In: Proceedings of International Symposium on Embedded Computing and System Design (2018)
16. Filippou, F., Keramidas, G., Mavropoulos, M., Nikolos, D.: A novel fault tolerant cache architecture based on orthogonal Latin squares theory. In: International Conference on Design, Automation, and Test in Europe (2018)

17. Ganapathy, S., Kalamatianos, J., Kasprak, K., Raasch, S.: On characterizing near-threshold SRAM failures in FinFET technology. In: Proceedings of Design Automation Conference (2017)
18. Gustafsson, J., Betts, A., Ermedahl, A., Lispe, B.: The Mälardalen WCET benchmarks: past, present and future. In: Workshop on Worst-Case Execution Time Analysis (2010)
19. Kulkarni, J.P., Roy, K.: Ultralow-voltage process-variation-tolerant Schmitt-trigger-based SRAM design. IEEE Trans. Very Large Scale Integr. Syst. (2012)
20. Kumar, A., Pundir, S., Sharma, O.P.: Fault tolerant reconfigurable hardware design using BIST on SRAM: a review. In: International Conference on Intelligent Computing and Control (2017)
21. Lee, H., Cho, S., Childers, B.R.: DEFCAM: a design and evaluation framework for defect-tolerant cache memories. Trans. Archit. Code Optim. (2011)
22. Mahmood, T., Kim, S.: Realizing near-true voltage scaling in variation sensitive l1 caches via fault buffers. In: Proceedings of International Conference on Compilers, Architectures and Synthesis for Embedded Systems (2011)
23. Mavropoulos, M., Keramidas, G., Nikolos, D.: Improving the performance predictability of faulty data caches. In: International European Dependable Computing Conference (2024)
24. Mavropoulos, M., Keramidas, G., Nikolos, D.: Enabling efficient sub-block disabled caches using coarse grain spatial predictions. Microprocess. Microsyst. (2022)
25. Mavropoulos, M., Keramidas, G., Adamopoulos, G., Nikolos, D.: Reconfigurable self adaptive fault tolerant cache memory for DVS enabled systems. In: International Symposium of Great Lakes on VLSI (2015)
26. Mavropoulos, M., Keramidas, G., Nikolos, D.: A defect-aware reconfigurable cache architecture for low-vccmin DVFS-enabled systems. In: International Conference in Design, Automation, and Test in Europe (2015)
27. McNairy, C., Mayfield, J.: Montecito error protection and mitigation. In: HPCRI 2005: 1st Workshop on High Performance Computing Reliability Issues. in conjunction with HPCA 2005 (2005)
28. Mofrad, A.B., Homayoun, H., Dutt, N.: FFT-cache: a flexible fault tolerant cache architecture for ultra low voltage operation. In: Proceedings of International Conference on Compilers, Architectures and Synthesis for Embedded Systems (2011)
29. Nassif, S.R., Mehta, N., Cao, Y.: A resilience roadmap. In: Proceedings of Design, Automation & Test in Europe Conference & Exhibition (2010)
30. Nikolaou, P., Sazeides, Y., Michael, M.K.: INTERPLAY: an intelligent model for predicting performance degradation due to multi-cache way-disabling. In: International Symposium on Defect and Fault Tolerance in VLSI and Nanotechnology Systems (2022)
31. Semiconductor International Association. International Technology Roadmap for Semiconductors (2005 Edition). http://public.itrs.net edition
32. Shirvani, P.P., McCluskey, E.J.: PADded cache: new fault tolerance technique for cache memories. In: International VLSI Test Symposium (1999)
33. Sohi, G.S.: Cache memory organization to enhance the yield of high-performance VLSI processors. Trans. Comput. (1989)
34. Thoziyoor, S., Muralimanohar, N., Jouppi, N.P.: CACTI 5.0, Advanced Architecture Laboratory, HP Laboratories, HPL-2007-167, 19 October 2007
35. Vergos, H.T., Nikolos, D.: Performance recovery in direct mapped faulty caches via the use of a very small fully associative spare cache. In: Proceedings of Computer Performance and Dependability Symposium (1995)

36. Wilkerson, C., Alameldeen, A.R., Chishti, Z., Wu, W., Somasekhar, D., Lu, S.L.: Reducing cache power with low-cost, multi-bit error-correcting codes. In: ISCA 2010 (2010)
37. Wilkerson, C., Gao, H., Alameldeen, A., Chishti, Z., Khellah, M., Lu, S.-L.: Trading off cache capacity for reliability to enable low voltage operation. In: 35th International Symposium on Computer Architecture, ISCA 2008 (2008)

PhD Forum

A System Model for Flexible Multi-objective Adaptation Planning in Hybrid Self-Adaptive and Self-Organizing Systems

Pia Schweizer[✉] [ID]

Department of Food Informatics and Computational Science Hub,
University of Hohenheim, Stuttgart, Germany
`pia.schweizer@uni-hohenheim.de`

Abstract. Self-Adaptive and Self-Organizing (SASO) systems aim to tackle the challenges of information technology's growing complexity. While various control patterns exist to coordinate such systems, this Ph.D. project takes a fully centralized perspective as its starting point. The focus lies on developing a Central Control Unit (CCU) capable of multi-objective, self-aware optimization while balancing potentially conflicting local decisions. As part of the InHOSaS project, this research, along with a second Ph.D. project, will ultimately integrate the CCU with autonomous decision-making at the subsystem level, forming a hybrid approach. These methods are exemplified using the platooning use case, demonstrating the coordination of semi-automated or automated vehicles within the SASO framework to maintain both individual subsystem goals and overarching system constraints.

Keywords: Autonomous systems · Optimization · Coordination · Adaptation

1 Introduction

The field of Self-Adaptive and Self-Organizing (SASO) systems [13] emerged in response to the ever-growing complexity of information technology. The two attributes, self-adaptation and self-organization, are—among further self-* properties like self-healing, self-protection, or self-optimization—naturally occurring phenomena [25]. Inspired by biological systems, Organic Computing leverages these principles to develop systems capable of adapting dynamically to changes in both their environment and the system itself – such as SASO systems [12]. A SASO system consists of multiple subsystems that operate on a local level, with control either issued globally by a central entity or locally by each autonomous subsystem. While a global optimization mechanism that takes control over all contained subsystems represents a potential single point of failure or a performance bottleneck as it does not incorporate individual constraints, a fully local and autonomous decision mechanism that can use machine learning to improve individual behavior can lead to uncoordinated adaptation decisions and miss a global optimum. In contrast, an integrated hybrid approach requires a combination of global optimization with autonomous subsystems. The InHOSaS project argues for a fundamentally different way of developing and deploying SASO systems based on the idea of integrating macro-level planning under longer time requirements with micro-level decisions that are subject to autonomous learning.

This paper describes the aspects of central adaptation planning following the *planning as optimization* [7] approach. The approach starts with the assumption that all participants will follow the optimized solution and then relaxes these assumptions. This will lead to a hybrid solution for maintaining individual subsystem's goals and constraints. In specific, this Ph.D. project focuses on macro-level planning and the development of a robust, multi-objective Central Control Unit (CCU) with implemented degrees of freedom. The developed approaches will be exemplarily shown in the use case of platooning, the coordinated driving of (semi-)automated vehicles in convoys [19]. Platooning coordination, in particular, represents a complex multi-level, multi-objective optimization problem that requires balancing the objectives of individual drivers, platoons, and overarching system goals. As such, it serves as an ideal first use case.

The remainder of the paper is structured as follows. First, Sect. 2 provides a brief introduction to the architecture of SASO systems and the platooning concept, while Sect. 3 provides an overview of related work. Section 4 outlines the key challenges in developing the CCU, followed by its architecture, which is detailed in Sect. 5. For a comprehensive evaluation of the final hybrid SASO system and all intermediate steps, Sect. 6 elucidates the respective simulation environment for platooning and introduces possible scenarios and metrics. Finally, this paper closes with a forecast of the next steps in Sect. 7.

2 Background

The InHOSaS project strives for a hybrid SASO system model. In the following, first, the underlying fundamental concepts of SASO systems will be explained briefly before presenting the platooning use case as an application scenario.

2.1 Coordinated SASO Systems

The design of a coordinated SASO system requires several assumptions [16]. A general SASO architecture, as shown in Fig. 1, is constituted of an adaptation manager AM_{SASO} (not explicitly shown in the figure) with a set of goals G_{SASO}. Depending on the level of control, the AM_{SASO} can be separated into multiple $AM_{ext,l}$ implemented with a structured functionality, e.g., a MAPE-K model (Monitor-Analyze-Plan-Execute-Knowledge) [12]. The managed resources MR_j, composed of various soft- and hardware elements mr_k, are grouped into subsystems S_j. If the subsystem follows its own goals G_j, an internal adaptation manager $AM_{int,j}$ takes control of the managed resources MR_j. The subsystems can, in turn, be combined into coordinated resource groups CR_i, where the position of the subsystem and the properties of the group directly influence the local as well as global goal achievement. In the case of a fully centralized control of the MR_j by the AM_{ext}, the intercalated AM_{int} forwards the respective signals of control. Conversely, the AM_{int} will act as the sole decision maker in a decentralized approach, with the AM_{ext} being non-existent. By combining both techniques in a hybrid approach, AM_{ext} and AM_{int} collaboratively coordinate the SASO system.

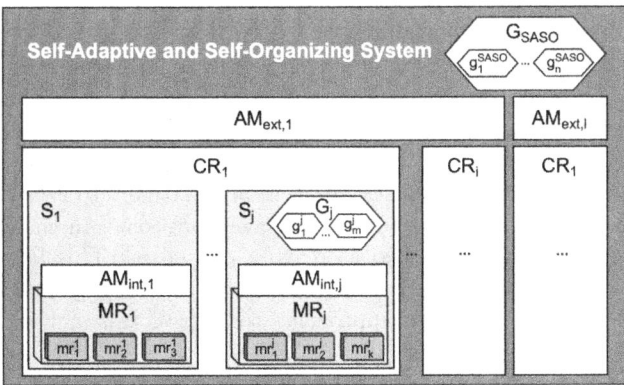

Fig. 1. System architecture for a coordinated self-adaptive and self-organizing system; adapted from [16].

2.2 Motivating Scenario: Platooning

Platooning refers to the coordinated driving of vehicles in convoys. Close inter-vehicle distance is enabled through a communication-based Cooperative Adaptive Cruise Control [20]. Benefits of platooning include improved fuel efficiency through aerodynamic drag reduction, increased safety as communication enables faster reaction, and an enhanced traffic flow through coordination [19].

By transferring the concept of the coordinated SASO system (see Section 2.1) to the platooning example, a single platoon depicts a Coordinated Resource CR_i, composed of numerous subsystems S_j. The subsystems represent the individual vehicles assigned to adequate platoons by the Platooning Coordination System (PCS), constituting the AM_{ext}. Whereas the PCS aims at optimizing global goals, e.g., energy efficiency, global safety, road capacity, and traffic flow [14], the autonomous vehicles target optimizing their individual goals, balancing their cost and travel time. Consequently, the $AM_{int,j}$ as local adaptation control might not be interested in platooning if the estimated benefits are not sufficient. Balancing those global optimization goals while considering local constraints and goals is the main objective of the project—and platooning coordination, which inherently requires this trade-off, an optimal application example.

3 Related Work

This PhD project deals with a hybrid organization of SASO systems that combine the advantages of global optimization with local autonomous learning.

3.1 Autonomous Self-Coordination

Works about autonomous self-coordination focus on resource allocation without external intervention to find an ordering of requesters by optimizing a specific goal (e.g., priorities, cost, or fairness) [2,6]. The InHOSaS project considers three classes of autonomous self-coordination.

a) Centralized approaches use algorithms such as leader election for choosing one specific node that acts on behalf of the group (see, e.g., [5] for an overview of algorithms). Afterward, the resource allocation or coordination problem is handled centrally.

b) Negotiation-based approaches are used alternatively to a centralized solution [26], especially in the context of multi-agent systems. In certain scenarios, agents may disagree yet still need to reach a consensus. This helps to achieve overall system reliability in the presence of some disagreeing agents, referred to as a "consensus problem". Current approaches to address this include protocols [2] or mechanisms such as auctions [10].

c) Emergent-based approaches avoid explicit coordination or management. In turn, fully decentralized agents act autonomously without explicit coordination or negotiation [3]. Coordination is established with simple scheduling schemes, for example, first-come-first-served.

However, none of the approaches considered so far explicitly aim to establish a hybrid optimization that is robust to changing conditions and reacts on different time scales while simultaneously respecting the autonomy of individual subsystems.

3.2 Hybrid SASO Systems

Hybrid SASO systems are usually designed in one of two ways. While bottom-up attempts usually focus on more practical concepts, they lack clear conceptual separation in the design. As a result, the developed mechanisms are very specific for the underlying tasks. In contrast, top-down approaches usually try to achieve clear responsibilities and encapsulation, making the approach more generally applicable. However, this easily results in solutions that are less efficient for a specific solution. There are only a few contributions in literature where both perspectives are combined to find a trade-off. One particular example is the goal-oriented holonic system design concept [4], where the strict hierarchical composition of a system is replaced by holonic system organization with goals as the primary coupling point. In general, hybrid SASO architectures integrate elements with different scopes w.r.t. the centrality of their responsibilities. Literature distinguishes between (i) layered structures (e.g., [24]), (ii) cascaded structures (e.g., [12]), and (iii) hybrid coordination patterns (e.g., [27]). All solutions of the three classes offer either complete autonomy, i.e., instances are responsible for their (uncoordinated) planning, or central planning, i.e., providing a global, static plan. Accordingly, planning of adaptations is either optimized for individual preferences but uncoordinated—resulting in potentially contradicting decisions—or coordinated but forces instances to obey a plan that might neglect individual preferences. In contrast, we propose to combine central adaptation planning with decentralized decision-making based on learning from previous decisions.

3.3 Planning as Optimization

The *planning as optimization* approach for SASO systems involves treating the planning process as a mathematical optimization problem [7]. The central planner is designed to compute optimal or near-optimal solutions for system adaptation by solving an optimization problem that balances global objectives with subsystem constraints. In [9], the authors analyzed optimization techniques within SASO systems for adaptation planning. 71 different techniques were identified in 115 publications, including probabilistic, combinatorial, evolutionary, stochastic, mathematical, and meta-heuristic optimization techniques. However, the approaches target optimization in centralized systems with only minor focus (less than 30%) to decentralized optimization. None combines central with local planning.

4 Research Challenges

The implementation of fully central coordination is computationally intensive, time-consuming, and introduces a single point of failure, while decentralized decision-making can lead to conflicting adaptations and suboptimal solutions. To address these challenges, the InHOSaS research project aims to develop a hybrid collaborating SASO system divided into two branches, further discussed in [22]. The first branch, led by the Intelligent Systems Group at the University of Kiel, adopts a bottom-up approach with autonomous local decision-making. The second branch, the focus of this Ph.D. project, explores a top-down approach centered on the following research question: **How should the central planner be constructed to allow for a many-objective, self-aware optimization at runtime while robustly handling the introduction of local decisions that possibly interfere with its global plan?**

By integrating both branches, the goal is to create a robust hybrid SASO system that balances micro-level objectives with global optimization through a CCU. The development of the CCU and its integration with local preferences involves several research challenges, which are outlined below and discussed in more depth in [21].

RC 1 – System-wide, situation-aware, single-objective optimization. The CCU provides adaptation instructions using a modular architecture for runtime optimization [7], ensuring flexibility and independence from specific optimization techniques. Based on the 'No Free Lunch' theorem [28], which implies an objective-dependent behavior of optimization techniques, and studies on situation-dependent optimization algorithms [17], a taxonomy will guide the selection of single-objective techniques (e.g., stochastic, evolutionary, and mathematical). An automated runtime selection and meta-adaptation logic [15] will enable self-aware, global optimization.

RC 2 – Robust multi-objective optimization. To address unfair contributions among subsystems (e.g., higher fuel consumption for platoon leaders), a compensation scheme will be developed. Multi-objective optimization will replace single-objective optimization, allowing a simultaneous focus on diverse goals.

RC 3 – Many-objective hybrid optimization with degrees of freedom. While the central planner focuses on global optimization, subsystems learn autonomous decision-making via reinforcement learning. The integration of these perspectives introduces degrees of freedom in adaptation plans, enabling local systems to select actions that align with their goals within boundaries. This transition from multi- to many-objective optimization allows systems to target goals individually rather than as compromises.

5 System Model

The CCU represents the AM_{ext} of Fig. 1. Its design shall enable a situation-aware runtime optimization of the coordination process. Figure 2 shows the design of its architecture, which is further structured into a *CCU Manager*, a *Situation Detector*, and an *Optimization Unit*.

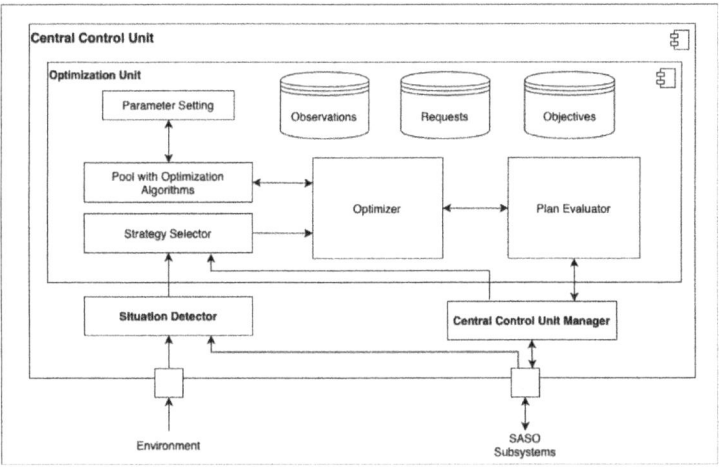

Fig. 2. System architecture for the Central Control Unit.

5.1 CCU Manager and Situation Detector

The CCU Manager acts as a coordinating instance for subsystem requests. It receives data regarding the status of the SASO system's subsystems, which includes both their objectives and any adaptation requests they may have. These inquiries are use-case specific—for example, they might involve the interest in joining a Coordinated Resource or switching to a different one. The primary function of the CCU Manager is to classify these requests into valid and invalid. In particular, any request from a subsystem that has already received an adaptation within the last time step—or within a defined recent period—is marked as invalid. All valid requests, along with the associated subsystem objectives, are then forwarded to the Plan Evaluator, a component of the Optimization Unit. Simultaneously, the Strategy Selector—also part of the Optimization Unit—is triggered. In parallel with the CCU Manager's sorting operations, the Situation Detector periodically gathers observations from the system's environment and the system itself. It then analyzes this data to classify the SASO subsystems' current state, considering external conditions as well as internal factors—such as a hardware failure. When a significant change in the situation is detected—one that is not noise or within the expected range for deviations—the Strategy Selector within the Optimization Unit is triggered, thereby receiving the updated situation and corresponding specifications.

5.2 Optimization Unit

The Optimization Unit processes data from the SASO subsystems—including subsystem requests, objectives, and observations from the environment—to generate adaptation action plans. Therefore, it consists of several components that interact with each other.

As soon as the Situation Detector identifies a significant change in the situation, it forwards its observations to the Strategy Selector. This component, if additionally triggered by the CCU Manager, evaluates whether to retain the current coordination strategy or to switch to an alternative one that already exists. A coordination strategy is essentially a rule defined by several strategy-dependent input parameters. Depending on the situation, the parameters of the strategy are initially set based on knowledge the system collected in similar situations in the past. If a strategy switch is warranted, the new strategy along with the observations from the Situation Detector are sent to the Optimizer. The Optimizer then retrieves a set of situation-suited optimization techniques from the Pool with Optimization Algorithms. To take into account the situation- and objective-dependent behavior of optimization algorithms, this pool offers a variety of algorithm types that are selected based on the current situation and coordination strategy. The pool not only provides the relevant algorithms but also gathers their necessary parameters from the Parameter Setting component and passes them along to the Optimizer. Utilizing these algorithms, the Optimizer fine-tunes and determines (quasi-)optimal input parameters for the selected strategy, thereby relying on historical data for the retraining process.

The resulting solutions—each comprising the strategy with a distinct set of parameters—are then forwarded to the Plan Evaluator. The Plan Evaluator's task is to select the best solution by considering the subsystems' objectives (i.e., their local preferences and concerns) and to convert the subsystem requests into concrete adaptation actions that align with the coordination strategy and the objectives of the individual subsystems.

Finally, these assembled adaptation actions are returned to the CCU Manager, that gathers all actions from the Plan Evaluator with the previously outsorted rejected requests. Afterwards, the CCU Manager forwards the complete set to the SASO subsystems. For any rejected request, the corresponding subsystem is advised to continue with its current behavior. When the Situation Detector is inactive or doesn't identify a new situation, the CCU Manager still forwards any available, valid subsystem request to the Plan Evaluator. The Plan Evaluator then triggers the Optimizer to update the strategy parameters based on the latest observations to continuously improve the system.

6 Evaluation Concept

Platooning is the first example of evaluating and comparing the fully centralized, fully decentralized, and hybrid SASO system setups. In the following, the simulation environment, scenarios, and applied metrics are presented.

Simulation Environment: The simulation environment is based on the one of Lesch et al. [17]. We apply the SUMO simulation [18] with the Plexe [23] extension that enables platooning behavior. Various traffic situations will be simulated to analyze the effects that global, local, and hybrid implementations of the adaptation logic have within the platooning use case.

Scenarios: Variations of the considered traffic volumes, route length, number of lanes, and speed limits will create different situations to help analyzing the claim of the requirement of situation-awareness. Additionally, the analysis focuses on specific dynamics that will trigger adaptation, which are represented by disturbances such as construction sites, traffic accidents, or sensor problems.

Metrics: Various metrics can be observed when determining the performance of SASO systems [8]. The two properties, self-adaptation and self-organization, are typically assessed independently. Key self-adaptation metrics include but are not limited to runtime metrics, the situation performance metric, as well as the decision benefit metric, e.g., [11]. To evaluate the self-organizing aspect of the systems, interaction metrics, but also graph-theoretic metrics, and the metric of entropy are relevant, e.g., [1].

7 Conclusion

The InHOSaS project aims to develop a framework and methodology for developing hybrid SASO systems that integrate centralized adaptation planning with decentralized decision-making. This approach addresses the growing complexity of modern software systems by combining top-down optimization with bottom-up learning strategies for enabling individual sub-systems optimization.

The part of the joint research project, described in this paper, focuses on the centralized adaptation planning functionality. It proposes three research challenges that need to be tackled for establishing the situation-aware, multi-objective central planner that considers the local preferences upon a merge with the decentralized setup. This includes the implementation of a CCU equipped with optimization algorithms and a meta-adaptation logic, followed by a focus shift towards multiple-differing goals, and finally, consideration of the local preferences. The initial evaluation domain for the distributed multi-agent system will be platooning. The project's first steps will involve the design of relevant traffic scenarios and the establishment of metrics. Additionally, the described system model will be integrated into the existing simulation framework.

Acknowledgments. The InHOSaS project is funded by the Deutsche Forschungsgemeinschaft (DFG, German Research Foundation) – 516601628. I thank Jun.-Prof. Dr. Christian Krupitzer for his supervision, advice, and support in my Ph.D. project. Further, I thank Jonas Lange and Prof. Dr.-Ing. Sven Tomforde for the close cooperation within the InHOSaS project, as well as Elia Henrichs for his support during revision.

References

1. Birdsey, L., Szabo, C., Falkner, K.: Identifying self-organization and adaptability in complex adaptive systems. In: IEEE SASO, pp. 131–140 (2017)
2. Bracha, G.: Asynchronous byzantine agreement protocols. Inf. Comput. **75**(2), 130–143 (1987)
3. Diaconescu, A., et al.: Architectures for collective self-aware computing systems. Self-Aware Comput. Syst. 191–235 (2017)
4. Diaconescu, A., Frey, S., Müller-Schloer, C., Pitt, J., Tomforde, S.: Goal-oriented holonics for complex system (self-)integration: concepts and case studies. In: Proceedings of the SASO (2016)
5. Dolev, S., Israeli, A., Moran, S.: Uniform dynamic self-stabilizing leader election. IEEE TPDS **8**(4), 424–440 (1997)
6. Edenhofer, S., et al.: Trust communities: an open, self-organised social infrastructure of autonomous agents. In: Trustworthy Open Self-Organising Systems, pp. 127–152 (2016)
7. Fredericks, E.M., Gerostathopoulos, I., Krupitzer, C., Vogel, T.: Planning as optimization: dynamically discovering optimal configurations for runtime situations. In: SASO, pp. 1–10 (2019)
8. Goller, J.M.: A measurement framework for the assessment of self-adaptation and self-organisation in systems with decentralised configurations. Ph.D. thesis, Kiel University (2023)
9. Henrichs, E., Lesch, V., Straesser, M., Kounev, S., Krupitzer, C.: A literature review on optimization techniques for adaptation planning in adaptive systems: State of the art and research directions. Inf. Softw. Technol. **149** (2022)

10. Jennings, N.R., Faratin, P., Lomuscio, A.R., Parsons, S., Sierra, C., Wooldridge, M.: Automated negotiation: prospects, methods and challenges. Int. J. Group Decis. Negotiation **10**(2), 199–215 (2001)
11. Kaddoum, E., Raibulet, C., George, J.P., Picard, G., Gleizes, M.P.: Criteria for the evaluation of self-* systems. In: ICSE SEAMS, pp. 29–38 (2010)
12. Kephart, J., Chess, D.: The vision of autonomic computing. Computer **36**(1), 41–50 (2003)
13. Krupitzer, C., Roth, F.M., VanSyckel, S., Schiele, G., Becker, C.: A survey on engineering approaches for self-adaptive systems. Pervasive Mob. Comput. **17**(PB), 184–206 (2015)
14. Krupitzer, C., Segata, M., Breitbach, M., El-Tawab, S., Tomforde, S., Becker, C.: Towards infrastructure-aided self-organized hybrid platooning. In: GCIoT, pp. 1–6 (2018)
15. Lesch, V., Hadry, M., Krupitzer, C., Kounev, S.: Self-aware optimization of adaptation planning strategies. ACM TAAS **18**(3) (2023)
16. Lesch, V., Krupitzer, C., Tomforde, S.: Multi-objective optimisation in hybrid collaborating adaptive systems. In: ARCS Workshop, pp. 1–8. VDE (2019)
17. Lesch, V., Noack, T., Hefter, J., Kounev, S., Krupitzer, C.: Towards situation-aware meta-optimization of adaptation planning strategies. In: ACSOS, pp. 177–187 (2021)
18. Lopez, P.A., et al.: Microscopic traffic simulation using SUMO. In: ITSC. IEEE (2018)
19. Mushtaq, A., Haq, I., Nabi, W., Khan, A., Shafiq, O.: Traffic flow management of autonomous vehicles using platooning and collision avoidance strategies. Electronics **10**(10) (2021)
20. Robinson, T., Chan, E., Coelingh, E.: Operating platoons on public motorways: an introduction to the SARTRE platooning programme. In: ITS World Congress, vol. 1, p. 12 (2010)
21. Schweizer, P.: Multi-objective adaptation planning with degrees of freedom in hybrid self-adaptive and self-organizing systems. In: Organic Computing: Doctoral Dissertation Colloquium 2024 (2025)
22. Schweizer, P., Lange, J., Henrichs, E., Tomforde, S., Krupitzer, C.: Towards a hybrid architecture for self-adaptive and self-organizing systems. In: ACSOS-C, pp. 41–46 (2024)
23. Segata, M., et al.: Multi-technology cooperative driving: an analysis based on PLEXE. IEEE TMC **22**(8), 4792–4806 (2023)
24. Tomforde, S., et al.: Observation and control of organic systems. In: Organic Computing-A Paradigm Shift for Complex Systems, pp. 325–338 (2011)
25. Tomforde, S., Sick, B., Müller-Schloer, C.: Organic computing in the spotlight. CoRR (2017)
26. Weißbach, M., Chrszon, P., Springer, T., Schill, A.: Decentrally coordinated execution of adaptations in distributed self-adaptive software systems. In: Proceedings of the SASO, pp. 111–120 (2017)
27. Weyns, D., et al.: On patterns for decentralized control in self-adaptive systems. In: de Lemos, R., Giese, H., Müller, H.A., Shaw, M. (eds.) Software Engineering for Self-Adaptive Systems II. LNCS, vol. 7475, pp. 76–107. Springer, Heidelberg (2013). https://doi.org/10.1007/978-3-642-35813-5_4
28. Wolpert, D., Macready, W.: No free lunch theorems for optimization. TEVC **1**(1), 67–82 (1997)

Dynamic Multimodal Cyclist Behaviour Modelling: From Representation Insights to Federated Collaboration

Shang Gao[✉]

Intelligent Embedded Systems, University of Kassel, Kassel, Germany
sgao@uni-kassel.de
https://www.uni-kassel.de/eecs/ies/startseite

Abstract. In the field of intelligent transportation systems, accurately modelling cyclist behaviour is crucial to enhancing traffic safety and efficiency, particularly as road environments are increasingly shared with automated vehicles. Modelling cyclist behaviour is intrinsically complex due to its dynamic, context-dependent nature, shaped by diverse environmental and individual factors. These complexities pose significant challenges for traditional centralized learning approaches, particularly regarding data privacy concerns and heterogeneity across distributed data sources. Federated Learning (FL), as an emerging framework, offers the potential to address these challenges by enabling collaborative model training without sharing raw data. However, in real-world traffic scenarios, FL must tackle the complexities of non-independent and identically distributed data and the need for real-time adaptability in dynamic traffic environments. This work explores an uncertainty-aware FL framework, incorporating multimodal data fusion, to support modelling cyclist behaviour in traffic environments. This research addresses key challenges in FL for cyclist behaviour modelling and explores potential solutions, offering both theoretical and practical insights for future applications in intelligent transportation systems.

Keywords: Federated Learning · Uncertainty Estimation · Representation Learning · Multimodal Data Fusion · Collaborative Model Training · Data Privacy Protection · Intelligent Transportation Systems

1 Introduction

Modern intelligent transportation systems (ITS) are evolving into highly interconnected, decentralized networks of vehicles, infrastructure, and road users [21]. As technology advances, data-driven approaches are increasingly being leveraged to improve traffic efficiency, enhance safety, and reduce carbon emissions. However, the complexity and dynamic nature of real-world traffic, coupled with growing concerns about data privacy, call for innovative solutions that can adapt to diverse scenarios and protect sensitive information. This paper focuses on one particularly challenging and essential component of ITS: modelling the behaviour of bicycle riders.

Bicycle riders play a critical role in contemporary urban transportation systems. As cities prioritize eco-friendly and health-oriented commuting, the number of cyclists on the road continues to surge. This trend helps to alleviate congestion and lower emissions but introduces new safety and coordination challenges. Unlike vehicles, which are relatively standardized, cyclists vary widely in terms of speed, skill, and adherence to road rules. Understanding the behaviour of this rapidly growing user group is crucial for designing traffic-flow strategies, optimizing infrastructure planning, and ensuring the well-being of all road users.

Cyclist behaviour is notoriously difficult to capture due to its high variability and dependence on context. Environmental conditions, personal riding habits, and interactions with other road users can all drastically affect a cyclist's decisions and trajectories [17]. Furthermore, the lack of standardized protective equipment, such as vehicle-grade sensors and communication systems, leads to irregularities in the available data. These factors make it challenging to develop robust predictive models that generalize effectively across different cities, climates, and infrastructure setups.

Many existing models for traffic behaviour were originally designed for cars and public transport, which typically follow more predictable, rule-bound movement patterns. However, the decentralized and adaptive nature of modern ITS [21] complicates centralized modelling approaches that assume data homogeneity and stable conditions. This leads to fundamental limitations when capturing the stochastic and context-dependent riding behaviours of cyclists [30]. Relying on a single, centralized data repository also raises issues with latency and privacy, as personal location data and riding patterns become consolidated in one place.

FL has emerged as a promising paradigm to address the limitations of traditional centralized approaches. Instead of pooling raw data in a central server, FL allows local nodes–such as smartphones, edge devices, or in-vehicle units–to train models on their own data and share only intermediate updates [4]. This decentralized method not only preserves privacy but also makes efficient use of localized computation and storage resources. In the context of intelligent transportation, where data is inherently distributed and sensitive, FL provides a practical approach to tapping into rich and diverse real-world datasets while respecting data ownership and confidentiality.

The distinctive strengths of FL are particularly beneficial for modelling cyclist behaviour. By enabling each node to learn from locally observed riding patterns, FL can accommodate the vast heterogeneity in cyclist data–varying across locations, infrastructure, weather, and individual preferences–without requiring a one-size-fits-all model. Moreover, aggregating updates from multiple clients allows the global model to capture broader traffic trends and rare events, such as near-miss incidents or sudden manoeuvres. FL can also incorporate adaptive aggregation mechanisms to mitigate the impact of noisy or low-quality data, improving the robustness and reliability of predictive models.

Despite the promise of FL, several technical hurdles must be overcome to realize its full potential for cyclist behaviour modelling. The non-independent and identically distributed (Non-IID) nature of cycling data shaped by region-specific infrastructure, regulatory differences, and rider profiles can disrupt standard federated training protocols. The dynamic conditions of real-world traffic systems also demand methods capable of adapting to time-varying distributions and shifting road conditions. Finally, ensuring adequate representation of rare but critical events (e.g., abrupt turning manoeuvres or close calls) remains essential for building models that can safeguard rider safety. Addressing these challenges will be key to the successful deployment of FL in advanced ITS applications. This work aligns with the principles of **organic computing (OC)**, which emphasize self-organization and context awareness [26].

2 Related Work

Modelling cyclist behaviour in the context of autonomous driving has seen significant advancements in recent years. A major focus is on trajectory prediction, where deep learning models forecast a cyclist's future path by accounting for interactions with other road users [16]. Gao et al. combine a dynamic Bayesian network (DBN) for inferring a cyclist's motion intention with an LSTM encoder-decoder for trajectory forecasting, improving both prediction accuracy and timeliness [9]. In the field of object detection, Wang et al. [27] utilized Fast R-CNN [10] for joint pedestrian and cyclist detection. They introduced improvements such as multilayer feature fusion and hard example mining to enhance detection accuracy, demonstrating strong stability and robustness, particularly in complex urban environments. Another key challenge is intention estimation âĂŞ predicting the cyclist's intent (e.g., to turn or cross) before it manifests in the trajectory. For instance, Kress et al. [15] utilized Long Short-Term Memory (LSTM) networks for cyclist intention prediction, achieving notable accuracy and generalization. Nevertheless, current cyclist behaviour models address trajectory forecasting, intent recognition, and anomaly detection, but challenges remain in handling the high uncertainty and variability inherent to human cyclists [17].

Autonomous vehicles rely on multiple sensors, such as cameras, LiDAR, radar, and IMUs, to perceive cyclists and understand their behaviour. To improve detection and prediction accuracy, researchers have proposed various sensor fusion approaches at the raw data, feature, or decision level. For instance, Huang et al. [14] adopted a late fusion strategy, where sensor data was processed independently before being combined at a higher level, improving cyclist behaviour prediction while potentially losing fine-grained complementary information. To overcome these limitations, Chang et al. [3] optimized cyclist orientation estimation by fusing visual pose features with 3D LiDAR point clouds. Overall, multi-sensor fusion holds great potential for cyclist behaviour modelling, but further improvements in fusion architectures are needed to effectively integrate heterogeneous data sources.

Uncertainty estimation in FL has gained attention due to the heterogeneity of decentralized data. Dempster-Shafer theory has been applied in FL to quantify uncertainty in missing features and resolve conflicting evidence across clients [29]. Bayesian approaches, such as variational inference and deep ensembles, have been adapted to FL, where each client maintains a local posterior approximation that is aggregated at the server to provide confidence-aware predictions [18]. Monte Carlo (MC) Dropout, introduced by Gal [8], has also been leveraged in FL for computationally efficient uncertainty estimation, enabling clients to generate local uncertainty measures through multiple stochastic forward passes before aggregation [18]. These methods enhance FL robustness by mitigating unreliable predictions and improving decision-making in safety-critical applications like autonomous driving.

A core challenge in FL for cyclist behaviour modelling is the heterogeneity of data across clients: each vehicle or city may encounter distinct cyclist habits or contextual factors. To mitigate this, researchers leverage representation learning to capture a shared feature space. For instance, Collins et al. [6] show that even with non-i.i.d. data, clients often benefit from learning global, universal features of cyclist behaviour (e.g., common motion patterns or typical reactions to traffic signals), significantly reducing the amount of local data required. Building on these shared representations, personalization strategies then tailor parts of the model to each client. Qi et al. [23] introduced a global feature extractor combined with a locally fine-tuned layer, allowing adaptation to client-specific behaviour patterns while maintaining generalization across clients. Ma et al. [19] proposed federated multi-task learning, where task-specific adaptations enable personalized model updates for different client distributions. To further enhance adaptability, Alsulaimawi et al. [1] leveraged meta-learning in FL, enabling new clients to fine-tune their models with only a few gradient steps, significantly improving convergence in non-IID settings. Additionally, Mansour et al. [31] explored cluster-based FL, where clients with similar data distributions are grouped to share tailored global models, reducing the bias introduced by heterogeneous data. These approaches collectively improve ability of FL to handle diverse cycling behaviours and road conditions while maintaining scalability and efficiency.

The integration of multi-sensor data in FL is an emerging area with significant potential for cyclist behaviour modelling. Yuan et al. [28] propose FedMFS, which introduces a modality-specific gating mechanism, each client communicates only the most salient sensor information, thereby reducing bandwidth and handling missing modalities. Fusion can occur at data level, feature level, or decision level, often employing attention modules or ensemble methods to combine multiple sensor streams effectively. Feng et al. [7] highlight that decision-level fusion can be particularly robust when dealing with noisy or partially missing sensor data. Additionally, causal inference [22] has begun to play a role in multi-sensor FL, helping to distinguish genuine cause-effect relationships from spurious correlations that can arise when training is distributed. Tang et al. [25] show that sharing intermediate representations among clients can serve as a form of causal intervention, improving generalization across heterogeneous data sources. For cyclist behaviour, this might mean identifying crucial cues–such as a cyclist's hand signals in camera data combined with LiDAR-detected distance changes–that reliably indicate upcoming manoeuvres, rather than relying on correlations present only in a single client's local dataset.

3 Research Proposal

This section presents a FL-based approach for cyclist behaviour modelling, emphasizing *multi-sensor data fusion, robust representation learning, uncertainty estimation*, and *adaptive federated aggregation strategies*. The objective is to capture the complex, context-dependent nature of cyclist behaviour in dynamic traffic environments while addressing key challenges such as heterogeneous and non-IID data, noisy observations, and limited labelling resources. The following discussion outlines the research objectives, methodological framework, and essential technical components required to achieve these goals, along with strategies to bridge the performance gap between FL and centralized learning (CL).

3.1 Proposed Methodology

Representation Learning for Heterogeneous Data. A key focus of this research is developing representation learning techniques that are resilient to heterogeneous and non-IID data distributions. The following approaches will be explored:

- **Autoencoder-Based Pretraining:** Masked Autoencoders (MAEs) [12] will be evaluated for their effectiveness in handling sensor noise and missing data. By reconstructing partially corrupted inputs, these models learn robust latent features that encode cyclist appearance, motion, and contextual cues.
- **Contrastive and Causal Representation Learning:** Contrastive learning objectives [5,13], will be extended to FL to enhance feature disentanglement, separating relevant information from spurious correlations. Additionally, causal representation learning will be explored to identify key causal factors influencing abrupt manoeuvres or near-miss incidents, improving model interpretability and generalization.
- **Diffusion-Based Generative Models:** Recent advancements in diffusion models [11], suggest their potential for learning more flexible latent spaces. These models will be investigated for their ability to enhance underrepresented scenarios (e.g., rare conflict events) by generating synthetic samples, improving both local and federated training.

Uncertainty Estimation. Uncertainty estimation is integral to improving model robustness and decision-making in safety-critical scenarios. This study will incorporate the following techniques:

- **Dempster-Shafer Evidence Theory:** Evidential Learning [2,24], which based on evidence theory, will be applied to assess the reliability of sensor inputs and local model updates, particularly when handling missing or corrupted data.
- **Bayesian Neural Networks and MC Dropout:** Bayesian methods will be employed to quantify epistemic uncertainty, providing insights into model confidence when predicting cyclist intentions. MC Dropout offers a computationally scalable approximation to Bayesian inference, making it suitable for real-world FL deployments.
- **Direct Modelling of Aleatoric Uncertainty:** Explicit modules will be designed to capture aleatoric uncertainty arising from sensor variability and environmental factors. This will enable the model to appropriately downweight inherently noisy data points during federated aggregation, reducing the impact of unreliable observations.

FL and Adaptive Aggregation. Standard FL will be enhanced with novel aggregation strategies that account for data quality and heterogeneity:

- **Adaptive Weighting with Uncertainty:** A dynamic weighting mechanism will be incorporated into FedAvg [20], adjusting client contributions based on epistemic and aleatoric uncertainties. Clients with higher data quality and confidence will exert greater influence on the global model.
- **Representation-Level Aggregation:** Rather than naively averaging model parameters, alternative aggregation strategies will be explored, including fusing intermediate representations or encoder modules. This can mitigate disparities in local updates, particularly in cases of highly heterogeneous data distributions.
- **Local Fine-Tuning and Personalization:** To improve performance on rare or geographically specific cyclist behaviours, clients will perform local fine-tuning on top of the globally trained representation. These personalized adjustments will help refine behaviour prediction models based on region-specific riding patterns and environmental conditions.

Multi-Sensor Fusion in FL. Capturing the complexity of cyclist behaviour requires effective fusion of multi-sensor data. Two complementary architectures will be examined:

- **Sensor-Stack FL:** Each sensor modality (e.g., camera, LiDAR, IMU) will be treated as a separate client or client cluster, and their intermediate representations will be fused in a federated manner. This enables each modality to leverage global knowledge from other modalities while maintaining privacy by avoiding raw data exchange.

– **Unified Encoder FL:** Alternatively, all sensors within a single device will feed into a shared encoder, generating a holistic representation of the cyclist and surrounding environment. These multi-sensor encoders will then be aggregated across devices in the FL loop, ensuring consistency in fused feature spaces.

Balancing these two strategies will be essential to achieving robust, cross-modal feature extraction while maintaining communication efficiency in large-scale intelligent transportation system deployments.

3.2 Addressing Key Challenges

Low-Quality and Noisy Data: By modelling uncertainty (epistemic and aleatoric), our FL framework can automatically prioritize updates from high-quality data. Clients generating sparse or noisy samples will have diminished influence on the global model. In parallel, our representation learning objectives, particularly AEs–are designed to handle data corruption and missing sensor inputs by reconstructing clean signals.

Rare Events and Edge Cases: Learning from infrequent yet high-impact scenarios, such as sudden braking or cyclist-vehicle conflicts, requires an uncertainty-guided data selection strategy. Since rare events typically exhibit higher epistemic uncertainty, their contribution to global training will be amplified. This will be achieved through synthetic oversampling using diffusion models or by assigning higher weights in the loss function. Ensuring adequate representation of these critical corner cases in the federated model enhances predictive robustness in safety-critical situations.

Bridging the FL-CL Performance Gap: The limited local dataset on each client often slows down convergence and affects the final accuracy of FL. Two key strategies will be explored to mitigate this issue: (i) leveraging self-supervised representation learning techniques, such as contrastive learning and MAE, to improve feature extraction from limited data, and (ii) adopting alternative aggregation methods beyond naive parameter averaging. Representation-level or encoder-level aggregation will be investigated to stabilize training in highly non-IID scenarios, potentially reducing the performance gap between FL and CL.

Labelling Constraints in Realistic ITS Settings: Addressing the challenge of limited labelled data will involve self-supervised and weakly supervised learning strategies. Local encoders will be pre-trained using tasks such as masked reconstruction and instance discrimination (contrastive learning) before being aggregated at a global level. This approach minimizes dependence on manually labelled data while enabling the model to learn a rich feature space that captures essential cyclist traits. Once the global encoder is established, a small amount of labelled or pseudo-labelled data can be utilized for downstream tasks, including cyclist detection, trajectory prediction, and intention recognition.

3.3 Expected Contributions

This research aims to provide both scientific advancements and practical contributions in the field of intelligent transportation systems:

- **FL Framework for Non-IID Cyclist Data:** A FL solution specifically designed to handle the inherent heterogeneity of cyclist data, integrating uncertainty estimation at both local and global levels.
- **Enhanced Multi-Sensor Fusion in FL:** A systematic integration of camera, LiDAR, and IMU data, evaluating multiple fusion strategies (sensor-stack vs. unified encoder) that address privacy constraints while improving modelling accuracy.
- **Robust Representation Learning for Rare Events:** The application of causal and contrastive learning techniques, as well as diffusion-based generative models, to enhance the detection and modelling of rare but safety-critical cyclist behaviours.
- **Scalable and Efficient Deployment Strategies:** The adoption of self-supervised training and adaptive aggregation techniques to reduce reliance on high-quality labelled data while ensuring seamless scalability in large, distributed ITS environments with minimal data-sharing overhead.
- **Empirical Validation of FL in ITS:** Extensive benchmarking against centralized and existing federated baselines using real-world cyclist datasets, providing insights into the practical deployment of FL in sensor-rich traffic ecosystems.

4 Conclusion

By unifying multi-sensor fusion, robust representation learning, and adaptive federated aggregation, this research aims to enhance cyclist behaviour modelling in modern ITS. The integration of uncertainty estimation and causal reasoning is expected to improve the reliability and interpretability of predictions, which is crucial for safety-critical scenarios. The next phase of this research will involve extensive empirical evaluations on datasets representing diverse weather conditions, road infrastructures, and traffic environments. Additionally, domain adaptation techniques will be explored to enable knowledge transfer across cities with varying cycling cultures and regulatory frameworks. Ultimately, this study seeks to advance FL to a level where it can match or even surpass centralized approaches, offering privacy-preserving, high-precision behavioural models that contribute to safer and more efficient transportation systems.

Acknowledgments. This work was supervised by Prof. Dr. Bernhard Sick and Dr. Franz Götz-Hahn. It was supported by the project "DyNaMo: Sichere und Nachhaltige MobilitÃďt in der Stadt von morgen – Wie hilft KÃijnstliche Intelligenz der Radverkehrssicherheit?", funded by the Hessian State Ministry for Higher Education, Research, Science and the Arts (HMWK) as part of the LOEWE program (Kapitel 15 02, Förderbuchungskreis 2995, Förderprodukt 11 - Landes-Offensive zur Entwicklung Wissenschaftlich-ökonomischer Exzellenz).

References

1. Alsulaimawi, Z.A.H.: Meta-fl: a novel meta-learning framework for optimizing heterogeneous model aggregation in federated learning (2024). https://doi.org/10.48550/arXiv.2406.16035
2. Amini, A., Schwarting, W., Soleimany, A., Rus, D.: Deep evidential regression (2020). https://arxiv.org/abs/1910.02600
3. Chang, H., Gu, Y., Goncharenko, I., Hsu, L.T., Premachandra, C.: Cyclist orientation estimation using lidar data. Sensors **23**, 3096 (2023). https://doi.org/10.3390/s23063096
4. Chellapandi, V.P., Yuan, L., Brinton, C.G., Zak, S.H., Wang, Z.: Federated learning for connected and automated vehicles: a survey of existing approaches and challenges (2023). https://arxiv.org/abs/2308.10407
5. Chen, T., Kornblith, S., Norouzi, M., Hinton, G.: A simple framework for contrastive learning of visual representations (2020). https://arxiv.org/abs/2002.05709
6. Collins, L., Hassani, H., Mokhtari, A., Shakkottai, S.: Exploiting shared representations for personalized federated learning (2021). https://doi.org/10.48550/arXiv.2102.07078
7. Feng, T., et al.: Fedmultimodal: a benchmark for multimodal federated learning (2023). https://doi.org/10.1145/3580305.3599825
8. Gal, Y., Ghahramani, Z.: Dropout as a bayesian approximation: Representing model uncertainty in deep learning. In: Proceedings of The 33rd International Conference on Machine Learning (2015)
9. Gao, H., et al.: Trajectory prediction of cyclist based on dynamic Bayesian network and long short-term memory model at unsignalized intersections. Science China Inf. Sci. **64**(7), 1–13 (2021). https://doi.org/10.1007/s11432-020-3071-8
10. Girshick, R.: Fast r-cnn (2015). https://doi.org/10.1109/ICCV.2015.169
11. de Goede, M., Cox, B., Decouchant, J.: Training diffusion models with federated learning (2024). https://arxiv.org/abs/2406.12575
12. He, K., Chen, X., Xie, S., Li, Y., Dollár, P., Girshick, R.: Masked autoencoders are scalable vision learners (2021). https://doi.org/10.48550/arXiv.2111.06377
13. He, K., Fan, H., Wu, Y., Xie, S., Girshick, R.: Momentum contrast for unsupervised visual representation learning (2020). https://arxiv.org/abs/1911.05722
14. Huang, K., Shi, B., Li, X., Li, X., Huang, S., Li, Y.: Multi-modal sensor fusion for auto driving perception: a survey (2022). https://doi.org/10.48550/arXiv.2202.02703
15. Kress, V., Jung, J., Zernetsch, S., Doll, K., Sick, B.: Start intention detection of cyclists using an lstm network (2019). https://doi.org/10.18420/inf2019_ws25
16. Li, M., Chen, T., Du, H.: Trajectory prediction of cyclist based on spatialâĂŘtemporal multiâĂŘgraph network in crowded scenarios. Electron. Lett. **58** (2021).https://doi.org/10.1049/ell2.12374
17. Li, X., Afghari, A., Oviedo-Trespalacios, O., Kaye, S.A., Haworth, N.: Cyclists perception and self-reported behaviour towards interacting with fully automated vehicles. Transp. Res. Part A Policy Practice **173**, 103713 (2023). https://doi.org/10.1016/j.tra.2023.103713
18. Linsner, F., Adilova, L., Däubener, S., Kamp, M., Fischer, A.: Approaches to uncertainty quantification in federated deep learning, pp. 128–145 (2021). https://doi.org/10.1007/978-3-030-93736-2_12

19. Ma, H., Yuan, X., Ding, Z., Fan, D., Fang, J.: Over-the-air federated multi-task learning via model sparsification, random compression, and turbo compressed sensing. IEEE Trans. Wireless Commun. **PP**, 1–1 (2022).https://doi.org/10.1109/TWC.2022.3231088
20. McMahan, H.B., Moore, E., Ramage, D., Hampson, S., y Arcas, B.A.: Communication-efficient learning of deep networks from decentralized data (2023). https://arxiv.org/abs/1602.05629
21. Pokhrel, S., Choi, J.: A decentralized federated learning approach for connected autonomous vehicles (2020). https://doi.org/10.1109/WCNCW48565.2020.9124733
22. Prosperi, M., et al.: Causal inference and counterfactual prediction in machine learning for actionable healthcare. Nat. Mach. Intell. **2**, 1–7 (2020). https://doi.org/10.1038/s42256-020-0197-y
23. Qi, J., Luan, Z., Huang, S., Fung, C., Yang, H., Qian, D.: Fdlora: personalized federated learning of large language model via dual lora tuning (2024). https://doi.org/10.48550/arXiv.2406.07925
24. Sensoy, M., Kaplan, L., Kandemir, M.: Evidential deep learning to quantify classification uncertainty (2018). https://arxiv.org/abs/1806.01768
25. Tang, Z., et al.: Fusefl: one-shot federated learning through the lens of causality with progressive model fusion (2024). https://doi.org/10.48550/arXiv.2410.20380
26. Tomforde, S., Sick, B., Müller-Schloer, C.: Organic computing in the spotlight (2017). https://arxiv.org/abs/1701.08125
27. Wang, K., Zhou, W.: Pedestrian and cyclist detection based on deep neural network fast r-CNN. Int. J. Adv. Robot. Syst. **16** (2019). https://doi.org/10.1177/1729881419829651
28. Yuan, L., Han, D.J., Pandi, V., Zak, S., Brinton, C.: Fedmfs: federated multimodal fusion learning with selective modality communication, pp. 287–292 (2024). https://doi.org/10.1109/ICC51166.2024.10622194
29. Zeng, Y., Liu, L., Liu, S., Dou, H., Wu, B., Liu, L.: Reliable imputed-sample assisted vertical federated learning (2025). https://doi.org/10.48550/arXiv.2501.06429
30. Zhang, R., Wang, H., Li, B., Cheng, X., Yang, L.: A survey on federated learning in intelligent transportation systems (2024). https://arxiv.org/abs/2403.07444
31. Zhang, S., et al.: Cluster-hsfl: a cluster-based hybrid split and federated learning, pp. 1–2 (2023). https://doi.org/10.1109/ICCC57788.2023.10233408

Self-Explanation of System Behaviour in Organic Computing Systems

Svea Wisy[✉][iD]

Intelligent Systems Group, Kiel University, Kiel, Germany
svea.wisy@informatik.uni-kiel.de

Abstract. Self-explainability is seen as an enabler for a broad acceptance of Organic Computing (OC) systems and the overarching field of self-adaptive and self-organising (SASO) systems within industry and society. Organic Traffic Control (OTC) is a system following the OC design principles to establish a self-adaptive and self-learning traffic management of intersection controllers in urban environments. Nevertheless, it is missing the self-explanation property. A step-by-step approach to self-explanation includes detecting the necessity for an explanation, then finding a cause for the observed behaviour, and finally translating the results in a good explanation for the different groups of users. We propose our research plan to utilise incident detection and classification to enable self-explainability in OTC. Additionally, we aim to generalise from our findings to enable self-explainability in multiple different SASO systems.

Keywords: self-explainability · SASO systems · traffic control · organic computing

1 Introduction

Technical systems become increasingly complex [18]. This results in problems with their overall controllability and maintainability. Especially, the effort for configuring these systems increases with their complexity. Researchers provide self-adaptive and self-organising (SASO) systems to solve these problems by adding autonomous behaviour [14] like self-adaptation, which is often also called self-configuration [26]. The SASO capabilities of these systems allow for the system to adapt itself during runtime, lowering the pressure on engineers to foresee every possible circumstance at design time [18]. This self-adaptation releases some of the pressure when configuring a complex system, but it does not necessarily help the controllability and maintainability of the system. The Organic Computing (OC) community argues that SASO systems are designed to be robust due to their self-management characteristic. Additionally, there are more self-* properties [26] that can reduce the need for maintenance in complex systems such as self-healing, self-protecting, and self-stabilising.

During the past years, multiple authors in the domain of OC expressed the need for self-explainability in complex systems [2,6,9,10]. While some of the works express the need for self-explainability rather implicitly [9], especially the work of Calinescu et al. [6] summarises the call for self-explainability from multiple of the respondents of their survey in a very direct manner. Additionally, self-explainability is seen as an enabler for broader acceptance of complex systems within industry and society [1,4,5,7,8,10].

Due to its complexity, traffic management is a challenging scenario for OC systems as it is highly dynamic, and considers mutual influences, such as local intersection-oriented objectives and global town-wide objectives. Systems that are robust to these influences and dynamics are crucial for traffic safety. Thus, self-adaptivity as seen in SASO systems and, more specific OC systems, is a reasonable way to face the dynamics of traffic control. One prominent example system from the OC domain is Organic Traffic Control (OTC) [24].

OTC is a fully decentralised intelligent traffic management system founded on the principles of OC [16]. The system optimises the signalling of traffic light controllers at run-time with respect to the current traffic conditions. This includes not only optimisation at single junctions but also communication between neighbouring junctions to establish a Progressive Signaling System (PSS) which result in "Green Waves" [25]. Additionally, OTC includes a prediction mechanism to predict future traffic patterns, making OTC faster in adapting to upcoming congestion [20].

We plan to enable self-explanation in intelligent traffic management systems by utilising anomaly detection and classification. Here, we use anomaly detection to detect abnormal situations which require an explanation. Causes for anomalies in traffic scenarios include full or partial lane closure but also closed intersections. Often, these abnormal situations in urban traffic management scenarios are caused by incidents. Hence, anomaly detection in traffic scenarios is also referred to as incident detection [23]. We propose six steps to enable self-explanations in intelligent traffic management systems:

- Observing the system
- Detecting abnormal situations
- Deciding if a situation needs an explanation
- Finding causes
- Generating a self-explanation
- Transmitting the explanation to the relevant users

The remainder of this paper is structured as follows: Sect. 2 gives a preliminary literature review on related work in the field of explainability in SASO systems. Section 3 presents our over all research plan, structured into the main challenges we are facing and the actual research questions we are considering. Section 4 introduces our evaluation scenario system, OTC, in more detail. Finally, we conclude this paper with a concise summary in Sect. 5.

2 Related Work

Multiple authors identify explainability as a desirable characteristic for complex systems such as SASO systems. They motivate explainability of systems for different scenarios. Some of them are autonomous service robots [7], vacuum robots and a flood detecting grid [4], autonomous racing vehicles [28], intelligent traffic control [27], and smart homes [8,10]. Accordingly, there are multiple different approaches to enable explainability in systems where most of the approaches are model-based [4,7,8,10,13,27] while the authors of [28] propose a data-driven approach using anomaly detection and classification.

There are different domains that approach explainability from the different points of their current research. For example, in [4,5,12] the authors use requirement models of their systems to explain their systems' behaviour. Additionally, the authors of [5,8,10] propose approaches using causality models. Both of the approaches in [5] need developers to know all possible causes for explanations at design time. Differently, the authors of [8] build an adaptive causal model from an initial hard-coded model which is used by the Local Explanation Components (LECs) in another approach named Spotlight [10]. Another approach is offered by the authors of [7]. They propose a design flow for self-explainable systems, which uses an abstract model and a formal model of the system to derive explanations from, with the intention to use self-explanations as an intermediate step to finally enable self-verification.

The approach of Ziesche et al. [28] uses anomaly detection to detect system states where the system under observation performs abnormal. They use the output of the anomaly detection algorithm to trigger a classifier which categorises input parameters into classes of causes. These input parameters need to be selected cautiously because too many parameters increase the complexity of the classifier, while a too small amount of different parameters might not be able to represent the system's behaviour and its context.

While any model of an intelligent traffic management system might grow large due to the complexity of the system, anomaly detection and classification seem feasible. Nevertheless, traffic control is a more complex scenario than the scenario used in [28]. Their approach also highlights the necessity to foresee every possible class of causes at design time and additionally, the necessity to perform the feature selection in a way that is highly specific to the application.

Overall, to the best of our knowledge, there is no common uniform approach in the literature for self-explainability in neither OC systems nor SASO systems. Moreover, there is also no common definition or uniform understanding of self-explainability, making it hard to discuss the topic over multiple contributions from different authors.

3 Research Design

Since SASO systems and their control problems are very diverse in themselves, we restrict our focus to urban traffic control and management in the first place and then aim at transferring the insights and technology to related domains with the vision of partial generalisation.

The goal of this doctoral project is to research ways on how to establish self-explanation for SASO systems while providing an accurate mapping of abnormal conditions to probable causes.

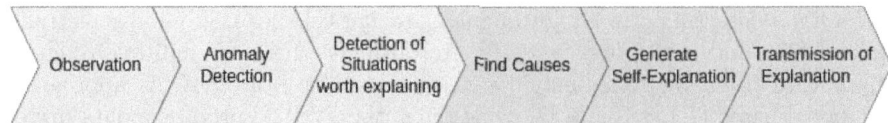

Fig. 1. Six steps to self-explanation, where the left blue block corresponds to the research challenge "Detect Behaviour' and the right violet block corresponds to the research challenge "From Behaviour to Self-Explanations".(Color figure online)

To reach this goal, one needs an increased self-reflection of the SASO system. We approach this by enabling them to automatically identify reasons for their behaviour, and restrict ourselves to explaining the system behaviour from observations and reflection, rather than analysing the underlying machine learning model. Hence, we aim to find causes for the system behaviour from observation and reflection, and then turn these causes into self-explanations of the performed actions.

3.1 Research Challenges

We identify four groups of research challenges to address the research problem:

State of the Art. For the start, we want to systematically analyse the current technical state in the field. As pointed out in [15], keywords in the context of interpretability are not well-defined and used inconsistently by different authors throughout the literature. The keywords in the context of interpretability are similar to the ones used in the context of explainability and self-explainability. According to Arrieta et al. [3] the terms interpretability and explainability are often used interchangeably in the literature regarding eXplainable Artificial Intelligence (XAI). Although we do not aim for classical XAI, we encounter the same problem of heavily but at least partially differently used vocabulary when searching the literature for the state of the art concerning self-explanations of behaviour in SASO systems.

Detect Behaviour. To enable explanations of SASO systems, one needs to detect conditions and behaviour that need an explanation. This is usually the case when a system performs differently than expected. Therefore, we plan on doing incident detection in the existing SASO system OTC [21]. According to Thomsen et al. [22], incident detection in OTC affects the decisions of the PSS algorithm. The algorithm establishes"Green Waves" between multiple crossings in an urban traffic network [25]. Thus, we aim to detect incidents in order to explain the difference in its decision. We marked the necessary steps in blue in Fig. 1.

From Behaviour to Self-Explanations. Once we detect the conditions and the behaviour that need an explanation, we aim to establish an accurate mapping between the behaviour and the corresponding cause. By that time, we need to know our precise definition of a self-explanation in our context, and what a self-explanation should be composed of. We then use these causes and possibly additional components to build a self-explanation from within our SASO system. We marked these steps violet in Fig. 1.

Self-Explainability Framework. The final goal is a robust self-explainability framework that can be used with SASO systems in different domains. The OC community utilises the implementation of self-* properties in their systems to make the system robust to dynamic changes. Thus, we aim to implement self-* properties in our final self-explainability framework. One of them is self-adaption, or self-configuration, as we want our system to adapt to dynamics in the environment. Additionally, a self-explanation framework should be self-stabilising because frequently changing the explanation for similar behaviour may lead to distrust of users into our framework.

3.2 Research Questions

These challenges lead us to more detailed research questions, starting with the first research challenge as the first two questions:

Question 1. What is the state of the art concerning self-explanation of the behaviour of SASO systems?

Question 2. Which components are necessary to build a good self-explanation?

Both research questions represent the state of the art. While the first one directly asks for the state of the art, the second one asks for the definition or the building blocks of a self-explanation. Answering both questions enables following a more straight line to the final research goal, because they let us summarise the main similarities and differences between the existing approaches, and let us clarify which of the existing approaches go in the direction of our problem.

In the next research challenge, we focus on detecting conditions and behaviour that need explanations. Therefore, we plan to observe the system, detect abnormal conditions, and decide if the conditions require an explanation. Essentially, this challenge leaves us with the following questions:

Question 3. What are conditions and behaviour of a traffic control system that need an explanation?

Question 4. How can these conditions be detected automatically and adapted dynamically in response to external feedback?

Question 5. How to decide if a condition requires an explanation for a user?

Questions 5 can also be seen as a part of the next challenge, because it not only answers if specific conditions require an explanation, but it also implicitly includes that different users may require explanations for different conditions. For example, a human driving a car might need explanations regarding a red light, while the human administrator of the system needs an explanation why the system did or did not generate an explanation for the other human user. From our initial six steps, this maps to transmitting the self-explanation to the relevant users, which is one of the three steps we conclude in the third challenge block. The other two steps are: Finding causes, and generating a self-explanation. Here, the answers for question 2 come in handy. As we already know which components build a self-explanation and which user groups need which explanations, there are two questions left:

Question 6. How to map causes to behaviour that needs to be explained?

Question 7. How can this process of generating self-explanations be optimised using experiences?

Finally, we are left with one additional question, highlighting the desire to generalise from our findings:

Question 8. Which characteristics of intelligent traffic management define a class of systems where we can apply our (adapted) approach?

Here, we want to generalise from our approach by finding a class of SASO systems apart from intelligent traffic management scenarios where our approach is applicable or is applicable if it is slightly adapted.

4 Evaluation Scenario

Urban traffic is very complex and dynamic due to multiple different participants with different objectives and large interdependent networks. This makes predictions of future traffic states of the network hard to achieve, and hardens the problem on finding the best fitting traffic control strategy [11]. Hence, urban traffic control is an interesting field for research projects. Accordingly, there are multiple centralised and decentralised approaches to urban traffic control. One of the decentralised approaches with roots in the OC community is OTC [21].

OTC is a decentralised but not strictly local approach which follows the Multi-Level Observer/Controller (MLOC) architecture as described in [24] and shown in Fig. 2. It consists of a fully local component [17] and collaboration mechanisms with neighbouring intersection controllers [24]. The fully local component can make decisions about the intersection's signal plan based on the situation at the intersection. Therefore, non-conflicting turnings of an intersection are combined into one signal group, as illustrated in Fig. 3 [24]. This, on the one hand, reduces the action space of OTC but on the other hand the signal groups add safety to the system. Induction loops in the lanes, or video cameras, serve as a base to the situation description in the observer at Layer 1. This enables the controller in Layer 1 of OTC to optimise the signal plan of the traffic light controller at Layer 0 according to the current traffic conditions. In Layer 2 of the MLOC architecture, OTC includes an evolutionary algorithm and the Aimsun traffic simulator [19] to generate new rules for the Learning Classifier System (LCS) in Layer 1 if necessary [21].

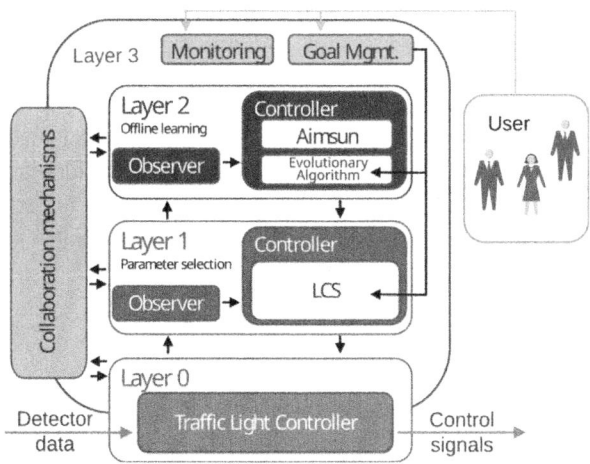

Fig. 2. MLOC architecture as adapted for OTC. The figure is adapted from [24].

The collaboration mechanisms allow for some integration of the neighbourhood into the decision on a local intersection, and add collaboration and coordination between the neighbouring intersections. Those collaboration mechanisms include two mechanisms which together establish PSSs over multiple intersections. Additionally, the third layer of OTC provides a mechanism for driver information and a route guidance mechanism to the users of OTC [24].

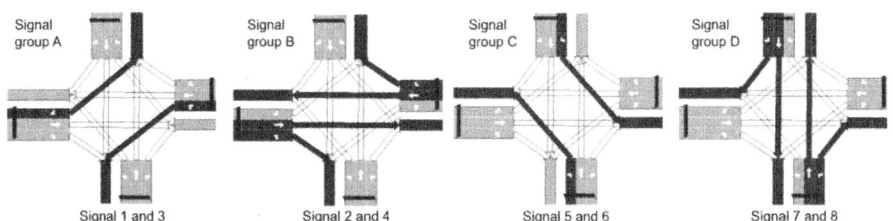

Fig. 3. An exemplary intersection with four signal groups from [24]. The darker connected turnings are the ones that receive the right of way together. The smaller dark rectangles on the lanes represent the detectors in the lanes.

The route guidance and driver information components enable direct interaction with users that have a very limited understanding of the underlying system.

Thus, they are a good reason to enhance OTC by adding self-explainability to the system. But also the fully local main component of OTC affects the participants in the urban traffic. Here, it may be even harder for the users to anticipate why an intersection controller behaves in a certain way. For example, they might wonder why the red phase on their lane is a lot longer compared to the red phase on another lane. This might be due to a lot of traffic coming from another direction, but it could also be due to a prioritised stream over multiple intersections that leads to the effect. Another user group that might need explanations are traffic engineers that manage traffic in a city. They might wonder why OTC creates a certain PSS in a specific situation instead of some other PSS that they would have created. So there are multiple different user groups, for example there are drivers, bikers, pedestrian, traffic engineers, and local residents. Those groups have different needs for explanations, e.g. when and how they want to perceive an explanation. Correspondingly, the target group of a system's self-explanation can have an impact on the way we create the explanation.

5 Summary

The task of enabling self-explanation in SASO systems with a focus on intelligent traffic management requires a concept that can handle complex distributed technical systems. Finding the research we are going for in the literature is hard, as the same keywords are used differently by different authors within the domain and are additionally used outside our domain as well. We propose our vision on how to enable self-explanation in SASO systems to improve their acceptance by human users and to decrease the weight on system administrators when maintaining the system. Therefore, we provided our eight research questions in Sect. 3.2 corresponding to the four core challenges we discussed in Sect. 3.1 and representing the six steps we introduced in Sect. 1 plus two additional steps.

For our next steps, we approach the first challenge with a comprehensive literature review in order to derive some of the core definitions needed for the future research. Additionally, we plan on sorting the existing literature into meaningful categories. Then, we can easier move on to the next challenges on anomaly detection, classification, and generating explanations for the behaviour of OTC, and other SASO systems.

References

1. Afchar, D., Melchiorre, A.B., Schedl, M., Hennequin, R., Epure, E.V., Moussallam, M.: Explainability in music recommender systems. AI Mag. **43**(2), 190–208 (2022). https://doi.org/10.1002/aaai.12056
2. Al-Falouji, G., Haschke, L., Nowotka, D., Tomforde, S.: Self-explanation as a basis for self-integration - the autonomous passenger ferry scenario. In: 2023 IEEE International Conference on Autonomic Computing and Self-Organizing Systems Companion (ACSOS-C), pp. 65–70 (2023). https://doi.org/10.1109/ACSOS-C58168.2023.00038

3. Barredo Arrieta, A., et al.: Explainable artificial intelligence (XAI): Concepts, taxonomies, opportunities and challenges toward responsible AI. Inform. Fusion **58**, 82–115 (2020). https://doi.org/10.1016/j.inffus.2019.12.012
4. Bencomo, N., Welsh, K., Sawyer, P., Whittle, J.: Self-explanation in adaptive systems. In: 2012 IEEE 17th International Conference on Engineering of Complex Computer Systems, pp. 157–166 (2012). https://doi.org/10.1109/ICECCS20050.2012.6299211
5. Blumreiter, M., et al.: Towards self-explainable cyber-physical systems (2019). https://doi.org/10.48550/arXiv.1908.04698
6. Calinescu, R., Mirandola, R., Perez-Palacin, D., Weyns, D.: Understanding uncertainty in self-adaptive systems. In: 2020 IEEE International Conference on Autonomic Computing and Self-Organizing Systems (ACSOS), pp. 242–251 (2020). https://doi.org/10.1109/ACSOS49614.2020.00047
7. Drechsler, R., Lüth, C., Fey, G., Güneysu, T.: Towards self-explaining digital systems: a design methodology for the next generation. In: 2018 IEEE 3rd International Verification and Security Workshop (IVSW), pp. 1–6 (2018). https://doi.org/10.1109/IVSW.2018.8494900
8. Fadiga, K., Houzé, E., Diaconescu, A., Dessalles, J.L.: To do or not to do: finding causal relations in smart homes. In: 2021 IEEE International Conference on Autonomic Computing and Self-Organizing Systems (ACSOS), pp. 110–119 (2021). https://doi.org/10.1109/ACSOS52086.2021.00030
9. Goller, M., Tomforde, S.: Identifying adaptation changes in collections of self-adaptive systems. In: 2022 IEEE International Conference on Autonomic Computing and Self-Organizing Systems Companion (ACSOS-C), pp. 101–106 (2022). https://doi.org/10.1109/ACSOSC56246.2022.00041
10. Houzé, E., Diaconescu, A., Dessalles, J.L., Menga, D.: A generic and modular reference architecture for self-explainable smart homes. In: 2022 IEEE International Conference on Autonomic Computing and Self-Organizing Systems (ACSOS), pp. 101–110 (2022). https://doi.org/10.1109/ACSOS55765.2022.00028
11. Ji, Q., Wen, X., Jin, J., Zhu, Y., Lv, Y.: Urban traffic control meets decision recommendation system: a survey and perspective. IEEE/CAA J. Automatica Sinica **11**(10), 2043–2058 (2024). https://doi.org/10.1109/JAS.2024.124659
12. Khalid, N., Qureshi, N.A.: Towards Self-Explainable Adaptive Systems (SEAS): A Requirements Driven Approach. REFSQ Workshops 2021 (2021)
13. Kounev, S., et al.: The Notion of Self-aware Computing (2017). https://doi.org/10.1007/978-3-319-47474-8_1
14. Krupitzer, C., Roth, F.M., VanSyckel, S., Schiele, G., Becker, C.: A survey on engineering approaches for self-adaptive systems. Pervasive Mob. Comput. **17**, 184–206 (2015). https://doi.org/10.1016/j.pmcj.2014.09.009
15. Lipton, Z.C.: In machine learning, the concept of interpretability is both important and slippery. Mach. Learn. (2018)
16. Prothmann, H., et al.: Decentralised route guidance in organic traffic control. In: 2011 IEEE Fifth International Conference on Self-Adaptive and Self-Organizing Systems, pp. 219–220 (2011). https://doi.org/10.1109/SASO.2011.34, iSSN: 1949-3681
17. Prothmann, H., et al.: Organic control of traffic lights. In: Rong, C., Jaatun, M.G., Sandnes, F.E., Yang, L.T., Ma, J. (eds.) ATC 2008. LNCS, vol. 5060, pp. 219–233. Springer, Heidelberg (2008). https://doi.org/10.1007/978-3-540-69295-9_19
18. Sheard, S., et al.: A complexity primer for systems engineers. INCOSE Complex Systems Working Group White Paper **1**(1), 1–10 (2015)

19. SLU, A.: Aimsun Home (2025). https://www.aimsun.com/de/
20. Sommer, M., Tomforde, S., Hähner, J.: Using a neural network for forecasting in an organic trafiñĄc control management system. In: International Workshop on Embedded Self-Organizing Systems (ESOS '13), June 2l5, 2013, San Jose, CA, part of the 10th International Comference on Autonomic Computing (ICAC '13) (2013)
21. Sommer, M., Tomforde, S., Hähner, J.: An organic computing approach to resilient traffic management. In: McCluskey, T.L., Kotsialos, A., Müller, J.P., Klügl, F., Rana, O., Schumann, R. (eds.) Autonomic Road Transport Support Systems. AS, pp. 113–130. Springer, Cham (2016). https://doi.org/10.1007/978-3-319-25808-9_7
22. Thomsen, I., Tomforde, S.: Decision tree based incident detection for distributed progressive signal system in an organic traffic control system. In: Klein, C., Jarke, M., Ploeg, J., Berns, K., Vinel, A., Gusikhin, O. (eds.) Smart Cities, Green Technologies, and Intelligent Transport Systems, pp. 167–183. Springer Nature Switzerland, Cham (2025). https://doi.org/10.1007/978-3-031-70966-1_8
23. Thomsen, I., Zapfe, Y., Tomforde, S.: Urban traffic incident detection for organic traffic control: a density-based clustering approach. In: Proceedings of the 7th International Conference on Vehicle Technology and Intelligent Transport Systems, pp. 152–160. SCITEPRESS - Science and Technology Publications, Online Streaming, — Select a Country — (2021). https://doi.org/10.5220/0010454101520160
24. Tomforde, S.: An architectural framework for self-configuration and self-improvement at runtime. Südwestdeutscher Verlag für Hochschulschriften (2012)
25. Tomforde, S., et al.: Decentralised progressive signal systems for organic traffic control. In: 2008 Second IEEE International Conference on Self-Adaptive and Self-Organizing Systems, pp. 413–422 (2008). https://doi.org/10.1109/SASO.2008.31, iSSN: 1949-3681
26. Tomforde, S., Sick, B., Müller-Schloer, C.: Organic Computing in the Spotlight (2017). https://arxiv.org/abs/1701.08125v1
27. Wollenstein-Betech, S., Muise, C., Cassandras, C.G., Paschalidis, I.C., Khazaeni, Y.: Explainability of intelligent transportation systems using knowledge compilation: a traffic light controller case. In: 2020 IEEE 23rd International Conference on Intelligent Transportation Systems (ITSC), pp. 1–6 (2020). https://doi.org/10.1109/ITSC45102.2020.9294213
28. Ziesche, F., Klös, V., Glesner, S.: Anomaly detection and classification to enable self-explainability of autonomous systems. In: 2021 Design, Automation & Test in Europe Conference & Exhibition (DATE), pp. 1304–1309 (2021). https://doi.org/10.23919/DATE51398.2021.9474232, iSSN: 1558-1101

Enhancing Dynamic Scene Understanding in Manual Assembly Processes

Chenxi Guo

University of Applied Sciences Aschaffenburg, Würzburger Straße 45,
Aschaffenburg 63743, Germany
Chenxi.Guo@th-ab.de

Abstract. In modern industrial manufacturing, manual assembly remains essential. Expert assistance systems have been developed for some areas but lack flexibility and the ability to perceive dynamic working scenes. A deeper and more comprehensive understanding of the entire working scene within an assembly cell enables the development of more complex and advanced assistance features. By integrating promising deep learning techniques, the expert assistance system will automatically capture and analyze assembly operations, providing appropriate guidance and error detection. This paper focuses on leveraging advanced large models and multiple data modalities, enhancing the expert systems' ability to understand complex and dynamic assembly scenes.

Keywords: Scene Understanding · Manual assembly · Expert Assistance Systems · Representation Learning · Semi-Supervised Learning

1 Introduction

Manual assembly plays a crucial role in modern manufacturing by enabling flexible, small-batch production to meet diverse customer demands. Unlike large-scale industrial assembly systems designed for specific tasks, it fits high-variance, low-volume production scenarios, requiring operators to adapt to varying components and procedures. However, frequent changes in assembly content increase workers' cognitive burden [13]. Normally, workers only undergo short training, even for complex tasks. However, assembly speed, quality, and loss of parts significantly affect the product competitiveness [12]. Therefore, a smart assistance system is needed to monitor, perceive, and characterize work scenarios and assist workers in improving efficiency and reducing errors in complex tasks. An accurate understanding of the working context is particularly critical. Camera-captured scenes provide a wealth of visual information, but relying solely on video recordings to monitor and manage the entire assembly process is impractical, as manually reviewing full video recordings is time-consuming and labor-intensive. Thus, an expert system must be able to accurately perceive and understand scenes, automatically track assembly progress, and prevent potential errors. Current research typically focuses on the worker's upper body, especially hand movement recognition during assembly tasks [28]. Recent advancements in Vision Language Models (VLMs) and Large Language Models (LLMs) offer the potential for more intelligent and efficient scene understanding, including but not limited to automatically tracking specific regions of interest, analyzing human-object interactions, and verifying the actual steps in the assembly process. Therefore, our research aims to address the following limitations:

(1) Despite the zero-shot capabilities of VLMs, the high computational cost severely limits their applicability in real-world, high-resolution industrial scenarios.
(2) The complexity of diverse assembly environments limits the generalization of visual models, which often rely on task-specific training conditions, making it hard to understand human actions and assembly states in various real-world settings.
(3) Understanding human-object interactions (HOI) and predicting future actions remain challenging. Human actions are highly continuous and complex, making it difficult to analyze behaviors from a single image. Moreover, models struggle to effectively utilize the spatial and temporal context of actions, limiting their ability to comprehensively understand the dynamic assembly process and anticipate future steps.
(4) Typical assembly expert systems employ predefined operational instructions and rely on a single source of information. When confronted with complex assembly tasks with limited guidance capability, they are incapable of providing adaptive, validated, and optimized operational instructions.

2 Relation to Organic Computing

The paper is related to organic computing (OC) and provides a foundation for two key domains. The first is Adaptability, the expert assistance system should adapt to different assembly tasks, user habits or preferences, and changes in the workspace. For example, if a work step or component in the assembly process changes, the system should be able to update its computational approaches accordingly without the need for a complete reprogramming. The second is Self-Organization, inspired by OC, the assistance system uses self-supervised and unsupervised learning methods to automatically organize data, extract patterns from unstructured, unlabeled data. An accurate understanding of complex and dynamic real-world scenes is crucial for both tasks.

3 State of the Art

Scene Understanding in Industry. Scene understanding is a core task in computer vision, essential for recognizing and comprehending elements in a scene. Beyond its critical role in robotics, autonomous driving, and smart cities, it also benefits expert assistance systems and industrial production. By leveraging advanced sensing technologies, expert assistance systems enhance human behavior analysis, boosting efficiency, accuracy, and adaptability in customized industrial manufacturing. Recent deep learning methods have driven notable progress in 2D and 3D scene understanding. Below are some cutting-edge systems for vision-based understanding from different levels in industrial scenarios:

Object perception: Studies such as [8,11,36] aim to classify objects like tools and industrial parts and identify their affordances based on their usage and attributes. Meanwhile, CNN-based detection models, including the YOLO series [6] and R-CNN series, perform well in locating objects of interest and extracting their positions in industrial settings. Furthermore, research in [4,33,38], etc., promotes 6-DoF pose estimation, which enables precise postures estimation of industrial parts by mapping between 3D object models and sensory observations.

Human recognition: Based on data captured by RGB-Depth cameras, studies such as [3,14,23] utilize both spatial and temporal information to distinguish actions with similar poses but differing in velocity or orientation. Meanwhile, [17,18] focuses on fine-grained human posture analysis, particularly dynamic hand gesture recognition.

Environment parsing: To achieve comprehensive workspace perception, 2D maps [9] and 3D representations, such as 3D point clouds in [18], provide abundant environmental information for finer-grained environment parsing.

Visual reasoning: Integrating object, human, and environment perception can provide a holistic understanding of industrial scenes. Recent studies, such as [1,37], introduce human language as a reasoning cue, combining linguistic and visual features for workspace image parsing. Meanwhile, [35] addresses explanatory Visual Question Answering (VQA) in industrial scenarios, while [32] leverages the reasoning ability of VLMs to accelerate multimodal perception and commonsense cognition.

Expert Assistance Systems. Modern commercial assistance systems in the market improve productivity and accuracy in the manufacturing process. For example, RFID and code scanning enable quick and accurate component identification, while tool integration, such as screwdriver control and localization, ensures precise and consistent fastening. Interactive work instructions and Pick-to-light functionality further streamline workflow guidance, and Real-time visualization tools provide immediate feedback to workers. Based on existing commercial systems, AI-powered assistance systems could integrate scene understanding mentioned in Sect. 3 for better working environments parsing and human behavior analysis and deploying sensor networks to enable real-time workflow analysis and error detection. Techniques like semantic segmentation and template matching automate assembly verification, improving detection efficiency and traceability. The following is an overview of promising state-of-the-art assistance systems for manual assembly cells:

Digital Twin Verification Systems [21]: These systems construct a Physical Twin (PT) to represent the real-world assembly and a Digital Twin (DT) for its ideal state. A part is mapped to the DT only if it is correctly assembled, with PT–DT mismatches indicating errors. This part-centric, verification-driven approach enhances accuracy and efficiency in manual assembly.

Augmented Reality (AR) Assistance Systems [24]: AR systems use depth cameras to track worker movements and provide real-time guidance through projection-based, wearable, or handheld displays. By reducing errors and boosting productivity, these systems support both training and on-site assembly tasks.

Collaborative Robots (Cobots) [7]: Cobots are designed to collaborate with humans, supporting them in manual assembly tasks. They can handle repetitive or physically strenuous work, allowing humans to concentrate on more complex tasks that require critical thinking and decision-making skills.

Wearable Assistance Systems [22]: Wearable systems provide workers with sensory feedback or haptic cues. Leveraging technologies such as vibrotactile stimulation or auditory prompts, these systems enhance precision and efficiency by offering real-time guidance.

Computer Vision Assistance Systems (CVAS) [40]: Computer vision systems can recognize and track objects and assist workers in assembling them. These systems utilize different technologies, including depth sensors and RGB cameras, to detect objects.

4 Research Questions

This section outlines the research gaps and corresponding key questions, focusing on scene understanding challenges in complex assembly environments and potential solutions to improve visual perception (see RQ1, RQ2, RQ3) and the effectiveness of expert assistance systems (see RQ4).

4.1 RQ1: How to Accelerate VLM-Based Scene Understanding in Assembly Processes by Preserving Task-Relevant Visual Details While Reducing Redundant Information?

VLMs like CLIP and DINOv2 [20,25] have attracted significant attention for their ability to generate robust visual features for unseen data without task-specific training, making them well-suited for flexible, undefined scenarios beyond pre-defined workflows. However, VLMs require intensive computation to generate high-quality representations, especially for high-resolution images. Vision Transformers take an image as input and convert it into a sequence of N non-overlapping patches, each patch is linearly embedded into a token of dimension d, the cost is roughly $O(N^2 \cdot d)$ [19]. Higher resolutions increase N, and since attention scales quadratically with N, the computation grows rapidly. This poses challenges for real-time cases, such as the application in real-time Chatbot. In assembly scenes, the operation area where hands interact with tools is key for understanding the task, while background clutter and unrelated tools add redundancy, increasing computation without adding useful information. Enhancing VLMs' focus on local details while reducing such interference remains a key challenge for improving efficiency.

Approach. One possible solution is to downsample the background while preserving the resolution of key regions, thus accelerating inference by focusing more on local details. This approach retains essential information and reduces redundancy. Prior work [26] defines regions of interest using query points in the initial frame and applies point-tracking to generate segmentation masks across frames. However, query points must be manually selected and may require reinitialization if lost during tracking. Combining studies in [16,31] propose deep learning-based systems to detect hand-object interactions, we propose an integrated system: Hands are first identified by a pre-trained hand detector in video frames, and interaction frames are then determined based on hand-tool proximity and motion. Positive query points are placed on hands and tools, and negative points in the background. These queries are passed to the SAM-PT model [26], which propagates the queries across frames, preserving foreground details while downsampling the background. System performance will be evaluated through:

(1) Query Point Evaluation: Assessing accuracy and coverage, ensuring positive points cover interaction regions and negatives exclude them.
(2) Inference Time Evaluation: Comparing feature extraction efficiency across VLMs on various assembly datasets at original vs. downsampled resolutions.

4.2 RQ2: How to Generate the General Visual Embeddings that Are Environment-Independent and Task-Relevant for Assembly Processes?

Traditional end-to-end learning methods often require extensive task-specific training under fixed environmental settings, limiting their adaptability and scene transferability [27]. The diversity of environmental variability, such as lighting changes (natural vs. artificial), background clutter, and unpredictable worker actions (hand occlusion, component movement) further complicates perception, as existing specific data-based trained methods struggle to generalize across varying environments. Visual embeddings compress high-dimensional visual data into low-dimensional representations and capture essential content and semantic relationships within images. Ideally, such embeddings should be task-relevant, invariant to environmental changes, and generalizable across different settings to minimize the need for fine-tuning in new environments.

Approach. Based on prior research [2,39], we adopt an adaptive multi-contrast learning strategy to construct $< anchor - positive - negative >$ triplets based on temporal distances, aiming to generate environment-independent, task-relevant visual embeddings. Positive samples are chosen from frames that are temporally close to the anchor point in the same assembly task, while negative samples are chosen from frames that are temporally far from the anchor point and possess significantly different actions.

Frozen pre-trained vision encoders are used to get initial visual embeddings, while multi-scene data augmentation enhances generalization ability and training efficiency. Training data covers diverse manual assembly scenarios, varying in lighting, background, operators, and assembly speeds. Augmentations, such as contrast, brightness, and rotation variations, further improve the model's robustness. The proposed self-supervised approach integrates adaptive training parameters to enhance embedding's distinctiveness and consistency across assembly steps and different environmental settings. We also creatively integrate this machine learning approach into the expert system to identify working stages.

With the goal that the vision embeddings should be task-related and independent to environmental variation, the model's performance will be evaluated from the following aspects:

(1) Intra-scene consistency: The visual embeddings within the same assembly step should be highly similar in both identical and comparable scenes. Conversely, the visual embedding representations at different stages of the assembly process should exhibit significant differences.
(2) Inter-scene consistency: To ensure the model's generalization capability in various scenarios, the visual embedding representations of the same assembly process should be highly similar across different environments. Embeddings of the same assembly process will be extracted from different working environments, and the similarity between them will be measured to evaluate consistency across environments.

4.3 RQ3: How Can We Leverage Spatiotemporal Information for Accurately Detecting Human-Object Interaction (HOI)?

The expert system should be able to recognize and predict human-tool interactions to provide crucial information for operation and safety tips. For example, in a manual assembly process, the system can predict subsequent assembly steps and provide real-time guidance or warnings if a safety risk arises. Existing HOI detection methods primarily rely on the analysis of single image [10] or egocentric videos [29]. However, single-frame approaches lack temporal information between consecutive frames, limiting their ability to predict future actions. While egocentric video methods leverage spatial-temporal cues and capture direct hand-object interactions, manual assembly environments typically rely on fixed, third-person cameras, and the presence of numerous tools in the real world further increases uncertainty in predicting workers' future actions. Effectively utilizing full spatio-temporal information from third-person views to understand scenes, detect interactions, and anticipate actions remains a key challenge. Moreover, most existing approaches focus on specific actions or limited object categories. Integrating VLMs with HOI detection may enable open-set HOI, offering a promising solution for recognizing novel action-object combinations.

Approach. Based on approaches in [15,30], etc., we propose the method of taking video clips just before interactions as inputs, extracting spatio-temporal features using a 3D convolutional backbone, and predicting the future hands' trajectory (i.e., motor attention) with probabilistic models. The method identifies the most probable future interactions, where motor attention represents the probability distribution of future hand positions over time and space.

By integrating visual information from both past frames and frames to be predicted, the model fully exploits contextual cues. The final observable frame offers critical spatial hints for detecting interaction hotspots, such as possible tools and regions, while temporal information refines action prediction (e.g., distinguishing "picking up" from "putting down").

VLMs further enhance scene understanding by extracting visual and textual embeddings from frames and action descriptions, focusing on action-related verbs. This semantic information improves generalization to unseen actions and objects, enabling more precise interaction anticipation. Evaluation is based on metrics such as Mean Top-5 Recall and Mean Accuracy. Top-1 Accuracy with different anticipation gaps used to evaluate the verb, noun, and action anticipation across different time gaps.

4.4 RQ4: How Can LLM Agents Assist in Assembly Scenes to Enhance Efficiency, Improve Worker Performance, and Reduce Error Rates?

Conventional expert assistance systems often lack advanced data analysis capabilities for identifying trends and recurring issues in working scenes, rely on time-consuming manual error documentation and analysis, and offer rigid, non-adaptive training programs that can't fit individuals' needs, limiting their intelligence and flexibility in complex assembly tasks. Advances in LLMs and VLMs offer promising solutions to this dilemma. With powerful natural language processing and reasoning capabilities, LLMs such as ChatGPT and LLaMA can understand and generate highly complex textual information [34]. This enables personalized training based on workers' skill levels and learning paces, large-scale data analysis can identify trends and recurring issues. The combination of VLMs and LLMs improves the system's capability to interpret visual data and generate actionable insights.

Approach. We propose an LLM-based agent assembly assistance system. Without retraining LLMs, the system can generate clear and detailed operating guidance by incorporating a local knowledge base of specific manual assembly instructions. By aligning visual feature embeddings with the textual embeddings in the descriptions, the system generates initial predictions for human-object interactions in the working scene. These predictions are then passed to the multi-LLM agents; the collaborative reasoning framework assigns specialized roles (e.g., common sense, spatial, and temporal reasoning) to multiple LLM agents, while a debate mechanism integrates and compares their responses for refined final predictions. Cross-validation through the debate mechanism, combined with a local knowledge base, ensures optimal guidance [5]. This approach emulates human-like reasoning, ensuring more comprehensive decision-making. LLMs also provide insightful analysis and summarization of the assembly process, helping with workflow optimization and identifying potential improvement. Model performance is evaluated by measuring the proportion of correct HOI predictions within the top K results and the consistency of LLM-generated guidance with the knowledge base.

5 Conclusion

Focusing on enhancing the expert assistance systems' ability to understand complex manual assembly scenes, this paper proposes several research questions. RQ1 (Sect. 4.1) and RQ2 (Sect. 4.2) introduce pre-trained large Vision-Language Models, which significantly reduce the need for intensive manual annotations while improving the model's consistency and robustness across diverse environments. RQ3 (Sect. 4.3) focuses on modeling dynamic interactions between humans and objects by leveraging both spatial and temporal information, enabling analysis beyond single-frame understanding. RQ4 (Sect. 4.4) incorporates advanced LLMs as the "brain" of the expert assistance system, capable of integrating sensory data with expert prompts for effective reasoning and decision-making. As a result, the expert assistance system can adapt to more complex and dynamic real-world scenarios.

In the future, we will implement and validate the proposed methods in practical environments and explore their integration into related domains, such as Human-Robot Collaboration and Industrial Cobots.

References

1. Ahn, H., Choi, S., Kim, N., Cha, G., Oh, S.: Interactive text2pickup networks for natural language-based human-robot collaboration. IEEE Robot. Automation Lett. **3**(4), 3308–3315 (2018)
2. Brüggemann, D., Sakaridis, C., Brödermann, T., Van Gool, L.: Contrastive model adaptation for cross-condition robustness in semantic segmentation. In: Proceedings of the IEEE/CVF International Conference on Computer Vision, pp. 11378–11387 (2023)
3. Carreira, J., Zisserman, A.: Quo vadis, action recognition? a new model and the kinetics dataset. In: Proceedings of the IEEE Conference on Computer Vision and Pattern Recognition, pp. 6299–6308 (2017)
4. Castro, P., Kim, T.K.: Crt-6d: fast 6d object pose estimation with cascaded refinement transformers. In: Proceedings of the IEEE/CVF Winter Conference on Applications of Computer Vision, pp. 5746–5755 (2023)
5. Chan, C.M., et al.: Chateval: towards better LLM-based evaluators through multi-agent debate. arXiv preprint arXiv:2308.07201 (2023)
6. Diwan, T., Anirudh, G., Tembhurne, J.V.: Object detection using yolo: Challenges, architectural successors, datasets and applications. Multimedia Tools and Applications **82**(6), 9243–9275 (2023)
7. Djuric, A.M., Urbanic, R., Rickli, J.: A framework for collaborative robot (cobot) integration in advanced manufacturing systems. SAE Int. J. Mater. Manufacturing **9**(2), 457–464 (2016)

8. D'Avella, S., Tripicchio, P., Avizzano, C.A.: A study on picking objects in cluttered environments: exploiting depth features for a custom low-cost universal jamming gripper. Robot. Comput. Integrated Manufacturing **63**, 101888 (2020)
9. Hu, Z., Pan, J., Fan, T., Yang, R., Manocha, D.: Safe navigation with human instructions in complex scenes. IEEE Robot. Autom. Lett. **4**(2), 753–760 (2019)
10. Ji, J., Desai, R., Niebles, J.C.: Detecting human-object relationships in videos. In: Proceedings of the IEEE/CVF International Conference on Computer Vision, pp. 8106–8116 (2021)
11. Keller, I., Lohan, K.S.: On the illumination influence for object learning on robot companions. Front. Robot. AI **6**, 154 (2020)
12. Lai, Z.H., Tao, W., Leu, M.C., Yin, Z.: Smart augmented reality instructional system for mechanical assembly towards worker-centered intelligent manufacturing. J. Manuf. Syst. **55**, 69–81 (2020)
13. Li, W., Xu, A., Wei, M., Zuo, W., Li, R.: Deep learning-based augmented reality work instruction assistance system for complex manual assembly. J. Manuf. Syst. **73**, 307–319 (2024)
14. Li, Z., Gavrilyuk, K., Gavves, E., Jain, M., Snoek, C.G.: Videolstm convolves, attends and flows for action recognition. Comput. Vis. Image Underst. **166**, 41–50 (2018)
15. Liu, M., Tang, S., Li, Y., Rehg, J.M.: Forecasting human-object interaction: joint prediction of motor attention and actions in first person video. In: Computer Vision–ECCV 2020: 16th European Conference, Glasgow, UK, August 23–28, 2020, Proceedings, Part I 16, pp. 704–721. Springer (2020)
16. Lu, Y., Liu, Y.: Egocentric hand-object interaction detection. In: 2022 IEEE Smartworld, Ubiquitous Intelligence & Computing, Scalable Computing & Communications, Digital Twin, Privacy Computing, Metaverse, Autonomous & Trusted Vehicles (SmartWorld/UIC/ScalCom/DigitalTwin/PriComp/Meta), pp. 25–32. IEEE (2022)
17. Miah, A.S.M., Hasan, M.A.M., Shin, J.: Dynamic hand gesture recognition using multi-branch attention based graph and general deep learning model. IEEE Access **11**, 4703–4716 (2023)
18. Miah, A.S.M., Hasan, M.A.M., Shin, J., Okuyama, Y., Tomioka, Y.: Multistage spatial attention-based neural network for hand gesture recognition. Computers **12**(1), 13 (2023)
19. Nauen, T.C., Palacio, S., Raue, F., Dengel, A.: Which transformer to favor: a comparative analysis of efficiency in vision transformers. arXiv preprint arXiv:2308.09372 (2023)
20. Oquab, M., et al.: Dinov2: learning robust visual features without supervision. arXiv preprint arXiv:2304.07193 (2023)
21. Pang, J., Zheng, P., Li, S., Liu, S.: A verification-oriented and part-focused assembly monitoring system based on multi-layered digital twin. J. Manuf. Syst. **68**, 477–492 (2023)
22. Patel, V., Chesmore, A., Legner, C.M., Pandey, S.: Trends in workplace wearable technologies and connected-worker solutions for next-generation occupational safety, health, and productivity. Adv. Intell. Syst. **4**(1), 2100099 (2022)
23. Piergiovanni, A., Ryoo, M.S.: Representation flow for action recognition. In: Proceedings of the IEEE/CVF Conference on Computer Vision and Pattern Recognition, pp. 9945–9953 (2019)
24. Pilati, F., Faccio, M., Gamberi, M., Regattieri, A.: Learning manual assembly through real-time motion capture for operator training with augmented reality. Procedia Manufacturing **45**, 189–195 (2020)

25. Radford, A., et al.: Learning transferable visual models from natural language supervision. In: International Conference on Machine Learning, pp. 8748–8763. PMLR (2021)
26. Rajič, F., Ke, L., Tai, Y.W., Tang, C.K., Danelljan, M., Yu, F.: Segment anything meets point tracking. arXiv preprint arXiv:2307.01197 (2023)
27. Ren, A., Veer, S., Majumdar, A.: Generalization guarantees for imitation learning. In: Conference on Robot Learning, pp. 1426–1442. PMLR (2021)
28. Riedel, A., Brehm, N., Pfeifroth, T.: Hand gesture recognition of methods-time measurement-1 motions in manual assembly tasks using graph convolutional networks. Appl. Artif. Intell. **36**(1), 2014191 (2022)
29. Roy, D., Rajendiran, R., Fernando, B.: Interaction visual transformer for egocentric action anticipation. arXiv preprint arXiv:2211.14154 (2022)
30. Roy, D., Rajendiran, R., Fernando, B.: Interaction region visual transformer for egocentric action anticipation. In: Proceedings of the IEEE/CVF Winter Conference on Applications of Computer Vision, pp. 6740–6750 (2024)
31. Shan, D., Geng, J., Shu, M., Fouhey, D.F.: Understanding human hands in contact at internet scale. In: Proceedings of the IEEE/CVF Conference on Computer Vision and Pattern Recognition, pp. 9869–9878 (2020)
32. Shao, Z., Yu, Z., Wang, M., Yu, J.: Prompting large language models with answer heuristics for knowledge-based visual question answering. In: Proceedings of the IEEE/CVF Conference on Computer Vision and Pattern Recognition, pp. 14974–14983 (2023)
33. Shugurov, I., Li, F., Busam, B., Ilic, S.: Osop: A multi-stage one shot object pose estimation framework. In: Proceedings of the IEEE/CVF Conference on Computer Vision and Pattern Recognition, pp. 6835–6844 (2022)
34. Singh, A.: Exploring language models: a comprehensive survey and analysis. In: Proceedings 2023 International Conference Research Methodologies in Knowledge Management, Artificial Intelligence and Telecommunication Engineering (RMKMATE), pp. 1–4. (2023). https://doi.org/10.1109/RMKMATE59243.2023.10369423
35. Tan, H.L., et al.: Task-oriented multi-modal question answering for collaborative applications. In: 2020 IEEE International Conference on Image Processing (ICIP), pp. 1426–1430. IEEE (2020)
36. Thermos, S., Potamianos, G., Daras, P.: Joint object affordance reasoning and segmentation in RGB-d videos. IEEE Access **9**, 89699–89713 (2021)
37. Venkatesh, S.G., Biswas, A., Upadrashta, R., Srinivasan, V., Talukdar, P., Amrutur, B.: Spatial reasoning from natural language instructions for robot manipulation. In: 2021 IEEE International Conference on Robotics and Automation (ICRA), pp. 11196–11202. IEEE (2021)
38. Wang, G., Manhardt, F., Tombari, F., Ji, X.: Gdr-net: geometry-guided direct regression network for monocular 6d object pose estimation. In: Proceedings of the IEEE/CVF Conference on Computer Vision and Pattern Recognition, pp. 16611–16621 (2021)
39. Xing, J., Bauersfeld, L., Song, Y., Xing, C., Scaramuzza, D.: Contrastive learning for enhancing robust scene transfer in vision-based agile flight. arXiv preprint arXiv:2309.09865 (2023)
40. Zhou, L., Zhang, L., Konz, N.: Computer vision techniques in manufacturing. IEEE Trans. Syst. Man Cybern. Syst. **53**(1), 105–117 (2022)

Situational Awareness by Audio Signals in Maritime Application

Paria Vali Zadeh

Intelligent Systems Group, Kiel University, Kiel, Germany
pvz@informatik.uni-kiel.de

Abstract. Maritime surveillance and safety rely heavily on situational awareness, often hindered by limitations in traditional visual and radar-based systems under challenging environmental conditions. This research proposes a self-adaptive system based on organic computing principles to enhance perception in autonomous ships through audio classification and localization. By leveraging advanced machine learning algorithms, the system autonomously detects, classifies, and localizes sound sources, such as vessel signals and environmental sounds, even if characterized by high noise and dynamic conditions. Integrating this adaptive layer into existing frameworks for perception models offers a robust approach to improving situational awareness, demonstrating how organic computing principles can address complex, evolving challenges in maritime environments.

Keywords: Organic Computing · Situational Awareness · Autonomous Behavior · Audio processing · Maritime application

1 Introduction

Advancements in technology have revolutionized the analysis and interpretation of sensory data, enabling innovative applications in various fields. Signal processing, a foundational component of modern technology, is instrumental in extracting meaningful insights from complex sensor information and datasets. Its applications range from speech recognition to environmental monitoring, underscoring its versatility and importance [11,21].

In parallel, machine learning (ML) has emerged as a transformative tool in data analysis. Deep learning (DL), a subset of ML, has gained significant traction due to its capacity to model intricate data relationships and learn robust representations. Integrating ML and DL with advanced hardware has driven progress in natural language processing, visual data analysis, and audio processing, opening new frontiers in sound localization, speech processing, autonomous systems, and navigation [19].

Within the maritime sector, these advances are particularly significant. ML-powered audio signal processing offers unique advantages in enhancing situational awareness in challenging environments. Unlike visual or radar systems, which can be limited by environmental factors such as fog or darkness, sound-based approaches leverage the propagation characteristics of acoustic waves to detect and classify signals from distant or obscured sources. This capability is invaluable for vessel navigation and collision avoidance applications, which directly contribute to maritime safety.

However, the complexity and variability of real-world sensory signals present significant challenges. This is especially true in maritime environments, where background noise, dynamic conditions, and diverse signal sources complicate audio-based situational awareness. To address these challenges, this PhD concept proposes a novel framework for improving situational awareness through adaptive audio signal classification and localization techniques, guided by the principles of organic computing (OC).

OC provides a paradigm for designing systems that adapt, self-organize and operate autonomously in dynamic and unpredictable environments. Applying this approach to maritime applications enables the development of robust systems capable of addressing the unique demands of this domain [13].

1.1 Paper Structure

This paper is structured as follows: Sect. 2 reviews the relevant background and technological foundations. Section 3 defines the main research challenges addressed in this study. Section 4 formulates the guiding research questions. Section 5 outlines the strategic roadmap and details the research methodology and key milestones planned for the progress of the PhD project. Finally, Sect. 6 concludes with a summary of the research concept and the current status of the work.

2 Related Work

Over the years, various acoustic detection, classification, and localization methods have been developed, making their categorization challenging [4]. This section focuses on literature relevant to maritime applications, particularly in classification and localization.

Building on the foundations laid by these studies, this research aims to develop an audio dataset of ship sounds to classify ship types and their associated messages based on the international regulations for preventing collisions at sea, 1972 (COLREGs) [15]. In addition, this study will focus on localizing ships using audio data and classifying audio-based maneuver signals, contributing to the enhancement of situational awareness and safety in maritime environments.

2.1 Audio Classification for Maritime Applications

Hydroacoustic sensors (passive sonar) have been widely used to capture and classify vessel noise. Traditional feature extraction methods, such as low frequency analysis and recording, mel frequency cepstral coefficients, and gammatone frequency cepstral coefficients, often face limitations in complex ocean environments. To address this, learning-based techniques leveraging ML have gained prominence [1].

Li et al. [6] introduced a multiscale auditory system inspired deep convolutional neural network (CNN) for the classification of ship noise, outperforming traditional models. Similarly, Luo and Feng [10] used a depth clustering algorithm with a restricted Boltzmann machine autoencoder and back propagation neural network, showing superior adaptability. Despite advancements, balancing accuracy and computational efficiency remains a challenge, as seen in Chen et al. [2], who combined multiple time-frequency (T-F)-based features in a CNN model but struggled with computational complexity.

Time-domain and T-F-based methods continue to be prominent. Tian et al. [26] combined wave and T-F features with a lightweight multiscale residual deep neural network, while Liu et al. [9] used a multi-dimensional T-F spectrogram with a convolutional recurrent neural network model, achieving strong results on the ShipsEar dataset.

Efforts to improve model efficiency include Yang et al. [30], who developed a lightweight ResNet10-based approach using features of 3D mel frequency cepstral coefficients. However, some models, such as Wang et al. [29], still face high computational complexity. Lingzhi et al. [8] addressed dataset limitations with a semi-supervised completion-attention based on ladder network, improving accuracy with limited labeled samples.

Environmental factors such as pressure, temperature, and turbulence affect the performance of hydroacoustic sensors. While research has focused on these sensors, few studies have explored conventional microphones or audio from videos for maritime monitoring. Tuncer and Aydemir [28] introduced a lightweight classification method using a ship sound dataset, and Yildirim [31] used frequency-domain features with DL.

In summary, progress in underwater acoustic recognition through ML has improved accuracy and efficiency, but challenges remain in computational complexity, dataset availability, and adaptability. Exploring novel sensing methods, such as conventional microphones, could enhance future maritime monitoring systems.

2.2 Audio Localization for Maritime Applications

Acoustic localization of moving sound sources presents unique challenges, including the Doppler effect [17]. Techniques are broadly categorized into classical and artificial intelligence (AI)-based methods, with further divisions by application [4].

In maritime contexts, Oudompheng et al. [16] improved array signal processing methods for ship noise localization, while Jiang et al. [5] enhanced time difference of arrival (TDOA) techniques to mitigate multipath errors in deep-sea environments. Sun et al. [24] optimized time-delay estimation using a triangular array, addressing multipath challenges.

Traditional methods such as time of arrival, TDOA, and direction of arrival rely on precise synchronization and high-precision measurements, often impractical in scenarios such as locating black boxes. To overcome these limitations, Sun et al. [23] introduced a second-order TDOA-based method, which offers high localization precision without requiring exact knowledge of the signal period.

Recent advances focus on improving accuracy under challenging conditions. Tian et al. [27] achieved superior accuracy in low signal to noise ratio environments with an azimuth-only triangular localization method. Sun et al. [22] developed a high-rate direct signal selection algorithm that combines time of arrival, bandwidth, and Doppler frequency for robust localization.

Localization techniques also support environmental conservation. Hung et al. [3] employed hydrophone-equipped unmanned surface vehicles to estimate underwater source locations. Similar methods have been adapted for other environments, such as Lin et al. [7], who applied deep neural network models in large cavitation tunnels.

Beyond maritime applications, AI-based methods have gained traction in gunshot localization. Raponi et al. [20] introduced a CNN-based approach for gunshot classification without prior knowledge of recording setups, while Park et al. [18] enhanced real-world performance using datasets derived from first-person shooter game recordings.

In summary, advances in localization methods continue to address challenges such as multipath errors, low signal to noise ratio conditions, and high precision requirements, with applications that extend beyond maritime to environmental conservation and public safety.

3 Problem Statement

This PhD project covers autonomous ships as an example of an OC system and explores how situational awareness can be enriched through the classification and localization of audio signals. The core challenge is accurately identifying diverse signals and pinpointing their exact spatial origins. These capabilities are essential for navigation safety, wildlife monitoring, and industrial operations. To address this, the study sets the following objectives:

- *Efficient Classification of Maritime Audio Signals*: Develop a system for accurately identifying diverse maritime audio signatures.
- *Robust Localization Framework*: Design a comprehensive approach for determining audio signal sources in heterogeneous environments.
- *Optimization of ML Models for Maritime Audio Signals*: Systematically evaluate and refine ML models to enhance classification and localization performance.

Building on the proven success of ML in domains such as image and speech recognition, this research employs a flexible, iterative approach to optimize audio signal processing in maritime contexts. The outcomes are expected to advance environmental monitoring, safety, and industrial applications, with potential benefits for urban noise monitoring and acoustic event detection.

3.1 Organic Computing Perspective

OC is a design paradigm for building systems that can adapt, self-organize, and operate autonomously in dynamic environments. It aims to reduce the risks associated with operating multitudes of intelligent devices in environments with some uncertainty about potential changes with respect to behavioral requirements [12]. Inspired by natural systems, OC introduces principles such as self-organization, self-optimization, and self-awareness to enhance robustness and adaptability [13].

This research leverages OC principles to address the challenges of audio-based situational awareness in noisy and unpredictable maritime environments. The system features self-organization, self-optimization, and self-awareness, enabling adaptability and continuous performance improvement. Based on the OC layered architecture [13], it comprises a productive layer for audio processing, a reflective layer for monitoring, and a meta layer for strategic adaptation—ensuring robust operation in complex scenarios.

4 Research Questions

This research proposal aims to answer the following research questions:

RQ1 *What acoustic features are essential for distinguishing between different maritime objects and their activities in dynamic and complex environments?*

RQ2 *How can signal processing techniques be optimized to enhance the detection and classification of acoustic signals in maritime environments?*

RQ3 *What are the most effective deep learning architectures for classifying ship types based on acoustic data – and how can they be tailored to maritime conditions?*

RQ4 *How can ships be localized in real-time using their acoustic signatures to monitor their existence and motion relative to an ego ship?*

RQ5 *How can the integration of advanced hardware and software systems improve the localization precision of ships using acoustic signals?*

RQ6 *What methodologies can be developed to evaluate and improve situational awareness in automated maritime navigation systems using acoustic data?*

In conclusion, this research seeks to harness the power of ML to tackle the challenges of sound localization and classification. By adopting a flexible approach for method selection and focusing on practical maritime applications, such as safety and navigation, this study aims to contribute meaningfully to both the scientific community and real-world challenges.

5 Research Design and Methodology

To address the identified challenges, this PhD project proposes using conventional microphones as a cost-effective, versatile alternative to hydroacoustic sensors. Their simplicity, ease of deployment, and integration make them suitable for diverse applications beyond the maritime domain. The research follows a structured methodology across three milestones:

- *Data Acquisition and Preprocessing*: Build a robust maritime dataset.
- *Algorithm Development*: Develop and optimize ML models for classification and localization.
- *System Testing*: Evaluate system performance in real-world scenarios.

This approach aims to advance audio signal processing for applications such as automated ship navigation, wildlife monitoring, and smart technologies. Section 5 outlines the methodology and experimental design corresponding to these milestones. Section 5.1 introduces the hardware and data acquisition setup, Sect. 5.2 focuses on object localization, and Sect. 5.3 addresses acoustic signal classification.

5.1 Experimental Design

This section presents the experimental design for sound source localization, focusing on the two primary objectives outlined in RQ5.

Target 1. *Hardware design. We will investigate the most promising microphone arrangement for marine applications and design a corresponding laboratory test.*

Target 2. *Field data acquisition (ship sounds). Our designed data acquisition scheme will be implemented and tested to collect real-world data in marine environments.*

5.2 Object Localization

The Doppler effect describes the frequency shift of sound waves emitted by a moving source relative to an observer. This phenomenon is widely applied in velocity measurements using radar and ultrasound [25]. In object localization, variations in the source-microphone distance introduce Doppler-induced frequency shifts and amplitude fluctuations, which complicate accurate localization [17]. Therefore, mitigating Doppler distortion is crucial for effective localization. This section addresses RQ4 and RQ6 through two primary targets.

Target 3. *Estimating location and object number (neglecting the Doppler effect). Target 3 assumes that the Doppler effect is negligible, focusing on estimating the location and the number of objects. This assumption simplifies the problem in RQ4, enabling its decomposition into smaller, sequential sub-problems.*

Target 4. *Recognizing object status, identity, and optionally speed (considering the Doppler effect). This target addresses RQ4 by recognizing whether objects are stationary or moving, identifying them, and optionally estimating their speed using the Doppler effect for enhanced localization accuracy.*

5.3 Object Classification

This section aims to address RQ1–3 and complete the response to RQ6. Upon completing milestone 1 (Sect. 5.2), we focus on targets 5, 6, and 7 to finalize our response to these research questions. As introduced earlier, a detailed understanding of ship and COLREGs sound signals is crucial for maritime object classification. This study groups vessel-related sounds into three categories: (1) standard ship sounds (e.g., bell, horn), (2) COLREGs-defined signal patterns for maneuvers and warnings, and (3) other dynamic or unidentified sounds (e.g., high-speed vessels). The following subsections outline their technical characteristics and related classification targets.

Ship Sound Types. COLREGs [15] provide rules governing the use of sound signals to ensure maritime safety. Key rules relevant to this study include:

Sound Signals. They are defined by their type and duration:

a) Whistle: A sound signaling device designed to produce prescribed tones.
b) Short tone: A tone lasting approximately one second.
c) Long tone: A tone lasting four to six seconds.

Required Sound Equipment. They are based on vessel size:

a) Vessels 12 meters (m) or longer must carry a whistle, those 20 m or longer must also carry a bell, and vessels 100 m or longer must include a gong distinguishable from the bell.
b) Smaller vessels (less than 12 m) must carry an alternative sound device capable of producing powerful signals.

Frequency and Range Specifications. Annex III of COLREGs specifies the technical characteristics of sound signals:

- Whistles: Operate within 70–700 Hz for all vessels, with frequency ranges varying by vessel size:
  a) 70–200 Hz for vessels 200 m or longer.
  b) 130–350 Hz for vessels 75–200 m.
  c) 250–700 Hz for vessels under 75 m.
- Bell or Gong: These devices must produce sound levels of at least 110 dB at a distance of 1 m.

Target 5. *Vessels' sound type classification (bell, horn, etc.). It focuses on classifying vessel sounds like bells and horns, aiding in identifying activities and improving maritime monitoring.*

COLREGs Messages. Specific sound signals defined by COLREGs are used in scenarios such as maneuvering, danger warnings, or reduced visibility, both day and night [15]. Figure 1 summarizes these signals for different situations.

Target 6. *COLREGs messages classification. This classifies standardized sound signals defined by COLREGs for scenarios like maneuvering and danger warnings, enabling automated interpretation for safer navigation.*

Target 7. *Sound type classification (optional) for sounds identified as originating from other sources, such as a passing ship at high speed (object type).*

This research will address all Research Questions (RQs) by achieving the proposed milestones.

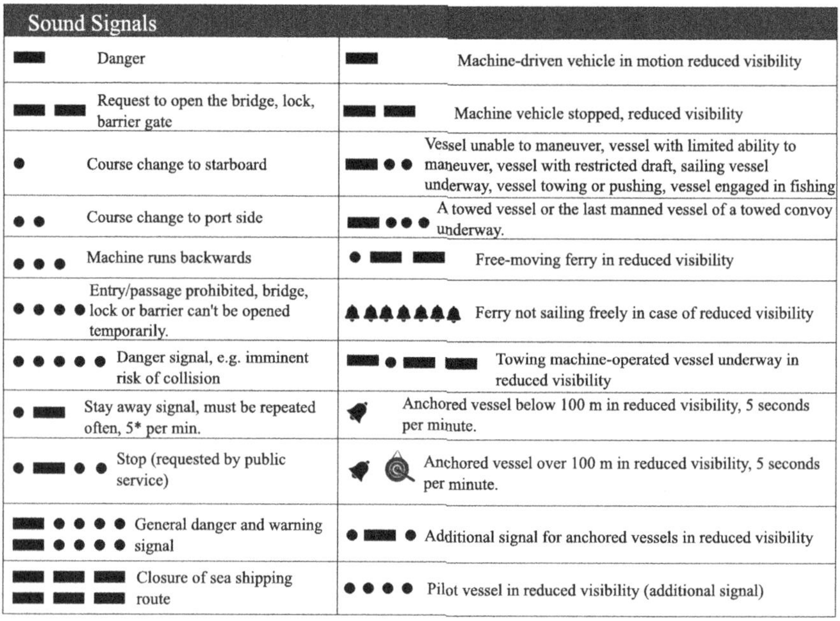

Sound Signals			
▬	Danger	▬	Machine-driven vehicle in motion reduced visibility
▬ ▬	Request to open the bridge, lock, barrier gate	▬ ▬	Machine vehicle stopped, reduced visibility
●	Course change to starboard	▬ ● ●	Vessel unable to maneuver, vessel with limited ability to maneuver, vessel with restricted draft, sailing vessel underway, vessel towing or pushing, vessel engaged in fishing
● ●	Course change to port side	▬ ● ● ●	A towed vessel or the last manned vessel of a towed convoy underway.
● ● ●	Machine runs backwards	● ▬ ▬	Free-moving ferry in reduced visibility
● ● ● ●	Entry/passage prohibited, bridge, lock or barrier can't be opened temporarily.	▲▲▲▲▲▲▲	Ferry not sailing freely in case of reduced visibility
● ● ● ● ●	Danger signal, e.g. imminent risk of collision	▬ ● ▬ ▬	Towing machine-operated vessel underway in reduced visibility
● ▬	Stay away signal, must be repeated often, 5* per min.	⚓	Anchored vessel below 100 m in reduced visibility, 5 seconds per minute.
● ▬ ● ●	Stop (requested by public service)	⚓ ⊚	Anchored vessel over 100 m in reduced visibility, 5 seconds per minute.
▬ ● ● ● ● General danger and warning ▬ ● ● ● signal		● ▬ ●	Additional signal for anchored vessels in reduced visibility
▬ ▬ ▬ Closure of sea shipping ▬ ▬ ▬ route		● ● ● ●	Pilot vessel in reduced visibility (additional signal)

Fig. 1. Sound signals for various scenarios [14].

6 Conclusion

Maritime surveillance relies on situational awareness, often hindered by the limitations of visual and radar systems in challenging conditions. This PhD concept addresses these gaps through adaptive audio signal classification and localization guided by OC principles. The PhD project is in its early phase, and it currently focuses on designing optimal microphone arrangements for marine applications and developing a laboratory test setup to validate these configurations. Upcoming works will involve finalizing the test setup and conducting experiments to optimize signal clarity and noise resilience, with insights guiding the refinement of a practical and reliable hardware design for maritime use.

References

1. Aslam, M.A., et al.: Underwater sound classification using learning based methods: a review. Expert Syst. Appl. **255**, 124498 (2024). https://doi.org/10.1016/j.eswa.2024.124498
2. Chen, L., Liu, F., Li, D., Shen, T., Zhao, D.: Underwater acoustic target classification with joint learning framework and data augmentation. In: 2022 5th International Conference on Artificial Intelligence and Big Data (ICAIBD), pp. 23–28. IEEE (2022). https://doi.org/10.1109/ICAIBD55127.2022.9820117
3. Hung, C.T., Zhang, Y.C., Chen, C.F.: Autonomous underwater acoustic localization through multiple unmanned surface vehicle. In: OCEANS 2022, Hampton Roads, pp. 1–5. IEEE (2022). https://doi.org/10.1109/OCEANS47191.2022.9977104
4. Jekateryńczuk, G., Piotrowski, Z.: A survey of sound source localization and detection methods and their applications. Sensors **24**(1), 68 (2023). https://doi.org/10.3390/s24010068
5. Jiang, F., Zhang, Z., Sabahi, M.F.: An acoustic source localization algorithm based on maximum or minimum value screening in deep sea multipath environment. In: 2019 IEEE Canadian Conference of Electrical and Computer Engineering (CCECE), pp. 1–4. IEEE (2019). https://doi.org/10.1109/CCECE43985.2019.9052388
6. Li, J., Yang, H., Shen, S., Xu, G.: The learned multi-scale deep filters for underwater acoustic target modeling and recognition. In: OCEANS 2019-Marseille, pp. 1–4. IEEE (2019). https://doi.org/10.1109/OCEANSE.2019.8867169
7. Lin, B.J., Guan, P.C., Chang, H.T., Hsiao, H.W., Lin, J.H.: Application of a deep neural network for acoustic source localization inside a cavitation tunnel. J. Marine Sci. Eng. **11**(4), 773 (2023). https://doi.org/10.3390/jmse11040773
8. Lingzhi, X., Xiangyang, Z., Xiang, Y., Shuang, Y.: Completion-attention ladder network for few-shot underwater acoustic recognition. Neural Process. Lett. **55**(7), 9563–9579 (2023). https://doi.org/10.1007/s11063-023-11214-3
9. Liu, F., Shen, T., Luo, Z., Zhao, D., Guo, S.: Underwater target recognition using convolutional recurrent neural networks with 3-d mel-spectrogram and data augmentation. Appl. Acoust. **178**, 107989 (2021). https://doi.org/10.1016/j.apacoust.2021.107989
10. Luo, X., Feng, Y.: An underwater acoustic target recognition method based on restricted boltzmann machine. Sensors **20**(18), 5399 (2020). https://doi.org/10.3390/s20185399
11. Mulgrew, B., Grant, P., Thompson, J.: Digital signal processing: concepts and applications (2002)
12. Müller-Schloer, C., Schmeck, H., Ungerer, T.: Organic Computing - A Paradigm Shift for Complex Systems. Springer-Verlag, Berlin, Heidelberg, 1st edn. (2011). https://doi.org/10.1007/978-3-0348-0130-0
13. Organic Computing – Technical Systems for Survival in the Real World. Springer, Cham (2017). https://doi.org/10.1007/978-3-319-68477-2

14. Neumann, I.I.: SKS licence. http://www.nautik-trainer.de/bilder/tafeln-sbf-see.pdf, Accessed 17 Jan 2025
15. Organization, I.M.: Convention on the international regulations for preventing collisions at sea, 1972 (COLREGs), https://www.imo.org/en/About/Conventions/Pages/COLREG.aspx, Accessed 17 Jan 2025
16. Oudompheng, B., Nicolas, B., Lamotte, L.: Localization and contribution of underwater acoustical sources of a moving surface ship. IEEE J. Oceanic Eng. **43**(2), 536–546 (2017). https://doi.org/10.1109/JOE.2017.2699260
17. Ouyang, K., Xiong, W., He, Q., Peng, Z.: Doppler distortion removal in wayside circular microphone array signals. IEEE Trans. Instrum. Meas. **68**(5), 1238–1251 (2019). https://doi.org/10.1109/TIM.2018.2886921
18. Park, J., Cho, Y., Sim, G., Lee, H., Choo, J.: Enemy spotted: in-game gun sound dataset for gunshot classification and localization. In: 2022 IEEE Conference on Games (CoG), pp. 56–63. IEEE (2022). https://doi.org/10.1109/CoG51982.2022.9893670
19. Pouyanfar, S., et al.: A survey on deep learning: algorithms, techniques, and applications. ACM Comput. Surv. (CSUR) **51**(5), 1–36 (2018). https://doi.org/10.1145/3234150
20. Raponi, S., Oligeri, G., Ali, I.M.: Sound of guns: digital forensics of gun audio samples meets artificial intelligence. Multimedia Tools and Applications **81**(21), 30387–30412 (2022). https://doi.org/10.1007/s11042-022-12612-w
21. Smith, S.W., et al.: The scientist and engineer's guide to digital signal processing (1997)
22. Sun, S., Liu, T., Wang, Y., Zhang, G., Liu, K., Wang, Y.: High-rate underwater acoustic localization based on the decision tree. IEEE Trans. Geosci. Remote Sens. **60**, 1–12 (2021). https://doi.org/10.1109/TGRS.2021.3127919
23. Sun, S., Zhang, X., Zheng, C., Fu, J., Zhao, C.: Underwater acoustical localization of the black box utilizing single autonomous underwater vehicle based on the second-order time difference of arrival. IEEE J. Oceanic Eng. **45**(4), 1268–1279 (2019). https://doi.org/10.1109/JOE.2019.2950954
24. SUN, X.y., LI, N.s., Xiao, L.: Three-dimensional passive localization method for underwater target using regular triangular array. In: 2019 13th Symposium on Piezoelectrcity, Acoustic Waves and Device Applications (SPAWDA). pp. 1–7. IEEE (2019). https://doi.org/10.1109/SPAWDA.2019.8681844
25. Tey, W.Y.: Review on klinaku-berisha equation via numerical modelling for acoustical doppler effect. Appl. Acoust. **180**, 108080 (2021). https://doi.org/10.1016/j.apacoust.2021.108080
26. Tian, S.Z., Chen, D.B., Fu, Y., Zhou, J.L.: Joint learning model for underwater acoustic target recognition. Knowl.-Based Syst. **260**, 110119 (2023). https://doi.org/10.1016/j.knosys.2022.110119
27. Tian, T., Xiao, J., Sun, H., Feng, X.: Underwater acoustic source localization via an improved triangular method. In: 2022 14th International Conference on Communication Software and Networks (ICCSN), pp. 174–181. IEEE (2022). https://doi.org/10.1109/ICCSN55126.2022.9817574
28. Tuncer, T., Aydemir, E.: An automated local binary pattern ship identification method by using sound. Acta Infologica **4**(1), 57–63 (2020). https://doi.org/10.26650/acin.762809
29. Wang, B., Zhang, W., Zhu, Y., Wu, C., Zhang, S.: An underwater acoustic target recognition method based on amnet. IEEE Geosci. Remote Sens. Lett. **20**, 1–5 (2023). https://doi.org/10.1109/LGRS.2023.3235659

30. Yang, S., Xue, L., Hong, X., Zeng, X.: A lightweight network model based on an attention mechanism for ship-radiated noise classification. J. Marine Sci. Eng. **11**(2), 432 (2023). https://doi.org/10.3390/jmse11020432
31. Yıldırım, M.E.: Ship type recognition using deep learning with fft spectrums of audio signals. El-Cezeri **10**(1), 57–65 (2023). https://doi.org/10.31202/ecjse.1149363

A Vision for Deep Reinforcement Learning with a Classifier System

Connor Schönberner(✉)

Intelligent Systems Group, Kiel University, Kiel, Germany
cos@informatik.uni-kiel.de

Abstract. XCS is seen as the most investigated Michigan-style Learning Classifier System (LCS). It is typically integrated in Organic Computing systems as their self-adaptive learning component. Despite its attractiveness for Organic Computing due to its interpretability and maturity, XCS has well-known weaknesses in multi-step Reinforcement Learning problems. Reasons for this are the curse of dimensionality of Michigan- style LCSs, a weakness against long action chains and learning stability issues. In the meanwhile, modern Deep Reinforcement Learning methods have left classic Reinforcement Learning methods including XCS far behind. The PhD project outlined in this paper aims to create Deep Learning-XCS-hybrids leveraging the computational and representational abilities of Deep Learning to improve the Reinforcement Learning capabilities of XCS. Hereby, it aims to narrow or close the gap between Deep Reinforcement Learning and LCS. Furthermore, this paper discusses the key concepts behind this vision, resulting research questions, the results so far and the road ahead.

Keywords: XCS · Learning Classifier Systems · Rule-based Machine Learning · Reinforcement Learning · Deep Learning · Organic Computing

1 Introduction

Organic Computing (OC) aims to cope with the increasing complexity of intelligent systems with increasing autonomy and increasing amount of intelligent sub-systems by organising them and by taking inspiration from biological systems [31]. The hereby created OC systems follow the OC paradigm by achieving so-called self-* properties [31] including self-adaptivity and self-learning capabilities [19]. These capabilities are usually implemented via Machine Learning (ML) methods. In-fact, OC systems usually integrate a variant of XCS Classifier System (XCS) for realising self-adaptation and self-learning [29]. XCS belongs to the so-called Learning Classifier Systems (LCSs), rule-based ML systems, which learn by training a population of so-called classifiers or rules housing their learnable parameters. More precisely, those systems learn utilising a combination of an evolutionary-based discovery method and a life-time learning method.

For XCS, this is a Genetic Algorithm (GA) for the discovery component and a Q-learning like Reinforcement Learning (RL) component. One key advantage of LCSs including XCS variants is their reputation as interpretable systems. This includes their ability to learn interpretable knowledge [30] and to generate interpretable decisions [26] due to their reliance on well-understood classic ML methods explaining their attractiveness for OC.

Originally, XCS was designed for learning RL problems, which can be understood as problems intended to be learned in an interactive fashion. However, most later research on XCS variants primarily focused on supervised learning and are seen as more suitable for this ML paradigm [9]. This is a consequence of well known weaknesses in multi-step RL problems such as a weakness to long action chains in multi-step problems [1] and a tendency to evolve overgeneral classifiers [32]. However, in particular multi-step RL problems are of special interest for OC demanding more capable improvements for XCS learners. In addition to that, the curse of dimensionality of LCS [8] immensely limits the application scenarios of XCS variants and related systems in general. This is true regardless of whether it is applied to multi-step RL or supervised learning.

In the meanwhile, the Deep Learning revolution has also revolutionised RL methods turning them into Deep Reinforcement Learning (DRL) methods. Even its first representative Deep Q Network (DQN) was already noticeably more capable than classic RL methods [18] sparking the aforementioned revolution. Nowadays, the gap between state-of-the-art DRL methods is arguably even wider. Despite the shortcomings of the system, applying XCS variants to RL has regained attention in recent research [10,26]. As Deep Learning has drastically increased the capabilities of classic RL, this suggests that hybridising XCS with Deep Learning could similarly improve its capabilities.

2 The Objective

It is noteworthy that there has been research hybridising LCSs with shallow (ANNs) by integrating the latter into classifiers for at least two decades largely preceding the DRL revolution. It began with Bull et al. [3] and effectively ceased with Howard et al. [12]. Another branch of research combines XCS with deep autencoders for dimensionality reduction as a countermeasure to the curse of dimensionality. They apply this hybrid approach to supervised learning directly benefiting from Deep Learning [17,25,37]. Aside from our previous work [23,24] no additional advances for hybridising Deep Learning (DL) with XCS for RL application have been contributed, yet.

As a result, the area of Deep LCS and Deep Learning LCS hybrids is rather recent and especially under-explored for RL problems. One of the disadvantages of this approach arguably would be a loss of interpretability by combining XCS with largely black-box-like Deep Neural Networks (DNNs). Appropriate hybridisation and Deep Learning interpretability as well as XAI methods could allow to limit the damage to the interpretability. While there has been work on improving the over-generality issues of XCS such as Wagner et al. [32], these usually do not focus on multi-step problems leaving additional space for improvements. In the meanwhile, research on related LCSs has not been stagnant raising the question how XCS variants might be able to benefit from findings of other LCSs, motivating research on additional LCS-centric improvements. Facing these open problems, the here outlined PhD project has the following objective:

Research Objective. Advance the research on XCS variants in order to significantly improve their RL capabilities by hybridising them with Deep Learning in order narrow or close the gap to DRL without severely harming its systemic advantages and interpretability.

Consequently, such systems could be applied to more complex RL scenarios and complex real-world problems in the context of OC.

3 Background

This PhD project focuses on variants of XCS or related systems. Important aspects of XCS and subsequent extensions are re-iterated in Sect. 3.1. Prior work in neural LCS is examined in Sect. 3.2.

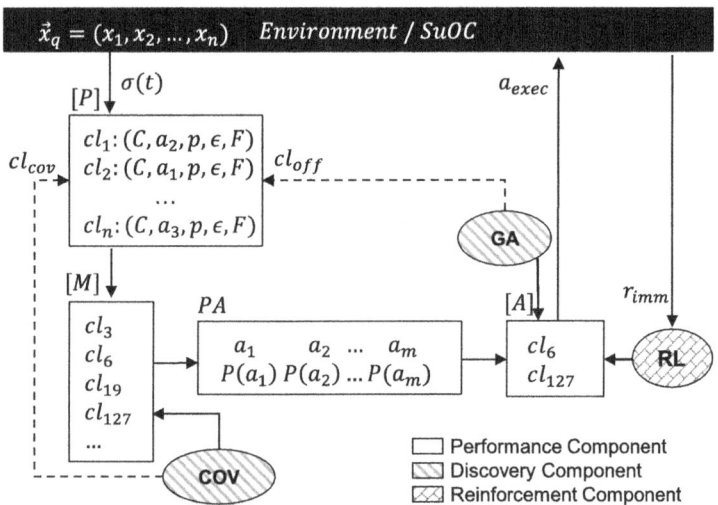

Fig. 1. Schematic of the general XCS architecture, cf. [29]. For simplicity's sake, only the variant for single-step problems is given.

3.1 XCS and Common Extensions

XCS is a Michigan-style LCS [30]. From the perspective of meta-heuristic systems XCS and its derivatives are online single-solution LCS, meaning that the system updates itself using single datapoints or experiences and the whole population forms the solution [9]. XCS combines a population-based evolutionary algorithm (EA), more specifically a GA, with a Q-learning-like RL scheme that is used to update subsets of the population sharing the same selected action called action-sets. Due to the combined and intertwined work of the GA and RL components of XCS, we additionally categorise XCS and related LCS using both components as Evolutionary Reinforcement Learning (ERL) methods.

Classifiers, also called rules or localised models, are the core elements of XCS. One such classifier is defined as $cl = (C, a, p, \varepsilon, F, \dots)$ and consists of a *condition* C, the *action* a it advocates, the *prediction* p of the payoff, the current prediction *error* ε as an error estimation for the previous predictions, its accuracy-based fitness value F, which is defined an inverse relationship to the prediction error [33], and additional bookkeeping parameters. All currently alive classifiers are collected in the population $[P]$. From an ML perspective, the population corresponds to the global model consisting of local models in form of the classifiers containing the learnable parameters of the system.

The original XCS utilised ternary conditions restricting it to binary input. Wilson [34] alleviated this with (XCSR) by introducing hyperrectangle conditions making XCS applicable to real-valued problems. Furthermore, the constant prediction of XCS was replaced with a computed prediction in XCSF [35] allowing it to learn more complex problems. Later, the Recursive Linear Least Squares (RLS) update was introduced improving computed prediction [15].

Figure 1 shows a schema of XCS' structure and sketches its main loop with arrows. For each new time-step t, XCS forms a *match set* $[M]$ out of all classifiers whose condition matches the current observation $\sigma(t)$. If $|[M]| = 0$ or the number of unique actions in $[M]$ is less than the given threshold θ_{mna}, the *covering* mechanism adds new classifiers to $[P]$ and $[M]$ matching $\sigma(t)$. Following this, the match set is used to calculate the *prediction array* PA. It has one entry per action. The entry of an action a, called *system prediction* for a, is computed as a fitness-weighted average of all prediction values of those classifiers advocating a. PA is utilised to select the system response, more precisely the action for the current time step, following an exploration/exploitation strategy which is also called an *action selection regime*. This strategy usually corresponds to epsilon greedy, selecting the best or a random action with a certain probability ε, or alternating between exploration, selection a random action, and exploitation, selecting the currently best action, episodes.

All actions that advocate the selected action are then collected in the *action set* $[A]$. The same action is passed to the environment. The latter executes it and passes the resulting reward back to the XCS. Next, the RL component updates the classifiers of the current action set $[A]$ or the preceding action set depending on whether XCS is faced with a single- or multi-step problem. The steady-state niche GA of XCS operates on action sets and is usually activated after the RL update. It is roughly called if the mean time difference to its last call exceeds the given threshold θ_{GA}. It follows the same case distinction as the RL update. First, the GA (usually) selects two parent classifiers using roulette or tournament selection, copies them and applies to a certain probability a crossover and a mutation operator on them. By doing this, the GA exerts evolutionary pressure on the population of XCS, which enables the system to evolve maximally general and accurate classifiers. This is encompassed by Wilson's generalisation hypothesis [33]. In their formal investigations, Butz et al. [4] identified several pressures active within the population and confirmed the hypothesis theoretically.

For more details about the implementation of a canonical XCS, including update formulas, the GA, and hyperparameters, the reader is referred to the algorithmic description of Butz et al. [5]. For simplicity sake, we treat XCS as an umbrella term for all XCS variants.

3.2 Related Work in Neural LCSs

As aforementioned, there exists prior research on the idea of integrating ANNs into the classifiers of an LCS.

The historically most covered variant of this idea are so-called neural rules originally introduced by Bull et al. [3] corresponding to integrating an ANN into each classifier. It replaces the condition and computes the action. The follow-up research on neural rules improving the concept eventually
ceased after Howard et al. [12] extended their approach of neural rules using spiking neural networks. If solely the condition is replaced by an ANN, we call this neural condition following Preen et al. [21]. Applying neural conditions to RL problems was so far covered sparingly by publications. Our initial experiments on neural conditions [23] stated not favourable results.

One related approach originally of Dam et al. [7] replaces the action of sUpervised Classifier System (UCS) with a shallow ANN. The condition of the system remains unchanged. Note that actions in UCS correspond to classes or other labels, but not to actions in the original sense derived from RL. Recent works built on this approach replacing the shallow ANN with DNNs [2,13].

Building on XCSF, Lanzi et al. [14] proposed neural prediction. It replaces the weight vector of a classifier with a sigmoid-activated shallow ANN with one output and updates it with Stochastic Gradient Descent (SGD). Preen et al. [20,21] integrated neural conditions and neural prediction with DNNs with multiple outputs into their classifiers for autoencoding and classification. We [23,24] re-examined a modernised variant of the original single output neural prediction for RL.

3.3 Perspective on OC

This paper follows the notion of OC defined by Tomforde et al. [31], already outlined in Sect. 1. OC augments technical system with life-like or self-* properties such as self-organisation, self-healing, self-explaining, and self-adaptation creating OC systems with sensors allowing it to perceive its environment and actuators allowing to manipulate it. From a systemic point of view, an OC system consists of two complementary components: The first component fulfils the technical purpose of the system, while a second component implements the organic capabilities, i.e., adaptive capabilities of the system. Meaning a typical OC system can self-learn and self-adapt autonomously and dynamically to the perceived observations in its environment. These aspects are usually implemented using ML methods – predominately using an XCS variant [31].

Consequently, the PhD project described here aims to improve the XCS-based controller of an OC system, and thus its self-learning and self-adaptivity.

4 Research Questions

The research objective previously introduced in Sect. 2 is targeted by dividing it into Research Questions (RQs). How they affect the different components of XCS is visualised in Fig. 2.

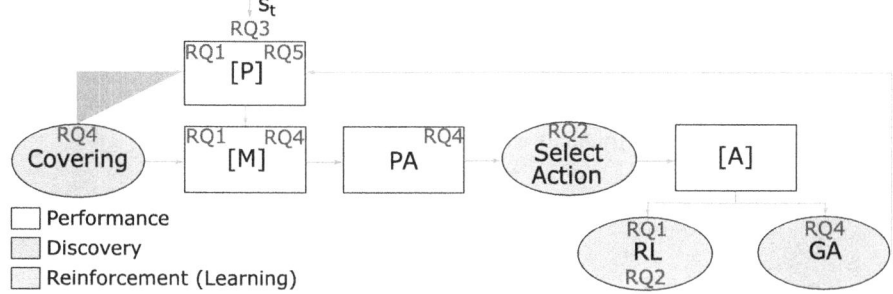

Fig. 2. Reduced schematic of the general XCS architecture annotated with which research question will affect them expectedly. For a better overview, see Fig. 1.

RQ1 What is the effect on the learning capabilities and performance of XCS when integrating DNNs into its classifiers?

DRL methods owe large amounts of their success to the computational and representational capabilities of ANNs. Analogously, XCS might benefit if its components are replaced by DNNs. Prior work before this PhD project doing this with shallow ANNs had similar to old RL methods no such effect. We intent to improve and modernise these approaches by using modern ANNs and DNNs. In addition, we plan to investigate further options to integrate DNNs into XCS.

RQ2 Can additional techniques of DRL or ERL be integrated into the components or classifiers of XCS? What is their impact on its learning capabilities and performance?

DRL methods faced similar issues as XCS including stability issues and sample efficiency. Given the close relationship between the RL component and Q-learning, it is conceivable that some solutions may be transferable to XCS variants. Experience Replay (ER) was already transferred to XCS and improved the single-step performance as well as the performance in at least one multi-step environment but also showed instability issues in others [28].

RQ3 Can hybridisation of XCS with Deep Learning or other methods, allow it to learn with higher-dimensional data than in its current state?

There have been no contributions in learning RL problems on images with XCS, yet. This is likely caused by the faced high-dimensionality, problematic for Michigan-style LCSs [8], when directly learning on the pixels of images, which was discussed for applying XCS variants [6] or related LCS such as UCS [27] to supervised learning. They addressed this by crafting problem-specific input states with smaller dimensionality [6] or by crafting image and statistics-based features [27]. Creating a Deep Learning and XCS hybrid, leveraging the representational capabilities of the former and combining them with the interpretability of the latter could allow the system to learn higher-dimensional state spaces. A recent branch of hybrid systems, pioneered by Matsumoto et al. [17], combines XCS or XCSR and deep autoencoders to allow XCS to learn on the lower dimensional latent representation of the input data. After this, most related approaches use the population of classifiers trained in latent space to bootstrap a population of human-readable classifiers in the data space [17,25,37].Such approaches were so far not applied to RL which is a promising option to allow XCS to learn on images and other high dimensional input.

RQ4 What are possible LCS-driven solutions to the weaknesses and limits of XCS in multi-step RL?

In general, Deep LCSs and hybrid systems would benefit from general systemic improvements and some of the weaknesses of XCS variants might only be solvable via this route. Since the introduction of XCS and XCSF research on LCSs has not been stagnant. Until now, there is nearly no published work transferring improvements from LCSs for supervised learning to XCS for RL. The line of UCS over ExSTraCS 2.0 to the recent Survival LCS are purely intended for supervised learning [36]. However, their relation to XCS suggests that some of their improvements might be transferable to XCS for improving its performance in RL problems. Additionally, concepts derived from innovative and systemically different LCS such as SuprRB [11] or the Phenotypic LCS [16] may offer additional potential for improving a RL focused approach for LCS.

RQ5 When hybridising XCS with Deep Learning, how can the system be augmented to mitigate a potential or be designed in a way that limits a loss of interpretability?

One of the often-addressed advantages of XCS is its interpretability. Hybridising Deep Learning with XCS or related LCS leading to a Deep XCS or hybrid system risks a loss of interpretability due to the near black-box nature of ANNs. Combining resulting systems with techniques from the field of XAI might be an option to partially mitigate such a loss in interpretability. Another approach could be to design a hybrid system in a way to limit the harm on its interpretability. In addition, this RQ should also include an investigation on how to quantify the interpretability of created LCSs, comparing it to classic XCS variants.

5 State of the PhD Project

In our already published works, we combined XCSF with neural prediction, neural conditions, and experience replay in order to gain first insights on RQ 1 and RQ 3. Neural prediction led to first favourable results and combining ER with neural prediction led to a performance improvement for the single-step problem, RMP-6. The results for neural conditions remained inconclusive. XCSF with neural conditions compared to hyperrectangle conditions achieved similar performance for Maze6 and substantially worse performance in deterministic Frozen Lake 8×8, meaning Frozen Lake without stochastic actions [23]. Following, we examined how XCSF with neural prediction performs with and without GA in several multi-step mazes and deterministic Frozen Lake 8×8 [24], providing insights for RQ1 and RQ4. It showed that neural prediction can lead to a better performance in Maze6 while leading to a very similar one in Frozen Lake. It also demonstrated that populations solely created by the covering operator for hyperrectangles in Unordered-Bound Representation (UBR) could learn the examined environments to a sometimes better, similar or slightly smaller extent than those with GA when using neural prediction. This showed that the GA of XCS requires a comparatively large amount of classifiers for an at best comparatively small performance gain when using neural prediction. It highlights the need for an improved GA. It should evolve smaller populations of better selected rules that either only contribute to the global solution if they contribute positively with some certainty.

In parallel to this paper, we submitted a now accepted paper [22] examining modernised neural rules and neural conditions for XCSF providing further insights to RQ1. Our results indicate that neural conditions are an adequate alternative condition representation outperforming hyperrectangles in almost all targeted environments. For details, we refer to the individual publications. There are two further papers currently under review: One investigates combining XCSF with two techniques analogous to DRL techniques, advancing our insights in RQ2. The other one marks our first contribution to RQ3. In the future, we plan to advance our research on RQ3 with the aim of allowing XCSF learning environments with high-dimensional state spaces such as images. In parallel to that, we want to investigate RQ1 further. This should include more insights to neural prediction and on the behaviour of neural conditions in an actual OC system and how they partition state spaces. Furthermore, we want to investigate applying our proposed systems to more varied RL environments reducing the reliance on grid-world tasks.

6 Conclusion

This paper outlined the intended path of the described PhD project to improve the RL capabilities of XCS variants by hybridising them with Deep Learning in order to close or narrow the gap to DRL. The background of the objective, the different research questions implied by it and possible directions to address them were described. This includes integrating ANNs into classifiers, combining Deep Learning and XCS to address its high-dimensionality issues, drawing inspiration from DRL and other LCSs as well as the question how to prevent or mitigate a loss of interpretability of hybrid systems. First contributions concentrated on neural prediction showing potential of the technique while not being fully able to leverage it. Also, the performance impact of the GA was investigated. Additional work is currently under review or work in progress. This includes further work on integrating ANNs into classifiers as well as taking inspiration from DRL and Deep Learning. In the near future, further contributions to integrating ANNs into classifiers and on how XCS variants might deal with environments featuring higher-dimensional input are planned.

Acknowledgments. Many thanks to Prof. Dr.-Ing. Sven Tomforde for supervising this PhD project.

References

1. Barry, A.: Limits in long path learning with XCS. In: Prod. of GECCO'03. Springer Berlin Heidelberg (2003)
2. Bu, S.J., Kang, H.B., Cho, S.B.: Ensemble of deep convolutional learning classifier system based on genetic algorithm for database intrusion detection. Electronics (2022)
3. Bull, L., O'Hara, T.: Accuracy-based neuro and neuro-fuzzy classifier systems. In: Prod. of GECCO '02. Morgan Kaufmann Publishers Inc. (2002)
4. Butz, M., Kovacs, T., Lanzi, P.L., Wilson, S.W.: Toward a Theory of Generalization and Learning in XCS. IEEE Trans. on Evol, Comput (2004)
5. Butz, M., Wilson, S.W.: An algorithmic description of XCS. In: Revised Papers from IWLCS '00. Springer-Verlag (2000)
6. Coombe, C., Howard, D., Browne, W.: Learning classifier systems as a solver for the abstraction and reasoning corpus. In: Prod. of GECCO-C '24. ACM (2024)
7. Dam, H., Abbass, H., Lokan, C.: Xin Yao: Neural-based learning classifier systems. IEEE Trans. Knowl. Data Eng. (2008)
8. Debie, E., Shafi, K.: Implications of the curse of dimensionality for supervised learning classifier systems: theoretical and empirical analyses. Patt. Analy. Appl. (2019)
9. Heider, M., Pätzel, D., Stegherr, H., Hähner, J.: A metaheuristic perspective on learning classifier systems. In: Metaheuristics for Machine Learning. Springer Nature Singapore (2023)
10. Heider, M., Pätzel, D., Wagner, A.R.M.: An overview of LCS research from 2021 to 2022. In: Prod. of GECCO-C '22. ACM (2022)
11. Heider, M., Stegherr, H., Sraj, R., Pätzel, D., et al.: Suprb in the Context of Rule-Based Machine Learning (2023)
12. Howard, D., Bull, L., Lanzi, P.L.: A cognitive architecture based on a learning classifier system with spiking classifiers. arXiv:1508.07700 [cs] (2015)
13. Kim, J.Y., Cho, S.B.: Exploiting deep convolutional neural networks for a neural-based learning classifier system (2019)
14. Lanzi, P.L., Loiacono, D.: XCSF with neural prediction. In: Prod. of ICEC '06. IEEE (2006)

15. Lanzi, P.L., Loiacono, D., Wilson, S.W., Goldberg, D.E.: Generalization in the XCSF classifier system: analysis, improvement, and extension. Evol. Comput. (2) (2007)
16. Liu, Y., Cui, Y., Cheng, W., Browne, W.N., et al.: A phenotypic learning classifier system for problems with continuous features. In: Prod. of GECCO '24. ACM (2024)
17. Matsumoto, K., Takano, R., Tatsumi, T., Sato, H., et al.: XCSR based on compressed input by deep neural network for high dimensional data. In: Prod. of GECCO-C '18'. ACM (2018)
18. Mnih, V., Kavukcuoglu, K., Silver, D., Rusu, A.A., et al.: Human-level control through deep reinforcement learning. Nature (2015)
19. Müller-Schloer, C., Tomforde, S.: Organic Computing - Technical Systems for Survival in the Real World. Birkhäuser (2017)
20. Preen, R.J., Bull, L.: Deep learning with a classifier system: initial results. arXiv:2103.01118 [cs] (2021)
21. Preen, R.J., Wilson, S.W., Bull, L.: Autoencoding with a classifier system. IEEE Trans. Evol. Comput. (2021)
22. Schönberner, C., Rothenburger, K.M., Mackensen, A., Tomforde, S.: Neural rules for reinforcement learning with XCSF as controller in organic computing systems. In: Prod. of ARCS '25. Springer Int. Publ. (2025)
23. Schönberner, C., Tomforde, S.: Deep reinforcement learning with a classifier system – first steps. In: Prod. of ARCS '22. Springer Int. Publ. (2022)
24. Schönberner, C., Tomforde, S.: XCS: Is covering all you need? In: Prod. of GECCO-C '24. ACM (2024)
25. Shiraishi, H., Tadokoro, M., Hayamizu, Y., Fukumoto, Y., et al.: Increasing accuracy and interpretability of high-dimensional rules for learning classifier system. In: Prod. of CEC'21. IEEE (2021)
26. Siddique, A., Heider, M., Iqbal, M., Shiraishi, H.: A survey on learning classifier systems from 2022 to 2024 (2024)
27. Siddique, A., Iqbal, M., Browne, W.N.: A comprehensive strategy for mammogram image classification using learning classifier systems. In: Prod. of CEC '16 (2016)
28. Stein, A., Maier, R., Rosenbauer, L., Hähner, J.: XCS classifier system with experience replay. In: Prod. of GECCO '20. ACM (2020)
29. Stein, A., Rauh, D., Tomforde, S., Hähner, J.: Interpolation in the eXtended classifier system: an architectural perspective. J. of Sys, Arch (2017)
30. Stein, A., Tomforde, S.: Reflective learning classifier systems for self-adaptive and self-organising agents. In: Prod. of ACSOS-C '21 (2021)
31. Tomforde, S., Sick, B., Müller-Schloer, C.: Organic computing in the spotlight. arXiv:1701.08125 [cs.MA] (2017)
32. Wagner, A.R.M., Stein, A.: Mechanisms to alleviate over-generalization in XCS for continuous-valued input spaces. SN Comput. Sci. (2022)
33. Wilson, S.W.: Classifier fitness based on accuracy. Evol. Comput (1995)
34. Wilson, S.W.: Get real! XCS with continuous-valued inputs. In: Learning Classifier Systems. Springer Berlin Heidelberg (2000)
35. Wilson, S.W.: Classifiers that approximate functions. Nat. Comput. (2002)
36. Woodward, A., Bandhey, H., Moore, J.H., Urbanowicz, R.J.: Survival-LCS: a rule-based machine learning approach to survival analysis. In: Prod. of GECCO '24. ACM (2024)
37. Yatsu, N., Shiraishi, H., Sato, H., Takadama, K.: Exploring high-dimensional rules indirectly via latent space through a dimensionality reduction for XCS. In: Prod. of GECCO'23. ACM (2023)

AI-Based Computer Vision Methods to Monitor Emission-Relevant Parameters in Livestock Barns

Simon Mielke

Department of Artificial Intelligence in Agricultural Engineering,
University of Hohenheim, Garbenstraße 9, 70599 Stuttgart, Germany
simon.mielke@uni-hohenheim.de

Abstract. In the context of climate change and the greenhouse effect, the source and cause of emissions is a well known and much debated issue. This includes the role that agriculture, and in particular livestock production, plays as a source of emissions. Measuring emissions in pig and dairy barns is therefore very important, but also very complex and expensive. This especially applies to free-ventilated barns, which are the preferred choice for animal welfare reasons and have a heterogeneous and dynamic distribution of gas concentrations. An alternative to measuring emissions is to model them using other parameters such as the size and temperature of emission sources. These parameters are mainly surfaces soiled with excrements such as urine or feces and can so far only be measured manually by humans. In this PhD project the research gap in the automated detection of emission sources and emission-relevant parameters will be addressed. For this purpose, both RGB and thermal infrared videos are recorded in several pig and dairy barns over a period of several weeks. The video data is then cut into frames, pre-processed and annotated. Subsequently, AI-based object detection models will be trained on the annotated data for different use cases. The focus is on real-time detection models such as YOLO and RT-DETR. Further the combined use of RGB and IR data modalities through fusion models and image fusion in pre-processing will be investigated. In addition to the ability to model emission dynamics more precisely, the automated detection contributes to an improved farm management in the barn and paves the way for a completely self-organized management in the future.

Keywords: Digital Agriculture · Object detection · Livestock farming · IR data

1 Introduction

Emissions from agriculture accounted for over 7,7% of total emissions in Germany in 2023. Around 68.1% of this is attributable to livestock farming [48]. The proportion of ammonia emissions in Germany due to agriculture is around 95% and the proportion caused by livestock farming is 70% [42]. Also 67 % of nitrous oxide (N_2O) and 76 % of total methane emissions (CH_4) in Germany came from agriculture in 2022 [43]. Agriculture, and in particular the livestock sector, is therefore an important source of emissions and greenhouse gases in Germany [48] and also worldwide [10]. The measurement of these emissions are complex and expensive processes for which cost-effective alternatives are being researched [21,34,53]. The measurement of airborne emissions from freely ventilated livestock buildings is associated with additional uncertainties [8]. Here, there is a very complex, heterogeneous and dynamic distribution of gas concentrations, which makes it impossible to clearly identify positions of the outgoing air (as in mechanically ventilated stables). An alternative to measure emissions is the mechanistic modeling of them [17,41]. To automatically observe the parameters required for a mechanistic model of emissions (e.g. the area of urine puddles on the floor) in a high spatial and temporal resolution, the use of computer vision tasks based on AI and machine learning (ML) such as object detection offers promising opportunities.

1.1 Problem Statement

In order to be able to model emissions instead of measuring them, other parameters must be measured. The most important parameters for this include the area and temperature of the floor contaminated with excrements (especially urine) [1,12,41]. Information on how many animals are present in which functional areas and what behavior they exhibit can also be used for modeling or predicting emissions. On the one hand, this can be due to a temporal or spatial correlation of the behavior with the emissions [22] or, on the other hand, through the direct detection of the elimination behavior and thus the formation of the emission sources. The challenge this PhD project addresses by leveraging AI and, is the fact that so far for the measurement or the observation of the necessary parameters (animals, urine puddles, feces) a human is needed continuously. But human resources for observation and monitoring tasks are limited due to time and cost reasons. The focus here is on dairy cows and fattening pigs. A unique feature is that, in addition to basic RGB images, thermal images in mid infrared range are used as a data basis.

1.2 Organic Computing

The PhD project is related to organic computing in two aspects. One consists in an application of the results of the PhD project, in an intelligent and self-organized barn. Referring to [33] the barn would be the organic system under observation and control with at least the animals as self-aware heterogeneous nodes. The automated detection of emission related objects will then be the analyzer component of the observer. In this scenario the controller can, for instance, send robots to the detected emission sources in order to remove them or activate reduction techniques such as modified ventilation, floor cooling or the application of urease inhibitors. The other aspect is that the used neural networks, described in Subsect. 3.2, have the ability to learn on their own and thus to self-adapt. This can be used together with the described system as Layer 2, whereby the system becomes self-reflective and can continually self-improve. This implies that the automated detection contributes to an improved barn management and paves the way for a completely self-organized management in the future.

2 Related Work

Research on emission dynamics in animal livestock farming has been conducted for several decades. Several studies exist on different methods of measuring emissions in pig and cattle barns with laser technologies [3,36,47] or other methods like fluorescence sensors, measuring the ammonia flux or tracer ratio methods [6,21,30,31,35]. There are also several research projects on the modeling of emissions [4,11,13,18,51], which parameters are required for this [1,5,28,41] and how these parameters can be measured [37–40]. AI and ML are already being used in livestock farming, but mainly for the detection and tracking of animals [2,16,29,49,50] and not for the detection of emission-relevant parameters. Another area of application is pose identification and behavior detection [14,26]. The use of AI was also investigated in connection with dairy cows and methane emissions [19]. However, this was about estimating herd and farm size based on aerial photographs. Furthermore, there are approaches for the use of AI in the modeling of methane emissions [15]. However, their use is limited to regressions and AI models that directly estimate emissions based on input parameters. The use of AI to directly capture the input parameters is not described. To conclude, there are gaps in research about the use of AI-based computer vision methods for recording emission-relevant parameters in livestock farming. The combined use of RGB and thermal IR images as a data basis for this purpose, which is also one of the objectives of this work, has also not been researched at all.

3 Doctoral Project

Based on this information and the identified research gaps, a doctoral project is conducted, which is described in more detail below.

3.1 Objectives and Research Questions

In particular, the PhD project will investigate whether, in what way and how well AI and especially Deep Learning (DL) can be used in conjunction with RGB and IR video data from livestock barns of pigs and cattle to detect the parameters necessary for modeling the occurring emissions. This includes the tasks of detecting and counting the animals, detecting and distinguishing the excrements (feces vs. urine) and detecting the start of the animals elimination behavior. The behavior is to be determined by combining the poses and the areas where the animals are staying (how many animals are where and in which pose). The aim thereby is to answer the following research questions:

- Is the precision of the detected process parameters high enough to use them as input for further steps such as mechanistic modeling of the emissions?
- Are there differences between the use of the techniques in dairy and pig husbandry?
- What are the advantages and disadvantages of using thermal infrared images compared to RGB images and to what extent can the information be used in a fused way?
- What are the minimum requirements regarding data modality, sensor setup and computational hardware for an implementation in practice?

3.2 Approach

The project can be structured into the following main work packages:

1. **Basic Analysis:** An analysis is carried out to determine the required parameters and the necessary precision for them. For instance, the number of animals and the soiled floor area.
2. **Literature research:** The next step is a detailed literature review of the current methods for determining the required parameters to detect. The analysis of results and experiences from other studies on object detection in animal stables will also be used to find out what needs to be taken into account during planning.
3. **Experimental setup:** This is followed by the planning, organization and execution of the data acquisition in pig and dairy barns. The data will collected with thermal infrared and RGB cameras in several positions in the barn or in several pens.
4. **Data processing:** After that, processing of the collected data takes place. This deals at least with the compression and decompression of the videos, a distortion correction and the selection and annotation of the video frames.
5. **Train/Eval Models:** With the annotated data different AI models and algorithms for real time object detection will be trained, validated and evaluated on two different use cases (excretion detection and functional area monitoring). Following the rapid developments in AI-based object detection at least a state of the art version of the You Only Look Once (YOLO) [32] model will be investigated, as well as of RT-DETR [52], representing a transformer architecture [9,44]. Also a hybrid or custom architecture and image fusion techniques will be included to use the combined information of thermal and RGB Data [20].

3.3 Papers and Milestones

At least three papers are planned, which represent the milestones of the doctoral project. One in the first half of 2025 on the detection of animals and excrements with different AI models in pig barns (Paper 1). Another in the second half of 2025 on a similar issue with dairy cattle with a comparison between models trained from scratch and a transfer learning of the models trained for the pigs (Paper 2). A third should address the topic of different methods to use fused IR and RGB information and is planned for 2026 (Paper 3). Papers on subsequent tasks such as object tracking and the implementation of a federated learning approach [24,25] are additionally or optionally possible. This could represent a further investigation and analysis of the data, but are mainly extensions and optimizations of the planned methods and processes. The use of AI methods, such as deep learning-based object detection, is very resource-intensive in terms of computing power and power consumption. This often goes hand in hand with the need for special non-standard hardware for the calculations. Therefore the practicability of using the AI in the barns, regarding needed computational resources and thus investments, is also aspect which will be investigated during the research and taken into account in the papers.

4 Current State and Discussion

The first steps of the doctoral project have already been completed. In the following, a brief overview of the current status is given and current challenges are discussed.

4.1 Progress Made

In the meantime, video data has already been collected in a pig barn. A pipeline for processing the data has been planned and the first steps have been taken. This includes the lossless compression of the data for more efficient storage, the automated cutting of frames from the video data using image difference hashing [7] and the a radial distortion correction without calibration target using discorpy [45]. Different methods were then tested using a first small data set for the annotation and a standardized method was defined. The labelme tool [46] is used by three people to annotate at segmentation level (polygons) with AI support. All annotations are then viewed again and checked (four-eyes concept). The polygons are then converted into bounding boxes in the style of the COCO format [23].

4.2 Preliminary Findings

The IR data collected differs fundamentally from standardized RGB video data. The video container is special and thus prevents the use of conventional compression methods. The data is also specially stored in the form of one channel with 16 bit singed integers. Based on this knowledge, a custom compression method was developed. In a preliminary study, the basic suitability of different AI architectures for the detection of excrements on infrared images out of pigsties has already been investigated and proven [27]. However, without the differentiation between feces and urine puddles and without the parallel detection of the animals. Figure 1 shows the annotated and predicted objects on a infrared image of a pig pen.

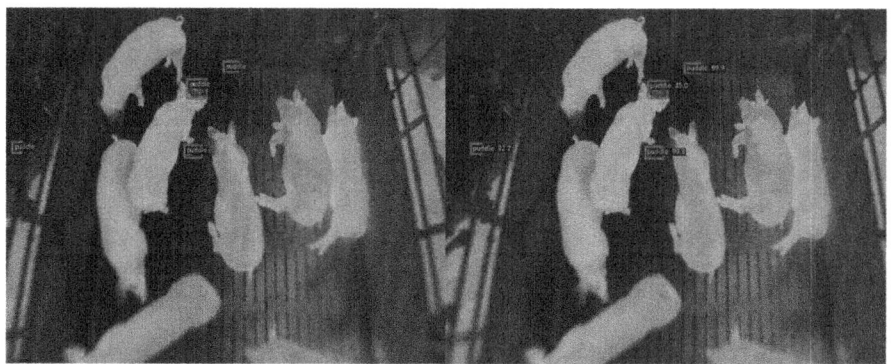

Fig. 1. Infrared image of a pen in a big barn from the preliminary study [27]. The annotations are on the left and the objects detected by a Faster R-CNN on the right.

4.3 Current Challenges

Current challenges include the adequate storage of large amounts of data (up to 100 TB) and the handling of different maximum and minimum temperature limits over the course of the year in the IR data (absolute vs. min-max normalization). Normalizing the data to the whole-year temperature limits offers the advantage, that in all images equally bright objects also have the same temperature. The disadvantage here is, that the images always have a gray blur or are darkened because they never reach the minimum and maximum values at the same time. Conversely, normalization to the current temperature limits of the images results in brighter images with clearer edges between different objects. But objects of the same temperature on different images will have different values.

Another challenge regarding the RGB data is the switch from color images to grayscale images at night. Here we consider several methods. One solution would be including the grayscale data in the same dataset as the daytime data to get a one network for day and night but with less performance. Therefore converting the RGB data into grayscale images to receive a uniform data set would be also a possible option. Another solution could be creating a separate dataset with only gray-scale images and train two AI models. One specifically for the night and one for the day.

Acknowledgments. This PhD project is financially supported by the Federal Ministry of Food and Agriculture (BMEL) based on a decision of the Parliament of the Federal Republic of Germany, granted by the Federal Office for Agriculture and Food (BLE); grant number 28N206507.

Special thanks to my supervisor Jun. Prof. Dr. rer. nat. Anthony Stein [0000-0002-1808-9758]

Disclosure of Interests. The author have no competing interests to declare that are relevant to the content of this article.

References

1. Aarnink, A.J.A., Elzing, A.: Dynamic model for ammonia volatilization in housing with partially slatted floors, for fattening pigs. Livestock Prod. Sci. **53**(2), 153–169 (1998). ISSN 0301-6226
2. Ariza-Sentís, M., et al.: Object detection and tracking in precision farming: a systematic review. Comput. Electron. Agric. **219**, 108757 (2024). ISSN 0168-1699
3. Baldé, H., et al.: Ammonia emissions measured using two different gas-finder open-path lasers. Atmosphere **10**(5) (2019)
4. Bjerg, B., et al.: Modelling of ammonia emissions from naturally ventilated livestock buildings: part 2, air change modelling. Biosyst. Eng. **116**(3), 246–258 (2013)
5. Bjerg, B., et al.: Modelling of ammonia emissions from naturally ventilated livestock buildings. Part 1: ammonia release modelling. Biosyst. Eng. **116**(3), 232–245 (2013)
6. Bjerg, B., et al.: Methane emission from naturally ventilated livestock buildings can be determined from gas concentration measurements. Environ. Monit. Assess. **184**(10), 5989–6000 (2012). ISSN 1573-2959
7. Buchner, J.: JohannesBuchner/Imagehash (2025)
8. Calvet, S., et al.: Measuring gas emissions from livestock buildings: a review on uncertainty analysis and error sources. Biosyst. Eng. Spec. Issue: Emissions Nat. Ventilated Livestock Build. **116**(3), 221–231 (2013). ISSN 1537-5110
9. Carion, N., Massa, F., Synnaeve, G., Usunier, N., Kirillov, A., Zagoruyko, S.: End-to-end object detection with transformers. In: Vedaldi, A., Bischof, H., Brox, T., Frahm, J.-M. (eds.) ECCV 2020. LNCS, vol. 12346, pp. 213–229. Springer, Cham (2020). https://doi.org/10.1007/978-3-030-58452-8_13. ISBN 978-3-030-58451-1
10. Caro, D., et al.: Global and regional trends in greenhouse gas emissions from livestock. Clim. Change **126**(1), 203–216 (2014). ISSN 1573-1480
11. Cortus, E.L., et al.: A dynamic model of ammonia emission from urine puddles. Biosyst. Eng. **99**(3), 390–402 (2008). ISSN 1537-5110
12. Elzing, A., Monteny, G.J.: Ammonia emission in a scale model of a dairy-cow house. Trans. Am. Soc. Agric. Eng. **40**(3), 713–720 (1997)
13. Elzing, A., Monteny, G.J.: Modeling and experimental determination of ammonia emissions rates from a scale model dairy-cow house. Trans. Am. Soc. Agric. Eng. **40**(3), 721–726 (1997)
14. Fan, Q., et al.: Bottom-up cattle pose estimation via concise multi-branch network. Comput. Electron. Agric. **211**, 107945 (2023). ISSN 0168-1699
15. Nejad, J.G., et al.: Advances in methane emission estimation in livestock: a review of data collection methods, model development and the role of AI technologies. Animals **14**(3), 435 (2024). ISSN 2076-2615
16. Guo, Q., et al.: Enhanced camera-based individual pig detection and tracking for smart pig farms. Comput. Electron. Agric. **211**, 108009 (2023). ISSN 0168-1699
17. Hempel, S., et al.: A nested semi-mechanistic model to predict the temporal dynamics of ammonia emissions from a solid floor naturally ventilated dairy cattle building parameter estimation and associated uncertainties. VDI Berichte **2022**(2406), 197–202 (2022)
18. Hempel, S., et al.: Ammonia emission prediction for dairy cattle housing from reaction kinetic modeling to the barn scale. Comput. Electron. Agric. **199**, 107168 (2022). ISSN 0168-1699
19. Jeong, S., et al.: Artificial intelligence approach for estimating dairy methane emissions. Environ. Sci. Technol. **56**(8), 4849–4858 (2022). ISSN 0013-936X

20. Kalamkar, S., Geetha, M.A.: Multimodal image fusion: a systematic review. Decis. Anal. J. **9**, 100327 (2023). ISSN 2772-6622
21. Kamp, J.N., et al.: Low-cost fluorescence sensor for ammonia measurement in livestock houses. Sensors **21**(5), 1701 (2021). ISSN 1424-8220
22. Lardy, Q., et al.: Effects of daytime or night-time grazing on animal performance, diurnal behaviour and enteric methane emissions from dairy cows at high latitudes. Acta Agric. Scand. Sect. A - Anim. Sci. **73**(1–2), 28–42 (2024). ISSN 0906- 4702
23. Lin, T.-Y., et al.: Microsoft COCO: common objects in context. In: Fleet, D., Pajdla, T., Schiele, B., Tuytelaars, T. (eds.) ECCV 2014. LNCS, vol. 8693, pp. 740–755. Springer, Cham (2014). https://doi.org/10.1007/978-3-319-10602-1_48. ISBN 978-3-319-10602-1
24. Liu, B., et al.: Recent advances on federated learning: a systematic survey. Neurocomputing **597**, 128019 (2024). ISSN 0925-2312
25. Mao, A., et al.: FedAAR: a novel federated learning framework for animal activity recognition with wearable sensors. Animals **12**(16), 2142 (2022). ISSN 2076-2615
26. Mao, R., et al.: An integrated gather-and-distribute mechanism and attention-enhanced deformable convolution model for pig behavior recognition. Animals **14**(9), 1316 (2024). ISSN 2076-2615
27. Mielke, S., Stein, A.: Excretion detection in pigsties using convolutional and transformerbased deep neural networks (2024). arXiv: 2412.00256 [cs]. Accessed 19 Feb 2025
28. Ni, J.: Mechanistic models of ammonia release from liquid manure: a review. J. Agric. Eng. Res. **72**(1), 1–17 (1999). ISSN 0021-8634
29. Parmiggiani, A., et al.: Don't get lost in the crowd: graph convolutional network for online animal tracking in dense groups. Comput. Electron. Agric. **212**, 108038 (2023). ISSN 0168-1699
30. Phillips, V.R., et al.: SE–structures and environment: a review of methods for measuring emission rates of ammonia from livestock buildings and slurry or manure stores, part 1: assessment of basic approaches. J. Agric. Eng. Res. **77**(4), 355–364 (2000). ISSN 0021-8634
31. Phillips, V.R., et al.: SE–structures and environment: a review of methods for measuring emission rates of ammonia from livestock buildings and slurry or manure stores, part 2: monitoring flux rates, concentrations and airflow rates. J. Agric. Eng. Res. **78**(1), 1–14 (2001). ISSN 0021-8634
32. Redmon, J., et al.: You only look once: unified, real-time object detection. In: 2016 IEEE Conference on Computer Vision and Pattern Recognition (CVPR), pp. 779–788 (2016)
33. Richter, U., et al: Towards a generic observer/controller architecture for organic computing. In: INFORMATIK 2006 – Informatik Für Menschen, Band 1, pp. 112–119. Gesellschaft für Informatik e.V., Bonn (2006). ISBN 978-3-88579-187-4
34. Rom, H.B., Zhang, G.-Q.: Time delay for aerial ammonia concentration measurements in livestock buildings. Senors **10**(5), 4634–4642 (2010). ISSN 1424-8220
35. Rumburg, B., et al.: Measurement and modeling of atmospheric flux of ammonia from dairy milking cow housing. Atmos. Environ. Agric. Air Qual.: State Sci. (AAQ-2006) **42**(14), 3364–3379 (2008). ISSN 1352-2310
36. Shen, F., et al.: Real-time monitoring of CH4 and N2O emissions from livestock using mid-infrared external cavity quantum cascade laser absorption spectroscopy. J. Quant. Spectrosc. Radiat. Transf. **327**, 109131 (2024). ISSN 0022-4073
37. Snoek, D.J.W., et al.: Assessing fresh urine puddle chemistry in commercial dairy cow houses. Biosyst. Eng. **159**, 143–153 (2017)

38. Snoek, D.J.W., et al.: Assessing fresh urine puddle physics in commercial dairy cow houses. Biosyst. Eng. **159**, 133–142 (2017)
39. Snoek, D.J.W., et al.: Measurement method for urine puddle depth in dairy cow houses as input variable for ammonia emission modelling. Agric. Eng. Int.: CIGR J. **2015**, 30–36 (2015)
40. Snoek, D., et al.: Dynamic behavior of ph in fresh urine puddles of dairy cows. Trans. ASABE (Am. Soc. Agric. Biol. Eng.) **59** (2016)
41. Snoek, D.J.W., et al.: Sensitivity analysis of mechanistic models for estimating ammonia emission from dairy cow urine puddles. Biosyst. Eng. **121**, 12–24 (2014). ISSN 1537-5110
42. Stoll, J.: Ammoniak, Geruch und Staub. Umweltbundesamt (2021). https://www.umweltbundesamt.de/themen/landwirtschaft/umweltbelastungen-der-landwirtschaft/ammoniak-geruch-staub. Accessed 22 July 2024
43. Stoll, J.: Lachgas und Methan. Umweltbundesamt (2024). https://www.umweltbundesamt.de/themen/landwirtschaft/umweltbelastungender-landwirtschaft/lachgas-methan. Accessed 22 July 2024
44. Vaswani, A., et al.: Attention is all you need. In: Advances in Neural Information Processing Systems, vol. 30, pp. 5998–6008. Curran Associates, Inc. (2017)
45. Vo, N.T., Atwood, R.C., Drakopoulos, M.: Radial lens distortion correction with sub-pixel accuracy for X-ray micro-tomography. Opt. Express **23**(25), 32859–32868 (2015). ISSN 1094-4087
46. KentaroWada. Labelme: Image Polygonal Annotation with Python (2024)
47. Wang, K., et al.: An open-path ammonia analyzer for eddy covariance flux measurement. Agric. For. Meteorol. 308–309 (2021)
48. Wilke, S.: Beitrag der Landwirtschaft zu den Treibhausgas-Emissionen. Umweltbundesamt (2024). https://www.umweltbundesamt.de/daten/land-forstwirtschaft/beitrag-der-landwirtschaft-zu-den-treibhausgas. Accessed 22 July 2024
49. Yang, W., et al.: Deformable convolution and coordinate attention for fast cattle detection. Comput. Electron. Agric. **211**, 108006 (2023). ISSN 0168-1699
50. Zhang, B., et al.: Pig eye area temperature extraction algorithm based on registered images. Comput. Electron. Agric. **217**, 108549 (2024). ISSN 0168-1699
51. Zhang, R.H., et al.: A computer model for predicting ammonia release rates from swine manure pits. J. Agric. Eng. Res. **58**(4), 223–229 (1994). ISSN 0021-8634
52. Zhao, Y., et al.: DETRs beat YOLOs on real-time object detection. In: 2024 IEEE/CVF Conference on Computer Vision and Pattern Recognition (CVPR), pp. 16965–16974 (2024)
53. Zhuang, S., et al.: Evaluation of a cost-effective ammonia monitoring system for continuous real-time concentration measurements in a fattening pig barn. Sensors **19**(17), 3669 (2019). ISSN 1424-8220

Open the Black Box: Self-Explainability of AI in Autonomous Marine Systems

Tom Beyer

Intelligent Systems Group, Kiel University, Kiel, Germany
tom.beyer@informatik.uni-kiel.de

Abstract. The rapid advancement of AI makes it ever more important to understand its decision-making—especially in safety-critical areas such as autonomous navigation. This PhD project investigates the self-explainability of autonomous systems using a self-driving ferry. It aims to develop a framework that enables the system to justify its decisions in a transparent manner.

Using Explainable AI, Explainable Reinforcement Learning, Inverse Reinforcement Learning and Causal Modeling, the ferry's expected behavior will be modeled, anomalies detected, causal relationships derived and self-explanations generated. This work could strengthen trust in autonomous systems and contribute to the general explainability of AI by opening the "black box" of its decision-making.

Keywords: Explainable Artificial Intelligence · Autonomous Systems · Autonomous Surface Vehicles · Organic Computing · Self-Explanation

1 Motivation

The capabilities of Artificial Intelligence (AI) are growing at a rapid pace, and its use is spreading to ever more areas of society [23]. It is, therefore, increasingly important to ensure the ability to manage this technology. Especially given the fact that these growing capabilities are accompanied by an ever-increasing complexity of the underlying models. Organic Computing (OC), in its ultimate goal of increasing the robustness of systems, relies at its core on those AI and Machine Learning (ML) mechanisms for decision-making [25]. At the same time, OC helps to deal with this growing complexity, ensuring that we can handle this advancing technology, whose limits yet remain to be seen.

An area in which AI significantly impacts human society is transportation [14]. Here, the trend towards ever greater autonomy continues to grow. In addition to the widely publicized advances in self-driving cars, a similar change is also emerging in shipping [12]. However, even though many decisions in this field are already being made with the help of technical systems, complete autonomy still remains a great challenge.

As in road traffic, the main focus here is on safety. Especially autonomous ships with people on board are an OC scenario that places high demands on resilience against disturbances in system behavior. To be considered safe, the decisive factor is human acceptance of the decisions made by the system [2]. This applies to nautical personnel (onboard, on land, or on nearby ships) and passengers. A high degree of trust in the reliability of the technology is necessary, as human lives are at stake. Safety and controllability will also likely be key to the pending legal approval and regulation of autonomous shipping.

To ensure manageability of autonomous systems it is vital to understand their decision-making processes [2]. This requires opening the "black box" of AI to provide transparency and reveal the rationale behind its choices. In other words, the autonomous system must be able to *self-explain*—one of the multiple self-* properties of OC [25]. It must be comprehensible to humans and other autonomous actors what the AI perceives, how it assesses the situation, and why it makes the corresponding decisions—or chooses not to make others. This approach seems to be the most promising way to assess the consequences of using this ever more powerful technology and build trust in it.

2 Problem Statement and Research Questions

Main Goal

To develop a concept for the self-explanation of system behavior resulting from (semi-)autonomous, self-adaptive, and self-organizing decisions, and to implement this concept using the example of an autonomous ferry.

Research Questions

RQ1: How can the normal behavior of an autonomous ferry on the Kiel Fjord be effectively modeled and recognized using sensor data (e.g., camera, lidar, radar) and contextual information (e.g., weather forecast, nautical charts, AIS data)?

RQ2: How can anomalous situations that deviate from normal behavior and require explanation be reliably identified and processed?

RQ3: How can causalities be derived from the trained behavior of the autonomous system?

RQ4: How can self-explanations be defined, what essential components must they contain, and what existing approaches can serve as a foundation for further development?

RQ5: How can comprehensible self-explanations be generated from the causal structures?

RQ6: How can these self-explanations be meaningfully evaluated and the success of the entire process be assessed?

RQ7: To what extent can techniques and insights be extracted from the developed framework that expand the general understanding of AI?

3 Background

To examine the background to this research, several key topics need to be explored. Much of what has to do with self-explainability of an autonomous ferry is based on young and still experimental research areas. This section therefore begins by clarifying the term explainability, then explores various techniques for establishing the explainability of AI, with explainable reinforcement learning as a key subtype for autonomous ferries. The next focus will be on causality, which is crucial in this context, as plausible explanations often rely on causal relationships. Finally, the section examines self-explainability and recent developments in this still under-researched field.

3.1 Explainability

The term *explanation* refers to different ways of providing information about a phenomenon to a recipient [24]. However, the term is philosophically controversial, and there is no uniform consensus on how exactly explanations should be defined [15,31]. In the context of this research, the above definition can be used tentatively: here, the phenomenon refers to the functionality of an autonomous system or the reasoning behind its decisions [24]. In a broader sense, it is therefore a matter of clarifying what causes a system to produce certain outputs or processes [28].

Two basic characteristics of explanations are *interpretability* and *completeness* [15]. Interpretability aims to describe the internal processes of a system adequately for a specific target group. Completeness focuses on how accurate this description is. The latter highlights a crucial point: in principle, all explanations are "wrong" to a certain extent. If they were perfect or complete, they would have to reproduce the internal processes of the original model in full—an impractical approach [24]. Instead, "good" explanations are heuristics that simplify these processes to make them understandable. Although there seems to be a trade-off between interpretability and completeness [15]. A very precise explanation may be too complex (e.g., a detailed mathematical representation of all the processes in a neural network), while a very simple one may be too shallow to predict system behavior accurately.

Explainability is essential for building trust in AI [3,29]. This is a major challenge for autonomous ships in particular, as critical decisions are made here that involve human lives [16]. To create trust, users must perceive the system as transparent [29]. At the same time, the respective context in which the system operates should be taken into account as well [16]. The explanations should also be adapted to the respective user groups, e.g., passengers, navigators, developers, or external agents [16,28]. The trade-off between interpretability (which ultimately depends on the user) and completeness can also be compensated here by the system providing explanations with varying degrees of detail (completeness)—depending on the target group [15].

In general, explainability is still underexplored in AI research; especially in the context of autonomous marine systems [16]. It can be assumed that a lack of explainability is a decisive hurdle for the broad acceptance of autonomous systems and AI in general [15]. This challenge is underscored by EU regulations on data protection (GDPR), which grant users a "right to explanation" of algorithmic decisions that affect them [18]. Ultimately, the use of autonomous systems will only be ethically justifiable if their decisions can be explained [1].

3.2 Explainable Artificial Intelligence (XAI)

The concept of XAI dates back to 1994, when an intelligent agent was designed to generate explanations in a flight simulation [32]. The term itself first appeared in 2004 in Van Lent et al. [1]. XAI encompasses methods that make AI model decisions transparent, interpretable, and comprehensible. In recent years, this field has grown rapidly [31].

XAI techniques can be classified by various criteria. First, there are two basic approaches: *intrinsic* XAI (sometimes also called transparent or similar) and *post-hoc* XAI [11,24,29]. The intrinsic approach is integrated into the model's architecture, making its functioning directly explainable (e.g., decision trees), while the post-hoc approach explains system behavior retrospectively from the outside (e.g., a different meta-model). This can be done within two scopes: *global* and *local* [11,29]. The global perspective aims to clarify the entire model's logic, so that all decisions are understandable, while the local approach focuses on explaining individual decisions [1]. Additionally, XAI methods can be divided into *model-specific* (applicable to specific models) and *model-agnostic* (applicable to all models); however, this distinction often aligns with the differentiation between intrinsic and post-hoc [11,29]. A comprehensive overview of various XAI techniques and their applications can be found in Adadi et al. [1], Barredo Arrieta et al. [5], and Phillips et al. [28].

Just as there is no consensus on how explanations should be defined, there is also no standardized way to evaluate them. Approaches can be broadly divided into *user-based* and more *objective* or *heuristic-based* metrics [31]. User-based evaluation depends on the respective target group and the extent to which given explanations meet their needs. Consequently, this metric is rather subjective and context-dependent. In contrast, objective/heuristic-based criteria use mathematical and statistical methods, such as estimating the complexity of a model by means of its size. The choice of evaluation method heavily depends on the use case. A detailed overview of different approaches is provided in Phillips et al. [28].

3.3 Explainable Reinforcement Learning (XRL)

Reinforcement Learning (RL) is often a key component of the control mechanism in OC systems, which lies at their core. It is frequently used in robotics and the control of autonomous vehicles. Safety and trust are particularly important here [32], which makes explainability a crucial factor. A key challenge in XRL, as a branch of XAI, is that individual decisions usually cannot be considered in isolation. Instead, they form interdependent sequences of actions. Furthermore,

RL agents are typically trained without labeled data, meaning that explanations cannot be derived directly from training data, but must be generated from scratch [32].

Various techniques address these challenges, such as reward function decomposition [20] or summarizing agent behavior: a global technique that attempts to gain a general overview of the agent's behavior by simulating it [3]. A detailed survey of various XRL techniques can be found in Puiutta et al. [29] and Wells et al. [32]. In general, however, these techniques face similar problems [32]: they often only deal with specific, simplified "toy samples", making scalability difficult. Additionally, many explanations generated by these methods are overly complex and not easily interpretable by humans. Consequently, XRL remains an experimental field.

A promising technique for explanations—not strictly limited to XRL—is Inverse Reinforcement Learning (IRL) [4]. This method aims to infer an agent's underlying preferences by deriving its reward function from observed behavior. This approach could distill the complexity of an already existing autonomous system into a single function, which could then serve as a basis for generating explanations (especially in combination with causality; see Sect. 3.4).

However, IRL also comes with certain challenges [4]. There are always multiple reward functions that can "explain" the same behavior. Furthermore, as problem complexity increases, IRL also becomes increasingly computationally demanding. It also remains questionable whether IRL can always yield clear and understandable rules for a given target group. This depends significantly on the quality and quantity of the sample data for system behavior. Despite these challenges, IRL appears to be a promising heuristic for modeling and explaining complex autonomous systems.

3.4 Causality

A central aspect of human explanations is causality. And while this concept is also philosophically complex, like "explanation" itself, for the purpose of research here it can be understood pragmatically as the establishment of cause-effect relationships [9]. Causality is therefore essential for the explainability of AI, as "good" explanations should mimic human reasoning [9,22]. This is particularly important for action-centered systems, such as autonomous ferries. Here, any meaningful explanation of the interdependent action sequences should inherently account for causality [6].

There are two basic ways of discovering causality [17]: first, by passively inferring correlations and patterns from observations, and second, by actively manipulating factors and analyzing how other features of the observed system react to them. In practice, these approaches are often combined.

There are various methods that attempt to formalize these principles mathematically and transfer them technically. Potential Outcome (PO) frameworks from statistics attempt to establish probabilistic relationships from observations [13]. Causal Graphical Models (CGMs) use directed graphs to quantify causal relationships between various system features in an understandable way.

Structural Causal Models (SCMs) [27] integrate graphical models, structural equations, and interventional logic. An adaptation of this to RL is the Action Influence Model (AIM) [22], which explicitly accounts for actions. Counterfactual algorithms simulate hypothetical changes in system variables to determine how a different decision could have been reached in the overall system [9]. A comprehensive overview of causality models can be found in Ganguly et al. [13].

However, discovering causalities algorithmically is not trivial. This is often only achieved to a limited extent, as algorithms inherently tend to capture correlations, which do not necessarily imply causation [9]. On the other hand, it can convincingly be argued that the "lack of causality" is currently one of the biggest obstacles on the way to powerful XAI [8].

3.5 Self-Explainability

A self-explanatory system must be capable of autonomously giving reasons for its behavior [33]. Ideally, making the past, present, and future of its behavior understandable [7]. However, just as explainability itself is still in the early stages of research, this is even more true for the sub-field of self-explainability. At the moment, many applications are not able to provide users with appropriate explanations [19].

Nevertheless, some approaches already exist. An early framework uses Recurrent Neural Networks (RNNs) for anomaly detection and classifies them into reason categories [33]. Another basic framework [10] suggests that self-explainability requires a model-like abstraction of the underlying system in order to generate explanations at runtime that are based on cause-effect chains. This should be complemented by self-verification (checking correctness at runtime) as well as reconfiguration (adaptation in case of attacks). Another related concept is Self-Aware Computing [21], which involves learning a model where the system accumulates knowledge about itself and its environment, in order to reason about its own behavior. A more detailed approach is the MAB-Ex framework [7], which describes a structured methodology: *Monitor, Analyze, Build* and *Explain*. It first monitors the system and its environment, then analyzes the collected data. Based on an internal explanation model (which relies on causal relationships), it generates an explanation and finally presents it in a target-specific way.

One of the most advanced frameworks addresses self-explainability for Cyber-Physical Systems (CPSs), like smart homes [19]. This involves overcoming three challenges: heterogeneity of the devices and sensors involved, changes in the system configuration during runtime, and shifts in the explanation context over time (e.g., linguistic variations: "cold" does not always have the same meaning). To overcome these challenges, a generic, standardized communication between devices, a modularized system architecture, and the ability for dynamic self-assessment are required. The proposed system configuration that considers these factors employs decentralized Local Explanatory Components (LECs), each of which monitors specific Observable Components (ObCs) and interprets them accordingly. These local findings are then collected and integrated by a central coordinator (Spotlight), which operates independently of the ObCs. This approach could potentially circumvent limitations of MAB-Ex [7], which, due to its purely centralized explanation model, might encounter issues with scalability and maintenance [19].

Despite these promising approaches, significant challenges remain. Currently, many explainability techniques only work for a specific model or scenario and do not target end users, but provide abstract benchmarks or rough verbalization [19]. This could probably be significantly improved by the rapid advancements in Large Language Models (LLMs).

4 Approach

Based on the foundational concepts outlined in the background, this section sketches the methodological approach of the PhD project. The aim is to develop a concept for the self-explainability of an autonomous system using the example of a self-driving ferry. To achieve this, several methodological steps are necessary, which are oriented on the research questions.

I. Modeling the Expected Behavior of the Ferry. First, the normal behavior of the autonomous ferry needs to be defined and modeled as a baseline (RQ 1). This involves incorporating various sensor data (camera, lidar, radar) and contextual information (e.g., weather data, nautical charts, AIS data), using both real and synthetic sources. A central aspect is quantifying the uncertainty of the model in order to assess its reliability. Technically, this will be carried out within the framework of the CAPTN (Clean Autonomous Public Transport Network) initiative, which, among other goals, aims to develop an autonomous ferry and is already operating a test platform on the Kiel Fjord, whose capacity and preliminary work can be built upon [2].

II. Identifying Situations Requiring Explanation. Beyond normal behavior, anomalies must be identified in a second step (RQ 2). These are likely to include situations that require explanation. In addition to the obligatory anomaly detection, this step also includes classification, the evaluation of the classification quality, and an analysis of the most important underlying features. From the latter, it should be possible to derive initial correlations and influencing factors of the features on the decision-making processes of the overall system. This approach could build on the pipeline in Ziesche et al. [33], which could be refined through specialized anomaly detection for autonomous ships using autoencoders [26].

III. Causal Modeling. To make autonomous decisions explainable, causal relationships between various influencing variables and system behavior must be derived (RQ 3). This is done using various techniques mentioned in the background (see Sect. 3.4), whereby AIM [22] and counterfactuals [9] seem particularly promising. In addition, an inverse analysis of the relationships using IRL [4] will support this process in order to draw further conclusions about the underlying decision-making processes from observed behavior and to consolidate already suspected relationships. This should provide insights into the relevant contextual conditions that can form the basis for explanations.

IV. Generating Self-Explanations. The identified causal relationships serve as the basis for the automatic generation of self-explanations. First, it is necessary to define the essential components of such explanations (RQ 4) before a mechanism can be developed to generate them from the derived causal structures in conjunction with various XAI or XRL techniques (see Sects. 3.2, 3.3) (RQ 5). The result may include visual components as well as linguistic explanations, for which the integration of LLMs might be considered. Starting points are the MAB-Ex framework [7] and the advanced approaches for CPSs [19] mentioned.

V. Evaluation of Explanations. The quality of the generated explanations must be assessed in terms of their comprehensibility and correctness, based on criteria that are yet to be defined. To this end, an evaluation framework for self-explanations must be developed that includes both objective metrics and subjective user perceptions (RQ 6). Impulses for this can be found in the work of Gilpin et al. [15] and Sokol et al. [30].

VI. General Insights for AI. Finally, it will be examined to what extent the methods developed can be transferred to other autonomous systems—especially those operating in dynamic, safety-critical environments (RQ 7). This might include other marine systems such as cargo ships or underwater vehicles, and also other (potentially) autonomous systems such as trains, drones, or self-driving cars. Greater explainability in all these areas could make an essential contribution to strengthening trust in AI decision-making.

5 Conclusion

Since self-explainability of AI is still a relatively young area of research, the corresponding methods and approaches are still in their early stages and are quite experimental. It will therefore be important in this PhD project to test, expand, and adapt various approaches from XAI, XRL, IRL, and causal modeling to develop a framework that is as effective as possible for the respective challenges. Ultimately, this may be a way to generally shed some light on the supposed darkness of the "black box" of AI.

Acknowledgments.. The author thanks Prof. Dr.-Ing. Sven Tomforde for his supervision, valuable advice, and support in this PhD project.

This work is part of the project "CAPTN X-FERRY - Self-Explanatory Behavior of an Autonomous Ferry" (FK: 03SX612A). We would like to thank the German Federal Ministry for Climate Action and Economics for funding in the context of the maritime research program.

References

1. Adadi, A., Berrada, M.: Peeking inside the black-box: a survey on explainable artificial intelligence (XAI). IEEE Access **6**, 52138–52160 (2018)
2. Al-Falouji, G., Haschke, L., Nowotka, D., Tomforde, S.: Self-explanation as a basis for self-integration - the autonomous passenger ferry scenario. In: 2023 IEEE International Conference on Autonomic Computing and Self-Organizing Systems Companion (ACSOS-C), pp. 65–70 (2023)
3. Amir, D., Amir, O.: Highlights: summarizing agent behavior to people. In: Proceedings of the 17th International Conference on Autonomous Agents and Multiagent Systems, AAMAS 2018, Richland, SC, pp. 1168–1176 (2018)
4. Arora, S., Doshi, P.: A survey of inverse reinforcement learning: challenges, methods and progress. Artif. Intell. **297**, 103500 (2021)
5. Barredo Arrieta, A., et al.: Explainable artificial intelligence (XAI): concepts, taxonomies, opportunities and challenges toward responsible AI. Inf. Fusion **58**(C), 82–115 (2020)
6. Beckers, S.: Causal explanations and XAI. In: Schölkopf, B., Uhler, C., Zhang, K. (eds.) Proceedings of the First Conference on Causal Learning and Reasoning. Proceedings of Machine Learning Research, vol. 177, pp. 90–109 (2022)
7. Blumreiter, M., et al.: Towards self-explainable cyber-physical systems. In: 2019 ACM/IEEE 22nd International Conference on Model Driven Engineering Languages and Systems Companion (MODELS-C), pp. 543–548 (2019)
8. Carloni, G., Berti, A., Colantonio, S.: The role of causality in explainable artificial intelligence (2023). https://arxiv.org/abs/2309.09901
9. Chou, Y.L., Moreira, C., Bruza, P., Ouyang, C., Jorge, J.: Counterfactuals and causability in explainable artificial intelligence: theory, algorithms, and applications. Inf. Fusion **81**, 59–83 (2022)
10. Drechsler, R., Lüth, C., Fey, G., Güneysu, T.: Towards self-explaining digital systems: a design methodology for the next generation. In: 2018 IEEE 3rd International Verification and Security Workshop (IVSW), pp. 1–6 (2018)
11. Du, M., Liu, N., Hu, X.: Techniques for interpretable machine learning. Commun. ACM **63**(1), 68–77 (2019)
12. Felski, A., Zwolak, K.: The ocean-going autonomous ship–challenges and threats. J. Marine Sci. Eng. **8**, 41 (2020)
13. Ganguly, N., et al.: A review of the role of causality in developing trustworthy AI systems (2023)
14. Garikapati, D., Shetiya, S.S.: Autonomous vehicles: evolution of artificial intelligence and the current industry landscape. Big Data Cogn. Comput. **8**(4) (2024)
15. Gilpin, L.H., Bau, D., Yuan, B.Z., Bajwa, A., Specter, M., Kagal, L.: Explaining explanations: an overview of interpretability of machine learning. In: 2018 IEEE 5th International Conference on Data Science and Advanced Analytics (DSAA), pp. 80–89 (2018)
16. Glomsrud, J., Ødegårdstuen, A., Clair, A., Smogeli, O.: Trustworthy versus explainable AI in autonomous vessels. In: Proceedings of the International Seminar on Safety and Security of Autonomous Vessels (ISSAV) and European STAMP Workshop and Conference (ESWC) 2019, pp. 37–47 (2019)
17. Glymour, C., Zhang, K., Spirtes, P.: Review of causal discovery methods based on graphical models. Front. Genet. **10** (2019)
18. Goodman, B., Flaxman, S.: European union regulations on algorithmic decision making and a "right to explanation". AI Mag. **38**(3), 50–57 (2017)

19. Houzé, É., Diaconescu, A., Dessalles, J.L., Menga, D.: A generic and modular reference architecture for self-explainable smart homes. In: 2022 IEEE International Conference on Autonomic Computing and Self-Organizing Systems (ACSOS), pp. 101–110. IEEE Computer Society (2022)
20. Juozapaitis, Z., Koul, A., Fern, A., Erwig, M., Doshi-Velez, F.: Explainable reinforcement learning via reward decomposition. In: Proceedings at the International Joint Conference on Artificial Intelligence. A Workshop on Explainable Artificial Intelligence (2019)
21. Kounev, S., Kephart, J.O., Milenkoski, A., Zhu, X.: Self-Aware Computing Systems. Springer, Cham (2017)
22. Madumal, P., Miller, T., Sonenberg, L., Vetere, F.: Explainable reinforcement learning through a causal lens. In: Proceedings of the AAAI Conference on Artificial Intelligence, vol. 34, no. 03, pp 2493–2500 (2020)
23. Maslej, N., et al.: Artificial intelligence index report 2024 (2024)
24. Mittelstadt, B., Russell, C., Wachter, S.: Explaining explanations in AI. In: Proceedings of the Conference on Fairness, Accountability, and Transparency, FAT* 2019, pp. 279–288. ACM (2019)
25. Müller-Schloer, C., Tomforde, S.: Organic Computing - Technical Systems for Survival in the Real World. Birkhäuser (2017)
26. Murray, B., Røstum Bellingmo, P., Lied, T., Hagaseth, M.: Autoencoder-based anomaly detection for safe autonomous ship operations. In: Proceedings of the 33rd European Safety and Reliability Conference (ESREL 2023), pp. 2885–2892 (2023)
27. Pearl, J.: The seven tools of causal inference, with reflections on machine learning. Commun. ACM **62**(3), 54–60 (2019)
28. Phillips, P.J., et al.: Four principles of explainable artificial intelligence (2021)
29. Puiutta, E., Veith, E.M.S.P.: Explainable reinforcement learning: a survey. In: Holzinger, A., Kieseberg, P., Tjoa, A.M., Weippl, E. (eds.) CD-MAKE 2020. LNCS, vol. 12279, pp. 77–95. Springer, Cham (2020). https://doi.org/10.1007/978-3-030-57321-8_5
30. Sokol, K., Vogt, J.E.: What does evaluation of explainable artificial intelligence actually tell us? In: Extended Abstracts of the CHI Conference on Human Factors in Computing Systems, CHI 2024, pp. 1–8. ACM (2024)
31. Vilone, G., Longo, L.: Notions of explainability and evaluation approaches for explainable artificial intelligence. Inf. Fusion **76**, 89–106 (2021)
32. Wells, L., Bednarz, T.: Explainable AI and reinforcement learning—a systematic review of current approaches and trends. Front. Artif. Intell. **4** (2021)
33. Ziesche, F., Klös, V., Glesner, S.: Anomaly detection and classification to enable self-explainability of autonomous systems. In: 2021 Design, Automation & Test in Europe Conference & Exhibition (DATE), pp. 1304–1309 (2021)

Leveraging Application-Specific Knowledge for Energy-Efficient Deep Learning Accelerators on Resource-Constrained FPGAs

Chao Qian(✉)

Intelligent Embedded Systems Lab, University of Duisburg-Essen, Duisburg, Germany
chao.qian@uni-due.de

Abstract. The growing adoption of Deep Learning (DL) applications in the Internet of Things has increased the demand for energy-efficient accelerators. Field Programmable Gate Arrays (FPGAs) offer a promising platform for such acceleration due to their flexibility and power efficiency. However, deploying DL models on resource-constrained FPGAs remains challenging because of limited resources, workload variability, and the need for energy-efficient operation.

This paper presents a framework for generating energy-efficient DL accelerators on resource-constrained FPGAs. The framework systematically explores design configurations to enhance energy efficiency while meeting requirements for resource utilization and inference performance in diverse application scenarios.

The contributions of this work include: (1) analyzing challenges in achieving energy efficiency on resource-constrained FPGAs; (2) proposing a methodology for designing DL accelerators with integrated Register Transfer Level (RTL) optimizations, workload-aware strategies, and application-specific knowledge; and (3) conducting a literature review to identify gaps and demonstrate the necessity of this work.

Keywords: FPGA · Deep Learning · Energy-Efficient · Accelerator

1 Introduction

The rapid growth of *Deep Learning* (DL) in the *Internet of Things* (IoT) has revolutionized domains such as smart homes, healthcare, and industrial automation [1]. By enabling IoT devices to process complex data and make intelligent decisions, DL has unlocked new possibilities for autonomous and real-time operations. However, these advancements are constrained by the physical size, power, and energy limitations of IoT devices, which challenge the deployment of computationally intensive DL models on *Microcontrollers* (MCUs). This creates a critical need for compact, energy-efficient hardware accelerators that balance computational performance with these constraints.

Field Programmable Gate Arrays (FPGAs) have emerged as a promising solution for deploying DL models on embedded platforms. They offer high flexibility for hardware customization and significant power efficiency, making them suitable for resource-constrained IoT devices. However, deploying DL models on FPGAs presents several challenges. Limited on-chip resources and high memory demands must be addressed while maintaining energy efficiency and performance. Additionally, selecting an appropriate FPGA size involves trade-offs: larger FPGAs consume more static power, while smaller FPGAs may lack the capacity to accommodate complex models. Frequent reconfiguration in duty-cycled operation modes, where the FPGA is turned off when not needed, introduces additional inefficiencies and makes energy-efficient DL inference even more difficult.

My PhD research focuses on the following questions to improving the energy efficiency of DL accelerators on FPGAs:

(RQ1) How can hardware accelerators be designed at the Register Transfer Level (RTL) to effectively utilize model-level optimizations, such as selecting suitable activation function implementations, to achieve energy-efficient inference on FPGAs?

(RQ2) What workload-aware strategies can be implemented to adapt inference efficiency dynamically to various workload demands?

(RQ3) How can application-specific knowledge be utilized to combine RTL optimizations and workload-aware strategies to derive the most energy-efficient DL accelerator?

Guided by the above questions, this paper proposes a systematic methodology for designing energy-efficient, problem-specific DL accelerators tailored to resource-constrained FPGAs. The approach integrates optimized RTL templates, workload-adapted execution strategies, and application-specific knowledge within a flexible framework. This methodology aims to maximize system energy efficiency while meeting the constraints defined by the application.

The remainder of this paper is structured as follows: Sect. 2 presents the proposed methodology, detailing the steps used to address the research questions. Section 3 discusses my current progress and findings. Section 4 outlines the planned work for completing my PhD. Section 5 positions my work within the context of related research. Finally, Sect. 6 summarizes the key findings and contributions.

2 Research Methodology

This section outlines my research methodology to design energy-efficient DL accelerators for FPGAs, guided by the conceptual framework depicted in Fig. 1. The methodology integrates three key steps: (1) preparing optimized RTL templates, workload-aware strategies, and application-specific knowledge as inputs; (2) combining these inputs within a *Generator* to produce optimized accelerator candidates; and (3) evaluating the candidates to identify the most efficient design.

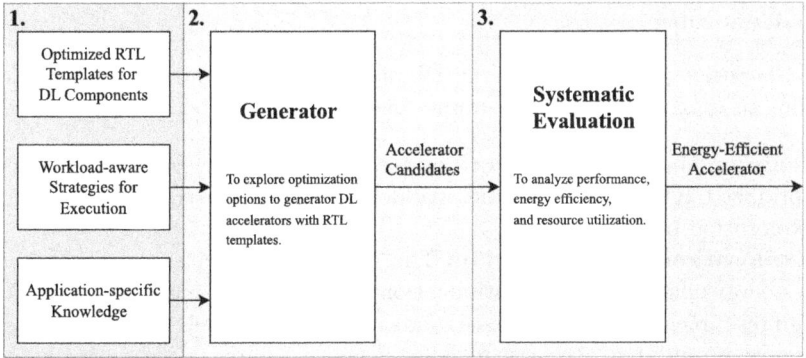

Fig. 1. Conceptual framework illustrating how RTL templates, workload-aware strategies, and application requirements are utilized to generate and evaluate energy-efficient DL accelerator designs.

2.1 Inputs for Accelerator Generation

The framework begins with three key inputs, as illustrated in Fig. 1:

- **Optimized RTL Templates for DL Components:** These templates provide reusable hardware designs for core DL operations, such as activation functions, fully connected layers, and *Long Short-Term Memory* (LSTM) layers. Each operation can be implemented in multiple ways to achieve different optimization goals, such as minimizing resource usage or maximizing clock frequency. Selecting the most suitable implementation depends on application-specific needs and resource availability.
- **Workload-aware Strategies:** Workload-aware strategies manage the unique characteristics of IoT devices, where sensor data collection is often slower than FPGA inference. Strategies include powering off FPGA with reconfiguration overhead or keeping it active to avoid reconfiguration overhead, which can be used to minimize energy consumption during idle periods. Alternatively, the inference speed can be reduced to align the inference time with the request period, preventing idle states and reconfiguration inefficiencies.
- **Application-Specific Knowledge:** Application-specific knowledge defines optimization goals (e.g., maximizing energy efficiency) and constraints (e.g., latency thresholds or resource limits). By aligning optimization goals with constraints, the framework ensures accelerators are efficient and practical for deployment.

These inputs lay the groundwork for the *Generator*, which will be detailed in the following sections.

2.2 Generator

The *Generator* produces optimized DL accelerators by systematically exploring the design space defined by the inputs in Sect. 2.1. Its process includes:

- **Defining the Design Space:** The *Generator* uses performance profiles from optimized RTL templates and workload adaptation strategies to establish exploration boundaries.
- **Exploration and Estimation:** The *Generator* prioritizes one metric, such as energy efficiency, as the optimization goal while treating others, like latency and resource utilization, as constraints. Analytical models estimate the performance of candidate accelerators, allowing early pruning of suboptimal designs.
- **Generating Outputs:** Multiple accelerator candidates are produced, each representing a unique configuration that meets the defined constraints. These candidates are evaluated in the next phase to identify the most suitable design.

This structured exploration ensures an efficient traversal of the design space, focusing on configurations most likely to meet energy efficiency and performance requirements.

2.3 Systematic Evaluation

The evaluation phase validates the impacts of individual inputs and their combination on the final accelerators. It employs the following tools and methods:

- **Evaluation Tools:**
  - **Behavior Simulation:** Tools like GHDL verify the mathematical correctness and functionality of accelerators and calculate inference time in clock cycles.
  - **Electronic Design Automation (EDA) Tool Analysis:** FPGA vendor tools, such as AMD Vivado and Lattice Radiant, generate reports on resource utilization, power consumption, and timing performance. Besides, these estimations can be conveniently replicated by other researchers, thanks to the widespread availability and adoption of these tools.
  - **Real Hardware Measurements:** Hardware platforms measure energy consumption, throughput, and latency under practical conditions.
- **Progressive Evaluation:**
  - **Standalone Input Evaluation:** Each input, such as RTL templates or workload-aware strategies, is evaluated independently to isolate its contribution to energy efficiency and performance, answering RQ1 and RQ2.
  - **Combined Optimization Evaluation:** Accelerators generated using all inputs are evaluated to address RQ3, verifying whether their combination results in superior energy efficiency and performance.

Including simulation with EDA tools and testing on real hardware offers a chance for cross-checking. Furthermore, the progressive evaluation approach allows adjustments to inputs and the *Generator*, enabling refinement of the design process and minimizing the risk of unresolved research questions.

3 Current State of Research

This section outlines my progress toward developing energy-efficient DL accelerators for FPGAs. Substantial advancements have been achieved in three key areas: optimized RTL templates for DL components, workload-aware strategies, and evaluation infrastructure.

3.1 Optimized RTL Templates

To address RQ1, I have made progress in developing optimized RTL templates for core DL operations, including LSTM cells, Convolutional layers, fully connected layers, and attention modules in Transformer models. These templates are designed to improve energy efficiency while ensuring high performance.

For the LSTM accelerator [2], notable improvements were achieved in both latency and energy efficiency through pipelining and activation function optimization at the RTL level. Latency was reduced from 53.32 µs to 28.07 µs, representing a 47.37% reduction. Energy efficiency improved from 5.57 GOPS/s/W to 12.98 GOPS/s/W, marking a 2.33× increase.

Similarly, accelerators for *Convolutional Neural Networks* [3] and *Multilayer Perceptrons* (MLPs) [4] with template optimizations have been validated through analytical models and hardware tests. These results further demonstrate the capability of optimized RTL templates to improve performance and energy efficiency, meeting the stringent constraints of resource-constrained FPGAs.

Additionally, activation functions such as Sigmoid, Tanh, HardSigmoid, and HardTanh have been optimized to provide multiple implementation options [2, 5]. These variations enable trade-offs between precision, resource usage, and throughput, allowing designers to select the most suitable implementation for specific application requirements.

3.2 Workload-Aware Optimization

To address RQ2 of my research, I have focused on workload-aware optimization, which tackles runtime inefficiencies by adapting accelerators to varying workload conditions. By optimizing the FPGA configuration phase and implementing the Idle-waiting strategy [6], substantial energy savings and improved workload management have been achieved.

For regular request periods, the Idle-Waiting strategy demonstrated superior energy efficiency compared to the traditional On-Off approach [6]. During a 40 ms request period, this strategy processed 12.39× more workload items within the same energy budget, effectively extending the system lifetime and addressing challenges posed by shorter request intervals.

To address irregular workloads, I have developed an adaptive strategy-switching mechanism using predefined and learnable thresholds [7]. The learnable threshold method outperformed the predefined approach with a 6% performance improvement, providing a robust and efficient solution for dynamic workload management.

These advancements indicate the feasibility of utilizing workload-awareness to improve the system energy efficiency for FPGA-based platforms.

3.3 Evaluation Infrastructure

The evaluation of accelerators begins with software-based analysis using tools such as AMD Vivado and Lattice Radiant. EDA tools provide reports with insights into resource utilization, power estimations, and timing performance.

Based on these software-based insights, the *Elastic Node* platform has been iterated within our research group over the past five years as a dedicated hardware testbed [8,9]. This platform is used for real-world validation. It measures metrics such as energy consumption, throughput, and latency under practical conditions, further validating the reports from EDA tools.

By combining software insights with hardware measurements [9], this approach ensures realistic evaluations of accelerator designs and enables accessible performance comparisons.

4 Future Work

Future work will address the remaining challenges to fully validate the research questions and further enhance the methodology for designing energy-efficient DL accelerators on FPGAs. Key focus areas include integrating and identifying inputs, implementing search algorithms, and rigorously evaluating the proposed framework.

The next step will fully integrate optimized RTL templates, workload-aware strategies, and application-specific knowledge into the *Generator* framework. Prioritizing inputs based on their impact on energy efficiency and developing adaptive mechanisms for dynamic inclusion will ensure that the *Generator* remains flexible and adaptable to varying requirements.

In parallel, I will implement search algorithms to explore combinations of inputs, such as RTL templates and workload strategies, while considering application-specific constraints. Finally, thorough evaluations will quantify the impact of application-specific knowledge on energy efficiency improvement.

This process includes assessing the individual and combined contributions of inputs to overall system performance and demonstrating energy efficiency improvements by comparing the designs generated by my methodology against baseline implementations under diverse workload conditions.

5 Related Work

Developing energy-efficient DL accelerators for resource-constrained FPGAs involves three key research areas: hardware optimization, workload adaptation, and search algorithms. This section reviews contributions in these areas and positions this work within the broader context of energy-efficient acceleration.

5.1 Hardware Optimization for Deep Learning Components

My PhD research builds on an earlier study in resource reuse techniques aimed at developing energy-efficient accelerators. Schiele et al. [10] introduced an MLP accelerator implemented on Spartan-6 LX9 FPGAs, delivering significant energy efficiency improvements over low-power MCUs. This design supported model training on the FPGA but was limited to an operating frequency of 50 MHz due to the backward propagation complex of the design. Subsequent efforts simplified the design by removing backward propagation, limiting it to feedforward propagation. Utilizing the newer Spartan-7 XC7S15 FPGA, the updated MLP accelerator achieved a clock frequency of 100 MHz for a soft sensor application [11].

Research on LSTM accelerators has evolved significantly, with distinct approaches to arithmetic unit allocation. Some studies focused on parallelizing all *Arithmetic Logic Units* (ALUs), maximizing throughput but resulting in inefficient resource utilization [12,13]. Conversely, other works prioritized resource efficiency by implementing minimal ALUs and reusing them over time [14,15]. While the latter showcased superior resource efficiency, its energy efficiency suffered due to prolonged execution times.

Within neural networks, particularly LSTMs, activation functions play a crucial role. Early studies [16–19] explored implementing functions like Sigmoid and Tanh on FPGAs, emphasizing resource efficiency and precision. As quantization-aware training gained traction, recent works demonstrated the viability of simplified activation functions, such as HardSigmoid and HardTanh, which achieve no precision loss between software definitions and hardware implementations while significantly reducing computational overhead [14,20].

The impact of precision on energy efficiency has also been studied as a key factor in FPGA-based accelerator optimization. Rybalkin et al. [13] systematically explored the design space concerning precision for Bidirectional Long Short-Term Memory (BiLSTM) neural networks. Their study highlights that significantly reducing precision enhances hardware efficiency, improving memory usage, energy consumption, and throughput. However, to our knowledge, no existing work has systematically prioritized energy efficiency as the primary optimization goal while exploring the design space for accelerators.

5.2 Workload-Aware Optimization

Studies in Sect. 5.1 focus on optimizing inference phases for continuous processing tasks where the FPGA remains busy. However, in practical IoT applications,

DL tasks often involve discontinuous workloads, resulting in idle periods. One method is to power off the FPGA during these periods to avoid idle power consumption. However, it introduces configuration overhead because the FPGA must be reconfigured each time it powers back on, which adds time and energy costs, potentially offsetting the overall energy efficiency.

Some researchers have explored optimizing the FPGA configuration process to address this challenge. Fritzsch et al. [21] proposed compressing the bitstream by 1.05× to 12.2× to reduce configuration time, but they did not evaluate its impact on energy efficiency. Similarly, Cichiwskyj et al. [22] introduced Temporal Accelerators, showing that even when the accelerator is split into two bitstreams, requiring to configuring the FPGA two times, a smaller FPGA (Spartan-7 XC7S6) could achieve greater energy efficiency than a larger one (Spartan-7 XC7S15) for a single inference. However, these studies have not utilized the workload intensity to change the configuration behavior, which can be applied to improve the system's energy efficiency.

5.3 Research Gap and Positioning

Despite progress in hardware optimization and workload-aware strategies, key gaps persist. Existing methods often lack integration of application requirements into the accelerator design process and fail to effectively address dynamic workload adaptation in heterogeneous platforms combining MCUs and FPGAs. Additionally, efficient exploration of optimal configurations under constraints such as resource constraints and workload variability remains underexplored.

My PhD aims to address these challenges through a systematic methodology, utilizing a *Generator* that leverages application-specific knowledge to guide design space exploration and maximize the energy efficiency of DL accelerators.

6 Conclusion

This research hypothesizes incorporating application-specific knowledge into a generator framework can produce DL accelerators with enhanced energy efficiency. The achievements to date include the development of efficient hardware templates for DL components, implementing workload-aware strategies, and establishing a robust evaluation platform. Preliminary progress has been demonstrated in enhancing energy efficiency for LSTM accelerators and developing strategies to manage both regular and irregular workloads effectively.

This study has also identified key gaps in existing research, including the limited integration of application-specific knowledge and the lack of systematic exploration algorithms for optimal accelerator design.

The next steps will focus on completing the proposed methodology and validating the feasibility of applying application-specific knowledge to derive optimal accelerator configurations automatically.

Acknowledgement. The author gratefully acknowledges the supervision of Prof. Dr. Gregor Schiele.

References

1. Cheng, L., Gu, Y., Liu, Q., Yang, L., Liu, C., Wang, Y.: Advancements in accelerating deep neural network inference on AIoT devices: a survey. IEEE Trans. Sustain. Comput. (2024)
2. Qian, C., Ling, T., Schiele, G.: Exploring energy efficiency of LSTM accelerators: a parameterized architecture design for embedded FPGAs. J. Syst. Architect. **152**, 103181 (2024)
3. Burger, A., Qian, C., Schiele, G., Helms, D.: An embedded CNN implementation for on-device ECG analysis. In: 2020 IEEE International Conference on Pervasive Computing and Communications Workshops, pp. 1–6. IEEE (2020)
4. Ling, T., Qian, C., Klann, T.M., Hoever, J., Einhaus, L., Schiele, G.: Configurable multi-layer perceptron-based soft sensors on embedded field programmable gate arrays: targeting diverse deployment goals in fluid flow estimation. Sens. (Basel Switz.) **25**(1), 83 (2024)
5. Qian, C., Ling, T., Schiele, G.: Enhancing energy-efficiency by solving the throughput bottleneck of LSTM cells for embedded FPGAs. In: Koprinska, I., et al. (eds.) ECML PKDD 2022. CCIS, vol. 1752, pp. 594–605. Springer, Cham (2023). https://doi.org/10.1007/978-3-031-23618-1_40
6. Qian, C., Cichiwskyj, C., Ling, T., Schiele, G.: Idle is the new sleep: configuration-aware alternative to powering off FPGA-based DL accelerators during inactivity. In: Fey, D., Stabernack, B., Lankes, S., Pacher, M., Pionteck, T. (eds.) ARCS 2024. LNCS, vol. 14842, pp. 161–176. Springer, Cham (2024). https://doi.org/10.1007/978-3-031-66146-4_11
7. Qian, C., Ling, T., Cichiwskyj, C., Schiele, G.: Configuration-aware approaches for enhancing energy efficiency in FPGA-based Deep Learning accelerators. J. Syst. Archit. (2025). (Under review)
8. Burger, A., Cichiwskyj, C., Schmeißer, S., Schiele, G.: The elastic internet of things-a platform for self-integrating and self-adaptive IoT-systems with support for embedded adaptive hardware. Futur. Gener. Comput. Syst. **113**, 607–619 (2020)
9. Qian, C., Ling, T., Schiele, G.: ElasticAI: creating and deploying energy-efficient deep learning accelerator for pervasive computing. In: 2023 IEEE International Conference on Pervasive Computing and Communications Workshops and other Affiliated Events, pp. 297–299. IEEE (2023)
10. Schiele, G., Burger, A., Cichiwskyj, C.: The elastic node: an experimentation platform for hardware accelerator research in the internet of things. In: IEEE International Conference on Autonomic Computing, pp. 84–94. IEEE (2019)
11. Ling, T., Qian, C., Schiele, G.: On-device soft sensors: real-time fluid flow estimation from level sensor data. In: Zaslavsky, A., Ning, Z., Kalogeraki, V., Georgakopoulos, D., Chrysanthis, P.K. (eds.) MobiQuitous 2023. LNICT, vol. 594, pp. 529–537. Springer, Cham (2024). https://doi.org/10.1007/978-3-031-63992-0_36
12. Cao, S., et al.: Efficient and effective sparse LSTM on FPGA with bank-balanced sparsity. In: Proceedings of the 2019 ACM/SIGDA International Symposium on Field-Programmable Gate Arrays, pp. 63–72 (2019)
13. Rybalkin, V., Pappalardo, A., Ghaffar, M.M., Gambardella, G., Wehn, N., Blott, M.: FINN-L: library extensions and design trade-off analysis for variable precision LSTM networks on FPGAs. In: International Conference on Field Programmable Logic and Applications, pp. 89–897 IEEE (2018)
14. Manjunath, N.K., Paneliya, H., Hosseini, M., Hairston, W.D., Mohsenin, T., et al.: A low-power LSTM processor for multi-channel brain EEG artifact detection. In: International Symposium on Quality Electronic Design, pp. 105–110. IEEE (2020)

15. Chen, J., Hong, S., He, W., Moon, J., Jun, S.-W.: Eciton: very low-power LSTM neural network accelerator for predictive maintenance at the edge. In: 2021 31st International Conference on Field-Programmable Logic and Applications, pp. 1–8. IEEE (2021)
16. Li, Z., Zhang, Y., Sui, B., Xing, Z., Wang, Q.: FPGA implementation for the Sigmoid with piecewise linear fitting method based on curvature analysis. Electronics **11**(9), 1365 (2022)
17. Pan, Z., Gu, Z., Jiang, X., Zhu, G., Ma, D.: A modular approximation methodology for efficient fixed-point hardware implementation of the Sigmoid function. IEEE Trans. Industr. Electron. **69**(10), 10 694–10 703 (2022)
18. Pogiri, R., Ari, S., Mahapatra, K.: Design and FPGA implementation of the LUT based Sigmoid function for DNN applications. In: 2022 IEEE International Symposium on Smart Electronic Systems, pp. 410–413. IEEE (2022)
19. Shatravin, V., Shashev, D., Shidlovskiy, S.: Sigmoid activation implementation for neural networks hardware accelerators based on reconfigurable computing environments for low-power intelligent systems. Appl. Sci. **12**(10), 5216 (2022)
20. Qian, C., Ling, T., Schiele, G.: Energy efficient LSTM accelerators for embedded FPGAs through parameterised architecture design. In: Goumas, G., Tomforde, S., Brehm, J., Wildermann, S., Pionteck, T. (eds.) ARCS 2023. LNCS, vol. 13949, pp. 3–17. Springer, Cham (2023). https://doi.org/10.1007/978-3-031-42785-5_1
21. Fritzsch, C., Hoffmann, J., Bogdan, M.: Reduction of bitstream size for low-cost iCE40 FPGAs. In:2022 32nd International Conference on Field-Programmable Logic and Applications, pp. 117–122. IEEE (2022)
22. Cichiwskyj, C., Qian, C., Schiele, G.: Time to learn: temporal accelerators as an embedded deep neural network platform. In: Gama, J., et al. (eds.) ITEM/IoT Streams -2020. CCIS, vol. 1325, pp. 256–267. Springer, Cham (2020). https://doi.org/10.1007/978-3-030-66770-2_19

Research Groups

FORnanoSatellites - Innovations in Nano-satellites - A Bavarian Research Alliance

Dietmar Fey[1(✉)], K. Schilling[2], J. Franke[3], M. Schmidt[4], and C. Fuchs[5]

[1] Computer Science 3 (Computer Architecture), Friedrich-Alexander-University (FAU) Erlangen-Nürnberg, 91058 Erlangen, Germany
dietmar.fey@fau.de
[2] Zentrum für Telematik e.V., 97074 Würzburg, Germany
[3] Chair FAPS, FAU Erlangen-Nürnberg, 91058 Erlangen, Germany
[4] Informatik VII, Julius-Maximilian-University Würzburg, 97074 Würzburg, Germany
[5] DLR Oberpfaffenhofen, 82234 Weßling, Germany
http://www3.cs.fau.de

Abstract. The research alliance "FORnanoSatellites - Innovations in nano-satellites - Advanced assembly and mounting technology (AMT), packaging, computing technology, and applications", funded by the Bavarian Research Foundation, pursues the design a new generation of nano-satellites, which have a spatial dimension of a few dm^3 and mass of only a few kilograms. In the 'New Space' sector, nano-satellites are already opening up a wide range of applications in telecommunications, earth observation, and navigation in a cost-effective manner, e.g. in multisatellite networks. Standardization approaches are intended to support a cost-efficient production of hundreds of satellites.

FORnanoSatellites intends to carry out research work to boost the development of small-scale production of nano-satellites in the long term. Open research challenges are in (i) the area of computer architecture for processing data. Furthermore, for the success of this technology (ii) a new mounting and interconnection 3D stacking technology of all components is required and a web configurator is foreseen to support the design of nano-satellites. To ensure reliable operation under harsh space conditions, (iii) appropriate redundancy concepts must be considered in hardware and software. Furthermore, we a (iv) new optical communication in nano-satellites and a new concept for a satellite bus is aspired. As already discussed at NASA and ESA for larger satellites, the computer architecture should also open up RISC-V and FPGA processor technology for nano-satellites.

Keywords: Nano-satellites · computer architecture · RISC-V and FPGA technology in space

1 Introduction

The aim of the "FORnanoSatellites" research alliance is to design a new generation of small satellites, hereinafter referred to as nano-satellites, weighing just a few kilograms, including a feasibility analysis for a fully digitalized value creation process, which should lead to the automated production of such satellites in Bavaria in the long term.

In the "New Space" sector, nano-satellites are already being used cost-effectively in multi-satellite networks for a wide range of applications in telecommunications, earth observation and navigation. Standardization approaches support the cost-efficient production of hundreds of satellites to them also economically interesting for industry and science. Current market analyses assume that the satellite market will grow to 2,700 billion US dollars by 2040. This corresponds to ten times the volume of the global automotive industry in 2020.

FORnanosatellites is an alliance of five Bavarian research institutions, namely the Chairs of Computer Architecture and of Factory Automation and Production Systems (FAPS) at FAU Erlangen-Nuremberg, the Chair of Embedded Systems and Sensors for Earth Observation at the University of Würzburg, the Center for Telematics in Würzburg and the DLR in Oberpfaffenhofen, as well as 15 companies from Bavaria, Baden-Württemberg and Hesse.

The paper will start with a brief introduction to nano-satellites in Sect. 2. In Sect. 3, focuses in particular on the aspect of computer architecture. However, reference will also be made to other research topics addressed in FORnanoSatellites in Sect. 4, e.g. a web configurator, special 3D AMT for developing customer-specific applications using adapted nano-satellite technology, the world smallest commercially available optical laser terminal, the standardization of the satellite bus, and applications particularly suitable for nano-satellites.

2 What are Nano-satellites?

2.1 Definition of Cubesats and Example for Nano-satellites

The outer dimensions of nano-satellites are based on the so-called CubeSat design specification of California Polytechnic State University from 2014 [1], which should allow other universities, colleges and private companies to launch small satellites into space at low cost [2]. Figure 1, left, shows a cube nano-satellite measuring $10 \times 10 \times 10$ cm, a so-called unit, as it was built under the name UWE-1 at University Würzburg in 2005 as first Cubesat from Germany. Three of such CubeSats form a so-called 3U+. Figure 1 right shows four of such 3U+ from the Zentrum für Telematik (ZfT) in Würzburg. Such an assembly is brought to space where each 3U+ is released. Satellite systems can be assembled according to a modular system. In addition to standardized sizes, standardized interfaces between subsystems will be handled in FORnanoSatellites to reduce the costs not only by the low weight, but also by standardized form factors. The nano-satellites MOVE and MOVE-II are current examples which are built for ESA misions.

Fig. 1. CubeSat UWE-1 during vibration test, left; CubeSat Deployer with four NetSat satellites, right.

2.2 Essential Components in a Nano-satellite

Inside the standardized form of a nano-satellite, or a CubeSat in general, we will find the following components. The *On-board Computer (OBC)* is the heart of the satellite. It is responsible for controlling all other subsystems. It is designed to be cold-redundant and consists e.g. of two energy-efficient microcontrollers that shall operate with a power of few tens of units at 10 mW. The microcontrollers monitor each other due to redundancy, so that the software is available multiple times. A watchdog and a power cycling unit complete the redundancy concept. The *Attitude Determination and Control System* (ADCS) provides highly accurate attitude information to all subsystems ($< 1°$ in sunlight). The *Electrical Power System* (EPS) contains space-hard batteries. The *Satellite Power Management* is controlled by the OBC. A *propulsion system* is based, e.g., on Field-Emission Electric Propulsion technology to generate up to $350\,\mu N$ thrust to change the orbit altitude. The *Communication System* provides high data rate to transmit the earth observation data to the ground.

In addition to these basic satellite systems for maintenance and control, the *Payload Computer*. It is the interface between the satellite bus and the payload. It is necessary to process the payload and receive data from it. The use of AI accelerators for the payload computer to preprocess data directly on the satellite using AI methods has also recently been discussed [5]. Furthermore, nano-satellites can contain *GNSS receiver* for geodetic applications and particular *multispectral cameras* for high-resolution earth observation and acceleration sensors or pressure sensors for a precise determination of the nano-satellite in the VLEO (very low earth orbit, between 250 and 400 km).

3 Future Challenges for Computer Architectures in Nano-satellites

3.1 State-of-the-Art

In a collaboration of University of Leuven and Cobham Gaisler [3], the "creator" of SPARC compatible architectures for space applications, the alternative use of open RISC-V processors vs. SPARC was investigated for ESA. Thousands of

SPARC processors are flying in space today. However, the loss of importance of SPARC restricts its use in space whereas RISC-V is driven by a large community. In a study from TU Delft and ESA [4] a roadmap for RISC-V use for ESA was created [4]. According to different applications and different requirements in satellites four different types of processors were identified: 1) general-purpose processors for payloads, 2) OBC controllers for the main platform, 3) microcontrollers (μCs) with a small footprint and low power consumption, 4) advanced payload processors with support for artificial intelligence (AI). The roadmap postulates a "computing architecture" paradigm shift, which says: "go away from the decades-long focus on SPARC architectures and turn towards RISC-V".

In July 2023, the Fraunhofer Institute IIS developed an from earth reconfigurable Fraunhofer On-Board Processor (FOBP) [5] for a Heinrich Hertz satellite mission for flexible communication payloads in digital signal processing. NASA and SiFive will establish a RISC-V-based ecosystem for future NASA missions [6]. Building on a SiFive multi-core CPU and a RISC-V based vector processor, SiFive is designing the next-generation High-Performance Spaceflight Computing (HPSC) processor. All these examples show that RISC-V and also FPGA technology are a hot topic for future computer architectures for space applications and are addresses by FAU, JMU, and ZfT in FORnanoSatellites,

3.2 Challenges on Computer Architecture in FORnanoSatellites

In FORnanoSatellites, our aim is initially to develop a fault-tolerant single core based on the NOEL-V processor architecture specification, published by the Geisler Group in VHDL [7]. This architecture offers extensive, inherently redundant components inside the processor, e.g. secured caches, and is primarily focused for use in large satellite systems far away from the VLEO. Therefore, we will not need these power-hungry redundant components in a small nano-satellite since in the VLEO there are much fewer error-causing radiation sources. Which of these are relevant for a miniature satellite is the subject of the planned investigations in FORnanoSatellites. At the end, we will get a"NOEL-V light" that is already inherently redundant. However, in order to increase the reliability, a multi-core architecture is planned to achieve radiation-hardness by software.

According to the philosophy of a modular design in nano-satellites the OBC and the payload computer shall be designed as chiplets as well as accelerator cores based on systolic arrays to carry out future sensor data processing directly in the satellite. Finally, also based on a RISC-V ISA we aspire to implement a high-performance controller with the DLR as controller for their optical communication laser terminal. The RISC-V based OBC, the payload computer and the accelerator cores shall be integrated in an FPGA technology made in Germany by CologneChip [8] to boost technology independence.

4 Further Design Challenges for Nano-satellites and Applications

FORnanoSatellites pursues a number of further scientific, technical and economic objectives. In general, FORnanoSatellites aims to design a new generation of nano-satellites characterized by innovations in the following areas: (i) 3D AMT for the components of a nano-satellite, (ii) new applications to be developed specifically for nano-satellites, (iii) a new miniaturized optical communication, and (iv) a contributing to new standardization approaches for nano-satellites.

For (i) a new process chain for the assembly of miniaturized 3D microsystems in system-in-package (SiP) technology shall be developed, which combines various innovative individual processes to combine antenna, electronic and ADCS devices in a small as possible size by means of electronic circuit carriers and housings by selected ceramic materials. Finally, to promote the production of future nano-satellites, the partner FAPS will create a Web configurator to configure a nano-satellite for own user purposes. For (ii) we selected applications specially appropriate for nano-satellites like weather forecasting, water monitoring and the generation of warning signals for large aircraft. All these special applications benefit from the VLEO altitude. They could not be carried out in large satellites. The ZfT will carry out mission studies for these scenarios. For (iii) to handle enormous amounts of data and high data rates, optical communication in combination with RF systems is favoured. In FORnanoSatellites, DLR is to advance such an optical communication system. For (iv) the University Würzburg will extend the Unisec bus standard and standardize the software and the logical separation of real-time operating system and middleware for a publish-subscribe framework for nano-satellites.

5 Conclusion

With the system envisaged in FORnanoSatellites, it will be possible to implement innovative and new applications within a very short time with a customized satellite fleet. E.g., while the development of a dedicated satellite bus has so far taken several years, a new satellite bus could then be configured and produced according to the modular principle. The same holds for the computer architecture and the AMT of the nano-satellites components.

References

1. CubeSat Design specification. https://static1.squarespace.com/static/5418c831e4b0fa4ecac1bacd/t/5f24997b6deea10cc52bb016/1596234122437/CDS+REV14+2020-07-31+DRAFT.pdf. Accessed 26 Mar 2025
2. Heidt, H., et al.: CubeSat: a new generation of picosatellite for education and industry low-cost space experimentation (2000)
3. RISC-V: High-Performance Fault-Tolerant Computing for Space. https://activities.esa.int/4000131253. Accessed 26 Mar 2025

4. Furano, G., et al.: A European roadmap to leverage RISC-V in space applications. In: 2022 IEEE AERO, Big Sky, MT, USA, pp. 1–7. IEEE (2022). https://doi.org/10.1109/AERO53065.2022.9843361
5. Das Satellitenkommunikationslabor im All. https://www.iis.fraunhofer.de/de/ff/kom/satkom/obp/fobp.html. Accessed 26 Mar 2025
6. Powell, W.: NASA's vision for spaceflight computing. Presented Remotely ADCSS 2022, Noordwijk, NL (2022)
7. NOEL-V. https://www.gaisler.com/index.php/products/processors/noel-v. Accessed 26 Mar 2025
8. GateMate FPGA. https://colognechip.com/programmable-logic/gatemate/. Accessed 27 Mar 2025

Feedback-Guided Dataset Shaping for Automated Downstream Task Optimization

Lukas Nolte[1](✉), Marten J. Finck[2](✉), Sören Pirk[2](✉), and Sven Tomforde[1](✉)

[1] Intelligent Systems, Kiel University, Hermann-Rodewald-Straße 3, 24118 Kiel, Germany
{Lukas.Nolte,st}@informatik.uni-kiel.de
[2] Visual Computing and Artificial Intelligence, Kiel University, Neufeldtstraße 6, 24118 Kiel, Germany
{mafi,sp}@informatik.uni-kiel.de

Abstract. Self-learning agents in open-world environments often face data scarcity due to the diversity and unpredictability of real-world conditions. Traditional datasets often over-represent common cases while under-representing rare but critical events, leading to biased learning and poor generalization. To address this, we propose dataset shaping. Dataset shaping aims to use generative models, such as multi-task diffusion models (MTDMs), to generate and refine synthetic data-label pairs through a feedback loop. By dynamically adjusting the data composition according to the performance of a self-learning agent-based downstream task model (DSTM), generative models expose agents to diverse and challenging scenarios, which leads to increased robustness and adaptability. Consequently, dataset shaping enhances generalization, particularly in applications, such as autonomous driving and robotics, where reliable performance in novel conditions is essential.

Keywords: dataset shaping · generative AI · agentic AI · computer vision · multi-task diffusion models · active learning

1 Introduction

In open-world scenarios, self-learning agents (e.g. as core of Organic Computing systems [7]) often struggle from data scarcity due to the vast diversity and unpredictability of real-world environments. Unlike controlled settings where curated datasets provide the required coverage of relevant situations, open-world agents must generalize across a vast range of conditions, many of which are rare or difficult to capture. For example, in autonomous driving, training data can include common urban scenes, but they lack sufficient examples of extreme weather conditions, unusual lighting, or rare road events, leading to performance gaps in real-world deployments. Data collection in open-world settings is often constrained by ethical, logistical, and financial challenges, making it infeasible to manually gather and annotate the necessary volume of training data. Moreover, traditional datasets often do not include data points of the long-tail of a distribution – usually common examples dominate, while critical yet infrequent edge cases remain underrepresented. Without sufficient exposure to these rare but crucial data points, self-learning agents are prone to biased learning, poor generalization, and failure in novel or unexpected situations. Overcoming this data shortage is therefore essential to ensure that agents can operate reliably and safely in open-world environments.

We aim to address the data bottleneck by introducing dataset shaping. Dataset shaping aims to leverage generative models that generate synthetic data-label pairs, which are continuously refined through a feedback loop (Fig. 1). Thereby, the synthetic data is used to train a self-learning agent-based downstream task model (DSTM). After every epoch, the agent's action decisions are evaluated on a target dataset. Data points for which the agent does not perform well are used to request new data by generating text prompts to shape the generation of synthetic data. Thus, a targeted exploration of the agent is established. This process ensures that self-learning agents are exposed to a progressively challenging and diverse set of training samples, addressing common issues like class imbalance and the long-tail distribution problem. Hence, through dataset shaping, the training curriculum of self-learning agents evolves dynamically, allowing them to generalize better to novel situations and ultimately achieve higher performance with minimal reliance on manually curated datasets.

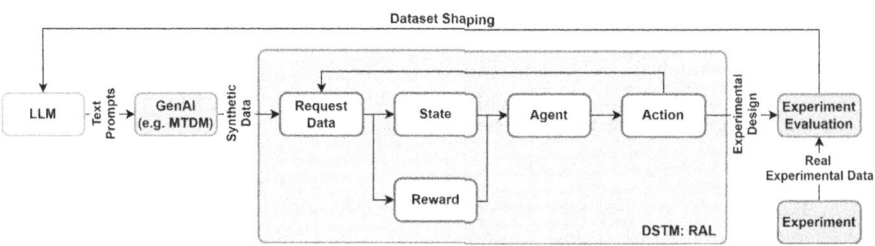

Fig. 1. Overview of the proposed agentic AI-based feedback-guided dataset shaping framework. Text-prompts are generated to produce labeled synthetic datasets with a generative model (GenAI). A reinforcement active learning-based downstream task model (DSTM: RAL) is trained on this generated synthetic data and evaluated on a real dataset. Based on the agent's decision, new prompts are generated, dynamically reshaping the synthetic data distribution to refine the DSTM training process. This iterative dataset shaping enables a targeted exploration, allowing the agent to systematically adjust and optimize data characteristics for improved downstream performance.

2 State of the Art

Self-learning agents face various challenges related to the scarcity of data in open-world scenarios. Analogous, computer vision tasks, such as classification, segmentation, and depth prediction, often require large-scale, carefully annotated datasets. While synthetic data generated through computer graphics techniques has been used to mitigate this challenge, achieving photorealism and accurately modeling physical properties remains computationally demanding [1]. Recent advances in generative neural networks offer an alternative approach, enabling the synthesis of new images [11] through models such as BigGAN [2]. However, these methods suffer from limitations such structural inconsistencies [3,5] or lack of pixel-precise alignment between images and their corresponding labels [13]. Only a few methods directly generate multiple data modalities, with Dataset-GAN [12] and BigDatasetGAN [6] being notable examples that facilitate multi-task generative modeling for dataset creation. Finally, diffusion models [10] have recently emerged as the leading approach, excelling in image generation tasks [8]. Another approach to addressing data scarcity is active learning, which dynamically adapts models by implementing a feedback loop and selecting the most informative samples while minimizing the amount of labeled data required [9].

3 Research Agenda

Our working hypothesis is that generative AI models, such as Stable Diffusion, produce smoother and more uniform data distributions for solving the problem of inherently imbalanced long-tail distributions present in real-world training datasets, compared to existing methods targeting this challenge.

To address this problem, our aim is to employ novel AI techniques with targeted balancing strategies, such as LoRA adaptors or active learning-inspired approaches such as ActGen [4]. State-of-the-art generative models can synthesize data conditioned on textual prompts and their content. The goal of this proposal is to leverage the text-based synthetic data generation for dataset shaping and apply it as a tool for targeted exploration of a self-learning agent in a DSTM. Once trained, the generative model is integrated into the DSTM training loop. During training of the DSTM, the generative model generates batches of data based on text prompts that are changed during exploration and training of the DSTM agent. With the objective to automatically shape datasets for training self-learning agents the key goals of this project are: (1) to develop generative models, e.g. multi-task diffusion models (MTDMs), that allow synthesizing real-world-like data, along with their labels; (2) to generate a diverse set of text prompts by a pretrained large language model (LLM) for shaping a dataset with generative models; (3) to employ generative models as data generator for training DSTMs with a focus on creating diverse and balanced data distributions; (4) to validate the DSTM agent's decision based on a real datasets to assess its performance; (5) to define a feedback loop that generates new text prompts based on the training outcome of the DTSM agent – the training data distribution is automatically refined for the next stage of training.

With dataset shaping we aim to define a training curriculum for self-learning agent-based DSTMs that leads to optimal performance and robustness for real world applications. For example, when training a depth prediction model for a self-driving car, the generative model, such as a MTDM, may initially be configured to predict depth for standard urban scenes ("An urban scene with several cars on the street"). When training the DSTM, text prompts are used to generate more complex data with the MTDM ("A rainy urban scene with cars on the street", "A night-time urban scene with complex lighting", "An intersection with several pedestrians"). The goal is to define a training curriculum that progressively shapes the data in a way that the variance of the data distribution is increased and rare observations (long-tail data distribution) are generated. To enable dataset shaping we plan to address the following open research challenges:

1. We aim to explore the use of existing LLMs for text prompt engineering to automatically produce varied distributions of data. Whether existing LLMs can be controlled in a way to generate distributions of data with specific features is an open research question.
2. To use generative models as data generators for agent-based DSTMs we need to extend existing approaches to not only predict synthetic data, but also the required label for a downstream task, such as the training of a self-learning agent. Some computer vision approaches show initial success in multi-task image generation, but reliably predicting different types of labels (e.g., depth, surface normal, semantic segmentation) with the quality required for downstream training remains a challenging problem.
3. To automatically shape datasets, we aim to define a feedback loop that guides the generation of text prompts according to the performance of an agent-based DSTM. To define this loop, we need to identify how the validation loss of a DSTM can be used to adjust text prompts in a meaningful manner.
4. As generative models produce new data-label tuples, for which no ground truth exist, validating the quality of the synthesized data and labels is challenging. Our goal is to identify new ways to assess the quality of the generated data and labels.

More generally, the goal of this project is to explore generating synthetic data for training neural networks. The use of synthetic data has recently gained momentum as automatically generated images are a cost-efficient alternative to manually annotated datasets. Most commonly computer graphics algorithms are used to model and render scenes to generate photorealistic imagery. Once defined, the advantage of this process is that the required labels can be generated at low computational costs. Generative neural networks (e.g., GANs or diffusion models) on the other hand can be leveraged to generate photorealistic images of objects and scenes, however, only a few methods exist to generate images jointly with the required labels. By defining generative models, such as MTDMs, we aim to contribute to the landscape of methods for automatically generating synthetic data for training neural networks and particularly self-learning agents for different tasks, such as computer vision.

4 Conclusion

As outlined, our goal is to address the challenge of data scarcity in open-world scenarios and propose dataset shaping – the adaptive generation of data – as a solution to improve the training of self-learning agents. By leveraging generative models, such as MTDMs, we want to investigate generating diverse and visually complex synthetic datasets that dynamically adapt based on the performance of a given downstream task model. Our approach focuses on defining a feedback loop to progressively refine training data distributions that allow us to enhance generalization and robustness in real-world applications such as autonomous driving and robotics. By addressing key research questions related to prompt engineering, multi-modal image generation, dataset validation, and feedback-driven optimization, this research will contribute to fields of generative AI, active learning, self-learning agents and synthetic data generation. With automated dataset generation methods, we enable self-learning agents to better navigate in complex environments with minimal manual intervention.

Acknowledgements. This work was supported by the IDIR-Project (Digital Implant Research), a cooperation financed by Kiel University, University Hospital Schleswig-Holstein and Helmholtz Zentrum Hereon.

References

1. Borkman, S., et al.: Unity perception: generate synthetic data for computer vision. CoRR abs/2107.04259 (2021)
2. Brock, A., Donahue, J., Simonyan, K.: Large scale GAN training for high fidelity natural image synthesis. In: ICLR (2019)
3. Chen, Q., Koltun, V.: Photographic image synthesis with cascaded refinement networks. In: ICCV, pp. 1520–1529 (2017)
4. Huang, T., Liu, J., You, S., Xu, C.: Active generation for image classification. In: ECCV, pp. 270–286 (2024)
5. Isola, P., Zhu, J.-Y., Zhou, T., Efros, A.: Image-to-image translation with conditional adversarial networks, pp. 5967–5976
6. Li, D., et al.: Synthesizing imagenet with pixel-wise annotations, Bigdatasetgan (2022)
7. Müller-Schloer, C.: Organic Computing - Technical Systems for Survival in the Real World. Birkhäuser (2017)
8. Rombach, R., Blattmann, A., Lorenz, D., Esser, P., Ommer, B.: High-resolution image synthesis with latent diffusion models. CVPR (2021)
9. Settles, B.: Active learning literature survey
10. Song, Y., Ermon, S.: Generative modeling by estimating gradients of the data distribution (2019)
11. Wu, X., Xu, K., Hall, P.: A survey of image synthesis and editing with generative adversarial networks. Tsinghua Sci. Technol. **22**, 6 (2017)
12. Zhang, Y.: Fidler, S, pp. 10140–10150. Efficient labeled data factory with minimal human effort. CVPR, Datasetgan (2021)
13. Zhu, J.Y., Park, T., Isola, P., Efros, A.A.: Unpaired image-to-image translation using cycle-consistent adversarial networks. ICCV, 2242–2251 (2017)

Disruptive Memory Technologies: An Overview of DFG Priority Program 2377

Marcel Köppen(✉) and Olaf Spinczyk

Universität Osnabrück, Wachsbleiche 27, 49090 Osnabrück, Germany
{marcel.koeppen,olaf.spinczyk}@uos.de

Abstract. Memory is a central component in every computer system. Hardware evolution has led to greater capacities and higher speeds, but essential properties of its hardware/software interface have been unchanged for decades: Main memories used to be passive, largely homogeneous, and volatile. These properties are now so firmly anchored in the expectations of software developers that they manifest in their products. However, a wave of innovations is currently shattering these assumptions. In this sense, several new memory technologies are disruptive for the entire software industry. For example, new servers combine "high-bandwidth memory" with classic memory modules and CXL enables even more hybrid architectures (non-homogeneous). The "in-/near-memory" computing approaches abandon the Von Neumann architecture and promise huge performance improvements by allowing CPU-independent processing of data objects in or close to the memory (non-passive). Finally, "persistent memory" is available for servers and embedded systems (non-volatile).

Overall, the expectations are high. Computers could have lower energy consumption, more performance, improved reliability, and reduced costs. However, from the (system) software perspective it is largely unclear how to use the novel memory technology efficiently. The DFG priority program 2377 addresses this problem. This overview discusses the state and potential of disruptive memory technologies, the challenges for system and application software, and important research directions.

Keywords: HW/SW Stack · HBM/CXL/PIM/NMC/NVM/RDMA

1 Introduction

The memory technology landscape is changing dramatically. A prominent example was the introduction of "Data Center Persistent Memory Modules" (DCP-MMs) by Intel in 2019. This byte-addressable memory can be used in combination or in place of ordinary DRAM, has higher capacities, a lower price, and keeps stored data safe even while the system is turned off. Soon after the first prototypes were available, success stories were published. For example, the startup time of an SAP HANA database could be reduced by a factor of 12.5, because the database is already in memory when the system is turned on[1]. However, DCP-MMs are slower than ordinary DRAM DIMMs and keeping software objects in this memory is not trivial, because consistency in case of a crash or power loss must be guaranteed. Hence, logging and checkpointing frameworks, specialized data structures, or partial/whole-system persistence mechanisms have to be used. Therefore, rewriting existing software to make use of this persistent memory is quite difficult. This led to slow adoption. Meanwhile, Intel has discontinued the development of DCPMMs in favor of a more flexible architecture based on the new Compute Express Link (CXL) technology. There are three lessons to learn from this example:

- Persistent memory technology is already mature enough for commercial products. For example, we also see persistent memory products in the area of embedded systems and CXL-based persistent memory is expected soon.
- Memory technologies can change the characteristics of computer systems significantly. For example, after the initial boot individual processes or the whole system could retain their state forever. Yet, this also holds for undesired state, for instance, created by bugs or attacks.
- Disruptive memory technologies might be unsuccessful, because system and application software is not ready, yet. There is a real danger that software is falling further behind the pace of hardware innovation.

Besides persistent memory there are more similar developments going on. For example, "Processing in Memory" (PIM) and "Near-Memory Computing" (NMC) are two concepts that avoid the communication bottleneck between memory and the central CPU cores. The idea is to either make the memory itself capable of computing simple tasks or to attach many small CPU cores directly to the memory. This changes the programming model a lot. Instead of building software with passive data objects and a small number of active threads, one could envision systems composed of many active data objects. In 2021 the French company UPMEM started selling the first commercial PIM solution. They claim that some applications can be executed by several orders of magnitude faster than on ordinary systems. Again, appropriate software support and the availability of success stories will determine the level of success.

Finally, memory subsystems tend to become more heterogeneous and even distributed. "High-Bandwidth Memory" (HBM) is closely integrated with CPU cores in a 2.5D or 3D stacking process. While this technology has been used for high-performance GPUs for some time, we now see several CPUs being equipped with HBM as well. For example, Fujitsu's A64FX processor with HBM held place 1 of the top 500 supercomputer list for a long time without using GPUs and the latest Intel server processors "Xeon Max" also contain HBM. Furthermore, on the consumer market Apple's M-Series CPUs have astonishing benchmark results with a wide interface to a unified memory. Again, the potential for performance improvements and energy savings is big.

---

[1] Source: "Intel®OptaneTM DC Persistent Memory and SAP HANA®2.0 SPS 03", Technical Brief, Intel.

Yet, on the software side methods have to be developed to fully exploit it. This becomes even more difficult with technologies such as CXL and RDMA. The latter allows remote machines to access local memory and vice versa. CXL will enable cache coherent access to memory modules on PCIe cards, such as FPGA-based accelerators, smart NICs, "memory semantic" SSDs, AI accelerators, and general-purpose GPUs. It even enables "disaggregated memory" architectures where memory pools can be shared between multiple machines.

All this affects various application domains from small embedded systems to huge cloud data centers. Computer scientists could help to make systems more efficient and reliable by exploring proper software support for these new "disruptive" memory technologies.

Therefore, new research programs are being started. For example, a parallel initiative to our priority program is the PRISM program[2] in the USA. Furthermore, the SOSP conference had a new "Workshop on Disruptive Memory Systems", the CASES conference had a special session in this context, and ARCS 2023 had a focus on "next-generation memory".

Current research in the area of disruptive memory technologies is carried out across different communities, for example using in-memory processing in databases [2] and combining near-data processing with persistent memory [3], using tiered DRAM and persistent memory connected via CXL for virtual machines [4], using microkernels for efficient checkpointing to achieve whole-system persistence on persistent memory [5], and discussing programming models for disaggregated systems [1]. We are convinced that now is the time to bring together experts of this research area.

In the German DFG priority program 2377 "Disruptive Memory Technologies"[3] we conduct research on improving the whole software stack, especially operating systems, DBMS, compilers, and algorithms in general, so that the benefits of the aforementioned memory technologies become effective. By joining forces across the boundaries of different communities, new perspectives and opportunities for collaboration are opening up.

2 Research Topics

Research on how to deal with disruptive memory technologies from a software and computer architecture perspective can be structured along the four topics that will be introduced below. The overall goal is to come up with cleaner (system) software and hardware architectures, and thereby improve efficiency in a general sense.

2.1 Models and Benchmarks

The development of system software or efficient application-level algorithms with dedicated support for disruptive memory technologies depends on assumptions

---

[2] For more information on PRISM visit https://prism.ucsd.edu/.
[3] For more information on DFG priority program 2377 visit https://spp2377.uos.de.

about the static and dynamic properties of the hardware. Therefore, having proper hardware models is an essential foundation for research on all layers of the hardware/software stack. Benchmarks are a pragmatic approach to gather the necessary data to parameterize such models. Besides models and benchmarks for hardware, it is also important to have means to analyze and predict how software interacts with disruptive memory technologies. Models and benchmarks are, thus, also crucial to describe software usage patterns. The following research questions are worth a more detailed investigation:

- Are the hardware and software models that are implicitly or explicitly used in research and industry good enough? Are all relevant features taken into account?
- Would it be possible to create unified models and benchmarks for different purposes on all software layers?
- What are the costs of hardware models at runtime and how can they be minimized?
- Do we need to update models at runtime and re-run benchmarks? If so, how could the overhead be minimized?

2.2 Software Challenges from Cross-Layer Perspective

Research papers on how to exploit disruptive memory technologies have been published in various communities. Often authors tackle a specific use case or problem that is of particular interest of the respective community, but the developed solutions and insights could be relevant for a wider audience. It is necessary to revisit the responsibilities of the various software layers and their interfaces to use the new hardware efficiently and without increasing complexity for all software developers.

- How do disruptive memory technologies affect the classic system software layers, namely the OS, DBMS, Middleware, and compiler, as well as application development? What new abstractions are needed and how can each layer benefit from the new technology?
- Can the interfaces between the system software layers be improved in order to deal with the cross-cutting nature of disruptive memory technologies more efficiently?
- What feedback can the software community give to hardware architects? Could simple changes on the hardware level positively affect software development complexity?

2.3 Migration Paths for Legacy Software

Software development is slow and expensive. There are software products and open source projects with a lifetime of decades. For disruptive memory technologies to be successful it is necessary to find cheap migration paths for legacy software to modern hardware platforms.

- Can the heterogeneity and complexity of disruptive memory technologies be hidden from legacy software without wasting potential benefits? What is the role of system software abstractions in this context?
- Would it be possible to automatically adapt legacy software to disruptive memory technologies? Could smarter compilers or language runtimes help?

2.4 Innovative Software Architectures

If we could redesign the whole software stack from scratch for modern hardware platforms that come with a combination of disruptive memory technologies, the outcome might be different from the stack that we use today. A thought experiment like this could help to answer interesting questions.

- What are best practices for developing new software with respect to disruptive memory technologies?
- How to redesign existing software to fully exploit the features of disruptive memory technologies?

3 Summary

There are many interesting research opportunities related to disruptive memory technologies. In the DFG priority program 2377 there are 14 research projects with 22 PIs from all over Germany tackling many of these challenges. After two of six years program runtime there are still more open questions than answers, but first results can be presented.

Acknowledgments. This work was funded by the Deutsche Forschungsgemeinschaft (DFG, German Research Foundation) – 502616169.

References

1. Anneser, C., Vogel, L., Gruber, F., Bandle, M., Giceva, J.: Programming fully disaggregated systems. In: Proceedings of the 19th Workshop on Hot Topics in Operating Systems, pp. 188–195. ACM (2023). 10.1145/3593856.3595889
2. Kang, H., et al.: PIM-Tree: A Skew-Resistant Index for Processing-in-Memory. Proc. VLDB Endowment **16**(4), 946–958 (2022). 10.14778/3574245.3574275
3. Seneviratne, Y., Seemakhupt, K., Liu, S., Khan, S.: NearPM: A Near-Data Processing System for Storage-Class Applications. In: Proceedings of the Eighteenth European Conference on Computer Systems, pp. 751–767. ACM (2023). 10.1145/3552326.3587456
4. Sha, S., Li, C., Luo, Y., Wang, X., Wang, Z.: vTMM: Tiered Memory Management for Virtual Machines. In: Proceeding of the Eighteenth European Conference on Computer Systems, pp. 283–297. ACM (2023). 10.1145/3552326.3587449
5. Wu, F., Dong, M., Mo, G., Chen, H.: TreeSLS: A Whole-system Persistent Microkernel with Tree-structured State Checkpoint on NVM. In: Proceedings of the 29th Symposium on Operating Systems Principles, pp. 1–16. ACM (2023). 10.1145/3600006.3613160

Author Index

A
Ali, Mohammad Wazed 205
Ali, Muhammad 94

B
Baunach, Marcel 109
Behrens, Alexander Benedict 347
Beyer, Tom 449
Bjørling, Matias 125
Boysen, Jonas 252
Brinkmann, André 125

C
Cabaret, Laurent 18

D
Dreimann, Marcel Lütke 79

F
Fey, Dietmar 34, 471
Finck, Marten J. 477
Franke, J. 471
Freitag, Florian 156
Frenkel, Wiebke 236
Friesenborg, Mika 220
Fuchs, C. 471

G
Gao, Shang 330, 389
Geißler, Daniel 140
Göhringer, Diana 94
Gössel, Michael 347
Götz-Hahn, Franz 330
Guo, Chenxi 409

H
Hahn, Tobias 48
Hähner, Jörg 283
Halder, Linus 156
Hannig, Frank 172

H
He, Xubin 125
Heider, Michael 283
Henrichs, Elia 298
Herglotz, Christian 94
Hernández Morales, José Juan 172
Herzog, Henriette 63
Hofmann, Jan 48
Hönig, Timo 63
Huber, Benedikt 156
Hübner, Michael 94
Hudelot, Céline 18

K
Kaendler, Luna 298
Kasper, Benjamin 156
Keramidas, Georgios 362
Kissich, Meinhard 109
Köppen, Marcel 482
Krall, Andreas 156
Krupitzer, Christian 298
Küble, Roman 283

L
Lange, Jonas 298
Liu, Mengxi 140
Lukowicz, Paul 140

M
Mackensen, Armin 268
Mavropoulos, Michail 362
Mielke, Simon 440
Modak, Sourav 314
Muñoz-Hernandez, Hector Gerardo 94
Mustafa, Mohammad Asif Ibna 205

N
Nestler, Michael 156
Nikolos, Dimitris 362
Nolte, Lukas 477

O
Oğuz Saltık, Ahmet 314

P
Per, Kevin 156
Pierrard, Régis 18
Pirk, Sören 477
Poli, Jean-Philippe 18

Q
Qian, Chao 459

R
Raoofy, Amir 3
Raschhofer, Matthias 156
Reichenbach, Marc 94
Renner, Bernd-Christian 236
Ripar, Alexander 156
Rothenburger, Kjell-Matti 268

S
Saleh, Ehab 3
Salkhordeh, Reza 125
Sass, Jan 125
Schilling, K. 471
Schlögl, Thomas 34
Schmidt, M. 471
Schoeberl, Martin 189
Schönberner, Connor 268, 430

Schweizer, Pia 298, 379
Shahin, Keyvan 94
Shuvo, Md. Aukerul Moin 205
Sick, Bernhard 205, 330
Siyavashi, Alireza 94
Smirnov, Nikita 220
Spinczyk, Olaf 79, 482
Stein, Anthony 252, 314
Steinberger, Marco 283
Suh, Sungho 140
Szymanski, Matthias 63

T
Teich, Jürgen 48, 63, 172
Tomforde, Sven 220, 268, 298, 477

V
Vali Zadeh, Paria 419

W
Weidendorfer, Josef 3
Wilbert, Nils 63
Wildermann, Stefan 48, 63
Wisy, Svea 399

Z
Zhou, Bo 140
Zottele, Johannes 156

Made in the USA
Monee, IL
03 May 2026